IMPORTANT

W9-AUI-156

HERE IS YOUR REGISTRATION CODE TO ACCESS MCGRAW-HILL PREMIUM CONTENT AND MCGRAW-HILL ONLINE RESOURCES

For key premium online resources you need THIS CODE to gain access. Once the code is entered, you will be able to use the web resources for the length of your course.

Access is provided only if you have purchased a new book.

If the registration code is missing from this book, the registration screen on our website, and within your WebCT or Blackboard course will tell you how to obtain your new code. Your registration code can be used only once to establish access. It is not transferable

To gain access to these online resources

1. **USE** your web browser to go to: **http://www.mhhe.com/thompson2e**

2. **CLICK** on "First Time User"

3. **ENTER** the Registration Code printed on the tear-off bookmark on the right

4. After you have entered your registration code, click on "Register"

5. **FOLLOW** the instructions to setup your personal UserID and Password

6. **WRITE** your UserID and Password down for future reference. Keep it in a safe place.

If your course is using WebCT or Blackboard, you'll be able to use this code to access the McGraw-Hill content within your instructor's online course.

To gain access to the McGraw-Hill content in your instructor's WebCT or Blackboard course simply log into the course with the user ID and Password provided by your instructor. Enter the registration code exactly as it appears to the right when prompted by the system. You will only need to use this code the first time you click on McGraw-Hill content.

These instructions are specifically for student access. Instructors are not required to register via the above instructions.

The McGraw-Hill Companies

McGraw-Hill Irwin

Thank you, and welcome to your McGraw-Hill/Irwin Online Resources.

Thompson/Gamble/Strickland
Strategy: Winning in the Marketplace, 2/e
0-07-320104-9

JJI8-9OVO-96Y8-CYJY-GPFJ

REGISTRATION CODE
REGISTRATION CODE

The McGraw-Hill Companies
Mc Graw Hill **McGraw-Hill Irwin**

STRATEGY

STRATEGY

Core Concepts, Analytical Tools, Readings

Second Edition

Arthur A. Thompson, Jr.
University of Alabama

John E. Gamble
University of South Alabama

A. J. Strickland III
University of Alabama

Boston   Burr Ridge, IL   Dubuque, IA   Madison, WI   New York   San Francisco   St. Louis
Bangkok   Bogotá   Caracas   Kuala Lumpur   Lisbon   London   Madrid   Mexico City
Milan   Montreal   New Delhi   Santiago   Seoul   Singapore   Sydney   Taipei   Toronto

McGraw-Hill
Irwin

STRATEGY: CORE CONCEPTS, ANALYTICAL TOOLS, READINGS

Published by McGraw-Hill/Irwin, a business unit of The McGraw-Hill Companies, Inc., 1221 Avenue of the Americas, New York, NY, 10020. Copyright © 2006, 2004 by The McGraw-Hill Companies, Inc. All rights reserved. No part of this publication may be reproduced or distributed in any form or by any means, or stored in a database or retrieval system, without the prior written consent of The McGraw-Hill Companies, Inc., including, but not limited to, in any network or other electronic storage or transmission, or broadcast for distance learning.

Some ancillaries, including electronic and print components, may not be available to customers outside the United States.

This book is printed on acid-free paper.

1 2 3 4 5 6 7 8 9 0 DOW/DOW 0 9 8 7 6 5

ISBN 0-07-299946-2

Editorial director: *John E. Biernat*
Executive editor: *John Weimeister*
Managing developmental editor: *Laura Hurst Spell*
Senior marketing manager: *Lisa Nicks*
Media producer: *Benjamin Curless*
Project manager: *Harvey Yep*
Senior production supervisor: *Rose Hepburn*
Lead designer: *Matthew Baldwin*
Photo research coordinator: *Lori Kramer*
Media project manager: *Joyce J. Chappetto*
Supplement producer: *Gina F. DiMartino*
Developer, Media technology: *Brian Nacik*
Cover design: *Kiera Pohl*
Interior design: *Kiera Pohl*
Typeface: *10.5/12 Times New Roman*
Compositor: *Cenveo*
Printer: *R. R. Donnelley*

Photo Credits *For Chapter Openers:*
page 2, © Images.com/CORBIS; page 38, © Images.com/CORBIS; page 82, © Images.com/CORBIS; page 112, © Images.com/CORBIS; page 158, © Royalty Free/CORBIS/MHHE; page 190, © Images.com/CORBIS; page 238, © Royalty Free/CORBIS/MHHE; page 272, © Images.com/CORBIS; page 316, © Ed Bock/Corbis

Library of Congress Cataloging-in-Publication Data
Thompson, Arthur A., 1940–
    Strategy: core concepts, analytical tools, readings / Arthur A. Thompson, John E. Gamble, A.J. Strickland.—2nd ed.
        p. cm.
    Includes index.
    ISBN 0-07-299946-2 (alk. paper)
    1. Strategic planning. 2. Management. 3. Strategic planning—Case studies. 4. Management—Case studies. I. Gamble, John (John E.) II. Strickland, A.J. (Alonzo J.) III. Title.
HD30.28.T537 2006
658.4'012—dc22   2005041647

www.mhhe.com

To our families and especially our wives:
Hasseline, Debra, and Kitty

About the Authors

Arthur A. Thompson, Jr., earned his BS and PhD degrees in economics from the University of Tennessee in 1961 and 1965, respectively; spent three years on the economics faculty at Virginia Tech; and served on the faculty of the University of Alabama's College of Commerce and Business Administration for 24 years. In 1974 and again in 1982, Dr. Thompson spent semester-long sabbaticals as a visiting scholar at the Harvard Business School.

His areas of specialization are business strategy, competition and market analysis, and the economics of business enterprises. He has published over 30 articles in some 25 different professional and trade publications and has authored or coauthored five textbooks and four computer-based simulation exercises.

Dr. Thompson is a frequent speaker and consultant on the strategic issues confronting the electric utility industry, particularly as concerns the challenges posed by industry restructuring, reregulation, competition, and customers' freedom of choice. He spends much of his off-campus time giving presentations to electric utility groups and conducting management development programs for electric utility executives all over the world.

Dr. Thompson and his wife of 44 years have two daughters, two grandchildren, and a Yorkshire terrier.

John E. Gamble is currently Associate Dean and Professor of Management in the Mitchell College of Business at The University of South Alabama. His teaching specialty at USA is strategic management and he also conducts a course in strategic management in Germany through a collaborative MBA program sponsored by the University of Applied Sciences in Ludwigshafen/Worms, the State of Rhineland Westphalia, and the University of South Alabama.

Dr. Gamble's research interests center on strategic issues in entrepreneurial, health care, and manufacturing settings. His work has been published in such scholarly journals as *Journal of Business Venturing, Journal of Labor Research, Health Care Management Review,* and *Journal of Occupational and Organizational Psychology.* He is the author or co-author of more than 30 case studies published in various strategic management and strategic marketing texts. He has done consulting on industry and market analysis and strategy formulation and implementation issues with clients in public utilities, technology, non-profit, and entrepreneurial businesses.

Professor Gamble received his Ph.D. in management from the University of Alabama in 1995. Dr. Gamble also has a Bachelor of Science degree and a Master of Arts degree from The University of Alabama.

Dr. A. J. (Lonnie) Strickland, a native of North Georgia, attended the University of Georgia, where he received a bachelor of science degree in math and physics in 1965. Afterward he entered the Georgia Institute of Technology, where he received a master of science in industrial management. He earned a PhD in business administration from Georgia State University in 1969. He currently holds the title of Professor of Strategic Management in the Graduate School of Business at the University of Alabama.

Dr. Strickland's experience in consulting and executive development is in the strategic management area, with a concentration in industry and competitive analysis. He has developed strategic planning systems for such firms as the Southern Company, BellSouth, South Center Bell, American Telephone and Telegraph, Gulf States Paper, Carraway Methodist Medical Center, Delco Remy, Mark IV Industries, Amoco Oil Company, USA Group, General Motors, and Kimberly Clark Corporation (Medical Products). He is a very popular speaker on the subject of implementing strategic change and serves on several corporate boards.

He has served as director of marketing for BellSouth, where he had responsibility for $1 billion in revenues and $300 million in profits.

In the international arena, Dr. Strickland has done extensive work in Europe, the Middle East, Central America, Malaysia, Australia, and Africa. In France he developed a management simulation of corporate decision making that enables management to test various strategic alternatives.

In the area of research, he is the author of 15 books and texts. His management simulations, Tempomatic IV and Micromatic, were pioneering innovations that enjoyed prominent market success for two decades.

Recent awards for Dr. Strickland include the Outstanding Professor Award from the Graduate School of Business and the Outstanding Commitment to Teaching Award from the University of Alabama, in which he takes particular pride. He is a member of various honor leadership societies: Mortar Board, Order of Omega, Beta Gamma Sigma, Omicron Delta Kappa, and Jasons. He is a past national president of Pi Kappa Phi social fraternity.

Preface

The objective of this text is to effectively and interestingly cover what every senior-level or MBA student needs to know about crafting and executing business strategies. It features a *streamlined* and *substantive* presentation of core concepts and analytical techniques and a collection of 14 relatively short and quite current readings that amplify important topics in managing a company's strategy-making, strategy-executing process. This book is particularly suited for courses where the instructor wishes to provide students with a foundation in the core concepts and analytical tools of strategic management before having them tackle a customized set of cases and/or a simulation exercise.

We have covered the main elements of strategic thinking and strategic analysis in nine manageable chapters (348 pages), striving for a presentation that is appropriately rigorous but that also can be readily digested by students and comfortably covered in a single term. Skirting the temptation to incorporate too many topics and include too much detail (in a 12- to 16-chapter presentation) results, we think, in three very positive benefits for adopters and students: (1) It creates more leeway for case assignments and a select number of readings. (2) It provides more time for including a substantive, stimulating simulation exercise as a core element of the course—a simulation not only is a pedagogically powerful way for students to learn about strategy but also introduces a welcome degree of added excitement and instructional variety into the course. (3) It helps make the course workload less intimidating or overwhelming for students.

Like most authors of second editions, we are confident that the content of this edition represents a solid improvement over the first edition. It includes an all-new and very timely chapter entitled Strategy, Ethics, and Social Responsibility, a more stream-lined two-chapter treatment of strategy execution (down from three chapters), and a raft of improvements and updates of all the chapter presentations. Although the book is shorter than most leading texts, you'll find that the nine chapters cover the principles of crafting and executing strategy with plenty of depth and substance. There's a straightforward, integrated flow from one chapter to the next. The writing style aims squarely at making the discipline of business strategy relevant and professionally interesting to students.

A Text with On-Target Content

In our view, for a senior-level/MBA strategy text to qualify as having on-target content, it must:

- Explain core concepts in language that students can grasp and provide examples of their relevance and use by actual companies.
- Take care to thoroughly describe the tools of strategic analysis, how they are used, and where they fit into the managerial process of crafting and executing strategy.

- Be up-to-date and comprehensive, with solid coverage of the landmark changes in competitive markets and company strategies being driven by globalization and Internet technology.

- Focus squarely on what every student needs to know about crafting, implementing, and executing business strategies in today's market environments.

The 9 text chapters and the 14 supplemental readings (which can be assigned in whole or part) do all these things without posing a formidable number of pages for instructors to cover and students to absorb in one semester. Chapter discussions cut straight to the chase. Our explanations of core concepts and analytical tools are covered in enough depth to make them understandable and usable, the rationale being that a shallow explanation carries little punch and has almost no instructional value. All the chapters are flush with convincing examples of strategy in action, and we made a point of choosing current examples that students can easily relate to. We have striven to incorporate all relevant state-of-the-art research pertinent to a first course in strategy.

Organization, Content, and Features of the Text Chapters

The inclusion of the all-new chapter on strategy, ethics, and social responsibility and the combining of the former three-chapter presentation on the managerial aspects of executing strategy into two chapters give this edition a different texture and feel. We think this new chapter will (1) better alert students to the role and importance of incorporating business ethics and social responsibility into decision-making and (2) address the accreditation requirements of the AACSB, which mandate that business ethics be visibly and thoroughly embedded in the core curriculum. In addition to making these two highly visible changes, we have thoroughly overhauled the opening chapter, which introduces the concept of strategy and the managerial process of crafting and executing strategy; added a host of current examples and new Company Spotlights; and embellished and refined the presentation of numerous topics and concepts throughout the chapters.

No other text comes close to matching our coverage of the resource-based theory of the firm and business ethics. The resource-based view of the firm is *prominently* and *comprehensively* integrated into our coverage of crafting both single-business and multibusiness strategies. Chapters 2, 3, 4, 5, and 6 emphasize that a company's strategy must be matched both to its external market circumstances and to its internal resources and competitive capabilities. Moreover, Chapters 8 and 9 have a strong resource-based perspective that makes it unequivocally clear how and why the tasks of assembling intellectual capital and building core competencies and competitive capabilities are absolutely critical to successful strategy execution and operating excellence. The all-new, 34-page Chapter 7 contains a very meaty and comprehensive treatment of business ethics and socially responsible behavior as it applies to crafting and executing company strategies.

As always, we have endeavored to highlight the latest developments in the theory and practice of strategic management and to keep the chapter presentations solidly in the mainstream of contemporary strategic thinking. You'll find up-to-date coverage of the continuing march of industries and companies to wider globalization, the growing scope and strategic importance of collaborative alliances, the spread of high-velocity change to more industries and company environments, and the way implementation of Internet technology applications in countries all across the world is driving fundamental changes in both strategy and internal operations.

The following rundown summarizes the noteworthy chapter features and topical emphasis in this edition:

- Chapter 1 continues to focus squarely on the central questions of "what is strategy and why is it important?" It introduces and defines a host of core concepts—strategy, business model, strategic visions and business missions, strategic versus financial objectives, strategic plans, strategic intent, strategy crafting, and strategy execution. Clear distinction is made between a company's strategy and its business model. A section on strategic visions and mission statements hammers home the importance of clear direction setting and a motivating strategic vision; there's an accompanying discussion of how core values and ethics tie in to a company's vision and business purpose. Emphasis is placed on why companies have to rapidly adapt strategy to newly unfolding market conditions and why strategy life cycles are often short.

  Following Henry Mintzberg's pioneering research, we stress how and why a company's strategy emerges from (1) the deliberate and purposeful actions of management and (2) as-needed reactions to unanticipated developments and fresh competitive pressures. There's a section underscoring that a company's strategic plan is a collection of strategies devised by different managers at different levels in the organizational hierarchy. We've taken pains to explain why *all managers are on a company's strategy-making, strategy-implementing team,* why every manager is well advised to make the concepts and techniques of strategic management a basic part of his or her toolkit, and why the best companies want their personnel to be true "students of the business." The chapter concludes with a substantially expanded section on corporate governance and a discussion of why *good strategy-making + good strategy execution = good management.*

  The role of this first chapter is to give readers a solid grasp of what the term *strategy* means, pique their interest, and convince them that the ins and outs of crafting and executing a winning strategy are things every business student should know. We intend this chapter to be a perfect accompaniment for the instructor's first one or two lectures on what the course is all about and why it matters.

- Chapter 2 sets forth the now-familiar analytical tools and concepts of industry and competitive analysis and demonstrates the importance of tailoring strategy to fit the circumstances of a company's industry and competitive environment. The standout feature of this chapter is a presentation of Michael E. Porter's "five forces model of competition" that we think is the clearest, most straightforward discussion of this model in any text in the field. Globalization and Internet technology are treated as potent driving forces capable of reshaping industry competition—their roles as change agents have become factors that most companies in most industries must reckon with in forging winning strategies.

- Chapter 3 establishes the importance of doing solid company situation analysis as a basis for matching strategy to organizational resources, competencies, and competitive capabilities. The roles of core competencies and organizational resources and capabilities in creating customer value and helping build competitive advantage are *center stage* in the discussions of company resource strengths and weaknesses. SWOT analysis is cast as a simple, easy-to-use way to assess a company's resources and overall situation. There is solid coverage of the now-standard tools of value chain analysis, benchmarking, and competitive strength assessments—all of which, we believe, provide insight into a company's relative cost position and market standing vis-à-vis rivals. There's solid coverage of how company implementation of

Internet technology applications is altering company and industry value chains and the performance of specific value chain activities.

■ Chapter 4 deals with a company's quest for competitive advantage—the options for crafting a strategy that simultaneously holds good prospects for competitive advantage while also being well suited both to industry and competitive conditions and to its own resources and competitive circumstances. While the chapter is framed around the five generic competitive strategies—low-cost leadership, differentiation, best-cost provider, focused differentiation, and focused low cost—you'll also find important sections on what use to make of strategic alliances and collaborative partnerships, what use to make of mergers and acquisitions in strengthening the company's competitiveness, when to integrate backward or forward into more stages of the industry value chain, the merits of outsourcing certain value chain activities to outside specialists, whether and when to employ offensive and defensive moves, and the different types of Web site strategies that companies can employ to position themselves in the marketplace.

■ Chapter 5 explores a company's strategy options for expanding beyond its domestic boundary and competing in the markets of either a few or a great many countries—options ranging from an export strategy to licensing and franchising to multicountry strategies to global strategies to heavy reliance on strategic alliances and joint ventures. Four strategic issues unique to competing multinationally are given special attention: (1) whether to customize the company's offerings in each different country market to match the tastes and preferences of local buyers or whether to offer a mostly standardized product worldwide; (2) whether to employ essentially the same basic competitive strategy in the markets of all countries where the company operates or whether to modify the company's competitive approach country by country as may be needed to fit the specific market conditions and competitive circumstances it encounters; (3) locating production facilities, distribution centers, and customer service operations to maximum competitive advantage; and (4) efficient cross-border transfer of a company's resource strengths and capabilities to build competitive advantage. There's also coverage of the concepts of profit sanctuaries and cross-market subsidization, the special problems associated with entry into the markets of emerging countries, and strategies that local companies in such emerging countries as India, China, Brazil, and Mexico can use to defend against the invasion of opportunity-seeking, resource-rich global giants.

■ Our rather meaty treatment of diversification strategies for multibusiness enterprises in Chapter 6 begins by laying out the various paths for becoming diversified, explains how a company can use diversification to create or compound competitive advantage for its business units, and examines the strategic options an already-diversified company has to improve its overall performance. In the middle part of the chapter, the analytical spotlight is on the techniques and procedures for assessing the strategic attractiveness of a diversified company's business portfolio—the relative attractiveness of the various businesses the company has diversified into, a multiindustry company's competitive strength in each of its lines of business, and the *strategic fits* and *resource fits* among a diversified company's different businesses. The chapter concludes with a brief survey of a company's four main postdiversification strategy alternatives: (1) broadening the diversification base, (2) divesting some businesses and retrenching to a narrower diversification base, (3) restructuring the makeup of the company's business lineup, and (4) engaging in multinational diversification.

■ Our all-new Chapter 7, "Strategy, Ethics, and Social Responsibility," zeroes in on whether and why a company's strategy should pass the test of moral scrutiny. Students usually acknowledge that a company and its personnel have a legal duty to obey the law and play by the rules of fair competition. But today's students seem to be much less clear on (1) whether a company has a *duty* to operate according to ethical standards and (2) whether a company has a *duty* or *obligation* to contribute to the betterment of society independent of the needs and preferences of the customers it serves. Is it in the best interests of shareholders for a company to operate ethically and/or to operate in a socially responsible manner? There is substantive discussion of what linkage, if any, there should be between a company's efforts to craft and execute a winning strategy and its duties to (1) conduct its activities in an ethical manner and (2) demonstrate socially responsible behavior by being a committed corporate citizen and attending to the needs of nonowner stakeholders—employees, the communities in which it operates, the disadvantaged, and society as a whole. The chapter reflects the very latest in the literature. The opening section of the chapter addresses whether ethical standards are universal (as maintained by the school of ethical universalism) or dependent on local norms and situational circumstances (as maintained by the school of ethical relativism) or a combination of both (as maintained by integrative social contracts theory). Following this is a section on the three categories of managerial morality (moral, immoral, and amoral), a section on the drivers of unethical strategies and shady business behavior, a section on the approaches to managing a company's ethical conduct, a section on linking a company's strategy to its ethical principles and core values, a section on the concept of a "social responsibility strategy," and sections that explore the business case for ethical and socially responsible behavior. The chapter gives students some serious ideas to chew on and, hopefully, will make them far more ethically conscious. It has been written as a stand-alone chapter that can be assigned in the early, middle, or late part of the course.

■ The two-chapter module on executing strategy (Chapters 8 and 9) is anchored around a solid, compelling conceptual framework: (1) building the resource strengths and organizational capabilities needed to execute the strategy in competent fashion; (2) allocating ample resources to strategy-critical activities; (3) ensuring that policies and procedures facilitate rather than impede strategy execution; (4) instituting best practices and pushing for continuous improvement in how value chain activities are performed; (5) installing information and operating systems that enable company personnel to better carry out their strategic roles proficiently; (6) tying rewards and incentives directly to the achievement of performance targets and good strategy execution; (7) shaping the work environment and corporate culture to fit the strategy; and (8) exerting the internal leadership needed to drive execution forward. The recurring theme of these two chapters is that implementing and executing strategy entails figuring out the specific actions, behaviors, and conditions that are needed for a smooth strategy-supportive operation and then following through to get things done and deliver results—the goal here is to ensure that students understand that the strategy-implementing/strategy-executing phase is a make-things-happen and make-them-happen-right kind of managerial exercise.

Our top priority has been to ensure that the nine chapters of text hit the bull's-eye with respect to content and represent the best thinking of both academics and practitioners. But, at the same time, we've gone the extra mile to stay on message with clear, crisp explanations laced with enough relevant examples and Company Spotlights to make the presentation convincing, pertinent, and worthwhile to readers preparing for careers in management and business. We have gone all out to create chapter discussions and compile a readings lineup capable of persuading students that the discipline of strategy merits their rapt attention.

The Collection of Readings

In selecting a set of readings to accompany the chapter presentations, we opted for readings that (1) were current (most appeared in 2004), (2) extended the chapter coverage and expanded on a topic of strategic importance, and (3) were quite readable and relatively short. At the same time, we endeavored to be highly selective, deciding that a small number of on-target readings was a better fit with the teaching/learning objectives of a first course in strategy than a more sweeping collection of readings. The readings are drawn from the *Harvard Business Review, the Academy of Management Executive,* the *Business Strategy Review, Strategy & Leadership, TQM Magazine,* and the *Ivey Business Journal.*

Aside from providing an introductory look at the literature of strategic management, the readings offer nice variety. For instance, Constantos Markides' article, "What Is Strategy and How Do You Know If You Have One?" expands on the various notions of what strategy is, the conflicting definitions that exist, and the reason why strategy is mainly about making some very difficult decisions on a *few* parameters. Mark Lipton's essay, "Walking the Talk (Really!): Why Visions Fail," describes why it is important for company executives to move beyond articulating a vision and actually push company personnel to weave the vision into the fabric of how the company conducts its operations. Gary Latham's article, "The Motivational Benefits of Goal-Setting," explains why setting stretch goals has such a positive effect on organizations.

The next four articles complement the coverage in Chapters 2 through 5. The *HBR* article by Anita McGahan, "How Industries Change," describes the various trajectories that industries follow and explains why taking the patterns of change into account can make a company's investments in innovation be more likely to pay off. The article by George Stalk and Rob Lachenauer, "Five Killer Strategies for Trouncing the Competition," is must reading and will open eyes about how companies play competitive hardball in the marketplace. The Markides and Geroski article, "Racing to Be Second: Conquering the Industries of the Future," provides excellent insight into first-mover disadvantages and fast-follower advantages. The timely reading "Outsourcing Strategies: Opportunities and Risks" provides useful perspectives on when outsourcing makes strategic sense and when it doesn't.

Zook's article on growth via diversification discusses why pursuing strategic fits in adjacent businesses usually is most advantageous. We chose this reading to accompany the coverage in Chapter 6.

Bruch and Ghoshal's intriguing article, "Management Is the Art of Doing and Getting Done," emphasizes the critical nature of effective strategy execution and purposeful action taking by managers. There are timely articles on the pros and cons of six sigma initiatives and on linking the achievement of objectives to the payment of monetary incentives, plus a very provocative article by Sidney Finkelstein: "The Seven Habits of Spectacularly Unsuccessful Executives." The last reading concerns corporate social responsibility and delves into why good people sometimes behave badly in organizations—you can assign the reading in conjunction with either Chapter 7 or the strategic leadership section of Chapter 9. The last reading by Jeffrey Sonnenfeld is a very thoughtful article on corporate governance; it can be used to complement the governance section in Chapter 1 or the strategic leadership section in Chapter 9.

Two Accompanying Online, Fully Automated Simulation Exercises—GLO-BUS and The Business Strategy Game

GLO-BUS: Developing Winning Competitive Strategies and *The Business Strategy Game* (the online eighth edition)—two strategy-related simulations that are available online and that feature automatic processing of student decisions—are being marketed by the publisher as companion supplements for use with this and other texts in the field. *The Business Strategy Game* is the world's leading strategy simulation, having been played by well over 350,000 students at universities throughout the world. *GLO-BUS*, a somewhat less complicated online simulation that was introduced in fall 2003, has been played by over 10,000 students at more than 100 universities worldwide and is equally suitable for courses in business strategy. All activity for *GLO-BUS* occurs at www.glo-bus.com and all activity for *The Business Strategy Game* takes place at www.bsg-online.com. The industry setting for *GLO-BUS* is the global digital camera industry, and the setting for *The Business Strategy Game* is the global athletic footwear industry—see Table 1 for a comparison of the two simulations.

Both simulations have attractive operating and administrative characteristics that make them a breeze to utilize in giving students valuable practice in thinking strategically and applying basic strategy concepts and analytical tools:

■ *Time requirements for instructors to administer the simulations are minimal.* Instructors must go through Industry Set-up and specify a decision schedule and desired scoring weights (which can be altered later). Setting up the simulation for the course is done online and takes about 10 to 15 minutes. Once set-up is completed, no other administrative actions are required beyond moving participants to a different team (should the need arise) and monitoring the progress of the simulation (to whatever extent desired). Instructors who wish to do so can track happenings in the simulation by printing copies of the Industry and Company reports (done online), change selected costs and rates to introduce different operating conditions (players are automatically notified of any changes if instructors so choose), and serve as a consultant to troubled companies.

■ *There's no software for students or administrators to download and no disks to fool with.* When participants log on to the Web site, the needed programming and company data are automatically transferred into Excel on the user's PC for the duration of the session and then automatically saved and uploaded back to the server on exit. All work must be done online, and the speed for participants using dial-up modems is quite satisfactory.

■ *Participant's guides for both simulations are available at the Web site*—students can read either guide on their monitors or print out a copy, as they prefer. The Participant's Guide for *GLO-BUS* is 25 pages, and the Participant's Guide for *The Business Strategy Game* is 33 pages.

■ *There are extensive built-in help screens* explaining (1) each decision entry, (2) the information on each page of the Industry Reports, and (3) the numbers presented in the Company Reports. The Help screens allow company comanagers to figure

Table 1   A COMPARISON OF *GLO-BUS* AND *THE BUSINESS STRATEGY GAME*

	GLO-BUS	The Business Strategy Game
Industry setting	Digital camera industry	Athletic footwear industry
Market scope	Worldwide. Production occurs at a single plant in Taiwan and sales are made to retailers in 4 regions: North America, Latin America, Europe-Africa, and Asia Pacific.	Worldwide. Both production and sales activities can be pursued in North America, Latin America, Europe-Africa, and Asia Pacific.
Number of market segments	A total of 8—4 geographic segments for entry-level cameras and 4 geographic segments for multifeatured cameras.	A total of 12—4 geographic segments each for branded footwear sales to retailers, for online footwear sales direct to consumers, and for private-label sales to multistore retailers.
Number of decision variables	■ Character and performance of the camera line (10 decisions) ■ Production operations and worker compensation (15 decisions) ■ Pricing and marketing (15 decisions in 4 geographic regions) ■ Financing of company operations (4 decisions)	■ Production operations and worker compensation (16 decisions each plant, with a maximum of 4 plants) ■ Shipping (up to 8 decisions each plant) ■ Pricing and marketing (13 decisions in 4 geographic regions) ■ Financing of company operations (5 decisions)
Competitive variables used to determine market share (All sales and market share differences are the result of differing competitive efforts among rival companies.)	■ Price ■ Performance/quality rating ■ Number of quarterly sales promotions ■ Length of promotions in weeks ■ Promotional discounts ■ Advertising ■ Number of camera models ■ Size of dealer network ■ Warranty period ■ Technical support	■ Price ■ Number of models/styles ■ Styling/quality rating ■ Advertising ■ Size of retailer network ■ Celebrity endorsements ■ Delivery time ■ Retailer support ■ Mail-in rebates ■ Shipping charges (Internet sales only)
Time frame of decisions	One year, with an option to update as many as 8 of the 44 decisions quarterly.	One year.
Strategy options (Which options deliver the best performance hinges on the interaction and competitive strength of the strategies employed by rival companies—not on "silver bullet" decision combinations that players are challenged to discover.)	Companies can pursue competitive advantage based on (1) low-cost or differentiation, (2) competing globally or in select segments, and (3) using largely the same strategy across all regions or strategies that are tailored to conditions in each market segment.	Companies have the widest possible strategy-making latitude—striving for competitive advantage based on (1) low-cost or differentiation, (2) competing globally or in select segments, and (3) using largely the same strategy across all regions or strategies that are tailored to conditions in each market segment.

Table 1   (CONCLUDED)

	GLO-BUS	The Business Strategy Game
Degree of complexity	• *GLO-BUS* Basic (easy to moderate) • *GLO-BUS* Plus (easy to moderate) • *GLO-BUS* Total (medium) Less complex than BSG because all production is in a single plant, there are no finished-goods inventories (newly assembled cameras are built to order and shipped directly to retailers), and sales forecasting is simpler.	More complex than *GLO-BUS* because companies can operate up to 4 plants, there are 12 market segments (as compared to 8 in *GLO-BUS*), finished-goods inventories have to be managed at 4 distribution centers, and players have to develop a sales forecast based on their competitive strategy and the expected competitive efforts of rivals.
Time required to make a complete decision	About 1.5 hours per decision (once players gain familiarity with software and reports). *GLO-BUS* Plus requires about 10 minutes more than *GLO-BUS* Basic per decision, and *GLO-BUS* Total can entail up to 30 minutes additional time per decision.	1.75 to 2.25 hours per decision (once players gain familiarity with software and reports).

things out for themselves, thereby curbing the need for students to always run to the instructor with questions about how things work.

■ *The results of each decision are processed automatically* on the simulation's server and are available to all participants *within one hour after the decision deadline* specified by the instructor or game administrator—typically the results are available 15 to 20 minutes after the decision deadline. The servers dedicated to hosting the two simulations have appropriate backup capability and are maintained by a prominent web-hosting service that guarantees 99.9 percent reliability on a 24/7 basis.

■ *Participants and instructors are notified via e-mail when the results are ready;* the e-mail contains highlights of the results.

■ *Decision schedules are determined by the instructor* (done online and automatically communicated to all players). Decisions can be made once per week, twice per week, or even twice daily, depending on how instructors want to conduct the exercise. One popular decision schedule involves 1 or 2 practice decisions, 6 to 10 regular decisions, and decisions made once a week across the whole term. A second popular schedule is 1 or 2 practice decisions, 6 to 8 regular decisions, and bi-weekly decisions, all made during the last four or five weeks of the course (when it can be assumed that students have pretty much digested the contents of Chapters 1 to 5, gotten somewhat comfortable with what is involved in crafting strategy for a single-business company situation, and have prepared several assigned cases).

■ *Instructors have the flexibility to prescribe 0, 1, or 2 practice decisions and from 3 to 10 regular decisions.*

- *Company teams can be composed of 1 to 5 players each, and the number of teams in a single industry can range from 4 to 12.* If your class size is too large for a single industry, then it is a simple matter to create two or more industries for a single class section. You'll find that having more than one industry per class presents no significant change in administrative requirements, because everything is processed automatically and all company and individual performances are automatically recorded in your online grade book. Thus it turns out not to be an extra administrative burden to divide a large class into two or more industries.

- *Following each decision, participants are provided with a complete set of reports*—a six-page Industry Report, a one-page Competitive Intelligence report for each geographic region that includes strategic group maps and bulleted lists of competitive strengths and weaknesses, and a set of Company Reports (income statement, balance sheet, cash flow statement, and assorted production, marketing, and cost statistics).

- *Two open-book multiple-choice tests of 20 questions* (optional, but strongly recommended) *are included as part of each of the two simulations.* The quizzes are taken online and automatically graded, with scores reported instantaneously to participants and automatically recorded in the instructor's electronic grade book. Quiz 1 has a time limit of 45 minutes and covers contents of the Participant's Guide. Quiz 2 has a time limit of 75 minutes and checks whether players understand what the numbers in the company reports mean and how they are calculated. Students are automatically provided with three sample questions for each test.

- At the end of the simulation exercises, *there are peer evaluations that instructors can have students complete.* The peer evaluations are optional but strongly recommended; they are completed online and automatically recorded in the instructor's electronic grade book. Results can be reviewed by clicking on each comanager's peer scores in the grade book.

Simulations now have a track record as a proven and very effective vehicle for giving students valuable practice in being active strategic thinkers, reading the signs of industry change, reacting to the moves of competitors, evaluating strengths and weaknesses in their company's competitive position, and deciding what to do to improve a company's financial performance.

Why Simulations Are Widely Used in Capstone Strategy Courses

All three coauthors of this book are avid, longtime simulation users. Our own experiences over the years, together with numerous discussions with colleagues around the world, have convinced us that competition-based simulation games are *the single most powerful pedagogical device for hammering home the core concepts and analytical techniques that constitute the discipline of business and competitive strategy.* We see three big reasons why simulations are rapidly growing in popularity and have earned a place in so many of today's strategy courses:

- Both *GLO-BUS* and *The Business Strategy Game* have been carefully designed to connect directly to the chapter material and give students the experience of putting what they read in the chapters into play. Company co-managers have to wrestle with charting a long-term direction for their company, setting strategic and financial objectives, and crafting strategies that produce good results and perhaps lead to competitive advantage. In crafting and executing a strategy, they can choose from a wide array of the strategic options discussed in the text chapters and they can practice using the tools of strategic analysis. In both *GLO-BUS* and *The Business Strategy Game*, students are provided with strategic group maps and lists of competitive strengths and weaknesses, as well as an assortment of cost benchmarks and comparative financial statistics, allowing them to diagnose their company's market standing vis-à-vis rivals and decide on a course of action to improve it. Moreover, simulations provide instructors with opportunity after opportunity to draw upon the industry and company circumstances in the simulation for examples to use in lectures on the text chapters—examples that all students in the class can relate to because of their personal experience in running their companies.

■ The market and competitive dynamics of an industry simulation—which make the simulation a "live case" in which class members are active managerial participants—give students valuable practice in thinking strategically and in making responsible, results-oriented decisions. Company comanagers can pursue a competitive advantage keyed to low cost/low price or to top-notch features and styling or to more value for the money. They can try to gain an edge over rivals with more advertising or wider product selection. They can focus on one or two geographic regions or strive for geographic balance. They can pursue essentially the same strategy worldwide or craft slightly or very different strategies for the Europe-Africa, Asia-Pacific, Latin America, and North America markets. Almost any well-conceived, well-executed competitive approach is capable of succeeding *provided it is not overpowered by the strategies of competitors or defeated by the presence of too many copycat strategies that dilute its effectiveness.* In other words, which company strategies end up delivering the best performance hinges on the interaction and competitive strength of the strategies employed by rival companies—not on "silver bullet" decision combinations that players are challenged to discover. Since, in a simulation, students have to live with all the decisions they make and the results they produce, they experience firsthand what is involved in crafting and executing a strategy that delivers good results—*it is this understanding that is the essence of a course in business strategy.*

■ Based on the classroom experiences of hundreds of instructors and the mushrooming use of simulations in strategy courses worldwide, incorporating a simulation as a centerpiece turns strategy courses into a livelier, richer, more powerful learning experience. A realistic, substantive, "learn by doing" simulation like *GLO-BUS* or *The Business Strategy Game* sparks a highly desirable degree of student excitement about the subject matter of crafting and executing strategy. More and more professors who teach strategy courses are finding that simulations are every bit as pedagogically effective as case analysis as the prime vehicle for showing students how to make use of core concepts and analytical techniques.

There are two other reasons why a simulation is a good exercise to include as an integral and featured part of the course:

■ A well-conceived simulation adds an enormous amount of student interest and excitement—a head-to-head competitive battle for market share and industry leadership is certain to stir students' competitive juices and emotionally involve them in the subject matter. Most students will enjoy the exercise, recognize its practical value, and learn a lot—all of which tends to result in higher instructor evaluations at the end of the course.

- Students will almost certainly learn more about the ins and outs of crafting and executing strategy from playing a simulation than they will learn from preparing two or three extra cases or doing a second or third written case analysis. Since use of *GLO-BUS* or *The Business Strategy Game* can add net time to the course requirements from a student perspective, instructors can compensate by trimming the total number of assigned cases or using a simulation as a substitute for a written case, an hour exam, or both. Happily, a simulation lightens the grading burden for instructors as compared to written cases or essay exams.

In sum, the value that a first-rate simulation adds to a strategy course boils down to two things:

1. The "WOW! This is great, plus I am learning a lot" reaction of students.
2. The contribution a good simulation exercise makes to better preparing students for a career in business and management—*a simulation makes courses in strategy much more of a true capstone experience* and puts students under the gun of competition to improve their business acumen and managerial judgment.

To learn more about *GLO-BUS* or *The Business Strategy Game*, please visit www.glo-bus.com or www.bsg-online.com and browse the wealth of information that is at your fingertips. There is a Guided Tour link on each of the Web sites that provides a quick bird's-eye view and takes about five minutes—enough to determine whether there's sufficient interest on your part to explore further. There are also instructor's guides and PowerPoint presentation slides that you can skim to preview the two simulations. If you call the senior author of this text at 205-348-8923, the simulation authors will be glad to provide you with a personal tour of either or both Web sites (while you are at your PC) and walk you through the many features that are built into the simulations. We think you'll be quite impressed with the capabilities that have been programmed into *The Business Strategy Game* and *GLO-BUS,* the simplicity with which both simulations can be administered, and their exceptionally tight connection to the text chapters, core concepts, and standard analytical tools.

Adopters of the text who want to incorporate use of either of the two simulation supplements should instruct their bookstores to order the "book-simulation package"—the publisher has a special ISBN number for this package that entails a discounted price; shrink-wrapped with each text is a special card that provides students with a prepaid access code for participating in either simulation.

Student Support Materials

Key Points Summaries

At the end of each chapter is a synopsis of the core concepts, analytical tools, and other key points discussed in the chapter. These chapter-end synopses, along with the margin notes scattered throughout each chapter, help students focus on basic strategy principles, digest the messages of each chapter, and prepare for tests.

Chapter-End Exercises

Each chapter contains a select number of exercises, most related to research on the Internet, that reinforce key concepts and topics covered in the chapters.

Web Site

The student section of www.mhhe.com/thompson2e features 20-question self-scoring chapter tests that students can take to measure their grasp of the material presented in each of the nine chapters. It also includes a select number of PowerPoint slides for each chapter.

PowerWeb

With each new copy of this text, students gain access to the publisher's PowerWeb site offering current news, articles from 6,300 premium sources, a Web research guide, current readings from annual editions, and links to related sites.

Instructor Support Materials

Instructor's Manual

The accompanying instructor's manual contains a section on suggestions for organizing and structuring your course, sample syllabi and course outlines, and a test bank prepared by the coauthors that contains about 700 multiple-choice questions and 100 short-answer and essay questions.

Computest

A computerized version of the test bank allows you to generate tests quite conveniently and to add your own questions.

PowerPoint Slides

To facilitate preparation of your lectures and to serve as chapter outlines, approximately 500 colorful and professional-looking slides are available. You'll have access to slides displaying core concepts, analytical procedures, key points, and all the figures in the text chapters. The slides are the creation of Professor Jana Kuzmicki of Troy State University.

Presentation CD-ROM

The instructor's manual, all of the PowerPoint slides and case teaching notes available with *Strategy: Winning in the Marketplace; Core Concepts, Analytical Tools, Cases* amd *Strategy: Core Concepts, Analytical Tools, Readings* have been installed on a CD that is made available to all adopters. The CD is a useful aid for compiling a syllabus and daily course schedule, preparing customized lectures, and developing tests on the text chapters.

The *GLO-BUS* and *Business Strategy Game* Online Simulations

Using one of the two companion simulations is a powerful and constructive way of emotionally connecting students to the subject matter of the course. We know of no more effective and interesting way to stimulate the competitive energy of students and prepare them for the rigors of real-world business decision-making than to have them match strategic wits with classmates as they run a company in head-to-head competition for global market leadership.

Acknowledgments

A great number of colleagues and students at various universities, business acquaintances, and people at McGraw-Hill provided inspiration, encouragement, and counsel during the course of this project. Like all text authors in the strategy field, we are intellectually indebted to the many academics whose research and writing have blazed new trails and advanced the discipline of strategic management. We are most grateful to the reviewers who made valuable suggestions that guided our preparation of the first edition: Seyda Deligonul, David Flanagan, Esmeralda Garbi, Mohsin Habib, Kim Hester, Jeffrey E. McGee, and Diana Wong. The following reviewers provided seasoned advice and suggestions for improving the chapters in this second edition:

Donald P. Austin, *Saint Michael's College of Vermont*

R. Ivan Blanco, *Emporia State University*

Debbie Gilliard, *Metropolitan State College–Denver*

Dale Henderson, *Radford University*

Matthew Howard, *Park University*

Tammy G. Hunt, *University of North Carolina at Wilmington*

Dennis M. Kripp, *Roosevelt University*

Thomas C. Leach, *University of New England*

Paul D. Maxell, *St. Thomas University*

Raza Mir, *William Paterson University*

Gordon Riggle, *University of Colorado*

Daniel A. Sauers, *Winona State University*

Srivatsa Seshadri, *University of Nebraska at Kearney*

As always, we value your recommendations and thoughts about the book. Your comments regarding coverage and contents will be taken to heart, and we always are grateful for the time you take to call our attention to printing errors, deficiencies, and other shortcomings. Please e-mail us at athompso@cba.ua.edu, jgamble@usouthal.edu, or astrickl@cba.ua.edu; fax us at 205-348-6695; or write us at PO Box 870225, Department of Management and Marketing, The University of Alabama, Tuscaloosa, AL 35487-0225.

Arthur A. Thompson
John E. Gamble
A. J. Strickland

Guided Tour

Chapter Structure and Overview of Readings

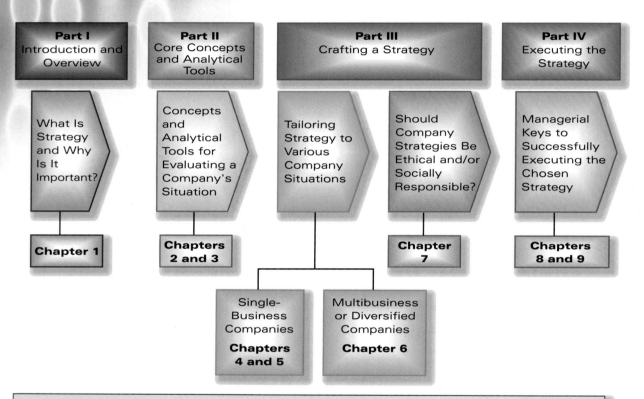

Part I
Introduction and Overview

What Is Strategy and Why Is It Important?

Chapter 1

Part II
Core Concepts and Analytical Tools

Concepts and Analytical Tools for Evaluating a Company's Situation

Chapters 2 and 3

Part III
Crafting a Strategy

Tailoring Strategy to Various Company Situations

Single-Business Companies
Chapters 4 and 5

Multibusiness or Diversified Companies
Chapter 6

Should Company Strategies Be Ethical and/or Socially Responsible?

Chapter 7

Part IV
Executing the Strategy

Managerial Keys to Successfully Executing the Chosen Strategy

Chapters 8 and 9

Part V Readings in Crafting and Executing Strategy

Section A: What Is Strategy and How Is the Process of Crafting and Executing Strategy Managed? (3 readings)

Section B: Crafting Strategy in Single-Business Companies (4 readings)

Section C: Crafting Strategy in Diversified Companies (1 readings)

Section D: Implementing and Executing Strategy (4 readings)

Section E: Strategy, Ethics, and Social Responsibility (2 readings)

Each chapter begins with a series of pertinent quotes and an introductory preview of its contents

CHAPTER 1

What Is Strategy and Why Is It Important?

A strategy is a commitment to undertake one set of actions rather than another.

—*Sharon Oster, professor, Yale University*

Without a strategy the organization is like a ship without a rudder.

—*Joel Ross and Michael Kami*

Unless we change our direction we are likely to end up where we are headed.

—*Ancient Chinese proverb*

If you don't know where you are going, any road will take you there.

—*The Koran*

Management's job is not to see the company as it is . . . but as it can become.

—*John W. Teets, former CEO, Greyhound Corp.*

COMPANY SPOTLIGHT 1.1
Comcast's Strategy to Revolutionize the Cable Industry

In 2004 cable TV giant Comcast was putting the finishing touches on a bold strategy to change the way people watched television and to grow its business by introducing Internet phone service. With revenues of $18 billion and almost 22 million of the 74 million U.S. cable subscribers, Comcast became the industry leader in the U.S. market in 2002 when it acquired AT&T Broadband and its 13 million cable subscribers for about $50 billion. Comcast's strategy in 2004 had the following elements:

- Roll out a new video-on-demand service that would allow customers to watch TV programs whenever they wanted to watch them. The service allowed customers to use their remotes to choose from a menu of thousands of programs, stored on Comcast's servers as they were first broadcast, and included network shows, news, sports, and movies; viewers had the ability to pause, stop, restart, and save programs, without having to remember to record them when they were broadcast. After only 18 months, Comcast had signed up close to 5 million of its subscribers for the service and it was introducing the service in additional geographic markets at a brisk pace.

service with many snazzy features, including call forwarding, caller ID, and conferencing.

- Use the video-on-demand and VOIP service offerings to differentiate Comcast's service offerings and combat mounting competition from direct-to-home satellite TV providers. Cable's two-way communications connection to homes enabled viewers to call up the programs they wanted with a few clicks of the remote; satellite TV had no such capability, nor did satellite providers yet have the capability to offer reliable high-speed Internet access. Satellite TV had been stealing customers away from cable TV because of its lower monthly fees—in the first six months of 2004, Direct TV and Echostar together added about 1.7 million new subscribers, whereas Comcast had lost 61,000 subscribers.

- Employ a sales force (currently numbering about 3,200 people) to sell advertising to businesses that were shifting some of their advertising dollars from sponsoring network programs to sponsoring cable programs. Ad sales generated revenues of $1.3 billion, and Comcast had cable operations in 21 of the 25 largest markets in the United States.

In-depth examples—**Company Spotlights** and **Global Spotlights**—appear in boxes throughout each chapter to illustrate important chapter topics, connect the text presentation to real-world companies, and convincingly demonstrate strategy in action.

GLOBAL SPOTLIGHT 5.1
Multicountry Strategies at Electronic Arts and Coca-Cola

Electronic Arts' Multicountry Strategy in Video Games

Electronic Arts (EA), the world's largest independent developer and marketer of video games, designs games that are suited to the differing tastes of game players in different countries and also designs games in multiple languages. EA has two major design studios—one in Vancouver, British Columbia, and one in Los Angeles—and smaller design studios in San Francisco, Orlando, London, and Tokyo. This dispersion of design studios helps EA to design games that are specific to different cultures—for example, the London studio took the lead in designing the popular FIFA Soccer game to suit European tastes and to replicate the stadiums, signage, and team rosters; a U.S. studio took the lead in designing games involving NFL football, NBA basketball, and NASCAR racing. No other game software company had EA's ability to localize games or to launch games on multiple platforms in multiple countries in multi-

ple languages. EA's Harry Potter and the Chamber of Secrets was released simultaneously in 75 countries, in 31 languages, and on 7 platforms.

Coca-Cola's Multicountry Strategy in Beverages

Coca-Cola strives to meet the demands of local tastes and cultures, offering 300 brands in some 200 countries. Its network of bottlers and distributors is distinctly local, and the company's products and brands are formulated to cater to local tastes. The ways in which Coca-Cola's local operating units bring products to market, the packaging that is used, and the advertising messages that are employed are all intended to match the local culture and fit in with local business practices. Many of the ingredients and supplies for Coca-Cola's products are sourced locally.

Source: www.ea.com and www.cocacola.com, accessed September 2004.

Regardless of whether a company's strategy changes gradually or swiftly, the important point is that a company's present strategy is always temporary and on trial, pending new ideas for improvement from management, changes in industry conditions, and any other new developments that management believes warrant strategic adjustments. Thus, a company's strategy at any given point is fluid, representing the temporary outcome of an ongoing process that, on the one hand, involves reasoned and intuitive management efforts to craft an effective strategy and, on the other hand, involves ongoing responses to market change and constant experimentation and tinkering. Adapting to new conditions and constantly learning what is working well enough to continue and what needs to be improved is consequently a normal part of the strategy-making process and results in an evolving strategy.

> A company's strategy is shaped partly by management analysis and choice and partly by the necessity of adapting and learning by doing.

Strategy and Ethics: Passing the Test of Moral Scrutiny

In choosing among strategic alternatives, company managers are well advised to embrace actions that are aboveboard and can pass the test of moral scrutiny. Just keeping a company's strategic actions within the bounds of what is legal does not make them ethical. Ethical and moral standards are not governed by what is legal. Rather, they involve issues of "right" versus "wrong" and *duty*—what one *should* do. A strategy is ethical only if it does not entail actions and behaviors that cross the line from "should do" to "should not do" (because such actions are "unsavory" or unconscionable, injurious to other people, or unnecessarily harmful to the environment).

> **Core Concept**
> A strategy cannot be considered ethical just because it involves actions that are legal. To meet the standard of being ethical, a strategy must entail actions that can pass moral scrutiny and that are aboveboard in the sense of not being shady or unconscionable, injurious to others, or unnecessarily harmful to the environment.

Admittedly, it is not always easy to categorize a given strategic behavior as definitely ethical or definitely unethical; many strategic actions fall in a gray zone in between. Whether they are deemed ethical or unethical hinges on how high one sets the bar. For example, is it ethical for advertisers of alcoholic products to place ads in media having an audience of as much as 50 percent underage viewers? (In 2003, growing concerns about underage drinking prompted some beer and distilled-spirits companies to agree to place ads in media with an audience at least 70 percent adult, up from a standard of 50 percent adult.) Is it ethical for an apparel retailer attempting to

Margin notes define core concepts and call attention to important ideas and principles.

Figures scattered throughout the chapters provide conceptual and analytical frameworks.

Figure 2.5   Factors Affecting the Threat of Entry

Entry threats are stronger when:
- The pool of entry candidates is large and some of the candidates have resources that would make them formidable market contenders.
- Entry barriers are low or can be readily hurdled by the likely entry candidates.
- Existing industry members are looking to expand their market reach by entering product segments or geographic areas where they currently do not have a presence.
- Newcomers can expect to earn attractive profits.
- Buyer demand is growing rapidly.
- Industry members are unable (or unwilling) to strongly contest the entry of newcomers.

Rivalry among Competing Sellers

Entry threats are weaker when:
- The pool of entry candidates is small.
- Entry barriers are high.
- Existing competitors are struggling to earn healthy profits.
- The industry's outlook is risky or uncertain.
- Buyer demand is growing slowly or is stagnant.
- Industry members will strongly contest the efforts of new entrants to gain a market foothold.

How strong are the competitive pressures associated with the entry threat from new rivals?

Potential New Entrants

The Key Points section at the end of each chapter provides a handy summary of essential ideas and things to remember.

Key Points

The tasks of crafting and executing company strategies are the heart and soul of managing a business enterprise and winning in the marketplace. A company's strategy consists of the competitive moves and business approaches that management is using to grow the business, stake out a market position, attract and please customers, compete successfully, conduct operations, and achieve organizational objectives. The central thrust of a company's strategy is undertaking moves to build and strengthen the company's long-term competitive position and financial performance and, ideally, gain a competitive advantage over rivals that then becomes a company's ticket to above-average profitability. A company's strategy typically evolves and re-forms over time, emerging from a blend of (1) proactive and purposeful actions on the part of company managers and (2) as-needed reactions to unanticipated developments and fresh market conditions.

Closely related to the concept of strategy is the concept of a company's business model. A company's business model is management's story line for how and why the company's product offerings and competitive approaches will generate a revenue stream and have an associated cost structure that produces attractive earnings and return on investment; in effect, a company's business model sets forth the economic logic for answering the question "How do we intend to make money in this business, given our current strategy?"

The managerial process of crafting and executing a company's strategy consists of five interrelated and integrated phases:

1. *Developing a strategic vision* of where the company needs to head and what its future product-customer-market-technology focus should be. This managerial step provides long term direction, infuses the organization with a sense of purposeful action, and communicates to stakeholders what management's aspirations for the company are.

2. *Setting objectives* and using the targeted results and outcomes as yardsticks for measuring the company's performance and progress. Objectives need to spell out *how much* of *what kind* of performance *by when,* and they need to require a significant amount of organizational stretch. A balanced-scorecard approach for measuring company performance entails setting both *financial objectives* and *strategic objectives.*

3. *Crafting a strategy to achieve the objectives* and move the company along the strategic course that management has charted. Crafting strategy is concerned principally with forming responses to changes under way in the external environment,

Exercises

1. Go to www.redhat.com and check the company's latest financial reports to determine how well the company's business model is working. Is the company profitable? Is its revenue stream from selling technical support services growing or declining as a percentage of total revenues? Does your review of the company's financial performance suggest that its business model and strategy are changing?

2. Go to www.levistrauss.com/about/vision and read what Levi Strauss & Company says about how its corporate values of originality, empathy, integrity, and courage are connected to its vision of clothing the world. Do you buy what the company says, or are its statements just a bunch of nice pontifications that represent the personal values of the CEO (and make for good public relations)? Explain.

3. Go to the investors' section of www.heinz.com and read the letter to the shareholders in the company's fiscal 2003 annual report. Is the vision for Heinz that is articulated by Chairman and CEO William R. Johnson sufficiently clear and well defined? Why or why not? If you were a shareholder, would you be satisfied with what Johnson has told you about the company's direction, performance targets, and strategy? Now read Johnson's letter to the shareholders in Heinz's 2004 annual report. Do the results he cites change your mind about Johnson's vision for Heinz and the caliber of his strategy?

Several short, mostly Internet-research-related exercises at the end of each chapter help reinforce core concepts and provide an alternative to case assignments.

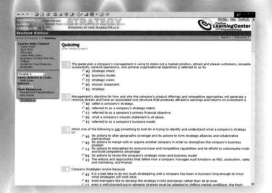

Web Site: <u>www.mhhe.com/ thompson2e</u>

The student portion of the Web site features 20-question self-scoring chapter tests and a select number of PowerPoint slides for each chapter.

The *GLO-BUS* Online Simulation and the Online Edition of *The Business Strategy Game*

Either of these course supplements emotionally connects you to the subject matter of the course by having teams of students manage companies in a head-to-head contest for global market leadership. A simulation puts you in a situation where you and comanagers have to make decisions relating to production operations, workforce compensation, pricing and marketing, and finance. It is your job to craft and execute a strategy for your company that is powerful enough to deliver good bottom-line performance despite the efforts of rival companies to take away your company's sales and market share. Each company competes in North America, Latin America, Europe-Africa, and Asia.

PowerWeb

With each new copy of this text, students gain access to the publisher's PowerWeb site offering current news, articles from 6,300 premium sources, a Web research guide, current readings from annual editions, and links to related sites.

Contents
in Brief

Contents

3 Analyzing a Company's Resources and Competitive Position 82

Part Three Crafting the Strategy

4 Crafting a Strategy: The Quest for Competitive Advantage 112

5 Competing in Foreign Markets 158

6 Diversification: Strategies for Managing a Group of Businesses 190

7 Strategy, Ethics, and Social Responsibility 238

What Do We Mean by Business Ethics? 239
Where Do Ethical Standards Come From—Are They Universal or Dependent on Local Norms and Situational Circumstances? 239
The School of Ethical Universalism 240
The School of Ethical Relativism 240
Ethics and Integrative Social Contracts Theory 244
The Three Categories of Management Morality 246

Part Four Executing the Strategy

8 Executing the Strategy: Building a Capable Organization and Instilling a Culture 272

9 Managing Internal Operations in Ways That Promote Good Strategy Execution 316

Part Five Readings in Strategy

STRATEGY

CHAPTER 1

What Is Strategy and Why Is It Important?

A strategy is a commitment to undertake one set of actions rather than another.

—*Sharon Oster, professor, Yale University*

Without a strategy the organization is like a ship without a rudder.

—*Joel Ross and Michael Kami*

Unless we change our direction we are likely to end up where we are headed.

—*Ancient Chinese proverb*

If you don't know where you are going, any road will take you there.

—*The Koran*

Management's job is not to see the company as it is . . . but as it can become.

—*John W. Teets, former CEO, Greyhound Corp.*

Managers

at all companies must address and have timely answers to three central questions: What's the company's present situation? Where does the company need to go from here? How should it get there? The question *"What's the company's present situation?"* pushes managers to evaluate industry conditions and competitive pressures, the company's current performance and market standing, its resource strengths and capabilities, and its competitive weaknesses. The question *"Where does the company need to go from here?"* forces management to think strategically about the direction the company should be headed in order to grow the business and strengthen the company's market standing and financial performance. The question *"How should it get there?"* challenges managers to craft and execute a strategy to move the company down the chosen strategic path and achieve the targeted outcomes.

What Is Strategy?

A company's **strategy** is management's game plan for growing the business, staking out a market position, attracting and pleasing customers, competing successfully, conducting operations, and achieving targeted objectives. In crafting a strategy, management is in effect saying, "Among all the strategic paths we could have chosen and all the strategic actions we could have taken, we have decided to focus on these markets and customer needs, compete in this fashion, allocate our resources and energies in these ways, and use these particular approaches to doing business." A company's strategy thus indicates the choices its managers have made about the specific actions it is taking and plans to take in order to move the company in the intended direction and achieve the targeted outcomes. It is partly the result of trial-and-error organizational learning about what worked in the past and what didn't and partly the product of managerial analysis and strategic thinking about what actions need to be taken in light of all the circumstances surrounding the company's situation.

> **Core Concept**
>
> A company's **strategy** consists of the competitive moves and business approaches that managers employ to grow the business, stake out a market position, attract and please customers, compete successfully, conduct operations, and achieve targeted objectives.

In most industries companies have considerable strategic freedom in choosing the hows of strategy.[1] Thus some rivals strive to improve their performance and market standing by driving down costs, while others pursue product superiority or personalized customer service or development of competencies and capabilities that rivals cannot match. Some target the high end of the market, while others go after the middle or low end; some opt for wide product lines, while others concentrate their energies on a narrow product lineup. Some competitors position themselves in only one part of the industry's chain of production/distribution activities (preferring to be just in manufacturing or wholesale distribution or retailing), while others are partially or fully integrated, with operations ranging from components production to manufacturing and assembly to wholesale distribution or retailing. Some rivals deliberately confine their operations to local or regional markets; others opt to compete nationally, internationally (several countries), or globally (as many countries as possible). Some companies decide to operate in only one industry, while others diversify broadly or narrowly, into related or unrelated industries, via acquisitions, joint ventures, strategic alliances, or internal start-ups.

At companies intent on gaining sales and market share at the expense of competitors, managers lean toward mostly offensive strategies, frequently launching fresh initiatives of one kind or another to make the company's product offering more distinctive and appealing to buyers. Conservative, risk-avoiding companies prefer a sound defense to an aggressive offense; their strategies emphasize making gradual gains in the marketplace, fortifying the company's market position, and defending against the latest maneuvering of rivals and other developments that threaten the company's well-being.

There is no shortage of opportunity to fashion a strategy that tightly fits a company's own particular situation and that is discernibly different from the strategies of rivals. Carbon-copy strategies among companies in the same industry are the exception rather than the rule.

For a concrete example of the actions and approaches that comprise strategy, see Company Spotlight 1.1, describing Comcast's strategy to revolutionize the cable TV business.

Strategy and the Quest for Competitive Advantage

> ### Core Concept
>
> A company achieves sustainable competitive advantage when an attractive number of buyers prefer its products or services over the offerings of competitors and when the basis for this preference is durable.

Typically, the central thrust of a company's strategy involves crafting moves to strengthen the company's long-term competitive position and financial performance. Indeed, what separates a powerful strategy from an ordinary or weak one is management's ability to forge a series of moves, both in the marketplace and internally, that makes the company *distinctive*, tilts the playing field in the company's favor by giving buyers reason to prefer its products or services, and produces a *sustainable competitive advantage* over rivals. With a durable competitive advantage, a company has good prospects for winning in the marketplace and realizing above-average profitability. Without competitive advantage, a company risks being outcompeted by stronger rivals and/or locked into mediocre financial performance.

Four of the most frequently used strategic approaches to setting a company apart from rivals and achieving a sustainable competitive advantage are:

1. *Striving to be the industry's low-cost provider, thereby aiming for a cost-based competitive advantage over rivals.* Wal-Mart and Southwest Airlines have earned strong market positions because of the low-cost advantages they have achieved over their rivals and their consequent ability to underprice their competitors.

2. *Outcompeting rivals on the basis of such differentiating features as higher quality, wider product selection, added performance, better service, more attractive styling, technological superiority, or unusually good value for the money.* Successful adopters of differentiation strategies include Johnson & Johnson in baby products (product reliability), Harley-Davidson (bad-boy image and king-of-the-road styling), Chanel and Rolex (top-of-the-line prestige), Mercedes and BMW (engineering design and performance), L.L. Bean (good value), and Amazon.com (wide selection and convenience).

3. *Focusing on a narrow market niche and winning a competitive edge by doing a better job than rivals of serving the special needs and tastes of buyers constituting the niche.* Prominent companies that enjoy competitive success in a specialized market niche include eBay in online auctions, Jiffy Lube International in quick oil

COMPANY SPOTLIGHT 1.1

Comcast's Strategy to Revolutionize the Cable Industry

In 2004 cable TV giant Comcast was putting the finishing touches on a bold strategy to change the way people watched television and to grow its business by introducing Internet phone service. With revenues of $18 billion and almost 22 million of the 74 million U.S. cable subscribers, Comcast became the industry leader in the U.S. market in 2002 when it acquired AT&T Broadband and its 13 million cable subscribers for about $50 billion. Comcast's strategy in 2004 had the following elements:

- *Roll out a new video-on-demand service that would allow customers to watch TV programs whenever they wanted to watch them.* The service allowed customers to use their remotes to choose from a menu of thousands of programs, stored on Comcast's servers as they were first broadcast, and included network shows, news, sports, and movies; viewers had the ability to pause, stop, restart, and save programs, without having to remember to record them when they were broadcast. After only 18 months, Comcast had signed up close to 5 million of its subscribers for the service and it was introducing the service in additional geographic markets at a brisk pace.

- *Partner with Sony, MGM, and others to expand Comcast's library of movie offerings.* In 2004, Comcast agreed to develop new cable channels using MGM and Sony libraries, which had a combined 7,500 movies and 42,000 TV shows—it took about 300 movies to feed a 24-hour channel for a month.

- *Continue to roll out high-speed Internet or broadband service to customers via cable modems.* Comcast was already America's number-one provider of broadband service with about 6 million customers that generated revenues of $3 billion annually.

- *Use "voice-over-Internet-protocol" (VOIP) technology to offer subscribers Internet-based phone service at a fraction of the cost charged by other providers.* VOIP is an appealing low-cost technology that is widely seen as the most significant new communication technology since the invention of the telephone, with the capability to alter the world's $750 billion voice communications industry. Comcast was planning on a VOIP service with many snazzy features, including call forwarding, caller ID, and conferencing.

- *Use the video-on-demand and VOIP service offerings to differentiate Comcast's service offering and combat mounting competition from direct-to-home satellite TV providers.* Cable's two-way communications connection to homes enabled viewers to call up the programs they wanted with a few clicks of the remote; satellite TV had no such capability, nor did satellite providers yet have the capability to offer reliable high-speed Internet access. Satellite TV had been stealing customers away from cable TV because of its lower monthly fees—in the first six months of 2004, Direct TV and Echostar together added about 1.7 million new subscribers, whereas Comcast had lost 61,000 subscribers.

- *Employ a sales force (currently numbering about 3,200 people) to sell advertising to businesses that were shifting some of their advertising dollars from sponsoring network programs to sponsoring cable programs.* Ad sales generated revenues of $1.3 billion, and Comcast had cable operations in 21 of the 25 largest markets in the United States.

- *Significantly improve Comcast's customer service.* Almost all cable subscribers were dissatisfied with the caliber of customer service offered by their local cable companies. Comcast management believed that service would be a big issue given the need to support video on demand, cable modems, high-definition TV, phone service, Internet access, and the array of customer inquiries and problems such services entailed. In 2004, Comcast employed about 12,500 people to answer an expected volume of 200 million phone calls. Newly hired customer service personnel were given five weeks of classroom training, followed by three weeks of taking calls while a supervisor listened in—it cost Comcast about $7 to handle each call. The company's goal was to answer 90 percent of calls within 30 seconds.

Sources: Marc Gunter, "Comcast Wants to Change the World, but Can It Learn to Answer the Phone?" *Fortune*, October 16, 2004, pp. 140–156, and Stephanie N. Mehta, "The Future Is on the Line," *Fortune*, July 26, 2004, pp. 121–130. ©2004 TIME INC. Reprinted by permission.

changes, McAfee in virus protection software, Starbucks in premium coffees and coffee drinks, Whole Foods Market in natural and organic foods, and Krispy Kreme in doughnuts.

4. *Developing expertise and resource strengths that give the company competitive capabilities that rivals can't easily imitate or trump with capabilities of their own.* FedEx has superior capabilities in next-day delivery of small packages, Walt Disney has hard-to-beat capabilities in theme park management and family entertainment, and IBM has wide-ranging capabilities in helping corporate customers develop information systems and effectively utilize information technology.

In established industries, most companies recognize that winning a durable competitive edge over rivals hinges more on building competitively valuable expertise and capabilities than it does on having a distinctive product. Rivals can nearly always copy the attributes of a popular or innovative product, but for rivals to match experience, know-how, and specialized competitive capabilities that a company has developed and perfected over a long period of time is substantially harder to do and takes much longer—despite years of trying, discounters like Kmart and Target have struck out trying to match Wal-Mart's sophisticated distribution systems and its finely honed merchandising expertise. Company initiatives to build competencies and capabilities that rivals don't have and cannot readily match can relate to greater product innovation capabilities than rivals (3M Corporation), better mastery of a complex technological process (Michelin in making radial tires), expertise in defect-free manufacturing (Toyota and Honda), specialized marketing and merchandising know-how (Coca-Cola), global sales and distribution capability (Black & Decker in power tools), superior e-commerce capabilities (Dell Computer), unique ability to deliver personalized customer service (Ritz Carlton and Four Seasons hotels), or anything else that constitutes a competitively valuable strength in creating, producing, distributing, or marketing the company's product or service.

But there's also another way to achieve a dramatic and durable competitive advantage: by abandoning efforts to beat out competitors in existing markets and, instead, inventing a new industry or distinctive market segment that makes existing competitors largely irrelevant and allows a company to create and capture altogether new demand.[2] To understand this approach a bit better, think of the business universe as consisting of two distinct types of market space. In one, industry boundaries are defined and accepted, the competitive rules of the game are well understood by all industry members, and companies try to outperform rivals by capturing a bigger share of existing demand; in such markets, lively competition constrains a company's prospects for rapid growth and superior profitability since rivals move quickly to either imitate or counter the successes of competitors. In the other type of market space, the industry does not really exist yet, is untainted by competition, and offers wide-open opportunity for profitable and rapid growth if a company can come up with a product offering and strategy that allows it to create new demand rather than fight over existing demand. A terrific example of the latter is eBay's creation and domination of the online auction industry. Another example is Cirque du Soleil, which has increased its revenues by 22 times during the 1993–2003 period in the circus business, an industry that has been in long-term decline for 20 years. How did Cirque du Soleil pull this off against long-time industry leader Ringling Bros. and Barnum & Bailey? By "reinventing the circus," creating a distinctively different market space for its performances (Las Vegas nightclubs and theater-type settings), and pulling in a whole new group of customers—adults and corporate clients—who were noncustomers of traditional circuses and were willing to pay several times more than the price of a conventional circus ticket to have an "entertainment experience" featuring sophisticated clowns and star-quality acrobatic acts in a comfortable, tentlike atmosphere—Cirque studiously avoided the use of animals because of costs and concerns over the treatment of circus animals; Cirque's market research led management to conclude that the lasting allure of the traditional circus came down to just three factors: the clowns, classic acrobatic acts, and a tentlike stage. As of 2004, Cirque du Soleil had nine different touring shows (each with its own theme and story line) running on three continents, was performing before audiences of about 7 million people annually, and had performed 250 engagements in 90 cities before 40 million spectators since its formation in 1984. Other examples of companies that have achieved competitive advantages by creating new market spaces include AMC via its pioneering of megaplex movie theaters, IBM with its invention of the business computer industry in the 1950s, CNN and The Weather Channel in cable TV, Home Depot in "big-box" retailing of hardware and building supplies, and FedEx in overnight package delivery. Companies that create new market spaces can usually sustain their initially won competitive advantage without encountering major competitive challenge for 10 to 15 years because of barriers to imitation and the strong brand-name awareness that their strategies produce.

Identifying a Company's Strategy

A company's strategy is reflected in its actions in the marketplace and the statements of senior managers about the company's current business approaches, future plans, and efforts to strengthen its competitiveness and performance. Figure 1.1 shows what to look for in identifying the substance of a company's overall strategy.

Once it is clear what to look for, the task of identifying a company's strategy is mainly one of researching information about the company's actions in the marketplace and its business approaches. In the case of publicly owned enterprises, the strategy is often openly discussed by senior executives in the company's annual report and 10-K report, in press releases and company news (posted on the company's Web site), and in the information provided to investors at the company's Web site. To maintain the confidence of investors and Wall Street, most public companies have to be fairly open about their strategies. Company executives typically lay out key elements of their strategies in presentations to securities analysts (such presentations are usually posted in the investor relations section of the company's Web site). Hence, except for some about-to-be-launched moves and changes that remain under wraps and in the planning stage, there's usually nothing secret or undiscoverable about what a company's present strategy is.

Strategy Is Partly Proactive and Partly Reactive

A company's strategy is typically a blend of (1) proactive actions on the part of managers to improve the company's market position and financial performance and (2) as-needed reactions to unanticipated developments and fresh market conditions—see Figure 1.2.[3] The biggest portion of a company's current strategy flows from previously initiated actions and business approaches that are working well enough to merit continuation and newly launched managerial initiatives to strengthen the company's overall position and performance. This part of management's game plan is deliberate and proactive, standing as the product of management's analysis and strategic thinking

Figure 1.1   Identifying a Company's Strategy—What to Look For

Actions to gain sales and market share via lower prices, more performance features, more appealing design, better quality or customer service, wider product selection, or other such actions

Actions to diversify the company's revenues and earnings by entering new businesses

Actions to respond to changing market conditions or other external circumstances

Actions to strengthen competitive capabilities and correct competitive weaknesses

Actions to enter new geographic or product markets or exit existing ones

The pattern of actions and business approaches that define a company's strategy

Actions and approaches that define how R&D, production, sales and marketing, finance, and other key activities are being managed

Actions to pursue new market opportunities and defend against threats to the company's well-being

Actions to form strategic alliances and collaborative partnerships

Actions to merge with or acquire rival companies

about the company's situation and its conclusions about how to position the company in the marketplace and compete for buyer patronage.

But not every strategic move is the result of proactive plotting and deliberate management design. Things happen that cannot be fully anticipated or planned for. When market and competitive conditions take an unexpected turn or certain aspects of a company's strategy hit a stone wall, some kind of strategic reaction or adjustment is required. Hence, a portion of a company's strategy is always developed on the fly, coming as a reasoned response to fresh strategic maneuvers on the part of rival firms, shifting customer requirements and expectations, new technologies and market opportunities, a changing political or economic climate, or other unanticipated happenings in the surrounding environment. But apart from adapting strategy to changing conditions, there is also a need to adapt strategy as new learning emerges about which pieces

Figure 1.2   A Company's Actual Strategy Is Partly Proactive and Partly Reactive

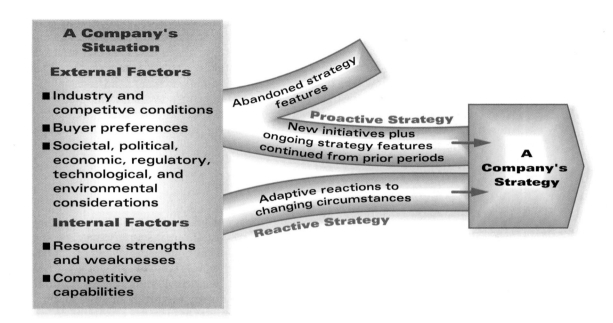

of the strategy are working well and which aren't and as management hits upon new ideas for improving the strategy. Crafting a strategy thus involves stitching together a *proactive/intended strategy* and then adapting first one piece and then another as circumstances surrounding the company's situation change or better options emerge—which results in same portion of the overall strategy being *reactive/adaptive*. In short, a company's actual strategy is something managers shape and reshape as circumstances dictate and as managers learn from experience what has worked well enough to continue and what needs to be changed.

A Company's Strategy Evolves over Time   A company's strategy should always be viewed as a work in progress. Most of the time a company's strategy evolves incrementally from management's ongoing efforts to fine-tune this or that piece of the strategy and to adjust certain strategy elements in response to unfolding events. On occasion, fine-tuning the existing strategy is not enough and major strategy shifts are called for, such as when a strategy is clearly failing and the company faces a financial crisis, when market conditions or buyer preferences change significantly and new opportunities arise, when competitors do something unexpected, or when important technological breakthroughs occur. Some industries are more volatile than others. Industry environments characterized by *high-velocity change* require companies to rapidly adapt their strategies.[4] For example, in high-technology industries and industries where buyer demand moves up and down very quickly, companies find it essential to revise demand forecasts, adjust key elements of their strategies, and update their financial projections every few months.

> **Core Concept**
>
> Changing circumstances and ongoing management efforts to improve the strategy cause a company's strategy to evolve over time—a condition that makes the task of crafting a strategy a work in progress, not a one-time event.

Regardless of whether a company's strategy changes gradually or swiftly, the important point is that a company's present strategy is always temporary and on trial, pending new ideas for improvement from management, changes in industry conditions, and any other new developments that management believes warrant strategic adjustments. Thus, a company's strategy at any given point is fluid, representing the temporary outcome of an ongoing process that, on the one hand, involves reasoned and intuitive management efforts to craft an effective strategy and, on the other hand, involves ongoing responses to market change and constant experimentation and tinkering. Adapting to new conditions and constantly learning what is working well enough to continue and what needs to be improved is consequently a normal part of the strategy-making process and results in an evolving strategy.

> A company's strategy is shaped partly by management analysis and choice and partly by the necessity of adapting and learning by doing.

Strategy and Ethics: Passing the Test of Moral Scrutiny

In choosing among strategic alternatives, company managers are well advised to embrace actions that are aboveboard and can pass the test of moral scrutiny. Just keeping a company's strategic actions within the bounds of what is legal does not make them ethical. Ethical and moral standards are not governed by what is legal. Rather, they involve issues of "right" versus "wrong" and *duty*—what one *should* do. A strategy is ethical only if it does not entail actions and behaviors that cross the line from "should do" to "should not do" (because such actions are "unsavory" or unconscionable, injurious to other people, or unnecessarily harmful to the environment).

> **Core Concept**
>
> A strategy cannot be considered ethical just because it involves actions that are legal. To meet the standard of being ethical, a strategy must entail actions that can pass moral scrutiny and that are aboveboard in the sense of not being shady or unconscionable, injurious to others, or unnecessarily harmful to the environment.

Admittedly, it is not always easy to categorize a given strategic behavior as definitely ethical or definitely unethical; many strategic actions fall in a gray zone in between. Whether they are deemed ethical or unethical hinges on how high one sets the bar. For example, is it ethical for advertisers of alcoholic products to place ads in media having an audience of as much as 50 percent underage viewers? (In 2003, growing concerns about underage drinking prompted some beer and distilled-spirits companies to agree to place ads in media with an audience at least 70 percent adult, up from a standard of 50 percent adult.) Is it ethical for an apparel retailer attempting to keep prices attractively low to source clothing from foreign manufacturers that pay substandard wages, utilize child labor, or engage in unsavory sweatshop practices? Many people would say no, but some might argue that a company is not unethical simply because it does not police the business practices of its suppliers. Is it ethical for pharmaceutical manufacturers to charge higher prices for life-saving drugs in some countries than they charge in others? (This is a fairly common practice that has recently come under scrutiny because it raises the costs of health care for consumers who are charged higher prices.) Is it ethical for a pharmaceutical company to downplay issues about the safety of a best-selling drug until more conclusive studies are done (which is apparently what Merck did before it decided to recall Vioxx, which had been taken by some 80 million people)? Is it ethical for a company to turn a blind eye to the damage its operations do to the environment even though they are in compliance with current environmental regulations—especially if it has the know-how and the means to prevent such damage by utilizing different technologies or operating practices?

Senior executives with strong ethical convictions are generally proactive in linking strategic action and ethics; they forbid the pursuit of ethically questionable business opportunities and insist that all aspects of company strategy reflect high ethical standards.[5] They make it clear that all company personnel are expected to act with integrity, and they put organizational checks and balances into place to monitor behavior, enforce ethical codes of conduct, and provide guidance to employees regarding any gray areas. Their commitment to conducting the company's business in an ethical manner is genuine, not hypocritical lip service.

Recent instances of corporate malfeasance, ethical lapses, and fraudulent accounting practices at Enron, WorldCom, Tyco, Adelphia, HealthSouth, and other companies leave no room to doubt the damage to a company's reputation and business that can result from ethical misconduct, corporate misdeeds, and even criminal behavior on the part of company personnel. Aside from just the embarrassment and black marks that accompany headline exposure of a company's unethical practices, the hard fact is that many customers and many suppliers are wary of doing business with a company that engages in sleazy practices or that turns a blind eye to illegal or unethical behavior on the part of employees. They are turned off by unethical strategies or behavior, and rather than become victims or get burned themselves, wary customers will quickly take their business elsewhere and wary suppliers will tread carefully. Moreover, employees with character and integrity do not want to work for a company whose strategies are shady or whose executives lack character and integrity. There's little lasting benefit to unethical strategies and behavior, and the downside risks can be substantial. Besides, such actions are plain wrong.

The Relationship between a Company's Strategy and Its Business Model

Closely related to the concept of strategy is the concept of a company's **business model.** While the word *model* conjures up images of ivory-tower ideas that may be loosely connected to the real world, such images do not apply here. A company's business model sets forth the economic logic of how an enterprise's strategy can deliver value to customers at a price and cost that yields acceptable profitability.[6]

A company's business model thus is management's story line for how and why the company's product offerings and competitive approaches will generate a revenue stream and have an associated cost structure that produces attractive earnings and return on investment. The nitty-gritty issue surrounding a company's business model is whether the chosen strategy makes good business sense from a money-making perspective. The concept of a company's business model is, consequently, more narrowly focused than the concept of a company's business strategy. A company's strategy *relates broadly to its competitive initiatives and business approaches (irrespective of the financial outcomes it produces),* while a company's business model *deals with how and why the revenues and costs flowing from the strategy will result in attractive profits and return on investment*—without the ability to deliver good profits, the strategy and the business are not viable. Companies that have been in business for a while and are making acceptable profits have a "proven" business model—because there is hard evidence that their strategies are capable of profitability and that they are viable business enterprises. Companies that are in a start-up mode or that are losing money have a "questionable" business model; their current strategies have yet to produce good

> **Core Concept**
>
> A company's **business model** deals with how and why the revenues and costs flowing from its strategy will result in attractive profits and return on investment. Without the ability to deliver profitability, the strategy is not viable and the survival of the business is in doubt.

bottom-line results, putting their story line about how they intend to make money and their viability as business enterprises in doubt. Company Spotlight 1.2 discusses the contrasting business models of Microsoft and Red Hat Linux.

What Makes a Strategy a Winner?

Three questions can be used to test the merits of one strategy versus another and distinguish a winning strategy from a losing or mediocre strategy:

1. *How well does the strategy fit the company's situation?* To qualify as a winner, a strategy has to be well matched to industry and competitive conditions, a company's best market opportunities, and other aspects of the enterprise's external environment. At the same time, it has to be tailored to the company's resource strengths and weaknesses, competencies, and competitive capabilities. Unless a strategy exhibits tight fit with both the external and the internal aspects of a company's overall situation, it is likely to produce less than the best possible business results.

2. *Is the strategy helping the company achieve a sustainable competitive advantage?* Winning strategies enable a company to achieve a competitive advantage that is durable. The bigger and more durable the competitive edge that a strategy helps build, the more powerful and appealing the strategy is.

3. *Is the strategy resulting in better company performance?* A winning strategy boosts company performance. Two kinds of performance improvements tell the most about the caliber of a company's strategy: (1) gains in profitability and financial strength and (2) gains in the company's competitive strength and market standing.

speech), and, in some cases, because they are anti-Microsoft and want to have a part in undoing what they see as a Microsoft monopoly.

- Collect and test enhancements and new applications submitted by the open-source community of volunteer programmers. Linux's originator, Linus Torvalds, and a team of more than 300 Red Hat engineers and software developers evaluate which incoming submissions merit inclusion in new releases of Red Hat Linux—the evaluation and integration of new submissions are Red Hat's only up-front product development costs.

- Market the upgraded and tested family of Red Hat Linux products to large enterprises and charge them a subscription fee that includes a limited number of days of service, support, and patches. Provide subscribers with updated versions of Red Hat Linux every 12 to 18 months.

- Make the source code open and available to all users, allowing them to create a customized version of Linux.

- Capitalize on the specialized expertise required to use Linux in multiserver, multiprocessor applications by providing fee-based training, consulting, support, engineering, and content management services to Red Hat Linux users. Red Hat offers Linux certification training programs at all skill levels at more than 60 global locations—Red Hat certification in the use of Linux is considered the best in the world.

Microsoft's business model—sell proprietary code software and give service away free—is a proven moneymaker that generates billions in profits annually. On the other hand, the jury is still out on Red Hat's business model of selling subscriptions to open-source software to large corporations and depending heavily on sales of technical support services, training, and consulting to generate revenues sufficient to cover costs and yield a profit. Red Hat posted losses of $140 million on revenues of $79 million in fiscal year 2002 and losses of $6.6 million on revenues of $91 million in fiscal year 2003, but it earned $14 million on revenues of $126 million in fiscal 2004. And the profits came from a shift in Red Hat's business model that involved putting considerably more emphasis on selling subscriptions to the latest Red Hat Linux updates to large enterprises.

Source: Company documents and information posted on their Web sites.

Once a company commits to a particular strategy and enough time elapses to assess how well it fits the situation and whether it is actually delivering competitive advantage and better performance, the company can determine what grade to assign its strategy. Strategies that come up short on one or more of the above questions are plainly less appealing than strategies passing all three test questions with flying colors. Managers can use the same questions to pick and choose among alternative strategic actions. A company determining which of several strategic options to employ can evaluate how well each option measures up against each of the three questions. The strategic option with the highest prospective passing scores on all three questions can be regarded as the best or most attractive strategic alternative.

Other criteria for judging the merits of a particular strategy include internal consistency and unity among all the pieces of the strategy, the degree of risk the strategy poses as compared to alternative strategies, and the degree to which it is flexible and adaptable to changing circumstances. These criteria are relevant and merit consideration, but they seldom override the importance of the three test questions posed above.

What Does the Strategy-Making, Strategy-Executing Process Entail?

The managerial process of crafting and executing a company's strategy consists of five interrelated and integrated phases:

1. *Developing a strategic vision* of where the company needs to head and what its future product-customer-market-technology focus should be.

Figure 1.3   The Strategy-Making, Strategy-Executing Process

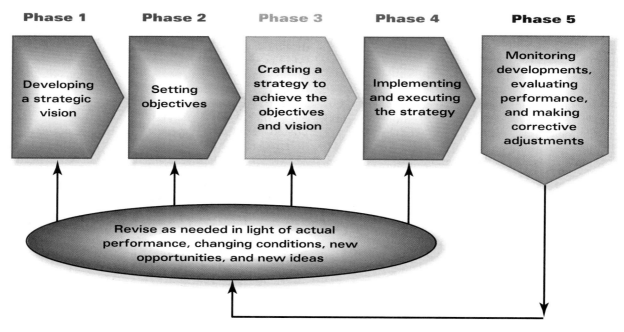

2. *Setting objectives* and using them as yardsticks for measuring the company's performance and progress.

3. *Crafting a strategy to achieve the objectives* and move the company along the strategic course that management has charted.

4. *Implementing and executing the chosen strategy efficiently and effectively.*

5. *Evaluating performance and initiating corrective adjustments* in the company's long-term direction, objectives, strategy, or execution in light of actual experience, changing conditions, new ideas, and new opportunities.

Figure 1.3 displays this five-task process. Let's examine each task in enough detail to set the stage for the forthcoming chapters and give you a bird's-eye view of what this book is about.

Developing a Strategic Vision: Phase 1 of the Strategy-Making, Strategy-Executing Process

Very early in the strategy-making process, a company's senior managers must wrestle with the issue of what directional path the company should take and what changes in the company's product-market-customer-technology focus would improve its current market position and future prospects. Deciding to commit the company to one path versus another pushes managers to draw some carefully reasoned conclusions about how to try to modify the company's business makeup and the market position it should

Table 1.1   FACTORS TO CONSIDER IN DECIDING TO COMMIT THE COMPANY TO ONE DIRECTIONAL PATH VERSUS ANOTHER

External Considerations	Internal Considerations
■ Is the outlook for the company promising if it simply maintains its present product-market-customer-technology focus—does sticking with the company's present strategic course present attractive growth opportunities?	■ What are our ambitions for the company—what industry standing do we want the company to have?
■ Are changes that are under way in the market and competitive landscape acting to enhance or weaken the outlook for the company's present business?	■ Will our present business generate sufficient growth and profitability in the years ahead to please shareholders?
■ What, if any, new customer groups and/or geographic markets should the company get in position to serve?	■ What organizational strengths ought we be trying to leverage in terms of adding new products/services and/or getting into new businesses?
■ Which emerging market opportunities should the company pursue, and which ones should not be pursued?	■ Is the company stretching its resources too thinly by trying to compete in too many markets or segments, some of which are unprofitable?
■ Should we plan to abandon any of the markets, market segments, or customer groups we are currently serving?	■ Is the company's technological focus too broad or too narrow? Are any changes needed?

stake out. A number of direction-shaping factors need to be considered in deciding where to head and why such a direction makes good business sense—see Table 1.1.

Top management's views and conclusions about the company's direction and future product-customer-market-technology focus constitute a **strategic vision** for the company. A strategic vision delineates management's aspirations for the business, providing a panoramic view of "where we are going" and a convincing rationale for why this makes good business sense for the company. A strategic vision thus points an organization in a particular direction, charts a strategic path for it to follow in preparing for the future, and molds organizational identity. A clearly articulated strategic vision communicates management's aspirations to stakeholders and helps steer the energies of company personnel in a common direction. For instance, Henry Ford's vision of a car in every garage had power because it captured the imagination of others, aided internal efforts to mobilize the Ford Motor Company's resources, and served as a reference point for gauging the merits of the company's strategic actions.

> **Core Concept**
>
> A **strategic vision** describes the route a company intends to take in developing and strengthening its business. It paints a picture of a company's destination and provides a rationale for going there.

Well-conceived visions are distinctive and specific to a particular organization; they avoid generic, feel-good statements like "We will become a global leader and the first choice of customers in every market we choose to serve"—which could apply to any of hundreds of organizations.[7] And they are not the product of a committee charged with coming up with an innocuous but well-meaning one-sentence vision that wins consensus approval from various stakeholders. Nicely worded vision statements with no specifics about the company's product-market-customer-technology focus are suspect. A strategic vision proclaiming management's quest "to be the market leader" or "to be the first choice of customers" or "to be the most innovative" or "to be recognized as the best company in the industry" offers scant guidance about a company's direction and what management intends to do to get there.

For a strategic vision to function as a valuable managerial tool, it must provide understanding of what management wants the company's business to look like and provide managers with a reference point in making strategic decisions and preparing the company for the future. It must say something definitive about how the company's leaders

Table 1.2   CHARACTERISTICS OF AN EFFECTIVELY-WORDED VISION STATEMENT

Graphic: Paints a picture of the kind of company that management is trying to create and the market position the company is striving to stake out.

Directional: Says something about the company's journey or destination and signals the kinds of business and strategic changes that will be forthcoming.

Focused: Is specific enough to provide managers with guidance in making decisions and allocating resources.

Flexible: Is not a once and for all time statement—visions about a company's future state and directional path may need to change as events unfold and circumstances change.

Feasible: Is within the realm of what the company can reasonably expect to achieve in due time.

Desirable: Appeals to the long-term interests of stakeholders—particularly shareowners, employees, and customers.

Easy to communicate: Is explainable in 5 to 10 minutes and, ideally, can be reduced to a simple, memorable "slogan" (like Henry Ford's famous vision of "a car in every garage").

Source: Based partly on John P. Kotter, *Leading Change* (Boston: Harvard Business School Press, 1996), p. 72, and Hugh Davidson, *The Committed Enterprise* (Oxford: Butterworth Heinemann, 2002), Chapters 1 and 2.

Table 1.3   COMMON SHORTCOMINGS IN COMPANY VISION STATEMENTS

1. Vague or incomplete—short on specifics about where the company is headed, what kind of company management is trying to create, and whether or how management intends to alter the company's current product-market-customer-technology focus.
2. Bland or lacking in motivational power.
3. Not distinctive—could apply to almost any company (or at least several others in the same industry).
4. Too reliant on such superlatives as *best, most successful, recognized leader, global* or *worldwide leader,* or *first choice of customers.*
5. Fails to identify what business or industry the vision applies to—the vision is so generic that it could apply to companies in any of several industries.
6. So broad that it doesn't rule out almost any opportunity that management might opt to pursue.

Source: Adapted from Hugh Davidson, *The Committed Enterprise* (Oxford: Butterworth Heinemann, 2002), Chapter 2, and Michel Robert, *Strategy Pure and Simple II* (New York: McGraw-Hill, 1998), Chapters 2, 3, and 6.

intend to position the company beyond where it is today. A good vision always needs to be a bit beyond a company's reach, but progress toward the vision is what unifies the efforts of company personnel. Table 1.2 lists some characteristics of an effective vision statement.

A sampling of vision statements currently in use shows a range from strong and clear to overly general and generic. A surprising number of the vision statements found on company Web sites and in annual reports are vague and unrevealing—some are nice-sounding but say little, others read like something written by a committee and worded to win the support of different stakeholders, and some are so generic and short on specifics as to apply to almost any company in any industry. Many read like a public relations statement—high-sounding words that someone came up with because it is fashionable for companies to have an official vision statement.[8] Table 1.3 provides a list of the most common shortcomings in company vision statements. The one- or two-sentence vision statements most companies make available to the public, of course, provide only a glimpse of what company executives are really thinking and the strategic course they have charted—company personnel nearly always have a much better understanding of the ins and outs of where the company is headed and why than is revealed in the official vision statement. But the real purpose of a vision statement is to serve as a management tool for giving the organization a sense of direction. Like any tool, it can be used properly or improperly, either clearly conveying a company's strategic course or not doing so.

Company Spotlight 1.3 provides examples of strategic visions of several prominent companies and nonprofit organizations. See if you can tell which ones are mostly meaningless or nice-sounding and which ones are managerially useful in communicating "where we are headed and the kind of company we are trying to become."

A Strategic Vision Is Different from a Mission Statement

Whereas the chief concern of a strategic vision is "where we are going and why," a company mission statement usually deals with a company's *present* business scope and purpose—"who we are, what we do, and why we are here." *A company's mission is defined by the buyer needs it seeks to satisfy, the customer groups and market segments it is endeavoring to serve, and the resources and technologies it is deploying in trying to please its customers.* (Many companies prefer the term *business purpose* to *mission statement,* but the two phrases are essentially conceptually identical and are used interchangeably.) A typical example is the mission statement of Trader Joe's (a unique grocery chain):

> The mission of Trader Joe's is to give our customers the best food and beverage values that they can find anywhere and to provide them with the information required for informed buying decisions. We provide these with a dedication to the highest quality of customer satisfaction delivered with a sense of warmth, friendliness, fun, individual pride, and company spirit.

> The distinction between a strategic vision and a mission statement is fairly clear-cut: A *strategic vision* portrays a company's future business scope ("where we are going") whereas a company's *mission* typically describes its present business scope and purpose ("who we are, what we do, and why we are here").

The mission statements that one finds in company annual reports or on company Web sites typically provide a brief overview of the company's present business purpose and raison d'être and sometimes its geographic coverage or standing as a market leader. They may or may not single out the company's present products/services, the buyer needs it is seeking to satisfy, the customer groups it serves, or its technological and business capabilities. But rarely do company mission statements say anything about where the company is headed, the anticipated changes in its business, or its aspirations; hence they lack the essential quality of a strategic vision in defining a company's future product-customer-market-technology focus.

Occasionally, companies couch their mission in terms of making a profit. This is misguided. Profit is more correctly an *objective* and a *result* of what a company does. Moreover, earning a profit is the obvious intent of every commercial enterprise. Such companies as BMW, Google, Caterpillar, Nintendo, and Nokia are each striving to earn a profit for shareholders; but plainly the fundamentals of their business are substantially different when it comes to "who we are and what we do." It is management's answer to "make a profit doing what and for whom?" that reveals a company's true substance and business purpose. A well-conceived mission statement distinguishes a company's business makeup from that of other profit-seeking enterprises in language specific enough to give the company its own identity.

Communicating the Strategic Vision

Effectively communicating the strategic vision down the line to lower-level managers and employees is as important as the strategic soundness of the long-term direction top management has chosen. People have a need to believe that senior management knows where it's trying to take the company and is planning for what changes lie ahead both externally and internally. Unless frontline employees understand why the strategic course that management has charted is reasonable and beneficial, they are unlikely to unite behind managerial efforts to get the organization moving in the intended direction.

Core Concept

An effectively communicated vision is a valuable management tool for enlisting the commitment of company personnel to actions that get the company moving in the intended direction.

Winning the support of organization members for the vision nearly always means putting "where we are going and why" in writing, distributing the statement organizationwide, and having executives personally explain the vision and its rationale to as many people as feasible. Ideally, executives should present their vision for the company in a manner that reaches out and grabs people. An engaging and convincing strategic vision has enormous motivational value—for the same reason that a stonemason is more inspired by building a great cathedral for the ages than by simply laying stones to create floors and walls. When managers articulate a vivid and compelling case for where the company is headed, organization members begin to say, "This is interesting and has a lot of merit. I want to be involved and do my part to help make it happen." The more that a vision evokes positive support and excitement, the greater its impact in terms of arousing a committed organizational effort and getting people to move in a common direction.[9] Thus executive ability to paint a convincing and inspiring picture of a company journey and destination is an important element of effective strategic leadership.

Expressing the Essence of the Vision in a Slogan   The task of effectively conveying the vision to company personnel is assisted when management can capture the vision of where to head in a catchy or easily remembered slogan. A number of organizations have summed up their vision in a brief phrase:

- *Levi Strauss & Company:* "We will clothe the world by marketing the most appealing and widely worn casual clothing in the world."
- *Nike:* "To bring innovation and inspiration to every athlete in the world."
- *Mayo Clinic:* "The best care to every patient every day."
- *Scotland Yard:* "To make London the safest major city in the world."
- *Greenpeace:* "To halt environmental abuse and promote environmental solutions."
- *Charles Schwab:* "To provide customers with the most useful and ethical financial services in the world."

> Strategic visions become real only when the vision statement is imprinted in the minds of organization members and then translated into hard objectives and strategies.

Creating a short slogan to illuminate an organization's direction and purpose and then using it repeatedly as a reminder of "where we are headed and why" helps rally organization members to hurdle whatever obstacles lie in the company's path and to maintain their focus.

Linking the Vision with Company Values

In the course of deciding "who we are and where we are going," many companies also come up with a statement of values to guide the company's pursuit of its vision. By *values,* we mean the beliefs, business principles, and ways of doing things that govern company operations and the behavior of organization members. Values, good and bad, exist in every organization. They relate to such things as fairness, integrity, ethics, innovativeness, teamwork, quality, customer service, social responsibility, and community citizenship. Company value statements tend to contain between four and eight values, which, ideally, are tightly connected to and reinforce the company's vision, strategy, and operating practices. Home Depot embraces eight values (entrepreneurial spirit, excellent customer service, giving back to the community, respect for all people, doing the

> **Core Concept**
>
> A company's *values* are the beliefs, business principles, and practices that guide the conduct of its business, the pursuit of its strategic vision, and the behavior of company personnel.

right thing, taking care of people, building strong relationships, and creating shareholder value) in its quest to become the world's largest home improvement retailer by operating warehouse stores filled with a wide assortment of products at the lowest prices and staffed with trained associates giving absolutely the best customer service in the industry. Du Pont stresses four values—safety, ethics, respect for people, and environmental stewardship; the first three have been in place since the company was founded 200 years ago by the Du Pont family. Loblaw, a major grocery chain in

Canada, focuses on just two main values in operating its stores—competence and honesty; it expects employees to display both, and top management strives to promote only those employees who are smart and honest. At Johnson & Johnson, the two core values are teamwork and manufacturing the highest-quality products.

Company managers connect values to the strategic vision in one of two ways. In companies with long-standing and deeply entrenched values, managers go to great lengths to explain how the vision matches the company's values, sometimes reinterpreting the meaning of existing values to indicate their relevance to the strategic vision. In new companies or companies having weak or incomplete sets of values, top management considers what values, beliefs, and operating principles will help drive the vision forward. Then new values that fit the vision are drafted and circulated among managers and employees for discussion and possible modification. A final value statement that connects to the vision and that reflects the beliefs and principles the company wants to uphold is then officially adopted. Some companies combine their vision and values into a single statement or document provided to all organization members and often posted on the company's Web site.

Of course, a wide gap sometimes opens between a company's stated values and its business practices. Enron, for example, touted its four corporate values—respect, integrity, communication, and excellence—but some top officials did not behave in accordance with those values and the $100 billion high-profile company imploded in late 2000 when executive failure to "walk the talk" was exposed. Once one of the world's Big Five public accounting firms, Arthur Andersen was renowned for its commitment to the highest standards of audit integrity, but its audit failures at Enron, WorldCom, and other companies led to Andersen's rapid demise.

Setting Objectives: Phase 2 of the Strategy-Making, Strategy-Executing Process

The managerial purpose of setting **objectives** is to convert the strategic vision into specific performance targets—results and outcomes the company's management wants to achieve—and then use these objectives as yardsticks for tracking the company's progress and performance. Well-stated objectives are *quantifiable,* or *measurable,* and contain a *deadline for achievement.* As Bill Hewlett, cofounder of Hewlett-Packard, shrewdly observed, "You cannot manage what you cannot measure. . . . And what gets measured gets done."[10] The experiences of countless companies and managers teach that precisely spelling out *how much* of *what kind* of performance *by when* and then pressing forward with actions and incentives calculated to help achieve the targeted outcomes greatly improve a company's actual performance. It definitely beats setting vague targets like "maximize profits," "reduce costs," "become more efficient," or "increase sales," which specify neither how much nor when, or exhorting company personnel to try hard to do the best they can and then living with whatever results they deliver.

> **Core Concept**
>
> **Objectives** are an organization's performance targets—the results and outcomes management wants to achieve. They function as yardsticks for measuring how well the organization is doing.

Ideally, managers ought to use the objective-setting exercise as a tool for *stretching an organization to reach its full potential.* Challenging company personnel to go all out and deliver big gains in performance pushes an enterprise to be more inventive, to exhibit some urgency in improving both its financial performance and its business position, and to be more intentional and focused in its actions. *Stretch objectives* spur exceptional performance and help build a firewall against contentment with slow, incremental improvements in organizational performance. As Mitchell Leibovitz, former CEO of the auto parts and service retailer Pep Boys, once said, "If you want to have ho-hum results, have ho-hum objectives."

What Kinds of Objectives to Set— The Need for a Balanced Scorecard

> **Core Concept**
>
> *Financial objectives* relate to the financial performance targets management has established for the organization to achieve. *Strategic objectives* relate to target outcomes that indicate a company is strengthening its market standing, competitive vitality, and future business prospects.

Two very distinct types of performance yardsticks are required: those relating to *financial performance* (outcomes relating to profitability, creditworthiness, and shareholder well-being) and those relating to *strategic performance* (outcomes that indicate a company is strengthening its marketing standing, competitive vitality, and future business prospects). Examples of commonly used financial and strategic objectives include the following:

Financial Objectives	**Strategic Objectives**
■ An *x* percent increase in annual revenues	■ Winning an *x* percent market share
■ Annual increases in after-tax profits of *x* percent	■ Achieving lower overall costs than rivals
■ Annual increases in earnings per share of *x* percent	■ Overtaking key competitors on product performance or quality or customer service
■ Annual dividend increases	■ Deriving *x* percent of revenues from the sale of new products introduced within the past five years
■ Larger profit margins	
■ An *x* percent return on capital employed (ROCE) or shareholder investment (ROE)	■ Achieving technological leadership
	■ Having better product selection than rivals
■ Increased shareholder value—in the form of an upward-trending stock price and annual dividend increases	■ Strengthening the company's brand-name appeal
■ Strong bond and credit ratings	■ Having stronger national or global sales and distribution capabilities than rivals
■ Sufficient internal cash flows to fund new capital investment	
■ Stable earnings during periods of recession	■ Consistently getting new or improved products to market ahead of rivals

Achieving acceptable financial results is a must. Without adequate profitability and financial strength, a company's pursuit of its strategic vision, as well as its long-term health and ultimate survival, is jeopardized. Further, subpar earnings and a weak balance sheet alarm shareholders and creditors and put the jobs of senior executives at risk. But good financial performance, by itself, is not enough. Of equal or greater importance is a company's strategic performance—outcomes that indicate whether a company's market position and competitiveness are deteriorating, holding steady, or improving.

The Case for a Balanced Scorecard: Improved Strategic Performance Fosters Better Financial Performance

A company's financial performance measures are really *lagging indicators* that reflect the results of past decisions and organizational activities. But a company's past or current financial performance is not a reliable indicator of its future prospects—poor financial performers often turn things around and do better, while good financial performers can fall upon hard times. The best and most reliable *leading indicators* of a company's future financial performance and business prospects are strategic outcomes that indicate whether the company's competitiveness and market position are stronger or weaker. For instance, if a company has set aggressive strategic objectives and is achieving them—such that its competitive strength and market position are on the rise—then there's reason to expect that its *future* financial performance will be better than its current or past performance. If a company is losing ground to competitors and its market position is slipping—outcomes that reflect weak strategic performance (and, very likely, failure to achieve its strategic objectives)—then its ability to maintain its present profitability is highly suspect. Hence the degree to which a company's managers set, pursue, and achieve stretch strategic objectives tends to be a reliable leading indicator of its ability to generate higher profits from business operations.

> **Core Concept**
>
> A company that pursues and achieves strategic outcomes that boost its competitiveness and strength in the marketplace is in a much better position to improve its future financial performance.

Thus, a balanced scorecard for measuring company performance—one that includes both financial objectives and strategic objectives—is essential. Just setting financial objectives overlooks the fact that what ultimately enables a company to deliver better financial results from its operations is the achievement of strategic objectives that improve its competitiveness and market strength. Indeed, *the surest path to boosting company profitability quarter after quarter and year after year is to relentlessly pursue strategic outcomes that strengthen the company's market position and produce a growing competitive advantage over rivals.*

Company Spotlight 1.4 shows selected objectives of several prominent companies.

Both Short-Term and Long-Term Objectives Are Needed

As a rule, a company's set of financial and strategic objectives ought to include both near-term and longer-term performance targets. Having quarterly or annual objectives focuses attention on delivering immediate performance improvements. Targets to be achieved within three to five years prompt considerations of what to do *now* to put the company in position to perform better later. If trade-offs have to be made between achieving long-run objectives and achieving short-run objectives, the long-run objectives should generally take precedence. A company rarely prospers from repeated management actions that put better short-term performance ahead of better long-run performance.

The Concept of Strategic Intent

A company's objectives sometimes play another role: Very ambitious or aggressive objectives often signal **strategic intent** to stake out a particular business position and be a winner in the marketplace, often against long odds.[11] A company's strategic intent can entail becoming the recognized industry leader, unseating the existing industry leader, delivering the best customer service of any company in the industry (or the world), or turning a new technology into products capable of changing the way people work and live. Nike's strategic intent during the 1960s was to overtake Adidas (which connected nicely with Nike's core purpose "to experience the emotion of competition, winning, and crushing competitors"). Canon's strategic intent in

> **Core Concept**
>
> A company exhibits **strategic intent** when it relentlessly pursues an ambitious strategic objective, concentrating the full force of its resources and competitive actions on achieving that objective.

COMPANY SPOTLIGHT 1.4
Examples of Company Objectives

Nissan
(Strategic and Financial Objectives)

Increase sales to 4.2 million cars and trucks by 2008 (up from 3 million in 2003); cut purchasing costs 20 percent and halve the number of suppliers; have zero net debt; maintain a return on invested capital of 20 percent; maintain a 10 percent or better operating margin.

The Kroger Company
(Strategic and Financial Objectives)

Narrow the retail price gap with major discounters (like Wal-Mart) and widen the price advantage over traditional supermarket competitors. Use one-third of the company's cash flow for debt reduction and two-thirds for stock repurchase and dividend payments. Reduce operating and administrative costs by $500 million; leverage Kroger's $51 billion size to achieve greater economies of scale; and grow earnings per share by 13 to 15 percent annually starting in 2004.

DuPont
(Financial and Strategic Objectives)

To achieve annual revenue growth of 5 to 6 percent and annual earnings-per-share growth averaging 10 percent. Grow per-share profits faster than revenues by (a) increasing productivity, (b) selling enough new products each year that average prices and average margins rise, and (c) using surplus cash to buy back shares. Sell the company's low-margin textiles and interiors division (with sales of $6.6 billion and operating profits of only $114 million); this division makes Lycra and other synthetic fibers for carpets and clothes.

Heinz
(Financial and Strategic Objectives)

Achieve earnings per share in the range of $2.15 to $2.25 in 2004; increase operating cash flow by 45 percent to $750 million; reduce net debt by $1.3 billion in 2003 and further strengthen the company's balance sheet in 2004; continue to introduce new and improved food products; remove the clutter in company product offerings by reducing the number of SKUs (stock-keeping units); increase spending on trade promotion and advertising by $200 million to strengthen the recognition and market shares of the company's core brands; and divest noncore underperforming product lines.

Seagate Technology
(Strategic Objectives)

Solidify the company's number-one position in the overall market for hard-disk drives; get more Seagate drives into popular consumer electronics products (i.e., video recorders); take share away from Western Digital in providing disk drives for Microsoft's Xbox; and capture a 10 percent share of the market for 2.5-inch hard drives for notebook computers by 2004.

3M Corporation
(Financial and Strategic Objectives)

To achieve long-term sales growth of 5 to 8 percent organic plus 2 to 4 percent from acquisitions; annual growth in earnings per share of 10 percent or better, on average; a return on stockholders' equity of 20 to 25 percent; a return on capital employed of 27 percent or better; to double the number of qualified new 3M product ideas and triple the value of products that win in the marketplace; to have at least 30 percent of sales come from products introduced in the past four years; and to build the best sales and marketing organization in the world.

Source: Company documents; *Business Week,* July 28, 2003, p. 106; *Business Week,* September 8, 2003, p. 108.

---

copying equipment was to "beat Xerox." For some years, Toyota has been driving to overtake General Motors as the world's largest motor vehicle producer (and it surpassed Ford Motor Company in total vehicles sold in 2003, to move into second place); Toyota has expressed its strategic intent in the form of a global market share objective of 15 percent by 2010, up from 5 percent in 1980 and 10 percent in 2003. Starbucks strategic intent is to make the Starbucks brand the world's most recognized and respected brand. Ambitious companies almost invariably begin with strategic intents that are out of proportion to their immediate capabilities and market positions. But they set aggressive stretch objectives and pursue them relentlessly, sometimes even obsessively. Capably managed, up-and-coming enterprises with strategic intents exceeding their present reach and resources often prove to be more formidable competitors over time than larger, cash-rich rivals with modest market ambitions.

The Need for Objectives at All Organizational Levels   Objective setting should not stop with top management's establishing of companywide performance targets. Company objectives need to be broken down into performance targets for each of the organization's separate businesses, product lines, functional departments, and individual work units. Company performance can't reach full potential unless each area of the organization does its part and contributes directly to the desired companywide outcomes and results. This means setting performance targets for each organizational unit that support—rather than conflict with or negate—the achievement of companywide strategic and financial objectives.

The ideal situation is a team effort in which each organizational unit strives to produce results in its area of responsibility that contribute to the achievement of the company's performance targets and strategic vision. Such consistency signals that organizational units know their strategic role and are on board in helping the company move down the chosen strategic path and produce the desired results.

Crafting a Strategy: Phase 3 of the Strategy-Making, Strategy-Executing Process

The task of stitching a strategy together entails addressing a series of hows: *how* to grow the business, *how* to please customers, *how* to outcompete rivals, *how* to respond to changing market conditions, *how* to manage each functional piece of the business and develop needed organizational capabilities, *how* to achieve strategic and financial objectives. It also means exercising astute entrepreneurship—proactively searching for opportunities to do new things or to do existing things in new or better ways.[12] The faster a company's business environment is changing, the more critical the need for its managers to be good entrepreneurs in diagnosing the direction and force of the changes under way and in responding with timely adjustments in strategy. Strategy makers have to pay attention to early warnings of future change and be willing to experiment with dare-to-be-different ways to establish a market position in that future. When obstacles unexpectedly appear in a company's path, it is up to management to adapt rapidly and innovatively. *Masterful strategies come partly (maybe mostly) by doing things differently from competitors where it counts—outinnovating them, being more efficient, being more imaginative, adapting faster—rather than running with the herd.* Good strategy making is therefore inseparable from good business entrepreneurship. One cannot exist without the other.

Who Participates in Crafting a Company's Strategy?

A company's senior executives obviously have important strategy-making roles. The chief executive officer (CEO), as captain of the ship, carries the mantles of chief direction setter, chief objective setter, chief strategy maker, and chief strategy implementer for the total enterprise. Ultimate responsibility for *leading* the strategy-making, strategy-executing process rests with the CEO. In some enterprises the CEO or owner functions as strategic visionary and chief architect of strategy, personally deciding which of several strategic options to pursue, although others may well assist with data gathering and analysis and the CEO may seek the advice of other senior managers and key employees on which way to go. Such an approach to strategy development is characteristic of small owner-managed companies and sometimes large corporations that have been founded by the present CEO or that have strong CEOs—Meg Whitman at eBay, Andrea Jung at Avon, Jeffrey Immelt at General Electric, and Howard Schultz at Starbucks are prominent examples of corporate CEOs who maintain a heavy hand in shaping their company's strategy.

In most companies, however, the heads of business divisions and major product lines, the chief financial officer, and vice presidents for production, marketing, human resources, and other functional departments have influential strategy-making roles. Normally, a company's chief financial officer is in charge of devising and implementing an appropriate financial strategy; the production vice president takes the lead in developing and executing the company's production strategy; the marketing vice president orchestrates sales and marketing strategy; a brand manager is in charge of the strategy for a particular brand in the company's product lineup; and so on.

But it is a mistake to view strategy making as exclusively a top-management function, the province of owner-entrepreneurs, CEOs, and other senior executives. The more wide-ranging a company's operations are, the more that strategy making is a collaborative team effort involving managers (and sometimes key employees) down through the whole organizational hierarchy. Take a company like Toshiba—a $43 billion corporation with 300 subsidiaries, thousands of products, and operations extending across the world. It would be a far-fetched error to assume that a few senior executives in Toshiba headquarters have either the expertise or a sufficiently detailed understanding of all the relevant factors to wisely craft all the strategic initiatives taken in Toshiba's numerous and diverse organizational units. Rather, it takes involvement on the part of Toshiba's whole management team to craft and execute the thousands of strategic initiatives that constitute the whole of Toshiba's strategy.

> **Core Concept**
>
> Every company manager has a role in the strategy-making, strategy-executing process; it is flawed thinking to view crafting and executing strategy as something only high-level managers do.

Major organizational units in a company—business divisions, product groups, functional departments, plants, geographic offices, distribution centers—normally have a leading or supporting role in the company's strategic game plan. Because senior executives in the corporate office seldom know enough about the situation in every geographic area and operating unit to direct every strategic move made in the field, it is common practice for top-level managers to delegate strategy-making authority to middle- and lower-echelon managers who head the organizational subunits where specific strategic results must be achieved. The more that a company's operations cut across different products, industries, and geographic areas, the more that headquarters executives are prone to delegate considerable strategy-making authority to on-the-scene personnel who have firsthand knowledge of customer requirements, can better evaluate market opportunities, and are better able to keep the strategy responsive to changing market and competitive conditions. While managers further down in the managerial hierarchy obviously have a narrower, more specific strategy-making, strategy-executing role than managers closer to the top, the important understanding here is that in most of today's companies *every company manager typically has a strategy-making, strategy-executing role—ranging from minor to major—for the area he or she heads.* Hence any notion that an organization's strategists are at the top of the management hierarchy and that mid-level and frontline personnel merely carry out the strategic directives of senior managers needs to be cast aside.

With decentralized decision making becoming common at companies of all stripes, it is now typical for key pieces of a company's strategy to originate in a company's middle and lower ranks.[13] In some companies, top management makes a regular practice of encouraging individuals and teams to develop and champion proposals for new product lines and new business ventures. The idea is to unleash the talents and energies of promising "corporate intrapreneurs," letting them try out untested business ideas and giving them the room to pursue new strategic initiatives. Executives judge which proposals merit support, give the chosen intrapreneurs the organizational and budgetary support they need, and let them run with the ball. Thus important pieces of company strategy can originate with those intrapreneurial individuals and teams who succeed in championing a proposal through the approval stage and then end up being charged with the lead role in launching new products, overseeing the company's entry into new geographic markets, or heading up new business ventures. W. L. Gore and Associates, a privately owned company famous for its Gore-Tex waterproofing film, is an avid and highly successful practitioner of the corporate intrapreneur approach to strategy making. Gore expects all employees to initiate improvements and to display innovativeness. Each employee's intrapreneurial contributions are prime considerations in determining raises, stock option bonuses, and promotions. W. L. Gore's commitment to intrapreneurship has produced a stream of product innovations and new strategic initiatives that has kept the company vibrant and growing for nearly two decades.

A Company's Strategy-Making Hierarchy

It thus follows that *a company's overall strategy is a collection of strategic initiatives and actions* devised by managers and key employees up and down the whole organizational hierarchy. The larger and more diverse the operations of an enterprise, the more points of strategic initiative it has and the more managers and employees at more levels of management there are who have a relevant strategy-making role. Figure 1.4 shows who is generally responsible for devising what pieces of a company's overall strategy.

In diversified, multibusiness companies where the strategies of several different businesses have to be managed, the strategy-making task involves four distinct types or levels of strategy, each of which involves different facets of the company's overall strategy:

1. *Corporate strategy* consists of the kinds of initiatives the company uses to establish business positions in different industries, the approaches corporate executives pursue to boost the combined performance of the set of businesses the company has diversified into, and the means of capturing cross-business synergies and turning them into competitive advantage. Senior corporate executives normally have lead responsibility for devising corporate strategy and for choosing among whatever recommended actions bubble up from the organization below. Key business-unit heads may also be influential, especially in strategic decisions affecting the businesses they head. Major strategic decisions are usually reviewed and approved by the company's board of directors. We will look deeper into the strategy-making process at diversified companies when we get to Chapter 6.

Figure 1.4   A Company's Strategy-Making Hierarchy

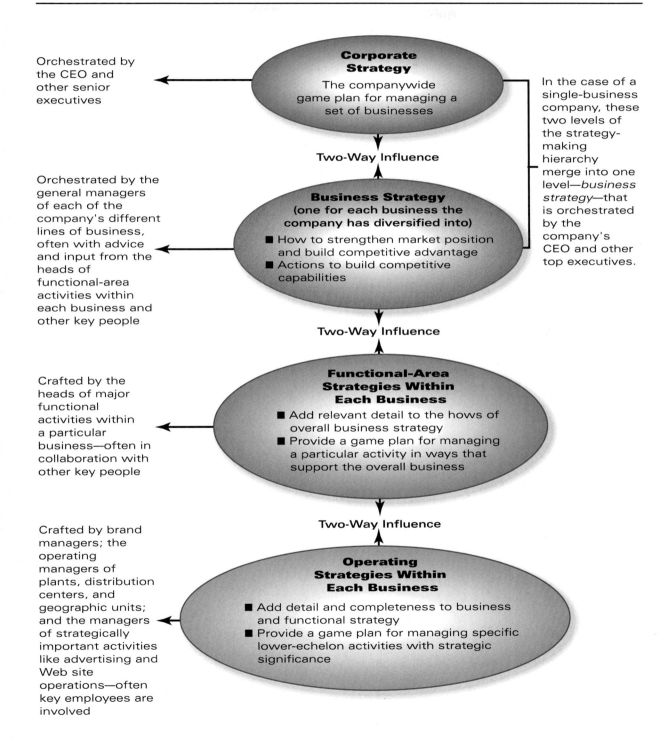

Orchestrated by the CEO and other senior executives

Orchestrated by the general managers of each of the company's different lines of business, often with advice and input from the heads of functional-area activities within each business and other key people

Crafted by the heads of major functional activities within a particular business—often in collaboration with other key people

Crafted by brand managers; the operating managers of plants, distribution centers, and geographic units; and the managers of strategically important activities like advertising and Web site operations—often key employees are involved

Corporate Strategy

The companywide game plan for managing a set of businesses

Two-Way Influence

Business Strategy (one for each business the company has diversified into)

■ How to strengthen market position and build competitive advantage
■ Actions to build competitive capabilities

Two-Way Influence

Functional-Area Strategies Within Each Business

■ Add relevant detail to the hows of overall business strategy
■ Provide a game plan for managing a particular activity in ways that support the overall business

Two-Way Influence

Operating Strategies Within Each Business

■ Add detail and completeness to business and functional strategy
■ Provide a game plan for managing specific lower-echelon activities with strategic significance

In the case of a single-business company, these two levels of the strategy-making hierarchy merge into one level—*business strategy*—that is orchestrated by the company's CEO and other top executives.

2. *Business strategy* concerns the actions and the approaches crafted to produce successful performance in one specific line of business. The key focus is crafting responses to changing market circumstances and initiating actions to strengthen market position, build competitive advantage, and develop strong competitive capabilities. Orchestrating the development of business-level strategy is the responsibility of the manager in charge of the business. The business head has at least two other strategy-related roles: (1) seeing that lower-level strategies are well conceived, consistent, and adequately matched to the overall business strategy, and (2) getting major business-level strategic moves approved by corporate-level officers (and sometimes the board of directors) and keeping them informed of emerging strategic issues. In diversified companies, business-unit heads may have the additional obligation of making sure business-level objectives and strategy conform to corporate-level objectives and strategy themes.

3. *Functional-area strategies* concern the actions, approaches, and practices to be employed in managing particular functions or business processes or key activities within a business. A company's marketing strategy, for example, represents the managerial game plan for running the sales and marketing part of the business. A company's product development strategy represents the managerial game plan for keeping the company's product lineup fresh and in tune with what buyers are looking for. Functional strategies add specifics to the hows of business-level strategy. Plus, they aim at establishing or strengthening a business unit's competencies and capabilities in performing strategy-critical activities so as to enhance the business's market position and standing with customers. The primary role of a functional strategy is to *support* the company's overall business strategy and competitive approach.

   Lead responsibility for functional strategies within a business is normally delegated to the heads of the respective functions, with the general manager of the business having final approval and perhaps even exerting a strong influence over the content of particular pieces of the strategies. To some extent, functional managers have to collaborate and coordinate their strategy-making efforts to avoid uncoordinated or conflicting strategies. For the overall business strategy to have maximum impact, a business's marketing strategy, production strategy, finance strategy, customer service strategy, product development strategy, and human resources strategy should be compatible and mutually reinforcing rather than each serving its own narrower purposes. If inconsistent functional-area strategies are sent up the line for final approval, the business head is responsible for spotting the conflicts and getting them resolved.

4. *Operating strategies* concern the relatively narrow strategic initiatives and approaches for managing key operating units (plants, distribution centers, geographic units) and specific operating activities with strategic significance (advertising campaigns, the management of specific brands, supply chain–related activities, and Web site sales and operations). A plant manager needs a strategy for accomplishing the plant's objectives, carrying out the plant's part of the company's overall manufacturing game plan, and dealing with any strategy-related problems that exist at the plant. A company's advertising manager needs a strategy for getting maximum audience exposure and sales impact from the ad budget. Operating strategies, while of limited scope, add further detail and completeness to functional strategies and to the overall business strategy. Lead responsibility for

operating strategies is usually delegated to frontline managers, subject to review and approval by higher-ranking managers.

Even though operating strategy is at the bottom of the strategy-making hierarchy, its importance should not be downplayed. A major plant that fails in its strategy to achieve production volume, unit cost, and quality targets can undercut the achievement of company sales and profit objectives and wreak havoc with strategic efforts to build a quality image with customers. Frontline managers are thus an important part of an organization's strategy-making team because many operating units have strategy-critical performance targets and need to have strategic action plans in place to achieve them. One cannot reliably judge the strategic importance of a given action simply by the strategy level or location within the managerial hierarchy where it is initiated.

In single-business enterprises, the corporate and business levels of strategy making merge into one level—business strategy—because the strategy for the whole company involves only one distinct line of business. Thus a single-business enterprise has three levels of strategy: business strategy for the company as a whole, functional-area strategies for each main area within the business, and operating strategies undertaken by lower-echelon managers to flesh out strategically significant aspects for the company's business and functional-area strategies. Proprietorships, partnerships, and owner-managed enterprises may have only one or two strategy-making levels since their strategy-making, strategy-executing process can be handled by just a few key people.

Uniting the Strategy-Making Effort Ideally, the pieces of a company's strategy should fit together like a jigsaw puzzle. To achieve such unity, the strategizing process must generally proceed from the corporate level to the business level and then from the business level to the functional and operating levels. *Mid-level and frontline managers cannot do good strategy making without understanding the company's long-term direction and higher-level strategies.* The strategic disarray that occurs in an organization when senior managers don't exercise strong top-down direction setting and set forth a clearly articulated companywide strategy is akin to what would happen to a football team's offensive performance if the quarterback decided not to call a play for the team but instead let each player pick whatever play he thought would work best at his respective position. In business, as in sports, all the strategy makers in a company are on the same team, and the many different pieces of the overall strategy crafted at various organizational levels need to be in sync and united. Anything less than a unified collection of strategies weakens company performance.

> **Core Concept**
>
> A company's strategy is at full power only when its many pieces are united.

Achieving unity is partly a function of communicating the company's basic strategy themes effectively across the organization and establishing clear strategic principles and guidelines for lower-level strategy making. Cohesive strategy making becomes easier to achieve when company strategy is distilled into pithy, easy-to-grasp terminology that can be used to drive consistent strategic action down through the hierarchy.[14] The greater the numbers of company personnel who know, understand, and buy into the company's basic direction and strategy, the smaller the risk that people and organization units will go off in conflicting strategic directions when decision making is pushed down to frontline levels and many people are given strategy-making, strategy-executing roles. Good communication of long-term direction and higher-level strategic themes thus serves a valuable strategy-unifying purpose.

Merging the Strategic Vision, Objectives, and Strategy into a Strategic Plan

Developing a strategic vision and mission, setting objectives, and crafting a strategy are basic direction-setting tasks. They map out where a company is headed, its short-range and long-range performance targets, and the competitive moves and internal action approaches to be used in achieving the targeted business results. Together, they constitute a **strategic plan** for coping with industry and competitive conditions, the expected actions of the industry's key players, and the challenges and issues that stand as obstacles to the company's success.[15]

> **Core Concept**
>
> A company's **strategic plan** lays out its future direction, performance targets, and strategy.

In companies committed to regular strategy reviews and the development of explicit strategic plans, the strategic plan may take the form of a written document that is circulated to most managers and perhaps selected employees. In small, privately owned companies, strategic plans usually take the form of oral understandings and commitments among managers and key employees about where to head, what to accomplish, and how to proceed. Near-term performance targets are the part of the strategic plan most often spelled out explicitly and communicated to managers and employees. A number of companies summarize key elements of their strategic plans in the company's annual report to shareholders, in postings on their Web site, or in statements provided to the business media, whereas others, perhaps for reasons of competitive sensitivity, make only vague, general statements about their strategic plans.

Implementing and Executing the Strategy: Phase 4 of the Strategy-Making, Strategy-Executing Process

Managing the implementation and execution of strategy is an operations-oriented, make-things-happen activity aimed at shaping the performance of core business activities in a strategy-supportive manner. It is easily the most demanding and time-consuming part of the strategy management process. Converting strategic plans into actions and results tests a manager's ability to direct organizational change, motivate people, build and strengthen company competencies and competitive capabilities, create a strategy-supportive work climate, and meet or beat performance targets. Initiatives have to be launched and managed on many organizational fronts.

Management's action agenda for implementing and executing the chosen strategy emerges from assessing what the company will have to do differently or better, given its particular operating practices and organizational circumstances, to execute the strategy proficiently and achieve the targeted performance. Each company manager has to think through the answer to "What has to be done in my area to execute my piece of the strategic plan, and what actions should I take to get the process under way?" How much internal change is needed depends on how much of the strategy is new, how far internal practices and competencies deviate from what the strategy requires, and how well the present work climate/culture supports good strategy execution. Depending on the amount of internal change involved, full implementation and proficient execution of company strategy (or important new pieces thereof) can take several months to several years.

In most situations, managing the strategy execution process includes the following principal aspects:

- Staffing the organization with the needed skills and expertise, consciously building and strengthening strategy-supportive competencies and competitive capabilities, and organizing the work effort.

- Creating a company culture and work climate conducive to successful strategy implementation and execution.

- Developing budgets that steer ample resources into those activities critical to strategic success.

- Ensuring that policies and operating procedures facilitate rather than impede effective execution.

- Using the best-known practices to perform core business activities and pushing for continuous improvement. Organizational units have to periodically reassess how things are being done and diligently pursue useful changes and improvements.

- Installing information and operating systems that enable company personnel to better carry out their strategic roles day in and day out.

- Motivating people to pursue the target objectives energetically and, if need be, modifying their duties and job behavior to better fit the requirements of successful strategy execution.

- Tying rewards and incentives directly to the achievement of performance objectives and good strategy execution.

- Exerting the internal leadership needed to drive implementation forward and keep improving on how the strategy is being executed. When stumbling blocks or weaknesses are encountered, management has to see that they are addressed and rectified on a timely basis.

Good strategy execution requires creating strong fits between strategy and organizational capabilities, between strategy and the organization's work climate and culture, between strategy and the reward structure, and between strategy and internal operating systems. The stronger these fits—that is, the more that the company's capabilities, culture, reward structure, and internal operating systems facilitate and promote proficient strategy execution—the better the execution and the higher the company's odds of achieving its performance targets. Furthermore, deliberately shaping the performance of core business activities around the strategy helps unite the organization.

Evaluating Performance and Initiating Corrective Adjustments: Phase 5 of the Strategy-Making, Strategy-Executing Process

The fifth phase of the strategy management process—evaluating the company's progress, assessing the impact of new external developments, and making corrective adjustments—is the trigger point for deciding whether to continue or change the company's vision, objectives, strategy, and/or strategy execution methods. As long as the company's direction and strategy seem well matched to industry and competitive conditions and performance targets are being met, company executives may well decide to stay the course. Simply fine-tuning the strategic plan and continuing with efforts to improve strategy execution are sufficient.

But whenever a company encounters disruptive changes in its environment, questions need to be raised about the appropriateness of its direction and strategy. If a company experiences a downturn in its market position or shortfalls in performance, then company managers are obligated to ferret out the causes—do they relate to poor strategy, poor strategy execution, or both?—and take timely corrective action. A company's direction, objectives, and strategy have to be revisited anytime external or internal conditions warrant. It is to be expected that a company will modify its strategic vision, direction, objectives, and strategy over time.

Likewise, it is not unusual for a company to find that one or more aspects of its strategy implementation and execution are not going as well as intended. Proficient strategy execution is always the product of much organizational learning. It is achieved unevenly—coming quickly in some areas and proving nettlesome in others. It is both normal and desirable to periodically assess strategy execution to determine which aspects are working well and which need improving. Successful strategy execution entails vigilantly searching for ways to improve and then making corrective adjustments whenever and wherever it is useful to do so.

Corporate Governance: The Role of the Board of Directors in the Strategy-Making, Strategy-Executing Process

Although senior managers have *lead responsibility* for crafting and executing a company's strategy, it is the duty of the board of directors to exercise strong oversight and see that the five tasks of strategic management are done in a manner that benefits shareholders (in the case of investor-owned enterprises) or stakeholders (in the case of not-for-profit organizations). In watching over management's strategy-making, strategy-executing actions and making sure that executive actions are not only proper but also aligned with the interests of stakeholders, the members of a company's board of directors have four important obligations to fulfill:

1. *Be inquiring critics and oversee the company's direction, strategy, and business approaches.* Board members must ask probing questions and draw on their business acumen to make independent judgments about whether strategy proposals have been adequately analyzed and whether proposed strategic actions appear to have greater promise than alternatives. If executive management is bringing well-supported and reasoned strategy proposals to the board, there's little reason for board members to aggressively challenge and try to pick apart everything put before them. Asking incisive questions is usually sufficient to test whether the case for management's proposals is compelling and to exercise vigilant oversight. However, when the company's strategy is failing or is plagued with faulty execution, and certainly when there is a precipitous collapse in profitability, board members have a duty to be proactive, expressing their concerns about the validity of the strategy and/or operating methods, initiating debate about the company's strategic path, having one-on-one discussions with key executives and other board

members, and perhaps directly intervening as a group to alter the company's executive leadership and, ultimately, its strategy and business approaches.

2. *Evaluate the caliber of senior executives' strategy-making and strategy-executing skills.* The board is always responsible for determining whether the current CEO is doing a good job of strategic leadership (as a basis for awarding salary increases and bonuses and deciding on retention or removal). Boards must also exercise due diligence in evaluating the strategic leadership skills of other senior executives in line to succeed the CEO. When the incumbent CEO steps down or leaves for a position elsewhere, the board must elect a successor, either going with an insider or deciding that an outsider is needed to perhaps radically change the company's strategic course.

3. *Institute a compensation plan for top executives that rewards them for actions and results that serve stakeholder interests, most especially those of shareholders.* A basic principle of corporate governance is that the owners of a corporation delegate operating authority and managerial control to top management in return for compensation. In their role as *agents* of shareholders, top executives have a clear and unequivocal duty to make decisions and operate the company in accord with shareholder interests (but this does not mean disregarding the interests of other stakeholders, particularly those of employees, with whom they also have an agency relationship). Most boards of directors have a compensation committee, composed entirely of outside directors, to develop a salary and incentive compensation plan that motivates executives to operate the business in a manner that benefits the owners; the compensation committee's recommendations are presented to the full board for approval. But in addition to creating compensation plans intended to align executive actions with owner interests, it is incumbent on the board of directors to put a halt to self-serving executive perks and privileges that simply enrich the personal welfare of executives. Numerous media reports have recounted instances in which boards of directors have gone along with opportunistic executive efforts to secure excessive, if not downright obscene, compensation of one kind or another (multimillion-dollar interest-free loans, personal use of corporate aircraft, excessive severance and retirement packages, outsized stock incentive awards, and so on).

4. *Oversee the company's financial accounting and financial reporting practices.* While top management, particularly the company's CEO and CFO (chief financial officer), is primarily responsible for seeing that the company's financial statements fairly and accurately report the results of the company's operations, it is well established that board members have a fiduciary duty to protect shareholders by exercising oversight of the company's financial practices, ensuring that generally accepted accounting principles are properly used in preparing the company's financial statements, and determining whether proper financial controls are in place to prevent fraud and misuse of funds. Virtually all boards of directors monitor the financial reporting activities by appointing an audit committee, always composed entirely of outside directors. The members of the audit committee have lead responsibility for overseeing the company's financial officers and consulting with both internal and external auditors to ensure accurate financial reporting and adequate financial controls.

Every corporation should have a strong, independent board of directors that (1) is well-informed about the company's performance, (2) guides and judges the CEO and other top executives, (3) has the courage to curb management actions it believes are inappropriate or unduly risky, (4) certifies to shareholders that the CEO is doing what the board expects, (5) provides insight and advice to management, and (6) is intensely involved in debating the pros and cons of key decisions and actions.[16] Boards of directors that lack the backbone to challenge a strong-willed or "imperial" CEO or that rubber-stamp almost anything the CEO recommends without probing inquiry and debate (perhaps because the board is stacked with the CEO's cronies) abdicate their duty to represent and protect shareholder interests. The whole fabric of effective corporate governance is undermined when boards of directors shirk their responsibility to maintain ultimate control over the company's strategic direction, the major elements of its strategy, the business approaches management is using to implement and execute the strategy, executive compensation, and the financial reporting process. Boards of directors thus have a very important oversight role in the strategy-making, strategy-executing process even though *lead responsibility* for crafting and executing strategy falls to top executives.

The number of prominent companies that have fallen on hard times because of the actions of scurrilous or out-of-control CEOs and CFOs, the growing propensity of disgruntled stockholders to file lawsuits alleging director negligence, and the escalating costs of liability insurance for directors all underscore the responsibility that a board of directors has for overseeing a company's strategy-making, strategy-executing process and ensuring that management actions are proper and responsible. Moreover, holders of large blocks of shares (mutual funds and pension funds), regulatory authorities, and the financial press consistently urge that board members, especially outside directors, be active and diligent in their oversight of company strategy and maintain a tight rein on executive actions.

Why Crafting and Executing Strategy Are Important Tasks

Crafting and executing strategy are top-priority managerial tasks for two very big reasons. First, there is a compelling need for managers to *proactively shape*, or *craft*, how the company's business will be conducted. A clear and reasoned strategy is management's prescription for doing business, its road map to competitive advantage, its game plan for pleasing customers and achieving performance targets. Winning in the marketplace requires implementing a well-conceived, opportunistic strategy, usually one characterized by strategic offensives to outinnovate and outmaneuver rivals and secure sustainable competitive advantage, and then using this market edge to achieve superior financial performance. A powerful strategy that delivers a home run in the marketplace can propel a firm from a trailing position into one of leadership, often making the firm's products/services the industry standard. High-achieving enterprises are nearly always the product of shrewd strategy making—companies don't get to the top of the industry rankings or stay there with strategies built around timid efforts to do better. And only a handful of companies can boast of strategies that hit home runs in the marketplace due to lucky breaks or the good fortune of having stumbled into the right market at the right time with the right product. So there can be little argument that the caliber of a company's strategy matters—and matters a lot.

Second, a *strategy-focused organization* is more likely to be a strong bottom-line performer than an organization that views strategy as secondary and puts its priorities elsewhere. The quality of managerial strategy making and strategy execution has a highly positive impact on earnings, cash flow, and return on investment. A company that lacks clear-cut direction, has vague or undemanding performance targets, has a muddled or flawed strategy, or can't seem to execute its strategy competently is a company whose financial performance is probably suffering, whose business is at long-term risk, and whose management is sorely lacking. On the other hand, when the five phases of the strategy-making, strategy-executing process drive management's whole approach to managing the company, the odds are much greater that the initiatives and activities of different divisions, departments, managers, and work groups will be unified into a *coordinated, cohesive effort.* Mobilizing the full complement of company resources in a total team effort behind good execution of the chosen strategy and achievement of the targeted performance allows a company to operate at full power. The chief executive officer of one successful company put it well when he said:

> In the main, our competitors are acquainted with the same fundamental concepts and techniques and approaches that we follow, and they are as free to pursue them as we are. More often than not, the difference between their level of success and ours lies in the relative thoroughness and self-discipline with which we and they develop and execute our strategies for the future.

Good Strategy + Good Strategy Execution = Good Management

Crafting and executing strategy are thus core management functions. Among all the things managers do, nothing affects a company's ultimate success or failure more fundamentally than how well its management team charts the company's direction, develops competitively effective strategic moves and business approaches, and pursues what needs to be done internally to produce good day-in, day-out strategy execution. Indeed, *good strategy and good strategy execution are the most trustworthy signs of good management.* Managers don't deserve a gold star for designing a potentially brilliant strategy but failing to put the organizational means in place to carry it out in high-caliber fashion—weak implementation and execution undermine the strategy's potential and pave the way for shortfalls in customer satisfaction and company performance. Competent execution of a mediocre strategy scarcely merits enthusiastic applause for management's efforts either. The rationale for using the twin standards of good strategy making and good strategy execution to determine whether a company is well managed is therefore compelling: *The better conceived a company's strategy and the more competently it is executed, the more likely that the company will be a standout performer in the marketplace.*

> **Core Concept**
> Excellent execution of an excellent strategy is the best test of managerial excellence—and the most reliable recipe for turning companies into standout performers.

Throughout the text chapters to come and the accompanying case collection, the spotlight is trained on the foremost question in running a business enterprise: What must managers do, and do well, to make a company a winner in the marketplace? The answer that emerges, and that becomes the message of this book, is that doing a good job of managing inherently requires good strategic thinking and good management of the strategy-making, strategy-executing process.

The mission of this book is to explore what "good strategic thinking" entails, to present the core concepts and tools of strategic analysis, to describe the ins and outs of crafting and executing strategy, and, through the cases that are included, to help you build your skills both in diagnosing how well the five aspects of managing strategy are being performed in actual companies and in making analysis-based recommendations for improvement. At the very least, we hope to convince you that capabilities in crafting and executing strategy are basic to managing successfully and have a prominent place in a manager's toolkit.

As you tackle the following pages, ponder an observation made by Ralph Waldo Emerson: "Commerce is a game of skill which many people play, but which few play well." If the content of this book helps you become a more savvy player and better equips you to succeed in business, then your journey through the following pages will indeed be time well spent.

Key Points

The tasks of crafting and executing company strategies are the heart and soul of managing a business enterprise and winning in the marketplace. A company's strategy consists of the competitive moves and business approaches that management is using to grow the business, stake out a market position, attract and please customers, compete successfully, conduct operations, and achieve organizational objectives. The central thrust of a company's strategy is undertaking moves to build and strengthen the company's long-term competitive position and financial performance and, ideally, gain a competitive advantage over rivals that then becomes a company's ticket to above-average profitability. A company's strategy typically evolves and re-forms over time, emerging from a blend of (1) proactive and purposeful actions on the part of company managers and (2) as-needed reactions to unanticipated developments and fresh market conditions.

Closely related to the concept of strategy is the concept of a company's business model. A company's business model is management's story line for how and why the company's product offerings and competitive approaches will generate a revenue stream and have an associated cost structure that produces attractive earnings and return on investment; in effect, a company's business model sets forth the economic logic for answering the question "How do we intend to make money in this business, given our current strategy?"

The managerial process of crafting and executing a company's strategy consists of five interrelated and integrated phases:

1. *Developing a strategic vision* of where the company needs to head and what its future product-customer-market-technology focus should be. This managerial step provides long term direction, infuses the organization with a sense of purposeful action, and communicates to stakeholders what management's aspirations for the company are.

2. *Setting objectives* and using the targeted results and outcomes as yardsticks for measuring the company's performance and progress. Objectives need to spell out *how much* of *what kind* of performance *by when,* and they need to require a significant amount of organizational stretch. A balanced-scorecard approach for measuring company performance entails setting both *financial objectives* and *strategic objectives.*

3. *Crafting a strategy to achieve the objectives* and move the company along the strategic course that management has charted. Crafting strategy is concerned principally with forming responses to changes under way in the external environment,

devising competitive moves and market approaches aimed at producing sustainable competitive advantage, building competitively valuable competencies and capabilities, and uniting the strategic actions initiated in various parts of the company.

4. *Implementing and executing the chosen strategy efficiently and effectively.* Managing the implementation and execution of strategy is an operations-oriented, make-things-happen activity aimed at shaping the performance of core business activities in a strategy-supportive manner.

5. *Evaluating performance and initiating corrective adjustments in vision, long-term direction, objectives, strategy, or execution* in light of actual experience, changing conditions, new ideas, and new opportunities. This phase of the strategy management process is the trigger point for deciding whether to continue or change the company's vision, objectives, strategy, and/or strategy execution methods.

Developing a strategic vision and mission, setting objectives, and crafting a strategy are the basic direction-setting tasks that together constitute a *strategic plan* for coping with industry and competitive conditions, the actions of rivals, and the challenges and issues that stand as obstacles to the company's success.

Boards of directors have a duty to shareholders to play a vigilant supervisory role in a company's strategy-making, strategy-executing process. They are obligated to (1) critically appraise and ultimately approve strategic action plans, (2) evaluate the strategic leadership skills of the CEO and others in line to succeed the incumbent CEO, (3) institute a compensation plan for top executives that rewards them for actions and results that serve stakeholder interests, most especially those of shareholders, and (4) ensure that the company issues accurate financial reports and has adequate financial controls.

Exercises

1. Go to www.redhat.com and check the company's latest financial reports to determine how well the company's business model is working. Is the company profitable? Is its revenue stream from selling technical support services growing or declining as a percentage of total revenues? Does your review of the company's financial performance suggest that its business model and strategy are changing?

2. Go to www.levistrauss.com/about/vision and read what Levi Strauss & Company says about how its corporate values of originality, empathy, integrity, and courage are connected to its vision of clothing the world. Do you buy what the company says, or are its statements just a bunch of nice pontifications that represent the personal values of the CEO (and make for good public relations)? Explain.

3. Go to the investors' section of www.heinz.com and read the letter to the shareholders in the company's fiscal 2003 annual report. Is the vision for Heinz that is articulated by Chairman and CEO William R. Johnson sufficiently clear and well defined? Why or why not? If you were a shareholder, would you be satisfied with what Johnson has told you about the company's direction, performance targets, and strategy? Now read Johnson's letter to the shareholders in Heinz's 2004 annual report. Do the results he cites change your mind about Johnson's vision for Heinz and the caliber of his strategy?

CHAPTER 2

Analyzing a Company's External Environment

Analysis is the critical starting point of strategic thinking.

—*Kenichi Ohmae, consultant and author*

Things are always different—the art is figuring out which differences matter.

—*Laszlo Birinyi, investments manager*

Competitive battles should be seen not as one-shot skirmishes but as a dynamic multiround game of moves and countermoves.

—*Anil K. Gupta, professor*

Managers

are not prepared to act wisely in steering a company in a different direction or altering its strategy until they have a deep understanding of the company's situation. Two facets of the company's situation are particularly pertinent: (1) the industry and competitive environment in which the company operates and the forces acting to reshape this environment and (2) the company's own market position and competitiveness—its resources and capabilities, its strengths and weaknesses vis-à-vis rivals, and its windows of opportunity.

A probing, analysis-based diagnosis of a company's external and internal environments is a prerequisite for managers to succeed in crafting a strategy that is an excellent fit with the company's situation, is capable of building competitive advantage, and holds good prospect for boosting company performance—the three criteria of a winning strategy. Developing a strategy begins with an appraisal of the company's external and internal situation (to form a strategic vision of where the company needs to head), then moves toward an evaluation of the most promising alternative strategies and business models, and finally culminates in choosing a specific strategy (see Figure 2.1).

This chapter presents the concepts and analytical tools for assessing a single-business company's external environment. Attention centers on the competitive arena in which a company operates, together with the technological, societal, regulatory, or demographic influences in the larger macroenvironment that are acting to reshape the company's future market arena. In Chapter 3 we explore the methods of evaluating a company's internal circumstances and competitiveness.

Figure 2.1 From Thinking Strategically to Choosing a Strategy

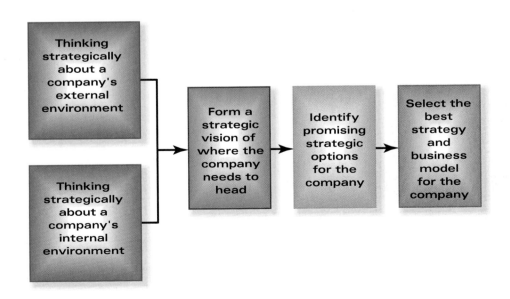

The Strategically Relevant Components of a Company's External Environment

All companies operate in a "macroenvironment" shaped by influences emanating from the economy at large; population demographics; societal values and lifestyles; governmental legislation and regulation; technological factors; and, closer to home, the industry and competitive arena in which the company operates (see Figure 2.2). Strictly speaking, a company's macroenvironment includes *all relevant factors and influences* outside the company's boundaries; by *relevant,* we mean important enough to have a

Figure 2.2   The Components of a Company's Macroenvironment

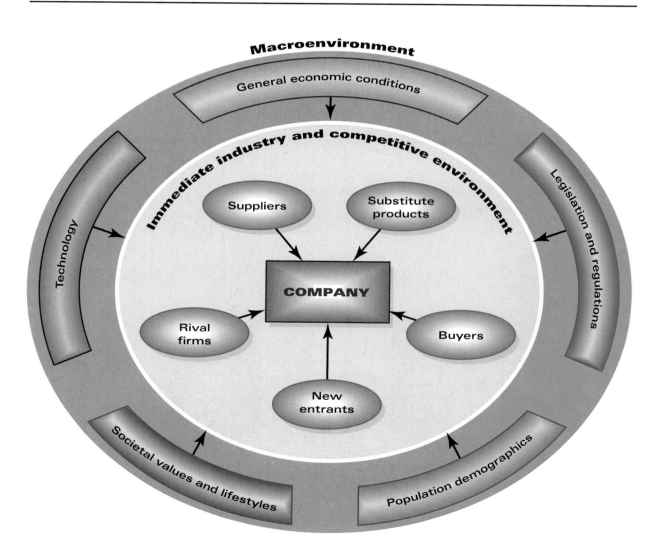

bearing on the decisions the company ultimately makes about its direction, objectives, strategy, and business model. For the most part, influences coming from the outer ring of the macroenvironment have a low impact on a company's business situation and shape only the edges of the company's direction and strategy. (There are notable exceptions, though. The strategic opportunities of cigarette producers to grow their business are greatly reduced by antismoking ordinances and the growing cultural stigma attached to smoking; the market growth potential for health care and prescription drug companies is quite favorably affected by the demographics of an aging population and longer life expectancies; and companies in almost all industries have to craft strategies that are responsive to environmental regulations, ups and downs in the level of economic activity, changing interest rates, and energy prices.) But while the strategy-shaping impact of outer-ring influences is normally low, there are enough strategically relevant trends and developments in the outer ring of the macroenvironment to justify a watchful eye. As company managers scan the external environment, they must be alert for potentially important outer-ring forces, assess their impact and influence, and adapt the company's direction and strategy as needed.

The factors and forces in a company's macroenvironment having the biggest strategy-shaping impact almost always pertain to the company's immediate industry and competitive environment. Consequently, it is on these factors that we concentrate our attention in this chapter.

Thinking Strategically about a Company's Industry and Competitive Environment

To gain a deep understanding of a company's industry and competitive environment, managers do not need to gather all the information they can find and spend lots of time digesting it. Rather, the task is much more focused. Thinking strategically about a company's industry and competitive environment entails using some well-defined concepts and analytical tools to get clear answers to seven questions:

1. What are the industry's strategy-shaping economic features?
2. What kinds of competitive forces are industry members facing, and how strong is each force?
3. What forces are driving changes in the industry, and what impact will these changes have on competitive intensity and industry profitability?
4. What market positions do industry rivals occupy—who is strongly positioned and who is not?
5. What strategic moves are rivals likely to make next?
6. What are the key factors for future competitive success?
7. Does the outlook for the industry present the company with sufficiently attractive prospects for profitability?

Analysis-based answers to these questions provide managers with a solid diagnosis of the industry and competitive environment. The remainder of this chapter is devoted to describing the methods of analyzing a company's industry and competitive environment.

Identifying Strategically Relevant Industry Features

Because industries differ so significantly in their basic character and structure, analyzing a company's industry and competitive environment begins with an overview of the industry's dominant economic features. The following economic features and corresponding questions need to be considered:

Economic Feature	Strategically Relevant Issues and Considerations
■ Market size and growth rate	■ How big is the industry, and how fast is it growing? ■ What does the industry's position in the growth cycle (early development, rapid growth and takeoff, early maturity, maturity, saturation and stagnation, decline) indicate about the industry's growth prospects?
■ Number of buyers	■ Is the number of buyers of the industry's product large enough that no one buyer accounts for a significant fraction of overall market demand, or do a fairly small number of buyers account for a big fraction of total sales?
■ Buyer needs and requirements	■ Are buyer needs or requirements changing, and, if so, what is driving such changes? ■ What are buyers looking for—what attributes prompt buyers to choose one brand over another?
■ Number of rivals	■ Is the industry fragmented into many small companies or concentrated and dominated by a few large companies? ■ Is the industry going through a period of consolidation to a smaller number of competitors? ■ Is the industry big enough or growing fast enough to attract the attention of opportunity-seeking new entrants?
■ Scope of competitive rivalry	■ Is the geographic area over which most companies compete local, regional, national, multinational, or global? ■ Is having a presence in the foreign-country markets becoming more important to a company's long-term competitive success?
■ Degree of product differentiation	■ Are the products of rival sellers strongly differentiated, weakly differentiated, or mostly identical? ■ Are the products of rivals becoming more differentiated or less differentiated? ■ Are increasingly "look-alike" products of rivals causing heightened price competition?

■ Product innovation	■ Is the industry characterized by rapid product innovation and short product life cycles?
	■ How important are R&D and product innovation?
	■ Are there opportunities to overtake key rivals by being first to market with next-generation products?
■ Production capacity	■ Is a surplus of capacity pushing prices and profit margins down?
	■ Is the industry overcrowded with too many competitors?
■ Pace of technological change	■ What role does advancing technology play in this industry?
	■ Are ongoing upgrades of facilities/equipment essential because of rapidly advancing production process technologies?
	■ Do most industry members have or need strong technological capabilities? Why?
■ Vertical integration	■ Do most industry members operate in only one stage of the industry (parts and components production, manufacturing and assembly, wholesale distribution, retailing), or are some or many partially or fully integrated?
	■ Does being fully integrated, partially integrated, or nonintegrated appear to result in a competitive advantage or disadvantage?
■ Economies of scale	■ Is the industry characterized by important economies of scale in purchasing, manufacturing, advertising, shipping, or other activities?
■ Learning- and experience-curve effects	■ Are certain industry activities characterized by strong learning and experience effects ("learning by doing") such that unit costs decline as a company's experience in performing the activity builds?[1]

Identifying an industry's economic features not only sets the stage for the analysis to come but also promotes understanding of the kinds of strategic moves that industry members are likely to employ. For example, in an industry characterized by important scale economies and/or learning- and experience-curve effects, industry members are strongly motivated to go after increased sales volumes and capture the cost-saving economies of larger-scale operations; small-scale firms are under considerable pressure to grow sales in order to become more cost-competitive with large-volume rivals. In industries characterized by one product advance after another, companies must invest in R&D and develop strong product innovation capabilities; a strategy of continuous product innovation becomes a condition of survival. An industry that has recently passed through the rapid-growth stage and is looking at single-digit percentage increases in buyer demand is likely to be experiencing a competitive shakeout and much stronger strategic emphasis on cost reduction and improved customer service.

Analyzing the Nature and Strength of Competitive Forces

The character, mix, and subtleties of the competitive forces operating in a company's industry are never the same from one industry to another. Far and away the most powerful and widely used tool for systematically diagnosing the principal competitive pressures in a market and assessing the strength and importance of each is the *five-forces model of competition*.[2] This model, depicted in Figure 2.3, holds that the state of competition in an industry is a composite of competitive pressures operating in five areas of the overall market:

1. Competitive pressures associated with the market maneuvering and jockeying for buyer patronage that goes on among *rival sellers* in the industry.

2. Competitive pressures associated with the threat of *new entrants* into the market.

3. Competitive pressures coming from the attempts of companies in other industries to win buyers over to their own *substitute products*.

4. Competitive pressures stemming from *supplier* bargaining power and supplier-seller collaboration.

5. Competitive pressures stemming from *buyer* bargaining power and seller-buyer collaboration.

The way one uses the five-forces model to determine what competition is like in a given industry is to build the picture of competition in three steps or stages. Step 1 is to identify the specific competitive pressures associated with each of the five forces. Step 2 is to evaluate how strong the pressures composing each of the five forces are (fierce, strong, moderate to normal, or weak). Step 3 is to determine whether the collective strength of the five competitive forces is conducive to earning attractive profits.

The Rivalry among Competing Sellers

The strongest of the five competitive forces is nearly always the market maneuvering and jockeying for buyer patronage that goes on among rival sellers of a product or service. In effect, *a market is a competitive battlefield* where it is customary for rival sellers to employ whatever weapons they have in their business arsenal to improve their market positions and performance. The strategy-making challenge of managers is to craft a competitive strategy that, at the very least, allows their company to hold its own against rivals and that, ideally, strengthens the company's standing with buyers, delivers good profitability, and *produces a competitive edge over rivals*. But when one firm makes a strategic move that produces good results, its rivals often react and respond with offensive or defensive counter-moves, shifting their strategic emphasis from one combination of product attributes, marketing tactics, and capabilities to another. This pattern of action and reaction, move and countermove, adjust and readjust is what makes competitive rivalry a combative, ever-changing contest. Market battles for buyer patronage involve a continually evolving competitive landscape as industry rivals initiate new rounds of market maneuvers, with one or more rivals gaining or losing momentum in the marketplace according to whether their adjustments succeed or fail.

> **Core Concept**
>
> Competitive jockeying among industry rivals is ever-changing, as rivals initiate fresh offensive and defensive moves and emphasize first one mix of competitive weapons and then another in efforts to improve their market positions.

Figure 2.3   The Five-Forces Model of Competition:
A Key Tool for Diagnosing the Competitive Environment

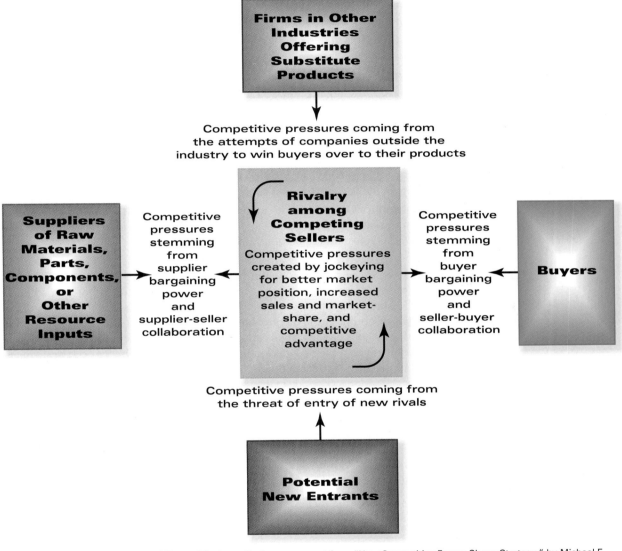

Figure 2.4 shows a sampling of competitive weapons that firms can deploy in battling rivals and indicates the factors that influence the intensity of their rivalry. A brief discussion of some of the factors that influence the tempo of rivalry among industry competitors is in order:[3]

■   *Rivalry among competing sellers intensifies the more frequently and more aggressively that industry members undertake fresh actions to boost their market standing and performance—perhaps at the expense of rivals.* Rivalry tends to be fairly intense whenever sellers actively compete on price—lively price competition pressures rival companies to aggressively pursue ways to drive costs out of the business; high-cost companies are hard-pressed to survive. Other indicators of the intensity of rivalry among industry members include:

- Whether industry members are racing to offer better performance features, higher quality, improved customer service, or a wider product selection.

- How frequently rivals resort to such marketing tactics as special sales promotions, heavy advertising, rebates, or low-interest-rate financing to drum up additional sales.

- How actively industry members are pursuing efforts to build stronger dealer networks, establish positions in foreign markets, or otherwise expand their distribution capabilities and market presence.

- How frequently rivals introduce new and improved products (and thus are competing on the basis of their product innovation capabilities).

- How hard companies are striving to gain a market edge over rivals by developing valuable expertise and capabilities.

Normally, industry members are proactive in drawing on their arsenal of competitive weapons and deploying their organizational resources in a manner calculated to strengthen their market positions and performance.

- ■ *Rivalry intensifies as the number of competitors increases and as competitors become more equal in size and capability.* Competition is not as strong in PC operating systems, where Linux is one of the few challengers to Microsoft, as it is in fast-food restaurants, where buyers have many choices. Up to a point, the greater the number of competitors, the greater the probability of fresh, creative strategic initiatives. In addition, when rivals are nearly equal in size and capability, they can usually compete on a fairly even footing, making it harder for one or two firms to win the competitive battle and dominate the market.

- ■ *Rivalry is usually weaker when there are fewer than five competitors or else so many rivals that the impact of any one company's actions is spread thinly across all industry members.* When an industry contains only a few rival sellers, each company tends to recognize that its actions can have an immediate and significant impact on the others and, if aggressive, may provoke direct retaliation. Although occasional warfare can break out, competition among the few tends to produce a live-and-let-live approach to competing and thus a restrained use of competitive weaponry. Rivalry also tends to be weak when an industry is fragmented with so many competitors that successful moves by one have little discernible adverse impact on the others and thus may provoke no immediate response or countermove on the part of its rivals.

- ■ *Rivalry is usually stronger in slow-growing markets and weaker in fast-growing markets.* Rapidly expanding buyer demand produces enough new business for all industry members to grow. Indeed, in a fast-growing market, a company may find itself stretched just to keep abreast of incoming orders, let alone devote resources to stealing customers away from rivals. But in markets where growth is sluggish or where buyer demand drops off unexpectedly, expansion-minded firms and/or firms with excess capacity often are quick to cut prices and initiate other sales-increasing tactics, thereby igniting a battle for market share that can result in a shakeout of weak, inefficient firms.

Figure 2.4   Weapons for Competing and Factors Affecting the Strength of Rivalry

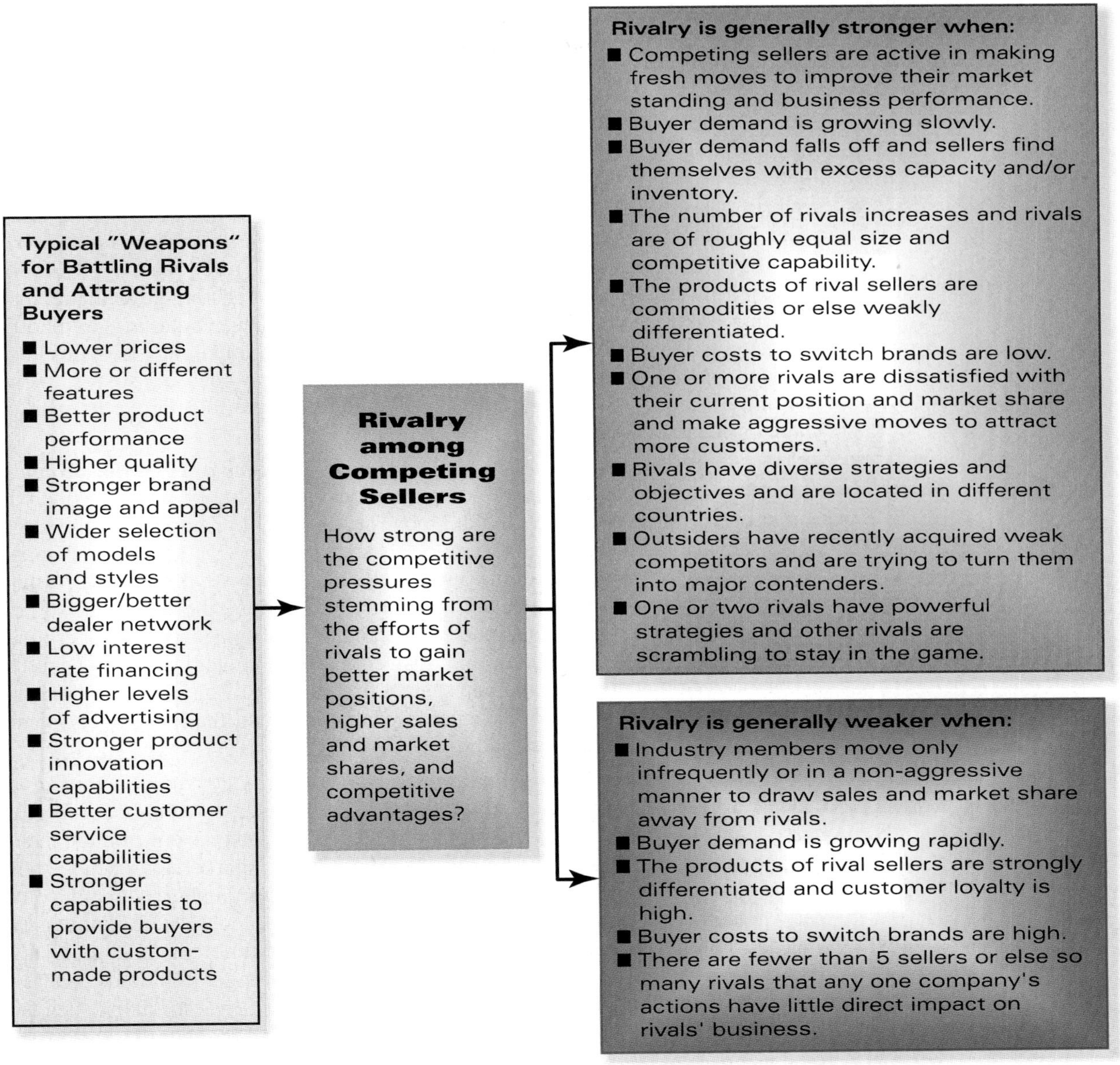

Typical "Weapons" for Battling Rivals and Attracting Buyers

- Lower prices
- More or different features
- Better product performance
- Higher quality
- Stronger brand image and appeal
- Wider selection of models and styles
- Bigger/better dealer network
- Low interest rate financing
- Higher levels of advertising
- Stronger product innovation capabilities
- Better customer service capabilities
- Stronger capabilities to provide buyers with custom-made products

Rivalry among Competing Sellers

How strong are the competitive pressures stemming from the efforts of rivals to gain better market positions, higher sales and market shares, and competitive advantages?

Rivalry is generally stronger when:

- Competing sellers are active in making fresh moves to improve their market standing and business performance.
- Buyer demand is growing slowly.
- Buyer demand falls off and sellers find themselves with excess capacity and/or inventory.
- The number of rivals increases and rivals are of roughly equal size and competitive capability.
- The products of rival sellers are commodities or else weakly differentiated.
- Buyer costs to switch brands are low.
- One or more rivals are dissatisfied with their current position and market share and make aggressive moves to attract more customers.
- Rivals have diverse strategies and objectives and are located in different countries.
- Outsiders have recently acquired weak competitors and are trying to turn them into major contenders.
- One or two rivals have powerful strategies and other rivals are scrambling to stay in the game.

Rivalry is generally weaker when:

- Industry members move only infrequently or in a non-aggressive manner to draw sales and market share away from rivals.
- Buyer demand is growing rapidly.
- The products of rival sellers are strongly differentiated and customer loyalty is high.
- Buyer costs to switch brands are high.
- There are fewer than 5 sellers or else so many rivals that any one company's actions have little direct impact on rivals' business.

- *Rivalry increases as the products of rival sellers become more standardized and/or when buyer costs to switch from one brand to another are low.* When the offerings of rivals are quite similar, it is usually easy and inexpensive for buyers to switch their purchases from one seller to another. Strongly differentiated products raise the probability that buyers will find it costly to switch brands.

- *Rivalry is more intense when industry conditions tempt competitors to use price cuts or other competitive weapons to boost unit volume.* When a product is perishable, seasonal, or costly to hold in inventory, or when demand slacks off, competitive pressures build quickly anytime one or more firms decide to cut prices and dump excess supplies on the market. Likewise, whenever fixed costs account for a large fraction of total cost and thus unit costs tend to be lowest at or near full capacity, then firms come under significant pressure to cut prices or otherwise try to boost sales. Unused capacity imposes a significant cost-increasing penalty because there are fewer units over which to spread fixed costs. The pressure of high fixed costs can push rival firms into price concessions, special discounts, rebates, low-interest-rate financing, and other volume-boosting tactics.

- *Rivalry increases when one or more competitors become dissatisfied with their market position and launch moves to bolster their standing at the expense of rivals.* Firms that are losing ground or in financial trouble often react aggressively by acquiring smaller rivals, introducing new products, boosting advertising, discounting prices, and so on. Such actions heighten rivalry and can trigger a hotly contested battle for market share. The market maneuvering among rivals usually heats up when a competitor makes new offensive moves—because it sees an opportunity to better please customers or is under pressure to improve its market share or profitability.

- *Rivalry increases in proportion to the size of the payoff from a successful strategic move.* The greater the benefits of going after a new opportunity, the more likely it is that one or more rivals will initiate moves to capture it. Competitive pressures nearly always intensify when several rivals start pursuing the same opportunity. For example, competition in online music sales heated up with the entries of Amazon.com, Barnesandnoble.com, and Buy.com. Furthermore, the size of the strategic payoff can vary with the speed of retaliation. When competitors respond slowly (or not at all), the initiator of a fresh competitive strategy can reap benefits in the intervening period and perhaps gain a first-mover advantage that is not easily surmounted. The greater the benefits of moving first, the more likely some competitor will accept the risk and try it.

- *Rivalry becomes more volatile and unpredictable as the diversity of competitors increases in terms of visions, strategic intents, objectives, strategies, resources, and countries of origin.* A diverse group of sellers often contains one or more mavericks willing to try novel or high-risk or rule-breaking market approaches, thus generating a livelier and less predictable competitive environment. Globally competitive markets often contain rivals with different views about where the industry is headed and a willingness to employ perhaps radically different competitive approaches. Attempts by cross-border rivals to gain stronger footholds in each other's domestic markets usually boost the intensity of rivalry, especially when the aggressors have lower costs or products with more attractive features.

- *Rivalry increases when strong companies outside the industry acquire weak firms in the industry and launch aggressive, well-funded moves to transform their newly acquired competitors into major market contenders.* A concerted effort to turn a weak rival into a market leader nearly always entails launching well-financed strategic initiatives to dramatically improve the competitor's product offering, excite buyer interest, and win a much bigger market share—actions that, if successful, put added pressure on rivals to counter with fresh strategic moves of their own.

■ *A powerful, successful competitive strategy employed by one company greatly
intensifies the competitive pressures on its rivals to develop effective strategic
responses or be relegated to also-ran status.*

Rivalry can be characterized as *cutthroat* or *brutal* when competitors engage in
protracted price wars or habitually employ other aggressive tactics that are mutually
destructive to profitability. Rivalry can be considered *fierce* to *strong* when the battle
for market share is so vigorous that the profit margins of most industry members are
squeezed to bare-bones levels. Rivalry can be characterized as *moderate* or *normal*
when the maneuvering among industry members, while lively and healthy, still allows
most industry members to earn acceptable profits. Rivalry is *weak* when most companies in the industry are relatively well satisfied with their sales growth and market
shares, rarely undertake offensives to steal customers away from one another, and have
comparatively attractive earnings and returns on investment.

The Potential Entry of New Competitors

Several factors affect the strength of the competitive threat of potential entry in a particular industry (see Figure 2.5). One factor relates to the size of the pool of likely entry candidates and the resources at their command. As a rule, competitive pressures
intensify the bigger the pool of entry candidates. This is especially true when some of
the likely entry candidates have ample resources and the potential to become formidable contenders for market leadership. Frequently, the strongest competitive pressures
associated with potential entry come not from outsiders but from current industry participants looking for growth opportunities. *Existing industry members are often strong
candidates to enter market segments or geographic areas where they currently do not
have a market presence.* Companies already well established in certain product categories or geographic areas often possess the resources, competencies, and competitive
capabilities to hurdle the barriers of entering a different market segment or new geographic area.

   A second factor concerns whether the likely entry candidates face high or low entry barriers. The most widely encountered barriers that entry candidates must hurdle
include:[4]

■ *The presence of sizable economies of scale in production or other areas of operation:* When incumbent companies enjoy cost advantages associated with large-
scale operation, outsiders must either enter on a large scale (a costly and perhaps
risky move) or accept a cost disadvantage and consequently lower profitability.
Trying to overcome the disadvantages of small size by entering on a large scale at
the outset can result in long-term overcapacity problems for the new entrant (until
sales volume builds up), and it can so threaten the market shares of existing firms
that they launch strong defensive maneuvers (price cuts, increased advertising and
sales promotion, and similar blocking actions) to maintain their positions and
make things hard on a newcomer.

■ *Cost and resource disadvantages not related to size:* Existing firms may have low
unit costs as a result of experience or learning-curve effects, key patents, partnerships with the best and cheapest suppliers of raw materials and components, proprietary technology know-how not readily available to newcomers, favorable
locations, and low fixed costs (because they have older plants that have been
mostly depreciated).

Figure 2.5   **Factors Affecting the Threat of Entry**

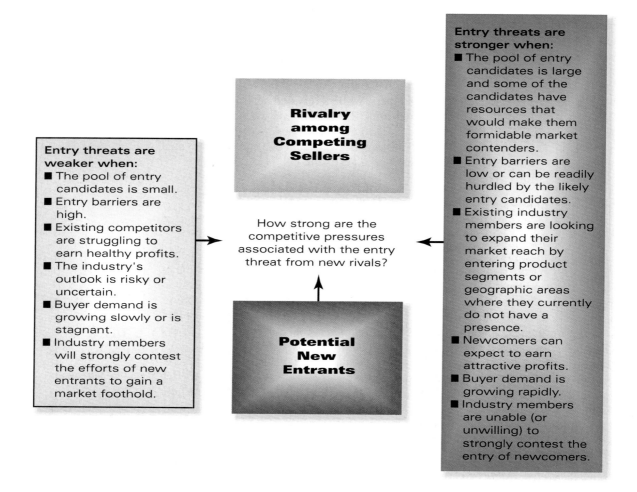

* *Brand preferences and customer loyalty:* In some industries, buyers are strongly attached to established brands. Japanese consumers, for example, are fiercely loyal to Japanese brands of motor vehicles, electronics products, cameras, and film. European consumers have traditionally been loyal to European brands of major household appliances. High brand loyalty means that a potential entrant must commit to spending enough money on advertising and sales promotion to overcome customer loyalties and build its own clientele. Establishing brand recognition and building customer loyalty can be a slow and costly process. In addition, if it is difficult or costly for a customer to switch to a new brand, a new entrant must persuade buyers that its brand is worth the switching costs. To overcome switching-cost barriers, new entrants may have to offer buyers a discounted price or an extra margin of quality or service. All this can mean lower expected profit margins for new entrants, which increases the risk to start-up companies dependent on sizable early profits to support their new investments.

- *Capital requirements:* The larger the total dollar investment needed to enter the market successfully, the more limited the pool of potential entrants. The most obvious capital requirements for new entrants are those associated with investing in the necessary manufacturing facilities and equipment, being able to finance the introductory advertising and sales promotion campaigns to build brand awareness and establish a clientele, securing the working capital to finance inventories and customer credit, and having sufficient cash reserves to cover start-up losses.

- *Access to distribution channels:* In consumer goods industries, a potential entrant may face the barrier of gaining adequate access to consumers. Wholesale distributors may be reluctant to take on a product that lacks buyer recognition. A network of retail dealers may have to be set up from scratch. Retailers have to be convinced to give a new brand ample display space and an adequate trial period. Entry is tough when existing producers have strong, well-functioning distributor-dealer networks and a newcomer must struggle to squeeze its way into existing distribution channels. To overcome the barrier of gaining adequate access to consumers, potential entrants may have to "buy" their way into wholesale or retail channels by cutting their prices to provide dealers and distributors with higher markups and profit margins or by giving them big advertising and promotional allowances. As a consequence, a potential entrant's own profits may be squeezed unless and until its product gains enough consumer acceptance that distributors and retailers want to carry it.

- *Regulatory policies:* Government agencies can limit or even bar entry by requiring licenses and permits. Regulated industries like cable TV, telecommunications, electric and gas utilities, radio and television broadcasting, liquor retailing, and railroads entail government-controlled entry. In international markets, host governments commonly limit foreign entry and must approve all foreign investment applications. Stringent government-mandated safety regulations and environmental pollution standards are entry barriers because they raise entry costs.

- *Tariffs and international trade restrictions:* National governments commonly use tariffs and trade restrictions (antidumping rules, local content requirements, quotas, etc.) to raise entry barriers for foreign firms and protect domestic producers from outside competition.

Whether an industry's entry barriers ought to be considered high or low and how hard it is for new entrants to compete on a level playing field depend on the resources and competencies possessed by the pool of potential entrants. Entry barriers can be formidable for newly formed enterprises that have to find some way to gain a market foothold and then over time make inroads against well-established companies. But opportunity-seeking companies in other industries, if they have suitable resources, competencies, and brand-name recognition, may be able to hurdle an industry's entry barriers rather easily. In evaluating the potential threat of entry, company managers must look at (1) how formidable the entry barriers are for each type of potential entrant—start-up enterprises, specific candidate companies in other industries, and current industry participants looking to expand their market reach—and (2) how attractive the growth and profit prospects are for new entrants. *Rapidly growing market demand and high potential profits act as magnets, motivating potential entrants to commit the resources needed to hurdle entry barriers.*[5]

However, even if a potential entrant has or can acquire the needed competencies and resources to attempt entry, it still faces the issue of how existing firms will react.[6] Will incumbent firms offer only passive resistance, or will they aggressively defend their market positions using price cuts, increased advertising, product improvements, and whatever else they can think of to give a new entrant (as well as other rivals) a hard time? A potential entrant can have second thoughts when financially strong incumbent firms send clear signals that they will stoutly defend their market positions against newcomers. A potential entrant may also turn away when incumbent firms can leverage distributors and customers to retain their business.

> The threat of entry is stronger when entry barriers are low, when there's a sizable pool of entry candidates, when industry growth is rapid and profit potentials are high, and when incumbent firms are unable or unwilling to vigorously contest a newcomer's entry.

The best test of whether potential entry is a strong or weak competitive force in the marketplace is to ask if the industry's growth and profit prospects are strongly attractive to potential entry candidates. When the answer is no, potential entry is a weak competitive force. When the answer is yes and there are actively interested entry candidates with sufficient expertise and resources, then potential entry adds significantly to competitive pressures in the marketplace. The stronger the threat of entry, the more that incumbent firms are driven to seek ways to fortify their positions against newcomers, pursuing strategic moves not only to protect their market shares but also to make entry more costly or difficult.

One additional point: *The threat of entry changes as the industry's prospects grow brighter or dimmer and as entry barriers rise or fall.* For example, in the pharmaceutical industry the expiration of a key patent on a widely prescribed drug virtually guarantees that one or more drug makers will enter with generic offerings of their own. Use of the Internet for shopping is making it much easier for e-tailers to enter into competition against some of the best-known retail chains. In international markets, entry barriers for foreign-based firms fall as tariffs are lowered, as host governments open up their domestic markets to outsiders, as domestic wholesalers and dealers seek out lower-cost foreign-made goods, and as domestic buyers become more willing to purchase foreign brands.

Competitive Pressures from the Sellers of Substitute Products

Companies in one industry come under competitive pressure from the actions of companies in a closely adjoining industry whenever buyers view the products of the two industries as good substitutes. For instance, the producers of sugar experience competitive pressures from the sales and marketing efforts of the makers of artificial sweeteners. Similarly, the producers of eyeglasses and contact lenses are currently facing mounting competitive pressures from growing consumer interest in corrective laser surgery. Newspapers are feeling the competitive force of the general public's turning to cable news channels for late-breaking news and using Internet sources to get information about sports results, stock quotes, and job opportunities.

Just how strong the competitive pressures are from the sellers of substitute products depends on three factors: (1) whether substitutes are readily available and attractively priced; (2) whether buyers view the substitutes as being comparable or better in terms of quality, performance, and other relevant attributes; and (3) how much it costs end users to switch to substitutes. Figure 2.6 lists factors affecting the strength of competitive pressures from substitute products and lists signs that indicate substitutes are a strong competitive force.

The presence of readily available and attractively priced substitutes creates competitive pressure by placing a ceiling on the prices industry members can charge without giving customers an incentive to switch to substitutes and risking sales erosion.[7]

Figure 2.6   Factors Affecting Competition from Substitute Products

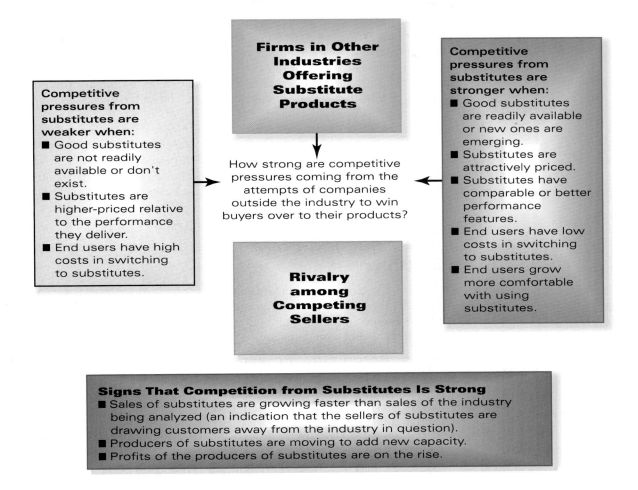

This price ceiling, at the same time, puts a lid on the profits that industry members can earn unless they find ways to cut costs. When substitutes are cheaper than an industry's product, industry members come under heavy competitive pressure to reduce their prices and find ways to absorb the price cuts with cost reductions.

The availability of substitutes inevitably invites customers to compare performance, features, ease of use, and other attributes as well as price. For example, ski boat manufacturers are experiencing strong competition from personal water-ski craft because water sports enthusiasts are finding that personal water skis are fun to ride and less expensive. The users of paper cartons constantly weigh the performance trade-offs of plastic containers and metal cans. Competition from good-performing substitute products pushes industry participants to incorporate new performance features and heighten efforts to convince customers their product has attributes that are superior to those of substitutes.

The strength of competition from substitutes is significantly influenced by how difficult or costly it is for the industry's customers to switch to a substitute.[8] Typical switching costs include the time and inconvenience that may be involved, the costs of additional equipment, the time and cost spent on testing the quality and reliability of the substitute, the psychological costs of severing old supplier relationships and establishing new ones, payments for technical help in making the changeover, and employee retraining costs. When buyers incur high costs in switching to substitutes, the competitive pressures that industry members experience from substitutes are usually lessened unless the sellers of substitutes begin offering price discounts or major performance benefits that entice the industry's customers away. When switching costs are low, it's much easier for sellers of substitutes to convince buyers to change to their products.

As a rule, then, the lower the price of substitutes, the higher their quality and performance, and the lower the user's switching costs, the more intense the competitive pressures posed by substitute products. Good indicators of the competitive strength of substitute products are the rate at which their sales and profits are growing, the market inroads they are making, and their plans for expanding production capacity.

Competitive Pressures Stemming from Supplier Bargaining Power and Seller-Supplier Collaboration

Whether supplier-seller relationships represent a weak or strong competitive force depends on (1) whether the major suppliers can exercise sufficient bargaining power to influence the terms and conditions of supply in their favor and (2) the nature and extent of supplier-seller collaboration in the industry.

How Supplier Bargaining Power Can Create Competitive Pressures

Whenever the major suppliers to an industry have considerable leverage in determining the terms and conditions of the item they are supplying, then they are in a position to exert competitive pressure on one or more rival sellers. For instance, Microsoft and Intel, both of whom supply PC makers with products that most PC users consider essential, are known for using their dominant market status not only to charge PC makers premium prices but also to leverage PC makers in other ways. Microsoft pressures PC makers to load only Microsoft products on the PCs they ship and to position the icons for Microsoft software prominently on the screens of new computers that come with factory-loaded software. Intel pushes greater use of Intel microprocessors in PCs by granting PC makers sizable advertising allowances on PC models equipped with "Intel Inside" stickers; it also tends to give PC makers who use the biggest percentages of Intel chips in their PC models top priority in filling orders for newly introduced Intel chips. Being on Intel's list of preferred customers helps a PC maker get an allocation of the first production runs of Intel's latest and greatest chips and thus get new PC models equipped with these chips to market ahead of rivals who are heavier users of chips made by Intel's rivals. The ability of Microsoft and Intel to pressure PC makers for preferential treatment of one kind or another in turn affects competition among rival PC makers.

Several other instances of supplier bargaining power are worth citing. Small-scale retailers must often contend with the power of manufacturers whose products enjoy prestigious and well-respected brand names; when a manufacturer knows that a retailer needs to stock the manufacturer's product because consumers expect to find the product on the shelves of retail stores where they shop, the manufacturer usually has some degree of pricing power and can also push hard for favorable shelf displays. Motor vehicle manufacturers typically exert considerable power over the terms and conditions with which they supply new vehicles to their independent automobile dealerships. The operators of franchised units of such chains as Krispy Kreme Doughnuts, Burger King, Pizza Hut, and Hampton Inns must frequently agree not only to source some of their supplies from the franchisor at prices and terms favorable to that franchisor but also to operate their facilities in a manner largely dictated by the franchisor. Strong supplier bargaining power is a competitive factor in industries where unions have been able to organize the workforces of some industry members but not others; those industry members that must negotiate wages, fringe benefits, and working conditions with powerful unions (which control the supply of labor) often find themselves with higher labor costs than their competitors with nonunion labor forces. The bigger the gap between union and nonunion labor costs in an industry, the more that unionized industry members must scramble to find ways to relieve the competitive pressure associated with their disadvantage on labor costs. High labor costs are proving a huge competitive liability to unionized supermarket chains like Kroger and Safeway in trying to combat the market share gains being made by Wal-Mart in supermarket retailing—Wal-Mart has a nonunion workforce and the prices for supermarket items at its supercenters tend to run 5 to 20 percent lower than those at unionized supermarket chains.

The factors that determine whether any of the suppliers to an industry are in a position to exert substantial bargaining power or leverage are fairly clear-cut:[9]

- *Whether the item being supplied is a commodity that is readily available from many suppliers at the going market price.* Suppliers have little or no bargaining power or leverage whenever industry members have the ability to source their requirements at competitive prices from any of several alternative and eager suppliers, perhaps dividing their purchases among two or more suppliers to promote lively competition for orders. The suppliers of commoditylike items have market power only when supplies become quite tight and industry members are so eager to secure what they need that they agree to terms more favorable to suppliers.

- *Whether a few large suppliers are the primary sources of a particular item.* The leading suppliers may well have pricing leverage unless they are plagued with excess capacity and are scrambling to secure additional orders for their products. Major suppliers with good reputations and strong demand for the items they supply are harder to wring concessions from than struggling suppliers striving to broaden their customer base or more fully utilize their production capacity.

- *Whether it is difficult or costly for industry members to switch their purchases from one supplier to another or to switch to attractive substitute inputs.* High switching costs signal strong bargaining power on the part of suppliers, whereas low switching costs and ready availability of good substitute inputs signal weak bargaining power. Soft-drink bottlers, for example, can counter the bargaining power of aluminum-can suppliers by shifting or threatening to shift to greater use of plastic containers and introducing more attractive plastic-container designs.

- *Whether certain needed inputs are in short supply.* Suppliers of items in short supply have some degree of pricing power, whereas a surge in the availability of particular items greatly weakens supplier pricing power and bargaining leverage.

- *Whether certain suppliers provide a differentiated input that enhances the performance or quality of the industry's product.* The more valuable a particular input is in terms of enhancing the performance or quality of the products of industry members or of improving the efficiency of their production processes, the more bargaining leverage its suppliers are likely to possess.

■ *Whether certain suppliers provide equipment or services that deliver valuable cost-saving efficiencies to industry members in operating their production processes.* Suppliers that provide cost-saving equipment or other valuable or necessary production-related services are likely to possess bargaining leverage. Industry members that do not source from such suppliers may find themselves at a cost disadvantage and thus under competitive pressure to do so (on terms that are favorable to the suppliers).

■ *Whether suppliers provide an item that accounts for a sizable fraction of the costs of the industry's product.* The bigger the cost of a particular part or component, the more opportunity for the pattern of competition in the marketplace to be affected by the actions of suppliers to raise or lower their prices.

■ *Whether industry members are major customers of suppliers.* As a rule, suppliers have less bargaining leverage when their sales to members of one industry constitute a big percentage of their total sales. In such cases, the well-being of suppliers is closely tied to the well-being of their major customers. Suppliers then have a big incentive to protect and enhance their customers' competitiveness via reasonable prices, exceptional quality, and ongoing advances in the technology of the items supplied.

■ *Whether it makes good economic sense for industry members to integrate backward and self-manufacture items they have been buying from suppliers.* The make-or-buy issue generally boils down to whether suppliers that specialize in the production of a particular part or component and make it in volume for many different customers have the expertise and scale economies to supply an as-good or better component at a lower cost than industry members could achieve via self-manufacture. Frequently, it is difficult for industry members to self-manufacture parts and components more economically than they can obtain them from suppliers that specialize in making such items. For instance, most producers of outdoor power equipment (lawn mowers, rotary tillers, leaf blowers, etc.) find it cheaper to source the small engines they need from outside manufacturers that specialize in small-engine manufacture than to make their own engines because the quantity of engines they need is too small to justify the investment in manufacturing facilities, master the production process, and capture scale economies. Specialists in small-engine manufacture, by supplying many kinds of engines to the whole power equipment industry, can obtain a big-enough sales volume to fully realize scale economies, become proficient in all the manufacturing techniques, and keep costs low. As a rule, suppliers are safe from the threat of self-manufacture by their customers *until* the volume of parts a customer needs becomes large enough for the customer to justify backward integration into self-manufacture of the component. Suppliers also gain bargaining power when they have the resources and profit incentive to integrate forward into the business of the customers they are supplying and thus become a strong rival.

Figure 2.7 summarizes the conditions that tend to make supplier bargaining power strong or weak.

How Seller-Supplier Collaboration Can Create Competitive Pressures   In more and more industries, sellers are forging strategic partnerships with select suppliers in efforts to (1) reduce inventory and logistics costs (e.g., through just-in-time deliveries), (2) speed the availability of next-generation components, (3) enhance the quality of the parts and components being supplied and reduce defect

Figure 2.7   Factors Affecting the Bargaining Power of Suppliers

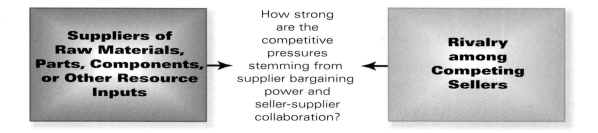

| Suppliers of Raw Materials, Parts, Components, or Other Resource Inputs | → How strong are the competitive pressures stemming from supplier bargaining power and seller-supplier collaboration? ← | Rivalry among Competing Sellers |

Supplier bargaining power is stronger when:
- Industry members incurs high costs in switching their purchases to alternative suppliers.
- Needed inputs are in short supply (which gives suppliers more leverage in setting prices).
- A supplier has a differentiated input that enhances the quality or performance of sellers' products or is a valuable or critical part of sellers' production processes.
- There are only a few suppliers of a particular input.
- Some suppliers threaten to integrate forward into the business of industry members and perhaps become a powerful rival.

Supplier bargaining power is weaker when:
- The item being supplied is a commodity that is readily available from many suppliers at the going market price.
- Seller switching costs to alternative suppliers are low.
- Good substitute inputs exist or new ones emerge.
- There is a surge in the availability of supplies (thus greatly weakening supplier pricing power).
- Industry members account for a big fraction of suppliers' total sales and continued high volume purchases are important to the well-being of suppliers.
- Industry members are a threat to integrate backward into the business of suppliers and to self-manufacture their own requirements.
- Seller collaboration or partnering with selected suppliers provides attractive win-win opportunities.

rates, and (4) squeeze out important cost savings for both themselves and their suppliers. Numerous Internet technology applications are now available that permit real-time data sharing, eliminate paperwork, and produce cost savings all along the supply chain. The many benefits of effective seller-supplier collaboration can translate into competitive advantage for industry members who do the best job of managing supply chain relationships.

Dell Computer has used strategic partnering with key suppliers as a major element in its strategy to be the world's lowest-cost supplier of branded PCs, servers, and workstations. Because Dell has managed its supply chain relationships in ways that contribute to a low-cost, high-quality competitive edge in components supply, it has put enormous pressure on its PC rivals to try to imitate its supply chain management practices. Effective partnerships with suppliers on the part of one or more industry members can thus become a major source of competitive pressure for rival firms.

The more opportunities that exist for win-win efforts between a company and its suppliers, the less their relationship is characterized by who has the upper hand in bargaining with the other. As long as the relationship is producing valuable benefits for both parties, it will last; only if a supply partner is falling behind alternative suppliers is a company likely to switch suppliers and incur the costs and trouble of building close working ties with a different supplier.

Competitive Pressures Stemming from Buyer Bargaining Power and Seller–Buyer Collaboration

Whether seller-buyer relationships represent a weak or strong competitive force depends on (1) whether some or many buyers have sufficient bargaining leverage to obtain price concessions and other favorable terms and conditions of sale and (2) the extent and competitive importance of seller-buyer strategic partnerships in the industry.

How Buyer Bargaining Power Can Create Competitive Pressures   As with suppliers, the leverage that certain types of buyers have in negotiating favorable terms can range from weak to strong. Individual consumers, for example, rarely have much bargaining power in negotiating price concessions or other favorable terms with sellers; the primary exceptions involve situations in which price haggling is customary, such as the purchase of new and used motor vehicles, homes, and certain big-ticket items like luxury watches, jewelry, and pleasure boats. For most consumer goods and services, individual buyers have no bargaining leverage—their option is to pay the seller's posted price or take their business elsewhere.

In contrast, large retail chains like Wal-Mart, Circuit City, Target, and Home Depot typically have considerable negotiating leverage in purchasing products from manufacturers because of manufacturers' need for broad retail exposure and the most appealing shelf locations. Retailers may stock two or three competing brands of a product but rarely all competing brands, so competition among rival manufacturers for visibility on the shelves of popular multistore retailers gives such retailers significant bargaining strength. Major supermarket chains like Kroger, Safeway, and Royal Ahold, which provide access to millions of grocery shoppers, have sufficient bargaining power to demand promotional allowances and lump-sum payments (called *slotting fees*) from food products manufacturers in return for stocking certain brands or putting them in the best shelf locations. Motor vehicle manufacturers have strong bargaining power in negotiating to buy original-equipment tires from Goodyear, Michelin, Bridgestone/Firestone, Continental, and Pirelli not only because they buy in large quantities but also because tire makers believe they gain an advantage in supplying replacement tires to vehicle owners if their tire brand is original equipment on the vehicle. "Prestige" buyers have a degree of clout in negotiating with sellers because a seller's reputation is enhanced by having prestige buyers on its customer list.

Even if buyers do not purchase in large quantities or offer a seller important market exposure or prestige, they gain a degree of bargaining leverage in the following circumstances:[10]

■ *If buyers' costs of switching to competing brands or substitutes are relatively low.* Buyers who can readily switch brands or source from several sellers have more negotiating leverage than buyers who have high switching costs. When the products of rival sellers are virtually identical, it is relatively easy for buyers to switch from seller to seller at little or no cost and anxious sellers may be willing to make concessions to win or retain a buyer's business.

- *If the number of buyers is small or if a customer is particularly important to a seller.* The smaller the number of buyers, the less easy it is for sellers to find alternative buyers when a customer is lost to a competitor. The prospect of losing a customer not easily replaced often makes a seller more willing to grant concessions of one kind or another.

- *If buyer demand is weak and sellers are scrambling to secure additional sales of their products.* Weak or declining demand creates a "buyers' market"; conversely, strong or rapidly growing demand creates a "sellers' market" and shifts bargaining power to sellers.

- *If buyers are well-informed about sellers' products, prices, and costs.* The more information buyers have, the better bargaining position they are in. The mushrooming availability of product information on the Internet is giving added bargaining power to individuals. Buyers can easily use the Internet to compare prices and features of vacation packages, shop for the best interest rates on mortgages and loans, and find the best prices on big-ticket items such as digital cameras. Bargain-hunting individuals can shop around for the best deal on the Internet and use that information to negotiate a better deal from local retailers; this method is becoming commonplace in buying new and used motor vehicles. Further, the Internet has created opportunities for manufacturers, wholesalers, retailers, and sometimes individuals to join online buying groups to pool their purchasing power and approach vendors for better terms than could be gotten individually. A multinational manufacturer's geographically scattered purchasing groups can use Internet technology to pool their orders with parts and components suppliers and bargain for volume discounts. Purchasing agents at some companies are banding together at third-party Web sites to pool corporate purchases to get better deals or special treatment.

- *If buyers pose a credible threat of integrating backward into the business of sellers.* Companies like Anheuser-Busch, Coors, and Heinz have integrated backward into metal-can manufacturing to gain bargaining power in obtaining the balance of their can requirements from otherwise powerful metal-can manufacturers. Retailers gain bargaining power by stocking and promoting their own private-label brands alongside manufacturers' name brands. Wal-Mart, for example, competes against Procter & Gamble, its biggest supplier, with its own brand of laundry detergent, called Sam's Choice, which is priced 25 to 30 percent lower than P&G's Tide. Wal-Mart also markets over 2,000 other grocery items under its Sam's Choice and Great Value private labels—its growing strategic emphasis on private-label products adds to its bargaining power with name-brand manufacturers.

- *If buyers have discretion in whether and when they purchase the product.* Many consumers, if they are unhappy with the present deals offered on major appliances or hot tubs or home entertainment centers, may be in a position to delay purchase until prices and financing terms improve. If business customers are not happy with the prices or security features of bill-payment software systems, they can either delay purchase until next-generation products become available or attempt to develop their own software in-house. If college students believe that the prices of new textbooks are too high, they can purchase used copies.

Figure 2.8 summarizes the circumstances that make for strong or weak bargaining power on the part of buyers.

Figure 2.8   Factors Affecting the Bargaining Power of Buyers

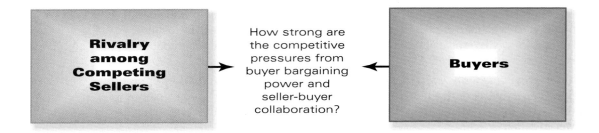

Buyer bargaining power is stronger when:
■ Buyer switching costs to competing brands or substitute products are low.
■ Buyers are large and can demand concessions when purchasing large quantities.
■ Large-volume purchases by buyers are important to sellers.
■ Buyer demand is weak or declining.
■ There are only a few buyers—so each one's business is important to sellers.
■ Identity of buyer adds prestige to the seller's list of customers.
■ Quantity and quality of information available to buyers improve.
■ Buyers have the ability to postpone purchases until later if they do not like the present deals being offered by sellers.
■ Some buyers are a threat to integrate backward into the business of sellers and become an important competitor.

Buyer bargaining power is weaker when:
■ Buyers purchase the item infrequently or in small quantities.
■ Buyer switching costs to competing brands are high.
■ There is a surge in buyer demand that creates a "sellers' market."
■ A seller's brand reputation is important to a buyer.
■ A particular seller's product delivers quality or performance that is very important to buyer and that is not matched in other brands.
■ Buyer collaboration or partnering with selected sellers provides attractive win-win opportunities.

A final point to keep in mind is that *not all buyers of an industry's product have equal degrees of bargaining power with sellers,* and some may be less sensitive than others to price, quality, or service differences. For example, independent tire retailers have less bargaining power in purchasing tires than do Honda, Ford, and Daimler-Chrysler (which buy in much larger quantities), and they are also less sensitive to quality. Motor vehicle manufacturers are very particular about tire quality and tire performance because of the effects on vehicle performance, and they drive a hard bargain with tire manufacturers on both price and quality. Apparel manufacturers confront significant bargaining power when selling to retail chains like JCPenney, Sears, or Macy's, but they can command much better prices selling to small owner-managed apparel boutiques.

How Seller-Buyer Collaboration Can Create Competitive Pressures   Partnerships between sellers and buyers are an increasingly important element of the competitive picture in *business-to-business relationships* (as opposed to business-to-consumer relationships). Many sellers that provide items to business customers have found it in their mutual interest to collaborate closely on such matters as just-in-time deliveries, order processing, electronic invoice payments, and data sharing. Wal-Mart, for example, provides the manufacturers with which it does business (like Procter & Gamble) with daily sales data from each of its stores so that the manufacturers can maintain sufficient inventories at Wal-Mart's distribution centers to keep the shelves at each Wal-Mart store amply stocked. Dell Computer has partnered with its largest customers to create online systems for over 50,000 corporate customers, providing their employees with information on approved product configurations, global pricing, paperless purchase orders, real-time order tracking, invoicing, purchasing history, and other efficiency tools. Dell also loads a customer's software at the factory and installs asset tags so that customer setup time is minimal; it also helps customers upgrade their PC systems to next-generation hardware and software. Dell's partnerships with its corporate customers have put significant competitive pressure on other PC makers.

Determining Whether the Collective Strength of the Five Competitive Forces Is Conducive to Good Profitability

Scrutinizing each of the five competitive forces one by one provides a powerful diagnosis of what competition is like in a given market. Once the strategist has gained an understanding of the specific competitive pressures composing each force and determined whether these pressures constitute a strong or weak competitive force, the next step is to evaluate the collective strength of the five forces and determine whether the state of competition is conducive to good profitability. Is the collective impact of the five competitive forces stronger than "normal"? Are some of the competitive forces sufficiently strong to undermine industry profitability? Can companies in this industry reasonably expect to earn decent profits in light of the prevailing competitive forces?

Are Competitive Pressures Conducive to Good Profitability?

As a rule, the stronger the collective impact of the five competitive forces, the lower the combined profitability of industry participants. The most extreme case of a "competitively unattractive" industry is one in which all five forces are producing strong competitive pressures: rivalry among sellers is vigorous, low entry barriers allow new rivals to gain a market foothold, competition from substitutes is intense, and both suppliers and customers are able to exercise considerable bargaining leverage. Fierce to strong competitive pressures coming from all five directions nearly always drive industry profitability to unacceptably low levels, frequently producing losses for many industry members and forcing some out of business. But an industry can be competitively unattractive without all five competitive forces being strong. Intense competitive pressures from just two or three of the five forces may suffice to destroy the conditions for good profitability and prompt some companies to exit the business. The manufacture of disk drives, for example, is brutally competitive; IBM recently announced the sale of its disk drive business to Hitachi, taking a loss of over $2 billion on its exit from the business. Especially intense competitive conditions seem to be the norm in tire manufacturing and apparel, two industries where profit margins have historically been thin.

> **Core Concept**
>
> The stronger the forces of competition, the harder it becomes for industry members to earn attractive profits.

In contrast, when the collective impact of the five competitive forces is moderate to weak, an industry is competitively attractive in the sense that industry members can reasonably expect to earn good profits and a nice return on investment. The ideal competitive environment for earning superior profits is one in which both suppliers and customers are in weak bargaining positions, there are no good substitutes, high barriers block further entry, and rivalry among present sellers generates only moderate competitive pressures. Weak competition is the best of all possible worlds for also-ran companies because even they can usually eke out a decent profit—if a company can't make a decent profit when competition is weak, then its business outlook is indeed grim.

In most industries, the collective strength of the five competitive forces is somewhere near the middle of the two extremes of very intense and very weak, typically ranging from slightly stronger than normal to slightly weaker than normal and typically allowing well-managed companies with sound strategies to earn attractive profits.

> A company's strategy is increasingly effective the more it provides some insulation from competitive pressures and shifts the competitive battle in the company's favor.

Matching Company Strategy to Competitive Conditions Working through the five-forces model step by step not only aids strategy makers in assessing whether the intensity of competition allows good profitability but also promotes sound strategic thinking about how to better match company strategy to the specific competitive character of the marketplace. Effectively matching a company's strategy to the particular competitive pressures and competitive conditions that exist has two aspects:

1. Pursuing actions to shield the firm from the prevailing competitive pressures as much as possible.

2. Initiating actions calculated to produce sustainable competitive advantage, thereby shifting the competitive battle in the company's favor, putting added competitive pressure on rivals, and perhaps even defining the business model for the industry.

But making headway on these two fronts first requires identifying competitive pressures, gauging the relative strength of each, and gaining a deep enough understanding of the state of competition in the industry to know which strategy buttons to push.

The Drivers of Industry Change: What Impacts Will They Have?

An industry's present conditions don't necessarily reveal much about the strategically relevant ways in which the industry environment is changing. All industries are characterized by trends and new developments that gradually or speedily produce changes important enough to require a strategic response from participating firms. The popular hypothesis that industries go through a life cycle of takeoff, rapid growth, early maturity, market saturation, and stagnation or decline helps explain industry change—but it is far from complete.[11] There are more causes of industry change than an industry's normal progression through the life cycle.

The Concept of Driving Forces

Although it is important to judge what growth stage an industry is in, there's more analytical value in identifying the specific factors causing fundamental industry and competitive adjustments. Industry and competitive conditions change because forces are enticing or pressuring certain industry participants (competitors, customers, suppliers) to alter their actions in important ways.[12] **Driving forces** are those that have the biggest influence on the changes under way in the industry's structure and competitive environment. Some driving forces originate in the outer ring of the company's macroenvironment (see Figure 2.2), but most usually originate in the company's more immediate industry and competitive environment. Driving-forces analysis has two steps: (1) identifying what the driving forces are and (2) assessing the impact they will have on the industry.

> **Core Concept**
>
> Industry conditions change because important forces are *driving* industry participants to alter their actions; the **driving forces** in an industry are the *major underlying causes* of changing industry and competitive conditions—some driving forces originate in the macroenvironment and some originate within a company's immediate industry and competitive environment.

Identifying the Industry's Driving Forces

Many events can affect an industry powerfully enough to qualify as driving forces—as shown in Table 2.1. Some are unique and specific to a particular industry situation, but most drivers of change fall into one of the following categories:[13]

- *Growing use of the Internet and adoption of emerging new Internet technology applications:* Over the past 10 years, the Internet and the adoption of Internet technology applications have been major drivers of change in industry after industry. As cases in point, consider how downloading music from the Internet is reshaping the music industry and the business of traditional brick-and-mortar retailers and how the use of e-mail is affecting the business of providing fax services and the revenues of governmental postal services worldwide. The Internet has proved to be an important new distribution channel in a growing number of industries, enabling manufacturers to access customers directly rather than distribute exclusively through traditional wholesale and retail channels, and also allowing companies of all types to extend their geographic reach and vie for sales in areas where they formerly did not have a presence. The ability of companies to reach

Table 2.1   THE MOST COMMON DRIVING FORCES

1. Growing use of the Internet and emerging new Internet technology applications.
2. Increasing globalization of the industry.
3. Changes in the industry's long-term growth rate.
4. Changes in who buys the product and how they use it.
5. Product innovation.
6. Technological change and manufacturing process innovation.
7. Marketing innovation.
8. Entry or exit of major firms.
9. Diffusion of technical know-how across more companies and more countries.
10. Changes in cost and efficiency.
11. Growing buyer preferences for differentiated products instead of standardized commodity products (or for a more standardized product instead of strongly differentiated products).
12. Reductions in uncertainty and business risk.
13. Regulatory influences and government policy changes.
14. Changing societal concerns, attitudes, and lifestyles.

consumers via the Internet increases the number of rivals a company faces and often escalates rivalry by pitting pure online sellers against combination brick-and-click sellers against pure brick-and-mortar sellers. The Web sites of rival sellers are only a few clicks apart and are open for business 24 hours a day every day of the year, giving buyers unprecedented ability to research the product offerings of competitors and shop the market for the best value. Companies are increasingly using online technology to (1) collaborate closely with suppliers and streamline their supply chains and (2) revamp internal operations and squeeze out cost savings. Internet technology has so many business applications that companies across the world are pursuing its operational benefits and making online systems a normal part of everyday operations. But the impacts vary from industry to industry and company to company, and the industry and competitive implications are continuously evolving. The challenges here are to assess precisely how the Internet and Internet technology applications are altering a particular industry's landscape and to factor these impacts into the strategy-making equation.

- *Increasing globalization:* Competition begins to shift from primarily a regional or national focus to an international or global focus when industry members begin seeking customers in foreign markets or when production activities begin to migrate to countries where costs are lowest. Globalization of competition really starts to take hold when one or more ambitious companies precipitate a race for worldwide market leadership by launching initiatives to expand into more and more country markets. Globalization can also be precipitated by the blossoming of consumer demand in more and more countries and by the actions of government officials in many countries to reduce trade barriers or open up once-closed markets to foreign competitors, as is occurring in many parts of Europe, Latin America, and Asia. Significant differences in labor costs among countries give manufacturers a strong incentive to locate plants for labor-intensive products in low-wage countries and use these plants to supply market demand across the world. Wages in China, India, Singapore, Mexico, and Brazil, for example, are about one-fourth those in the United States, Germany, and Japan. The forces of globalization are sometimes such a strong driver that companies find it highly advantageous, if not necessary, to spread their operating reach into more and more country markets. Globalization is very much a driver of industry change in such industries as credit cards, mobile phones, motor vehicles, steel, refined petroleum products, public accounting, and textbook publishing.

- *Changes in the long-term industry growth rate:* Shifts in industry growth up or down are a driving force for industry change, affecting the balance between industry supply and buyer demand, entry and exit, and the character and strength of competition. An upsurge in buyer demand triggers a race among established firms and newcomers to capture the new sales opportunities; ambitious companies with trailing market shares may see the upturn in demand as a golden opportunity to broaden their customer base and move up several notches in the industry standings to secure a place among the market leaders. A slowdown in the rate at which demand is growing nearly always portends mounting rivalry and increased efforts by some firms to maintain their high rates of growth by taking sales and market share away from rivals. If industry sales suddenly turn flat or begin to shrink after years of rising steadily, competition is certain to intensify as industry members scramble for the available business and as mergers and acquisitions result in industry consolidation to a smaller number of competitively stronger participants. Dimming sales prospects usually prompt both competitively weak and growth-oriented companies to sell their business operations to those industry members that elect to stick it out; as demand for the industry's product continues to shrink, the remaining industry members may be forced to close inefficient plants and retrench to a smaller production base—all of which results in a much-changed competitive landscape.

■ *Changes in who buys the product and how they use it:* Shifts in buyer demographics and new ways of using the product can alter the state of competition by opening the way to market an industry's product through a different mix of dealers and retail outlets, prompting producers to broaden or narrow their product lines, bringing different sales and promotion approaches into play, and forcing adjustments in customer service offerings (credit, technical assistance, maintenance and repair). The mushrooming popularity of downloading music from the Internet, storing music files on PC hard drives, and burning custom discs has forced recording companies to reexamine their distribution strategies and raised questions about the future of traditional retail music stores; at the same time, it has stimulated sales of disc burners and blank discs. Longer life expectancies and growing percentages of relatively well-to-do retirees are driving changes in such industries as health care, prescription drugs, recreational living, and vacation travel. The growing percentage of households with PCs and Internet access is opening opportunities for banks to expand their electronic bill-payment services and for retailers to move more of their customer services online.

■ *Product innovation:* Competition in an industry is always affected by rivals racing to be first to introduce one new product or product enhancement after another. An ongoing stream of product innovations tends to alter the pattern of competition in an industry by attracting more first-time buyers, rejuvenating industry growth, and/or creating wider or narrower product differentiation among rival sellers. Successful new product introductions strengthen the market positions of the innovating companies, usually at the expense of companies that stick with their old products or are slow to follow with their own versions of the new product. Product innovation has been a key driving force in such industries as digital cameras, golf clubs, video games, toys, and prescription drugs.

■ *Technological change and manufacturing process innovation:* Advances in technology can dramatically alter an industry's landscape, making it possible to produce new and better products at lower cost and opening up whole new industry frontiers. For instance, growing use of Voice Over Internet Protocol technology (VOIP) has given rise to an Internet-based phone network and is rapidly eroding the business of AT&T and other long-distance providers worldwide. Flat-screen technology for PC monitors is killing the demand for conventional CRT monitors. LCD and plasma-screen technology and high-definition technology are precipitating a revolution in the television industry. MP3 technology is altering the shape of the music industry. Digital technology is driving huge changes in the camera and film industries. Technological developments can also produce competitively significant changes in capital requirements, minimum efficient plant sizes, distribution channels and logistics, and experience or learning-curve effects. In the steel industry, ongoing advances in electric-arc minimill technology (which involve recycling scrap steel to make new products) have allowed steelmakers with state-of-the-art minimills to gradually expand into the production of more and more steel products, steadily taking sales and market share from higher-cost integrated producers (which make steel from scratch using iron ore, coke, and traditional blast furnace technology). Nucor, the leader of the minimill technology revolution in the United States, began operations in 1970 and has ridden the wave of technological advances in minimill technology to become the biggest U.S. steel producer (as of 2004) and rank among the lowest-cost producers in the world. In a space of 30 years, advances in minimill technology have changed the face of the steel industry worldwide.

■ *Marketing innovation:* When firms are successful in introducing new ways to market their products, they can spark a burst of buyer interest, widen industry demand, increase product differentiation, and lower unit costs—any or all of which can alter the competitive positions of rival firms and force strategy revisions. In today's world, Internet marketing is shaking up competition in such industries as electronics retailing, stock brokerage (where online brokers have taken significant business away from traditional brokers), and office supplies (where Office Depot, Staples, and Office Max are using their Web sites to market office supplies to corporations, small businesses, schools and universities, and government agencies). Increasing numbers of music artists are marketing their recordings at their own Web sites rather than entering into contracts with recording studios that distribute through music retailers and online music stores.

■ *Entry or exit of major firms:* The entry of one or more foreign companies into a geographic market once dominated by domestic firms nearly always shakes up competitive conditions. Likewise, when an established domestic firm from another industry attempts entry either by acquisition or by launching its own start-up venture, it usually applies its skills and resources in some innovative fashion that pushes competition in new directions. Entry by a major firm thus often produces a new ball game, not only with new key players but also with new rules for competing. Similarly, exit of a major firm changes the competitive structure by reducing the number of market leaders (perhaps increasing the dominance of the leaders that remain) and causing a rush to capture the exiting firm's customers.

■ *Diffusion of technical know-how across more companies and more countries:* As knowledge about how to perform a particular activity or execute a particular manufacturing technology spreads, the competitive advantage held by firms originally possessing this know-how erodes. Knowledge diffusion can occur through scientific journals, trade publications, on-site plant tours, word of mouth among suppliers and customers, employee migration, and Internet sources. It can also occur when those possessing technological know-how license others to use it for a royalty fee or team up with a company interested in turning the technology into a new business venture. Quite often, technological know-how can be acquired by simply buying a company that has the wanted skills, patents, or manufacturing capabilities. In recent years, *rapid technology transfer across national boundaries has been a prime factor in causing industries to become more globally competitive.* As companies worldwide gain access to valuable technical know-how, they upgrade their manufacturing capabilities in a long-term effort to compete head-on with established companies. Cross-border technology transfer has made the once domestic industries of automobiles, tires, consumer electronics, telecommunications, computers, and others increasingly global.

■ *Changes in cost and efficiency:* Widening or shrinking differences in the costs among key competitors tend to dramatically alter the state of competition. The low cost of e-mail and fax transmission has put mounting competitive pressure on the relatively inefficient and high-cost operations of the U.S. Postal Service—sending a one-page fax is cheaper and far quicker than sending a first-class letter; sending e-mail is faster and cheaper still. In the electric power industry, sharply lower costs to generate electricity at newly constructed combined-cycle generating plants during 1998–2001 forced older coal-fired and gas-fired plants to lower their production costs to remain competitive. Shrinking cost differences in producing multifeatured mobile phones is turning the mobile phone market into a commodity business and causing more buyers to base their purchase decisions on price.

■   *Growing buyer preferences for differentiated products instead of a commodity product (or for a more standardized product instead of strongly differentiated products):* When buyer tastes and preferences start to diverge, sellers can win a loyal following with product offerings that stand apart from those of rival sellers. In recent years, beer drinkers have grown less loyal to a single brand and have begun to drink a variety of domestic and foreign beers; as a consequence, beer manufacturers have introduced a host of new brands and malt beverages with different tastes and flavors. Buyer preferences for motor vehicles are becoming increasingly diverse, with few models generating sales of more than 250,000 units annually. When a shift from standardized to differentiated products occurs, the driver of change is the contest among rivals to cleverly differentiate themselves.

However, buyers sometimes decide that a standardized, budget-priced product suits their requirements as well as or better than a premium-priced product with lots of snappy features and personalized services. Online brokers, for example, have used the lure of cheap commissions to attract many investors willing to place their own buy-sell orders via the Internet; growing acceptance of online trading has put significant competitive pressures on full-service brokers whose business model has always revolved around convincing clients of the value of asking for personalized advice from professional brokers and paying their high commission fees to make trades. Pronounced shifts toward greater product standardization usually spawn lively price competition and force rival sellers to drive down their costs to maintain profitability. The lesson here is that competition is driven partly by whether the market forces in motion are acting to increase or decrease product differentiation.

■   *Reductions in uncertainty and business risk:* An emerging industry is typically characterized by much uncertainty over potential market size, how much time and money will be needed to surmount technological problems, and what distribution channels and buyer segments to emphasize. Emerging industries tend to attract only risk-taking entrepreneurial companies. Over time, however, if the business model of industry pioneers proves profitable and market demand for the product appears durable, more conservative firms are usually enticed to enter the market. Often, these later entrants are large, financially strong firms looking to invest in attractive growth industries.

Lower business risks and less industry uncertainty also affect competition in international markets. In the early stages of a company's entry into foreign markets, conservatism prevails and firms limit their downside exposure by using less risky strategies like exporting, licensing, joint marketing agreements, or joint ventures with local companies to accomplish entry. Then, as experience accumulates and perceived risk levels decline, companies move more boldly and more independently, making acquisitions, constructing their own plants, putting in their own sales and marketing capabilities to build strong competitive positions in each country market, and beginning to link the strategies in each country to create a more globalized strategy.

■ *Regulatory influences and government policy changes:* Government regulatory actions can often force significant changes in industry practices and strategic approaches. Deregulation has proved to be a potent procompetitive force in the airline, banking, natural gas, telecommunications, and electric utility industries. Government efforts to reform Medicare and health insurance have become potent driving forces in the health care industry. In international markets, host governments can drive competitive changes by opening their domestic markets to foreign participation or closing them to protect domestic companies. Note that this driving force is spawned by forces in a company's macroenvironment.

■ *Changing societal concerns, attitudes, and lifestyles:* Emerging social issues and changing attitudes and lifestyles can be powerful instigators of industry change. Growing antismoking sentiment has emerged as a major driver of change in the tobacco industry; concerns about terrorism are having a big impact on the travel industry. Consumer concerns about salt, sugar, chemical additives, saturated fat, cholesterol, carbohydrates, and nutritional value have forced food producers to revamp food-processing techniques, redirect R&D efforts into the use of healthier ingredients, and compete in developing nutritious, good-tasting products. Safety concerns have driven product design changes in the automobile, toy, and outdoor power equipment industries, to mention a few. Increased interest in physical fitness has spawned new industries in exercise equipment, biking, outdoor apparel, sports gyms and recreation centers, vitamin and nutrition supplements, and medically supervised diet programs. Social concerns about air and water pollution have forced industries to incorporate expenditures for controlling pollution into their cost structures. Shifting societal concerns, attitudes, and lifestyles alter the pattern of competition, usually favoring those players that respond quickly and creatively with products targeted to the new trends and conditions. As with the preceding driving force, this driving force springs from factors at work in a company's macroenvironment.

That there are so many different *potential driving forces* explains why it is too simplistic to view industry change only in terms of moving through the different stages in an industry's life cycle and why a full understanding of the *causes* underlying the emergence of new competitive conditions is a fundamental part of industry analysis. However, while many forces of change may be at work in a given industry, no more than three or four are likely to be true driving forces powerful enough to qualify as the *major determinants* of why and how the industry is changing. Thus company strategists must resist the temptation to label every change they see as a driving force; the analytical task is to evaluate the forces of industry and competitive change carefully enough to separate major factors from minor ones.

Assessing the Impact of the Driving Forces

The second phase of driving-forces analysis is to determine whether the driving forces are, on the whole, acting to make the industry environment more or less attractive. Answers to three questions are needed here:

1. Are the driving forces causing demand for the industry's product to increase or decrease?

2. Are the driving forces acting to make competition more or less intense?

3. Will the driving forces lead to higher or lower industry profitability?

Getting a handle on the collective impact of the driving forces usually requires looking at the likely effects of each force separately, since the driving forces may not all be pushing change in the same direction. For example, two driving forces may be acting to spur demand for the industry's product while one driving force may be working to curtail demand. Whether the net effect on industry demand is up or down hinges on which driving forces are the more powerful. The analyst's objective here is to get a good grip on what external factors are shaping industry change and what difference these factors will make.[14]

The Link between Driving Forces and Strategy

Sound analysis of an industry's driving forces is a prerequisite to sound strategy making. Without understanding the forces driving industry change and the impacts these forces will have on the character of the industry environment and on the company's business over the next one to three years, managers are ill-prepared to craft a strategy tightly matched to emerging conditions. Similarly, if managers are uncertain about the implications of each driving force, or if their views are incomplete or off-base, it's difficult for them to craft a strategy that is responsive to the drivers of industry change. So driving-forces analysis is not something to take lightly; it has practical value and is basic to the task of thinking strategically about where the industry is headed and how to prepare for the changes.

Diagnosing the Market Positions of Industry Rivals: Who Is Strongly Positioned and Who Is Not?

Since competing companies commonly sell in different price/quality ranges, emphasize different distribution channels, incorporate product features that appeal to different types of buyers, have different geographic coverage, and so on, it stands to reason that some companies enjoy stronger or more attractive market positions than other companies. Understanding which companies are strongly positioned and which are weakly positioned is an integral part of analyzing an industry's competitive structure. The best technique for revealing the market positions of industry competitors is **strategic group mapping**.[15] This analytical tool is useful for comparing the market positions of each firm separately or for grouping them into like positions when an industry has so many competitors that it is not practical to examine each one in depth.

> **Core Concept**
>
> **Strategic group mapping** is a technique for displaying the different market or competitive positions that rival firms occupy in the industry.

Using Strategic Group Maps to Assess the Market Positions of Key Competitors

A **strategic group** consists of those industry members with similar competitive approaches and positions in the market.[16] Companies in the same strategic group can resemble one another in any of several ways: they may have comparable product-line breadth, sell in the same price/quality range, emphasize the same distribution channels,

> **Core Concept**
>
> A **strategic group** is a cluster of industry rivals that have similar competitive approaches and market positions.

use essentially the same product attributes to appeal to similar types of buyers, depend on identical technological approaches, or offer buyers similar services and technical assistance.[17] An industry contains only one strategic group when all sellers pursue essentially identical strategies and have comparable market positions. At the other extreme, an industry may contain as many strategic groups as there are competitors when each rival pursues a distinctively different competitive approach and occupies a substantially different market position.

The procedure for constructing a *strategic group map* is straightforward:

- Identify the competitive characteristics that differentiate firms in the industry; typical variables are price/quality range (high, medium, low), geographic coverage (local, regional, national, global), degree of vertical integration (none, partial, full), product-line breadth (wide, narrow), use of distribution channels (one, some, all), and degree of service offered (no-frills, limited, full).

- Plot the firms on a two-variable map using pairs of these differentiating characteristics.

- Assign firms that fall in about the same strategy space to the same strategic group.

- Draw circles around each strategic group, making the circles proportional to the size of the group's share of total industry sales revenues.

This produces a two-dimensional diagram like the one for the retailing industry in Company Spotlight 2.1.

Several guidelines need to be observed in mapping the positions of strategic groups in the industry's overall strategy space.[18] First, the two variables selected as axes for the map should *not* be highly correlated; if they are, the circles on the map will fall along a diagonal and strategy makers will learn nothing more about the relative positions of competitors than they would by considering just one of the variables. For instance, if companies with broad product lines use multiple distribution channels while companies with narrow lines use a single distribution channel, then looking at broad versus narrow product lines reveals just as much about who is positioned where as looking at single versus multiple distribution channels; that is, one of the variables is redundant. Second, the variables chosen as axes for the map should expose big differences in how rivals position themselves to compete in the marketplace. This, of course, means analysts must identify the characteristics that differentiate rival firms and use these differences as variables for the axes and as the basis for deciding which firm belongs in which strategic group. Third, the variables used as axes don't have to be either quantitative or continuous; rather, they can be discrete variables or defined in terms of distinct classes and combinations. Fourth, drawing the sizes of the circles on the map proportional to the combined sales of the firms in each strategic group allows the map to reflect the relative sizes of each strategic group. Fifth, if more than two good competitive variables can be used as axes for the map, several maps can be drawn to give different exposures to the competitive positioning relationships present in the industry's structure. Because there is not necessarily one best map for portraying how competing firms are positioned in the market, it is advisable to experiment with different pairs of competitive variables.

What Can Be Learned from Strategic Group Maps?

One thing to look for is to what extent *industry driving forces and competitive pressures favor some strategic groups and hurt others.*[19] Firms in adversely affected strategic

Comparative Market Positions of Selected Retail Chains: A Strategic Group Map Application

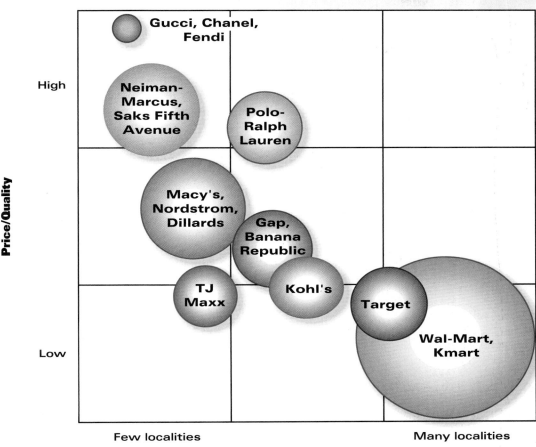

Geographic Coverage

Note: Circles are drawn roughly proportional to the sizes of the chains, based on revenues.

groups may try to shift to a more favorably situated group; how hard such a move proves to be depends on whether entry barriers for the target strategic group are high or low. Attempts by rival firms to enter a new strategic group nearly always increase competitive pressures. If certain firms are known to be trying to change their competitive positions on the map, then attaching arrows to the circles showing the targeted direction helps clarify the picture of competitive maneuvering among rivals.

> Driving forces and competitive pressures do not affect all strategic groups evenly. Profit prospects vary from group to group based on the relative attractiveness of their market positions.

Another consideration is to what extent *the profit potential of different strategic groups varies due to the strengths and weaknesses in each group's market position.* Differences in profitability can occur because of differing degrees of bargaining leverage or collaboration with suppliers and/or customers, differing degrees of exposure to competition from substitute products outside the industry, differing degrees of competitive rivalry within strategic groups, and differing growth rates for the principal buyer segments served by each group.

Generally speaking, *the closer strategic groups are to each other on the map, the stronger the cross-group competitive rivalry tends to be.* Although firms in the same strategic group are the closest rivals, the next closest rivals are in the immediately adjacent groups.[20] Often, firms in strategic groups that are far apart on the map hardly compete at all. For instance, Tiffany & Co. and Wal-Mart both sell gold and silver jewelry, but their clientele and the prices and quality of their products are much too different to justify calling them competitors. For the same reason, Timex is not a meaningful competitive rival of Rolex, and Subaru is not a close competitor of Lincoln or Mercedes-Benz.

Predicting the Next Strategic Moves Rivals Are Likely to Make

Unless a company pays attention to what competitors are doing and knows their strengths and weaknesses, it ends up flying blind into competitive battle. As in sports, scouting the opposition is essential. **Competitive intelligence** about rivals' strategies, their latest actions and announcements, their resource strengths and weaknesses, the efforts being made to improve their situation, and the thinking and leadership styles of their executives is valuable for predicting or anticipating the strategic moves competitors are likely to make next in the marketplace. Having good information to predict the strategic direction and likely moves of key competitors allows a company to prepare defensive countermoves, to craft its own strategic moves with some confidence about what market maneuvers to expect from rivals, and to exploit any openings that arise from competitors' missteps or strategy flaws.

> Good scouting reports on rivals provide a valuable assist in anticipating what moves rivals are likely to make next and outmaneuvering them in the marketplace.

Identifying Competitors' Strategies and Resource Strengths and Weaknesses

Keeping close tabs on a competitor's strategy entails monitoring what the rival is doing in the marketplace, what its management is saying in company press releases, information posted on the company's Web site (especially press releases and the presentations management has recently made to securities analysts), and such public documents as annual reports and 10-K filings, articles in the business media, and reports of securities analysts. (Figure 1.1 in Chapter 1 indicates what to look for in identifying a company's strategy.) Company personnel may be able to pick up useful information from a rival's exhibits at trade shows and from conversations with a rival's customers, suppliers, and former employees.[21] Many companies have a competitive intelligence unit that sifts through the available information to construct up-to-date strategic profiles of rivals—their current strategies, their resource strengths and competitive capabilities, their competitive shortcomings, and the latest pronouncements and leadership styles of their executives. Such profiles are typically updated regularly and made available to managers and other key personnel.

Those who gather competitive intelligence on rivals, however, can sometimes cross the fine line between honest inquiry and unethical or even illegal behavior. For example, calling rivals to get information about prices, the dates of new product introductions, or wage and salary levels is legal, but misrepresenting one's company affiliation during such calls is unethical. Pumping rivals' representatives at trade shows is ethical only if one wears a name tag with accurate company affiliation indicated. Avon Products at one point secured information about its biggest rival, Mary Kay Cosmetics (MKC), by having its personnel search through the garbage bins outside MKC's headquarters.[22] When MKC officials learned of the action and sued, Avon claimed it did nothing illegal, since a 1988 Supreme Court case had ruled that trash left on public property (in this case, a sidewalk) was anyone's for the taking. Avon even produced a videotape of its removal of the trash at the MKC site. Avon won the lawsuit—but Avon's action, while legal, scarcely qualifies as ethical.

In sizing up the strategies and the competitive strengths and weaknesses of competitors, it makes sense for company strategists to make three assessments:

1. Which competitor has the best strategy? Which competitors appear to have flawed or weak strategies?

2. Which competitors are poised to gain market share, and which ones seem destined to lose ground?

3. Which competitors are likely to rank among the industry leaders five years from now? Do one or more up-and-coming competitors have powerful strategies and sufficient resource capabilities to overtake the current industry leader?

The industry's *current* major players are generally easy to identify, but some of the leaders may be plagued with weaknesses that are causing them to lose ground; others may lack the resources and capabilities to remain strong contenders given the superior strategies and capabilities of up-and-coming companies. In evaluating which competitors are favorably or unfavorably positioned to gain market ground, company strategists need to focus on why there is potential for some rivals to do better or worse than other rivals. Usually, a competitor's prospects are a function of its vulnerability to driving forces and competitive pressures, whether its strategy has resulted in competitive advantage or disadvantage, and whether its resources and capabilities are well suited for competing on the road ahead.

Predicting Competitors' Next Moves

Predicting the next strategic moves of competitors is the hardest yet most useful part of competitor analysis. Good clues about what actions a specific company is likely to undertake can often be gleaned from how well it is faring in the marketplace, the problems or weaknesses it needs to address, and how much pressure it is under to improve its financial performance. Content rivals are likely to continue their present strategy with only minor fine-tuning. Ailing rivals can be performing so poorly that fresh strategic moves are virtually certain. Ambitious rivals looking to move up in the industry ranks are strong candidates for launching new strategic offensives to pursue emerging market opportunities and exploit the vulnerabilities of weaker rivals.

Since the moves a competitor is likely to make are generally predicated on the views their executives have about the industry's future and their beliefs about their firm's situation, it makes sense to closely scrutinize the public pronouncements of rival company executives about where the industry is headed and what it will take to be successful, what they are saying about their firm's situation, information from the grapevine about what they are doing, and their past actions and leadership styles. Other considerations in trying to predict what strategic moves rivals are likely to make next include the following:

- Which rivals badly need to increase their unit sales and market share? What strategic options are they most likely to pursue: lowering prices, adding new models and styles, expanding their dealer networks, entering additional geographic markets, boosting advertising to build better brand-name awareness, acquiring a weaker competitor, or placing more emphasis on direct sales via their Web site?

- Which rivals have a strong incentive, along with the resources, to make major strategic changes, perhaps moving to a different position on the strategic group map? Which rivals are probably locked in to pursuing the same basic strategy with only minor adjustments?

- Which rivals are good candidates to be acquired? Which rivals may be looking to make an acquisition and are financially able to do so?

- Which rivals are likely to enter new geographic markets?

- Which rivals are strong candidates to expand their product offerings and enter new product segments where they do not currently have a presence?

> Managers who fail to study competitors closely risk being caught napping by the new strategic moves of rivals.

To succeed in predicting a competitor's next moves, company strategists need to have a good feel for each rival's situation, how its managers think, and what its best options are. Doing the necessary detective work can be tedious and time-consuming, but scouting competitors well enough to anticipate their next moves allows managers to prepare effective countermoves (perhaps even beat a rival to the punch) and to take rivals' probable actions into account in crafting their own best course of action.

Pinpointing the Key Factors for Future Competitive Success

An industry's **key success factors (KSFs)** are those competitive factors that most affect industry members' ability to prosper in the marketplace—the particular strategy elements, product attributes, resources, competencies, competitive capabilities, and market achievements that spell the difference between being a strong competitor and a weak competitor and sometimes between profit and loss. KSFs by their very nature are so important to future competitive success that *all firms* in the industry must pay close attention to them or risk becoming an industry also-ran. To indicate the significance of KSFs another way, how well a company's product offering, resources, and capabilities measure up against an industry's KSFs determines just how financially and competitively successful that company will be. Identifying KSFs, in light of the prevailing and anticipated industry and competitive conditions, is therefore always a top-priority analytical and strategy-making consideration. Company strategists

> **Core Concept**
>
> **Key success factors** are the product attributes, competencies, competitive capabilities, and market achievements with the greatest impact on future competitive success in the marketplace.

need to understand the industry landscape well enough to separate the factors most important to competitive success from those that are less important.

In the beer industry, the KSFs are full utilization of brewing capacity (to keep manufacturing costs low), a strong network of wholesale distributors (to get the company's brand stocked and favorably displayed in retail outlets where beer is sold), and clever advertising (to induce beer drinkers to buy the company's brand and thereby pull beer sales through the established wholesale/retail channels). In apparel manufacturing, the KSFs are appealing designs and color combinations (to create buyer interest) and low-cost manufacturing efficiency (to permit attractive retail pricing and ample profit margins). In tin and aluminum cans, because the cost of shipping empty cans is substantial, one of the keys is having can-manufacturing facilities located close to end-use customers. Key success factors thus vary from industry to industry, and even from time to time within the same industry, as driving forces and competitive conditions change. Table 2.2 lists the most common types of key success factors.

An industry's key success factors can usually be deduced from what was learned from the previously described analysis of the industry and competitive environment. The factors that are most important to future competitive success flow directly from the industry's dominant characteristics, the nature of the competition, the impacts of the driving forces, the comparative market positions of industry members, and the likely next moves of key rivals. In addition, the answers to three questions help identify an industry's key success factors:

1. On what basis do buyers of the industry's product choose between the competing brands of sellers? That is, what product attributes are crucial?

2. Given the nature of competitive rivalry and the competitive forces prevailing in the marketplace, what resources and competitive capabilities does a company need to have to be competitively successful?

3. What shortcomings are almost certain to put a company at a significant competitive disadvantage?

Only rarely are there more than five or six key factors for future competitive success. And even among these, two or three usually outrank the others in importance. Managers should therefore bear in mind the purpose of identifying key success factors—to determine which factors are most important to future competitive success—and resist the temptation to label a factor that has only minor importance a KSF. To compile a list of every factor that matters even a little bit defeats the purpose of concentrating management attention on the factors truly critical to long-term competitive success.

Correctly diagnosing an industry's KSFs raises a company's chances of crafting a sound strategy. The goal of company strategists should be to design a strategy aimed at stacking up well on all of the industry's future KSFs and trying to be *distinctively better* than rivals on one (or possibly two) of the KSFs. Indeed, companies that stand out or excel on a particular KSF are likely to enjoy a stronger market position—*being distinctively better than rivals on one or two key success factors tends to translate into competitive advantage.* Hence, using the industry's KSFs as *cornerstones* for the company's strategy and trying to gain sustainable competitive advantage by excelling at one particular KSF is a fruitful competitive strategy approach.[23]

> **Core Concept**
>
> A sound strategy incorporates the intent to stack up well on all of the industry's key success factors and to excel on one or two KSFs.

Table 2.2   COMMON TYPES OF INDUSTRY KEY SUCCESS FACTORS

Technology-related KSFs	■ Expertise in a particular technology or in scientific research (important in pharmaceuticals, Internet applications, mobile communications, and most "high-tech" industries) ■ Proven ability to improve production processes (important in industries where advancing technology opens the way for higher manufacturing efficiency and lower production costs)
Manufacturing-related KSFs	■ Ability to achieve scale economies and/or capture experience-curve effects (important to achieving low production costs) ■ Quality control know-how (important in industries where customers insist on product reliability) ■ High utilization of fixed assets (important in capital-intensive/high-fixed-cost industries) ■ Access to attractive supplies of skilled labor ■ High labor productivity (important for items with high labor content) ■ Low-cost product design and engineering (reduces manufacturing costs) ■ Ability to manufacture or assemble products that are customized to buyer specifications
Distribution-related KSFs	■ A strong network of wholesale distributors/dealers ■ Strong direct-sales capabilities via the Internet and/or company-owned retail outlets ■ Ability to secure favorable display space on retailer shelves
Marketing-related KSFs	■ Breadth of product line and product selection ■ A well-known and well-respected brand name ■ Fast, accurate technical assistance ■ Courteous, personalized customer service ■ Accurate filling of buyer orders (few back orders or mistakes) ■ Customer guarantees and warranties (important in mail-order and online retailing, big-ticket purchases, new product introductions) ■ Clever advertising
Skills- and capability-related KSFs	■ A talented workforce (superior talent is important in professional services like accounting and investment banking) ■ National or global distribution capabilities ■ Product innovation capabilities (important in industries where rivals are racing to be first to market with new product attributes or performance features) ■ Design expertise (important in fashion and apparel industries) ■ Short delivery time capability ■ Supply chain management capabilities ■ Strong e-commerce capabilities—a user-friendly Web site and/or skills in using Internet technology applications to streamline internal operations
Other types of KSFs	■ Overall low costs (not just in manufacturing) so as to be able to meet low-price expectations of customers ■ Convenient locations (important in many retailing businesses) ■ Ability to provide fast, convenient after-the-sale repairs and service ■ A strong balance sheet and access to financial capital (important in newly emerging industries with high degrees of business risk and in capital-intensive industries) ■ Patent protection

Deciding Whether the Industry Presents an Attractive Opportunity

The final step in evaluating the industry and competitive environment is to use the preceding analysis to decide whether the outlook for the industry presents the company with a sufficiently attractive business opportunity. The important factors on which to base such a conclusion include:

- The industry's growth potential.

- Whether powerful competitive forces are squeezing industry profitability to subpar levels and whether competition appears destined to grow stronger or weaker.

- Whether industry profitability will be favorably or unfavorably affected by the prevailing driving forces.

- The degrees of risk and uncertainty in the industry's future.

- Whether the industry as a whole confronts severe problems—regulatory or environmental issues, stagnating buyer demand, industry overcapacity, mounting competition, and so on.

- The company's competitive position in the industry vis-à-vis rivals. (Being a well-entrenched leader or strongly positioned contender in a lackluster industry may present adequate opportunity for good profitability; however, having to fight a steep uphill battle against much stronger rivals may hold little promise of eventual market success or good return on shareholder investment, even though the industry environment is attractive.)

- The company's potential to capitalize on the vulnerabilities of weaker rivals (perhaps converting a relatively unattractive *industry* situation into a potentially rewarding *company* opportunity).

- Whether the company has sufficient competitive strength to defend against or counteract the factors that make the industry unattractive.

- Whether continued participation in this industry adds importantly to the firm's ability to be successful in other industries in which it may have business interests.

As a general proposition, *if an industry's overall profit prospects are above average, the industry environment is basically attractive; if industry profit prospects are below average, conditions are unattractive.* However, it is a mistake to think of a particular industry as being equally attractive or unattractive to all industry participants and all potential entrants. Attractiveness is relative, not absolute, and conclusions one way or the other have to be drawn from the perspective of a particular company. Industries attractive to insiders may be unattractive to outsiders. Companies on the outside may look at an industry's environment and conclude that it is an unattractive business for them to get into, given the prevailing entry barriers, the difficulty of challenging current market leaders with their particular resources and competencies, and the opportunities they have elsewhere. Industry environments unattractive to weak competitors may be attractive to strong competitors. A favorably positioned company may survey a business environment and see a host of opportunities that weak competitors cannot capture.

> **Core Concept**
> The degree to which an industry is attractive or unattractive is not the same for all industry participants and all potential entrants; the attractiveness of the opportunities an industry presents depends heavily on whether a company has the resource strengths and competitive capabilities to capture them.

When a company decides an industry is fundamentally attractive and presents good opportunities, a strong case can be made that it should invest aggressively to capture the opportunities it sees and to improve its long-term competitive position in the business. When a strong competitor concludes an industry is relatively unattractive and lacking in opportunity, it may elect to simply protect its present position, investing cautiously, if at all, and looking for opportunities in other industries. A competitively weak company in an unattractive industry may see its best option as finding a buyer, perhaps a rival, to acquire its business.

Key Points

Thinking strategically about a company's external situation involves probing for answers to the following seven questions:

1. *What are the industry's strategy-shaping economic features?* Industries differ significantly on such factors as market size and growth rate, the geographic scope of competitive rivalry, the number and relative sizes of both buyers and sellers, the ease of entry and exit, the extent of vertical integration, how fast basic technology is changing, the extent of scale economies and learning-curve effects, the degree of product standardization or differentiation, and overall profitability. In addition to setting the stage for the analysis to come, identifying an industry's economic features also promotes understanding of the kinds of strategic moves that industry members are likely to employ.

2. *What kinds of competitive forces are industry members facing, and how strong is each force?* The strength of competition is a composite of five forces: the rivalry among competing sellers, the presence of attractive substitutes, the potential for new entry, the competitive pressures stemming from supplier bargaining power and supplier-seller collaboration, and the competitive pressures stemming from buyer bargaining power and seller-buyer collaboration. These five forces have to be examined one by one to identify the specific competitive pressures they each comprise and to decide whether these pressures constitute a strong or weak competitive force. The next step in competition analysis is to evaluate the collective strength of the five forces and determine whether the state of competition is conducive to good profitability. Working through the five-forces model step by step not only aids strategy makers in assessing whether the intensity of competition allows good profitability but also promotes sound strategic thinking about how to better match company strategy to the specific competitive character of the marketplace. Effectively matching a company's strategy to the particular competitive pressures and competitive conditions that exist has two aspects: (a) pursuing avenues that shield the firm from as many of the prevailing competitive pressures as possible, and (b) initiating actions calculated to produce sustainable competitive advantage, thereby shifting competition in the company's favor, putting added competitive pressure on rivals, and perhaps even defining the business model for the industry.

3. *What forces are driving changes in the industry, and what impact will these changes have on competitive intensity and industry profitability?* Industry and competitive conditions change because forces are in motion that create incentives or pressures for change. The first phase is to identify the forces that are driving change in the industry; the most common driving forces include the Internet and

Internet technology applications, globalization of competition in the industry, changes in the long-term industry growth rate, changes in buyer composition, product innovation, entry or exit of major firms, changes in cost and efficiency, changing buyer preferences for standardized versus differentiated products or services, regulatory influences and government policy changes, changing societal and lifestyle factors, and reductions in uncertainty and business risk. The second phase of driving-forces analysis is to determine whether the driving forces, taken together, are acting to make the industry environment more or less attractive. Are the driving forces causing demand for the industry's product to increase or decrease? Are the driving forces acting to make competition more or less intense? Will the driving forces lead to higher or lower industry profitability?

4. *What market positions do industry rivals occupy—who is strongly positioned and who is not?* Strategic group mapping is a valuable tool for understanding the similarities, differences, strengths, and weaknesses inherent in the market positions of rival companies. Rivals in the same or nearby strategic groups are close competitors, whereas companies in distant strategic groups usually pose little or no immediate threat. The lesson of strategic group mapping is that some positions on the map are more favorable than others. The profit potential of different strategic groups varies due to strengths and weaknesses in each group's market position. Often, industry driving forces and competitive pressures favor some strategic groups and hurt others.

5. *What strategic moves are rivals likely to make next?* This analytical step involves identifying competitors' strategies, deciding which rivals are likely to be strong contenders and which are likely to be weak, evaluating rivals' competitive options, and predicting their next moves. Scouting competitors well enough to anticipate their actions can help a company prepare effective countermoves (perhaps even beating a rival to the punch) and allows managers to take rivals' probable actions into account in designing their own company's best course of action. Managers who fail to study competitors risk being caught unprepared by the strategic moves of rivals.

6. *What are the key factors for competitive success?* An industry's key success factors (KSFs) are the particular strategy elements, product attributes, competitive capabilities, and business outcomes that spell the difference between being a strong competitor and being a weak competitor—and sometimes between profit and loss. KSFs by their very nature are so important to competitive success that *all firms* in the industry must pay close attention to them or risk becoming an industry also-ran. Correctly diagnosing an industry's KSFs raises a company's chances of crafting a sound strategy. The goal of company strategists should be to design a strategy aimed at stacking up well on all of the industry KSFs and trying to be *distinctively better* than rivals on one (or possibly two) of the KSFs. Indeed, using the industry's KSFs as *cornerstones* for the company's strategy and trying to gain sustainable competitive advantage by excelling at one particular KSF is a fruitful competitive strategy approach.

7. *Does the outlook for the industry present the company with sufficiently attractive prospects for profitability?* The answer to this question is a major driver of company strategy. An assessment that the industry and competitive environment is fundamentally attractive typically suggests employing a strategy calculated to build a stronger competitive position in the business, expanding sales efforts, and

investing in additional facilities and equipment as needed. If the industry is relatively unattractive, outsiders considering entry may decide against it and look elsewhere for opportunities, weak companies in the industry may merge with or be acquired by a rival, and strong companies may restrict further investments and employ cost-reduction strategies or product innovation strategies to boost long-term competitiveness and protect their profitability. On occasion, an industry that is unattractive overall is still very attractive to a favorably situated company with the skills and resources to take business away from weaker rivals.

A competently conducted industry and competitive analysis generally tells a clear, easily understood story about the company's external environment. Different analysts can have different judgments about competitive intensity, the impacts of driving forces, how industry conditions will evolve, how good the outlook is for industry profitability, and the degree to which the industry environment offers the company an attractive business opportunity. However, while no method can guarantee a single conclusive diagnosis about the state of industry and competitive conditions and an industry's future outlook, this doesn't justify shortcutting hard-nosed strategic analysis and relying instead on opinion and casual observation. Managers become better strategists when they know what questions to pose and what tools to use. This is why this chapter has concentrated on suggesting the right questions to ask, explaining concepts and analytical approaches, and indicating the kinds of things to look for. There's no substitute for staying on the cutting edge of what's happening in the industry—anything less weakens managers' ability to craft strategies that are well matched to the industry and competitive situation.

Exercises

1. As the owner of a new fast-food enterprise seeking a loan from a bank to finance the construction and operation of three new store locations, you have been asked to provide the loan officer with a brief analysis of the competitive environment in fast food. Draw a five-forces diagram for the fast-food industry, and briefly discuss the nature and strength of each of the five competitive forces in fast food.

2. Based on the strategic group map in Company Spotlight 2.1, (a) who are Wal-Mart's two closest competitors? (b) between which two strategic groups is competition the weakest? and (c) which strategic group faces the weakest competition from the members of other strategic groups?

3. Based on your knowledge of the ice-cream industry, which of the following factors might qualify as possible driving forces capable of causing fundamental change in the industry's structure and competitive environment?

   a) Increasing sales of frozen yogurt and frozen sorbets.

   b) The potential for additional makers of ice cream to enter the market.

   c) Growing consumer interest in low-calorie/low-fat/low-carb/sugar-free dessert alternatives.

d) A slowdown in consumer purchases of ice-cream products.

e) Rising prices for milk, sugar, and other ice-cream ingredients.

f) A decision by Häagen-Dazs to increase its prices by 10 percent.

g) A decision by Ben & Jerry's to add five new flavors to its product line.

h) A trend on the part of several prominent ice-cream manufacturers to introduce low-fat, low-carb, sugar-free ice-cream products in response to consumer interest in healthier ice-cream alternatives.

CHAPTER 3

Analyzing a Company's Resources and Competitive Position

Before executives can chart a new strategy, they must reach common understanding of the company's current position.

—W. Chan Kim and Rene Mauborgne

The real question isn't how well you're doing today against your own history, but how you're doing against your competitors.

—Donald Kress

Organizations succeed in a competitive marketplace over the long run because they can do certain things their customers value better than can their competitors.

—Robert Hayes, Gary Pisano, and David Upton

Only firms who are able to continually build new strategic assets faster and cheaper than their competitors will earn superior returns over the long term.

—C. C. Markides and P. J. Williamson

In Chapter 2 we described how to use the tools of industry and competitive analysis to assess a company's external environment and lay the groundwork for matching a company's strategy to its external situation. In this chapter we discuss the techniques of evaluating a company's internal circumstances and competitiveness—its resource capabilities, relative cost position, and competitive strength versus rivals. The analytical spotlight will be trained on five questions:

1. How well is the company's present strategy working?
2. What are the company's resource strengths and weaknesses and its external opportunities and threats?
3. Are the company's prices and costs competitive?
4. Is the company competitively stronger or weaker than key rivals?
5. What strategic issues and problems merit front-burner managerial attention?

In probing for answers to these questions, four analytical tools—SWOT analysis, value chain analysis, benchmarking, and competitive strength assessment—will be used. All four are valuable techniques for revealing a company's competitiveness and for helping company managers match their strategy to the company's own particular circumstances.

Evaluating How Well a Company's Present Strategy Is Working

In determining how well a company's present strategy is working, a manager has to start with what the strategy is. Figure 3.1 shows the key components of a single-business company's strategy. The first thing to pin down is the company's competitive approach. Is the company striving to be a low-cost leader *or* stressing ways to differentiate its product offering from rivals? Is it concentrating its efforts on serving a broad spectrum of customers *or* a narrow market niche? Another strategy-defining consideration is the firm's competitive scope within the industry—what its geographic market coverage is and whether it operates in just a single stage of the industry's production/distribution chain or is vertically integrated across several stages. Another good indication of the company's strategy is whether the company has made moves recently to improve its competitive position and performance—for instance, by cutting prices, improving design, stepping up advertising, entering a new geographic market (domestic or foreign), or merging with a competitor. The company's functional strategies in R&D, production, marketing, finance, human resources, information technology, and so on, further characterize company strategy.

While there's merit in evaluating the strategy from a *qualitative* standpoint (its completeness, internal consistency, rationale, and relevance), the best *quantitative* evidence of how well a company's strategy is working comes from its results. The two best empirical indicators are (1) whether the company is achieving its stated financial and strategic objectives and (2) whether the company is an above-average industry performer. Persistent shortfalls in meeting company performance targets and weak performance relative to rivals are reliable warning signs that the company suffers from

Figure 3.1   Identifying the Components of a Single-Business Company's Strategy

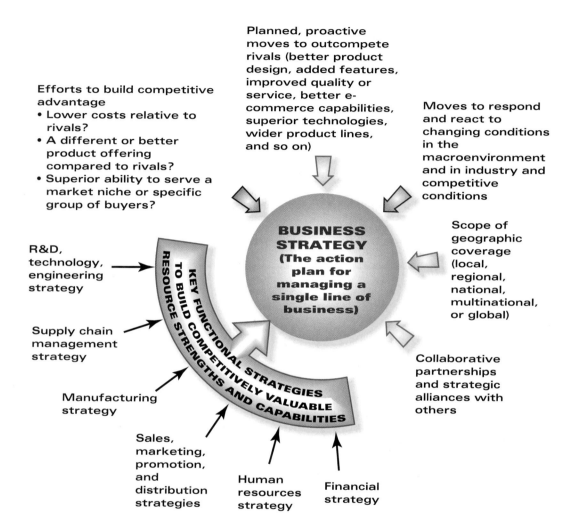

poor strategy making, less-than-competent strategy execution, or both. Other indicators of how well a company's strategy is working include:

- Whether the firm's sales are growing faster than, slower than, or about the same pace as the market as a whole, thus resulting in a rising, eroding, or stable market share.

- Whether the company is acquiring new customers at an attractive rate as well as retaining existing customers.

- Whether the firm's profit margins are increasing or decreasing and how well its margins compare to rival firms' margins.

- Trends in the firm's net profits and return on investment and how these compare to the same trends for other companies in the industry.

■ Whether the company's overall financial strength and credit rating are improving or declining.

■ Whether the company can demonstrate continuous improvement in such internal performance measures as days of inventory, employee productivity, unit cost, defect rate, scrap rate, misfilled orders, delivery times, warranty costs, and so on.

■ How shareholders view the company based on trends in the company's stock price and shareholder value (relative to the stock price trends at other companies in the industry).

■ The firm's image and reputation with its customers.

■ How well the company stacks up against rivals on technology, product innovation, customer service, product quality, delivery time, price, speed in getting newly developed products to market, and other relevant factors on which buyers base their choice of brands.

The stronger a company's current overall performance, the less likely the need for radical changes in strategy. The weaker a company's financial performance and market standing, the more its current strategy must be questioned. Weak performance is almost always a sign of weak strategy, weak execution, or both.

> The stronger a company's financial performance and market position, the more likely it has a well-conceived, well-executed strategy.

Sizing Up a Company's Resource Strengths and Weaknesses and Its External Opportunities and Threats

Appraising a company's resource *strengths* and *weaknesses* and its external *opportunities* and *threats*, commonly known as **SWOT analysis**, provides a good overview of whether its overall situation is fundamentally healthy or unhealthy. Just as important, a first-rate SWOT analysis provides the basis for crafting a strategy that capitalizes on the company's resources, aims squarely at capturing the company's best opportunities, and defends against the threats to its well-being.

> **SWOT analysis** is a simple but powerful tool for sizing up a company's resource capabilities and deficiencies, its market opportunities, and the external threats to its future well-being.

Identifying Company Resource Strengths and Competitive Capabilities

A *strength* is something a company is good at doing or an attribute that enhances its competitiveness. A strength can take any of several forms:

■ *A skill or important expertise*—low-cost manufacturing capabilities, technological know-how, strong e-commerce expertise, skills in improving production processes, a proven track record in defect-free manufacture, expertise in providing consistently good customer service, excellent mass-merchandising skills, or unique advertising and promotional talents.

■ *Valuable physical assets*—state-of-the-art plants and equipment, attractive real estate locations, worldwide distribution facilities, or ownership of valuable natural resource deposits.

■ *Valuable human assets*—an experienced and capable workforce, talented employees in key areas, cutting-edge knowledge and intellectual capital, collective learning embedded in the organization and built up over time, or proven managerial know-how.[1]

■ *Valuable organizational assets*—proven quality control systems, proprietary technology, key patents, mineral rights, a cadre of highly trained customer service representatives, sizable amounts of cash and marketable securities, a strong balance sheet and credit rating (thus giving the company access to additional financial capital), or a comprehensive list of customers' e-mail addresses.

■ *Valuable intangible assets*—a powerful or well-known brand name, a reputation for technological leadership, or strong buyer loyalty and goodwill.

■ *Competitive capabilities*—product innovation capabilities, short development times in bringing new products to market, a strong dealer network, cutting-edge supply chain management capabilities, quickness in responding to shifting market conditions and emerging opportunities, or state-of-the-art systems for doing business via the Internet.

■ *An achievement or attribute that puts the company in a position of market advantage*—low overall costs relative to competitors, market share leadership, a superior product, a wider product line than rivals, wide geographic coverage, a well-known brand name, superior e-commerce capabilities, or exceptional customer service.

■ *Competitively valuable alliances or cooperative ventures*—fruitful partnerships with suppliers that reduce costs and/or enhance product quality and performance; alliances or joint ventures that provide access to valuable technologies, competencies, or geographic markets.

> **Core Concept**
>
> A company is better positioned to succeed if it has a competitively valuable complement of resources at its command.

Taken together, a company's strengths determine the complement of competitively valuable *resources* with which it competes—a company's resource strengths represent *competitive assets*. The caliber of a firm's resource strengths and competitive capabilities, along with its ability to mobilize them in the pursuit of competitive advantage, is a big determinant of how well a company will perform in the marketplace.[2]

Company Competencies and Competitive Capabilities   Sometimes a company's resource strengths relate to fairly specific skills and expertise (like just-in-time inventory control), and sometimes they flow from pooling the knowledge and expertise of different organizational groups to create a company competence or competitive capability. Competence or capability in continuous product innovation, for example, comes from teaming the efforts of people and groups with expertise in market research, new product R&D, design and engineering, cost-effective manufacturing, and market testing. Company competencies can range from merely a competence in performing an activity to a core competence to a distinctive competence:

> **Core Concept**
>
> A **competence** is an activity that a company has learned to perform well.

1. A **competence** is something an organization is good at doing. It is nearly always the product of experience, representing an accumulation of learning and the buildup of proficiency in performing an internal activity. Usually a company competence originates with deliberate efforts to develop the organizational ability to do something, however imperfectly or inefficiently. Such efforts involve

selecting people with the requisite knowledge and skills, upgrading or expanding individual abilities as needed, and then molding the efforts and work products of individuals into a cooperative group effort to create organizational ability. Then, as experience builds, such that the company gains proficiency in performing the activity consistently well and at an acceptable cost, the ability evolves into a true competence and company capability. Examples of competencies include proficiency in merchandising and product display, the capability to create attractive and easy-to-use Web sites, expertise in a specific technology, proven capabilities in selecting good locations for retail outlets, and a proficiency in working with customers on new applications and uses of the product.

2. A **core competence** is a proficiently performed internal activity that is *central* to a company's strategy and competitiveness. A core competence is a more valuable resource strength than a competence because of the well-performed activity's core role in the company's strategy and the contribution it makes to the company's success in the marketplace. A core competence can relate to any of several aspects of a company's business: expertise in integrating multiple technologies to create families of new products, know-how in creating and operating systems for cost-efficient supply chain management, the capability to speed new or next-generation products to market, good after-sale service capabilities, skills in manufacturing a high-quality product at a low cost, or the capability to fill customer orders accurately and swiftly. A company may have more than one core competence in its resource portfolio, but rare is the company that can legitimately claim more than two or three core competencies. Most often, *a core competence is knowledge-based, residing in people and in a company's intellectual capital and not in its assets on the balance sheet.* Moreover, a core competence is more likely to be grounded in cross-department combinations of knowledge and expertise than to be the product of a single department or work group.

> **Core Concept**
>
> A **core competence** is a *competitively important* activity that a company performs better than other internal activities.

3. A **distinctive competence** is a competitively valuable activity that a company *performs better than its rivals.* A distinctive competence thus represents a *competitively superior resource strength.* A company may perform one competitively important activity well enough to claim that activity as a core competence, but what a company does best internally doesn't translate into a distinctive competence unless the company enjoys *competitive superiority in performing that activity.* For instance, most retailers believe they have core competencies in product selection and in-store merchandising, but many retailers run into trouble in the marketplace because they encounter rivals whose core competencies in product selection and in-store merchandising are better than theirs. Consequently, *a core competence becomes a basis for competitive advantage only when it rises to the level of a distinctive competence.* The distinctive competencies of Toyota and Honda in low-cost, high-quality manufacturing and in short design-to-market cycles for new models have proved to be considerable competitive advantages in the global market for motor vehicles. Toyota's production system is far superior to that of any other automaker's, and the company is pushing the boundaries of its production advantage with a new type of assembly line—the "Global Body line"—that costs 50 percent less to install and can be changed to accommodate a new model for 70 percent less

> **Core Concept**
>
> A **distinctive competence** is a competitively important activity that a company performs better than its rivals—it thus represents *a competitively superior resource strength.*

than its previous production system.[3] Intel's distinctive competence in rapidly developing new generations of ever-more-powerful semiconductor chips for PCs and network servers has helped give the company a dominating presence in the semiconductor industry. Starbucks' distinctive competence in store ambience and innovative coffee drinks has made it the leading coffee drink retailer.

The conceptual differences between a competence, a core competence, and a distinctive competence draw attention to the fact that competitive capabilities are not all equal.[4] Some competencies and competitive capabilities merely enable market survival because most rivals have them—indeed, not having a competence or capability that rivals have can result in competitive disadvantage. Core competencies are *competitively* more important than competencies because they add power to the company's strategy and have a bigger positive impact on its market position and profitability. A distinctive competence is even more important because it represents a *uniquely strong* competitive capability that holds the potential for yielding competitive advantage. It is always easier to build competitive advantage when a firm has a distinctive competence in performing an activity important to market success, when rival companies do not have offsetting competencies, and when it is costly and time-consuming for rivals to imitate the competence. A distinctive competence can thus be the mainspring of a company's success—unless it is trumped by more powerful resources of rivals.

> **Core Concept**
>
> The importance of a distinctive competence to strategy making rests with (1) the competitively valuable capability it gives a company, (2) its value as a cornerstone of strategy, and (3) the competitive edge it can produce in the marketplace.

What Is the Competitive Power of a Resource Strength?   It is not enough to simply compile a list of a company's resource strengths and competitive capabilities. What is most telling about a company's strengths, individually and collectively, is how powerful they are in the marketplace. The competitive power of a company strength is measured by how many of the following four tests it can pass:[5]

1. *Is the resource strength hard to copy?* The more difficult and more expensive it is to imitate a company's resource strength, the greater its potential competitive value. Resources tend to be difficult to copy when they are unique (a fantastic real estate location, patent protection), when they must be built over time in ways that are difficult to imitate (a brand name, mastery of a technology), and when they carry big capital requirements (a cost-effective plant to manufacture cutting-edge microprocessors). Wal-Mart's competitors have failed miserably in their attempts over the past two decades to match Wal-Mart's superefficient state-of-the-art distribution capabilities. Hard-to-copy strengths and capabilities are valuable competitive assets, adding to a company's market strength and contributing to sustained profitability.

2. *Is the resource strength durable—does it have staying power?* The longer the competitive value of a resource lasts, the greater the value of the resource. Some resources lose their clout in the marketplace quickly because of the rapid speeds at which technologies or industry conditions are moving. The value of Eastman Kodak's resources in film and film processing is rapidly being undercut by the growing popularity of digital cameras. The investments that commercial banks have made in branch offices are a rapidly depreciating asset because of growing use of direct deposits, automated teller machines, and telephone and Internet banking options.

3. *Is the resource really competitively superior?* Companies have to guard against pridefully believing that their core competences are distinctive competences or that their brand name is more powerful than the brand names of rivals. Who can really say whether Coca-Cola's consumer marketing prowess is better than PepsiCo's or whether the Mercedes-Benz brand name is more powerful than that of BMW or Lexus?

4. *Can the resource strength be trumped by the different resource strengths and competitive capabilities of rivals?* Many commercial airlines (American Airlines, Delta Airlines, Continental Airlines, Singapore Airlines) have attracted large numbers of passengers because of their resources and capabilities in offering safe, convenient, reliable air transportation services and in providing an array of amenities to passengers. However, Southwest Airlines has consistently been a more profitable air carrier because it provides safe, reliable, basic services at radically lower fares. The prestigious brand names of Cadillac and Lincoln have faded in the market for luxury cars because Mercedes, BMW, Audi, and Lexus have introduced the most appealing luxury vehicles in recent years. Amazon.com is putting a big dent in the business prospects of brick-and-mortar bookstores; likewise, Wal-Mart (with its lower prices) is putting major competitive pressure on Toys "R" Us, at one time the leading toy retailer in the United States.

The vast majority of companies are not well endowed with competitively valuable resources, much less with competitively superior resources capable of passing all four tests with high marks. Most firms have a mixed bag of resources—one or two quite valuable, some good, many satisfactory to mediocre. Only a few companies, usually the strongest industry leaders or up-and-coming challengers, possess a distinctive competence or competitively superior resource.

Even if a company doesn't possess a competitively superior resource, it can still marshal potential for winning in the marketplace if it has an assortment of good-to-adequate resources that *collectively* have competitive power in the marketplace. Toshiba's laptop computers were the market share leader throughout most of the 1990s—an indicator that Toshiba had competitively valuable resource strengths. Yet Toshiba's laptops were not demonstrably faster than rivals' laptops; nor did they have bigger screens, more memory, longer battery power, a better pointing device, or other superior performance features; nor did Toshiba provide clearly superior technical support services to buyers of its laptops. Further, Toshiba laptops were definitely not cheaper, model for model, than the comparable models of its rivals, and they seldom ranked first in the overall performance ratings done by various organizations. Rather, Toshiba's market share leadership stemmed from a *combination* of *good* resource strengths and capabilities—its strategic partnerships with suppliers of laptop components, efficient assembly capability, design expertise, skills in choosing quality components, a wide selection of models, the attractive mix of built-in performance

> Winning in the marketplace becomes more likely when a company has appropriate and ample resources with which to compete, and especially when it has strengths and capabilities with competitive advantage potential.

features found in each model when balanced against price, the better-than-average reliability of its models (based on buyer ratings), and very good technical support services (based on buyer ratings). The verdict from the marketplace was that PC buyers perceived Toshiba laptops as better, all things considered, than competing brands. (Shortly after 2000, however, Dell Computer overtook Toshiba as the global market leader in laptop PCs.)

Identifying Company Resource Weaknesses and Competitive Deficiencies

A *weakness,* or *competitive deficiency,* is something a company lacks or does poorly (in comparison to others) or a condition that puts it at a disadvantage in the marketplace. A company's weaknesses can relate to (1) inferior or unproven skills, expertise, or intellectual capital in competitively important areas of the business; (2) deficiencies in competitively important physical, organizational, or intangible assets; or (3) missing or competitively inferior capabilities in key areas. *Internal weaknesses are thus shortcomings in a company's complement of resources and represent competitive liabilities.* Nearly all companies have competitive liabilities of one kind or another. Whether a company's resource weaknesses make it competitively vulnerable depends on how much they matter in the marketplace and whether they are offset by the company's resource strengths.

> **Core Concept**
>
> A company's resource strengths represent competitive assets; its resource weaknesses represent competitive liabilities.

Table 3.1 lists the kinds of factors to consider in compiling a company's resource strengths and weaknesses. Sizing up a company's complement of resource capabilities and deficiencies is akin to constructing a *strategic balance sheet,* on which resource strengths represent *competitive assets* and resource weaknesses represent *competitive liabilities.* Obviously, the ideal condition is for the company's competitive assets to outweigh its competitive liabilities by an ample margin—a 50-50 balance is definitely not the desired condition!

Identifying a Company's Market Opportunities

Market opportunity is a big factor in shaping a company's strategy. Indeed, managers can't properly tailor strategy to the company's situation without first identifying its opportunities and appraising the growth and profit potential each one holds. Depending on the prevailing circumstances, a company's opportunities can be plentiful or scarce and can range from wildly attractive (an absolute "must" to pursue) to marginally interesting (because the growth and profit potential are questionable) to unsuitable (because there's not a good match with the company's strengths and capabilities). A checklist of potential market opportunities is included in Table 3.1.

In evaluating a company's market opportunities and ranking their attractiveness, managers have to guard against viewing every *industry* opportunity as a *company* opportunity. Not every company is equipped with the resources to successfully pursue each opportunity that exists in its industry. Some companies are more capable of going after particular opportunities than others, and a few companies may be hopelessly outclassed. *The market opportunities most relevant to a company are those that match up well with the company's financial and organizational resource capabilities, offer the best growth and profitability, and present the most potential for competitive advantage.*

> A company is well advised to pass on a particular market opportunity unless it has or can acquire the resources to capture it.

Identifying the Threats to a Company's Future Profitability

Often, certain factors in a company's external environment pose *threats* to its profitability and competitive well-being. Threats can stem from the emergence of cheaper or better technologies, rivals' introduction of new or improved products, the entry of

Table 3.1 WHAT TO LOOK FOR IN IDENTIFYING A COMPANY'S STRENGTHS, WEAKNESSES, OPPORTUNITIES, AND THREATS

Potential Resource Strengths and Competitive Capabilities	Potential Resource Weaknesses and Competitive Deficiencies
■ A powerful strategy ■ Core competencies in _____. ■ A distinctive competence in _____. ■ A product that is strongly differentiated from those of rivals ■ Competencies and capabilities that are well matched to industry key success factors ■ A strong financial condition; ample financial resources to grow the business ■ Strong brand-name image and/or company reputation ■ An attractive customer base ■ Economy of scale and/or learning and experience-curve advantages over rivals ■ Proprietary technology, superior technological skills, important patents ■ Superior intellectual capital relative to key rivals ■ Cost advantages over rivals ■ Strong advertising and promotion ■ Product innovation capabilities ■ Proven capabilities in improving production processes ■ Good supply chain management capabilities ■ Good customer service capabilities ■ Better product quality relative to rivals ■ Wide geographic coverage and/or strong global distribution capability ■ Alliances or joint ventures with other firms that provide access to valuable technology, competencies, and/or attractive geographic markets	■ No clear strategic direction ■ Resources that are not well matched to industry key success factors ■ No well-developed or proven core competencies ■ A weak balance sheet; burdensome debt ■ Higher overall unit costs relative to key competitors ■ Weak or unproven product innovation capabilities ■ A product/service with ho-hum attributes or features inferior to those of rivals ■ Too narrow a product line relative to rivals ■ Weak brand image or reputation ■ Weaker dealer network than key rivals and/or lack of adequate global distribution capability ■ Behind on product quality, R&D, and/or technological know-how ■ In the wrong strategic group ■ Losing market share because _____. ■ Lack of management depth ■ Inferior intellectual capital relative to leading rivals ■ Subpar profitability because _____. ■ Plagued with internal operating problems or obsolete facilities ■ Behind rivals in e-commerce capabilities ■ Short on financial resources to grow the business and pursue promising initiatives ■ Too much underutilized plant capacity

Potential Market Opportunities	Potential External Threats to a Company's Future Profitability
■ Openings to win market share from rivals ■ Sharply rising buyer demand for the industry's product ■ Serving additional customer groups or market segments ■ Expanding into new geographic markets ■ Expanding the company's product line to meet a broader range of customer needs ■ Utilizing existing company skills or technological know-how to enter new product lines or new businesses ■ Online sales via the Internet ■ Integrating forward or backward ■ Falling trade barriers in attractive foreign markets ■ Acquiring rival firms or companies with attractive technological expertise or capabilities ■ Entering into alliances or joint ventures to expand the firm's market coverage or boost its competitive capability ■ Openings to exploit emerging new technologies	■ Increasing intensity of competition among industry rivals—may squeeze profit margins ■ Slowdowns in market growth ■ Likely entry of potent new competitors ■ Loss of sales to substitute products ■ Growing bargaining power of customers or suppliers ■ A shift in buyer needs and tastes away from the industry's product ■ Adverse demographic changes that threaten to curtail demand for the industry's product ■ Vulnerability to industry driving forces ■ The introduction of restrictive trade policies in countries where the company does business ■ Costly new regulatory requirements ■ The emergence of cheaper or better technologies ■ Key rivals introduce innovative new products ■ Adverse changes in foreign exchange rates, interest rates, or energy prices

lower-cost foreign competitors into a company's market stronghold, new regulations that are more burdensome to a company than to its competitors, vulnerability to a rise in interest rates, the potential of a hostile takeover, unfavorable demographic shifts, adverse changes in foreign exchange rates, political upheaval in a foreign country where the company has facilities, and the like. External threats may pose no more than a moderate degree of adversity (all companies confront some threatening elements in the course of doing business), or they may be so imposing as to make a company's situation and outlook quite tenuous. It is management's job to identify the threats to the company's future well-being and to evaluate what strategic actions can be taken to neutralize or lessen their impact.

A list of potential threats to a company's future profitability and market position is included in Table 3.1.

What Do the SWOT Listings Reveal?

> Simply making lists of a company's strengths, weaknesses, opportunities, and threats is not enough; the payoff from SWOT analysis comes from the conclusions about a company's situation and the implications for strategy improvement that flow from the four lists.

SWOT analysis involves more than making four lists. The two most important parts of SWOT analysis are *drawing conclusions* from the SWOT listings about the company's overall situation and *acting on those conclusions* to better match the company's strategy to its resource strengths and market opportunities, to correct the important weaknesses, and to defend against external threats. Figure 3.2 shows the three steps of SWOT analysis.

What story the SWOT listings tell about the company's overall situation is often revealed in the answers to the following sets of questions:

- Does the company have an attractive set of resource strengths? Does it have any strong core competencies or a distinctive competence? Are the company's strengths and capabilities well matched to the industry key success factors? Do they add adequate power to the company's strategy, or are more or different strengths needed? Will the company's current strengths and capabilities matter in the future?

- How serious are the company's weaknesses and competitive deficiencies? Are they mostly inconsequential and readily correctable, or could one or more prove fatal if not remedied soon? Are some of the company's weaknesses in areas that relate to the industry's key success factors? Are there any weaknesses that, if uncorrected, would keep the company from pursuing an otherwise attractive opportunity? Does the company have important resource gaps that need to be filled for it to move up in the industry rankings and/or boost its profitability?

- Do the company's resource strengths and competitive capabilities (its competitive assets) outweigh its resource weaknesses and competitive deficiencies (its competitive liabilities) by an attractive margin?

- Does the company have attractive market opportunities that are well suited to its resource strengths and competitive capabilities? Does the company lack the resources and capabilities to pursue any of the most attractive opportunities?

- Are the threats alarming, or are they something the company appears able to deal with and defend against?

- All things considered, how strong is the company's overall situation? Where on a scale of 1 to 10 (where 1 is alarmingly weak and 10 is exceptionally strong) should the firm's position and overall situation be ranked? What aspects of the company's situation are particularly attractive? What aspects are of the most concern?

Figure 3.2   The Three Steps of SWOT Analysis: Identify, Draw Conclusions, Translate into Strategic Action

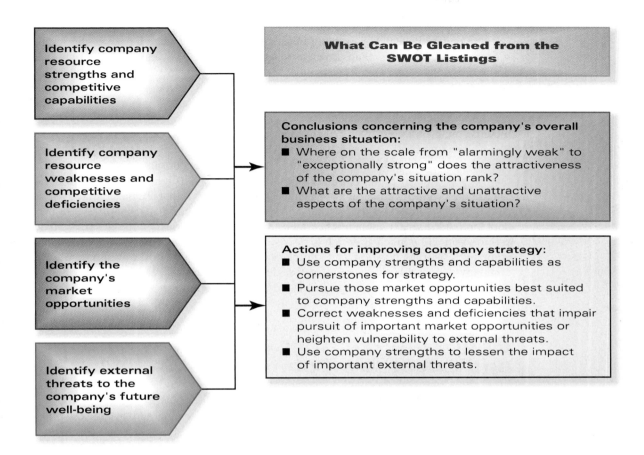

The final piece of SWOT analysis is to translate the diagnosis of the company's situation into actions for improving the company's strategy and business prospects. The following questions point to implications the SWOT listings have for strategic action:

■ Which competitive capabilities need to be strengthened immediately (so as to add greater power to the company's strategy and boost sales and profitability)? Do new types of competitive capabilities need to be put in place to help the company better respond to emerging industry and competitive conditions? Which resources and capabilities need to be given greater emphasis, and which merit less emphasis? Should the company emphasize leveraging its existing resource strengths and capabilities, or does it need to create new resource strengths and capabilities?

■ What actions should be taken to reduce the company's competitive liabilities? Which weaknesses or competitive deficiencies are in urgent need of correction?

■ Which market opportunities should be top priority in future strategic initiatives (because they are good fits with the company's resource strengths and competitive capabilities, present attractive growth and profit prospects, and/or offer the best potential for securing competitive advantage)? Which opportunities should be ignored, at least for the time being (because they offer less growth potential or are not suited to the company's resources and capabilities)?

■ What should the company be doing to guard against the threats to its well-being?

A company's resource strengths should generally form the cornerstones of strategy because they represent the company's best chance for market success.[6] As a rule, strategies that place heavy demands on areas where the company is weakest or has unproven ability are suspect and should be avoided. If a company doesn't have the resources and competitive capabilities around which to craft an attractive strategy, managers need to take decisive remedial action either to upgrade existing organizational resources and capabilities and add others as needed or to acquire them through partnerships or strategic alliances with firms possessing the needed expertise. Plainly, managers have to look toward correcting competitive weaknesses that make the company vulnerable, hold down profitability, or disqualify it from pursuing an attractive opportunity.

At the same time, sound strategy making requires sifting through the available market opportunities and aiming strategy at capturing those that are most attractive and suited to the company's circumstances. Rarely does a company have the resource depth to pursue all available market opportunities simultaneously without spreading itself too thin. How much attention to devote to defending against external threats to the company's market position and future performance hinges on how vulnerable the company is, whether there are attractive defensive moves that can be taken to lessen their impact, and whether the costs of undertaking such moves represent the best use of company resources.

Analyzing Whether a Company's Prices and Costs Are Competitive

Company managers are often stunned when a competitor cuts its price to "unbelievably low" levels or when a new market entrant comes on strong with a very low price.

> The higher a company's costs are above those of close rivals, the more competitively vulnerable it becomes.

The competitor may not, however, be "dumping" (an economic term for selling at prices that are below cost), buying market share, or waging a desperate move to gain sales; it may simply have substantially lower costs. One of the most telling signs of whether a company's business position is strong or precarious is whether its prices and costs are competitive with industry rivals. Price-cost comparisons are especially critical in a commodity-product industry where the value provided to buyers is the same from seller to seller, price competition is typically the ruling market force, and lower-cost companies have the upper hand. But even in industries where products are differentiated and competition centers on the different attributes of competing brands as much as on price, rival companies have to keep their costs *in line* and make sure that any added costs they incur, and any price premiums they charge, create ample buyer value.

For a company to compete successfully, its costs must be *in line* with those of close rivals. While some cost disparity is justified as long as the products or services of closely competing companies are sufficiently differentiated, a high-cost firm's market position becomes increasingly vulnerable the more its costs exceed those of close rivals.

Two analytical tools are particularly useful in determining whether a company's prices and costs are competitive and thus conducive to winning in the marketplace: value chain analysis and benchmarking.

The Concept of a Company Value Chain

Every company's business consists of a collection of activities undertaken in the course of designing, producing, marketing, delivering, and supporting its product or service. A company's **value chain** consists of the linked set of value-creating activities the company performs internally. As shown in Figure 3.3, the value chain consists of two broad categories of activities: the *primary activities* that are fore-most in creating value for customers and the requisite *support activities* that facilitate and enhance the performance of the primary activities.[7] The value chain includes a profit margin because a markup over the cost of performing the firm's value-creating activities is customarily part of the price (or total cost) borne by buyers—a fundamental objective of every enterprise is to create and deliver a value to buyers whose margin over cost yields an attractive profit.

> **Core Concept**
>
> A company's **value chain** identifies the primary activities that create customer value and the related support activities.

Disaggregating a company's operations into primary and secondary activities exposes the major elements of the company's cost structure. Each activity in the value chain gives rise to costs and ties up assets; assigning the company's operating costs and assets to each individual activity in the chain provides cost estimates and capital requirements. Quite often, there are links between activities such that the manner in which one activity is done can affect the costs of performing other activities. For instance, how a product is designed has a huge impact on the number and manufacturing costs of different parts and components and on the time and costs required to assemble it.

The combined costs of all the various activities in a company's value chain define the company's internal cost structure. Further, the cost of each activity contributes to whether the company's overall cost position relative to rivals is favorable or unfavorable. The tasks of value chain analysis and benchmarking are to develop the data for comparing a company's costs activity by activity against the costs of key rivals and to learn which internal activities are a source of cost advantage or disadvantage. A company's relative cost position is a function of how the overall costs of the activities it performs in conducting business compare to the overall costs of the activities performed by rivals.

Why the Value Chains of Rival Companies Often Differ

A company's value chain and the manner in which it performs each activity reflect the evolution of its own particular business and internal operations, its strategy, the approaches it is using to execute its strategy, and the underlying economics of the activities themselves.[8] Because these factors differ from company to company, the value chains of rival companies sometimes differ substantially—a condition that complicates the task of assessing rivals' relative cost positions. For instance, competing companies may differ in their degrees of vertical integration. Comparing the value chains of a fully integrated rival and a partially integrated rival requires adjusting for differences in the scope of activities performed. Clearly the internal costs for a manufacturer that *makes* all of its own parts and components will be greater than the internal costs of a producer that *buys* the needed parts and components from outside suppliers and performs only assembly operations.

Likewise, there is legitimate reason to expect value chain and cost differences between a company that is pursuing a low-cost/low-price strategy and a rival that is positioned on the high end of the market. The costs of certain activities along the low-cost company's value chain should indeed be relatively low, whereas the high-end firm may

Figure 3.3   A Representative Company Value Chain

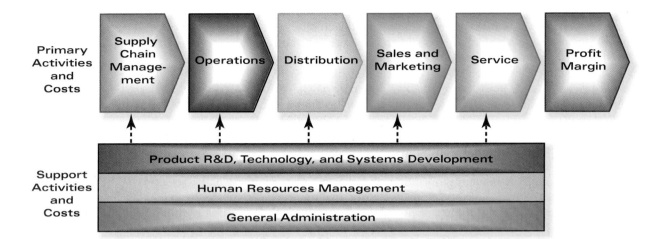

PRIMARY ACTIVITIES
- **Supply Chain Management**—activities, costs, and assets associated with purchasing fuel, energy, raw materials, parts, and components, merchandise, and consumable items from vendors; receiving, storing, and disseminating inputs from suppliers; inspection; and inventory management.
- **Operations**—activities, costs, and assets associated with converting inputs into final product form (production, assembly, packaging, equipment maintenance, facilities, operations, quality assurance, environmental protection).
- **Distribution**—activities, costs, and assets dealing with physically distributing the product to buyers (finished-goods warehousing, order processing, order picking and packing, shipping, delivery vehicle operations, establishing and maintaining a network of dealers and distributors).
- **Sales and Marketing**—activities, costs, and assets related to sales force efforts, advertising and promotion, market research and planning, and dealer/distributor support.
- **Service**—activities, costs, and assets associated with providing assistance to buyers, such as installation, spare parts delivery, maintenance and repair, technical assistance, buyer inquiries, and complaints.

SUPPORT ACTIVITIES
- **Product R&D, Technology, and Systems Development**—activities, costs, and assets relating to product R&D, process R&D, process design improvement, equipment design, computer software development, telecommunications systems, computer-assisted design and engineering, database capabilities, and development of computerized support systems.
- **Human Resources Management**—activities, costs, and assets associated with the recruitment, hiring, training, development, and compensation of all types of personnel; labor relations activities; and development of knowledge-based skills and core competencies.
- **General Administration**—activities, costs, and assets relating to general management, accounting and finance, legal and regulatory affairs, safety and security, management information systems, forming strategic alliances and collaborating with strategic partners, and other "overhead" functions.

understandably be spending relatively more to perform those activities that create the added quality and extra features of its products.

Moreover, cost and price differences among rival companies can have their origins in activities performed by suppliers or by distribution channel allies involved in getting the product to end users. Suppliers or wholesale/retail dealers may have excessively high cost structures or profit margins that jeopardize a company's cost-competitiveness even though its costs for internally performed activities are competitive. For example, when determining Michelin's cost-competitiveness vis-à-vis Goodyear and Bridgestone in supplying replacement tires to vehicle owners, we have to look at more than whether Michelin's tire manufacturing costs are above or below Goodyear's and Bridgestone's. Let's say that a buyer has to pay $400 for a set of Michelin tires and only $350 for a comparable set of Goodyear or Bridgestone tires; Michelin's $50 price disadvantage can stem not only from higher manufacturing costs (reflecting, perhaps, the added costs of Michelin's strategic efforts to build a better-quality tire with more performance features) but also from (1) differences in what the three tire makers pay their suppliers for materials and tire-making components and (2) differences in the operating efficiencies, costs, and markups of Michelin's wholesale-retail dealer outlets versus those of Goodyear and Bridgestone. Company value chains can also be different when different distribution channels are used to reach customers. In the music industry, music retailers like Blockbuster and Musicland that purchase CDs from recording studios and wholesale distributors have different value chains than online music stores like Apple's iTunes and Musicmatch that sell downloadable files. Thus, determining whether a company's prices and costs are competitive from an end user's standpoint requires looking at the activities and costs of competitively relevant suppliers and forward allies, as well as the costs of internally performed activities.

The Value Chain System for an Entire Industry

As the tire industry example makes clear, a company's value chain is embedded in a larger system of activities that includes the value chains of its suppliers and the value chains of whatever distribution channel allies it utilizes in getting its product or service to end users.[9] *Accurately assessing a company's competitiveness in end-use markets thus requires that company managers understand the entire value chain system for delivering a product or service to end users, not just the company's own value chain.* At the very least, this means considering the value chains of suppliers and forward channel allies (if any), as shown in Figure 3.4.

Suppliers' value chains are relevant because suppliers perform activities and incur costs in creating and delivering the purchased inputs used in a company's own value chain. The costs, performance features, and quality of these inputs influence a company's own costs and product differentiation capabilities. Anything a company can do to help its suppliers' take costs out of their value chain activities or improve the quality and performance of the items being supplied can enhance its own competitiveness—a powerful reason for working collaboratively with suppliers in managing supply chain activities.[10]

Forward channel and customer value chains are relevant because (1) the costs and margins of a company's distribution allies are part of the price the end user pays and (2) the activities that distribution allies perform affect the end user's satisfaction. For these reasons, companies normally work closely with their forward channel allies (who are their direct customers) to perform value chain activities in mutually

> A company's cost-competitiveness depends not only on the costs of internally performed activities (its own value chain) but also on costs in the value chains of its suppliers and forward channel allies.

Figure 3.4 A Representative Value Chain for an Entire Industry

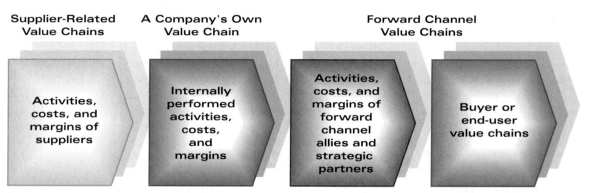

beneficial ways. For instance, some aluminum-can producers have constructed plants next to beer breweries and deliver cans on overhead conveyors directly to the breweries' can-filling lines; this has resulted in significant savings in production scheduling, shipping, and inventory costs for both container producers and breweries.[11] Many automotive parts suppliers have built plants near the auto assembly plants they supply to facilitate just-in-time deliveries, reduce warehousing and shipping costs, and promote close collaboration on parts design and production scheduling. Irrigation equipment companies, suppliers of grape-harvesting and winemaking equipment, and firms making barrels, wine bottles, caps, corks, and labels all have facilities in the California wine country to be close to the nearly 700 winemakers they supply.[12] The lesson here is that a company's value chain activities are often closely linked to the value chains of its suppliers and the forward allies or customers to whom it sells.

Although the value chains in Figures 3.3 and 3.4 are representative, actual value chains vary by industry and by company. The primary value chain activities in the pulp and paper industry (timber farming, logging, pulp mills, and papermaking) differ from the primary value chain activities in the home appliance industry (parts and components manufacture, assembly, wholesale distribution, retail sales). The value chain for the soft-drink industry (processing of basic ingredients and syrup manufacture, bottling and can filling, wholesale distribution, advertising, and retail merchandising) differs from that for the computer software industry (programming, disk loading, marketing, distribution). A producer of bathroom and kitchen faucets depends heavily on the activities of wholesale distributors and building supply retailers in winning sales to homebuilders and do-it-yourselfers; a producer of small gasoline engines internalizes its distribution activities by selling directly to the makers of lawn and garden equipment. A wholesaler's most important activities and costs deal with purchased goods, inbound logistics, and outbound logistics. A hotel's most important activities and costs are in operations—check-in and checkout, maintenance and housekeeping, dining and room service, conventions and meetings, and accounting. Outbound logistics is a crucial activity at Domino's Pizza but comparatively insignificant at Blockbuster. Advertising and promotion are dominant activities at Anheuser-Busch but only minor

Table 3.2   THE DIFFERENCE BETWEEN TRADITIONAL AND ACTIVITY-BASED COST ACCOUNTING: A PURCHASING DEPARTMENT EXAMPLE

Traditional Cost Accounting Categories in Purchasing Department Budget		Cost of Performing Specific Purchasing Department Activities Using Activity-Based Cost Accounting	
Wages and salaries	$340,000	Evaluate supplier capabilities	$100,300
Employee benefits	95,000	Process purchase orders	82,100
Supplies	21,500	Collaborate with suppliers on just-in-time deliveries	140,200
Travel	12,400		
Depreciation	19,000	Share data with suppliers	59,550
Other fixed charges (office space, utilities)	112,000	Check quality of items purchased	94,100
Miscellaneous operating expenses	40,250	Check incoming deliveries against purchase orders	48,450
	$640,150	Resolve disputes	15,250
		Conduct internal administration	100,200
			$640,150

Source: Adapted from information in Terence P. Par, "A New Tool for Managing Costs," *Fortune,* June 14, 1993, pp. 124–129.

activities at interstate gas-pipeline companies. Consequently, generic value chains like those in Figures 3.3 and 3.4 are illustrative, not absolute, and have to be drawn to fit the activities of a particular company or industry.

Developing the Data to Measure a Company's Cost-Competitiveness

Once the major value chain activities are identified, the next step in evaluating a company's cost-competitiveness involves breaking down departmental cost accounting data into the costs of performing specific activities.[13] The appropriate degree of disaggregation depends on the economics of the activities and how valuable it is to develop cross-company cost comparisons for narrowly defined activities as opposed to broadly defined activities. A good guideline is to develop separate cost estimates for activities having different economics and for activities representing a significant or growing proportion of cost.[14]

Traditional accounting identifies costs according to broad categories of expenses—wages and salaries, employee benefits, supplies, maintenance, utilities, travel, depreciation, R&D, interest, general administration, and so on. A newer method, *activity-based costing,* entails defining expense categories according to the specific activities being performed and then assigning costs to the activity responsible for creating the cost. An illustrative example is shown in Table 3.2.[15] Perhaps 25 percent of the companies that have explored the feasibility of activity-based costing have adopted this accounting approach. To fully understand the costs of activities all along the industry value chain, cost estimates for activities performed in the competitively relevant portions of suppliers' and customers' value chains also have to be developed—an advanced art in competitive intelligence. But despite the tediousness of developing cost estimates activity by activity and the imprecision of some of the estimates, the payoff in exposing the costs of particular activities makes activity-based

COMPANY SPOTLIGHT 3.1

Estimated Value Chain Costs for Recording and Distributing Music CDs through Traditional Music Retailers

The table below presents the representative costs and markups associated with producing and distributing a music CD retailing for $15 in music stores (as opposed to Internet sources).

Value Chain Activities and Costs in Producing and Distributing a CD		
1. Record company direct production costs:		$ 2.40
Artists and repertoire	$0.75	
Pressing of CD and packaging	1.65	
2. Royalties		.99
3. Record company marketing expenses		1.50
4. Record company overhead		1.50
5. Total record company costs		6.39
6. Record company's operating profit		1.86
7. Record company's selling price to distributor/wholesaler		8.25
8. Average wholesale distributor markup to cover distribution activities and profit margins		1.50
9. Average wholesale price charged to retailer		9.75
10. Average retail markup over wholesale cost		5.25
11. Average price to consumer at retail		$15.00

Source: Developed from information in "Fight the Power," a case study prepared by Adrian Aleyne, Babson College, 1999.

costing a valuable analytical tool.[16] Company Spotlight 3.1 shows representative costs for various activities performed by the producers and marketers of music CDs.

The most important application of value chain analysis is to expose how a particular firm's cost position compares with the cost positions of its rivals. What is needed are competitor-versus-competitor cost estimates for supplying a product or service to a well-defined customer group or market segment. The size of a company's cost advantage or disadvantage can vary from item to item in the product line, from customer group to customer group (if different distribution channels are used), and from geographic market to geographic market (if cost factors vary across geographic regions).

Benchmarking the Costs of Key Value Chain Activities

Many companies today are **benchmarking** their costs of performing a given activity against competitors' costs (and/or against the costs of a noncompetitor that efficiently and effectively performs much the same activity in another industry). Benchmarking is a tool that allows a company to determine whether the manner in which it performs particular functions and activities represents industry "best practices" when both cost and effectiveness are taken into account.

Benchmarking entails comparing how different companies perform various value chain activities—how materials are purchased, how suppliers are paid, how inventories are managed, how products are assembled, how fast the company can get new products to market, how the quality control function is performed, how customer orders are filled and shipped, how employees are trained, how payrolls are processed, and how maintenance is performed—and then making cross-company comparisons of the costs of these activities.[17] The objectives of benchmarking are to identify the best practices in performing an activity, to learn how other companies have actually achieved lower costs or better results in performing benchmarked activities, and to take action to improve a company's competitiveness whenever benchmarking reveals that its costs and results of performing an activity do not match those of other companies (either competitors or noncompetitors).

> **Core Concept**
>
> **Benchmarking** has proved to be a potent tool for learning which companies are best at performing particular activities and then using their techniques (or "best practices") to improve the cost and effectiveness of a company's own internal activities.

In 1979, Xerox became an early pioneer in the use of benchmarking when Japanese manufacturers began selling midsize copiers in the United States for $9,600 each—less than Xerox's production costs.[18] Although Xerox management suspected its Japanese competitors were dumping, it sent a team of line managers to Japan, including the head of manufacturing, to study competitors' business processes and costs. Fortunately, Xerox's joint-venture partner in Japan, Fuji-Xerox, knew the competitors well. The team found that Xerox's costs were excessive due to gross inefficiencies in the company's manufacturing processes and business practices; the study proved instrumental in Xerox's efforts to become cost-competitive and prompted Xerox to embark on a long-term program to benchmark 67 of its key work processes against companies identified as having the best practices in performing these processes. Xerox quickly decided not to restrict its benchmarking efforts to its office equipment rivals but to extend them to any company regarded as "world class" in performing *any activity* relevant to Xerox's business.

Thus, benchmarking has quickly come to be a tool for comparing a company against rivals not only on cost but on almost any relevant activity or competitively important measure. Toyota managers got their idea for just-in-time inventory deliveries by studying how U.S. supermarkets replenished their shelves. Southwest Airlines reduced the turnaround time of its aircraft at each scheduled stop by studying pit crews on the auto racing circuit. Over 80 percent of Fortune 500 companies reportedly engage in some form of benchmarking.

The tough part of benchmarking is not whether to do it but rather how to gain access to information about other companies' practices and costs. Sometimes benchmarking can be accomplished by collecting information from published reports, trade groups, and industry research firms and by talking to knowledgeable industry analysts, customers, and suppliers. On occasion, customers, suppliers, and joint-venture partners often make willing benchmarking allies. Usually, though, benchmarking requires field trips to the facilities of competing or noncompeting companies to observe how things are done, ask questions, compare practices and processes, and perhaps exchange data on productivity, staffing levels, time requirements, and other cost components. The problem is that because benchmarking involves competitively sensitive cost information, close rivals can't be expected to be completely open, even if they agree to host facilities tours and answer questions. Making reliable cost comparisons is complicated by the fact that participants often use different cost accounting systems.

> Benchmarking the costs of company activities against rivals provides hard evidence of whether a company is cost competitive.

However, the explosive interest of companies in benchmarking costs and identifying best practices has prompted consulting organizations (e.g., Accenture, A. T. Kearney,

Benchnet—The Benchmarking Exchange, Towers Perrin, and Best Practices) and several councils and associations (the International Benchmarking Clearinghouse, the Strategic Planning Institute's Council on Benchmarking) to gather benchmarking data, do benchmarking studies, and distribute information about best practices without identifying the sources. Having an independent group gather the information and report it in a manner that disguises the names of individual companies permits companies to avoid having to disclose competitively sensitive data to rivals and lessens the potential for unethical behavior on the part of company personnel in gathering their own data about competitors.

Strategic Options for Remedying a Cost Disadvantage

Value chain analysis and benchmarking can reveal a great deal about a firm's cost competitiveness. Examining the costs of a company's own value chain activities and comparing them to rivals' indicates who has how much of a cost advantage or disadvantage and which cost components are responsible. Such information is vital in strategic actions to eliminate a cost disadvantage or create a cost advantage. One of the fundamental insights of value chain analysis and benchmarking is that a company's competitiveness on cost depends on how efficiently it manages its value chain activities relative to how well competitors manage theirs.[19] There are three main areas in a company's overall value chain where important differences in the costs of competing firms can occur: a company's own activity segments, suppliers' part of the industry value chain, and the forward channel portion of the industry chain.

When the source of a firm's cost disadvantage is internal, managers can use any of the following nine strategic approaches to restore cost parity:[20]

1. Implement the use of best practices throughout the company, particularly for high-cost activities.

2. Try to eliminate some cost-producing activities altogether by revamping the value chain. Examples include cutting out low-value-added activities or bypassing the value chains and associated costs of distribution allies and marketing directly to end users (the approach used by Dell in PCs).

3. Relocate high-cost activities (such as R&D or manufacturing) to geographic areas where they can be performed more cheaply.

4. Attempt to squeeze out cost savings by greatly improving the company's supply chain.[21]

5. Search for activities that can be outsourced from vendors or performed by contractors more cheaply than they can be done internally.

6. Invest in productivity-enhancing, cost-saving technological improvements (robotics, flexible manufacturing techniques, state-of-the-art electronic networking).

7. Innovate around the troublesome cost components—computer chip makers regularly design around the patents held by others to avoid paying royalties; automakers have substituted lower-cost plastic and rubber for metal at many exterior body locations.

8. Simplify the product design so that it can be manufactured or assembled quickly and more economically.

9. Try to make up the internal cost disadvantage by achieving savings in the other two parts of the value chain system—usually a last resort.

Table 3.3   **OPTIONS FOR ATTACKING COST DISADVANTAGES ASSOCIATED WITH SUPPLY CHAIN ACTIVITIES OR FORWARD CHANNEL ALLIES**

Options for Attacking the High Costs of Items Purchased from Suppliers	Options for Attacking the High Costs of Forward Channel Allies
■ Negotiate more favorable prices with suppliers. ■ Work with suppliers on the design and specifications for what is being supplied to identify cost savings that will allow them to lower their prices. ■ Switch to lower-priced substitute inputs. ■ Collaborate closely with suppliers to identify mutual cost-saving opportunities. For example, just-in-time deliveries from suppliers can lower a company's inventory and internal logistics costs and may also allow its suppliers to economize on their warehousing, shipping, and production scheduling costs—a win-win outcome for both. ■ Integrate backward into the business of high-cost suppliers to gain control over the costs of purchased items—seldom an attractive option. ■ Try to make up the difference by cutting costs elsewhere in the chain—usually a last resort.	■ Push distributors and other forward channel allies to reduce their markups. ■ Work closely with forward channel allies to identify win-win opportunities to reduce costs. A chocolate manufacturer learned that by shipping its bulk chocolate in liquid form in tank cars instead of 10-pound molded bars, it could not only save its candy-bar manufacturing customers the costs associated with unpacking and melting but also eliminate its own costs of molding bars and packing them. ■ Change to a more economical distribution strategy, including switching to cheaper distribution channels (perhaps direct sales via the Internet) or perhaps integrating forward into company-owned retail outlets. ■ Try to make up the difference by cutting costs earlier in the cost chain—usually a last resort.

If a firm finds that it has a cost disadvantage stemming from costs in the supplier or forward channel portions of the industry value chain, then the task of reducing its costs to levels more in line with competitors usually has to extend beyond the firm's own in-house operations. Table 3.3 presents the strategy options for attacking high costs associated with supply chain activities or forward channel allies.

Translating Proficient Performance of Value Chain Activities into Competitive Advantage

A company that does a first-rate job of managing its value chain activities relative to competitors stands a good chance of leveraging its competitively valuable competencies and capabilities into sustainable competitive advantage. With rare exceptions, company attempts to achieve competitive advantage with unique attributes and performance features seldom result in a durable competitive advantage. It is too easy for resourceful competitors to clone, improve on, or find an effective substitute for any unique features of a product or service.[22] A more fruitful approach to achieving and sustaining a competitive edge over rivals is for a company to develop competencies and capabilities that please buyers and that rivals don't have or can't quite match.

The process of translating proficient company performance of value chain activities into competitive advantage is shown in Figure 3.5. The road to competitive advantage begins with management efforts to build more organizational expertise in performing certain competitively important value chain activities, deliberately striving to develop competencies and capabilities that add power to its strategy and competitiveness. If management begins to make one or two of these competencies and capabilities cornerstones of its strategy and continues to invest resources in building greater and greater proficiency in performing them, then over time one (or maybe

> Performing value chain activities in ways that give a company the capabilities to outmatch rivals is a source of competitive advantage.

Figure 3.5   Translating Company Performance of Value Chain Activities into Competitive Advantage

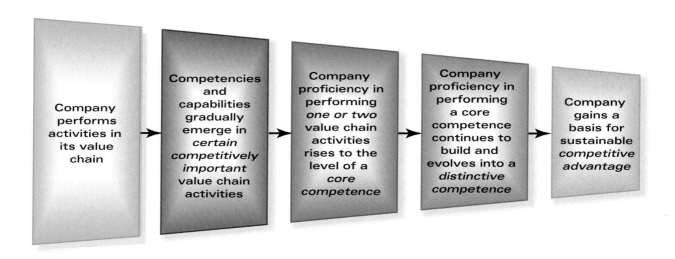

both) of the targeted competencies/capabilities may rise to the level of a core competence. Later, following additional organizational learning and investments in gaining still greater proficiency, the core competence could evolve into a distinctive competence, giving the company superiority over rivals. Such superiority, if it gives the company significant competitive clout in the marketplace, could produce an attractive competitive edge over rivals and, more important, prove difficult for rivals to match or offset with competencies and capabilities of their own making. As a general rule, it is substantially harder for rivals to achieve "best in industry" proficiency in performing a key value chain activity than it is for them to clone the features and attributes of a hot-selling product or service. This is especially true when a company with a distinctive competence avoids becoming complacent and works diligently to maintain its industry-leading expertise and capability.

There are numerous examples of companies that have gained a competitive edge by building competencies and capabilities that outmatch those of rivals. Merck and Glaxo, two of the world's most competitively capable pharmaceutical companies, built their business positions around expert performance of a few competitively crucial activities: extensive R&D to achieve first discovery of new drugs, a carefully constructed approach to patenting, skill in gaining rapid and thorough clinical clearance through regulatory bodies, and unusually strong distribution and sales force capabilities.[23] Federal Express has linked and integrated the performance of its aircraft fleet, truck fleet, support systems, and personnel so tightly and smoothly across the company's different value chain activities that it has created the capability to provide customers with guaranteed overnight delivery services. McDonald's can turn out identical-quality fast-food items at some 25,000-plus outlets around the world—an impressive demonstration of its capability to replicate its operating systems at many locations via an omnibus manual of detailed rules and procedures for each activity and intensive training of franchise operators and outlet managers.

Assessing a Company's Competitive Strength

Using value chain analysis and benchmarking to determine a company's competitiveness on price and cost is necessary but not sufficient. A more comprehensive assessment needs to be made of the company's overall competitive strength. The answers to two questions are of particular interest: First, how does the company rank relative to competitors on each of the important factors that determine market success? Second, all things considered, does the company have a net competitive advantage or disadvantage versus major competitors?

An easy-to-use method for answering the two questions posed above involves developing quantitative strength ratings for the company and its key competitors on each industry key success factor and each competitively decisive resource capability. Much of the information needed for doing a competitive strength assessment comes from previous analyses. Industry and competitive analysis reveals the key success factors and competitive capabilities that separate industry winners from losers. Benchmarking data and scouting key competitors provide a basis for judging the competitive strength of rivals on such factors as cost, key product attributes, customer service, image and reputation, financial strength, technological skills, distribution capability, and other competitively important resources and capabilities. SWOT analysis reveals how the company in question stacks up on these same strength measures.

Step 1 in doing a competitive strength assessment is to make a list of the industry's key success factors and most telling measures of competitive strength or weakness (6 to 10 measures usually suffice). Step 2 is to rate the firm and its rivals on each factor. Numerical rating scales (e.g., from 1 to 10) are best to use, although ratings of stronger (1), weaker (2), and about equal (5) may be appropriate when information is scanty and assigning numerical scores conveys false precision. Step 3 is to sum the strength ratings on each factor to get an overall measure of competitive strength for each company being rated. Step 4 is to use the overall strength ratings to draw conclusions about the size and extent of the company's net competitive advantage or disadvantage and to take specific note of areas of strength and weakness.

Table 3.4 provides two examples of competitive strength assessment, using the hypothetical ABC Company against four rivals. The first example employs an *unweighted rating system*. With unweighted ratings, each key success factor and competitive strength measure is assumed to be equally important (a rather dubious assumption). Whichever company has the highest strength rating on a given measure has an implied competitive edge on that factor; the size of its edge is mirrored in the margin of difference between its rating and the ratings assigned to rivals—a rating of 9 for one company versus ratings of 5, 4, and 3, respectively, for three other companies indicates a bigger advantage than a rating of 9 versus ratings of 8, 7, and 6. Summing a company's ratings on all the measures produces an overall strength rating. The higher a company's overall strength rating, the stronger its overall competitiveness versus rivals. The bigger the difference between a company's overall rating and the scores of *lower-rated* rivals, the greater its implied *net competitive advantage*. Conversely, the bigger the difference between a company's overall rating and the scores of *higher-rated* rivals, the greater its implied *net competitive disadvantage*. Thus, ABC's total score of 61 (see the top half of Table 3.4) signals a much greater net competitive advantage over rival 4 (with a score of 32) than over rival 1 (with a score of 58) but indicates a moderate net competitive disadvantage against rival 2 (with an overall score of 71).

Table 3.4   ILLUSTRATIONS OF UNWEIGHTED AND WEIGHTED COMPETITIVE STRENGTH ASSESSMENTS

A. Sample of an Unweighted Competitive Strength Assessment
(Rating scale: 1 = very weak; 10 = very strong)

Key Success Factor/ Strength Measure	ABC Co.	Rival 1	Rival 2	Rival 3	Rival 4
Quality/product performance	8	5	10	1	6
Reputation/image	8	7	10	1	6
Manufacturing capability	2	10	4	5	1
Technological skills	10	1	7	3	8
Dealer network/distribution capability	9	4	10	5	1
New product innovation capability	9	4	10	5	1
Financial resources	5	10	7	3	1
Relative cost position	5	10	3	1	4
Customer service capabilities	5	7	10	1	4
Unweighted overall strength rating	61	58	71	25	32

B. Sample of a Weighted Competitive Strength Assessment
(Rating scale: 1 = very weak; 10 = very strong)

Key Success Factor/ Strength Measure	Importance Weight	Rating/Score ABC Co.		Rival 1		Rival 2		Rival 3		Rival 4	
Quality/product performance	0.10	8	0.80	5	0.50	10	1.00	1	0.10	6	0.60
Reputation/image	0.10	8	0.80	7	0.70	10	1.00	1	0.10	6	0.60
Manufacturing capability	0.10	2	0.20	10	1.00	4	0.40	5	0.50	1	0.10
Technological skills	0.05	10	0.50	1	0.05	7	0.35	3	0.15	8	0.40
Dealer network/ distribution capability	0.05	9	0.45	4	0.20	10	0.50	5	0.25	1	0.05
New product innovation capability	0.05	9	0.45	4	0.20	10	0.50	5	0.25	1	0.05
Financial resources	0.10	5	0.50	10	1.00	7	0.70	3	0.30	1	0.10
Relative cost position	0.30	5	1.50	10	3.00	3	0.95	1	0.30	4	1.20
Customer service capabilities	0.15	5	0.75	7	1.05	10	1.50	1	0.15	4	0.60
Sum of importance weights	1.00										
Weighted overall strength rating		5.95		7.70		6.85		2.10		3.70	

However, a better method is a *weighted rating system* (shown in the bottom half of Table 3.4) because the different measures of competitive strength are unlikely to be equally important. In an industry where the products/services of rivals are virtually identical, for instance, having low unit costs relative to rivals is nearly always the most important determinant of competitive strength. In an industry with strong product differentiation, the most significant measures of competitive strength may be brand awareness, amount of advertising, product attractiveness, and distribution capability. In a weighted rating system each measure of competitive strength is assigned a weight based on its perceived importance in

> A weighted competitive strength analysis is conceptually stronger than an unweighted analysis because of the inherent weakness in assuming that all the strength measures are equally important.

shaping competitive success. A weight could be as high as 0.75 (maybe even higher) in situations where one particular competitive variable is overwhelmingly decisive, or a weight could be as low as 0.20 when two or three strength measures are more important than the rest. Lesser competitive strength indicators can carry weights of 0.05 or 0.10. Whether the differences between the importance weights are big or little, *the sum of the weights must add up to 1.0.*

Weighted strength ratings are calculated by rating each competitor on each strength measure (using the 1 to 10 rating scale) and multiplying the assigned rating by the assigned weight (a rating of 4 times a weight of 0.20 gives a weighted rating, or score, of 0.80). Again, the company with the highest rating on a given measure has an implied competitive edge on that measure, with the size of its edge reflected in the difference between its rating and rivals' ratings. The weight attached to the measure indicates how important the edge is. Summing a company's weighted strength ratings for all the measures yields an overall strength rating. Comparisons of the weighted overall strength scores indicate which competitors are in the strongest and weakest competitive positions and who has how big a net competitive advantage over whom.

Note in Table 3.4 that the unweighted and weighted rating schemes produce different orderings of the companies. In the weighted system, ABC Company drops from second to third in strength, and rival 1 jumps from third to first because of its high strength ratings on the two most important factors. Weighting the importance of the strength measures can thus make a significant difference in the outcome of the assessment.

Competitive strength assessments provide useful conclusions about a company's competitive situation. The ratings show how a company compares against rivals, factor by factor or capability by capability, thus revealing where it is strongest and weakest, and against whom. Moreover, the overall competitive strength scores indicate how all the different factors add up—whether the company is at a net competitive advantage or disadvantage against each rival. The firm with the largest overall competitive strength rating enjoys the strongest competitive position, with the size of its net competitive advantage reflected by how much its score exceeds the scores of rivals.

Knowing where a company is competitively strong and where it is weak in comparison to specific rivals is valuable in deciding on specific actions to strengthen its ability to compete. As a general rule, a company should try to leverage its competitive strengths (areas where it scores higher than rivals) into sustainable competitive advantage. Furthermore, it makes sense for the company to initiate actions to remedy its important competitive weaknesses (areas where its scores are below those of rivals); at the very least, it should try to narrow the gap against companies with higher strength ratings—when the leader is at 10, improving from a rating of 3 to a rating of 7 can be significant.

> High competitive strength ratings signal a strong competitive position and possession of competitive advantage; low ratings signal a weak position and competitive disadvantage.

In addition, the competitive strength ratings point to which rival companies may be vulnerable to competitive attack and the areas where they are weakest. When a company has important competitive strengths in areas where one or more rivals are weak, it makes sense to consider offensive moves to exploit rivals' competitive weaknesses.

Identifying the Strategic Issues That Merit Managerial Attention

The final and most important analytical step is to zero in on exactly what strategic issues company managers need to address—and resolve—for the company to be more

> Zeroing in on the strategic issues a company faces and compiling a "worry list" of problems and roadblocks creates a strategic agenda of problems that merit prompt managerial attention.

financially and competitively successful in the years ahead. This step involves drawing on the results of both industry and competitive analysis and the evaluations of the company's own competitiveness. The task here is to get a clear fix on exactly what strategic and competitive challenges confront the company, which of the company's competitive shortcomings need fixing, what obstacles stand in the way of improving the company's competitive position in the marketplace, and what specific problems merit front-burner attention by company managers. *Pinpointing the precise things that management needs to worry about sets the agenda for deciding what actions to take next to improve the company's performance and business outlook.*

The "worry list" of issues and problems that have to be wrestled with can include such things as *how* to stave off market challenges from new foreign competitors, *how* to combat the price discounting of rivals, *how* to reduce the company's high costs and pave the way for price reductions, *how* to sustain the company's present rate of growth in light of slowing buyer demand, *whether* to expand the company's product line, *whether* to correct the company's competitive deficiencies by acquiring a rival company with the missing strengths, *whether* to expand into foreign markets rapidly or cautiously, *whether* to reposition the company and move to a different strategic group, *what to do* about growing buyer interest in substitute products, and *what to do* about the aging demographics of the company's customer base.

> A good strategy must contain ways to deal with all the strategic issues and obstacles that stand in the way of the company's financial and competitive success in the years ahead.

If the worry list is relatively minor, thus suggesting the company's strategy is mostly on track and reasonably well matched to the company's overall situation, company managers seldom need to go much beyond fine-tuning of the present strategy. If, however, the issues and problems confronting the company are serious and indicate the present strategy is not well suited for the road ahead, the task of crafting a better strategy has got to go to the top of management's action agenda.

Key Points

There are five key questions to consider in analyzing a company's particular competitive circumstances and its competitive position vis-à-vis key rivals:

1. *How well is the present strategy working?* This involves evaluating the strategy from a qualitative standpoint (completeness, internal consistency, rationale, and suitability to the situation) and also from a quantitative standpoint (the strategic and financial results the strategy is producing). The stronger a company's current overall performance, the less likely the need for radical strategy changes. The weaker a company's performance and/or the faster the changes in its external situation (which can be gleaned from industry and competitive analysis), the more its current strategy must be questioned.

2. *What are the company's resource strengths and weaknesses and its external opportunities and threats?* A SWOT analysis provides an overview of a firm's situation and is an essential component of crafting a strategy tightly matched to the company's situation. The two most important parts of SWOT analysis are (1) drawing conclusions about what story the compilation of strengths, weaknesses, opportunities, and threats tells about the company's overall situation and (2) acting on those conclusions to better match the company's strategy to its resource

strengths and market opportunities to correct the important weaknesses and defend against external threats. A company's resource strengths, competencies, and competitive capabilities are strategically relevant because they are the most logical and appealing building blocks for strategy; resource weaknesses are important because they may represent vulnerabilities that need correction. External opportunities and threats come into play because a good strategy necessarily aims at capturing a company's most attractive opportunities and at defending against threats to its well-being.

3. *Are the company's prices and costs competitive?* One telling sign of whether a company's situation is strong or precarious is whether its prices and costs are competitive with those of industry rivals. Value chain analysis and benchmarking are essential tools in determining whether the company is performing particular functions and activities cost-effectively, learning whether its costs are in line with competitors, and deciding which internal activities and business processes need to be scrutinized for improvement. Value chain analysis teaches that how competently a company manages its value chain activities relative to rivals is a key to building valuable competencies and competitive capabilities and then leveraging them into sustainable competitive advantage.

4. *Is the company competitively stronger or weaker than key rivals?* The key appraisals here involve how the company matches up against key rivals on industry key success factors and other chief determinants of competitive success and whether and why the company has a competitive advantage or disadvantage. Quantitative competitive strength assessments, using the method presented in Table 3.4, indicate where a company is competitively strong and weak and provide insight into the company's ability to defend or enhance its market position. As a rule a company's competitive strategy should be built around its competitive strengths and should aim at shoring up areas where it is competitively vulnerable. Also, the areas where company strengths match up against competitor weaknesses represent the best potential for new offensive initiatives.

5. *What strategic issues and problems merit front-burner managerial attention?* This analytical step zeros in on the strategic issues and problems that stand in the way of the company's success. It involves using the results of both industry and competitive analysis and company situation analysis to identify a "worry list" of issues to be resolved for the company to be financially and competitively successful in the years ahead.

Good company situation analysis, like good industry and competitive analysis, is a valuable precondition for good strategy making. A competently done evaluation of a company's resource capabilities and competitive strengths exposes strong and weak points in the present strategy and how attractive or unattractive the company's competitive position is and why. Managers need such understanding to craft a strategy that is well suited to the company's competitive circumstances.

Exercises

Review the information in Company Spotlight 3.1 concerning the costs of the different value chain activities associated with recording and distributing music CDs through traditional brick-and-mortar retail outlets. Then answer the following questions:

1. Does the growing popularity of downloading music from the Internet give rise to a new music industry value chain that differs considerably from the traditional value chain? Explain why or why not.

2. What costs would be cut out of the traditional value chain or bypassed in the event that recording studios sell downloadable files of artists' recordings direct to online buyers and buyers make their own custom CDs, load them onto their MP3 players, or play music directly from their PCs?

3. What costs would be cut out of the traditional value chain or bypassed in the event that online music retailers (Apple, Sony, Microsoft, Musicmatch, Napster, Cdigix, and others) sell direct to online buyers and buyers load the music files directly onto their MP3 players, make their own custom CDs, or play music directly from their PCs? (Note: In 2004, online music stores were selling download-only titles for $0.79 to $0.99 per song and $9.99 for most albums.)

4. What will happen to the traditional value chain if more and more music lovers use peer-to-peer file-sharing software to download music from the Internet to play music on their PCs or MP3 players or make their own CDs? (Note: It was estimated in 2004 that about 1 billion songs were available for online trading and file sharing via such programs as Kazaa, Grokster, Shareaza, BitTorrent, and eDonkey, despite the fact that some 4,000 people had been sued by the Recording Industry Association of America for pirating copyrighted music via peer-to-peer file sharing.)

CHAPTER 4

Crafting a Strategy
The Quest for Competitive Advantage

The process of developing superior strategies is part planning, part trial and error, until you hit upon something that works.

—Costas Markides, professor, London Business School

Successful business strategy is about actively shaping the game you play, not just playing the game you find.

—Adam M. Brandenburger and Barry J. Nalebuff

The essence of strategy lies in creating tomorrow's competitive advantages faster than competitors mimic the ones you possess today.

—Gary Hamel and C. K. Prahalad

Competitive strategy is about being different. It means deliberately choosing to perform activities differently or to perform different activities than rivals to deliver a unique mix of value.

—Michael E. Porter

Winners in business play rough and don't apologize for it. The nicest part of playing hardball is watching your competitors squirm.

—George Stalk, Jr., and Rob Lachenauer

This chapter focuses on the primary options a company has in crafting a strategy to compete successfully in a particular industry and secure an attractive market position. The strategy-making challenge is to stitch together a winning strategy—one that fits industry and competitive conditions, capitalizes on the company's resources and competitive capabilities, builds a sustainable competitive advantage, and boosts company performance. We begin our survey of a company's menu of strategic options by describing the five *generic competitive strategy options*—what basic competitive approach to employ is a company's first and foremost choice in crafting an overall strategy. Next on a company's menu of strategic choices are the various *strategic actions* it can take to complement its choice of a basic competitive strategy:

- What use to make of strategic alliances and collaborative partnerships.
- What use to make of mergers and acquisitions.
- Whether to integrate backward or forward into more stages of the industry value chain.
- Whether to outsource certain value chain activities or perform them in-house.
- Whether and when to employ offensive and defensive moves.
- What Web site strategy to employ.

This chapter contains sections discussing the pros and cons of each of the above complementary strategic options. The next-to-last section in the chapter discusses the need for strategic choices in each functional area of a company's business (R&D, production, sales and marketing, finance, and so on) to support its basic competitive approach and complementary strategic moves. The chapter concludes with a brief look at the competitive importance of timing strategic moves—when it is advantageous to be a first-mover and when it is better to be a fast-follower or late-mover.

Figure 4.1 shows the menu of options a company has in crafting a strategy and the order in which the choices should generally be made. It also illustrates the structure of the chapter and the topics that will be covered.

The Five Generic Competitive Strategies

A company's **competitive strategy** deals exclusively with its plans for competing successfully—its specific efforts to please customers, its offensive and defensive moves to counter the maneuvers of rivals, its responses to whatever market conditions prevail at the moment, and its initiatives to strengthen its market position. Companies the world over are imaginative in conceiving competitive strategies to win customer favor. At most companies the aim, quite simply, is to gain a competitive advantage by doing a significantly better job than rivals of providing buyers with the best overall value. There are many routes to competitive advantage, but they all involve giving buyers what they perceive as superior value compared to the offerings of rival sellers. Superior value can mean a good product at a lower price, a superior product that is worth paying more for, or a best-value offering that represents an attractive combination of price, features, quality, service, and other appealing attributes. Delivering superior value—whatever form it

> **Core Concept**
>
> The objective of **competitive strategy** is to knock the socks off rival companies by doing a better job of providing a product offering that best satisfies buyer needs and preferences.

Figure 4.1   A Company's Menu of Strategy Options

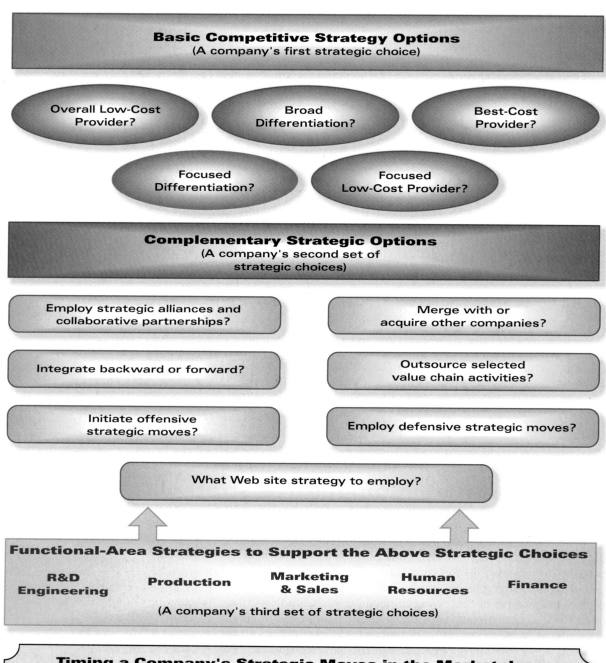

takes—nearly always requires performing value chain activities differently than rivals and building competencies and resource capabilities that are not readily matched.

There are countless variations in the competitive strategies that companies employ, mainly because each company's strategic approach entails custom-designed actions to fit its own circumstances and industry environment. The custom-tailored nature of each company's strategy makes the chances remote that any two companies—even companies in the same industry—will employ strategies that are exactly alike in every detail. Managers at different companies always have a slightly different spin on what future market conditions will be like and how to best align their company's strategy with these conditions; moreover, they have different notions of how they intend to outmaneuver rivals and what strategic options make the most sense for their particular company. However, when one strips away the details to get at the real substance, the biggest and most important differences among competitive strategies boil down to (1) whether a company's market target is broad or narrow and (2) whether the company is pursuing a competitive advantage linked to low costs or product differentiation. Five distinct competitive strategy approaches stand out:[1]

1. *A low-cost provider strategy*—striving to achieve lower overall costs than rivals and appealing to a broad spectrum of customers, usually by underpricing rivals.

2. *A broad differentiation strategy*—seeking to differentiate the company's product offering from rivals' in ways that will appeal to a broad spectrum of buyers.

3. *A best-cost provider strategy*—giving customers more value for the money by incorporating good-to-excellent product attributes at a lower cost than rivals; the target is to have the lowest (best) costs and prices compared to rivals offering products with comparable attributes.

4. *A focused (or market niche) strategy based on low costs*—concentrating on a narrow buyer segment and outcompeting rivals by having lower costs than rivals and thus being able to serve niche members at a lower price.

5. *A focused (or market niche) strategy based on differentiation*—concentrating on a narrow buyer segment and outcompeting rivals by offering niche members customized attributes that meet their tastes and requirements better than rivals' products.

Each of these five generic competitive approaches stakes out a different market position, as shown in Figure 4.2.

Low-Cost Provider Strategies

A company achieves low-cost leadership when it becomes the industry's lowest-cost provider rather than just being one of perhaps several competitors with comparatively low costs. A low-cost provider's strategic target is meaningfully lower costs than rivals—but not necessarily the absolutely lowest possible cost. In striving for a cost advantage over rivals, managers must take care to include features and services that buyers consider essential—*a product offering that is too frills-free sabotages the attractiveness of the company's product and can turn buyers off even if it is cheaper than competing products.* For maximum effectiveness, companies employing a low-cost provider strategy need to achieve their cost advantage in ways difficult for

> ### Core Concept
> A low-cost leader's basis for competitive advantage is lower overall costs than competitors. Successful low-cost leaders are exceptionally good at finding ways to drive costs out of their businesses.

Figure 4.2   The Five Generic Competitive Strategies:
Each Stakes Out a Different Market Position

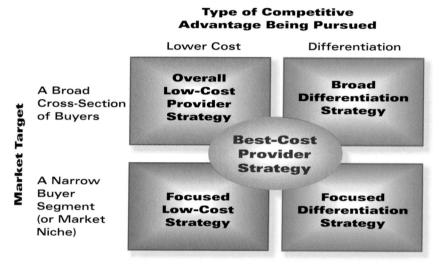

Source: Adapted with permission of the Free Press, a division of Simon & Schuster Adult Publishing Group, from *Competitive Advantage: Creating and Sustaining Superior Performance,* by Michael Porter, Copyright ©1995, 1998 by Michael E. Porter. All rights reserved.

rivals to copy or match. If rivals find it relatively easy or inexpensive to imitate the leader's low-cost methods, then the leader's advantage will be too short-lived to yield a valuable edge in the marketplace.

A company has two options for translating a low-cost advantage over rivals into attractive profit performance. Option 1 is to use the lower-cost edge to underprice competitors and attract price-sensitive buyers in great-enough numbers to increase total profits. The trick to profitably underpricing rivals is either to keep the size of the price cut smaller than the size of the firm's cost advantage (thus reaping the benefits of both a bigger profit margin per unit sold and the added profits on incremental sales) or to generate enough added volume to increase total profits despite thinner profit margins (larger volume can make up for smaller margins provided the underpricing of rivals brings in enough extra sales). Option 2 is to maintain the present price, be content with the present market share, and use the lower-cost edge to earn a higher profit margin on each unit sold, thereby raising the firm's total profits and overall return on investment.

Company Spotlight 4.1 describes Nucor Corporation's strategy for gaining low-cost leadership in manufacturing a variety of steel products.

The Two Major Avenues for Achieving a Cost Advantage   To achieve a cost advantage, a firm's cumulative costs across its overall value chain must be lower than competitors' cumulative costs. There are two ways to accomplish this:[2]

1. Outmanage rivals in the efficiently performing value chain activities and in controlling the factors that drive the costs of value chain activities.

2. Revamp the firm's overall value chain to eliminate or bypass some cost-producing activities.

COMPANY SPOTLIGHT 4.1
Nucor Corporation's Low-Cost Provider Strategy

Nucor Corporation is the world's leading minimill producer of such steel products as carbon and alloy steel bars, beams, sheet, and plate; steel joists and joist girders; steel deck; cold finished steel; steel fasteners; metal building systems; and light-gauge steel framing. In 2004 it had close to $10 billion in sales, 9,000 employees, and annual production capacity of nearly 22 million tons, making it the largest steel producer in the United States. The company has pursued a strategy that has made it among the lowest-cost producers of steel in the world and has allowed it to consistently outperform its rivals in terms of financial and market performance.

Nucor's low-cost strategy aims to give the company a cost and pricing advantage in the commoditylike steel industry and leaves no part of the company's value chain neglected. The key elements of the strategy include the following:

- Using electric-arc furnaces where scrap steel and directly reduced iron ore are melted and then sent to a continuous caster and rolling mill to be shaped into steel products, thereby eliminating an assortment of production processes from the value chain used by traditional integrated steel mills. Nucor's minimill value chain makes the use of coal, coke, and iron ore unnecessary, cuts investment in facilities and equipment (eliminating coke ovens, blast furnaces, basic oxygen furnaces, and ingot casters), and requires fewer employees than integrated mills.

- Striving hard for continuous improvement in the efficiency of its plants and frequently investing in state-of-the-art equipment to reduce unit costs. Nucor is known for its technological leadership and its aggressive pursuit of production process innovation.

- Carefully selecting plant sites to minimize inbound and outbound shipping costs and to take advantage of low rates for electricity (electric-arc furnaces are heavy users of electricity). Nucor tends to avoid locating new plants in geographic areas where labor unions are a strong influence.

- Hiring a nonunion workforce that uses team-based incentive compensation systems (often opposed by unions). Operating and maintenance employees and supervisors are paid weekly bonuses based on the productivity of their work group. The size of the bonus is based on the capabilities of the equipment employed and ranges from 80 to 150 percent of an employee's base pay; no bonus is paid if the equipment is not operating. Nucor's compensation program has boosted the company's labor productivity to levels nearly double the industry average while rewarding productive employees with annual compensation packages that exceed what their union counterparts earn by as much as 20 percent. Nucor has been able to attract and retain highly talented, productive, and dedicated employees. In addition, the company's healthy culture and results-oriented self-managed work teams allow Nucor to employ fewer supervisors than would be needed with an hourly union workforce.

- Heavily emphasizing consistent product quality and rigorous quality systems.

- Minimizing general and administrative expenses by maintaining a lean staff at corporate headquarters (fewer than 125 employees) and allowing only four levels of management between the CEO and production workers. Headquarters offices are modestly furnished and located in an inexpensive building. The company minimizes reports, paperwork, and meetings to keep managers focused on value-adding activities. Nucor is noted not only for its streamlined organizational structure but also for its frugality in travel and entertainment expenses—the company's top managers set the example by flying coach class, avoiding pricey hotels, and refraining from taking customers out for expensive dinners.

In 2001–2003, when many U.S. producers of steel products were in dire economic straits because of weak demand for steel and deep price discounting by foreign rivals, Nucor began acquiring state-of-the-art steelmaking facilities from bankrupt or nearly bankrupt rivals at bargain-basement prices, often at 20 to 25 percent of what it cost to construct the facilities. This has given Nucor much lower depreciation costs than rivals having comparable plants.

Nucor management's outstanding execution of its low-cost strategy and its commitment to driving down costs throughout its value chain has allowed it to compete aggressively on price, earn higher profit margins than rivals, and grow its business at a considerably faster rate than its integrated steel mill rivals.

Source: Company annual reports, news releases, and Web site.

Let's look at both of the approaches to securing a cost advantage.

Controlling the Cost Drivers   There are nine major cost drivers that come into play in determining a company's costs in each activity segment of the value chain:[3]

1. *Economies or diseconomies of scale:* The costs of a particular value chain activity are often subject to economies or diseconomies of scale. Economies of scale arise whenever activities can be performed more cheaply at larger volumes than at smaller volumes and whenever certain costs like R&D and advertising can be spread out over a greater sales volume. Astute management of activities subject to scale economies or diseconomies can be a major source of cost savings. For example, manufacturing economies can usually be achieved by simplifying the product line, scheduling longer production runs for fewer models, and using common parts and components in different models. In global industries, making separate products for each country market instead of selling a mostly standard product worldwide tends to boost unit costs because of lost time in model changeover, shorter production runs, and the inability to reach the most economic scale of production for each country model.

2. *Experience- and learning-curve effects:* The cost of performing an activity can decline over time as the learning and experience of company personnel build. Learning/experience economies can stem from debugging and mastering newly introduced technologies, finding ways to improve plant layout and work flows, making product design modifications that streamline the assembly process, and capitalizing on the added speed and knowledge that accrues from repeatedly siting and building new plants, retail outlets, or distribution centers. Aggressively managed low-cost providers pay diligent attention to capturing the benefits of learning and experience and to keeping the benefits proprietary to whatever extent possible.

3. *The cost of key resource inputs:* The cost of performing value chain activities depends in part on what a firm has to pay for key resource inputs. Competitors do not all incur the same costs for items purchased from suppliers or for other resources. How well a company manages the costs of acquiring key resource inputs is often a big driver of costs. Input costs are a function of four factors:

    a) *Union versus nonunion labor:* Avoiding the use of union labor is often a key to keeping labor input costs low, not just because unions demand high wages but also because union work rules can stifle productivity. Such highly regarded low-cost manufacturers as Nucor and Cooper Tire are noted for their incentive compensation systems that promote very high levels of labor productivity—at both companies, nonunion workers earn more than their unionized counterparts at rival companies but their high productivity results in lower labor costs per unit produced.

    b) *Bargaining power vis-à-vis suppliers:* Many large enterprises (e.g., Wal-Mart, Home Depot, the world's major motor vehicle producers) have used their bargaining clout in purchasing large volumes to wrangle good prices on their purchases from suppliers. Having greater buying power than rivals can be an important source of cost advantage.

    c) *Location variables:* Locations differ in their prevailing wage levels, tax rates, energy costs, inbound and outbound shipping and freight costs, and so on. Opportunities may exist for reducing costs by relocating plants, field offices, warehousing, or headquarters operations.

d) *Supply chain management expertise:* Some companies have more efficient supply chain expertise than others and are able to squeeze out cost savings via partnerships with suppliers that lower the costs of purchased materials and components, e-procurement systems, and inbound logistics.

4. *Links with other activities in the company or industry value chain:* When the cost of one activity is affected by how other activities are performed, costs can be managed downward by making sure that linked activities are performed in cooperative and coordinated fashion. For example, when a company's materials inventory costs or warranty costs are linked to the activities of suppliers, cost savings can be achieved by working cooperatively with key suppliers on the design of parts and components, quality-assurance procedures, just-in-time delivery, and integrated materials supply. The costs of new product development can often be managed downward by having cross-functional task forces (perhaps including representatives of suppliers and key customers) jointly work on R&D, product design, manufacturing plans, and market launch. Links with forward channels tend to center on location of warehouses, materials handling, outbound shipping, and packaging. Nail manufacturers, for example, learned that delivering nails in prepackaged 1-, 5-, and 10-pound assortments instead of 100-pound bulk cartons could reduce a hardware dealer's labor costs in filling individual customer orders. The lesson here is that effective coordination of linked activities anywhere in the value chain holds potential for cost reduction.

5. *Sharing opportunities with other organizational or business units within the enterprise:* Different product lines or business units within an enterprise can often share the same order processing and customer billing systems, utilize a common sales force to call on customers, share the same warehouse and distribution facilities, or rely on a common customer service and technical support team. Such combining of like activities and sharing of resources across sister units can create significant cost savings. Furthermore, there are times when the know-how gained in one division or geographic unit can be used to help lower costs in another; sharing know-how across organizational lines has significant cost-saving potential when cross-unit value chain activities are similar and know-how is readily transferred from one unit to another.

6. *The benefits of vertical integration versus outsourcing:* Partially or fully integrating into the activities of either suppliers or distribution channel allies can allow an enterprise to detour suppliers or buyers with considerable bargaining power. Vertical integration forward or backward also has potential if there are significant cost savings from having a single firm perform adjacent activities in the industry value chain. But more often it is cheaper to outsource certain functions and activities to outside specialists, who by virtue of their expertise and volume can perform the activity/function more cheaply.

7. *Timing considerations associated with first-mover advantages and disadvantages:* Sometimes the first major brand in the market is able to establish and maintain its brand name at a lower cost than later brand arrivals. Competitors looking to go head-to-head against such first-movers as eBay, Yahoo!, and Amazon.com have to spend heavily to come close to achieving the same brand awareness and name recognition. On other occasions, such as when technology is developing fast, late purchasers can benefit from waiting to install second- or third-generation equipment that is both cheaper and more efficient; first-generation users often incur

added costs associated with debugging and learning how to use an immature and unperfected technology. Likewise, companies that follow, rather than lead, new product development efforts sometimes avoid many of the costs that pioneers incur in performing pathbreaking R&D and opening up new markets.

8. *The percentage of capacity utilization:* Capacity utilization is a big cost driver for those value chain activities associated with substantial fixed costs. Higher rates of capacity utilization allow depreciation and other fixed costs to be spread over a larger unit volume, thereby lowering fixed costs per unit. The more capital intensive the business, or the higher the percentage of fixed costs as a percentage of total costs, the more important this cost driver becomes because there's such a stiff unit-cost penalty for underutilizing existing capacity. In such cases, finding ways to operate close to full capacity year-round can be an important source of cost advantage.

9. *Strategic choices and operating decisions:* A company's costs can be driven up or down by a fairly wide assortment of managerial decisions:

   a) Adding/cutting the services provided to buyers.

   b) Incorporating more/fewer performance and quality features into the product.

   c) Increasing/decreasing the number of different channels utilized in distributing the firm's product.

   d) Lengthening/shortening delivery times to customers.

   e) Putting more/less emphasis than rivals on the use of incentive compensation, wage increases, and fringe benefits to motivate employees and boost worker productivity.

   f) Raising/lowering the specifications for purchased materials.

> Outperforming rivals in controlling the factors that drive costs is a very demanding managerial exercise.

For a company to outmanage rivals in performing value chain activities cost-effectively, its managers must possess a sophisticated understanding of the factors that drive the costs of each activity. And then they must not only use their knowledge about the cost drivers to squeeze out cost savings all along the value chain but also be so much more ingenious and committed than rivals in achieving cost-saving efficiencies that the company ends up with a sustainable cost advantage.

Revamping the Value Chain   Dramatic cost advantages can emerge from finding innovative ways to eliminate or bypass cost-producing value chain activities. The primary ways companies can achieve a cost advantage by reconfiguring their value chains include:

■ *Making greater use of Internet technology applications:* In recent years the Internet and Internet technology applications have become powerful and pervasive tools for reengineering company and industry value chains. For instance, Internet technology has revolutionized supply chain management. Using software packages from any of several vendors, company procurement personnel can—with only a few mouse clicks within one seamless system—check materials inventories against incoming customer orders, check suppliers' stocks, check the latest prices for parts and components at auction and e-sourcing Web sites, and check Federal Express delivery schedules. Electronic data interchange software permits the relevant details of incoming customer orders to be instantly shared with the suppliers of needed parts and components. All this lays the foundation for just-in-time deliveries of parts and components, and for the production of parts and components, to be matched closely to assembly plant requirements and production schedules—

and such coordination produces savings for both suppliers and manufacturers. Via the Internet, manufacturers can collaborate closely with parts and components suppliers in designing new products and reducing the time it takes to get them into production. Warranty claims and product performance problems involving supplier components can be made available instantly to the relevant suppliers so that corrections can be expedited. Various e-procurement software packages streamline the purchasing process by eliminating much of the manual handling of data and by substituting electronic communication for paper documents such as requests for quotations, purchase orders, order acceptances, and shipping notices.

Manufacturers are using Internet applications to link customer orders to production at their plants and to deliveries of components from suppliers. Real-time sharing of customer orders with suppliers facilitates just-in-time deliveries of parts and slices parts inventory costs. It also allows both manufacturers and their suppliers to gear production to match demand for both components and finished goods. Online systems that monitor actual sales permit more accurate demand forecasting, thereby helping both manufacturers and their suppliers adjust their production schedules as swings in buyer demand are detected. Data sharing, starting with customer orders and going all the way back to components production, coupled with the use of enterprise resource planning (ERP) and manufacturing execution system (MES) software, can make custom manufacturing just as cheap as mass production—and sometimes cheaper. It can also greatly reduce production times and labor costs. Lexmark used ERP and MES software to cut its production time for inkjet printers from 4 hours to 24 minutes.

The instant communications features of the Internet, combined with all the real-time data sharing and information availability, have the further effect of breaking down corporate bureaucracies and reducing overhead costs. The whole "back-office" data management process (order processing, invoicing, customer accounting, and other kinds of transaction costs) can be handled quickly, accurately, and efficiently, with less paperwork and fewer personnel. The time savings and transaction cost reductions associated with doing business online has allowed companies in many industries to streamline their supply chains and has resulted in significant cost savings in the back-office activities of stock brokerages and banks.

- *Using direct-to-end-user sales and marketing approaches:* Costs in the wholesale/retail portions of the value chain frequently represent 35 to 50 percent of the price final consumers pay. Software developers are increasingly using the Internet to market and deliver their products directly to buyers; allowing customers to download software directly from the Internet eliminates the costs of producing and packaging CDs and cuts out the host of activities, costs, and markups associated with shipping and distributing software through wholesale and retail channels. By cutting all these costs and activities out of the value chain, software developers have the pricing room to boost their profit margins and still sell their products below levels that retailers would have to charge. The major airlines now sell most of their tickets directly to passengers via their Web sites, ticket counter agents, and telephone reservation systems, allowing them to save hundreds of millions of dollars in commissions once paid to travel agents.

- *Simplifying product design:* Using computer-assisted design techniques, reducing the number of parts, standardizing parts and components across models and styles, and shifting to an easy-to-manufacture product design can all simplify the value chain.

- *Stripping away the extras:* Offering only basic products or services can help a company cut costs associated with multiple features and options. Stripping extras is a favorite technique of the no-frills airlines like Southwest Airlines.

- *Shifting to a simpler, less capital-intensive, or more streamlined or flexible technological process:* Computer-assisted design and manufacture, or other flexible manufacturing systems, can accommodate both low-cost efficiency and product customization.

- *Bypassing the use of high-cost raw materials or component parts:* High-cost raw materials and parts can be designed out of the product.

- *Relocating facilities:* Moving plants closer to suppliers, customers, or both can help curtail inbound and outbound logistics costs.

- *Dropping the "something for everyone" approach:* Pruning slow-selling items from the product lineup and being content to meet the needs of most buyers, rather than all buyers, can eliminate activities and costs associated with numerous product versions.

Company Spotlight 4.2 describes how Wal-Mart has managed its value chain in the retail grocery portion of its business to achieve a dramatic cost advantage over rival supermarket chains and become the world's biggest grocery retailer.

> Success in achieving a low-cost edge over rivals comes from exploring all the avenues for cost reduction and pressing for continuous cost reductions across all aspects of the company's value chain year after year.

The Keys to Success in Achieving Low-Cost Leadership   To succeed with a low-cost provider strategy, company managers have to scrutinize each cost-creating activity and determine what drives its cost. Then they have to use this knowledge about the cost drivers to manage the costs of each activity downward, exhaustively pursuing cost savings throughout the value chain. They have to be proactive in restructuring the value chain to eliminate nonessential work steps and low-value activities. Normally, low-cost producers work diligently to create cost-conscious corporate cultures that feature broad employee participation in continuous cost improvement efforts and limited perks and frills for executives. They strive to operate with exceptionally small corporate staffs to keep administrative costs to a minimum.

But while low-cost providers are champions of frugality, they are usually aggressive in investing in resources and capabilities that promise to drive costs out of the business. Wal-Mart, one of the foremost practitioners of low-cost leadership, employs state-of-the-art technology throughout its operations—its distribution facilities are an automated showcase, it uses online systems to order goods from suppliers and manage inventories, it equips its stores with cutting-edge sales-tracking and checkout systems, and it operates a private satellite communications system that daily sends point-of-sale data to 4,000 vendors. Wal-Mart's information and communications systems and capabilities are more sophisticated than those of virtually any other retail chain in the world.

Other companies noted for their successful use of low-cost provider strategies include Lincoln Electric in arc welding equipment, Briggs & Stratton in small gasoline engines, Bic in ballpoint pens, Black & Decker in power tools, Stride Rite in footwear, Beaird-Poulan in chain saws, and General Electric and Whirlpool in major home appliances.

When a Low-Cost Provider Strategy Works Best   A competitive strategy predicated on low-cost leadership is particularly powerful when:

How Wal-Mart Managed Its Value Chain to Achieve a Huge Low-Cost Advantage over Rival Supermarket Chains

Wal-Mart has achieved a very substantial cost and pricing advantage over rival supermarket chains both by revamping portions of the grocery retailing value chain and by outmanaging its rivals in efficiently performing various value chain activities. Its cost advantage stems from a series of initiatives and practices:

- Instituting extensive information sharing with vendors via online systems that relay sales at its checkout counters directly to suppliers of the items, thereby providing suppliers with real-time information on customer demand and preferences (creating an estimated 6 percent cost advantage). It is standard practice at Wal-Mart to collaborate extensively with vendors on all aspects of the purchasing and store delivery process to squeeze out mutually beneficial cost savings. Procter & Gamble, Wal-Mart's biggest supplier, went so far as to integrate its enterprise resource planning (ERP) system with Wal-Mart's.

- Pursuing global procurement of some items and centralizing most purchasing activities so as to leverage the company's buying power (creating an estimated 2.5 percent cost advantage).

- Investing in state-of-the-art automation at its distribution centers, efficiently operating a truck fleet that makes daily deliveries to Wal-Mart stores, and putting various other cost-saving

practices into place at its headquarters, distribution centers, and stores (resulting in an estimated 4 percent cost advantage).

- Striving to optimize the product mix and achieve greater sales turnover (resulting in about a 2 percent cost advantage).

- Installing security systems and store operating procedures that lower shrinkage rates (producing a cost advantage of about 0.5 percent).

- Negotiating preferred real estate rental and leasing rates with real estate developers and owners of its store sites (yielding a cost advantage of 2 percent).

- Managing and compensating its workforce in a manner that produces lower labor costs (yielding an estimated 5 percent cost advantage).

Altogether, these value chain initiatives give Wal-Mart an approximately 22 percent cost advantage over Kroger, Safeway, and other leading supermarket chains. With such a sizable cost advantage, Wal-Mart has been able to underprice its rivals and become the world's leading supermarket retailer in little more than a decade.

Source: Reprinted by permission of *Harvard Business Review,* an excerpt from "Strategy as Ecology," by Marco Iansiti and Roy Levien, March 2004, Copyright ©2004 by the President and Fellows of Harvard College, all rights reserved.

---

1. *Price competition among rival sellers is especially vigorous.* Low-cost providers are in the best position to compete offensively on the basis of price, to use the appeal of lower price to grab sales (and market share) from rivals, to remain profitable in the face of strong price competition, and to survive price wars.

2. *The products of rival sellers are essentially identical, and supplies are readily available from any of several eager sellers.* Commoditylike products and/or ample supplies set the stage for lively price competition; in such markets, it is the less efficient, higher-cost companies whose profits get squeezed the most.

3. *There are few ways to achieve product differentiation that have value to buyers.* When the differences between brands do not matter much to buyers, buyers are nearly always very sensitive to price differences and shop the market for the best price.

4. *Most buyers use the product in the same way.* With common user requirements, a standardized product can satisfy the needs of buyers, in which case low selling price, not features or quality, becomes the dominant factor in causing buyers to choose one seller's product over another's.

5. *Buyers incur low costs in switching their purchases from one seller to another.* Low switching costs give buyers the flexibility to shift purchases to lower-priced

sellers having equally good products or to attractively priced substitute products. A low-cost leader is well positioned to use low price to induce its customers not to switch to rival brands or substitutes.

6. *Buyers are large and have significant power to bargain down prices.* Low-cost providers have partial profit-margin protection in bargaining with high-volume buyers, since powerful buyers are rarely able to bargain price down past the survival level of the next most cost-efficient seller.

7. *Industry newcomers use introductory low prices to attract buyers and build a customer base.* The low-cost leader can use price cuts of its own to make it harder for a new rival to win customers; the pricing power of the low-cost provider acts as a barrier for new entrants.

> A low-cost provider is in the best position to win the business of price-sensitive buyers, set the floor on market price, and still earn a profit.

As a rule, the more price sensitive buyers are, the more appealing a low-cost strategy becomes. A low-cost company's ability to set the industry's price floor and still earn a profit erects protective barriers around its market position.

The Pitfalls of a Low-Cost Provider Strategy   Perhaps the biggest pitfall of a low-cost provider strategy is getting carried away with overly aggressive price cutting and ending up with lower, rather than higher, profitability. A low-cost/low-price advantage results in superior profitability only if (1) prices are cut by less than the size of the cost advantage or (2) the added gains in unit sales are large enough to bring in a bigger total profit despite lower margins per unit sold. A company with a 5 percent cost advantage cannot cut prices 20 percent, end up with a volume gain of only 10 percent, and still expect to earn higher profits!

A second big pitfall is not emphasizing avenues of cost advantage that can be kept proprietary or that relegate rivals to playing catch-up. The value of a cost advantage depends on its sustainability. Sustainability, in turn, hinges on whether the company achieves its cost advantage in ways difficult for rivals to copy or match.

> A low-cost provider's product offering must always contain enough attributes to be attractive to prospective buyers—low price, by itself, is not always appealing to buyers.

A third pitfall is becoming too fixated on cost reduction. Low cost cannot be pursued so zealously that a firm's offering ends up being too features-poor to generate buyer appeal. Furthermore, a company driving hard to push its costs down has to guard against misreading or ignoring increased buyer interest in added features or service, declining buyer sensitivity to price, or new developments that start to alter how buyers use the product. A low-cost zealot risks losing market ground if buyers start opting for more upscale or features-rich products.

Even if these mistakes are avoided, a low-cost competitive approach still carries risk. Cost-saving technological breakthroughs or the emergence of still-lower-cost value chain models can nullify a low-cost leader's hard-won position. The current leader may have difficulty in shifting quickly to the new technologies or value chain approaches because heavy investments lock it in (at least temporarily) to its present value chain approach.

Differentiation Strategies

> **Core Concept**
> The essence of a broad differentiation strategy is to be unique in ways that are valuable to a wide range of customers.

Differentiation strategies are attractive whenever buyers' needs and preferences are too diverse to be fully satisfied by a standardized product or by sellers with identical capabilities. A company attempting to succeed through differentiation must study buyers' needs and behavior carefully to learn what buyers consider important, what they think has value, and what they are willing to pay for. Then the company has to incorporate buyer-desired attributes into its product or service offering that will clearly set it apart from rivals. Competitive advantage results once a sufficient number of buyers become strongly attached to the differentiated attributes.

Successful differentiation allows a firm to:

- Command a premium price for its product, and/or

- Increase unit sales (because additional buyers are won over by the differentiating features), and/or

- Gain buyer loyalty to its brand (because some buyers are strongly attracted to the differentiating features and bond with the company and its products).

Differentiation enhances profitability whenever the extra price the product commands outweighs the added costs of achieving the differentiation. Company differentiation strategies fail when buyers don't value the brand's uniqueness and/or when a company's approach to differentiation is easily copied or matched by its rivals.

Types of Differentiation Themes   Companies can pursue differentiation from many angles: a unique taste (Dr Pepper, Listerine); multiple features (Microsoft Windows, Microsoft Office); wide selection and one-stop shopping (Home Depot, Amazon.com); superior service (FedEx); spare parts availability (Caterpillar guarantees 48-hour spare parts delivery to any customer anywhere in the world or else the part is furnished free); engineering design and performance (Mercedes, BMW); prestige and distinctiveness (Rolex); product reliability (Johnson & Johnson in baby products); quality manufacture (Karastan in carpets, Michelin in tires, Honda in automobiles); technological leadership (3M Corporation in bonding and coating products); a full range of services (Charles Schwab in stock brokerage); a complete line of products (Campbell's soups); and top-of-the-line image and reputation (Ralph Lauren and Starbucks).

The most appealing approaches to differentiation are those that are hard or expensive for rivals to duplicate. Indeed, resourceful competitors can, in time, clone almost any product or feature or attribute. If Coca-Cola introduces a vanilla-flavored soft drink, so can PepsiCo; if Ford offers a 50,000-mile bumper-to-bumper warranty on its new vehicles, so can Volkswagen and Nissan. As a rule, differentiation yields a longer-lasting and more profitable competitive edge when it is based on product innovation, technical superiority, product quality and reliability, comprehensive customer service, and unique competitive capabilities. Such differentiating attributes tend to be tough for rivals to copy or offset profitably, and buyers widely perceive them as having value.

> Easy-to-copy differentiating features cannot produce sustainable competitive advantage.

Where along the Value Chain to Create the Differentiating Attributes   Differentiation is not something hatched in marketing and advertising departments, nor is it limited to the catchalls of quality and service. Differentiation opportunities can exist in activities all along an industry's value chain; possibilities include the following:

- *Supply chain activities* that ultimately spill over to affect the performance or quality of the company's end product. Starbucks gets high ratings on its coffees partly because it has very strict specifications on the coffee beans purchased from suppliers.

- *Product R&D activities* that aim at improved product designs and performance features, expanded end uses and applications, more frequent first-on-the-market victories, wider product variety and selection, added user safety, greater recycling capability, or enhanced environmental protection.

■ *Production R&D and technology-related activities* that permit custom-order manufacture at an efficient cost, make production methods safer for the environment, or improve product quality, reliability, and appearance. Many manufacturers have developed flexible manufacturing systems that allow different models to be made or different options to be added on the same assembly line. Being able to provide buyers with made-to-order products can be a potent differentiating capability.

■ *Manufacturing activities* that reduce product defects, prevent premature product failure, extend product life, allow better warranty coverages, improve economy of use, result in more end-user convenience, or enhance product appearance. The quality edge enjoyed by Japanese automakers stems partly from their distinctive competence in performing assembly-line activities.

■ *Outbound logistics and distribution activities* that allow for faster delivery, more accurate order filling, lower shipping costs, and fewer warehouse and on-the-shelf stockouts.

■ *Marketing, sales, and customer service activities* that result in superior technical assistance to buyers, faster maintenance and repair services, more and better product information for customers, more and better training materials for end users, better credit terms, quicker order processing, or greater customer convenience.

Managers need keen understanding of the sources of differentiation and the activities that drive uniqueness to devise a sound differentiation strategy and evaluate various differentiation approaches.

Achieving a Differentiation-Based Competitive Advantage

While it is easy enough to grasp that a successful differentiation strategy must entail creating buyer value in ways unmatched by rivals, the big question is which of four basic differentiating approaches to take in delivering unique buyer value. One approach is to *incorporate product attributes and user features that lower the buyer's overall costs of using the company's product.* Making a company's product more economical for a buyer to use can be done by reducing the buyer's raw materials waste (providing cut-to-size components), reducing a buyer's inventory requirements (providing just-in-time deliveries), increasing maintenance intervals and product reliability so as to lower a buyer's repair and maintenance costs, using online systems to reduce a buyer's procurement and order processing costs, and providing free technical support.

A second approach is to *incorporate features that raise product performance.*[4] This can be accomplished with attributes that provide buyers greater reliability, durability, convenience, or ease of use. Other performance-enhancing options include making the company's product or service cleaner, safer, quieter, or more maintenance-free than rival brands. A third approach is to *incorporate features that enhance buyer satisfaction in noneconomic or intangible ways.* Goodyear's Aquatread tire design appeals to safety-conscious motorists wary of slick roads. BMW, Ralph Lauren, and Rolex have differentiation-based competitive advantages linked to buyer desires for status, image, prestige, upscale fashion, superior craftsmanship, and the finer things in life. L.L. Bean makes its mail-order customers feel secure in their purchases by providing an unconditional guarantee with no time limit: "All of our products are guaranteed to give 100 percent satisfaction in every way. Return anything purchased from us

Core Concept

A differentiator's basis for competitive advantage is either a product/service offering whose attributes differ significantly from the offerings of rivals or competitive capabilities and resource strengths that set it apart from rivals.

at any time if it proves otherwise. We will replace it, refund your purchase price, or credit your credit card, as you wish."

A fourth approach is to differentiate on the basis of capabilities—*to deliver value to customers via competitive capabilities that rivals don't have or can't afford to match.*[5] Japanese automakers can bring new models to market faster than American and European automakers, thereby allowing the Japanese companies to satisfy changing consumer preferences for one vehicle style versus another. CNN has the capability to cover breaking news stories faster and more completely than the major networks. Microsoft has stronger capabilities to design, create, distribute, and advertise an array of software products for PC applications than any of its rivals.

Keeping the Cost of Differentiation in Line   Company efforts to achieve differentiation usually raise costs. The trick to profitable differentiation is either to keep the costs of achieving differentiation below the price premium the differentiating attributes can command in the marketplace (thus increasing the profit margin per unit sold) or to offset thinner profit margins with enough added volume to increase total profits. It usually makes sense to incorporate differentiating features that are not costly but that add to buyer satisfaction. Federal Express (FedEx) installed systems that allowed customers to track packages in transit by connecting to FedEx's Web site and entering the airbill number; some hotels and motels provide free continental breakfasts, exercise facilities, and in-room coffee-making amenities; publishers are using their Web sites to deliver complementary educational materials to the buyers of their textbooks.

When a Differentiation Strategy Works Best   Differentiation strategies tend to work best in market circumstances where:

- *There are many ways to differentiate the product or service, and many buyers perceive these differences as having value.* Unless buyers have strong preferences about certain features, profitable differentiation opportunities are very restricted.

- *Buyer needs and uses are diverse.* The more diverse buyer preferences are, the more room firms have to pursue different approaches to differentiation.

> **Core Concept**
> Any differentiating feature that works well tends to draw imitators.

- *Few rival firms are following a similar differentiation approach.* There is less head-to-head rivalry when differentiating rivals go separate ways in pursuing uniqueness and try to appeal to buyers on different combinations of attributes.

- *Technological change is fast-paced, and competition revolves around rapidly evolving product features.* Rapid product innovation and frequent introductions of next-version products help maintain buyer interest and provide space for companies to pursue separate differentiating paths.

The Pitfalls of a Differentiation Strategy   There are, of course, no guarantees that differentiation will produce a meaningful competitive advantage. If buyers see little value in the unique attributes or capabilities of a product, then the company's differentiation strategy will get a ho-hum market reception. In addition, attempts at differentiation are doomed to fail if competitors can quickly copy most or all of the appealing product attributes a company comes up with. Rapid imitation means that no rival achieves differentiation, since whenever one firm introduces some aspect of uniqueness that strikes the fancy of buyers, fast-following copycats quickly reestablish similarity. Thus, to build competitive advantage through differentiation, a firm must rely on sources of uniqueness that are time-consuming or burdensome for rivals to match. Other common pitfalls and mistakes in pursuing differentiation include:[6]

- Trying to differentiate on the basis of something that does not lower a buyer's cost or enhance a buyer's well-being, as perceived by the buyer.

- Overdifferentiating, so that the features and attributes incorporated end up exceeding buyers' needs.

- Trying to charge too high a price premium. (The bigger the price differential, the harder it is to keep buyers from switching to lower-priced competitors.)

A low-cost provider strategy can defeat a differentiation strategy when buyers are satisfied with a basic product and don't think "extra" attributes are worth a higher price.

Best-Cost Provider Strategies

Best-cost provider strategies aim at giving customers *more value for the money*. The objective is to deliver superior value to buyers by satisfying their expectations on key quality/service/features/performance attributes and beating their expectations on price (given what rivals are charging for much the same attributes). A company achieves best-cost status from an ability to incorporate attractive attributes at a lower cost than rivals. To become a best-cost provider, a company must have the resources and capabilities to achieve good-to-excellent quality, incorporate appealing features, match product performance, and provide good-to-excellent customer service—all at a lower cost than rivals.

As Figure 4.1 indicates, best-cost provider strategies stake out a middle ground between pursuing a low-cost advantage and pursuing a differentiation advantage and between appealing to the broad market as a whole and appealing to a narrow market niche. From a competitive positioning standpoint, best-cost strategies are a *hybrid,* balancing a strategic emphasis on low cost against a strategic emphasis on differentiation (superior value). *The target market is value-conscious buyers,* perhaps a very sizable part of the overall market. *The competitive advantage of a best-cost provider is lower costs than rivals* in incorporating good-to-excellent attributes, putting the company in a position to underprice rivals whose products have similar appealing attributes.

A best-cost provider strategy is very appealing in markets where buyer diversity makes product differentiation the norm *and* where many buyers are sensitive to price, product quality, and product performance. This is because a best-cost provider can position itself near the middle of the market with either a medium-quality product at a below-average price or a high-quality product at an average price. Often, substantial numbers of buyers prefer midrange products rather than the cheap, basic products of low-cost providers or the expensive products of top-of-the-line differentiators. But unless a company has the resources, know-how, and capabilities to incorporate upscale product or service attributes at a lower cost than rivals, this strategy is ill-advised.

Company Spotlight 4.3 describes how Toyota has used a best-cost approach with its Lexus models.

The Big Risk of a Best-Cost Provider Strategy   The danger of a best-cost provider strategy is that a company using it will get squeezed between the strategies of firms using low-cost and differentiation strategies. Low-cost leaders may be able to siphon customers away with the appeal of a lower price. High-end differentiators may be able to steal customers away with the appeal of better product attributes. Thus, to be successful, a best-cost provider must offer buyers *significantly* better product attributes in order to justify a price above what low-cost leaders are charging. Likewise, it

Toyota's Best-Cost Producer Strategy for Its Lexus Line

Toyota Motor Company is widely regarded as a low-cost producer among the world's motor vehicle manufacturers. Despite its emphasis on product quality, Toyota has achieved low-cost leadership because it has developed considerable skills in efficient supply chain management and low-cost assembly capabilities and because its models are positioned in the low-to-medium end of the price spectrum, where high production volumes are conducive to low unit costs. But when Toyota decided to introduce its new Lexus models to compete in the luxury-car market, it employed a classic best-cost provider strategy. Toyota took the following four steps in crafting and implementing its Lexus strategy:

- Designing an array of high-performance characteristics and upscale features into the Lexus models so as to make them comparable in performance and luxury to other high-end models and attractive to Mercedes, BMW, Audi, Jaguar, Cadillac, and Lincoln buyers.

- Transferring its capabilities in making high-quality Toyota models at low cost to making premium-quality Lexus models at costs below other luxury-car makers. Toyota's supply chain capabilities and low-cost assembly know-how allowed it to incorporate high-tech performance features and upscale quality into Lexus models at substantially less cost than Mercedes and BMW.

- Using its relatively lower manufacturing costs to underprice comparable Mercedes and BMW models. Toyota believed that with its cost advantage it could price attractively equipped Lexus cars low enough to draw price-conscious buyers away from Mercedes and BMW and perhaps induce dissatisfied Lincoln and Cadillac owners to move up to a Lexus.

- Establishing a new network of Lexus dealers, separate from Toyota dealers, dedicated to providing a level of personalized, attentive customer service unmatched in the industry.

Lexus models have consistently ranked first in the widely watched J. D. Power & Associates quality survey, and the prices of Lexus models are typically several thousand dollars below those of comparable Mercedes and BMW models—clear signals that Toyota has succeeded in becoming a best-cost producer with its Lexus brand.

---

has to achieve significantly lower costs in providing upscale features so that it can outcompete high-end differentiators on the basis of an attractively lower price.

Focused (or Market Niche) Strategies

What sets focused strategies apart from low-cost leadership or broad differentiation strategies is concentrated attention on a narrow piece of the total market. The target segment, or niche, can be defined by geographic uniqueness, by specialized requirements in using the product, or by special product attributes that appeal only to niche members. Examples of firms that concentrate on a well-defined market niche include eBay (in online auctions); Porsche (in sports cars); Cannondale (in top-of-the-line mountain bikes); Jiffy Lube International (a specialist in quick oil changes and simple maintenance for motor vehicles); Enterprise Rent-a-Car (specializing in providing rental cars to repair-garage customers); Pottery Barn Kids (a retail chain featuring children's furniture and accessories); E-Loan (in online consumer lending); and Bandag (a specialist in truck-tire recapping that promotes its recaps aggressively at over 1,000 truck stops). Microbreweries, local bakeries, bed-and-breakfast inns, and local owner-managed retail boutiques are all good examples of enterprises that have scaled their operations to serve narrow or local customer segments.

> Even though a focuser may be small, it still may have substantial competitive strength because of the attractiveness of its product offering and its strong expertise and capabilities in meeting the needs and expectations of niche members.

A Focused Low-Cost Strategy A focused strategy based on low cost aims at securing a competitive advantage by serving buyers in the target market niche at a lower cost and lower price than do rival competitors. This strategy has considerable attraction when a firm can lower costs significantly by limiting its customer base to a well-defined buyer segment. The avenues to achieving a cost advantage over rivals also serving the target market niche are the same as those for low-cost leadership—outmanage rivals in controlling the factors that drive costs and reconfigure the firm's value chain in ways that yield a cost edge over rivals.

Focused low-cost strategies are fairly common. Producers of private-label goods are able to achieve low costs in product development, marketing, distribution, and advertising by concentrating on making generic items imitative of name-brand merchandise and selling directly to retail chains wanting a basic house brand to sell to price-sensitive shoppers. Several small printer-supply manufacturers have begun making low-cost clones of the premium-priced replacement ink and toner cartridges sold by Hewlett-Packard, Lexmark, Canon, and Epson; the clone manufacturers dissect the cartridges of the name-brand companies and then reengineer a similar version that won't violate patents. The components for remanufactured replacement cartridges are acquired from various outside sources, and the clones are then marketed at prices as much as 50 percent below the name-brand cartridges. Cartridge remanufacturers have been lured to focus on this market because replacement cartridges constitute a multibillion-dollar business with considerable profit potential given their low costs and the premium pricing of the name-brand companies. Company Spotlight 4.4 describes how Motel 6 has kept its costs low in catering to budget-conscious travelers.

A Focused Differentiation Strategy A focused strategy based on differentiation aims at securing a competitive advantage by offering niche members a product they perceive as unusually well suited to their own unique tastes and preferences. Successful use of a focused differentiation strategy depends on the existence of a buyer segment that is looking for special product attributes or seller capabilities and on a firm's ability to stand apart from rivals competing in the same target market niche.

Companies like Godiva Chocolates, Chanel, Rolls-Royce, Häagen-Dazs, and W. L. Gore (the maker of Gore-Tex) employ successful differentiation-based focused

COMPANY SPOTLIGHT 4.5

Progressive Insurance's Focused Differentiation Strategy in Auto Insurance

Progressive Insurance has fashioned a strategy in auto insurance focused on people with a record of traffic violations who drive high-performance cars, drivers with accident histories, motorcyclists, teenagers, and other so-called high-risk categories of drivers that most auto insurance companies steer away from. Progressive discovered that some of these high-risk drivers are affluent and pressed for time, making them less sensitive to paying premium rates for their car insurance. Management learned that it could charge such drivers high-enough premiums to cover the added risks, plus it differentiated Progressive from other insurers by expediting the process of obtaining insurance and decreasing the annoyance that such drivers face in obtaining insurance coverage.

In further differentiating and promoting Progressive policies, management created teams of roving claims adjusters who arrive at accident scenes to assess claims and issue checks for repairs on the spot. Progressive also studied the market segments for insurance carefully enough to discover that some motorcycle owners are not especially risky (middle-aged suburbanites who sometimes commute to work or use their motorcycles mainly for recreational trips with their friends). Progressive's strategy allowed it to become a leader in the market for luxury-car insurance for customers who appreciate Progressive's streamlined approach to doing business.

strategies targeted at upscale buyers wanting products and services with world-class attributes. Indeed, most markets contain a buyer segment willing to pay a big price premium for the very finest items available, thus opening the strategic window for some competitors to pursue differentiation-based focused strategies aimed at the very top of the market pyramid. Another successful focused differentiator is a "fashion food retailer" called Trader Joe's, a 150-store East and West Coast chain that is a combination gourmet deli and food warehouse.[7] Customers shop Trader Joe's as much for entertainment as for conventional grocery items—the store stocks out-of-the-ordinary culinary treats like raspberry salsa, salmon burgers, and jasmine fried rice, as well as the standard goods normally found in supermarkets. What sets Trader Joe's apart is not just its unique combination of food novelties and competitively priced grocery items but also its capability to turn an otherwise mundane grocery excursion into a whimsical treasure hunt that is just plain fun. Company Spotlight 4.5 describes Progressive Insurance's focused differentiation strategy.

When Focusing Is Attractive A focused strategy aimed at securing a competitive edge based either on low cost or differentiation becomes increasingly attractive as more of the following conditions are met:

1. The target market niche is big enough to be profitable and offers good growth potential.

2. Industry leaders do not see that having a presence in the niche is crucial to their own success—in which case focusers can often escape battling head-to-head against some of the industry's biggest and strongest competitors.

3. It is costly or difficult for multisegment competitors to put capabilities in place to meet the specialized needs of the target market niche and at the same time satisfy the expectations of their mainstream customers.

4. The industry has many different niches and segments, thereby allowing a focuser to pick a competitively attractive niche suited to its resource strengths and capabilities.

Also, with more niches there is more room for focusers to avoid each other in competing for the same customers.

5. Few, if any, other rivals are attempting to specialize in the same target segment—a condition that reduces the risk of segment overcrowding.

6. The focuser can compete effectively against challengers by relying on its capabilities and resources to serve the targeted niche and the customer goodwill it may have built up.

The Risks of a Focused Strategy   Focusing carries several risks. One is the chance that competitors will find effective ways to match the focused firm's capabilities in serving the target niche—perhaps by coming up with more appealing product offerings or by developing expertise and capabilities that offset the focuser's strengths. A second is the potential for the preferences and needs of niche members to shift over time toward the product attributes desired by the majority of buyers. An erosion of the differences across buyer segments lowers entry barriers into a focuser's market niche and provides an open invitation for rivals in adjacent segments to begin competing for the focuser's customers. A third risk is that the segment may become so attractive it is soon inundated with competitors, intensifying rivalry and splintering segment profits.

The Five Generic Competitive Strategies Entail Different Operating Approaches

Deciding which generic competitive strategy should serve as the framework for the rest of the company's strategy is not a trivial matter. Each of the five generic competitive strategies positions the company differently in its market and competitive environment. Each establishes a central theme for how the company will endeavor to defeat rivals. Each creates some boundaries or guidelines for maneuvering as market circumstances unfold and as ideas for improving the strategy are debated. Each points to different ways of experimenting and tinkering with the basic strategy—for example, employing a low-cost leadership strategy means experimenting with ways that costs can be cut and value chain activities can be streamlined, whereas a broad differentiation strategy means exploring ways to add new differentiating features or to perform value chain activities differently if the result is to add value for customers in ways they are willing to pay for. Each entails differences in terms of product line, production emphasis, marketing emphasis, and means of sustaining the strategy. Thus a choice of which generic strategy to employ spills over to affect several aspects of the way the business will be operated and the manner in which value chain activities must be managed. Deciding which generic strategy to employ is perhaps the most important strategic commitment a company makes—it tends to drive the rest of the strategic actions a company decides to undertake.

One of the big dangers here is that managers, torn between the pros and cons of the various generic strategies, will opt for *"stuck in the middle" strategies* that represent compromises between lower costs and greater differentiation and between broad and narrow market appeal. Compromise or middle-ground strategies rarely produce sustainable competitive advantage or a distinctive competitive position—well-executed best-cost-producer strategies are the only exception where a compromise between low cost and differentiation succeeds. Usually, companies with compromise strategies end up with a middle-of-the-pack industry ranking—they have average costs, some but not a lot of product differentiation relative to rivals, an average image and reputation, and little prospect of industry leadership. Having a competitive edge over rivals is the single most dependable contributor to above-average company profitability. Hence, only if a company makes a strong and unwavering commitment to one of the five generic competitive strategies does it stand much chance of achieving the sustainable competitive advantage that such strategies can deliver if properly executed.

Collaborative Strategies: Strategic Alliances and Partnerships

During the past decade, companies in all types of industries and in all parts of the world have elected to form strategic alliances and partnerships to complement their own strategic initiatives and strengthen their competitiveness in domestic and international markets. This is an about-face from times past, when the vast majority of companies were content to go it alone, confident that they already had or could independently develop whatever resources and know-how were needed to be successful in their markets. But globalization of the world economy, revolutionary advances in technology across a broad front, and untapped opportunities in national markets in Asia, Latin America, and Europe that are opening up, deregulating, and/or undergoing privatization have made strategic partnerships of one kind or another integral to competing on a broad geographic scale.

Many companies now find themselves thrust into two very demanding competitive races: (1) *the global race to build a market presence in many different national markets* and join the ranks of companies recognized as global market leaders and (2) *the race to seize opportunities on the frontiers of advancing technology* and build the resource strengths and business capabilities to compete successfully in the industries and product markets of the future.[8] Even the largest and most financially sound companies have concluded that simultaneously running the races for global market leadership and for a stake in the industries of the future requires more diverse and expansive skills, resources, technological expertise, and competitive capabilities than they can assemble and manage alone. Such companies, along with others that are missing the resources and competitive capabilities needed to pursue promising opportunities, have determined that the fastest way to fill the gap is often to form alliances with enterprises having the desired strengths. Consequently, these companies form **strategic alliances** or collaborative partnerships in which two or more companies join forces to achieve mutually beneficial strategic outcomes. Typically, alliances are formed for such purposes as joint marketing, joint sales or distribution, joint production, design collaboration, joint research and development, and technology licensing. Strategic alliances may entail formal agreements to work together, but they usually stop short of full partnership with formal ownership ties; some strategic alliances, however, do involve arrangements whereby one or more allies have minority ownership in certain of the other alliance members. Five factors make an alliance "strategic," as opposed to just a convenient business arrangement:[9]

> **Core Concept**
>
> **Strategic alliances** are collaborative arrangements where two or more companies join forces to achieve mutually beneficial strategic outcomes.

1. It is critical to the company's achievement of an important objective.
2. It helps build, sustain, or enhance a core competence or competitive advantage.
3. It helps block a competitive threat.
4. It helps open up important new market opportunities.
5. It mitigates a significant risk to a company's business.

The Pervasive Use of Alliances   Companies in many different industries all across the world have made strategic alliances a core part of their overall strategy; U.S. companies alone announced nearly 68,000 alliances from 1996 through 2003.[10] In the personal computer industry, alliances are pervasive because the different components of PCs and the software to run them are supplied by so many different companies—one set of companies provides the microprocessors, another group makes the motherboards, another the monitors, another the disk drives, another the memory chips, and so on. Moreover, their facilities are scattered across the United States, Japan, Taiwan, Singapore, Malaysia, and parts of Europe. Strategic alliances among companies in the various parts of the PC industry facilitate the close cross-company collaboration required on next-generation product development, logistics, production, and the timing of new product releases.

Toyota has forged long-term strategic partnerships with many of its suppliers of automotive parts and components, both to achieve lower costs and to improve the quality and reliability of its vehicles. Microsoft collaborates very closely with independent software developers to ensure that their programs will run on the next-generation versions of Windows. Genentech, a leader in biotechnology and human genetics, has a partnering strategy to increase its access to novel biotherapeutic products and technologies and has formed alliances with over 30 companies to strengthen its research and development pipeline. During the 1998–2004 period, Samsung Electronics, a South Korean corporation with $54 billion in sales, entered into over 50 major strategic alliances involving such companies as Sony, Yahoo, Hewlett-Packard, Nokia, Motorola, Intel, Microsoft, Dell, Mitsubishi, Disney, IBM, Maytag, and Rockwell Automation; the alliances involved joint investments, technology transfer arrangements, joint R&D projects, and agreements to supply parts and components—all of which facilitated Samsung's strategic efforts to transform itself into a global enterprise and establish itself as a leader in the worldwide electronics industry.

Studies indicate that large corporations are commonly involved in 30 to 50 alliances and that a number have hundreds of alliances. One recent study estimated that about 35 percent of corporate revenues in 2003 came from activities involving strategic alliances, up from 15 percent in 1995.[11]

Why and How Strategic Alliances Are Advantageous

> The best alliances are highly selective, focusing on particular value chain activities and on a particular competitive benefit. They tend to enable a firm to build on its strengths and to learn.

The most common reasons why companies enter into strategic alliances are to expedite the development of promising new technologies or products, to overcome deficits in their own technical and manufacturing expertise, to bring together the personnel and expertise needed to create desirable new skill sets and capabilities, to improve supply chain efficiency, to gain economies of scale in production and/or marketing, and to acquire or improve market access through joint marketing agreements.[12] A company that is racing for *global market leadership* needs alliances to:

- *Get into critical country markets quickly* and accelerate the process of building a potent global market presence.

- *Gain inside knowledge about unfamiliar markets and cultures through alliances with local partners.* For example, U.S., European, and Japanese companies wanting to build market footholds in the fast-growing Chinese market have pursued partnership arrangements with Chinese companies to help in dealing with government regulations, to supply knowledge of local markets, to provide guidance on adapting their products to better match the buying preferences of Chinese consumers, to set up local manufacturing capabilities, and to assist in distribution, marketing, and promotional activities. The policy of the Chinese government has long been to limit foreign companies to a 50 percent ownership in local companies, making alliances with local Chinese companies a virtual necessity to gain market access.

- *Access valuable skills and competencies* that are concentrated in particular geographic locations (such as software design competencies in the United States, fashion design skills in Italy, and efficient manufacturing skills in Japan and China).

A company that is racing to *stake out a strong position in an industry of the future* needs alliances to:

- *Establish a stronger beachhead* for participating in the target industry.
- *Master new technologies and build new expertise and competencies* faster than would be possible through internal efforts.
- *Open up broader opportunities* in the target industry by melding the firm's own capabilities with the expertise and resources of partners.

Allies can learn much from one another in performing joint research, sharing technological know-how, and collaborating on complementary new technologies and products—sometimes enough to enable them to pursue other new opportunities on their own. Manufacturers typically pursue alliances with parts and components suppliers to gain the efficiencies of better supply chain management and to speed new products to market. By joining forces in components production and/or final assembly, companies may be able to realize cost savings not achievable with their own small volumes—Volvo, Renault, and Peugeot formed an alliance to join forces in making engines for their large car models because none of the three needed enough such engines to operate its own engine plant economically. Information systems consultant Accenture has developed strategic alliances with such leading technology providers as SAP, PeopleSoft, Oracle, Siebel, Microsoft, BEA, and Hewlett-Packard to give it greater capabilities in designing and integrating information systems for its corporate clients. Dell Computer entered into an alliance with IBM that involved Dell's purchasing $16 billion in parts and components from IBM for use in Dell's PCs, servers, and workstations over a three-year period; Dell determined that IBM's growing expertise and capabilities in PC components justified using IBM as a major supplier even though Dell and IBM competed in supplying laptop computers and servers to corporate customers. Johnson & Johnson and Merck entered into an alliance to market Pepcid AC; Merck developed the stomach distress remedy and Johnson & Johnson functioned as marketer—the alliance made Pepcid products the best-selling remedies for acid indigestion and heartburn. United Airlines, American Airlines, Continental, Delta, and Northwest created an alliance to form Orbitz, an Internet travel site designed to compete with Expedia and Travelocity to provide consumers with low-cost airfares, rental cars, lodging, cruises, and vacation packages.

Strategic cooperation is a much-favored, indeed necessary, approach in industries where new technological developments are occurring at a furious pace along many different paths and where advances in one technology spill over to affect others (often

> The competitive attraction of alliances is in allowing companies to bundle competencies and resources that are more valuable in a joint effort than when kept separate.

blurring industry boundaries). Whenever industries are experiencing high-velocity technological change in many areas simultaneously, firms find it virtually essential to have cooperative relationships with other enterprises to stay on the leading edge of technology and product performance even in their own area of specialization.

Why Many Alliances Are Unstable or Break Apart   The stability of an alliance depends on how well the partners work together, their success in responding and adapting to changing internal and external conditions, and their willingness to renegotiate the bargain if circumstances so warrant. A successful alliance requires real in-the-trenches collaboration, not merely an arm's-length exchange of ideas. Unless partners place a high value on the skills, resources, and contributions each brings to the alliance and the cooperative arrangement results in valuable win-win outcomes, it is doomed. A surprisingly large number of alliances never live up to expectations. A 1999 study by Accenture, a global business consulting organization, revealed that 61 percent of alliances were either outright failures or "limping along." In 2004, McKinsey & Co. estimated that the overall success rate of alliances was around 50 percent, based on whether the alliance achieved the stated objectives. Many alliances are dissolved after a few years. The high "divorce rate" among strategic allies has several causes—diverging objectives and priorities, an inability to work well together (the alliance between Disney and Pixar is a classic example of an alliance coming apart because of clashes between key managers), changing conditions that render the purpose of the alliance obsolete, the emergence of more attractive technological paths, and marketplace rivalry between one or more allies.[13] Experience indicates that alliances stand a reasonable chance of helping a company reduce competitive disadvantage but very rarely have they proved a durable device for achieving a competitive edge over rivals.

The Strategic Dangers of Relying Heavily on Alliances and Cooperative Partnerships   The Achilles heel of alliances and cooperative strategies is becoming dependent on other companies for *essential* expertise and capabilities. To be a market leader (and perhaps even a serious market contender), a company must ultimately develop its own capabilities in areas where internal strategic control is pivotal to protecting its competitiveness and building competitive advantage. Moreover, some alliances hold only limited potential because the partner guards its most valuable skills and expertise; in such instances, acquiring or merging with a company possessing the desired resources is a better solution.

Merger and Acquisition Strategies

Combining the operations of two companies, via merger or acquisition, is an attractive strategic option for achieving operating economies, strengthening the resulting company's competencies and competitiveness, and opening up avenues of new market opportunity.

Mergers and acquisitions are much-used strategic options—for example, from 1996 through 2003 U.S. companies alone made 90,000 acquisitions.[14] Mergers and acquisitions are especially suited for situations in which alliances and partnerships do not go far enough in providing a company with access to needed resources and capabilities.[15] Ownership ties are more permanent than partnership ties, allowing the operations of the merger/acquisition participants to be tightly integrated and creating more in-house control and autonomy. A *merger* is a pooling of equals, with the newly created company often taking on a new name. An *acquisition* is a combination in which one company, the acquirer, purchases and absorbs the operations of another, the acquired. The difference between a merger and an acquisition relates more to the details of ownership, management control, and financial arrangements than to strategy and competitive advantage. The resources, competencies, and competitive capabilities of the newly created enterprise end up much the same whether the combination is the result of acquisition or merger.

Many mergers and acquisitions are driven by strategies to achieve one of five strategic objectives:[16]

1. *To pave the way for the acquiring company to gain more market share and, further, create a more efficient operation out of the combined companies by closing high-cost plants and eliminating surplus capacity industrywide:* The merger that formed DaimlerChrysler was motivated in large part by the fact that the motor vehicle industry had far more production capacity worldwide than was needed; management at both Daimler Benz and Chrysler believed that the efficiency of the two companies could be significantly improved by shutting some plants and laying off workers, realigning which models were produced at which plants, and squeezing out efficiencies by combining supply chain activities, product design, and administration. Quite a number of acquisitions are undertaken with the objective of transforming two or more otherwise high-cost companies into one lean competitor with average or below-average costs.

2. *To expand a company's geographic coverage:* Many industries exist for a long time in a fragmented state, with local companies dominating local markets and no company having a significantly visible regional or national presence. Eventually, though, expansion-minded companies will launch strategies to acquire local companies in adjacent territories. Over time, companies with successful growth via acquisition strategies emerge as regional market leaders and later perhaps as companies with national coverage. Often the acquiring company follows up on its acquisitions with efforts to lower the operating costs and improve the customer service capabilities of the local businesses it acquires.

3. *To extend the company's business into new product categories or international markets:* PepsiCo acquired Quaker Oats chiefly to bring Gatorade into the Pepsi family of beverages, and PepsiCo's Frito-Lay division has made a series of acquisitions of foreign-based snack-food companies to begin to establish a stronger presence in international markets. Companies like Nestlé, Kraft, Unilever, and Procter & Gamble—all racing for global market leadership—have made acquisitions an integral part of their strategies to widen their geographic reach and broaden the number of product categories in which they compete.

4. *To gain quick access to new technologies and avoid the need for a time-consuming R&D effort* (which might not succeed): This type of acquisition strategy is a favorite of companies racing to establish attractive positions in emerging markets. Such companies need to fill in technological gaps, extend their technological capabilities along some promising new paths, and position themselves to launch next-wave products and services. Cisco Systems purchased over 75 technology companies to give it more technological reach and product breadth, thereby buttressing its standing as the world's biggest supplier of systems for building the infrastructure of the Internet. Intel has made over 300 acquisitions in the past five or so years to broaden its technological base, put it in a stronger position to be a major supplier of Internet technology, and make it less dependent on supplying microprocessors for PCs. This type of acquisition strategy enables a company to

build a market position in attractive technologies quickly and serves as a substitute for extensive in-house R&D programs.

5. *To try to invent a new industry and lead the convergence of industries whose boundaries are being blurred by changing technologies and new market opportunities:* Such acquisitions are the result of a company's management betting that a new industry is on the verge of being born and deciding to establish an early position in this industry by bringing together the resources and products of several different companies. Examples include the merger of AOL and media giant Time Warner and Viacom's purchase of Paramount Pictures, CBS, and Blockbuster—both of which reflected bold strategic moves predicated on beliefs that all entertainment content will ultimately converge into a single industry and be distributed over the Internet.

In addition to the above objectives, there are instances when acquisitions are motivated by a company's desire to fill resource gaps, thus allowing the new company to do things it could not do before. Global Spotlight 4.1 describes how Clear Channel Worldwide has used mergers and acquisitions to build a leading global position in outdoor advertising and radio and TV broadcasting.

All too frequently, mergers and acquisitions do not produce the hoped-for outcomes.[17] Combining the operations of two companies, especially large and complex ones, often entails formidable resistance from rank-and-file organization members, hard-to-resolve conflicts in management styles and corporate cultures, and tough problems of integration. Cost savings, expertise sharing, and enhanced competitive capabilities may take substantially longer than expected or, worse, may never materialize at all. Integrating the operations of two fairly large or culturally diverse companies is hard to pull off—only a few companies that use merger and acquisition strategies have proved they can consistently make good decisions about what to leave alone and what to meld into their own operations and systems. In the case of mergers between companies of roughly equal size, the management groups of the two companies frequently battle over which one is going to end up in control.

A number of previously applauded mergers/acquisitions have yet to live up to expectations—the merger of AOL and Time Warner, the merger of Daimler Benz and Chrysler, Hewlett-Packard's acquisition of Compaq Computer, and Ford's acquisition of Jaguar. The AOL–Time Warner merger has proved to be mostly a disaster, partly because AOL's rapid growth has evaporated, partly because of a huge clash of corporate cultures, and partly because most of the expected benefits have yet to materialize. Ford paid a handsome price to acquire Jaguar but has yet to make the Jaguar brand a major factor in the luxury-car segment in competition against Mercedes, BMW, and Lexus. Novell acquired WordPerfect for $1.7 billion in stock in 1994, but the combination never generated enough punch to compete against Microsoft Word and Microsoft Office—Novell sold WordPerfect to Corel for $124 million in cash and stock less than two years later. In 2001 electronics retailer Best Buy paid $685 million to acquire Musicland, a struggling 1,300-store music retailer that included stores operating under the Musicland, Sam Goody, Suncoast, Media Play, and On Cue names. But Musicland's sales, already declining, dropped even further. In June 2003 Best Buy "sold" Musicland to a Florida investment firm. No cash changed hands, and the "buyer" received shares of stock in Best Buy in return for assuming Musicland's liabilities.

Vertical Integration Strategies: Operating across More Stages of the Industry Value Chain

Vertical integration extends a firm's competitive and operating scope within the same industry. It involves expanding the firm's range of activities backward into sources of supply and/or forward toward end users. Thus, if a manufacturer invests in facilities to produce certain component parts that it formerly purchased from outside suppliers, it remains in essentially the same industry as before. The only change is that it has operations in two stages of the industry value chain. Similarly, if a paint manufacturer, Sherwin-Williams for example, elects to integrate forward by opening 100 retail stores to market its paint products directly to consumers, it remains in the paint business even though its competitive scope extends from manufacturing to retailing.

Vertical integration strategies can aim at *full integration* (participating in all stages of the industry value chain) or *partial integration* (building positions in selected stages of the industry's total value chain). A firm can pursue vertical integration by starting its own operations in other stages in the industry's activity chain or by acquiring a company already performing the activities it wants to bring in-house.

The Advantages of a Vertical Integration Strategy

> **Core Concept**
>
> A vertical integration strategy has appeal *only* if it significantly strengthens a firm's competitive position.

The two best reasons for investing company resources in vertical integration are to strengthen the firm's competitive position and/or boost its profitability.[18] Vertical integration has no real payoff unless it produces sufficient cost savings and/or profit increases to justify the extra investment, adds materially to a company's technological and competitive strengths, and/or helps differentiate the company's product offering.

Integrating Backward to Achieve Greater Competitiveness

Integrating backward generates cost savings only when the volume needed is big enough to capture the same scale economies suppliers have and when suppliers' production efficiency can be matched or exceeded with no drop-off in quality. The best potential for being able to reduce costs via backward integration exists in situations where suppliers have sizable profit margins, where the item being supplied is a major cost component, and where the needed technological skills are easily mastered or can be gained by acquiring a supplier with the desired technological know-how. Integrating backward can sometimes significantly enhance a company's technological capabilities and give it expertise needed to stake out positions in the industries and products of the future. Intel, Cisco, and many other Silicon Valley companies have been active in acquiring companies that will help them speed the advance of Internet technology and pave the way for next-generation families of products and services.

Backward vertical integration can produce a differentiation-based competitive advantage when a company, by performing in-house activities that were previously outsourced, ends up with a better-quality product/service offering, improves the caliber of its customer service, or in other ways enhances the performance of its final product. On occasion, integrating into more stages along the industry value chain can add to a company's differentiation capabilities by allowing it to build or strengthen its core competencies, better master key skills or strategy-critical technologies, or add features that deliver greater customer value. Other potential advantages of backward integration include sparing a company the uncertainty of being dependent on suppliers for crucial components or support services and lessening a company's vulnerability to powerful suppliers inclined to raise prices at every opportunity.

Integrating Forward to Enhance Competitiveness   The strategic impetus for forward integration is to gain better access to end users and better market visibility. In many industries, independent sales agents, wholesalers, and retailers

handle competing brands of the same product; having no allegiance to any one company's brand, they tend to push whatever sells and earns them the biggest profits. Half-hearted commitments by distributors and retailers can frustrate a company's attempt to boost sales and market share, give rise to costly inventory pileups and frequent under-utilization of capacity, and disrupt the economies of steady, near-capacity production. In such cases, it can be advantageous for a manufacturer to integrate forward into wholesaling or retailing via company-owned distributorships or a chain of retail stores. But often a company's product line is not broad enough to justify stand-alone distributorships or retail outlets. This leaves the option of integrating forward into the activity of selling directly to end users—perhaps via the Internet. Bypassing regular wholesale/retail channels in favor of direct sales and Internet retailing can have appeal if it lowers distribution costs, produces a relative cost advantage over certain rivals, and results in lower selling prices to end users.

The Disadvantages of a Vertical Integration Strategy

Vertical integration has some substantial drawbacks, however.[19] First, it boosts a firm's capital investment in the industry, increasing business risk (what if industry growth and profitability go sour?) and perhaps denying financial resources to more worthwhile pursuits. A vertically integrated firm has vested interests in protecting its technology and production facilities. Because of the high costs of abandoning such investments before they are worn out, fully integrated firms tend to adopt new technologies slower than partially integrated or nonintegrated firms. Second, integrating forward or backward locks a firm into relying on its own in-house activities and sources of supply (which later may prove more costly than outsourcing) and potentially results in less flexibility in accommodating buyer demand for greater product variety. In today's world of close working relationships with suppliers and efficient supply chain management systems, very few businesses can make a case for integrating backward into the business of suppliers to ensure a reliable supply of materials and components or to reduce production costs.

Third, vertical integration poses all kinds of capacity-matching problems. In motor vehicle manufacturing, for example, the most efficient scale of operation for making axles is different from the most economic volume for radiators, and different yet again for both engines and transmissions. Building the capacity to produce just the right number of axles, radiators, engines, and transmissions in-house—and doing so at the lowest unit costs for each—is much easier said than done. If internal capacity for making transmissions is deficient, the difference has to be bought externally. Where internal capacity for radiators proves excessive, customers need to be found for the surplus. And if by-products are generated—as occurs in the processing of many chemical products—they require arrangements for disposal.

Fourth, integration forward or backward often calls for radical changes in skills and business capabilities. Parts and components manufacturing, assembly operations, wholesale distribution and retailing, and direct sales via the Internet are different businesses with different key success factors. Managers of a manufacturing company should consider carefully whether it makes good business sense to invest time and money in developing the expertise and merchandising skills to integrate forward into wholesaling and retailing. Many manufacturers learn the hard way that company-owned wholesale/retail networks present many headaches, fit poorly with what they do best, and don't always add the kind of value to their core business they thought they would. Selling to customers via the Internet poses still another set of problems—it is usually easier to use the Internet to sell to business customers than to consumers.

Integrating backward into parts and components manufacture isn't as simple or profitable as it sounds either. Producing some or all of the parts and components needed for final assembly can reduce a company's flexibility to make desirable changes in using certain parts and components—it is one thing to design out a component made by a supplier and another to design out a component being made in-house. Companies that alter designs and models frequently in response to shifting buyer preferences often find outsourcing the needed parts and components cheaper and less complicated than making them in-house. Most of the world's automakers, despite their expertise in automotive technology and manufacturing, have concluded that purchasing many of their key parts and components from manufacturing specialists results in higher quality, lower costs, and greater design flexibility than does the vertical integration option.

Weighing the Pros and Cons of Vertical Integration

All in all, therefore, a strategy of vertical integration can have both important strengths and weaknesses. The tip of the scales depends on (1) whether vertical integration can enhance the performance of strategy-critical activities in ways that lower cost, build expertise, or increase differentiation; (2) the impact of vertical integration on investment costs, flexibility and response times, and the administrative costs of coordinating operations across more value chain activities; and (3) whether the integration substantially enhances a company's competitiveness. Vertical integration strategies have merit according to which capabilities and value chain activities truly need to be performed in-house and which can be performed better or cheaper by outsiders. Without solid benefits, integrating forward or backward is not likely to be an attractive competitive strategy option. In a growing number of instances, companies are proving that deintegrating (i.e., focusing on a narrower portion of the industry value chain) is a cheaper and more flexible competitive strategy.

Outsourcing Strategies

Core Concept

Outsourcing involves farming out certain value chain activities to outside vendors.

Over the past decade, **outsourcing** the performance of more value chain activities to outside suppliers and vendors has become increasingly popular. The two big drivers behind outsourcing are that (1) outsiders can often perform certain activities better or cheaper and (2) outsourcing allows a firm to focus its entire energies on those activities that are at the center of its expertise (its core competencies) and that are the most critical to its competitive and financial success. Outsourcing strategies thus involve a conscious decision to abandon or forgo attempts to perform certain value chain activities *internally* and, instead, to farm them out to outside specialists and strategic allies.

The outsourcing trend represents a big departure from the way that most companies used to deal with their suppliers and vendors. In years past, it was common for companies to maintain arm's-length relationships with suppliers and outside vendors, insisting on items being made to precise specifications and negotiating long and hard over price.[20] Although a company might place orders with the same supplier repeatedly, there was no expectation that this would be the case; price usually determined which supplier was awarded an order, and companies used the threat of switching suppliers to get the lowest possible prices. To enhance their bargaining power and to make the threat of switching credible, it was standard practice for companies to source key parts and components from several suppliers as opposed to dealing with only a single supplier. But today, most companies are abandoning such approaches in favor of forging alliances and strategic partnerships with a small number of highly capable suppliers. Collaborative relationships are replacing contractual, purely price-oriented relationships because companies have discovered that many of the advantages of performing value chain activities in-house can be captured and many of the disadvantages avoided by forging close, long-term cooperative partnerships with able suppliers and vendors and tapping into the expertise and capabilities that they have painstakingly developed.

Benefits of Outsourcing

Outsourcing pieces of the value chain to narrow the boundaries of a firm's business makes strategic sense whenever:

- *An activity can be performed better or more cheaply by outside specialists.* Many PC makers, for example, have shifted from assembling units in-house to using contract assemblers because of the sizable scale economies associated with purchasing PC components in large volumes and assembling PCs. By outsourcing the distribution of shoes made in its two plants in Germany to UPS, German shoemaker Birkenstock has cut the time for delivering orders to U.S. footwear retailers from seven weeks to three weeks.[21]

- *The activity is not crucial to the firm's ability to achieve sustainable competitive advantage and won't hollow out its core competencies, capabilities, or technical know-how.* Outsourcing of maintenance services, data processing and data storage, fringe benefit management, Web site operations, and similar administrative support activities to specialists has become commonplace. American Express, for instance, recently entered into a seven-year, $4 billion deal whereby IBM's Services division will host American Express's Web site, network servers, data storage, and help-desk support; American Express indicated that it would save several hundred million dollars by paying only for the services it needed when it needed them (as opposed to funding its own full-time staff). A number of companies have begun outsourcing their call center operations to foreign-based contractors that have access to lower-cost labor supplies and can employ lower-paid call center personnel to respond to customer inquiries or requests for technical support.

- *It reduces the company's risk exposure* to changing technology and/or changing buyer preferences. When a company outsources certain parts, components, and services, its suppliers must bear the burden of incorporating state-of-the-art technologies and/or undertaking redesigns and upgrades to accommodate a company's plans to introduce next-generation products. If what a supplier provides falls out of favor with buyers or is designed out of next-generation products, it is the supplier's business that suffers rather than a company's own internal operations.

- *It improves a company's ability to innovate.* Collaborative partnerships with world-class suppliers that have cutting-edge intellectual capital and are early adopters of the latest technology give a company access to ever better parts and components—such supplier-driven innovations, when incorporated into a company's own product offering, fuel a company's ability to introduce its own new and improved products.

> ### Core Concept
>
> A company should generally *not* perform any value chain activity internally that can be performed more efficiently or effectively by its outside business partners—the chief exception is a particular activity that is strategically crucial and over which internal control is deemed essential.

■ *It streamlines company operations* in ways that improve organizational flexibility and cut cycle time. Outsourcing gives a company the flexibility to switch suppliers in the event that its present supplier falls behind competing suppliers. To the extent that its suppliers can speedily get next-generation parts and components into production, then a company can get its own next-generation product offerings into the marketplace quicker. Moreover, seeking out new suppliers with the needed capabilities already in place is frequently quicker, easier, less risky, and cheaper than hurriedly retooling internal operations to replace obsolete capabilities or try to install and master new technologies.

■ *It allows a company to assemble diverse kinds of expertise speedily and efficiently.* A company can nearly always gain quicker access to first-rate capabilities and expertise by partnering with suppliers that already have them in place than it can by trying to build them from scratch with its own company personnel.

■ *It allows a company to concentrate on its core business and do what it does best.* A company is better able to build and develop its own competitively valuable competencies and capabilities when it concentrates its full resources and energies on performing those activities internally that it can perform better than outsiders and/or that it needs to have under its direct control. Cisco Systems, for example, devotes its energy to designing new generations of switches, routers, and other Internet-related equipment, opting to outsource the more mundane activities of producing and assembling its routers and switching equipment to contract manufacturers that together operate 37 factories, all closely monitored and overseen by Cisco personnel via online systems.

Dell Computer's partnerships with the suppliers of PC components have allowed it to operate with fewer than four days of inventory, to realize substantial savings in inventory costs, and to get PCs that are equipped with next-generation components into the marketplace in less than a week after the newly upgraded components start shipping. Cisco's contract suppliers work so closely with Cisco that they can ship Cisco products to Cisco customers without a Cisco employee ever touching the gear. This system of alliances saves $500 million to $800 million annually.[22] Hewlett-Packard, IBM, Silicon Graphics (now SGI), and others have sold plants to suppliers and then contracted to purchase the output. Starbucks finds purchasing coffee beans from independent growers far more advantageous than trying to integrate backward into the coffee-growing business.

When Outsourcing Can Be Disadvantageous

The biggest danger of outsourcing is that a company will farm out too many or the wrong types of activities and thereby hollow out its own capabilities.[23] In such cases, a company loses touch with the very activities and expertise that over the long run determine its success. Cisco Systems guards against loss of control and protects its manufacturing expertise by designing the production methods that its contract manufacturers must use. Cisco keeps the source code for its design proprietary and is thus the source of all improvements and innovations. Further, Cisco uses the Internet to monitor the factory operations of contract manufacturers around the clock and can therefore know immediately when problems arise and whether to get involved.

Offensive Strategies—Improving Market Position and Building Competitive Advantage

Almost every company must at times go on the offensive to improve its market position and try to build a competitive advantage or widen an existing one. Companies like Dell, Wal-Mart, and Toyota play hardball, aggressively pursuing competitive advantage and trying to reap the benefits its offers—a leading market share, excellent profit margins and rapid growth (as compared to rivals), and all the intangibles of being known as a company on the move and one that plays to win.[24] Offensive strategies are also important when a company has no choice but to try to whittle away at a strong rival's competitive advantage and when it is possible to gain profitable market share at the expense of rivals despite whatever resource strengths and capabilities they have. How long it takes for an offensive to yield good results varies with the competitive circumstances.[25] It can be short if buyers respond immediately (as can occur with a dramatic price cut, an imaginative ad campaign, or an especially appealing new product). Securing a competitive edge can take much longer if winning consumer acceptance of an innovative product will take some time or if the firm may need several years to debug a new technology, put new production capacity in place, or develop and perfect new competitive capabilities. Ideally, an offensive move will improve a company's market standing or result in a competitive edge fairly quickly; the longer it takes, the more likely it is that rivals will spot the move, see its potential, and begin a counterresponse.

> **Core Concept**
>
> It takes successful offensive strategies to build competitive advantage—good defensive strategies can help protect competitive advantage but rarely are the basis for creating it.

Several types of strategic offensives merit consideration:

1. *Offering an equally good or better product at a lower price:* This is the classic offensive for improving a company's market position vis-à-vis rivals. Advanced Micro Devices (AMD), wanting to grow its sales of microprocessors for PCs, has on several occasions elected to attack Intel head-on, offering a faster alternative to Intel's Pentium chips at a lower price. Believing that the company's survival depends on eliminating the performance gap between AMD chips and Intel chips, AMD management has been willing to risk that a head-on offensive might prompt Intel to counter with lower prices of its own and accelerated development of faster Pentium chips. Lower prices can produce market share gains if competitors don't respond with price cuts of their own and if the challenger convinces buyers that its product is just as good or better. However, such a strategy increases total profits only if the gains in additional unit sales are enough to offset the impact of lower prices and thinner margins per unit sold. General Motors, for instance, repeatedly attacked rival carmakers with aggressive rebates and 0 percent financing (at a cost of about $3,100 per vehicle sold) in 2001–2003, but it failed to gain more than 1 percent additional market share and such deals definitely cut into GM's profitability. Price-cutting offensives generally work best when a company *first achieves a cost advantage and then hits competitors with a lower price.*[26]

2. *Leapfrogging competitors by being the first adopter of next-generation technologies or being first to market with next-generation products:* In 2004–2005, Microsoft waged an offensive to get its next-generation Xbox to market four to six months ahead of Sony's PlayStation 3, anticipating that such a lead time would

help it convince video gamers to switch to the Xbox rather than wait for the new PlayStation to hit the market.

3. *Adopting and improving on the good ideas of other companies (rivals or otherwise):*[27] The idea of warehouse-type hardware and home improvement centers did not originate with Home Depot founders Arthur Blank and Bernie Marcus; they got the "big box" concept from their former employer Handy Dan Home Improvement. But they were quick to improve on Handy Dan's business model and strategy and take Home Depot to the next plateau in terms of product line breadth and customer service. Casket-maker Hillenbrand greatly improved its market position by adapting Toyota's production methods to casket making. Ryanair has succeeded as a low-cost airline in Europe by imitating many of Southwest Airlines' operating practices and applying them in a different geographic market.

4. *Deliberately attacking those market segments where a key rival makes big profits:*[28] Dell Computer's recent entry into printers and printer cartridges—the market arena where number-two PC maker Hewlett-Packard enjoys hefty profit margins and makes the majority of its profits—while mainly motivated by Dell's desire to broaden its product line and save its customers money (because of Dell's lower prices), nonetheless represented a hardball offensive calculated to weaken HP's market position in printers. To the extent that Dell might be able to use lower prices to woo away some of HP's printer customers, it would have the effect of eroding HP's "profit sanctuary," distracting HP's attention away from PCs, and reducing the financial resources HP has available for battling Dell in the global market for PCs.

5. *Attacking the competitive weaknesses of rivals:* Such offensives can include going after the customers of rivals whose products lag on quality, features, or product performance; making special sales pitches to the customers of rivals who provide subpar customer service; trying to win customers away from rivals with weak brand recognition (an attractive option if the aggressor has strong marketing skills and a recognized brand name); emphasizing sales to buyers in geographic regions where a rival has a weak market share or is exerting less competitive effort; and paying special attention to buyer segments that a rival is neglecting or is weakly equipped to serve.

6. *Maneuvering around competitors and concentrating on capturing unoccupied or less contested market territory:* Examples include launching initiatives to build strong positions in geographic areas where close rivals have little or no market presence and trying to create new market segments by introducing products with different attributes and performance features to better meet the needs of selected buyers.[29]

7. *Using hit-and-run tactics to grab sales and market share from complacent or distracted rivals:* Such "guerrilla offensives" include occasionally low-balling on price (to win a big order or steal a key account from a rival); surprising key rivals with sporadic but intense bursts of promotional activity (offering a 20 percent discount for one week to draw customers away from rival brands); or undertaking special campaigns to attract buyers away from rivals plagued with a strike or problems in meeting buyer demand.[30] Guerrilla offensives are particularly well suited to small challengers who have neither the resources nor the market visibility to mount a full-fledged attack on industry leaders.

8. *Launching a preemptive strike to secure an advantageous position that rivals are prevented or discouraged from duplicating:*[31] What makes a move preemptive is its one-of-a-kind nature—whoever strikes first stands to acquire competitive assets that rivals can't readily match. Examples of preemptive moves include (1) securing the best distributors in a particular geographic region or country; (2) moving to obtain the most favorable site along a heavily traveled thoroughfare, at a new interchange or intersection, in a new shopping mall, in a natural beauty spot, close to cheap transportation or raw material supplies or market outlets, and so on; (3) tying up the most reliable, high-quality suppliers via exclusive partnership, long-term contracts, or even acquisition; and (4) moving swiftly to acquire the assets of distressed rivals at bargain prices. To be successful, a preemptive move doesn't have to totally block rivals from following or copying; it merely needs to give a firm a prime position that is not easily circumvented.

Other offensives that may be attractive in the right circumstances include trying to trump the products of rivals by introducing new/improved products with features calculated to win customers away from rivals, running comparison ads, constructing major new plant capacity in a rival's backyard, expanding the product line to match one or more rivals model for model, and developing customer service capabilities that rivals don't have.

As a rule, challenging rivals on competitive grounds where they are strong is an uphill struggle.[32] Offensive initiatives that exploit competitor weaknesses stand a better chance of succeeding than do those that challenge competitor strengths, especially if the weaknesses represent important vulnerabilities and weak rivals can be caught by surprise with no ready defense. Strategic offensives should, as a general rule, be grounded in a company's competitive assets and strong points—its core competencies, competitive capabilities, and such resource strengths as a well-known brand name, a cost advantage in manufacturing or distribution, and a new or much-improved product. Otherwise, its prospects for success are dim unless its resources and competitive strengths amount to a competitive advantage over the targeted rivals.

Defensive Strategies—Protecting Market Position and Competitive Advantage

In a competitive market, all firms are subject to offensive challenges from rivals. The purposes of defensive strategies are to lower the risk of being attacked, weaken the impact of any attack that occurs, and influence challengers to aim their efforts at other rivals. While defensive strategies usually don't enhance a firm's competitive advantage, they can definitely help fortify its competitive position, protect its most valuable resources and capabilities from imitation, and defend whatever competitive advantage it might have. Defensive strategies can take either of two forms: actions to block challengers and signals to indicate the likelihood of strong retaliation.

> It is just as important to discern when to fortify a company's present market position with defensive actions as it is to seize the initiative and launch strategic offensives.

Blocking the Avenues Open to Challengers

The most frequently employed approach to defending a company's present position involves actions that restrict a challenger's options for initiating competitive attack.

> There are many ways to throw obstacles in the path of challengers.

There are any number of obstacles that can be put in the path of would-be challengers.[33] A defender can participate in alternative technologies as a hedge against rivals attacking with a new or better technology. A defender can introduce new features, add new models, or broaden its product line to close off gaps and vacant niches to opportunity-seeking challengers. It can thwart the efforts of rivals to attack with a lower price by maintaining economy-priced options of its own. It can try to discourage buyers from trying competitors' brands by lengthening warranties, offering free training and support services, developing the capability to deliver spare parts to users faster than rivals can, providing coupons and sample giveaways to buyers most prone to experiment, and making early announcements about impending new products or price changes to induce potential buyers to postpone switching. It can challenge the quality or safety of rivals' products. Finally, a defender can grant volume discounts or better financing terms to dealers and distributors to discourage them from experimenting with other suppliers, or it can convince them to handle its product line *exclusively* and force competitors to use other distribution outlets.

Signaling Challengers That Retaliation Is Likely

The goal of signaling challengers that strong retaliation is likely in the event of an attack is either to dissuade challengers from attacking at all or to divert them to less threatening options. Either goal can be achieved by letting challengers know the battle will cost more than it is worth. Would-be challengers can be signaled by:[34]

- Publicly announcing management's commitment to maintain the firm's present market share.
- Publicly committing the company to a policy of matching competitors' terms or prices.
- Maintaining a war chest of cash and marketable securities.
- Making an occasional strong counterresponse to the moves of weak competitors to enhance the firm's image as a tough defender.

Web Site Strategies: Which One to Employ?

> Companies today must wrestle with the strategic issue of how to use their Web sites in positioning themselves in the marketplace—whether to use their Web sites just to disseminate product information or whether to operate an e-store to sell direct to online shoppers.

Companies across the world are deep into the process of implementing a variety of Internet technology applications—the chief question companies face at this point is what additional Internet technology applications to incorporate into day-to-day operations. But the larger and much tougher *strategic* issue is just what role the company's Web site should play in a company's competitive strategy. In particular, to what degree should a company use the Internet as a distribution channel for accessing buyers? Should a company use its Web site *only as a means of disseminating product information* (with traditional distribution channel partners making all sales to end users), as a *secondary or minor channel for selling direct to buyers* of its product, as *one of several important distribution channels* for accessing customers, as *the primary distribution channel* for accessing customers, or as *the exclusive channel* for transacting sales with customers?[35] Let's look at each of these strategic options in turn.

Product-Information-Only Strategies— Avoiding Channel Conflict

Operating a Web site that contains extensive product information but that relies on click-throughs to the Web sites of distribution channel partners for sales transactions (or that informs site users where nearby retail stores are located) is an attractive market positioning option for manufacturers and/or wholesalers that have invested heavily in building and cultivating retail dealer networks and that face nettlesome channel conflict issues if they try to sell online in direct competition with their dealers. A manufacturer or wholesaler that aggressively pursues online sales to end users is signaling both a weak strategic commitment to its dealers and a willingness to cannibalize dealers' sales and growth potential. To the extent that strong partnerships with wholesale and/or retail dealers are critical to accessing end users, selling direct to end users via the company's Web site is a very tricky road to negotiate. A manufacturer's effort to use its Web site to sell around its dealers is certain to anger its wholesale distributors and retail dealers, who may respond by putting more effort into marketing the brands of rival manufacturers that don't sell online. As a consequence, the manufacturer may stand to lose more sales by offending its dealers than it gains from its own online sales effort. Moreover, dealers may be in a better position to employ a brick-and-click strategy than a manufacturer is because dealers have a local presence to complement their online sales approach (which consumers may find appealing). Consequently, in industries where the strong support and goodwill of dealer networks is essential, manufacturers may conclude that their Web sites should be designed to partner with dealers rather than compete with them—just as the auto manufacturers are doing with their franchised dealers.

Web Site E-Stores as a Minor Distribution Channel

A second strategic option is to use online sales as a relatively minor distribution channel for achieving incremental sales, gaining online sales experience, and doing marketing research. If channel conflict poses a big obstacle to online sales, or if only a small fraction of buyers can be attracted to make online purchases, then companies are well advised to pursue online sales with the strategic intent of gaining experience, learning more about buyer tastes and preferences, testing reaction to new products, creating added market buzz about their products, and boosting overall sales volume a few percentage points. Sony and Nike, for example, sell almost all of their products at their Web sites without provoking resistance from their retail dealers since most buyers of their products prefer to do their buying at retail stores rather than buying online. They use their Web sites not so much to make sales as to glean valuable marketing research data from tracking the browsing patterns of Web site visitors. The behavior and actions of Web surfers are a veritable gold mine of information for companies seeking to keep their finger on the market pulse and respond more precisely to buyer preferences and interests.

Despite the channel conflict that exists when a manufacturer sells directly to end users at its Web site in head-to-head competition with its distribution channel allies, manufacturers might still opt to pursue online sales at their Web sites and try to establish online sales as an important distribution channel because (1) their profit margins from online sales are bigger than those earned from selling to their wholesale/retail customers; (2) encouraging buyers to visit the company's Web site helps educate them to the ease and convenience of purchasing online and, over time, prompts more and more buyers to purchase online (where company profit margins are greater)—which makes incurring channel conflict in the short term and competing against traditional distribution allies potentially worthwhile; and (3) selling directly to end users allows a manufacturer to make greater use of build-to-order manufacturing and assembly, which, if met with growing buyer acceptance and satisfaction, would increase the rate at which sales migrate from distribution allies to the company's Web site—such migration could lead to streamlining the company's value chain and boosting its profit margins.

Brick-and-Click Strategies

Brick-and-click strategies have two big strategic appeals for wholesale and retail enterprises: they are an economic means of expanding a company's geographic reach, and they give both existing and potential customers an additional way of how to communicate with the company, shop for product information, make purchases, or resolve customer service problems. Software developers, for example, have come to rely on the Internet as a highly effective distribution channel to complement sales through brick-and-mortar wholesalers and retailers. Selling online directly to end users has the advantage of eliminating the costs of producing and packaging CDs and cutting out the costs and margins of software wholesalers and retailers (often 35 to 50 percent of the retail price). However, software developers are still strongly motivated to continue to distribute their products through wholesalers and retailers (to maintain broad access to existing and potential users who, for whatever reason, may be reluctant to buy online). Chain retailers like Wal-Mart and Circuit City operate online stores for their products primarily as a convenience to customers who want to buy online rather than making a shopping trip to nearby stores.

Many brick-and-mortar companies can enter online retailing at relatively low cost—all they need is a Web store and systems for filling and delivering individual customer orders. Brick-and-mortar distributors and retailers (as well as manufacturers with company-owned retail stores) can employ brick-and-click strategies by using their current distribution centers and/or retail stores for picking orders from on-hand inventories and making deliveries. Blockbuster, the largest chain of video and DVD rental stores, utilizes the inventories at its stores to fill orders for its online subscribers who pay a monthly fee for unlimited DVDs delivered by mail carrier; using local stores to fill orders typically allows delivery in 24 hours versus 48 hours for shipments made from a regional shipping center. Walgreen's, a leading drugstore chain, allows customers to order a prescription online and then pick it up at the drive-through window or inside counter of a local store. In banking, a brick-and-click strategy allows customers to use local branches and ATMs for depositing checks and getting cash while using online systems to pay bills, check account balances, and transfer funds. Many industrial distributors are finding it efficient for customers to place their orders over the Web rather than phoning them in or waiting for salespeople to call in person.

Strategies for Online Enterprises

A company that elects to use the Internet as its exclusive channel for accessing buyers is essentially an online business from the perspective of the customer. The Internet becomes the vehicle for transacting sales and delivering customer services; except for advertising, the Internet is the sole point of all buyer-seller contact. Many so-called pure dot-com enterprises have chosen this strategic approach—prominent examples include eBay, Amazon.com, Yahoo, Buy.com, and Priceline.com. For a company to succeed in using the Internet as its exclusive distribution channel, its product or service must be one for which buying online holds strong appeal.

A company that decides to use online sales as its exclusive method for sales transactions must address several strategic issues:

- *How it will deliver unique value to buyers:* Online businesses must usually attract buyers on the basis of low price, convenience, superior product information, build-to-order systems, or attentive online service.

- *Whether it will pursue competitive advantage based on lower costs, differentiation, or better value for the money:* For an online-only sales strategy to succeed in head-to-head competition with brick-and-mortar and brick-and-click rivals, an online seller's value chain approach must hold potential for low-cost leadership, competitively valuable differentiating attributes, or a best-cost provider advantage. If an online firm's strategy is to attract customers by selling at cut-rate prices, then it must possess cost advantages in those activities it performs, and it must outsource the remaining activities to low-cost specialists. If an online seller is going to differentiate itself on the basis of a superior buying experience and top-notch customer service, then it needs to concentrate on having an easy-to-navigate Web site, an array of functions and conveniences for customers, "Web reps" who can answer questions online, and logistical capabilities to deliver products quickly and accommodate returned merchandise. If it is going to deliver more value for the money, then it must manage value chain activities so as to deliver upscale products and services at lower costs than rivals.

- *Whether it will have a broad or a narrow product offering:* A one-stop shopping strategy like that employed by Amazon.com (which offers over 30 million items for sale at its Web sites in the United States, Britain, France, Germany, Denmark, and Japan) has the appealing economics of helping spread fixed operating costs over a wide number of items and a large customer base. Other e-tailers, such as E-Loan and Hotel.com, have adopted classic focus strategies and cater to a sharply defined target audience shopping for a particular product or product category.

- *Whether to perform order fulfillment activities internally or to outsource them:* Building central warehouses, stocking them with adequate inventories, and developing systems to pick, pack, and ship individual orders all require substantial start-up capital but may result in lower overall unit costs than would paying the fees of order fulfillment specialists who make a business of providing warehouse space, stocking inventories, and shipping orders for e-tailers. However, outsourcing order fulfillment activities is likely to be more economical unless an e-tailer has high unit volume and the capital to invest in its own order fulfillment capabilities. Buy.com, an online superstore consisting of some 30,000 items, obtains products from name-brand manufacturers and uses outsiders to stock and ship those products; thus, its focus is not on manufacturing or order fulfillment but, rather, on selling.

- *How it will draw traffic to its Web site:* Web sites have to be cleverly marketed. Unless Web surfers hear about the site, like what they see on their first visit, and are intrigued enough to return again and again, the site is unlikely to generate adequate revenues. Marketing campaigns that result only in heavy site traffic and lots of page views are seldom sufficient; the best test of effective marketing is the ratio at which page views are converted into revenues (the "look-to-buy" ratio). For example, in 2001 Yahoo's site traffic averaged 1.2 *billion* page views daily but generated only about $2 million in daily revenues; in contrast, the traffic at the Web site of brokerage firm Charles Schwab averaged only 40 *million* page views per day but resulted in an average of $5 million daily in online commission revenues.

Choosing Appropriate Functional-Area Strategies

A company's strategy is not complete until company managers have made strategic choices about how the various functional parts of the business—R&D, production, human resources, sales and marketing, finance, and so on—will be managed in support of its basic competitive strategy approach and the other important competitive moves being taken. Normally, functional-area strategy choices rank third on the menu of choosing among the various strategy options, as shown in Figure 4.1 (see page 114). But whether commitments to particular functional strategies are made before or after the choices of complementary strategic options shown in Figure 4.1 is beside the point—what's really important is what the functional strategies are and how they mesh to enhance the success of the company's higher-level strategic thrusts.

In many respects, the nature of functional strategies is dictated by the choice of competitive strategy. For example, a manufacturer employing a low-cost provider strategy needs an R&D and product design strategy that emphasizes cheap-to-incorporate features and facilitates economical assembly, a production strategy that stresses capture of scale economies and actions to achieve low-cost manufacture (such as high labor productivity, efficient supply chain management, and automated production processes), and a low-budget marketing strategy. A business pursuing a high-end differentiation strategy needs a production strategy geared to top-notch quality and a marketing strategy aimed at touting differentiating features and using advertising and a trusted brand name to "pull" sales through the chosen distribution channels. A company using a focused differentiation strategy (like Krispy Kreme) needs a marketing strategy that stresses growing the niche (getting more people hooked on Krispy Kreme doughnuts), keeping buyer interest at a high level, and protecting the niche against invasion by outsiders.

Beyond very general prescriptions, it is difficult to say just what the content of the different functional-area strategies should be without first knowing what higher-level strategic choices a company has made, the industry environment in which it operates, the resource strengths that can be leveraged, and so on. Suffice it to say here that company personnel—both managers and employees charged with strategy-making responsibility down through the organizational hierarchy—must be clear about which higher-level strategies top management has chosen and then must tailor the company's functional-area strategies accordingly.

First-Mover Advantages and Disadvantages

When to make a strategic move is often as crucial as *what* move to make. Timing is especially important when *first-mover advantages* or *disadvantages* exist.[36] Being first to initiate a strategic move can have a high payoff when (1) pioneering helps build a firm's image and reputation with buyers; (2) early commitments to new technologies, new-style components, new or emerging distribution channels, and so on, can produce an absolute cost advantage over rivals; (3) first-time customers remain strongly loyal to pioneering firms in making repeat purchases; and (4) moving first constitutes a preemptive strike, making imitation extra hard or unlikely. The bigger the first-mover advantages, the more attractive making the first move becomes.[37] In e-commerce, companies like America Online, Amazon.com, Yahoo, eBay, and Priceline.com that were first with a new technology, network solution, or business model enjoyed lasting first-mover advantages in gaining the visibility and reputation needed to remain market leaders. But just being a first-mover by itself is seldom enough to win a sustainable competitive advantage. A first-mover also needs to be a fast learner and continue to move aggressively to capitalize on any initial pioneering advantage, and it helps immensely if the first-mover has deep financial pockets, important competencies and competitive capabilities, and high-quality management. What makes being a first-mover strategically important is not being the first company to do something but, rather, being the first competitor to put together the precise combination of features, customer value, and sound revenue/ cost/profit economics that gives it an edge over rivals in the battle for market leadership.[38]

> ### Core Concept
> Because of first-mover advantages and disadvantages, competitive advantage can spring from *when* a move is made as well as from *what* move is made.

However, being a fast-follower or even a wait-and-see late-mover doesn't always carry a significant or lasting competitive penalty. There are times when a first-mover's skills, know-how, and actions are easily copied or even surpassed, allowing late-movers to catch or overtake the first-mover in a relatively short period. And there are times when there are actually *advantages* to being an adept follower rather than a first-mover. Late-mover advantages (or *first-mover disadvantages*) arise when (1) pioneering leadership is more costly than imitating followership and only negligible experience or learning-curve benefits accrue to the leader—a condition that allows a follower to end up with lower costs than the first-mover; (2) the products of an innovator are somewhat primitive and do not live up to buyer expectations, thus allowing a clever follower to win disenchanted buyers away from the leader with better-performing products; and (3) technology is advancing rapidly, giving fast-followers the opening to leapfrog a first-mover's products with more attractive and full-featured second- and third-generation products.

In weighing the pros and cons of being a first-mover versus a fast-follower versus a slow-mover, it matters whether the race to market leadership in a particular industry is a marathon or a sprint. In marathons, a slow-mover is not unduly penalized—first-mover advantages can be fleeting, and there's ample time for fast-followers and sometimes even late-movers to play catch-up.[39] For instance, it took 18 months for 10 million users to sign up for Hotmail, 5.5 years for worldwide mobile phone use to grow from 10 million to 100 million, 7 years for videocassette recorders to find their way into 1 million U.S. homes, and close to 10 years for the number of at-home broadband subscribers to grow to 100 million worldwide. The lesson here is that there is a market-penetration curve for every emerging opportunity; typically, the curve has an inflection point at which all the pieces of the business model fall into place, buyer demand explodes, and the market takes off. The inflection point can come early on a fast-rising curve (like use of e-mail) or later on a slow-rising curve (like use of broadband). Any company that seeks competitive advantage by being a first-mover thus needs to ask some hard questions: Does market takeoff depend on the development of complementary products or services that currently are not available? Is new infrastructure

COMPANY SPOTLIGHT 4.6

The Battle in Consumer Broadband: First-Movers versus Late-Movers

In 1988 an engineer at the Bell companies' research labs figured out how to rush signals along ordinary copper wire at high speed using digital technology, thus creating the digital subscriber line (DSL). But the regional Bells, which dominated the local telephone market in the United States, showed little interest over the next 10 years, believing it was more lucrative to rent T-1 lines to businesses that needed fast data transmission capability and rent second phone lines to households wanting an Internet connection that didn't disrupt their regular telephone service. Furthermore, telephone executives were skeptical about DSL technology—there were a host of technical snarls to overcome, and early users encountered annoying glitches. Many executives doubted that it made good sense to invest billions of dollars in the infrastructure needed to roll out DSL to residential and small business customers, given the success they were having with T-1 and second-line rentals. As a consequence, the Bells didn't seriously begin to market DSL until the late 1990s, two years after the cable TV companies began their push to market cable broadband.

Cable companies were more than happy to be the first-movers in marketing broadband service via their copper cable wires, chiefly because their business was threatened by satellite TV technology and they saw broadband as an innovative service they could provide that the satellite companies could not. (Delivering broadband service via satellite has yet to become a factor in the marketplace, winning only a 1 percent share in 2003.) Cable companies were able to deploy broadband on their copper wire economically because during the 1980s and early 1990s most cable operators had spent about $60 billion to upgrade their systems with fiber-optic technology in order to handle two-way traffic rather than just one-way TV signals and thereby make good on their promises to local governments to develop "interactive" cable systems if they were awarded franchises. Although the early interactive services were duds, technicians discovered in the mid-1990s that the

required before buyer demand can surge? Will buyers need to learn new skills or adopt new behaviors? Will buyers encounter high switching costs? Are there influential competitors in a position to delay or derail the efforts of a first-mover? When the answers to any of these questions are yes, then a company must be careful not to pour too many resources into getting ahead of the market opportunity—the race is likely going to be more of a 10-year marathon than a 2-year sprint. But being first out of the starting block is competitively important if it produces clear and substantial benefits to buyers and competitors will be compelled to follow.

While being an adept fast-follower has the advantages of being less risky and skirting the costs of pioneering, rarely does a company have much to gain from being a slow-follower and concentrating on avoiding the "mistakes" of first-movers. Habitual late-movers, while often able to survive, are usually fighting to retain their customers and scrambling to keep pace with more progressive and innovative rivals. For a habitual late-mover to catch up, it must count on first-movers to be slow learners and complacent in letting their lead dwindle. Plus it has to hope that buyers will be slow to gravitate to the products of first-movers, again giving it time to catch up. And it has to have competencies and capabilities that are sufficiently strong to allow it to close the gap fairly quickly once it makes its move. Counting on all first-movers to stumble or otherwise be easily overtaken is usually a bad bet that puts a late-mover's competitive position at risk.

Company Spotlight 4.6 describes the challenges that late-moving telephone companies have in winning the battle to supply at-home high-speed Internet access and overcoming the first-mover advantages of cable companies.

two-way systems enabled high-speed Internet hookups.

With Internet excitement surging in the late 1990s, cable executives saw high-speed Internet service as a no-brainer and began rolling it out to customers in 1998, securing about 362,000 customers by year-end versus only about 41,000 for DSL. Part of the early success of cable broadband was due to a cost advantage in modems—cable executives, seeing the potential of cable broadband several years earlier, had asked CableLabs to standardize the technology for cable modems, a move that lowered costs and made cable modems marketable in consumer electronics stores. DSL modems were substantially more complicated, and it took longer to drive the costs down from several hundred dollars each to under $100—in 2004, both cable and phone companies paid about $50 for modems, but cable modems got there much sooner.

As cable broadband began to attract more and more attention in the 1998–2002 period, the regional Bells continued to move slowly on DSL. The technical problems lingered, and early users were disgruntled by a host of annoying and sometimes horrendous installation difficulties and service glitches. Not only did providing users with convenient and reliable service prove to be a formidable challenge, but some regulatory issues stood in the way as well. Even in 2003 phone company executives found it hard to justify multibillion-dollar investments to install the necessary equipment and support systems to offer, market, manage, and maintain DSL service on the vast scale of a regional Bell company. SBC Communications figured it would cost at least $6 billion to roll out DSL to its customers. Verizon estimated that it would take 3.5 to 4 million customers to make DSL economics work, a number it would probably not reach until the end of 2005.

In 2003–2004, high-speed consumer access to the Internet was a surging business with a bright outlook—the number of U.S. Internet users upgrading to high-speed service was growing by close to 500,000 monthly. In the U.S., cable broadband was the preferred choice—70 percent of the market was opting for cable modems supplied by cable TV companies, and cable modem subscribers outnumbered DSL subscribers 40 million to 10.6 million. DSL's late start made it questionable whether DSL would be able to catch cable broadband in the U.S. marketplace. In the rest of the world, however, DSL was the broadband connection of choice.

Source: Wall Street Journal. Eastern Edition [staff produced copy only] by Shawn Young and Peter Grant. Copyright 2003 by Dow Jones & Co Inc. Reproduced with permission of Dow Jones & Co Inc in the format textbook via Copyright Clearance Center.

Key Points

A company competing in a particular industry or market has a varied menu of strategy options for seeking and securing a competitive advantage (see Figure 4.1). The first and foremost strategic choice is which of the five basic competitive strategies to employ—overall low-cost, broad differentiation, best-cost, focused low-cost, or focused differentiation.

Once a company has decided which of the five basic competitive strategies to employ in its quest for competitive advantage, then it must decide whether to supplement its choice of a basic competitive strategy approach with strategic actions relating to alliances and collaborative partnerships, mergers and acquisitions, integration forward or backward, outsourcing of certain value chain activities, offensive and defensive moves, and the use of the Internet in selling directly to end users, as shown in Figure 4.1.

Once all the higher-level strategic choices have been made, company managers can turn to the task of crafting functional and operating-level strategies to flesh out the details of the company's overall business and competitive strategy.

The timing of strategic moves also has relevance in the quest for competitive advantage. Because of the competitive importance that is sometimes associated with when a strategic move is made, company managers are obligated to carefully consider the advantages or disadvantages that attach to being a first-mover versus a fast-follower versus a wait-and-see late-mover. At the end of the day, though, the proper objective of a first-mover is that of being the first competitor to put together the precise combination of features, customer value, and sound revenue/cost/profit economics that puts it ahead of the pack in capturing an attractive market opportunity. Sometimes the company that first unlocks a profitable market opportunity is the first-mover and sometimes it is not—but the company that comes up with the key is surely the smart mover.

Exercises

1. Go to www.google.com and do a search for "low-cost producer." See if you can identify five companies that are pursuing a low-cost strategy in their respective industries.

2. Using the advanced search engine function at www.google.com, enter "best-cost producer" in the exact-phrase box and see if you can locate three companies that indicate they are employing a best-cost producer strategy.

3. Go to www.google.com and do a search on "strategic alliances." Identify at least two companies in different industries that are making a significant use of strategic alliances as a core part of their strategies. In addition, identify who their alliances are with and describe the purpose of the alliances.

4. Go to www.google.com and do a search on "acquisition strategy." Identify at least two companies in different industries that are using acquisitions to strengthen their market positions. Identify some of the companies that have been acquired, and research the purpose behind the acquisitions.

CHAPTER 5

Competing in Foreign Markets

You have no choice but to operate in a world shaped by globalization and the information revolution. There are two options: Adapt or die.

—*Andrew S. Grove, chairman, Intel Corporation*

You do not choose to become global. The market chooses for you; it forces your hand.

—*Alain Gomez, CEO, Thomson, S.A.*

Industries actually vary a great deal in the pressures they put on a company to sell internationally.

—*Niraj Dawar and Tony Frost, professors, Richard Ivey School of Business*

Any company that aspires to industry leadership in the 21st century must think in terms of global, not domestic, market leadership. The world economy is globalizing at an accelerating pace as countries previously closed to foreign companies open up their markets, as the Internet shrinks the importance of geographic distance, and as ambitious growth-minded companies race to build stronger competitive positions in the markets of more and more countries. Companies in industries that are already globally competitive or are in the process of becoming so are under the gun to come up with a strategy for competing successfully in foreign markets.

This chapter focuses on strategy options for expanding beyond domestic boundaries and competing in the markets of either a few or a great many countries. The spotlight will be on four strategic issues unique to competing multinationally:

1. Whether to customize the company's offerings in each different country market to match the tastes and preferences of local buyers or to offer a mostly standardized product worldwide.

2. Whether to employ essentially the same basic competitive strategy in all countries or modify the strategy country by country.

3. Where to locate the company's production facilities, distribution centers, and customer service operations so as to realize the greatest location advantages.

4. How to efficiently transfer the company's resource strengths and capabilities from one country to another in an effort to secure competitive advantage.

In the process of exploring these issues, we will introduce a number of core concepts—multicountry competition, global competition, profit sanctuaries, and cross-market subsidization. The chapter includes sections on cross-country differences in cultural, demographic, and market conditions; strategy options for entering and competing in foreign markets; the growing role of alliances with foreign partners; the importance of locating operations in the most advantageous countries; and the special circumstances of competing in such emerging markets as China, India, and Brazil.

Why Companies Expand into Foreign Markets

A company may opt to expand outside its domestic market for any of four major reasons:

1. *To gain access to new customers:* Expanding into foreign markets offers potential for increased revenues, profits, and long-term growth and becomes an especially attractive option when a company's home markets are mature. Firms like Cisco Systems, Dell, Sony, Nokia, Avon, and Toyota, which are racing for global leadership in their respective industries, are moving rapidly and aggressively to extend their market reach into all corners of the world.

2. *To achieve lower costs and enhance the firm's competitiveness:* Many companies are driven to sell in more than one country because domestic sales volume is not large enough to fully capture manufacturing economies of scale or learning-curve effects and thereby substantially improve the firm's cost-competitiveness. The relatively small size of country markets in Europe explains why companies like

Michelin, BMW, and Nestlé long ago began selling their products all across Europe and then moved into markets in North America and Latin America.

3. *To capitalize on its core competencies:* A company may be able to leverage its competencies and capabilities into a position of competitive advantage in foreign markets as well as domestic markets. Nokia's competencies and capabilities in mobile phones have propelled it to global market leadership in the wireless telecommunications business.

4. *To spread its business risk across a wider market base:* A company spreads business risk by operating in a number of different foreign countries rather than depending entirely on operations in its domestic market. Thus, if the economies of certain Asian countries turn down for a period of time, a company with operations across much of the world may be sustained by buoyant sales in Latin America or Europe.

In a few cases, companies in industries based on natural resources (e.g., oil and gas, minerals, rubber, and lumber) often find it necessary to operate in the international arena because attractive raw material supplies are located in foreign countries.

The Difference between Competing Internationally and Competing Globally

Typically, a company will start to compete internationally by entering just one or maybe a select few foreign markets. Competing on a truly global scale comes later, after the company has established operations on several continents and is racing against rivals for global market leadership. Thus, there is a meaningful distinction between the competitive scope of a company that operates in a few foreign countries (with perhaps modest ambitions to enter several more country markets) and a company that markets its products in 50 to 100 countries and is expanding its operations into additional country markets annually. The former is most accurately termed an *international competitor,* while the latter qualifies as a *global competitor.* In the discussion that follows, we'll continue to make a distinction between strategies for competing internationally and strategies for competing globally.

Cross-Country Differences in Cultural, Demographic, and Market Conditions

Regardless of a company's motivation for expanding outside its domestic markets, the strategies it uses to compete in foreign markets must be situation-driven. Cultural, demographic, and market conditions vary significantly among the countries of the world. Cultures and lifestyles are the most obvious areas in which countries differ; market demographics are close behind. Consumers in Spain do not have the same tastes, preferences, and buying habits as consumers in Norway; buyers differ yet again in Greece, Chile, New Zealand, and Taiwan. Less than 10 percent of the populations of Brazil, India, and China have annual purchasing power equivalent to $20,000. Middle-class consumers represent a much smaller portion of the population in these and other emerging countries than in North America, Japan, and much of Western Europe.[1] Sometimes, product designs suitable in one country are inappropriate in another—for example, in the United States electrical devices run on 110-volt electric systems, but in some European countries the standard is a 240-volt electric system, necessitating the use of different electric designs and components. In France consumers prefer top-loading washing machines, while in most other European countries consumers prefer front-loading machines. Northern Europeans want large refrigerators because they tend to shop once a week in supermarkets; southern Europeans can get by on small refrigerators because they shop daily. In parts of Asia refrigerators are a status symbol and may be placed in the living room, leading to preferences for stylish designs and colors—in India bright blue and red are popular colors. In other Asian countries household space is constrained and many refrigerators are only 4 feet high so that the top can be used for storage. In Hong Kong the preference is for compact European-style appliances, but in Taiwan large American-style appliances are more popular. In Italy, most people use automatic washing machines, but there is a strongly entrenched tradition and cultural preference for hanging the clothes out to dry on a clothesline and ironing them rather than using clothes dryers—the widespread belief that sun-dried clothes are fresher virtually shuts down any opportunities for appliance makers to market clothes dryers in Italy. In China, many parents are reluctant to purchase PCs even when they can afford them because of concerns that their children will be distracted from their schoolwork by surfing the Web, playing PC-based video games, and downloading and listening to pop music.

Similarly, market growth varies from country to country. In emerging markets like India, China, Brazil, and Malaysia, market growth potential is far higher than in the more mature economies of Britain, Denmark, Canada, and Japan. In automobiles, for example, the potential for market growth is explosive in China, where sales amount to only 1 million vehicles annually in a country with 1.3 billion people. In India there are efficient, well-developed national channels for distributing trucks, scooters, farm equipment, groceries, personal care items, and other packaged products to the country's 3 million retailers, whereas in China distribution is primarily local and there is no national network for distributing most products. The marketplace is intensely competitive in some countries and only moderately contested in others. Industry driving forces may be one thing in Spain, quite another in Canada, and different yet again in Turkey or Argentina or South Korea.

One of the biggest concerns of companies competing in foreign markets is whether to customize their offerings in each different country market to match the tastes and preferences of local buyers or whether to offer a mostly standardized product worldwide. While the products of a company that is responsive to local tastes will appeal to local buyers, customizing a company's products country by country may have the effect of raising production and distribution costs due to the greater variety of designs and components, shorter production runs, and the complications of added inventory handling and distribution logistics. Greater standardization of a global company's product offering, on the other hand, can lead to scale economies and learning-curve effects, thus contributing to the achievement of a low-cost advantage. The tension between the market pressures to customize and the competitive pressures to lower costs is one of the big strategic issues that participants in foreign markets have to resolve.

Aside from the basic cultural and market differences among countries, a company also has to pay special attention to location advantages that stem from country-to-country variations in manufacturing and distribution costs, the risks of shifting exchange rates, and the economic and political demands of host governments.

Gaining Competitive Advantage Based on Where Activities Are Located

Differences in wage rates, worker productivity, inflation rates, energy costs, tax rates, government regulations, and the like, create sizable variations in manufacturing costs from country to country. Plants in some countries have major manufacturing cost advantages because of lower input costs (especially labor), relaxed government regulations, the proximity of suppliers, or unique natural resources. In such cases, the low-cost countries become principal production sites, with most of the output being exported to markets in other parts of the world. Companies that build production facilities in low-cost countries (or that source their products from contract manufacturers in these countries) have a competitive advantage over rivals with plants in countries where costs are higher. The competitive role of low manufacturing costs is most evident in low-wage countries like China, India, Pakistan, Cambodia, Vietnam, Mexico, Brazil, Guatemala, the Philippines, and several countries in Africa that have become production havens for manufactured goods with high labor content (especially textiles and apparel). China is fast becoming the manufacturing capital of the world—virtually all of the world's major manufacturing companies now have facilities in China, and China attracted more foreign direct investment in 2002 and 2003 than any other country in the world. Likewise, concerns about short delivery times and low shipping costs make some countries better locations than others for establishing distribution centers.

The quality of a country's business environment also offers locational advantages—the governments of some countries are anxious to attract foreign investments and go all-out to create a business climate that outsiders will view as favorable. A good example is Ireland, which has one of the world's most pro-business environments. Ireland offers companies very low corporate tax rates, has a government that is responsive to the needs of industry, and aggressively recruits high-tech manufacturing facilities and multinational companies. Such policies were a significant force in making Ireland the most dynamic, fastest-growing nation in Europe during the 1990s. Ireland's policies were a major factor in Intel's decision to locate a $2.5 billion chip manufacturing plant in Ireland that employs over 4,000 people. Another locational advantage is the clustering of suppliers of components and capital equipment, infrastructure suppliers (universities, vocational training providers, research enterprises), trade associations, and makers of complementary products in a single geographic area—such clustering can be an important source of cost savings in addition to facilitating close collaboration with key suppliers.

The Risks of Adverse Exchange Rate Shifts

The volatility of exchange rates greatly complicates the issue of geographic cost advantages. Currency exchange rates often move up or down 20 to 40 percent annually. Changes of this magnitude can either totally wipe out a country's low-cost advantage or transform a former high-cost location into a competitive-cost location. For instance, in the mid-1980s, when the dollar was strong relative to the Japanese yen (meaning that $1 would purchase, say, 125 yen as opposed to only 100 yen), Japanese heavy-equipment maker Komatsu was able to undercut U.S.-based Caterpillar's prices by as much as 25 percent, causing Caterpillar to lose sales and market share. But starting in 1985, when exchange rates began to shift and the dollar grew steadily weaker against the yen (meaning that $1 was worth fewer and fewer yen), Komatsu had to raise its prices six times over two years as its yen-based costs in terms of dollars soared. With its competitiveness against Komatsu restored, Caterpillar regained sales and market share. The lesson of fluctuating exchange rates is that companies that export goods to foreign countries always gain in competitiveness when the currency of the country in which the goods are manufactured is weak. Exporters are disadvantaged when the currency of the country where goods are being manufactured grows stronger. Sizable long-term shifts in exchange rates thus shuffle the global cards of which rivals have the upper hand in the marketplace and which countries represent the low-cost manufacturing location.

As a further illustration of the risks associated with fluctuating exchange rates, consider the case of a U.S. company that has located manufacturing facilities in Brazil (where the currency is *reals*—pronounced "ray-alls") and that exports most of the Brazilian-made goods to markets in the European Union (where the currency is *euros*). To keep the numbers simple, assume that the exchange rate is 4 Brazilian reals for 1 euro and that the product being made in Brazil has a manufacturing cost of 4 Brazilian reals (or 1 euro). Now suppose that for some reason the exchange rate shifts from 4 reals per euro to 5 reals per euro (meaning that the real has declined in value and that the euro is stronger). Making the product in Brazil is now more cost-competitive because a Brazilian good costing 4 reals to produce has fallen to only 0.8 euro at the new exchange rate. If, in contrast, the value of the Brazilian real grows stronger in relation to the euro—resulting in an exchange rate of 3 reals to 1 euro—the same good costing 4 reals to produce now has a cost of 1.33 euros. Clearly, the attraction of manufacturing a good in Brazil and selling it in Europe is far greater when the euro is strong (an exchange rate of 1 euro for 5 Brazilian reals) than when the euro is weak and exchanges for only 3 Brazilian reals.

> **Core Concept**
> Companies with manufacturing facilities in a particular country are more cost-competitive in exporting goods to world markets when the local currency is weak (or declines in value relative to other currencies); their competitiveness erodes when the local currency grows stronger relative to the currencies of the countries to which the locally made goods are being exported.

Insofar as U.S.-based manufacturers are concerned, declines in the value of the U.S. dollar against foreign currencies reduce or eliminate whatever cost advantage foreign manufacturers might have over U.S. manufacturers and can even prompt foreign companies to establish production plants in the United States. Likewise, a weak euro enhances the cost-competitiveness of companies manufacturing goods in Europe for export to foreign markets; a strong euro versus other currencies weakens the cost-competitiveness of European plants that manufacture goods for export.

In 2002, when the Brazilian real declined in value by about 25 percent against the dollar, the euro, and several other currencies, the ability of companies with manufacturing plants in Brazil to compete in world markets was greatly enhanced—of course, in future years this windfall gain in cost advantage might well be eroded by sustained rises in the value of the Brazilian real against these same currencies. Herein lies the risk: Currency exchange rates are rather unpredictable, swinging first one way and then another way, so the competitiveness of any company's facilities in any country is partly dependent on whether exchange rate changes over time have a favorable or unfavorable cost impact. Companies making goods in one country for export to foreign countries always gain in competitiveness as the currency of that country grows weaker. Exporters are disadvantaged when the currency of the country where goods are being manufactured grows stronger. On the other hand, domestic companies that are under

> **Core Concept**
> Fluctuating exchange rates pose significant risks to a company's competitiveness in foreign markets. Exporters win when the currency of the country where goods are being manufactured grows weaker, and they lose when the currency grows stronger. Domestic companies under pressure from lower-cost imports are benefited when their government's currency grows weaker in relation to the countries where the imported goods are being made.

pressure from lower-cost imported goods gain in competitiveness when their currency grows weaker in relation to the currencies of the countries where the imported goods are made.

Host-Government Policies

National governments enact all kinds of measures affecting business conditions and the operation of foreign companies in their markets. Host governments may set local content requirements on goods made inside their borders by foreign-based companies, put restrictions on exports to ensure adequate local supplies, regulate the prices of imported and locally produced goods, and impose tariffs or quotas on the imports of certain goods. Until 2002, when it joined the World Trade Organization, China imposed a 100 percent tariff on motor vehicle imports. Governments may or may not have burdensome tax structures, stringent environmental regulations, or strictly enforced worker safety standards. Sometimes outsiders face a web of regulations regarding technical standards, product certification, prior approval of capital spending projects, withdrawal of funds from the country, and required minority (sometimes majority) ownership of foreign company operations by local citizens. A few governments may be hostile to or suspicious of foreign companies operating within their borders. Some governments provide subsidies and low-interest loans to domestic companies to help them compete against foreign-based companies. Other governments, anxious to obtain new plants and jobs, offer foreign companies a helping hand in the form of subsidies, privileged market access, and technical assistance. All of these possibilities explain why the managers of companies opting to compete in foreign markets have to take a close look at a country's politics and policies toward business in general, and foreign companies in particular, in deciding which country markets to participate in and which ones to avoid.

The Concepts of Multicountry Competition and Global Competition

There are important differences in the patterns of international competition from industry to industry.[2] At one extreme is **multicountry competition,** in which there's so much cross-country variation in market conditions and in the companies contending for leadership that the market contest among rivals in one country is not closely connected to the market contests in other countries. The standout features of multicountry competition are that (1) buyers in different countries are attracted to different product attributes, (2) sellers vary from country to country, and (3) industry conditions and competitive forces in each national market differ in important respects. Take the banking industry in Italy, Brazil, and Japan as an example— the requirements and expectations of banking customers vary among the three countries, the lead banking competitors in Italy differ from those in Brazil or in Japan, and the competitive battle going on among the leading banks in Italy is unrelated to the rivalry taking place in Brazil or Japan. Thus, with multicountry competition, rival firms battle for national championships and winning in one country does not necessarily signal the ability to fare well in other countries. In multicountry competition, the power of a company's strategy and resource capabilities in one country may not enhance its competitiveness

> **Core Concept**
>
> **Multicountry competition** exists when competition in one national market is not closely connected to competition in another national market—there is no global or world market, just a collection of self-contained country markets.

to the same degree in other countries where it operates. Moreover, any competitive advantage a company secures in one country is largely confined to that country; the spillover effects to other countries are minimal to nonexistent. Industries characterized by multicountry competition include radio and TV broadcasting, consumer banking, life insurance, apparel, metals fabrication, many types of food products (coffee, cereals, breads, canned goods, frozen foods), and retailing.

At the other extreme is **global competition,** in which prices and competitive conditions across country markets are strongly linked and the term *global* or *world market* has true meaning. In a globally competitive industry, much the same group of rival companies competes in many different countries, but especially so in countries where sales volumes are large and where having a competitive presence is strategically important to building a strong global position in the industry. Thus, a company's competitive position in one country both affects and is affected by its position in other countries. In global competition, a firm's overall competitive advantage grows out of its entire worldwide operations; the competitive advantage it creates at its home base is supplemented by advantages growing out of its operations in other countries (having plants in low-wage countries, being able to transfer expertise from country to country, having the capability to serve customers who also have multinational operations, and having brand-name recognition in many parts of the world). Rival firms in globally competitive industries vie for worldwide leadership. Global competition exists in motor vehicles, television sets, tires, mobile phones, personal computers, copiers, watches, digital cameras, bicycles, and commercial aircraft.

> **Core Concept**
>
> **Global competition** exists when competitive conditions across national markets are linked strongly enough to form a true international market and when leading competitors compete head-to-head in many different countries.

An industry can have segments that are globally competitive and segments in which competition is country by country.[3] In the hotel/motel industry, for example, the low- and medium-priced segments are characterized by multicountry competition—competitors mainly serve travelers within the same country. In the business and luxury segments, however, competition is more globalized. Companies like Nikki, Marriott, Sheraton, and Hilton have hotels at many international locations, use worldwide reservation systems, and establish common quality and service standards to gain marketing advantages in serving businesspeople and other travelers who make frequent international trips. In lubricants, the marine-engine segment is globally competitive—ships move from port to port and require the same oil everywhere they stop. Brand reputations in marine lubricants have a global scope, and successful marine-engine lubricant producers (ExxonMobil, BP Amoco, and Shell) operate globally. In automotive motor oil, however, multicountry competition dominates—countries have different weather conditions and driving patterns, production of motor oil is subject to limited scale economies, shipping costs are high, and retail distribution channels differ markedly from country to country. Thus, domestic firms—like Quaker State and Pennzoil in the United States and Castrol in Great Britain—can be leaders in their home markets without competing globally.

It is also important to recognize that an industry can be in transition from multicountry competition to global competition. In a number of today's industries—beer and major home appliances are prime examples—leading domestic competitors have begun expanding into more and more foreign markets, often acquiring local companies or brands and integrating them into their operations. As some industry members start to build global brands and a global presence, other industry members find themselves pressured to follow the same strategic path—especially if establishing multinational operations results in important scale economies and a powerhouse brand name. As the industry consolidates to fewer players, such that many of the same companies find themselves in head-to-head competition in more and more country markets, global competition begins to replace multicountry competition.

At the same time, consumer tastes in a number of important product categories are converging across the world. Less diversity of tastes and preferences opens the way for companies to create global brands and sell essentially the same products in almost all countries of the world. Even in industries where consumer tastes remain fairly diverse, companies are learning to use "custom mass production" to economically create different versions of a product and thereby satisfy the tastes of people in different countries.

In addition to taking the obvious cultural and political differences between countries into account, a company has to shape its strategic approach to competing in foreign markets according to whether its industry is characterized by multicountry competition, global competition, or a transition from one to the other.

Strategy Options for Entering and Competing in Foreign Markets

There are a host of generic strategic options for a company that decides to expand outside its domestic market and compete internationally or globally:

1. *Maintain a national (one-country) production base and export goods to foreign markets*, using either company-owned or foreign-controlled forward distribution channels.

2. *License foreign firms to use the company's technology or to produce and distribute the company's products.*

3. *Employ a franchising strategy.*

4. *Follow a multicountry strategy*, varying the company's strategic approach (perhaps a little, perhaps a lot) from country to country in accordance with local conditions and differing buyer tastes and preferences.

5. *Follow a global strategy*, using essentially the same competitive strategy approach in all country markets where the company has a presence.

6. *Use strategic alliances or joint ventures with foreign companies as the primary vehicle for entering foreign markets,* and perhaps also use them as ongoing strategic arrangements aimed at maintaining or strengthening the company's competitiveness.

The following sections discuss the first five options in more detail; the sixth option is discussed in a separate section later in the chapter.

Export Strategies

Using domestic plants as a production base for exporting goods to foreign markets is an excellent initial strategy for pursuing international sales. It is a conservative way to test the international waters. The amount of capital needed to begin exporting is often quite minimal; existing production capacity may well be sufficient to make goods for export. With an export strategy, a manufacturer can limit its involvement in foreign markets by contracting with foreign wholesalers experienced in importing to handle the entire distribution and marketing function in their countries or regions of the world. If it is more advantageous to maintain control over these functions, however, a manufacturer can establish its own distribution and sales organizations in some or all of the target foreign markets. Either way, a home-based production and export strategy helps the firm minimize its direct investments in foreign countries. Such strategies are commonly favored by Chinese, Korean, and Italian companies—products are designed and manufactured at home and then distributed through local channels in the importing countries; the primary functions performed abroad relate chiefly to establishing a network of distributors and perhaps conducting sales promotion and brand awareness activities.

Whether an export strategy can be pursued successfully over the long run hinges on the relative cost-competitiveness of the home-country production base. In some industries, firms gain additional scale economies and learning-curve benefits from centralizing production in one or several giant plants whose output capability exceeds demand in any one country market; obviously, a company must export to capture such economies. However, an export strategy is vulnerable when (1) manufacturing costs in the home country are substantially higher than in foreign countries where rivals have plants, (2) the costs of shipping the product to distant foreign markets are relatively high, or (3) adverse shifts occur in currency exchange rates. Unless an exporter can both keep its production and shipping costs competitive with rivals and successfully hedge against unfavorable changes in currency exchange rates, its success will be limited.

Licensing Strategies

Licensing makes sense when a firm with valuable technical know-how or a unique patented product has neither the internal organizational capability nor the resources to enter foreign markets. Licensing also has the advantage of avoiding the risks of committing resources to country markets that are unfamiliar, politically volatile, economically unstable, or otherwise risky. By licensing the technology or the production rights to foreign-based firms, the firm does not have to bear the costs and risks of entering foreign markets on its own, yet it is able to generate income from royalties. The big disadvantage of licensing is the risk of providing valuable technological know-how to foreign companies and thereby losing some degree of control over its use; monitoring licensees and safeguarding the company's proprietary know-how can prove quite difficult in some circumstances. But if the royalty potential is considerable and the companies to whom the licenses are being granted are both trustworthy and reputable, then licensing can be a very attractive option. Many software and pharmaceutical companies use licensing strategies.

Franchising Strategies

While licensing works well for manufacturers and owners of proprietary technology, franchising is often better suited to the global expansion efforts of service and retailing enterprises. McDonald's, Yum! Brands (the parent of Pizza Hut, KFC, and Taco Bell), the UPS Store, Jani-King International (the world's largest commercial cleaning franchisor), Roto-Rooter, 7-Eleven, and Hilton Hotels have all used franchising to build a presence in foreign markets. Franchising has much the same advantages as licensing. The franchisee bears most of the costs and risks of establishing foreign locations; a franchisor has to expend only the resources to recruit, train, support, and monitor franchisees. The big problem a franchisor faces is maintaining quality control; foreign franchisees do not always exhibit strong commitment to consistency and standardization, especially when the local culture does not stress the same kinds of quality concerns. Another problem that can arise is whether to allow foreign franchisees to make modifications in the franchisor's product offering so as to better satisfy the tastes and expectations of local buyers. Should McDonald's allow its franchised units in Japan to modify Big Macs slightly to suit Japanese tastes? Should the franchised KFC units in China be permitted to substitute spices that appeal to Chinese consumers? Or should the same menu offerings be rigorously and unvaryingly required of all franchisees worldwide?

Localized Multicountry Strategies or a Global Strategy?

The issue of whether to vary the company's competitive approach to fit specific market conditions and buyer preferences in each host country or whether to employ essentially the same strategy in all countries is perhaps the foremost strategic issue that companies must address when they operate in two or more foreign markets. Figure 5.1 shows a company's options for resolving this issue.

Think-Local, Act-Local Approaches to Strategy Making
The bigger the differences in buyer tastes, cultural traditions, and market conditions in different countries, the stronger the case for a "think-local, act-local" approach to strategy making, in which a company tailors its product offerings and perhaps its basic competitive strategy to fit buyer tastes and market conditions in each country where it opts to compete. The strength of employing a set of *localized* or *multicountry strategies* is that the company's actions and business approaches are deliberately crafted to accommodate the differing tastes and expectations of buyers in each country and to stake out the most attractive market positions vis-à-vis local competitors. A think-local, act-local approach means giving local managers considerable strategy-making latitude. It means having plants produce different product versions for different local markets and adapting marketing and distribution to fit local customs and cultures. The bigger the country-to-country variations, the more that a company's overall strategy is a collection of its localized country strategies rather than a common or "global" strategy.

> **Core Concept**
>
> A *localized* or *multicountry strategy* is one where a company varies its product offering and competitive approach from country to country in an effort to be responsive to differing buyer preferences and market conditions.

A think-local, act-local approach to strategy making is essential when there are significant country-to-country differences in customer preferences and buying habits, when there are significant cross-country differences in distribution channels and marketing methods, when host governments enact regulations requiring that products sold locally meet strict manufacturing specifications or performance standards, and when the trade restrictions of host governments are so diverse and complicated that they preclude a uniform, coordinated worldwide market approach. With localized strategies, a company often has different product versions for different countries and sometimes sells them under different brand names. Sony markets a different Walkman in Norway than in Sweden to better meet the somewhat different preferences and habits of the users in each market. Castrol, a specialist in oil lubricants, has over 3,000 different formulas of lubricants, many of which have been tailored for different climates, vehicle types and uses, and equipment applications that characterize different country markets. In the food products industry, it is common for companies to vary the ingredients in their products and sell the localized versions under local brand names in order to cater to country-specific tastes and eating preferences. Motor vehicle manufacturers routinely produce smaller, more fuel-efficient vehicles for markets in Europe, where roads are often narrower and gasoline prices two to three times higher, than they produce for the North American market; the models they manufacture for the Asian market are different yet again. DaimlerChrysler, for example, equips all of the Jeep Grand Cherokees and many of its Mercedes cars sold in Europe with fuel-efficient diesel engines. The

Figure 5.1   A Company's Strategic Options for Dealing with Cross-Country Variations in Buyer Preferences and Market Conditions

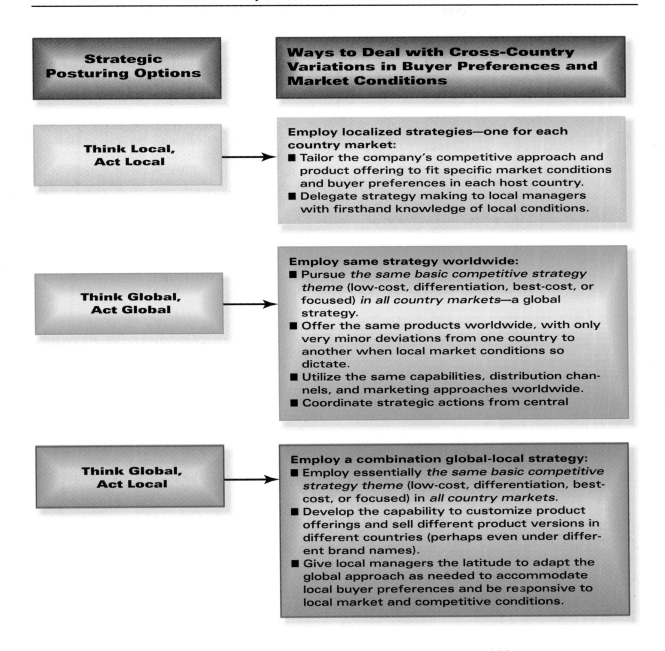

Strategic Posturing Options

Ways to Deal with Cross-Country Variations in Buyer Preferences and Market Conditions

Think Local, Act Local

Employ localized strategies—one for each country market:
- Tailor the company's competitive approach and product offering to fit specific market conditions and buyer preferences in each host country.
- Delegate strategy making to local managers with firsthand knowledge of local conditions.

Think Global, Act Global

Employ same strategy worldwide:
- Pursue *the same basic competitive strategy theme* (low-cost, differentiation, best-cost, or focused) *in all country markets*—a global strategy.
- Offer the same products worldwide, with only very minor deviations from one country to another when local market conditions so dictate.
- Utilize the same capabilities, distribution channels, and marketing approaches worldwide.
- Coordinate strategic actions from central

Think Global, Act Local

Employ a combination global-local strategy:
- Employ essentially *the same basic competitive strategy theme* (low-cost, differentiation, best-cost, or focused) in *all country markets*.
- Develop the capability to customize product offerings and sell different product versions in different countries (perhaps even under different brand names).
- Give local managers the latitude to adapt the global approach as needed to accommodate local buyer preferences and be responsive to local market and competitive conditions.

Buicks that General Motors sells in China are small compacts, whereas those sold in the United States are large family sedans and SUVs.

However, think-local, act-local strategies have two big drawbacks: they hinder transfer of a company's competencies and resources across country boundaries (since different competencies and capabilities may be used in different host countries), and they do not promote building a single, unified competitive advantage—especially one based on low cost. Companies employing highly localized or multicountry strategies face big hurdles in achieving low-cost leadership *unless* they find ways to customize their products and *still* be in a position to capture scale economies and learning-curve effects. Companies like Dell Computer and Toyota, because they have mass-customization production capabilities, can cost-effectively adapt their product offerings to local buyer tastes.

Think-Global, Act-Global Approaches to Strategy Making

While multicountry or localized strategies are best suited for industries where multicountry competition dominates and a fairly high degree of local responsiveness is competitively imperative, global strategies are best suited for globally competitive industries. A *global strategy* is one in which the company's approach is predominantly the same in all countries—it sells the same products under the same brand names everywhere, utilizes much the same types of distribution channels in all countries, and competes on the basis of the same capabilities and marketing approaches worldwide. Although the company's strategy or product offering may be adapted in very minor ways to accommodate specific situations in a few host countries, the company's fundamental competitive approach (low-cost, differentiation, best-cost, or focused) remains very much intact worldwide and local managers stick close to the global strategy. A "think-global, act-global" strategic theme prompts company managers to integrate and coordinate the company's strategic moves worldwide and to expand into most, if not all, nations where there is significant buyer demand. It puts considerable strategic emphasis on building a *global* brand name and aggressively pursuing opportunities to transfer ideas, new products, and capabilities from one country to another.[4] Indeed, with a think-global, act-global approach to strategy making, a company's operations in each country can be viewed as experiments that result in learning and in capabilities that may merit transfer to other country markets.

> **Core Concept**
>
> A *global strategy* is one in which a company employs the same basic competitive approach in all countries where it operates, sells much the same products everywhere, strives to build global brands, and coordinates its actions worldwide.

Whenever country-to-country differences are small enough to be accommodated within the framework of a global strategy, a global strategy is preferable to localized strategies because a company can more readily unify its operations and focus on establishing a brand image and reputation that is uniform from country to country. Moreover, with a global strategy a company is better able to focus its full resources on building the resource strengths and capabilities to secure a sustainable low-cost or differentiation-based competitive advantage over both domestic rivals and global rivals racing for world market leadership. Figure 5.2 summarizes the basic differences between a localized or multicountry strategy and a global strategy.

Think-Global, Act-Local Approaches to Strategy Making

Often, a company can accommodate cross-country variations in buyer tastes, local customs, and market conditions with a "think-global, act-local" approach to developing strategy. This middle-ground approach entails utilizing the same basic competitive theme (low-cost, differentiation, best-cost, or focused) in each country but allowing local managers the latitude to (1) incorporate whatever country-specific variations in product attributes are needed to best satisfy local buyers and (2) make whatever adjustments in production, distribution, and marketing are needed to be responsive to local market conditions and compete successfully against local rivals. Slightly different product versions sold under the same brand name may suffice to satisfy local tastes, and it may be feasible to accommodate these versions rather economically in the course of designing and manufacturing the company's product offerings. The build-to-order component of Dell Computer's strategy, for example, makes it simple for Dell to

Figure 5.2   **How a Localized or Multicountry Strategy Differs from a Global Strategy**

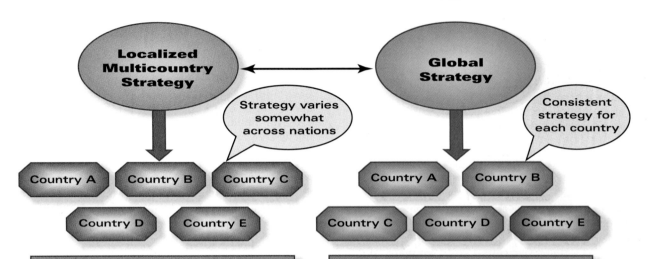

- Customize the company's competitive approach as needed to fit market and business circumstances in each host country—strong responsiveness to local conditions.
- Sell different product versions in different countries under different brand names—adapt product attributes to fit buyer tastes and preferences country by country.
- Scatter plants across many host countries, each producing product versions for local markets.
- Preferably use local suppliers (some local sources may be required by host government).
- Adapt marketing and distribution to local customs and culture of each country.
- Transfer competencies and capabilities from country to country where feasible.
- Give country managers fairly wide strategy-making latitude and autonomy over local operations.

- Pursue same basic competitive strategy worldwide (low-cost, differentiation, best-cost, focused low-cost, focused differentiation)-minimal responsiveness to local conditions.
- Sell same products under same brand name worldwide; focus efforts on building global brands as opposed to strengthening local/regional brands sold in local/regional markets.
- Locate plants on basis of maximum locational advantage, usually in countries where production costs are lowest but plants may be scattered if shipping costs are high or other locational advantages dominate.
- Use best suppliers from anywhere in world.
- Coordinate marketing and distribution worldwide; make minor adaptation to local countries where needed.
- Compete on basis of same technologies, competencies, and capabilities worldwide; stress rapid transfer of new ideas, products, and capabilities to other countries.
- Coordinate major strategic decisions worldwide; expect local managers to stick close to global strategy.

be responsive to how buyers in different parts of the world want their PCs equipped. However, Dell has not wavered in its strategy to sell direct to customers rather than through local retailers even though the majority of buyers in countries such as China are concerned about ordering online and prefer to personally inspect PCs at stores before making a purchase.

As a rule, most companies that operate multinationally endeavor to employ as global a strategy as customer needs and market conditions permit. Philips Electronics, the Netherlands-based electronics and consumer products company, operated successfully with localized strategies for many years but has recently begun moving more toward a unified strategy within the European Union and within North America.[5] Whirlpool has been globalizing its low-cost leadership strategy in home appliances for over 15 years, striving to standardize parts and components and move toward worldwide designs for as many of its appliance products as possible. But it has found it necessary to continue producing significantly different versions of refrigerators, washing machines, and cooking appliances for consumers in different regions of the world because the needs and tastes of local buyers for appliances of different sizes and designs have not converged sufficiently to permit standardization of Whirlpool's product offerings worldwide. General Motors began an initiative in 2004 to insist that its worldwide units share basic parts and work together to design vehicles that can be sold, with modest variations, anywhere in the world; by reducing the types of radios used in its cars and trucks from 270 to 50, it expected to save 40 percent in radio costs.

Global Spotlight 5.1 describes how two companies localize their strategies for competing in country markets across the world.

The Quest for Competitive Advantage in Foreign Markets

There are three important ways in which a firm can gain competitive advantage (or off-set domestic disadvantages) by expanding outside its domestic market.[6] One, it can use location to lower costs or achieve greater product differentiation. Two, it can transfer competitively valuable competencies and capabilities from its domestic markets to foreign markets. And three, it can use cross-border coordination in ways that a domestic-only competitor cannot.

Using Location to Build Competitive Advantage

To use location to build competitive advantage, a company must consider two issues: (1) whether to concentrate each activity it performs in a few select countries or to disperse performance of the activity to many nations and (2) in which countries to locate particular activities.[7]

> Companies that compete multinationally can pursue competitive advantage in world markets by locating their value chain activities in whatever nations prove most advantageous.

When to Concentrate Activities in a Few Locations   Companies tend to concentrate their activities in a limited number of locations in the following circumstances:

■ *When the costs of manufacturing or other activities are significantly lower in some geographic locations than in others:* For example, much of the world's athletic footwear is manufactured in Asia (China and Korea) because of low labor costs; much of the production of motherboards for PCs is located in Taiwan because of both low costs and the high-caliber technical skills of the Taiwanese labor force.

■ *When there are significant scale economies:* The presence of significant economies of scale in components production or final assembly means that a company can gain major cost savings from operating a few superefficient plants as opposed to a host of small plants scattered across the world. Important marketing and distribution economies associated with multinational operations can also yield low-cost leadership. In situations where some competitors are intent on global dominance, being the worldwide low-cost provider is a powerful competitive advantage. Achieving low-cost provider status often requires a company to have the largest worldwide manufacturing share, with production centralized in one or a few world-scale plants in low-cost locations. Some companies even use such plants to manufacture units sold under the brand names of rivals. Manufacturing share (as distinct from brand share or market share) is significant because it provides more certain access to production-related scale economies. Japanese makers of VCRs, microwave ovens, TVs, and DVD players have used their large manufacturing share to establish a low-cost advantage.[8]

■ *When there is a steep learning curve associated with performing an activity in a single location:* In some industries learning-curve effects in parts manufacture or assembly are so great that a company establishes one or two large plants from which it serves the world market. The key to riding down the learning curve is to concentrate production in a few locations to increase the accumulated volume at a plant (and thus the experience of the plant's workforce) as rapidly as possible.

■ *When certain locations have superior resources, allow better coordination of related activities, or offer other valuable advantages:* A research unit or a sophisticated production facility may be situated in a particular nation because of its pool of technically trained personnel. Samsung became a leader in memory chip technology by establishing a major R&D facility in Silicon Valley and transferring the know-how it gained back to headquarters and its plants in South Korea. Where just-in-time inventory practices yield big cost savings and/or where an assembly firm has long-term partnering arrangements with its key suppliers, parts manufacturing plants may be clustered around final assembly plants. An assembly plant may be located in a country in return for the host government's allowing freer import of components from large-scale, centralized parts plants located elsewhere. A customer service center or sales office may be opened in a particular country to help cultivate strong relationships with pivotal customers located nearby.

When to Disperse Activities across Many Locations   There are several instances when dispersing activities is more advantageous than concentrating them. Buyer-related activities—such as distribution to dealers, sales and advertising, and after-sale service—usually must take place close to buyers. This means physically locating the capability to perform such activities in every country market where a global firm has major customers (unless buyers in several adjoining countries can be served quickly from a nearby central location). For example, firms that make mining and oil-drilling equipment maintain operations in many international locations to support customers' needs for speedy equipment repair and technical assistance. The four biggest public accounting firms have numerous international offices to service the foreign operations of their multinational corporate clients. A global competitor that effectively disperses its buyer-related activities can gain a service-based competitive edge in world markets over rivals whose buyer-related activities are more concentrated—this is one reason the Big Four public accounting firms (PricewaterhouseCoopers, KPMG, Deloitte & Touche, and Ernst & Young) have been so successful relative to regional and national firms. Dispersing activities to many locations is also competitively advantageous when high transportation costs, diseconomies of large size, and trade barriers make it too expensive to operate from a central location. Many companies distribute their products from multiple locations to shorten delivery times to customers. In addition, it is strategically advantageous to disperse activities to hedge against the risks of fluctuating exchange rates; supply interruptions (due to strikes, mechanical failures, and transportation delays); and adverse political developments. Such risks are greater when activities are concentrated in a single location.

The classic reason for locating an activity in a particular country is low cost.[9] Even though multinational and global firms have strong reason to disperse buyer-related activities to many international locations, such activities as materials procurement, parts manufacture, finished-goods assembly, technology research, and new product development can frequently be decoupled from buyer locations and performed wherever advantage lies. Components can be made in Mexico; technology research done in Frankfurt; new products developed and tested in Phoenix; and assembly plants located in Spain, Brazil, Taiwan, or South Carolina. Capital can be raised in whatever country is available on the best terms.

Using Cross-Border Transfers of Competencies and Capabilities to Build Competitive Advantage

Expanding beyond domestic borders is a way for companies to leverage their core competencies and resource strengths, using them as a basis for competing successfully in additional country markets and growing sales and profits in the process. Transferring competencies, capabilities, and resource strengths from country to country contributes to the development of broader or deeper competencies and capabilities—ideally helping a company achieve dominating depth in some competitively valuable area. Dominating depth in a competitively valuable capability, resource, or value chain activity is a strong basis for sustainable competitive advantage over other multinational or global competitors and especially so over domestic-only competitors. A one-country customer base is often too small to support the resource buildup needed to achieve such depth; this is particularly true when the market is just emerging and sophisticated resources have not been required.

Whirlpool, the leading global manufacturer of home appliances, with plants in 14 countries and sales in 170 countries, has used the Internet to create a global information technology platform that allows the company to transfer key product innovations and production processes across regions and brands quickly and effectively. Wal-Mart is slowly but forcefully expanding its operations with a strategy that involves transferring its considerable domestic expertise in distribution and discount retailing to other countries. Its status as the largest, most resource-deep, and most sophisticated user of distribution-retailing know-how has served it well in building its foreign sales and profitability. But Wal-Mart is not racing madly to position itself in many foreign markets; rather, it is establishing a strong presence in select country markets and learning how to be successful in these before tackling entry into other major markets.

However, cross-border resource transfers are not a guaranteed recipe for success. Philips Electronics sells more color TVs and DVD recorders in Europe than any other company does; its biggest technological breakthrough was the compact disc, which it invented in 1982. Philips has worldwide sales of about 32 billion euros, but as of 2002 Philips had lost money for 15 consecutive years in its U.S. consumer electronics business. In the United States, the company's color TVs and DVD recorders (sold under the Magnavox and Philips brands) are slow sellers. Philips is notoriously slow in introducing new products into the U.S. market and has been struggling to develop an able sales force that can make inroads with U.S. electronics retailers and change its image as a clunky brand.

Using Cross-Border Coordination to Build Competitive Advantage

Coordinating company activities across different countries contributes to sustainable competitive advantage in several different ways.[10] Multinational and global competitors can choose where and how to challenge rivals. They may decide to retaliate against an aggressive rival in the country market where the rival has its biggest sales volume or its best profit margins in order to reduce the rival's financial resources for competing in other country markets. They may also decide to wage a price-cutting offensive against weak rivals in their home markets, capturing greater market share and subsidizing any short-term losses with profits earned in other country markets.

If a firm learns how to assemble its product more efficiently at, say, its Brazilian plant, the accumulated expertise can be quickly communicated via the Internet to assembly plants in other world locations. Knowledge gained in marketing a company's product in Great Britain can readily be exchanged with company personnel in New Zealand or Australia. A global or multinational manufacturer can shift production from a plant in one country to a plant in another to take advantage of exchange rate fluctuations, to enhance its leverage with host-country governments, and to respond to changing wage rates, components shortages, energy costs, or changes in tariffs and quotas. Production schedules can be coordinated worldwide; shipments can be diverted from one distribution center to another if sales rise unexpectedly in one place and fall in another.

Using Internet technology applications, companies can collect ideas for new and improved products from customers and sales and marketing personnel all over the world, permitting informed decisions about what can be standardized and what should be customized. Likewise, Internet technology can be used to involve the company's best design and engineering personnel (wherever they are located) in collectively coming up with next-generation products—it is becoming increasingly easy for company personnel in one location to use the Internet to collaborate closely with personnel in other locations in performing strategically relevant activities. Efficiencies can also be achieved by shifting workloads from locations where they are unusually heavy to locations where personnel are underutilized.

A company can enhance its brand reputation by consistently incorporating the same differentiating attributes in its products worldwide. The reputation for quality that Honda established worldwide first in motorcycles and then in automobiles gave it competitive advantage in positioning Honda lawn mowers at the upper end of the U.S. outdoor power equipment market—the Honda name gave the company instant credibility with U.S. buyers. Whirlpool's efforts to link its product R&D and manufacturing operations in North America, Latin America, Europe, and Asia allowed it to accelerate the discovery of innovative appliance features, coordinate the introduction of these features in the appliance products marketed in different countries, and create a cost-efficient worldwide supply chain. Whirlpool's conscious efforts to integrate and coordinate its various operations around the world have helped it become a low-cost producer and also speed product innovations to market, both of which have helped give Whirlpool advantages over rivals in designing and rapidly introducing innovative and attractively priced appliances worldwide.

Profit Sanctuaries, Cross-Market Subsidization, and Global Strategic Offensives

Core Concept

Companies with large, protected **profit sanctuaries** have competitive advantage over companies that don't have a protected sanctuary. Companies with multiple profit sanctuaries have a competitive advantage over companies with a single sanctuary.

Profit sanctuaries are country markets in which a company derives substantial profits because of its strong or protected market position. Japan, for example, is a profit sanctuary for most Japanese companies because trade barriers erected by the Japanese government effectively block foreign companies from competing for a large share of Japanese sales. Protected from the threat of foreign competition in their home market, Japanese companies can safely charge somewhat higher prices to their Japanese customers and thus earn attractively large profits on sales made in Japan. In most cases, a company's biggest and most

Figure 5.3 **Profit Sanctuary Potential of Domestic-Only, International, and Global Competitors** (profit sanctuary = 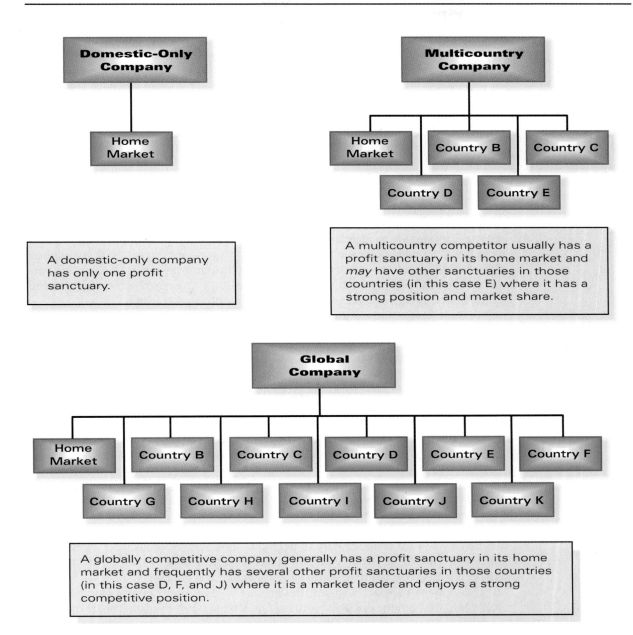)

A domestic-only company has only one profit sanctuary.

A multicountry competitor usually has a profit sanctuary in its home market and *may* have other sanctuaries in those countries (in this case E) where it has a strong position and market share.

A globally competitive company generally has a profit sanctuary in its home market and frequently has several other profit sanctuaries in those countries (in this case D, F, and J) where it is a market leader and enjoys a strong competitive position.

strategically crucial profit sanctuary is its home market, but international and global companies may also enjoy profit sanctuary status in other nations where they have a strong competitive position, big sales volume, and attractive profit margins. Companies that compete globally are likely to have more profit sanctuaries than companies that compete in just a few country markets; a domestic-only competitor, of course, can have only one profit sanctuary (see Figure 5.3).

Using Cross-Market Subsidization to Wage a Strategic Offensive

Profit sanctuaries are valuable competitive assets, providing the financial strength to support strategic offensives in selected country markets and aid a company's race for global market leadership. The added financial capability afforded by multiple profit sanctuaries gives a global or multicountry competitor the financial strength to wage a market offensive against a domestic competitor whose only profit sanctuary is its home market. Consider the case of a purely domestic company in competition with a company that has multiple profit sanctuaries and that is racing for global market leadership. The global company has the flexibility of lowballing its prices in the domestic company's home market and grabbing market share at the domestic company's expense, subsidizing razor-thin margins or even losses with the healthy profits earned in its profit sanctuaries—a practice called **cross-market subsidization.** The global company can adjust the depth of its price cutting to move in and capture market share quickly, or it can shave prices slightly to make gradual market inroads (perhaps over a decade or more) so as not to threaten domestic firms precipitously or trigger protectionist government actions. If the domestic company retaliates with matching price cuts, it exposes its entire revenue and profit base to erosion; its profits can be squeezed substantially and its competitive strength sapped, even if it is the domestic market leader.

> ## Core Concept
>
> **Cross-market subsidization**—supporting competitive offensives in one market with resources and profits diverted from operations in other markets—is a powerful competitive weapon.

Global Strategic Offensives

One of the most frequently used offensives is dumping goods at unreasonably low prices in the markets of foreign rivals. Such a strategy, if used repeatedly in the same country, can put domestic firms in dire financial straits or drive them out of business. Many governments have antidumping laws aimed at protecting domestic firms from unfair pricing by foreign rivals. In 2002, for example, the U.S. government imposed tariffs of up to 30 percent on selected steel products that Asian and European steel manufacturers were said to be selling at ultralow prices in the U.S. market.

But more usually the offensive strategies of companies that compete in multiple country markets with multiple products (several brands of cigarettes or different brands of food products) are more sophisticated. In deciding how to attack a multinational rival, a company needs to be alert to a competitor's incentive to react strongly and forcefully (often indicated by the size of the rival's market share or the growth potential of the market) and the rival's ability to defend its position (who has more clout in this arena—the attacker or the defender?).[11] The company also has to decide just how important it is to defeat the rival—how much is there to be gained?

If the offensive appears attractive, there are at least three options. One is a *direct onslaught*, in which the objective is to capture a major slice of market share and force the rival to retreat. Such onslaughts nearly always involve (1) price cutting (often without regard to immediate profits), (2) heavy expenditures on marketing, advertising, and promotion, and (3) attempts to gain the upper hand in one or more distribution channels. Direct onslaughts require a massive commitment of resources and make sense only if the market arena is highly attractive to the attacker.

A second type of offensive is the *contest*, which is more subtle and more focused than an onslaught. A contest offensive zeros in on a particular market segment that is unsuited to the capabilities and strengths of the defender and in which the attacker has a new next-generation or breakthrough product. Warner Brothers recently slashed the prices of its DVDs to such low levels that rivals were loath to follow suit; the move put enormous pressure on movie rental companies like Blockbuster. Warner Brothers' motive was to get people accustomed to buying DVDs instead of renting them. Such offensives often become a contest of whose strategy and business model will prevail.

A third offensive is the *feint*, a move designed to divert the defender's attention away from the attacker's main target. A good example of a feint offensive is Philip Morris's move in 1993 to reduce the U.S. price of its best-selling Marlboro cigarettes by 20 percent. Its rival R. J. Reynolds, which at the time was strapped for resources, was forced to institute matching price cuts on its Camel and Winston brands and scramble to defend its already eroding market share. But while Reynolds was busily engaged protecting its turf in the U.S. market, Philip Morris launched a major offensive into Russia and Eastern Europe (where cigarette sales were on the rise) and spent $800 million to get its brands established there. Philip Morris won the battle for market share in Eastern Europe hands down over Reynolds.

Strategic Alliances and Joint Ventures with Foreign Partners

Strategic alliances, joint ventures, and other cooperative agreements with foreign companies are a favorite and potentially fruitful means for entering a foreign market or strengthening a firm's competitiveness in world markets. Historically, export-minded firms in industrialized nations sought alliances with firms in less developed countries to import and market their products locally—such arrangements were often necessary to win approval for entry from the host country's government. More recently, companies from different parts of the world have formed strategic alliances and partnership arrangements to strengthen their mutual ability to serve whole continents and move toward more global market participation. Both Japanese and American companies are actively forming alliances with European companies to strengthen their ability to compete in the 25-nation European Union and to capitalize on the opening up of Eastern European markets. Many U.S. and European companies are allying with Asian companies in their efforts to enter markets in China, India, and other Asian countries.

Cooperative arrangements between domestic and foreign companies have strategic appeal for reasons besides gaining wider access to attractive country markets.[12] One is to capture economies of scale in production and/or marketing—cost reduction can be the difference that allows a company to be cost-competitive. By joining forces in producing components, assembling models, and marketing their products, companies can realize cost savings not achievable with their own small volumes. A second reason is to fill gaps in technical expertise and/or knowledge of local markets (buying habits and product preferences of consumers, local customs, and so on). Allies learn much from one another in performing joint research, sharing technological know-how, studying one another's manufacturing methods, and understanding how to tailor sales and marketing approaches to fit local cultures and traditions. A third reason is to share distribution facilities and dealer networks, thus mutually strengthening their access to buyers. Fourth, allied companies can direct their competitive energies more toward mutual rivals and less toward one another; teaming up may help them close the gap on leading companies. Fifth, companies opt to form

> Strategic alliances can help companies in globally competitive industries strengthen their competitive positions while still preserving their independence.

alliances with local companies (even where not legally required) because of the partner's local market knowledge and working relationships with key officials in the host-country government.[13] And, finally, alliances can be a particularly useful way to gain agreement on important technical standards—they have been used to arrive at standards for DVD players, assorted PC devices, Internet-related technologies, high-definition televisions, and mobile phones.

The Risks of Strategic Alliances with Foreign Partners

Alliances and joint ventures have their pitfalls, however. Achieving effective collaboration between independent companies, each with different motives and perhaps conflicting objectives, is not easy.[14] It requires many meetings of many people working in good faith over a period of time to iron out what is to be shared, what is to remain proprietary, and how the cooperative arrangements will work. Cross-border allies typically have to overcome language and cultural barriers; the communication, trust-building, and coordination costs are high in terms of management time. Often, once the bloom is off the rose, partners discover they have conflicting objectives and strategies and/or deep differences of opinion about how to proceed. Tensions build up, working relationships cool, and the hoped-for benefits never materialize.[15] Even if the alliance proves fruitful, there is the danger of becoming overly dependent on foreign partners for essential expertise and competitive capabilities. If a company is aiming for global market leadership and needs to develop capabilities of its own, then at some juncture cross-border merger or acquisition may have to be substituted for cross-border alliances and joint ventures.

Another major problem is getting alliance partners to make decisions fast enough to respond to rapidly advancing technological developments. Large telecommunications companies striving to achieve "global connectivity" have made extensive use of alliances and joint ventures with foreign counterparts, but they are encountering serious difficulty in reaching agreements on which of several technological approaches to employ and how to adapt to the swift pace at which all of the alternatives are advancing. AT&T and British Telecom, which formed a $10 billion joint venture to build an Internet-based global network linking 100 major cities, took eight months to find a CEO to head the project and even longer to come up with a name; the joint venture was abandoned in 2002.

Allies often find it difficult to collaborate effectively in competitively sensitive areas, thus raising questions about mutual trust and forthright exchanges of information

> Strategic alliances are more effective in helping establish a beachhead of new opportunity in world markets than in achieving and sustaining global leadership.

and expertise. There can also be clashes of egos and company cultures. The key people on whom success or failure depends may have little personal chemistry, be unable to work closely together or form a partnership, or be unable to come to consensus. For example, an alliance between Northwest Airlines and KLM Royal Dutch Airlines linking their hubs in Detroit and Amsterdam resulted in a bitter feud among both companies' top officials (who, according to some reports, refused to speak to each other) and precipitated a battle for control of Northwest engineered by KLM. The dispute was rooted in a clash of business philosophies (the American way versus the European way), basic cultural differences, and an executive power struggle.[16]

Global Spotlight 5.2 relates the experiences of various companies with cross-border strategic alliances.

GLOBAL SPOTLIGHT 5.2

Cross-Border Strategic Alliances and Joint Ventures: Five High-Profile Examples

Of late, the number of strategic alliances and co-operative agreements of one kind or another among companies from different parts of the world has exploded. Five high-profile alliances are highlighted below:

- Two auto firms, Renault of France and Nissan of Japan, formed a broad-ranging global partnership in 1999 and then strengthened and expanded the alliance in 2002. The initial objective was to gain sales for new Nissan vehicles introduced in the European market, but the alliance now extends to full cooperation in all major areas, including the use of common platforms, joint development and use of engines and transmissions, fuel cell research, purchasing and use of common suppliers, and exchange of best practices. When the alliance was formed in 1999, Renault acquired a 36.8 percent ownership stake in Nissan; this was extended to 44.4 percent in 2002 when the alliance was expanded. Also, in 2002, the partners formed a jointly and equally owned strategic management company, named Renault-Nissan, to coordinate cooperative efforts.

- Verizon Wireless, one of the two largest cell-phone carriers in the United States, is a joint venture between Verizon Communications and Vodafone AirTouch PLC (a leader in wireless communications in Europe). In February 2004, the alliance came close to unraveling when Vodafone made a $38 billion bid to acquire AT&T Wireless. The bid failed when Cingular Wireless (a joint venture between BellSouth Corp. and SBC Communications) bid $41 billion. But Vodafone's bid showed a desire to strike out on its own, control its destiny in the pivotal North American market, and further establish itself as a truly global cell-phone company.

- Microsoft and Fujitsu entered into an alliance in 2004 to collaborate on (1) the development of Fujitsu servers based on Intel's Itanium processors and (2) Microsoft's Windows Server 2003 and next-generation operating system (code-named "Longhorn"); the objective was to improve interoperability between their respective software applications.

- Toyota and First Automotive Works, China's biggest automaker, entered into an alliance in 2002 to make luxury sedans, sport-utility vehicles, and minivehicles for the Chinese market. The intent was to make as many as 400,000 vehicles annually by 2010, an amount equal to the number that Volkswagen, the company with the largest share of the Chinese market, was making as of 2002. The alliance envisioned a joint investment of about $1.2 billion. At the time of the announced alliance, Toyota was lagging behind Honda, General Motors, and Volkswagen in setting up production facilities in China. Capturing a bigger share of the Chinese market was seen as crucial to Toyota's success in achieving its strategic objective of having a 15 percent share of the world's automotive market by 2010.

- General Electric (GE) and SNECMA, a French maker of jet engines, have had a long-standing 50-50 partnership in two ventures, one called CFM International, which makes jet engines to power aircraft made by Boeing and Airbus Industrie, and a second called CFAN, which functions as the exclusive supply source for wide-chord blades for commercial jet engines made by GE. The GE/SNECMA alliance has enjoyed great success since the 1970s. SNECMA was an attractive alliance partner from GE's perspective because it gave GE a France-based connection to help market the alliance's products to Airbus Industrie; likewise, SNECMA found the alliance attractive because it could serve as an entrée for marketing the alliance's products to Boeing. CFM International has sold over 15,000 jet engines since the early 1980s, winning market shares for large commercial aircraft of about 35 percent through the 1980s and market shares approaching 50 percent since 1995. As of mid-2004, CFM had delivered some 14,200 jet engines for aircraft deployed by 390 customers.

Source: Company Web sites and press releases; and Yves L. Doz and Gary Hamel, *Alliance Advantage: The Art of Creating Value through Partnering* (Boston: Harvard Business School Press, 1998).

Making the Most of Strategic Alliances with Foreign Partners

Whether or not a company realizes the potential of alliances and collaborative partnerships with foreign enterprises seems to be a function of six factors:[17]

1. *Picking a good partner:* A good partner not only has the desired expertise and capabilities but also shares the company's vision about the purpose of the alliance. Experience indicates that it is generally wise to avoid a partnership in which there is strong potential of direct competition because of overlapping product lines or other conflicting interests—agreements to jointly market each other's products hold much potential for conflict unless the products are complements rather than substitutes and unless there is good chemistry among key personnel.

2. *Being sensitive to cultural differences:* Unless the outsider exhibits respect for the local culture and local business practices, productive working relationships are unlikely to emerge.

3. *Recognizing that the alliance must benefit both sides:* Information must be shared as well as gained, and the relationship must remain forthright and trustful. Many alliances fail because one or both partners grow unhappy with what they are learning. Also, if either partner plays games with information or tries to take advantage of the other, the resulting friction can quickly erode the value of further collaboration.

4. *Ensuring that both parties live up to their commitments:* Both parties have to deliver on their commitments for the alliance to produce the intended benefits. The division of work has to be perceived as fairly apportioned, and the caliber of the benefits received on both sides has to be perceived as adequate.

5. *Structuring the decision-making process so that actions can be taken swiftly when needed:* In many instances, the fast pace of technological and competitive changes dictates an equally fast decision-making process. If the parties get bogged down in discussion or in gaining internal approval from higher-ups, the alliance can turn into an anchor of delay and inaction.

6. *Managing the learning process and then adjusting the alliance agreement over time to fit new circumstances:* In today's fast-moving markets, few alliances can succeed by holding only to initial plans. One of the keys to long-lasting success is learning to adapt to change; the terms and objectives of the alliance must be adjusted as needed.

Most alliances with foreign companies that aim at technology sharing or providing market access turn out to be temporary, fulfilling their purpose after a few years because the benefits of mutual learning have occurred and because the businesses of both partners have developed to the point where they are ready to go their own ways. In such cases, it is important for the company to learn thoroughly and rapidly about a partner's technology, business practices, and organizational capabilities and then transfer valuable ideas and practices into its own operations promptly. Although long-term alliances sometimes prove mutually beneficial, most partners don't hesitate to terminate the alliance and go it alone when the payoffs run out.

Alliances are more likely to be long-lasting when (1) they involve collaboration with suppliers or distribution allies and each party's contribution involves activities in different portions of the industry value chain or (2) both parties conclude that continued collaboration is in their mutual interest, perhaps because new opportunities for learning are emerging or perhaps because further collaboration will allow each partner to extend its market reach beyond what it could accomplish on its own.

GLOBAL SPOTLIGHT 5.3

Coca-Cola's Strategy for Growing Its Sales in China and India

In 2004, Coca-Cola developed a strategy to dramatically boost its market penetration in such emerging countries as China and India, where annual growth had recently dropped from about 30 percent in 1994–1998 to 10 to 12 percent in 2001–2003. Prior to 2003 Coca-Cola had focused its marketing efforts in China and India on making its drinks attractive to status-seeking young people in urbanized areas (cities with populations of 500,000 or more), but as annual sales growth steadily declined in these areas during the 1998–2003 period, Coca-Cola management decided a new, bolder strategy aimed at more rural areas of these countries was needed. It began promoting the sales of small 6.5-ounce returnable glass bottles of Coke in smaller cities and outlying towns with populations in the 50,000 to 250,000 range. Returnable bottles (which could be reused about 20 times) were much cheaper than plastic bottles or aluminum cans, and the savings in packaging costs were enough to slash the price of single-serve bottles to 1 yuan in China and about 5 rupees in India, the equivalent in both cases of about 12 cents. Initial results were promising. Despite the fact that annual dispos-

able incomes in these rural areas were often less than $1,000 annually, the 1-yuan and 5-rupee prices proved attractive. Sales of the small bottles of Coke for one local Coca-Cola distributor in Anning, China, soon accounted for two-thirds of the distributor's total sales; a local distributor in India boosted sales from 9,000 cases in 2002 to 27,000 cases in 2003 and was expecting sales of 45,000 cases in 2004. Coca-Cola management expected that greater emphasis on rural sales would boost Coca-Cola's growth rate in Asia to close to 20 percent and help boost worldwide volume growth to the 3 to 5 percent range as opposed to the paltry 1 percent rate experienced in 2003.

However, PepsiCo, which had a market share of about 27 percent in China, versus Coca-Cola's 55 percent, was skeptical of Coca-Cola's rural strategy and continued with its all-urban strategy of marketing to consumers in China's 165 cities with populations greater than 1 million people.

Source: Wall Street Journal. Eastern Edition [staff produced copy only] by Gabriel Kahn and Eric Bellman. Copyright 2004 by Dow Jones & Co. Inc. Reproduced with permission of Dow Jones & Co. Inc. in the format textbook via Copyright Clearance Center.

Competing in Emerging Foreign Markets

Companies racing for global leadership have to consider competing in emerging markets like China, India, Brazil, Indonesia, and Mexico—countries where the business risks are considerable but where the opportunities for growth are huge, especially as their economies develop and living standards climb toward levels in the industrialized world.[18] With the world now comprising more than 6 billion people—fully one-third of whom are in India and China, and hundreds of millions more in other less developed countries of Asia and Latin America—a company that aspires to world market leadership (or to sustained rapid growth) cannot ignore the market opportunities or the base of technical and managerial talent such countries offer. For example, in 2003 China's population of 1.3 billion people consumed nearly 33 percent of the world's annual cotton production, 51 percent of the world's pork, 35 percent of all the cigarettes, 31 percent of worldwide coal production, 27 percent of the world's steel production, 19 percent of the aluminum, 23 percent of the TVs, 20 percent of the cell phones, and 18 percent of the washing machines.[19] China is the world's largest consumer of copper, aluminum, and cement and the second-largest importer of oil; it is the world's biggest market for mobile phones and the second biggest for PCs, plus it is on track to become the second-largest market for motor vehicles by 2010. No company that aspires to global market leadership can thus afford to ignore the strategic importance of establishing a competitive market position in China, India, other parts of the Asian Pacific, Latin America, and Eastern Europe. Global Spotlight 5.3 describes Coca-Cola's strategy to boost its sales and market share in China.

Tailoring products for big emerging markets, however, often involves more than making minor product changes and becoming more familiar with local cultures.[20] Ford's attempt to sell a Ford Escort in India at a price of $21,000—a luxury-car price, given that India's best-selling Maruti-Suzuki model sold at the time for $10,000 or less and that fewer than 10 percent of Indian households have annual purchasing power greater than $20,000—met with a less-than-enthusiastic market response. McDonald's has had to offer vegetable burgers in parts of Asia and to rethink its prices, which are often high by local standards and affordable only by the well-to-do. Kellogg has struggled to introduce its cereals successfully because consumers in many less developed countries do not eat cereal for breakfast—changing habits is difficult and expensive. Coca-Cola has found that advertising its world image does not strike a chord with the local populace in a number of emerging country markets. Single-serving packages of detergents, shampoos, pickles, cough syrup, and cooking oils are very popular in India because they allow buyers to conserve cash by purchasing only what they need immediately.

Strategy Implications

Consumers in emerging markets are highly focused on price, in many cases giving local low-cost competitors the edge. Companies wishing to succeed in these markets have to attract buyers with bargain prices as well as better products—an approach that can entail a radical departure from the strategy used in other parts of the world. If building a market for the company's products is likely to be a long-term process and involve reeducation of consumers, a company must not only be patient with regard to sizable revenues and profits but also be prepared in the interim to invest sizable sums to alter buying habits and tastes. Also, specially designed or packaged products may be needed to accommodate local market circumstances. For example, when Unilever entered the market for laundry detergents in India, it realized that 80 percent of the population could not afford the brands it was selling to affluent consumers there

> Profitability in emerging markets rarely comes quickly or easily—new entrants have to be very sensitive to local conditions, be willing to invest in developing the market for their products over the long term, and be patient in earning a profit.

(as well as in wealthier countries). To compete against a very low-priced detergent made by a local company, Unilever came up with a low-cost formula that was not harsh to the skin, constructed new low-cost production facilities, packaged the detergent (named Wheel) in single-use amounts so that it could be sold very cheaply, distributed the product to local merchants by handcarts, and crafted an economical marketing campaign that included painted signs on buildings and demonstrations near stores—the new brand quickly captured $100 million in sales and was the number-one detergent brand in India in 2004 based on dollar sales. Unilever later replicated the strategy with low-priced packets of shampoos and deodorants in India and in South America with a detergent brand named Ala.

Because managing a new venture in an emerging market requires a blend of global knowledge and local sensitivity to the culture and business practices, the management team must usually consist of a mix of expatriate and local managers. Expatriate managers are needed to transfer technology, business practices, and the corporate culture and to serve as conduits for the flow of information between the corporate office and local operations; local managers bring needed understanding of the area's nuances and deep commitment to its market.

Defending against Global Giants: Strategies for Local Companies in Emerging Markets

If large, opportunity-seeking, resource-rich companies are looking to enter emerging markets, what strategy options can local companies use to survive? As it turns out, the prospects for local companies facing global giants are by no means grim. Their optimal strategic approach hinges on (1) whether their competitive assets are suitable only for the home market or can be transferred abroad and (2) whether industry pressures to move toward global competition are strong or weak. The four generic options are shown in Figure 5.4.

Using Home-Field Advantages

When the pressures for global competition are low and a local firm has competitive strengths well suited to the local market, a good strategy option is to concentrate on the advantages enjoyed in the home market, cater to customers who prefer a local touch, and accept the loss of customers attracted to global brands.[21] A local company may be able to astutely exploit its local orientation—its familiarity with local preferences, its expertise in traditional products, its long-standing customer relationships. In many cases, a local company enjoys a significant cost advantage over global rivals (perhaps because of simpler product design or lower operating and overhead costs), allowing it

Figure 5.4   **Strategy Options for Local Companies in Competing against Global Companies**

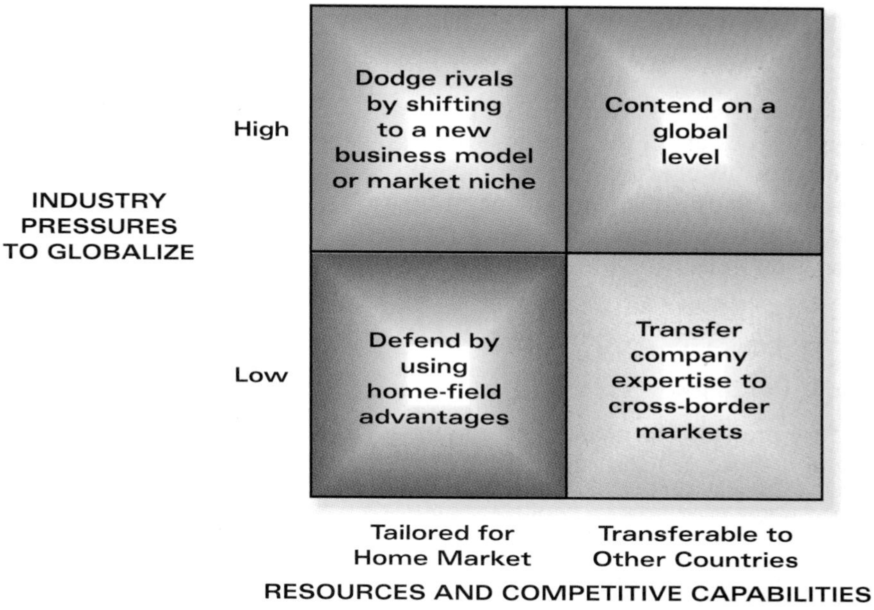

	Tailored for Home Market	Transferable to Other Countries
High	Dodge rivals by shifting to a new business model or market niche	Contend on a global level
Low	Defend by using home-field advantages	Transfer company expertise to cross-border markets

INDUSTRY PRESSURES TO GLOBALIZE

RESOURCES AND COMPETITIVE CAPABILITIES

to compete on the basis of price. Its global competitors often aim their products at upper- and middle-income urban buyers, who tend to be more fashion-conscious, more willing to experiment with new products, and more attracted to global brands.

Another competitive approach is to cater to the local market in ways that pose difficulties for global rivals. A small Middle Eastern cell-phone manufacturer competes successfully against industry giants Nokia, Samsung, and Motorola by selling a model designed especially for Muslims—it is loaded with the Koran, alerts people at prayer times, and is equipped with a compass that points them toward Mecca. Two Chinese PC makers, Lenovo and Founder Electronics, have been able to retain their market share lead in China over global leader Dell because Chinese PC buyers strongly prefer to personally inspect PCs before making a purchase; thus Dell with its build-to-order, sell-direct business model is at a competitive disadvantage against Lenovo and Founder, both of which have vast retail dealer networks across China that allow prospective buyers to check out their offerings in nearby stores. Bajaj Auto, India's largest producer of scooters, has defended its turf against Honda (which entered the Indian market with local joint-venture partner Hero Group to sell scooters, motorcycles, and other vehicles on the basis of its superior technology, quality, and brand appeal) by focusing on buyers who want low-cost, durable scooters and easy access to maintenance in the countryside. Bajaj designed a rugged, cheap-to-build scooter for India's rough roads, increased its investments in R&D to improve reliability and quality, and created an extensive network of distributors and roadside-mechanic stalls, a strategic approach that allowed it to remain the market leader with a 70 to 75 percent market share through 2004 despite growing unit sales of Hero Honda motorcycles and scooters.

Transferring the Company's Expertise to Cross-Border Markets

When a company has resource strengths and capabilities suitable for competing in other country markets, launching initiatives to transfer its expertise to cross-border markets becomes a viable strategic option.[22] Televisa, Mexico's largest media company, used its expertise in Spanish culture and linguistics to become the world's most prolific producer of Spanish-language soap operas. Jollibee Foods, a family-owned company with 56 percent of the fast-food business in the Philippines, combated Mc-Donald's entry first by upgrading service and delivery standards and then by using its expertise in seasoning hamburgers with garlic and soy sauce and making noodle and rice meals with fish to open outlets catering to Asian residents in Hong Kong, the Middle East, and California.

Shifting to a New Business Model or Market Niche

When industry pressures to globalize are high, any of the following three options makes the most sense: (1) shift the business to a piece of the industry value chain where the firm's expertise and resources provide competitive advantage, (2) enter into a joint venture with a globally competitive partner, or (3) sell out to (be acquired by) a global entrant into the home market that concludes the company would be a good entry vehicle.[23] When Microsoft entered China, local software developers shifted from cloning Windows products to developing Windows application software customized to the Chinese market. When the Russian PC market opened to IBM, Compaq, and

Hewlett-Packard, local Russian PC maker Vist focused on assembling very low-cost models, marketing them through exclusive distribution agreements with selected local retailers, and opening company-owned full-service centers in dozens of Russian cities. Vist focused on providing low-cost PCs, giving lengthy warranties, and catering to buyers who felt the need for local service and support. Vist's strategy allowed it to remain the market leader, with a 20 percent share. An India-based electronics company has been able to carve out a market niche for itself by developing an all-in-one business machine designed especially for India's 1.2 million small shopkeepers that tolerates heat, dust, and power outages and that sells for a modest $180 for the smallest of its three models.[24]

Contending on a Global Level

If a local company in an emerging market has transferable resources and capabilities, it can sometimes launch successful initiatives to meet the pressures for globalization head-on and start to compete on a global level itself.[25] When General Motors (GM) decided to outsource the production of radiator caps for all of its North American vehicles, Sundaram Fasteners of India pursued the opportunity; it purchased one of GM's radiator cap production lines, moved it to India, and became GM's sole supplier of radiator caps in North America—at 5 million units a year. As a participant in GM's supplier network, Sundaram learned about emerging technical standards, built its capabilities, and became one of the first Indian companies to achieve QS 9000 certification, a quality standard that GM now requires for all suppliers. Sundaram's acquired expertise in quality standards enabled it then to pursue opportunities to supply automotive parts in Japan and Europe. Chinese communications equipment maker Huawei has captured a 16 percent share in the global market for Internet routers because its prices are up to 50 percent lower than industry leaders like Cisco Systems; Huawei's success in low-priced Internet networking gear has allowed it to expand aggressively outside China, including such country markets as Russia and Brazil, and achieve the number-two worldwide market share in broadband networking gear.[26]

Key Points

Most issues in competitive strategy that apply to domestic companies apply also to companies that compete internationally. But there are four strategic issues unique to competing across national boundaries:

1. Whether to customize the company's offerings in each different country market to match the tastes and preferences of local buyers or offer a mostly standardized product worldwide.

2. Whether to employ essentially the same basic competitive strategy in all countries or modify the strategy country by country to fit the specific market conditions and competitive circumstances the company encounters.

3. Where to locate the company's production facilities, distribution centers, and customer service operations so as to realize the greatest locational advantages.

4. Whether and how to efficiently transfer the company's resource strengths and capabilities from one country to another in an effort to secure competitive advantage.

Multicountry competition exists when competition in one national market is independent of competition in another national market—there is no "international market," just a collection of self-contained country markets. Global competition exists when competitive conditions across national markets are linked strongly enough to form a true world market and when leading competitors compete head-to-head in many different countries.

In posturing to compete in foreign markets, a company has three basic options: (1) a think-local, act-local approach to crafting a strategy, (2) a think-global, act-global approach to crafting a strategy, and (3) a combination think-global, act-local approach. A think-local, act-local, or multicountry, strategy is appropriate for industries where multicountry competition dominates; a localized approach to strategy making calls for a company to vary its product offering and competitive approach from country to country in order to accommodate differing buyer preferences and market conditions. A think-global, act-global approach (or global strategy) works best in markets that are globally competitive or beginning to globalize; global strategies involve employing the same basic competitive approach (low-cost, differentiation, best-cost, focused) in all country markets and marketing essentially the same products under the same brand names in all countries where the company operates. A think-global, act-local approach can be used when it is feasible for a company to employ essentially the same basic competitive strategy in all markets but still customize its product offering and some aspect of its operations to fit local market circumstances.

Other strategy options for competing in world markets include maintaining a national (one-country) production base and exporting goods to foreign markets, licensing foreign firms to use the company's technology or produce and distribute the company's products, employing a franchising strategy, and using strategic alliances or other collaborative partnerships to enter a foreign market or strengthen a firm's competitiveness in world markets.

There are three ways in which a firm can gain competitive advantage (or offset domestic disadvantages) in global markets. One way involves locating various value chain activities among nations in a manner that lowers costs or achieves greater product differentiation. A second way involves efficient and effective transfer of competitively valuable competencies and capabilities from its domestic markets to foreign markets. A third way draws on a multinational or global competitor's ability to deepen or broaden its resource strengths and capabilities and to coordinate its dispersed activities in ways that a domestic-only competitor cannot.

Profit sanctuaries are country markets in which a company derives substantial profits because of its strong or protected market position. They are valuable competitive assets, providing the financial strength to support competitive offensives in one market with resources and profits diverted from operations in other markets, and aid a company's race for global market leadership. Companies with large, protected profit sanctuaries have a competitive advantage over companies that don't have a protected sanctuary. Companies with multiple profit sanctuaries have a competitive advantage over companies with a single sanctuary. The cross-market subsidization capabilities provided by multiple profit sanctuaries gives a global or international competitor a powerful offensive weapon.

The outlook for local companies in emerging markets wishing to survive against the entry of global giants is by no means grim. The optimal strategic approach hinges on whether a firm's competitive assets are suitable only for the home market or can be transferred abroad and on whether industry pressures to move toward global competition are strong or weak. Local companies can compete against global newcomers by

(1) defending on the basis of home-field advantages, (2) transferring their expertise to cross-border markets, (3) dodging large rivals by shifting to a new business model or market niche, or (4) launching initiatives to compete on a global level themselves.

Exercises

1. Log on to www.caterpillar.com and search for information about Caterpillar's strategy in foreign markets. Is the company pursuing a global strategy or a localized multicountry strategy? Support your answer.

2. Assume you are in charge of developing the strategy for a multinational company selling products in some 50 different countries around the world. One of the issues you face is whether to employ a multicountry strategy or a global strategy.

   a) If your company's product is personal computers, do you think it would make better strategic sense to employ a multicountry strategy or a global strategy? Why?

   b) If your company's product is dry soup mixes and canned soups, would a multicountry strategy seem to be more advisable than a global strategy? Why?

   c) If your company's product is washing machines, would it seem to make more sense to pursue a multicountry strategy or a global strategy? Why?

   d) If your company's product is basic work tools (hammers, screwdrivers, pliers, wrenches, saws), would a multicountry strategy or a global strategy seem to have more appeal? Why?

CHAPTER 6

Diversification
Strategies for Managing a Group of Businesses

To acquire or not to acquire: that is the question.

—*Robert J. Terry*

Fit between a parent and its businesses is a two-edged sword: a good fit can create value; a bad one can destroy it.

—*Andrew Campbell, Michael Goold, and Marcus Alexander*

Achieving superior performance through diversification is largely based on relatedness.

—*Philippe Very*

Make winners out of every business in your company. Don't carry losers.

—*Jack Welch, former CEO, General Electric*

We measure each of our businesses against strict criteria: growth, margin, and return-on-capital hurdle rate, and does it have the ability to become number one or two in its industry? We are quite pragmatic. If a business does not contribute to our overall vision, it has to go.

—*Richard Wambold, CEO, Pactiv*

In this chapter, we move up one level in the strategy-making hierarchy, from strategy making in a single-business enterprise to strategy making in a diversified enterprise. Because a diversified company is a collection of individual businesses, the strategy-making task is more complicated. In a one-business company, managers have to come up with a plan for competing successfully in only a single industry environment—the result is what we labeled in Chapter 1 as *business strategy* (or *business-level strategy*). But in a diversified company, the strategy-making challenge involves assessing multiple industry environments and developing a *set* of business strategies, one for each industry arena in which the diversified company operates. And top executives at a diversified company must still go one step further and devise a companywide or *corporate strategy* for improving the attractiveness and performance of the company's overall business lineup and for making a rational business whole out of its collection of individual businesses.

In most diversified companies, corporate-level executives delegate considerable strategy-making authority to the heads of each business, usually giving them the latitude to craft a business strategy suited to their particular industry and competitive circumstances and holding them accountable for producing good results. But the task of crafting a diversified company's overall or corporate strategy falls squarely in the lap of top-level executives and involves four distinct facets:

1. *Picking new industries to enter and deciding on the means of entry:* The first concerns in diversifying are what new industries to get into and whether to enter by starting a new business from the ground up, acquiring a company already in the target industry, or forming a joint venture or strategic alliance with another company. A company can diversify narrowly into a few industries or broadly into many industries. The choice of whether to enter an industry via a start-up operation, a joint venture, or the acquisition of an established leader, an up-and-coming company, or a troubled company with turnaround potential shapes what position the company will initially stake out for itself.

2. *Initiating actions to boost the combined performance of the businesses the firm has entered:* As positions are created in the chosen industries, corporate strategists typically zero in on ways to strengthen the long-term competitive positions and profits of the businesses the firm has invested in. Corporate parents can help their business subsidiaries by providing financial resources, by supplying missing skills or technological know-how or managerial expertise to better perform key value chain activities, and by providing new avenues for cost reduction. They can also acquire another company in the same industry and merge the two operations into a stronger business or acquire new businesses that strongly complement existing businesses. Typically, a company will pursue rapid-growth strategies in its most promising businesses, initiate turnaround efforts in weak-performing businesses with potential, and divest businesses that are no longer attractive or that don't fit into management's long-range plans.

3. *Pursuing opportunities to leverage cross-business value chain relationships and strategic fits into competitive advantage:* A company that diversifies into businesses with competitively important value chain matchups (pertaining to technology, supply chain logistics, production, overlapping distribution channels, or common customers) gains competitive advantage potential not open to a company that diversifies into businesses whose value chains are totally unrelated. Capturing this competitive advantage potential requires that corporate strategists spend considerable time trying to capitalize on such cross-business opportunities

as transferring skills or technology from one business to another, reducing costs via sharing use of common facilities and resources, and utilizing the company's well-known brand names and distribution muscle to grow the sales of newly acquired products.

4. *Establishing investment priorities and steering corporate resources into the most attractive business units:* A diversified company's different businesses are usually not equally attractive from the standpoint of investing additional funds. It is incumbent on corporate management to (a) decide on the priorities for investing capital in the company's different businesses, (b) channel resources into areas where earnings potentials are higher and away from areas where they are lower, and (c) divest business units that are chronically poor performers or are in an increasingly unattractive industry. Divesting poor performers and businesses in unattractive industries frees up unproductive investments either for redeployment to promising business units or for financing attractive new acquisitions.

The demanding and time-consuming nature of these four tasks explains why corporate executives generally refrain from becoming immersed in the details of crafting and implementing business-level strategies, preferring instead to delegate lead responsibility for business strategy to the heads of each business unit.

In the first portion of this chapter we describe the various paths through which a company can become diversified, and we explain how a company can use diversification to create or compound competitive advantage for its business units. The second part of the chapter surveys techniques and procedures for assessing the attractiveness of a diversified company's business lineup, evaluating its diversification strategy, and coming up with its next set of strategic moves. In the chapter's concluding section, we survey the strategic options open to already diversified companies.

When to Diversify

As long as a company has its hands full trying to capitalize on profitable growth opportunities in its present industry, there is no urgency to pursue diversification. The big risk of a single-business company, of course, is having all of the firm's eggs in one industry basket. If demand for the industry's product is eroded by the appearance of alternative technologies, substitute products, or fast-shifting buyer preferences, or if the industry becomes competitively unattractive and unprofitable, then a company's prospects can quickly dim. Consider, for example, what digital cameras are doing to companies dependent on making camera film and doing film processing, what CD and DVD technology have done to producers of cassette tapes and 3.5-inch disks, and what mobile phones are doing to AT&T's long-distance business and the need for groundline telephones in homes.

Thus, diversifying into new industries always merits strong consideration whenever a single-business company encounters diminishing market opportunities and stagnating sales in its principal business. But there are four other instances in which a company becomes a prime candidate for diversifying:[1]

1. When it spots opportunities for expanding into industries whose technologies and products complement its present business.

2. When it can leverage existing competencies and capabilities by expanding into businesses where these same resource strengths are key success factors and valuable competitive assets.

3. When diversifying into closely related businesses opens new avenues for reducing costs.

4. When it has a powerful and well-known brand name that can be transferred to the products of other businesses and thereby used as a lever for driving up the sales and profits of such businesses.

The decision to diversify presents wide-open possibilities. A company can diversify into closely related businesses or into totally unrelated businesses. It can diversify its present revenue and earning base to a small extent (such that new businesses account for less than 15 percent of companywide revenues and profits) or to a major extent (such that new businesses produce 30 or more percent of revenues and profits). It can move into one or two large new businesses or a greater number of small ones. It can achieve multibusiness/multiindustry status by acquiring an existing company already in a business/industry it wants to enter, starting up a new business subsidiary from scratch, or entering into a joint venture.

Building Shareholder Value: The Ultimate Justification for Diversifying

Diversification must do more for a company than simply spread its business risk across various industries. In principle, diversification cannot be considered a success unless it results in *added shareholder value*—value that shareholders cannot capture on their own by purchasing stock in companies in different industries or investing in mutual funds so as to spread their investments across several industries.

For there to be reasonable expectations that a company's diversification efforts can produce added value, a move to diversify into a new business must pass three tests:[2]

1. *The industry attractiveness test:* The industry to be entered must be attractive enough to yield consistently good returns on investment. Whether an industry is attractive depends chiefly on the presence of industry and competitive conditions that are conducive to earning as-good or better profits and return on investment than the company is earning in its present business(es). It is hard to justify diversifying into an industry where profit expectations are *lower* than those in the company's present businesses.

2. *The cost-of-entry test:* The cost to enter the target industry must not be so high as to erode the potential for good profitability. A catch-22 can prevail here, however. The more attractive an industry's prospects are for growth and good long-term profitability, the more expensive it can be to get into. Entry barriers for start-up companies are likely to be high in attractive industries; were barriers low, a rush of new entrants would soon erode the potential for high profitability. And buying a well-positioned company in an appealing industry often entails a high acquisition cost that makes passing the cost-of-entry test less likely. For instance, suppose that the price to purchase a company is $3 million and that the company is earning after-tax profits of $200,000 on an equity investment of $1 million (a 20 percent annual return). Simple arithmetic requires that the profits be tripled if the purchaser (paying $3 million) is to earn the same 20 percent return. Building the acquired

firm's earnings from $200,000 to $600,000 annually could take several years—and require additional investment on which the purchaser would also have to earn a 20 percent return. Since the owners of a successful and growing company usually demand a price that reflects their business's profit prospects, it's easy for such an acquisition to fail the cost-of-entry test.

3. *The better-off test:* Diversifying into a new business must offer potential for the company's existing businesses and the new business to perform better together under a single corporate umbrella than they would perform operating as independent, stand-alone businesses. For example, let's say that company A diversifies by purchasing company B in another industry. If A and B's consolidated profits in the years to come prove no greater than what each could have earned on its own, then A's diversification won't provide its shareholders with added value. Company A's shareholders could have achieved the same $1 + 1 = 2$ result by merely purchasing stock in company B. Shareholder value is not created by diversification unless it produces a $1 + 1 = 3$ effect, where the businesses perform better together as part of the same firm than they could have performed as independent companies.

> **Core Concept**
>
> Creating added value for shareholders via diversification requires building a multibusiness company where the whole is greater than the sum of its parts.

Diversification moves that satisfy all three tests have the greatest potential to grow shareholder value over the long term. Diversification moves that can pass only one or two tests are suspect.

Strategies for Entering New Businesses

Entry into new businesses can take any of three forms: acquisition, internal start-up, or joint ventures or strategic partnerships.

Acquisition of an Existing Business

Acquisition is the most popular means of diversifying into another industry. Not only is it quicker than trying to launch a brand-new operation, but it also offers an effective way to hurdle such entry barriers as acquiring technological know-how, establishing supplier relationships, becoming big enough to match rivals' efficiency and unit costs, having to spend large sums on introductory advertising and promotions, and securing adequate distribution. Buying an ongoing operation allows the acquirer to move directly to the task of building a strong market position in the target industry, rather than getting bogged down in going the internal start-up route and trying to develop the knowledge, resources, scale of operation, and market reputation necessary to become an effective competitor within a few years.

The big dilemma an acquisition-minded firm faces is whether to pay a premium price for a successful company or to buy a struggling company at a bargain price.[3] If the buying firm has little knowledge of the industry but ample capital, it is often better off purchasing a capable, strongly positioned firm—unless the price of such an acquisition is prohibitive and flunks the cost-of-entry test. However, when the acquirer sees promising ways to transform a weak firm into a strong one and has the resources, the know-how, and the patience to do so, a struggling company can be the better long-term investment.

Internal Start-Up

Achieving diversification through *internal start-up* involves building a new business subsidiary from scratch. This entry option takes longer than the acquisition option and poses some hurdles. A newly formed business unit not only has to overcome entry barriers but also has to invest in new production capacity, develop sources of supply, hire and train employees, build channels of distribution, grow a customer base, and so on. Generally, forming a start-up subsidiary to enter a new business has appeal only when (1) the parent company already has in-house most or all of the skills and resources it needs to piece together a new business and compete effectively; (2) there is ample time to launch the business; (3) internal entry has lower costs than entry via acquisition; (4) the targeted industry is populated with many relatively small firms such that the new start-up does not have to compete head-to-head against larger, more powerful rivals; (5) adding new production capacity will not adversely impact the supply-demand balance in the industry; and (6) incumbent firms are likely to be slow or ineffective in responding to a new entrant's efforts to crack the market.[4]

> The biggest drawbacks to entering an industry by forming an internal start-up are the costs of overcoming entry barriers and the extra time it takes to build a strong and profitable competitive position.

Joint Ventures and Strategic Partnerships

Joint ventures typically entail forming a new corporate entity owned by the partners, whereas strategic partnerships represent a collaborative arrangement that usually can be terminated whenever one of the partners so chooses. A strategic partnership or joint venture can be useful in at least three types of situations.[5] First, a strategic alliance or joint venture is a good way to pursue an opportunity that is too complex, uneconomical, or risky for a single organization to pursue alone. Second, strategic alliances and joint ventures make sense when the opportunities in a new industry require a broader range of competencies and know-how than any one organization can marshal. Many of the opportunities in satellite-based telecommunications, biotechnology, and network-based systems that blend hardware, software, and services call for the coordinated development of complementary innovations and the integration of a host of financial, technical, political, and regulatory factors. In such cases, pooling the resources and competencies of two or more independent organizations is essential to generate the capabilities needed for success.

Third, joint ventures are sometimes the only way to gain entry into a desirable foreign market, especially when the foreign government requires companies wishing to enter the market to secure a local partner. Alliances with local partners have become a favorite mechanism for global companies wanting to establish footholds in desirable foreign-country markets; local partners offer outside companies the benefits of local knowledge about market conditions, customs and cultural factors, and customer buying habits. They can also be a source of managerial and marketing personnel and provide access to distribution outlets. The foreign partner's role is usually to provide specialized skills, technological know-how, and other resources needed to crack the local market and serve it efficiently.

However, as discussed in Chapters 4 and 5, partnering with another company—in the form of either an alliance or a joint venture—has significant drawbacks due to the potential for conflicting objectives, disagreements over how to best operate the venture, and so on. Joint ventures are generally the least durable of the entry options, usually lasting only until the partners decide to go their own ways.

Figure 6.1   Strategy Alternatives for a Company Looking to Diversify

Choosing the Diversification Path: Related versus Unrelated Businesses

Core Concept

Related businesses possess competitively valuable cross-business value chain matchups; **unrelated businesses** have dissimilar value chains, containing no competitively useful cross-business relationships.

Once a company decides to diversify, its first big strategy decision is whether to diversify into **related businesses, unrelated businesses,** or some mix of both (see Figure 6.1). *Businesses are said to be related when their value chains possess competitively valuable cross-business relationships that present opportunities for the businesses to perform better under the same corporate umbrella than they could by operating as stand-alone entities.* The big appeal of related diversification is to build shareholder value by leveraging these cross-business relationships into competitive advantage, thus allowing the company as a whole to perform better than just the sum of its individual businesses. *Businesses are said to be unrelated when the activities constituting their respective*

Figure 6.2   Related Businesses Possess Related Value Chain Activities and Competitively Valuable Strategic Fits

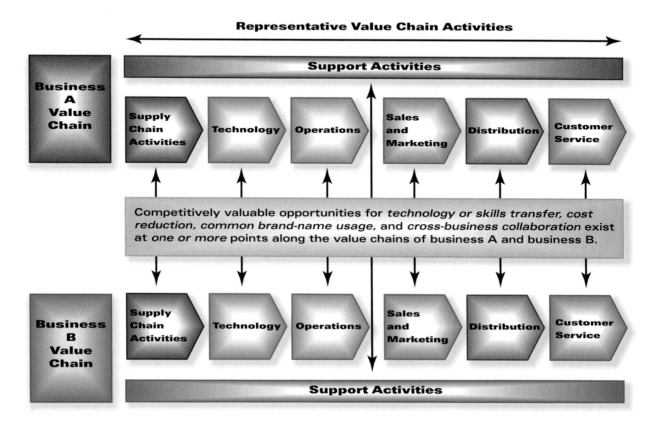

value chains are so dissimilar that no competitively valuable cross-business relationships are present.

The next two sections explore the ins and outs of related and unrelated diversification.

The Case for Diversifying into Related Businesses

A related diversification strategy involves building the company around businesses whose value chains possess competitively valuable strategic fits, as shown in Figure 6.2. **Strategic fit** exists whenever one or more activities constituting the value chains of different businesses are sufficiently similar as to present opportunities for:[6]

- Transferring competitively valuable expertise, technological know-how, or other capabilities from one business to another.
- Combining the related value chain activities of separate businesses into a single operation to achieve lower costs. For instance,

Core Concept

Strategic fit exists when the value chains of different businesses present opportunities for cross-business resource transfer, lower costs through combining the performance of related value chain activities, cross-business use of a potent brand name, and cross-business collaboration to build new or stronger competitive capabilities.

it is often feasible to manufacture the products of different businesses in a single plant or use the same warehouses for shipping and distribution or have a single sales force for the products of different businesses (because they are marketed to the same types of customers).

■ Exploiting common use of a well-known and potent brand name. For example, Honda's name in motorcycles and automobiles gave it instant credibility and recognition in entering the lawn-mower business, allowing it to achieve a significant market share without spending large sums on advertising to establish a brand identity for its lawn mowers. Canon's reputation in photographic equipment was a competitive asset that facilitated the company's diversification into copying equipment. Sony's name in consumer electronics made it easier and cheaper for Sony to enter the market for video games with its PlayStation console and lineup of PlayStation video games.

■ Collaborating across businesses to create competitively valuable resource strengths and capabilities.

Related diversification thus has strategic appeal from several angles. It allows a firm to reap the competitive advantage benefits of skills transfer, lower costs, a powerful brand name, and/or stronger competitive capabilities and still spread investor risks over a broad business base. Furthermore, the relatedness among the different businesses provides sharper focus for managing diversification and a useful degree of strategic unity across the company's various business activities.

Identifying Cross-Business Strategic Fits along the Value Chain

Cross-business strategic fits can exist anywhere along the value chain—in R&D and technology activities, in supply chain activities and relationships with suppliers, in manufacturing, in sales and marketing, in distribution activities, or in administrative support activities.[7]

Strategic Fits in R&D and Technology Activities   Diversifying into businesses where there is potential for sharing common technology, exploiting the full range of business opportunities associated with a particular technology and its derivatives, or transferring technological know-how from one business to another has considerable appeal. Businesses with technology-sharing benefits can perform better together than apart because of potential cost savings in R&D and potentially shorter times in getting new products to market; also, technological advances in one business can lead to increased sales for both. Technological innovations have been the driver behind the efforts of cable TV companies to diversify into high-speed Internet access (via the use of cable modems) and, further, to explore providing local and long-distance telephone service to residential and commercial customers in a single wire.

Strategic Fits in Supply Chain Activities   Businesses that have supply chain strategic fits can perform better together because of the potential for skills transfer in procuring materials, greater bargaining power in negotiating with common suppliers, the benefits of added collaboration with common supply chain partners, and/or added leverage with shippers in securing volume discounts on incoming parts and components. Dell Computer's strategic partnerships with leading suppliers of microprocessors, motherboards, disk drives, memory chips, monitors, modems, flat-panel displays, long-life batteries, and other PC-related components have been an important element of the company's strategy to diversify into servers, data storage devices, MP3 players, and LCD TVs—products that include many components common to PCs and that can be sourced from the same strategic partners that provide Dell with PC components.

Manufacturing-Related Strategic Fits Cross-business strategic fits in manufacturing-related activities can represent an important source of competitive advantage in situations where a diversifier's expertise in quality manufacture and cost-efficient production methods can be transferred to another business. When Emerson Electric diversified into the chain-saw business, it transferred its expertise in low-cost manufacture to its newly acquired Beaird-Poulan business division; the transfer drove Beaird-Poulan's new strategy—to be the low-cost provider of chain-saw products—and fundamentally changed the way Beaird-Poulan chain saws were designed and manufactured. Another benefit of production-related value chain matchups is the ability to consolidate production into a smaller number of plants and significantly reduce overall production costs. When snowmobile maker Bombardier diversified into motorcycles, it was able to set up motorcycle assembly lines in the same manufacturing facility where it was assembling snowmobiles. When Smucker's acquired Procter & Gamble's Jif peanut butter business, it was able to combine the manufacture of its own Smucker's peanut butter products with those of Jif, plus it gained greater leverage with vendors in purchasing its peanut supplies.

Distribution-Related Strategic Fits Businesses with closely related distribution activities can perform better together than apart because of potential cost savings in sharing the same distribution facilities or using many of the same wholesale distributors and retail dealers to access customers. When Sunbeam acquired Mr. Coffee, it was able to consolidate its own distribution centers for small household appliances with those of Mr. Coffee, thereby generating considerable cost savings. Likewise, since Sunbeam products were sold to many of the same retailers as Mr. Coffee products (Wal-Mart, Kmart, Target, department stores, home centers, hardware chains, supermarket chains, and drugstore chains), Sunbeam was able to convince many of the retailers carrying Sunbeam appliances to also take on the Mr. Coffee line and vice versa.

Strategic Fits in Sales and Marketing Activities Various cost-saving opportunities spring from diversifying into businesses with closely related sales and marketing activities. The same distribution centers can be utilized for warehousing and shipping the products of different businesses. When the products are sold directly to the same customers, sales costs can often be reduced by using a single sales force and avoiding having two different salespeople call on the same customer. The products of related businesses can be promoted at the same Web site and included in the same media ads and sales brochures. After-sale service and repair organizations for the products of closely related businesses can often be consolidated into a single operation. There may be opportunities to reduce costs by consolidating order processing and billing and using common promotional tie-ins (cents-off couponing, free samples and trial offers, seasonal specials, and the like). When global power-tool maker Black & Decker acquired General Electric's domestic small household appliance business, it was able to use its own global sales force and distribution facilities to sell and distribute the newly acquired GE line of toasters, irons, mixers, and coffeemakers because the types of customers that carried its power tools (discounters like Wal-Mart and Target, home centers, and hardware stores) also stocked small appliances. The economies Black & Decker achieved for both product lines were substantial.

A second category of benefits arises when different businesses use similar sales and marketing approaches; in such cases, there may be competitively valuable opportunities to transfer selling, merchandising, advertising, and product differentiation skills from one business to another. Procter & Gamble's product lineup includes Folgers coffee, Tide laundry detergent, Crest toothpaste, Ivory soap, Charmin toilet tissue, and Head & Shoulders shampoo. All of these have different competitors and different supply chain and production requirements, but they all move through the same wholesale distribution systems, are sold in common retail settings to the same shoppers, are advertised and promoted in much the same ways, and require the same marketing and merchandising skills.

Strategic Fits in Managerial and Administrative Support Activities   Often, different businesses require comparable types of managerial know-how, thereby allowing the know-how in one line of business to be transferred to another. At General Electric (GE), managers who were involved in GE's expansion into Russia were able to expedite entry because of information gained from GE managers involved in expansions into other emerging markets. The lessons GE managers learned in China were passed along to GE managers in Russia, allowing them to anticipate that the Russian government would demand that GE build production capacity in the country rather than enter the market through exporting or licensing. In addition, GE's managers in Russia were better able to develop realistic performance expectations and make tough up-front decisions since experience in China and elsewhere warned them (1) that there would likely be increased short-term costs during the early years of start-up and (2) that if GE committed to the Russian market for the long term and aided the country's economic development, it could eventually expect to be given the freedom to pursue profitable penetration of the Russian market.[8]

Likewise, different businesses can often use the same administrative and customer service infrastructure. For instance, an electric utility that diversifies into natural gas, water, appliance sales and repair services, and home security services can use the same customer data network, the same customer call centers and local offices, the same billing and customer accounting systems, and the same customer service infrastructure to support all of its products and services.

Company Spotlight 6.1 lists the businesses of five companies that have pursued a strategy of related diversification.

Strategic Fit, Economies of Scope, and Competitive Advantage

What makes related diversification an attractive strategy is the opportunity to convert cross-business strategic fits into a competitive advantage over business rivals whose operations do not offer comparable strategic-fit benefits. The greater the relatedness among a diversified company's businesses, the bigger a company's window for converting strategic fits into competitive advantage via (1) skills transfer, (2) combining related value chain activities to achieve lower costs, (3) leveraging use of a well-respected brand name, and/or (4) cross-business collaboration to create new resource strengths and capabilities.

> **Core Concept**
>
> **Economies of scope** are cost reductions that flow from operating in multiple businesses; such economies stem directly from strategic-fit efficiencies along the value chains of related businesses.

Economies of Scope: A Path to Competitive Advantage   One of the most important competitive advantages that a related diversification strategy can produce is lower costs than competitors. Related businesses often present opportunities to eliminate or reduce the costs of performing certain value chain activities; such cost savings are termed **economies of scope**—a concept distinct

COMPANY SPOTLIGHT 6.1

Related Diversification at Gillette, Darden Restaurants, L'Oréal, Johnson & Johnson, and PepsiCo

See if you can identify the value chain relationships which make the businesses of the following companies related in competitively relevant ways.

Gillette

- Blades and razors
- Toiletries (Right Guard, Foamy, Dry Idea, Soft & Dry, White Rain)
- Oral-B toothbrushes
- Braun shavers, coffeemakers, alarm clocks, mixers, hair dryers, and electric toothbrushes
- Duracell batteries

Darden Restaurants

- Olive Garden restaurant chain (Italian-themed)
- Red Lobster restaurant chain (seafood-themed)
- Bahama Breeze restaurant chain (Caribbean-themed)

L'Oréal

- Maybelline, Lancôme, Helena Rubenstein, Kiehl's, Garner, and Shu Uemura cosmetics
- L'Oréal and Soft Sheen/Carson hair care products
- Redken, Matrix, L'Oréal Professional, and Kerastase Paris professional hair care and skin care products
- Ralph Lauren and Giorgio Armani fragrances
- Biotherm skin care products
- La Roche-Posay and Vichy Laboratories dermo-cosmetics

Johnson & Johnson

- Baby products (powder, shampoo, oil, lotion)
- Band-Aids and other first-aid products
- Women's health and personal care products (Stayfree, Carefree, Sure & Natural)
- Neutrogena and Aveeno skin care products
- Nonprescription drugs (Tylenol, Motrin, Pepcid AC, Mylanta, Monistat)
- Prescription drugs
- Prosthetic and other medical devices
- Surgical and hospital products
- Accuvue contact lenses

PepsiCo, Inc.

- Soft drinks (Pepsi, Diet Pepsi, Pepsi One, Mountain Dew, Mug, Slice)
- Fruit juices (Tropicana and Dole)
- Sports drinks (Gatorade)
- Other beverages (Aquafina bottled water, SoBe, Lipton ready-to-drink tea, Frappucino—in partnership with Starbucks, international sales of 7UP)
- Snack foods (Fritos, Lay's, Ruffles, Doritos, Tostitos, Santitas, Smart Food, Rold Gold pretzels, Chee-tos, Grandma's cookies, Sun Chips, Cracker Jack, Frito-Lay dips and salsas)
- Cereals, rice, and breakfast products (Quaker oatmeal, Cap'n Crunch, Life, Rice-A-Roni, Quaker rice cakes, Aunt Jemima mixes and syrups, Quaker grits)

Source: Company annual reports.

---

from *economies of scale.* Economies of *scale* are cost savings that accrue directly from a larger-size operation; for example, unit costs may be lower in a large plant than in a small plant, lower in a large distribution center than in a small one, lower for large-volume purchases of components than for small-volume purchases. Economies of *scope*, however, stem directly from cost-saving strategic fits along the value chains of related businesses. Such economies are open only to a multibusiness enterprise and are the result of a related diversification strategy that allows sister businesses to share technology, perform R&D together, use common manufacturing or distribution facilities, share a common sales force or distributor/dealer network, use the same established brand name, and/or share the same administrative infrastructure. *The greater the cross-business economies associated with cost-saving strategic fits, the greater the potential for a related diversification strategy to yield a competitive advantage based on lower costs than rivals.*

From Competitive Advantage to Added Profitability and Gains in Shareholder Value   The competitive advantage potential that flows from economies of scope and the capture of other strategic-fit benefits is what

> **Core Concept**
>
> Diversifying into related businesses where competitively valuable strategic-fit benefits can be captured puts sister businesses in position to perform better financially as part of the same company than they could have performed as independent enterprises, thus providing a clear avenue for boosting shareholder value.

enables a company pursuing related diversification to achieve $1 + 1 = 3$ financial performance and the hoped-for gains in shareholder value. The strategic and business logic is compelling: capturing strategic fits along the value chains of its related businesses gives a diversified company a clear path to achieving competitive advantage over undiversified competitors and competitors whose own diversification efforts don't offer equivalent strategic-fit benefits.[9] Such competitive advantage potential provides a company with a dependable basis for earning profits and a return on investment that exceed what the company's businesses could earn as stand-alone enterprises. Converting the competitive advantage potential into greater profitability is what fuels $1 + 1 = 3$ gains in shareholder value—the necessary outcome for satisfying the better-off test and proving the business merit of a company's diversification effort.

There are two things to bear in mind here. One, capturing cross-business strategic fits via a strategy of related diversification builds shareholder value in ways that shareholders cannot undertake by simply owning a portfolio of stocks of companies in different industries. Two, the capture of cross-business strategic-fit benefits is possible only via a strategy of related diversification.

The Case for Diversifying into Unrelated Businesses

An unrelated diversification strategy discounts the merits of pursuing cross-business strategic fits and, instead, focuses squarely on entering and operating businesses in industries that allow the company as a whole to grow its revenues and earnings. Companies that pursue a strategy of unrelated diversification generally exhibit a willingness to diversify into *any industry* where senior managers see *opportunity* to realize consistently good financial results—*the basic premise of unrelated diversification is that any company or business that can be acquired on good financial terms and that has satisfactory growth and earnings potential represents a good acquisition and a good business opportunity.* With a strategy of unrelated diversification, the emphasis is on satisfying the attractiveness and cost-of-entry tests and each business's prospects for good financial performance. As indicated in Figure 6.3, there's no deliberate effort to satisfy the better-off test in the sense of diversifying only into businesses having strategic fits with the firm's other businesses.

Thus, with an unrelated diversification strategy, company managers spend much time and effort screening acquisition candidates and evaluating the pros and cons of keeping or divesting existing businesses, using such criteria as:

■   Whether the business can meet corporate targets for profitability and return on investment.

**Figure 6.3   Unrelated Businesses Have Unrelated Value Chains and
No Strategic Fits**

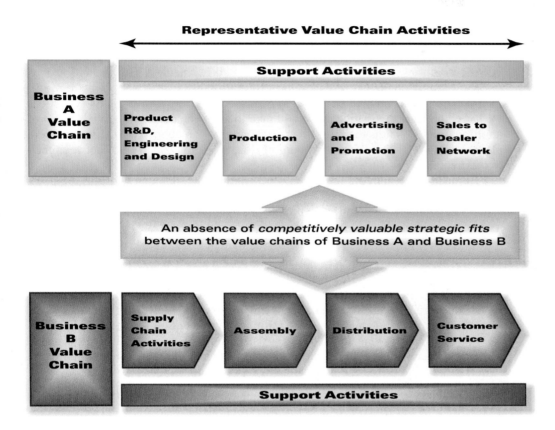

- Whether the business is in an industry with attractive growth potential.
- Whether the business is big enough to contribute *significantly* to the parent firm's bottom line.
- Whether the business has burdensome capital requirements (associated with replacing out-of-date plants and equipment, growing the business, and/or providing working capital).
- Whether the business is plagued with chronic union difficulties and labor problems.
- Whether there is industry vulnerability to recession, inflation, high interest rates, tough government regulations concerning product safety or the environment, and other potentially negative factors.

Companies that pursue unrelated diversification nearly always enter new businesses by acquiring an established company rather than by forming a start-up subsidiary within their own corporate structures. The premise of acquisition-minded corporations is that growth by acquisition can deliver enhanced shareholder value through upward-trending corporate revenues and earnings and a stock price that *on average* rises enough year after year to amply reward and please shareholders. Three types of acquisition candidates are usually of particular interest: (1) businesses that have bright growth prospects but are short on investment capital—cash-poor, opportunity-rich businesses are highly coveted acquisition targets for cash-rich companies scouting for good market opportunities; (2) undervalued companies that can be acquired at a bargain price; and (3) struggling companies whose operations can be turned around with the aid of the parent company's financial resources and managerial know-how.

A key issue in unrelated diversification is how wide a net to cast in building a portfolio of unrelated businesses. In other words, should a company pursuing unrelated diversification seek to have few or many unrelated businesses? How much business diversity can corporate executives successfully manage? A reasonable way to resolve the issue of how much diversification to pursue comes from answering two questions: "What is the least diversification it will take to achieve acceptable growth and profitability?" and "What is the most diversification that can be managed, given the complexity it adds?"[10] The optimal amount of diversification usually lies between these two extremes.

Company Spotlight 6.2 lists the businesses of three companies that have pursued unrelated diversification. Such companies are frequently labeled *conglomerates* because their business interests range broadly across diverse industries.

The Merits of an Unrelated Diversification Strategy

A strategy of unrelated diversification has appeal from several angles:

1. Business risk is scattered over a set of truly *diverse* industries. In comparison to related diversification, unrelated diversification more closely approximates *pure* diversification of financial and business risk because the company's investments are spread over businesses whose technologies and value chain activities bear no close relationship and whose markets are largely disconnected.[11]

2. The company's financial resources can be employed to maximum advantage by (a) investing in *whatever industries* offer the best profit prospects (as opposed to considering opportunities only in industries with related value chain activities) and (b) diverting cash flows from company businesses with lower growth and profit prospects to acquiring and expanding businesses with higher growth and profit potentials.

3. To the extent that corporate managers are exceptionally astute at spotting bargain-priced companies with big upside profit potential, shareholder wealth can be enhanced by buying distressed businesses at a low price, turning their operations around fairly quickly with infusions of cash and managerial know-how supplied by the parent company, and then riding the crest of the profit increases generated by the newly acquired businesses.

4. Company profitability may prove somewhat more stable over the course of economic upswings and downswings because market conditions in all industries don't move upward or downward simultaneously—in a broadly diversified company, there's a chance that market downtrends in some of the company's businesses will be partially offset by cyclical upswings in its other businesses, thus producing somewhat less earnings volatility. (In actual practice, however, there's no convincing evidence that the consolidated profits of firms with unrelated diversification strategies are more stable or less subject to reversal in periods of recession and economic stress than the profits of firms with related diversification strategies.)

Unrelated Diversification at General Electric, United Technologies, and Lancaster Colony

There are few competitively valuable cross-business relationships in the value chains of the businesses that make up General Electric, United Technologies, and Lancaster Colony. Peruse the business listings of each company below and see if you can confirm why it is fair to say that these three companies are pursuing unrelated diversification.

General Electric

- Advanced materials (engineering thermoplastics, silicon-based products and technology platforms, and fused quartz and ceramics)—revenues of $8.3 billion in 2004.

- Commercial and consumer finance (loans, operating leases, financing programs, and financial services provided to corporations, retailers, and consumers in 38 countries)—revenues of $39.2 billion in 2004.

- Major appliances, lighting, and integrated industrial equipment, systems, and services—revenues of $13.8 billion in 2004.

- Commercial insurance and reinsurance products and services for insurance companies, Fortune 1000 companies, self-insurers, health care providers, and other groups—revenues of $23.1 billion in 2004.

- Jet engines for military and civil aircraft, freight and passenger locomotives, motorized systems for mining trucks and drills, and gas turbines for marine and industrial applications—revenues of $15.6 billion in 2004.

- Electric power generation equipment, power transformers, high-voltage breakers, distribution transformers and breakers, capacitors, relays, regulators, substation equipment, metering products—revenues of $17.3 billion in 2004.

- Medical imaging and information technologies, medical diagnostics, patient monitoring systems, disease research, drug discovery and biopharmaceuticals—revenues of $13.5 billion in 2004.

- NBC Universal—owns and operates the NBC television network, a Spanish-language network (Telemundo), several news and entertainment networks (CNBC, MSNBC, Bravo, Sci-Fi Channel, USA Network), Universal Studios, various television production operations, a group of television stations, and theme parks—revenues of $12.9 billion in 2004).

- Chemical treatment programs for water and industrial process systems, precision sensors, security and safety systems for intrusion and fire detection, access and building control, video surveillance, explosives and drug detection, and real estate services—revenues of $3.4 billion in 2004.

- Equipment Services—Penske truck leasing; operating leases, loans, sales, and asset management services for owners of computer networks, trucks, trailers, railcars, construction equipment, and shipping containers—revenues of $8.5 billion in 2004.

United Technologies, Corp.

- Pratt & Whitney aircraft engines—2004 revenues of $8.3 billion.

- Carrier heating and air-conditioning equipment—2004 revenues of $10.6 billion.

- Otis elevators and escalators—2004 revenues of $9.0 billion.

- Sikorsky helicopters and Hamilton Sunstrand aerospace systems—2004 revenues of $6.4 billion.

- Chubb fire detection and security systems—2004 revenues of $2.9 billion.

Lancaster Colony Corp.

- Cardini, Marzetti, Girard's, and Pfeiffer salad dressings; Chatham Village croutons; New York Brand, Sister Schubert, and Mamma Bella frozen breads and rolls; Reames frozen noodles and pastas; Mountain Top frozen pies; and Romanoff caviar—fiscal 2004 revenues of $639 million.

- Candle-lite candles, Indiana Glass drinkware and tabletop items, Colony giftware, and Brody floral containers—fiscal 2004 revenues of $231 million.

- Automotive floor mats, Dee Zee aluminum accessories for light trucks, Koneta truck and trailer splash guards, Protecta truck bed mats, and Rubber Queen plastic accessories—fiscal 2004 revenues of $227 million.

Source: Company press releases.

Unrelated diversification certainly merits consideration when a firm is trapped in or overly dependent on an endangered or unattractive industry, especially when it has no competitively valuable resources or capabilities it can transfer to an adjacent industry. A case can also be made for unrelated diversification when a company has a strong preference for spreading business risks widely and not restricting itself to investing in a family of closely related businesses.

Building Shareholder Value via Unrelated Diversification
Given the absence of cross-business strategic fits with which to capture added competitive advantage, the task of building shareholder value via unrelated diversification ultimately hinges on the business acumen of corporate executives. To succeed in using a strategy of unrelated diversification to produce companywide financial results above and beyond what the businesses could generate operating as stand-alone entities, corporate executives must:

- Do a superior job of diversifying into new businesses that can produce consistently good earnings and returns on investment (thereby satisfying the attractiveness test).

- Do an excellent job of negotiating favorable acquisition prices (thereby satisfying the cost-of-entry test).

- Do such a good job of overseeing the firm's business subsidiaries and contributing to how they are managed—by providing expert problem-solving skills, creative strategy suggestions, and high-caliber decision-making guidance to the heads of the various business subsidiaries—that the subsidiaries perform at a higher level than they would otherwise be able to do through the efforts of the business-unit heads alone (a possible way to satisfy the better-off test).

- Be shrewd in identifying when to shift resources out of businesses with dim profit prospects and into businesses with above-average prospects for growth and profitability.

- Be good at discerning when a business needs to be sold (because it is on the verge of confronting adverse industry and competitive conditions and probable declines in long-term profitability) and also at finding buyers who will pay a price higher than the company's net investment in the business (so that the sale of divested businesses will result in capital gains for shareholders rather than capital losses).

To the extent that corporate executives are able to craft and execute a strategy of unrelated diversification that produces enough of the above outcomes to result in a stream of dividends and capital gains for stockholders greater than a $1 + 1 = 2$ outcome, a case can be made that shareholder value has truly been enhanced.

The Drawbacks of Unrelated Diversification

Unrelated diversification strategies have two important negatives that undercut the pluses: very demanding managerial requirements and limited competitive advantage potential.

Demanding Managerial Requirements Successfully managing a set of fundamentally different businesses operating in fundamentally different industry and competitive environments is a very challenging and exceptionally difficult proposition for corporate-level managers. It is difficult because key executives at the corporate level, while perhaps having personally worked in one or two of the company's businesses, rarely have the time and expertise to be sufficiently familiar with all the circumstances surrounding each of the company's businesses to be able to give high-caliber guidance to business-level managers. Indeed, the greater the number of businesses a company is in and the more diverse they are, the harder it is for corporate managers to (1) stay abreast of what's happening in each industry and each subsidiary and thus judge whether a particular business has bright prospects or is headed for trouble, (2) know enough about the issues and problems facing each subsidiary to pick business-unit heads having the requisite combination of managerial skills and know-how, (3) be able to tell the difference between those strategic proposals of business-unit managers

> **Core Concept**
>
> The two biggest drawbacks to unrelated diversification are the difficulties of competently managing many different businesses and being without the added source of competitive advantage that cross-business strategic fit provides.

that are prudent and those that are risky or unlikely to succeed, and (4) know what to do if a business unit stumbles and its results suddenly head downhill.[12]

In a company like General Electric (see Company Spotlight 6.2) or Tyco International (which acquired over 1,000 companies during the 1990–2001 period), corporate executives are constantly scrambling to stay on top of fresh industry developments and the strategic progress and plans of each subsidiary, often depending on briefings by business-level managers for many of the details. As a rule, the more unrelated businesses that a company has diversified into, the more that corporate executives are dependent on briefings from business-unit heads and "managing by the numbers"—that is, keeping a close track on the financial and operating results of each subsidiary and assuming that the heads of the various subsidiaries have most everything under control so long as the latest key financial and operating measures look good. Managing by the numbers works okay if the heads of the various business units are quite capable and consistently meet their numbers. But the problem comes when things start to go awry in a business despite the best efforts of business-unit managers and corporate management has to get deeply involved in turning around a business it does not know all that much about. As the former chairman of a Fortune 500 company advised, "Never acquire a business you don't know how to run." Because every business tends to encounter rough sledding, a good way to gauge the merits of acquiring a company in an unrelated industry is to ask, "If the business gets into trouble, is corporate management likely to know how to bail it out?" When the answer is no (or even a qualified yes or maybe), growth via acquisition into unrelated businesses is a chancy strategy.[13] Just one or two unforeseen declines or big strategic mistakes (misjudging the importance of certain competitive forces or the impact of driving forces or key success factors, encountering unexpected problems in a newly acquired business, or being too optimistic about turning around a struggling subsidiary) can cause a precipitous drop in corporate earnings and crash the parent company's stock price.

Hence, competently overseeing a set of widely diverse businesses can turn out to be much harder than it sounds. In practice, comparatively few companies have proved that they have top-management capabilities that are up to the task. There are far more companies whose corporate executives have failed at delivering consistently good financial results with an unrelated diversification strategy than there are companies with corporate executives who have been successful.[14] It is simply more difficult than it might seem for corporate executives to achieve $1 + 1 = 3$ gains in shareholder value based on their expertise in (1) picking which industries to diversify into and which companies in these industries to acquire, (2) shifting resources from low-performing businesses into high-performing businesses, and (3) giving high-caliber decision-making guidance to the general managers of their business subsidiaries. The odds are that the result of unrelated diversification will be $1 + 1 = 2$ or less.

> Relying solely on the expertise of corporate executives to wisely manage a set of unrelated businesses is *a much weaker foundation for enhancing shareholder value* than is a strategy of related diversification where corporate performance can be boosted by competitively valuable cross-business strategic fits.

Limited Competitive Advantage Potential   The second big negative is that *unrelated diversification offers no potential for competitive advantage beyond what each individual business can generate on its own.* Unlike a related diversification strategy, there are no cross-business strategic fits to draw on for reducing costs, beneficially transferring skills and technology, leveraging use of a powerful brand name, or collaborating to build mutually beneficial competitive capabilities and thereby *adding to any competitive advantage possessed by individual businesses.* Yes, a cash-rich corporate parent pursuing unrelated diversification can provide its subsidiaries with much-needed capital and maybe even the managerial know-how to help resolve problems in particular business units, but otherwise it has little to offer in the way of enhancing the competitive strength of its individual business units. *Without the competitive advantage potential of strategic fits, consolidated performance of an unrelated group of businesses stands to be little or no better than the sum of what the individual business units could achieve if they were independent.*

Combination Related-Unrelated Diversification Strategies

There's nothing to preclude a company from diversifying into both related and unrelated businesses. Indeed, in actual practice the business makeup of diversified companies varies considerably. Some diversified companies are really *dominant-business enterprises*—one major "core" business accounts for 50 to 80 percent of total revenues, and a collection of small related or unrelated businesses accounts for the remainder. Some diversified companies are *narrowly diversified* around a few (two to five) related or unrelated businesses. Others are *broadly diversified* around a wide-ranging collection of related businesses, unrelated businesses, or a mixture of both. And a number of multibusiness enterprises have diversified into unrelated areas but have a collection of related businesses within each area—thus giving them a business portfolio consisting of *several unrelated groups of related businesses.* There's ample room for companies to customize their diversification strategies to incorporate elements of both related and unrelated diversification, as may suit their own risk preferences and strategic vision.

Figure 6.4 indicates what to look for in identifying the main elements of a company's diversification strategy. Having a clear fix on the company's current corporate strategy sets the stage for evaluating how good the strategy is and proposing strategic moves to boost the company's performance.

Evaluating the Strategy of a Diversified Company

Strategic analysis of diversified companies builds on the concepts and methods used for single-business companies. But there are some additional aspects to consider and a couple of new analytical tools to master. The procedure for evaluating the pluses and minuses of a diversified company's strategy and deciding what actions to take to improve the company's performance involves six steps:

1. Assessing the attractiveness of the industries the company has diversified into, both individually and as a group.

2. Assessing the competitive strength of the company's business units and determining how many are strong contenders in their respective industries.

3. Checking the competitive advantage potential of cross-business strategic fits among the company's various business units.

4. Checking whether the firm's resources fit the requirements of its present business lineup.

5. Ranking the performance prospects of the businesses from best to worst and determining what the corporate parent's priority should be in allocating resources to its various businesses.

6. Crafting new strategic moves to improve overall corporate performance.

The core concepts and analytical techniques underlying each of these steps merit further discussion.

Figure 6.4   Identifying a Diversified Company's Strategy

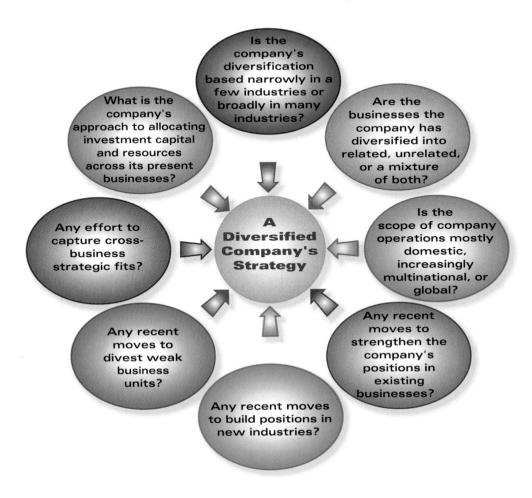

Step 1: Evaluating Industry Attractiveness

A principal consideration in evaluating a diversified company's business makeup and the caliber of its strategy is the attractiveness of the industries in which it has business operations. Answers to several questions are required:

1. *Does each industry the company has diversified into represent a good business for the company to be in?* Ideally, each industry in which the firm operates will pass the attractiveness test.

2. *Which of the company's industries are most attractive, and which are least attractive?* Comparing the attractiveness of the industries and ranking them from most to least attractive is a prerequisite to wise allocation of corporate resources across the various businesses.

3. *How appealing is the whole group of industries in which the company has invested?* The answer to this question points to whether the group of industries holds promise for attractive growth and profitability. A company whose revenues and profits come chiefly from businesses in relatively unattractive industries probably needs to look at divesting businesses in unattractive industries and entering industries that qualify as highly attractive.

The more attractive the industries (both individually and as a group) a diversified company is in, the better its prospects for good long-term performance.

Calculating Industry Attractiveness Scores for Each Industry into Which the Company Has Diversified   A simple and reliable analytical tool involves calculating quantitative industry attractiveness scores, which can then be used to gauge each industry's attractiveness, rank the industries from most to least attractive, and make judgments about the attractiveness of all the industries as a group.

The following measures are typically used to gauge an industry's attractiveness:

- *Market size and projected growth rate:* Big industries are more attractive than small industries, and fast-growing industries tend to be more attractive than slow-growing industries, other things being equal.

- *The intensity of competition:* Industries where competitive pressures are relatively weak are more attractive than industries where competitive pressures are strong.

- *Emerging opportunities and threats:* Industries with promising opportunities and minimal threats on the near horizon are more attractive than industries with modest opportunities and imposing threats.

- *The presence of cross-industry strategic fits:* The more the industry's value chain and resource requirements match up well with the value chain activities of other industries in which the company has operations, the more attractive the industry is to a firm pursuing related diversification. However, cross-industry strategic fits may be of no consequence to a company committed to a strategy of unrelated diversification.

- *Resource requirements:* Industries having resource requirements within the company's reach are more attractive than industries where capital and other resource requirements could strain corporate financial resources and organizational capabilities.

- *Seasonal and cyclical factors:* Industries where buyer demand is relatively steady year-round and not unduly vulnerable to economic ups and downs tend to be more attractive than industries where there are wide swings in buyer demand within or across years. However, seasonality may be a plus for a company that is in several seasonal industries, if the seasonal highs in one industry correspond to the lows in another industry, thus helping even out monthly sales levels. Likewise, cyclical market demand in one industry can be attractive if its up-cycle runs counter to the market down-cycles in another industry where the company operates, thus helping reduce revenue and earnings volatility.

■ *Social, political, regulatory, and environmental factors:* Industries that have significant problems in such areas as consumer health, safety, or environmental pollution or that are subject to intense regulation are less attractive than industries where such problems are not burning issues.

■ *Industry profitability:* Industries with healthy profit margins and high rates of return on investment are generally more attractive than industries where profits have historically been low or unstable.

■ *Industry uncertainty and business risk:* Industries with less uncertainty on the horizon and lower overall business risk are more attractive than industries whose prospects, for one reason or another, are quite uncertain, especially when the industry has formidable resource requirements.

After settling on a set of attractiveness measures that suit a diversified company's circumstances, each attractiveness measure is assigned a weight reflecting its relative importance in determining an industry's attractiveness—it is weak methodology to assume that the various attractiveness measures are equally important. The intensity of competition in an industry should nearly always carry a high weight (say, 0.20 to 0.30). Strategic-fit considerations should be assigned a high weight in the case of companies with related diversification strategies; for companies with unrelated diversification strategies, strategic fits with other industries may be given a low weight or even dropped from the list of attractiveness measures altogether. Seasonal and cyclical factors generally are assigned a low weight (or maybe even eliminated from the analysis) unless a company has diversified into industries strongly characterized by seasonal demand and/or heavy vulnerability to cyclical upswings and downswings. The importance weights must add up to 1.

Next, each industry is rated on each of the chosen industry attractiveness measures, using a rating scale of 1 to 10 (where a *high* rating signifies *high* attractiveness and a *low* rating signifies *low* attractiveness). Keep in mind here that the more intensely competitive an industry is, the *lower* the attractiveness rating for that industry. Likewise, the higher the capital and resource requirements associated with being in a particular industry, the lower the attractiveness rating. And an industry that is subject to stringent pollution control regulations or that causes societal problems (like cigarettes or alcoholic beverages) should be given a low attractiveness rating. Weighted attractiveness scores are then calculated by multiplying the industry's rating on each measure by the corresponding weight. For example, a rating of 8 times a weight of 0.25 gives a weighted attractiveness score of 2.00. The sum of the weighted scores for all the attractiveness measures provides an overall industry attractiveness score. This procedure is illustrated in Table 6.1.

Interpreting the Industry Attractiveness Scores   Industries with a score much below 5 probably do not pass the attractiveness test. If a company's industry attractiveness scores are all above 5, it is probably fair to conclude that the group of industries the company operates in is attractive as a whole. But the group of

Table 6.1   CALCULATING WEIGHTED INDUSTRY ATTRACTIVENESS SCORES

(Rating scale: 1 = very unattractive to company; 10 = very attractive to company.)

Industry Attractiveness Measure	Importance Weight	Rating/Score			
		Industry A	Industry B	Industry C	Industry D
Market size and projected growth rate	0.10	8/0.80	5/0.50	7/0.70	3/0.30
Intensity of competition	0.25	8/2.00	7/1.75	3/0.75	2/0.50
Emerging opportunities and threats	0.10	2/0.20	9/0.90	4/0.40	5/0.50
Cross-industry strategic fits	0.20	8/1.60	4/0.80	8/1.60	2/0.40
Resource requirements	0.10	9/0.90	7/0.70	10/1.00	5/0.50
Seasonal and cyclical influences	0.05	9/0.45	8/0.40	10/0.50	5/0.25
Societal, political, regulatory, and environmental factors	0.05	10/1.00	7/0.70	7/0.70	3/0.30
Industry profitability	0.10	5/0.50	10/1.00	3/0.30	3/0.30
Industry uncertainty and business risk	0.05	5/0.25	7/0.35	10/0.50	1/0.05
Sum of the assigned weights	1.00				
Overall industry attractiveness scores		**7.70**	**7.10**	**5.45**	**3.10**

industries takes on a decidedly lower degree of attractiveness as the number of industries with scores below 5 increases, especially if industries with low scores account for a sizable fraction of the company's revenues.

For a diversified company to be a strong performer, a substantial portion of its revenues and profits must come from business units with relatively high attractiveness scores. It is particularly important that a diversified company's principal businesses be in industries with a good outlook for growth and above-average profitability. Having a big fraction of the company's revenues and profits come from industries with slow growth, low profitability, or intense competition tends to drag overall company performance down. Business units in the least attractive industries are potential candidates for divestiture, unless they are positioned strongly enough to overcome the unattractive aspects of their industry environments or they are a strategically important component of the company's business makeup.

The Difficulties of Calculating Industry Attractiveness Scores   There are two hurdles to using this method of evaluating industry attractiveness. One is deciding on appropriate weights for the industry attractiveness measures. Not only may different analysts have different views about which weights are appropriate for the different attractiveness measures, but also different weightings may be appropriate for different companies—based on their strategies, performance targets, and financial circumstances. For instance, placing a low weight on industry resource requirements may be justifiable for a cash-rich company, whereas a high weight may be more appropriate for a financially strapped company. The second hurdle is gaining sufficient command of the industry to assign accurate and objective ratings. Generally, a company can come up with the statistical data needed to compare its industries on such factors as market size, growth rate, seasonal and cyclical influences, and industry profitability. Cross-industry fits and resource requirements are also fairly easy to judge. But the attractiveness measure where judgment weighs most heavily is that of intensity of competition. It is not always easy to conclude whether competition is stronger or weaker in one industry than in another industry because of the different types of competitive influences that prevail and the differences in their relative importance. In the event that the available information is too skimpy to confidently assign a rating value to an industry on a particular attractiveness measure, then it is usually best to use a score of 5, which avoids biasing the overall attractiveness score either up or down.

Despite the hurdles, calculating industry attractiveness scores is a systematic and reasonably reliable method for ranking a diversified company's industries from most to least attractive—numbers like those shown for the four industries in Table 6.1 help pin down the basis for judging which industries are more attractive and to what degree.

Step 2: Evaluating Business-Unit Competitive Strength

The second step in evaluating a diversified company is to appraise how strongly positioned each of its business units are in their respective industry. Doing an appraisal of each business unit's strength and competitive position in its industry not only reveals its chances for industry success but also provides a basis for ranking the units from competitively strongest to competitively weakest and sizing up the competitive strength of all the business units as a group.

Calculating Competitive Strength Scores for Each Business Unit Quantitative measures of each business unit's competitive strength can be calculated using a procedure similar to that for measuring industry attractiveness. The following factors are used in quantifying the competitive strengths of a diversified company's business subsidiaries:

- *Relative market share:* A business unit's *relative market share* is defined as the ratio of its market share to the market share held by the largest rival firm in the industry, with market share measured in unit volume, not dollars. For instance, if business A has a market-leading share of 40 percent and its largest rival has 30 percent, A's relative market share is 1.33. (Note that only business units that are market share leaders in their respective industries can have relative market shares greater then 1.) If business B has a 15 percent market share and B's largest rival has 30 percent, B's relative market share is 0.5. The further below 1 a business unit's relative market share is, the weaker its competitive strength and market position vis-à-vis rivals. A 10 percent market share, for example, does not signal much competitive strength if the leader's share is 50 percent (a 0.20 relative market share), but a 10 percent share is actually quite strong if the leader's share is only 12 percent (a 0.83 relative market share)—this is why a company's relative market share is a better measure of competitive strength than a company's market share based on either dollars or unit volume.

> Using relative market share to measure competitive strength is analytically superior to using straight-percentage market share.

- *Costs relative to competitors' costs*: Business units that have low costs relative to key competitors' costs tend to be more strongly positioned in their industries than business units struggling to maintain cost parity with major rivals. Assuming that the prices charged by industry rivals are about the same, there's reason to expect that business units with higher relative market shares have lower unit costs than competitors with lower relative market shares because their greater unit sales volumes offer the possibility of economies from larger-scale operations and the benefits of any experience- or learning-curve effects. Another indicator of low cost can be a business unit's supply chain management capabilities. The only time when a business unit's competitive strength may not be undermined by having higher costs than rivals is when it has incurred the higher costs to strongly differentiate its product offering and its customers are willing to pay premium prices for the differentiating features.

■ *Ability to match or beat rivals on key product attributes*: A company's competitiveness depends in part on being able to satisfy buyer expectations with regard to features, product performance, reliability, service, and other important attributes.

■ *Ability to benefit from strategic fits with sister businesses*: Strategic fits with other businesses within the company enhance a business unit's competitive strength and may provide a competitive edge.

■ *Ability to exercise bargaining leverage with key suppliers or customers*: Having bargaining leverage signals competitive strength and can be a source of competitive advantage.

■ *Caliber of alliances and collaborative partnerships with suppliers and/or buyers*: Well-functioning alliances and partnerships may signal a potential competitive advantage vis-à-vis rivals and thus add to a business's competitive strength. Alliances with key suppliers are often the basis for competitive strength in supply chain management.

■ *Brand image and reputation*: A strong brand name is a valuable competitive asset in most industries.

■ *Competitively valuable capabilities*: Business units recognized for their technological leadership, product innovation, or marketing prowess are usually strong competitors in their industry. Skills in supply chain management can generate valuable cost or product differentiation advantages. So can unique production capabilities. Sometimes a company's business units gain competitive strength because of their knowledge of customers and markets and/or their proven managerial capabilities. *An important thing to look for here is how well a business unit's competitive assets match industry key success factors.* The more a business unit's resource strengths and competitive capabilities match the industry's key success factors, the stronger its competitive position tends to be.

■ *Profitability relative to competitors*: Business units that consistently earn above-average returns on investment and have bigger profit margins than their rivals usually have stronger competitive positions. Moreover, above-average profitability signals competitive advantage, while below-average profitability usually denotes competitive disadvantage.

After settling on a set of competitive strength measures that are well matched to the circumstances of the various business units, weights indicating each measure's importance need to be assigned. A case can be made for using different weights for different business units whenever the importance of the strength measures differs significantly from business to business, but otherwise it is simpler just to go with a single set of weights and avoid the added complication of multiple weights. As before, the importance weights must add up to 1. Each business unit is then rated on each of the chosen strength measures, using a rating scale of 1 to 10 (where a *high* rating signifies competitive *strength* and a *low* rating signifies competitive *weakness*). In the event that the available information is too skimpy to confidently assign a rating value to a business unit on a particular strength measure, then it is usually best to use a score of 5, which avoids biasing the overall score either up or down. Weighted strength ratings are

Table 6.2   CALCULATING WEIGHTED COMPETITIVE STRENGTH SCORES FOR A DIVERSIFIED COMPANY'S BUSINESS UNITS

(Rating scale: 1 = very weak; 10 = very strong.)

Competitive Strength Measure	Importance Weight	Rating/Score			
		Business A in Industry A	Business B in Industry B	Business C in Industry C	Business D in Industry D
Relative market share	0.15	10/1.50	1/0.15	6/0.90	2/0.30
Costs relative to competitors' costs	0.20	7/1.40	2/0.40	5/1.00	3/0.60
Ability to match or beat rivals on key product attributes	0.05	9/0.45	4/0.20	8/0.40	4/0.20
Ability to benefit from strategic fits with company's other businesses	0.20	8/1.60	4/0.80	8/0.80	2/0.60
Bargaining leverage with suppliers/ buyers; caliber of alliances	0.05	9/0.90	3/0.30	6/0.30	2/0.10
Brand image and reputation	0.10	9/0.90	2/0.20	7/0.70	5/0.50
Competitively valuable capabilities	0.15	7/1.05	2/0.20	5/0.75	3/0.45
Profitability relative to competitors	0.10	5/0.50	1/0.10	4/0.40	4/0.40
Sum of the assigned weights	1.00				
Overall industry attractiveness scores		**8.30**	**2.35**	**5.25**	**3.15**

calculated by multiplying the business unit's rating on each strength measure by the assigned weight. For example, a strength score of 6 times a weight of 0.15 gives a weighted strength rating of 0.90. The sum of weighted ratings across all the strength measures provides a quantitative measure of a business unit's overall market strength and competitive standing. Table 6.2 provides sample calculations of competitive strength ratings for four businesses.

Interpreting the Competitive Strength Scores   Business units with competitive strength ratings above 6.7 (on a scale of 1 to 10) are strong market contenders in their industries. Businesses with ratings in the 3.3 to 6.7 range have moderate competitive strength vis-à-vis rivals. Businesses with ratings below 3.3 are in competitively weak market positions. If a diversified company's business units all have competitive strength scores above 5, it is fair to conclude that its business units are all fairly strong market contenders in their respective industries. But as the number of business units with scores below 5 increases, there's reason to question whether the company can perform well with so many businesses in relatively weak competitive positions. This concern takes on even more importance when business units with low scores account for a sizable fraction of the company's revenues.

Using a Nine-Cell Matrix to Simultaneously Portray Industry Attractiveness and Competitive Strength   The industry attractiveness and business strength scores can be used to portray the strategic positions of each business in a diversified company. Industry attractiveness is plotted on the vertical axis, and competitive strength on the horizontal axis. A nine-cell grid emerges from dividing the vertical axis into three regions (high, medium, and low attractiveness) and the horizontal axis into three regions (strong, average, and weak competitive strength). As shown in Figure 6.5, high attractiveness is associated with scores of 6.7 or greater

Figure 6.5   A Nine-Cell Industry Attractiveness–Competitive Strength Matrix

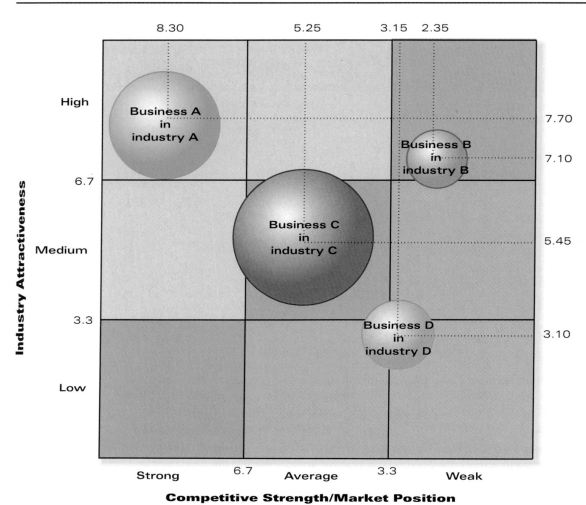

High priority for resource allocation
Medium priority for resource allocation
Low priority for resource allocation

Note: Circle sizes are scaled to reflect the percentage of companywide revenues generated by the business unit.

on a rating scale of 1 to 10; medium attractiveness, to scores of 3.3 to 6.7; and low attractiveness, to scores below 3.3. Likewise, high competitive strength is defined as scores greater than 6.7; average strength, as scores of 3.3 to 6.7; and low strength, as scores below 3.3. *Each business unit is plotted on the nine-cell matrix according to its overall attractiveness score and strength score and then shown as a "bubble."* The size of each bubble is scaled to what percentage of revenues the business generates relative to total corporate revenues. The bubbles in Figure 6.5 were located on the grid using the four industry attractiveness scores from Table 6.1 and the strength scores for the four business units in Table 6.2.

The locations of the business units on the attractiveness-strength matrix provide valuable guidance in deploying corporate resources to the various business units. In general, *a diversified company's prospects for good overall performance are enhanced by concentrating corporate resources and strategic attention on those business units having the greatest competitive strength and positioned in highly attractive industries*—specifically, businesses in the three cells in the upper left portion of the attractiveness-strength matrix, where industry attractiveness and competitive strength/market position are both favorable. The general strategic prescription for businesses falling into these three cells (for instance, business A in Figure 6.5) is "grow and build," with businesses in the high-strong cell standing first in line for resource allocations by the corporate parent.

Next in priority come businesses positioned in the three diagonal cells stretching from the lower left to the upper right (businesses B and C in Figure 6.5). Such businesses usually merit medium or intermediate priority in the parent's resource allocation ranking. However, some businesses in the medium-priority diagonal cells may have brighter or dimmer prospects than others. For example, a small business in the upper right cell of the matrix (like business B), despite being in a highly attractive industry, may occupy too weak a competitive position in its industry to justify the investment and resources needed to turn it into a strong market contender and shift its position leftward in the matrix over time. If, however, a business in the upper right cell has attractive opportunities for rapid growth and a good potential for winning a much stronger market position over time, it may merit a high claim on the corporate parent's resource allocation ranking and be given the capital it needs to pursue a grow-and-build strategy—the strategic objective here would be to move the business leftward in the attractiveness-strength matrix over time.

Businesses in the three cells in the lower right corner of the matrix (like business D in Figure 6.5) typically are weak performers and have the lowest claim on corporate resources. Most such businesses are good candidates for being divested (sold to other companies) or else managed in a manner calculated to squeeze out the maximum cash flows from operations—the cash flows from low-performing/low-potential businesses can then be diverted to financing expansion of business units with greater market opportunities. In exceptional cases where a business located in the three lower right cells is nonetheless fairly profitable (which it might be if it is in the low-average cell) or has the potential for good earnings and return on investment, the business merits retention and the allocation of sufficient resources to achieve better performance.

The nine-cell attractiveness-strength matrix provides clear, strong logic for why a diversified company needs to consider both industry attractiveness and business strength in allocating resources and investment capital to its different businesses. A good case can be made for concentrating resources in those businesses that enjoy higher degrees of attractiveness and competitive strength, being very selective in making investments in businesses with intermediate positions on the grid, and withdrawing resources from businesses that are lower in attractiveness and strength unless they offer exceptional profit or cash flow potential.

Step 3: Checking the Competitive Advantage Potential of Cross-Business Strategic Fits

While this step can be bypassed for diversified companies whose businesses are all unrelated (since, by design, no strategic fits are present), a high potential for converting strategic fits into competitive advantage is central to concluding just how good a

Core Concept

A company's related diversification strategy derives its power in large part from the presence of competitively valuable strategic fits among its businesses.

company's related diversification strategy is. Checking the competitive advantage potential of cross-business strategic fits involves searching for and evaluating how much benefit a diversified company can gain from value chain matchups that present (1) opportunities to combine the performance of certain activities, thereby reducing costs and capturing economies of scope, (2) opportunities to transfer skills, technology, or intellectual capital from one business to another, thereby leveraging use of existing resources, (3) opportunities to share use of a well-respected brand name, and (4) opportunities for the company's other businesses to collaborate in creating valuable new competitive capabilities (such as enhanced supply chain management capabilities, quicker first-to-market capabilities, or greater product innovation capabilities).

Figure 6.6 illustrates the process of comparing the value chains of a company's businesses and identifying competitively valuable cross-business strategic fits. *But more than just strategic-fit identification is needed. The real test is what competitive value can be generated from these fits.* To what extent can cost savings be realized? How much competitive value will come from cross-business transfer of skills, technology, or

Figure 6.6   Identifying the Competitive Advantage Potential of Cross-Business Strategic Fits

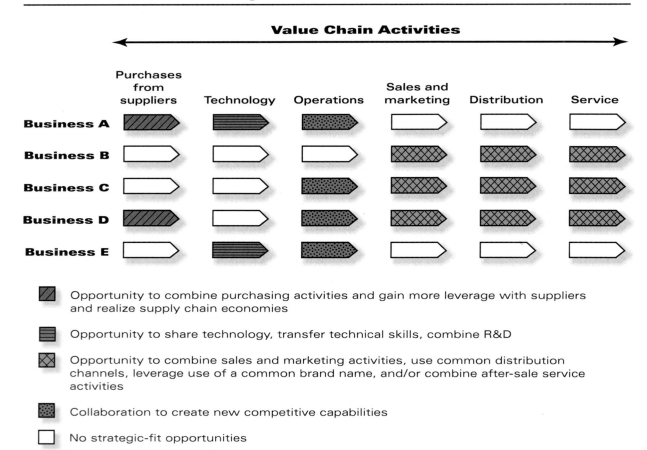

	Opportunity to combine purchasing activities and gain more leverage with suppliers and realize supply chain economies
	Opportunity to share technology, transfer technical skills, combine R&D
	Opportunity to combine sales and marketing activities, use common distribution channels, leverage use of a common brand name, and/or combine after-sale service activities
	Collaboration to create new competitive capabilities
	No strategic-fit opportunities

intellectual capital? Will transferring a potent brand name to the products of sister businesses grow sales significantly? Will cross-business collaboration to create or strengthen competitive capabilities lead to significant gains in the marketplace or in financial performance? Without significant strategic fits and dedicated company efforts to capture the benefits, one has to be skeptical about the potential for a diversified company's businesses to perform better together than apart.

Step 4: Checking for Resource Fit

The businesses in a diversified company's lineup need to exhibit good **resource fit.** Resource fit exists when (1) the businesses add to a company's overall resource strengths and (2) a company has the resources to adequately support its businesses as a group without spreading itself too thin. One important dimension of resource fit concerns whether a diversified company can generate the internal cash flows sufficient to fund the capital requirements of its businesses, pay its dividends, meet its debt obligations, and otherwise remain financially healthy.

> **Core Concept**
>
> A company's businesses exhibit **resource fit** when the various businesses, individually and collectively, add to the company's overall resource strengths and when the company's complement of resources is adequate to support the requirements of its business units.

Financial Resource Fits: Cash Cows versus Cash Hogs
Different businesses have different cash flow and investment characteristics. For example, business units in rapidly growing industries are often **cash hogs**—so labeled because the cash flows they are able to generate from internal operations aren't big enough to fund their expansion. To keep pace with rising buyer demand, rapid-growth businesses frequently need sizable annual capital investments—for new facilities and equipment, for new product development or technology improvements, and for additional working capital to support inventory expansion and a larger base of operations. A business in a fast-growing industry becomes an even bigger cash hog when it has a relatively low market share and is pursuing a strategy to become an industry leader. Because a cash hog's financial resources must be provided by the corporate parent, corporate managers have to decide whether it makes good financial and strategic sense to keep pouring additional money into a business that continually needs cash infusions.

> **Core Concept**
>
> A **cash hog** is a business whose internal cash flows are inadequate to fully fund its needs for working capital and new capital investment.

In contrast, business units with leading market positions in mature industries may, however, be **cash cows**—businesses that generate substantial cash surpluses over what is needed to adequately fund their operations. Market leaders in slow-growth industries often generate sizable positive cash flows *over and above what is needed for growth and reinvestment* because their industry-leading positions tend to give them the sales volumes and reputation to earn attractive profits and because the slow-growth nature of their industries often entails relatively modest annual investment requirements. Cash cows, though not always attractive from a growth standpoint, are valuable businesses from a financial resource perspective. The surplus cash flows they generate can be used to pay corporate dividends, finance acquisitions, and provide funds for investing in the company's promising cash hogs. It makes good financial and strategic sense for diversified companies to keep cash cows in healthy condition, fortifying and defending their market position so as to preserve their cash-generating capability over the long term and thereby have an ongoing source of financial resources to deploy elsewhere. The cigarette business is one of the world's biggest cash-cow businesses. General Electric, whose business lineup is

> **Core Concept**
>
> A **cash cow** is a business that generates cash flows over and above its internal requirements, thus providing a corporate parent with funds for investing in cash hog businesses, financing new acquisitions, or paying dividends.

shown in Company Spotlight 6.2 on page 205, considers that its advanced materials, equipment services, and appliance and lighting businesses are cash cow businesses.

Viewing a diversified group of businesses as a collection of cash flows and cash requirements (present and future) is a major step forward in understanding what the financial ramifications of diversification are and why having businesses with good financial resource fit is so important. For instance, *a diversified company's businesses exhibit good financial resource fit when the excess cash generated by its cash-cow businesses is sufficient to fund the investment requirements of promising cash-hog businesses.* Ideally, investing in promising cash-hog businesses over time results in growing the hogs into self-supporting *star businesses* that have strong or market-leading competitive positions in attractive, high-growth markets and have high levels of profitability. Star businesses are often the cash cows of the future—when the markets of star businesses begin to mature and their growth slows, their competitive strength should produce self-generated cash flows more than sufficient to cover their investment needs. The "success sequence" is thus cash hog to young star (but perhaps still a cash hog) to self-supporting star to cash cow.

If, however, a cash hog has questionable promise (either because of low industry attractiveness or a weak competitive position), then it becomes a logical candidate for divestiture. Pursuing an aggressive invest-and-expand strategy for a cash hog with an uncertain future seldom makes sense because it requires the corporate parent to keep pumping more capital into the business with only a dim hope of eventually turning the cash hog into a future star and realizing a good return on its investments. Such businesses are a financial drain and fail the resource-fit test because they strain the corporate parent's ability to adequately fund its other businesses. Divesting a less attractive cash-hog business is usually the best alternative unless (1) it has valuable strategic fits with other business units or (2) the capital infusions needed from the corporate parent are modest relative to the funds available and there's a decent chance of growing the business into a solid bottom-line contributor yielding a good return on invested capital.

Other Tests of Resource Fit   Aside from cash flow considerations, there are two other factors to consider in determining whether the businesses constituting a diversified company's portfolio exhibit good resource fit from a financial perspective:

- *Does the business adequately contribute to achieving companywide performance targets?* A business has good financial fit when it contributes to the achievement of corporate performance objectives (growth in earnings per share, above-average return on investment, recognition as an industry leader, etc.) and when it materially enhances shareholder value via helping drive increases in the company's stock price. A business exhibits poor financial fit if it soaks up a disproportionate share of the company's financial resources, makes subpar or inconsistent bottom-line contributions, is unduly risky and its failure would jeopardize the entire enterprise, or remains too small to make a material earnings contribution even though it performs well.

- *Does the company have adequate financial strength to fund its different businesses and still maintain a healthy credit rating?* A diversified company's strategy fails the resource-fit test when its financial resources are stretched across so many businesses that its credit rating is impaired. Severe financial strain sometimes occurs when a company borrows so heavily to finance new acquisitions that it has to trim way back on capital expenditures for existing businesses and use the big majority of its financial resources to meet interest obligations and to pay down debt. Time Warner, Royal Ahold, and AT&T, for example, have found themselves so financially overextended that they have had to sell off some of their business units to raise the money to pay down burdensome debt obligations and continue to fund essential capital expenditures for the remaining businesses.

■ *Does the company have or can it develop the specific resource strengths and competitive capabilities needed to be successful in each of its businesses?*[15] Sometimes the resource strengths a company has accumulated in its core or mainstay business prove to be a poor match with the key success factors and competitive capabilities needed to succeed in one or more businesses it has diversified into. For instance, BTR, a multibusiness company in Great Britain, discovered that its resources and managerial skills were quite well suited for parenting industrial manufacturing businesses but not for parenting its distribution businesses (National Tyre Services and Texas-based Summers Group); as a consequence, BTR decided to divest its distribution businesses and focus exclusively on diversifying around small industrial manufacturing.[16] One company with businesses in restaurants and retailing decided that its resource capabilities in site selection, control of operating costs, management selection and training, and supply chain logistics would enable it to succeed in the hotel business and in property management; but what management missed was that these businesses had some significantly different key success factors—namely, skills in controlling property development costs, maintaining low overheads, branding products (hotels), and recruiting a sufficient volume of business to maintain high levels of facility utilization.[17] Thus, a mismatch between the company's resource strengths and the key success factors in a particular business can be serious enough to warrant divesting an existing business or not acquiring a new business. In contrast, when a company's resources and capabilities are a good match with the key success factors of industries it is not presently in, it makes sense to take a hard look at acquiring companies in these industries and expanding the company's business lineup.

■ *Are recently acquired businesses acting to strengthen a company's resource base and competitive capabilities, or are they causing its competitive and managerial resources to be stretched too thinly?* A diversified company has to guard against overtaxing its resource strengths, a condition that can arise when (1) it goes on an acquisition spree and management is called upon to assimilate and oversee many new businesses very quickly or (2) it lacks sufficient resource depth to do a creditable job of transferring skills and competencies from one of its businesses to another (especially, a large acquisition or several lesser ones). The broader the diversification, the greater the concern about whether the company has sufficient managerial depth to cope with the diverse range of operating problems its wide business lineup presents. And the more a company's diversification strategy is tied to transferring its existing know-how or technologies to new businesses, the more it has to develop a big-enough and deep-enough resource pool to supply these businesses with sufficient capability to create competitive advantage.[18] Otherwise, its strengths end up being thinly spread across many businesses, and the opportunity for competitive advantage slips through the cracks.

A Cautionary Note about Transferring Resources from One Business to Another Just because a company has hit a home run in one business doesn't mean it can easily enter a new business with similar resource requirements and hit a second home run.[19] Noted British retailer Marks & Spencer, despite possessing a range of impressive resource capabilities (ability to choose excellent store locations, having a supply chain that gives it both low costs and high merchandise quality, loyal employees, an excellent reputation with consumers, and strong management expertise) that have made it one of Britain's premier retailers for 100 years, has failed repeatedly in its efforts to diversify into department store retailing in the United States. Even though Philip Morris (now named Altria) had built powerful consumer marketing capabilities in its cigarette and beer businesses, it floundered in soft drinks and ended up divesting its acquisition of 7UP after several frustrating years of competing against strongly entrenched and resource-capable rivals like Coca-Cola and PepsiCo. Then in 2002 it decided to divest its Miller Brewing business—despite its long-standing marketing successes in cigarettes and in its Kraft Foods subsidiary—because it was unable to grow Miller's market share in head-to-head competition against the considerable marketing prowess of Anheuser-Busch.

Step 5: Ranking the Performance Prospects of Business Units and Assigning a Priority for Resource Allocation

Once a diversified company's strategy has been evaluated from the perspective of industry attractiveness, competitive strength, strategic fit, and resource fit, the next step is to rank the performance prospects of the businesses from best to worst and determine which businesses merit top priority for resource support and new capital investments by the corporate parent.

The most important considerations in judging business-unit performance are sales growth, profit growth, contribution to company earnings, and return on capital invested in the business. Sometimes, cash flow is a big consideration. Information on each business's past performance can be gleaned from a company's financial records. While past performance is not necessarily a good predictor of future performance, it does signal whether a business already has good-to-excellent performance or has problems to overcome.

Furthermore, the industry attractiveness/business strength evaluations provide a solid basis for judging a business's prospects. Normally, strong business units in attractive industries have significantly better prospects than weak businesses in unattractive industries. And, normally, the revenue and earnings outlook for businesses in fast-growing industries is better than for businesses in slow-growing industries—one important exception occurs when a business in a slow-growing industry has the competitive strength to draw sales and market share away from its rivals and thus achieve much faster growth than the industry as a whole. As a rule, the prior analyses, taken together, signal which business units are likely to be strong performers on the road ahead and which are likely to be laggards. And it is a short step from ranking the prospects of business units to drawing conclusions about whether the company as a whole is capable of strong, mediocre, or weak performance in upcoming years.

The rankings of future performance generally determine what priority the corporate parent should give to each business in terms of resource allocation. The task here is to decide which business units should have top priority for corporate resource support and new capital investment and which should carry the lowest priority. *Business subsidiaries with the brightest profit and growth prospects and solid strategic and resource fits generally should head the list for corporate resource support.* More specifically, corporate executives need to consider whether and how corporate resources can be used to enhance the competitiveness of particular business units. And they must be diligent in steering resources out of low-opportunity areas into high-opportunity areas. Divesting marginal businesses is one of the best ways of freeing unproductive assets for redeployment. Surplus funds from cash cows also add to the corporate treasury.

Figure 6.7   The Chief Strategic and Financial Options for Allocating a
Diversified Company's Financial Resources

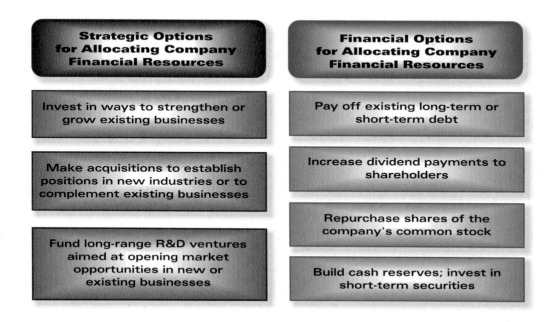

Figure 6.7 shows the chief strategic and financial options for allocating a diversified company's financial resources. Ideally, a company will have enough funds to do what is needed, both strategically and financially. If not, strategic uses of corporate resources should usually take precedence unless there is a compelling reason to strengthen the firm's balance sheet or divert financial resources to pacify shareholders.

Step 6: Crafting New Strategic Moves to Improve Overall Corporate Performance

The diagnosis and conclusions flowing from the five preceding analytical steps set the agenda for crafting strategic moves to improve a diversified company's overall performance. The strategic options boil down to five broad categories of actions:

1. Sticking closely with the existing business lineup and pursuing the opportunities these businesses present.
2. Broadening the company's business scope by making new acquisitions in new industries.
3. Divesting certain businesses and retrenching to a narrower base of business operations.
4. Restructuring the company's business lineup and putting a whole new face on the company's business makeup.
5. Pursuing multinational diversification and striving to globalize the operations of several of the company's business units.

The option of sticking with the current business lineup makes sense when the company's present businesses offer attractive growth opportunities and can be counted on to generate good earnings and cash flows. As long as the company's set of existing businesses puts it in good position for the future and these businesses have good strategic and/or resource fits, then rocking the boat with major changes in the company's business mix is usually unnecessary. Corporate executives can concentrate their attention on getting the best performance from each of its businesses, steering corporate resources into those areas of greatest potential and profitability. The specifics of "what to do" to wring better performance from the present business lineup have to be dictated by each business's circumstances and the preceding analysis of the corporate parent's diversification strategy.

However, in the event that corporate executives are not entirely satisfied with the opportunities they see in the company's present set of businesses and conclude that changes in the company's direction and business makeup are in order, they can opt for any of the four other strategic alternatives listed above. These options are discussed in the following section.

After a Company Diversifies: The Four Main Strategy Alternatives

Diversifying is by no means the final chapter in the evolution of a company's strategy. Once a company has diversified into a collection of related or unrelated businesses and concludes that some overhaul is needed in the company's present lineup and diversification strategy, there are four main strategic paths it can pursue (see Figure 6.8). To more fully understand the strategic issues corporate managers face in the ongoing process of managing a diversified group of businesses, we need to take a brief look at the central thrust of each of the four postdiversification strategy alternatives.

Strategies to Broaden a Diversified Company's Business Base

Diversified companies sometimes find it desirable to build positions in new industries, whether related or unrelated. There are several motivating factors. One is sluggish growth that makes the potential revenue and profit boost of a newly acquired business look attractive. A second is vulnerability to seasonal or recessionary influences or to threats from emerging new technologies. A third is the potential for transferring resources and capabilities to other related or complementary businesses. A fourth is rapidly changing conditions in one or more of a company's core businesses brought on by technological, legislative, or new product innovations that alter buyer requirements and preferences. For instance, the passage of legislation in the United States allowing banks, insurance companies, and stock brokerages to enter each other's businesses spurred a raft of acquisitions and mergers to create full-service financial enterprises capable of meeting the multiple financial needs of customers. Citigroup, already the largest U.S. bank with a global banking franchise, acquired Salomon Smith Barney to position itself in the investment banking and brokerage business and acquired insurance giant Travelers Group to enable it to offer customers insurance products.

A fifth, and often very important, motivating factor for adding new businesses is to complement and strengthen the market position and competitive capabilities of one or more of its present businesses. Viacom's acquisition of CBS strengthened and extended Viacom's reach into various media businesses—it was the parent of Paramount Pictures,

Figure 6.8   **A Company's Four Main Strategic Alternatives after It Diversifies**

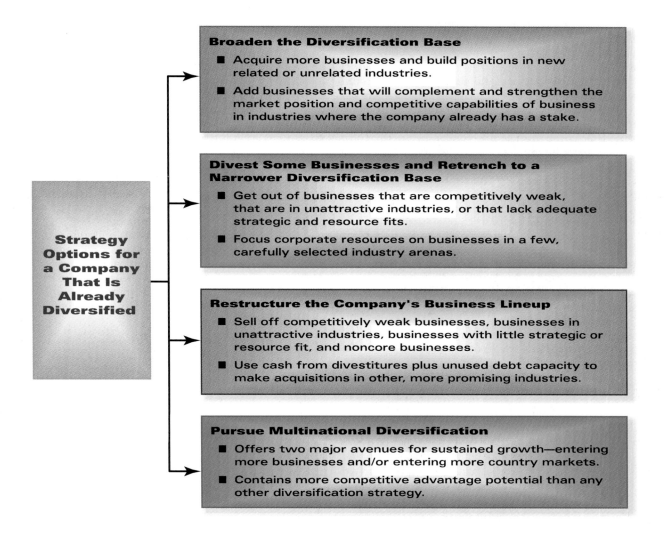

Strategy Options for a Company That Is Already Diversified

Broaden the Diversification Base
- Acquire more businesses and build positions in new related or unrelated industries.
- Add businesses that will complement and strengthen the market position and competitive capabilities of business in industries where the company already has a stake.

Divest Some Businesses and Retrench to a Narrower Diversification Base
- Get out of businesses that are competitively weak, that are in unattractive industries, or that lack adequate strategic and resource fits.
- Focus corporate resources on businesses in a few, carefully selected industry arenas.

Restructure the Company's Business Lineup
- Sell off competitively weak businesses, businesses in unattractive industries, businesses with little strategic or resource fit, and noncore businesses.
- Use cash from divestitures plus unused debt capacity to make acquisitions in other, more promising industries.

Pursue Multinational Diversification
- Offers two major avenues for sustained growth—entering more businesses and/or entering more country markets.
- Contains more competitive advantage potential than any other diversification strategy.

an assortment of cable TV networks (UPN, MTV, Nickelodeon, VH1, Showtime, The Movie Channel, Comedy Central), Blockbuster video stores, 2 movie theater chains, and 19 local TV stations. Unilever, a leading maker of food and personal care products, expanded its business lineup by acquiring SlimFast, Ben & Jerry's Homemade Ice Cream, and Bestfoods (whose brands included Knorr's soups, Hellman's mayonnaise, Skippy peanut butter, and Mazola cooking oils). Unilever saw these businesses as giving it more clout in competing against such other diversified food and household products companies as Nestlé, Kraft, Procter & Gamble, Campbell Soup, and General Mills.

Usually, expansion into new businesses is undertaken by acquiring companies already in the target industry. Some companies depend on new acquisitions to drive a major portion of their growth in revenues and earnings, and thus are always on the acquisition trail. Cisco Systems built itself into a worldwide leader in networking

COMPANY SPOTLIGHT 6.3

Managing Diversification at Johnson & Johnson—The Benefits of Cross-Business Strategic Fits

Johnson & Johnson (J&J), once a consumer products company known for its Band-Aid line and its baby care products, has evolved into a $47 billion diversified enterprise consisting of some 200-plus operating companies organized into three divisions: drugs, medical devices and diagnostics, and consumer products. Over the past decade J&J has acquired 54 businesses at a cost of about $30 billion; about 10 to 15 percent of J&J's annual growth in revenues has come from acquisitions. Much of the company's recent growth has been in the pharmaceutical division, which in 2004 accounted for 47 percent of J&J's revenues and 57 percent of its operating profits.

While each of J&J's business units sets its own strategies and operates with its own finance and human resources departments, corporate management strongly encourages cross-business cooperation and collaboration, believing that many of the advances in 21st-century medicine will come from applying advances in one discipline to another. J&J had 9,300 scientists working in 40 research labs in 2003, and the frequency of cross-disciplinary collaboration was increasing. One of J&J's new drug-coated stents grew out of a discussion between a drug researcher and a researcher in the company's stent business. (When stents are inserted to prop open arteries following angioplasty, the drug coating helps prevent infection.) A gene technology database compiled by the company's gene research lab was shared with personnel from the diagnostics division, who developed a test that the drug R&D people could use to predict which patients would most benefit from an experimental cancer therapy. J&J experts in various diseases have been meeting quarterly for the past five years to share information, and top management is setting up cross-disciplinary groups to focus on new treatments for particular diseases. J&J's new liquid Band-Aid product (a liquid coating applied to hard-to-cover places like fingers and knuckles) is based on a material used in a wound-closing product sold by the company's hospital products company.

J&J's corporate management maintains that close collaboration among people in its diagnostics, medical devices, and pharmaceutical businesses—where numerous cross-business strategic fits exist—gives J&J an edge on competitors, most of whom cannot match the company's breadth and depth of expertise.

Source: Amy Barrett, "Staying on Top," *BusinessWeek,* May 5, 2003, pp. 60–68, and www.jnj.com, accessed October 28, 2004 and January 25, 2005.

systems for the Internet by making 87 technology-based acquisitions during 1993–2004 to extend its market reach from routing and switching into voice and video over Internet protocol, optical networking, wireless, storage networking, security, broadband, and content networking. Tyco International, now recovering from charges of looting on the part of several top executives, transformed itself from an obscure company in the early 1990s into a $36 billion global manufacturing enterprise with operations in over 100 countries as of 2004 by making over 1,000 acquisitions; the company's far-flung diversification includes businesses in electronics, electrical components, fire and security systems, health care products, valves, undersea telecommunications systems, plastics, and adhesives. Tyco made over 700 acquisitions of small companies in the 1999–2001 period alone.

Company Spotlight 6.3 describes how Johnson & Johnson has used acquisitions to diversify far beyond its well-known Band-Aid and baby care businesses and become a major player in pharmaceuticals, medical devices, and medical diagnostics.

Divestiture Strategies Aimed at Retrenching to a Narrower Diversification Base

A number of diversified firms have had difficulty managing a diverse group of businesses and have elected to get out of some of them. Retrenching to a narrower diversification base is usually undertaken when top management concludes that its diversification strategy has ranged too far afield and that the company can improve long-term performance by concentrating on building stronger positions in a smaller number of core businesses and industries. Hewlett-Packard spun off its testing and measurement businesses into a stand-alone company called Agilent Technologies so that it could better concentrate on its PC, workstation, server, printer and peripherals, and electronics businesses. PepsiCo divested its cash-hog group of restaurant businesses, consisting of Kentucky Fried Chicken, Pizza Hut, Taco Bell, and California Pizza Kitchens, to provide more resources for strengthening its soft-drink business (which was losing market share to Coca-Cola) and growing its more profitable Frito-Lay snack foods business. Kmart divested OfficeMax, Sports Authority, and Borders Bookstores in order to refocus management attention and all of the company's resources on restoring luster to its distressed discount retailing business, which was (and still is) being totally outclassed in the marketplace by Wal-Mart and Target. In 2003–2004, Tyco International began a program to divest itself of some 50 businesses, including its entire undersea fiber-optics telecommunications network and an assortment of businesses in its fire and security division; the initiative also involved consolidating 219 manufacturing, sales, distribution, and other facilities and reducing its workforce of some 260,000 people by 7,200. Lucent Technology's retrenchment strategy is described in Company Spotlight 6.4.

> Focusing corporate resources on a few core and mostly related businesses avoids the mistake of diversifying so broadly that resources and management attention are stretched too thin.

But there are other important reasons for divesting one or more of a company's present businesses. Sometimes divesting a business has to be considered because market conditions in a once attractive industry have badly deteriorated. A business can become a prime candidate for divestiture because it lacks adequate strategic or resource fit, because it is a cash hog with questionable long-term potential, or because it is weakly positioned in its industry with little prospect that the corporate parent can realize a decent return on its investment in the business. Sometimes a company acquires businesses that, down the road, just do not work out as expected even though management has tried all it can think of to make them profitable—mistakes cannot be completely avoided because it is hard to foresee how getting into a new line of business will actually work out. Subpar performance by some business units is bound to occur, thereby raising questions of whether to divest them or keep them and attempt a turnaround. Other business units, despite adequate financial performance, may not mesh as well with the rest of the firm as was originally thought.

On occasion, a diversification move that seems sensible from a strategic-fit standpoint turns out to be a poor *cultural fit.*[20] Several pharmaceutical companies had just this experience. When they diversified into cosmetics and perfume, they discovered their personnel had little respect for the "frivolous" nature of such products compared to the far nobler task of developing miracle drugs to cure the ill. The absence of shared values and cultural compatibility between the medical research and chemical-compounding expertise of the pharmaceutical companies and the fashion/marketing orientation of the cosmetics business was the undoing of what otherwise was diversification into businesses with technology-sharing potential, product development fit, and some overlap in distribution channels.

Recent research indicates that pruning businesses and narrowing a firm's diversification base improve corporate performance.[21] Corporate parents often end up selling off businesses too late and at too low a price, sacrificing shareholder value.[22] A useful guide to determine whether or when to divest a business subsidiary is to ask, "If we were not in this business today, would we want to get into it now?"[23] When the answer

COMPANY SPOTLIGHT 6.4
Lucent Technology's Retrenchment Strategy

At the height of the telecommunication boom in 1999–2000, Lucent Technology was a company with $38.3 billion in revenues and 157,000 employees; it was the biggest maker of telecommunications equipment in the United States and a recognized leader worldwide. The company's strategy was to build positions in a number of blossoming technologies and industry arenas and achieve 20 percent annual revenue growth in each of 11 different business groups. But when customers' orders for new equipment began to evaporate in 2000–2001, Lucent's profits vanished and the once-growing company found itself battling to overcome bloated costs, deep price discounting, and customer defaults on the $7.5 billion in loans Lucent had made to finance their purchases. As it became clear that equipment sales and prices would never return to former levels, Lucent executives concluded that the company had over-extended itself trying to do too many things and needed to pare its lineup of businesses.

Alongside efforts to curtail lavish spending at the company's fabled Bell Labs research unit, make deep workforce cutbacks, streamline order-taking and billing systems, shore up the balance sheet, and conserve cash by ending dividend payments, management launched a series of retrenchment initiatives:

- In 2000, Lucent spun off the business which made gear for sending business calls through data networks as an independent company named Avaya, Inc.

- In 2002, still under intense financial pressure, Lucent exited the chip-making business by spinning

the operation off as a company named Agere Systems.

- Lucent ceased all manufacturing operations, opting to outsource everything.

- It stopped making gear for wireless phone networks based on a technology known as GSM (the dominant technology used in Europe and much of the world) in order to focus more fully on wireless gear using CMDA technology (a technology prevalent in the United States and some developing nations). As of 2004 Lucent had an estimated 45 percent share in the CMDA market, and the CMDA gear division was the company's chief revenue and profit producer.

- Of the 40 businesses Lucent acquired since 1996, 27 were sold, closed, or spun off.

These strategic moves to retrench stemmed a string of 13 straight money-losing quarters. Going into 2005, Lucent was a company with sales of about $9 billion and a workforce of 32,000. The company's stock price, which reached a high of $62 in 1999 before crashing to below $1 in 2002, was trading in the $3 to $4 range. In May 2004, Lucent announced its first acquisition in four years, buying a maker of Internet transmission technology for $300 million; the acquisition was intended to help Lucent become a leader in Internet telephone technology and grow the company's overall revenues.

Sources: Shawn Young, "Less May Be More," *The Wall Street Journal*, October 23, 2004, p. R10, and www.lucent.com, accessed October 28, 2004.

---

is no or probably not, divestiture should be considered. Another signal that a business should become a divestiture candidate is whether it is worth more to another company than to the present parent; in such cases, shareholders would be well served if the company sells the business and collects a premium price from the buyer for whom the business is a valuable fit.[24]

The Two Options for Divesting a Business: Selling It or Spinning It Off as an Independent Company   Selling a business outright to another company is far and away the most frequently used option for divesting a business. But sometimes a business selected for divestiture has ample resource strengths to compete successfully on its own. In such cases, a corporate parent may elect to spin the unwanted business off as a financially and managerially independent company, either by selling shares to the investing public via an initial public offering or by distributing shares in the new company to existing shareholders of the corporate parent. When a corporate parent decides to spin off one of its businesses as a separate company, there's the issue of whether or not to retain partial ownership. Retaining partial ownership makes sense when the business to be divested has a hot product or technological capabilities that give it good profit prospects. When 3Com elected to divest its PalmPilot business, which investors then saw as having very promising profit potential, it elected to retain a substantial ownership interest so as to provide 3Com shareholders a way of participating in whatever future market success PalmPilot (now Palm, Inc.) might have on its own. In 2001, when Philip Morris became concerned that its popular Kraft Foods subsidiary was suffering because of its affiliation with PM's cigarette business (antismoking groups were leading a national boycott of Kraft Macaroni & Cheese and a Harris poll revealed that about 16 percent of people familiar with Philip Morris had boycotted its products), Philip Morris executives opted to spin Kraft Foods off as an independent public company but retained a controlling ownership interest. R.J. Reynolds Tobacco was also spun off from Nabisco Foods in 1999 in an effort to distance the tobacco operations part of the company from the food operations part (Nabisco was then acquired by Philip Morris in 2000 and integrated into Kraft Foods).

Selling a business outright requires finding a buyer. This can prove hard or easy, depending on the business. As a rule, a company selling a troubled business should not ask, "How can we pawn this business off on someone, and what is the most we can get for it?"[25] Instead, it is wiser to ask, "For what sort of company would this business be a good fit, and under what conditions would it be viewed as a good deal?" Enterprises for which the business is a good fit are likely to pay the highest price. Of course, if a buyer willing to pay an acceptable price cannot be found, then a company must decide whether to keep the business until a buyer appears; spin it off as a separate company; or, in the case of a crisis-ridden business that is losing substantial sums, simply close it down and liquidate the remaining assets. Liquidation is obviously a last resort.

Strategies to Restructure a Company's Business Lineup

Restructuring strategies involve divesting some businesses and acquiring others so as to put a whole new face on the company's business lineup. Performing radical surgery on a company's group of businesses is an appealing strategy alternative when its financial performance is being squeezed or eroded by:

> **Core Concept**
>
> **Restructuring** involves divesting some businesses and acquiring others so as to put a whole new face on the company's business lineup.

- Too many businesses in slow-growth, declining, low-margin, or otherwise unattractive industries (a condition indicated by the number and size of businesses with industry attractiveness ratings below 5 and located on the bottom half of the attractiveness-strength matrix—see Figure 6.5).
- Too many competitively weak businesses (a condition indicated by the number and size of businesses with competitive strength ratings below 5 and located on the right half of the attractiveness-strength matrix).
- Ongoing declines in the market shares of one or more major business units that are falling prey to more market-savvy competitors.
- An excessive debt burden with interest costs that eat deeply into profitability.
- Ill-chosen acquisitions that haven't lived up to expectations.

Restructuring can also be mandated by the emergence of new technologies that threaten the survival of one or more of a diversified company's important businesses or by the appointment of a new CEO who decides to redirect the company. On occasion, restructuring can be prompted by special circumstances—like when a firm has a unique opportunity to make an acquisition so big and important that it has to sell several existing business units to finance the new acquisition or when a company needs to sell off some businesses in order to raise the cash for entering a potentially big industry with wave-of-the-future technologies or products.

Candidates for divestiture in a corporate restructuring effort typically include not only weak or up-and-down performers or those in unattractive industries but also business units that lack strategic fit with the businesses to be retained, businesses that are cash hogs or that lack other types of resource fit, and businesses incompatible with the company's revised diversification strategy (even though they may be profitable or in an attractive industry). As businesses are divested, corporate restructuring generally involves aligning the remaining business units into groups with the best strategic fits and then redeploying the cash flows from the divested business to either pay down debt or make new acquisitions to strengthen the parent company's business position in the industries it has chosen to emphasize.[26]

Over the past decade, corporate restructuring has become a popular strategy at many diversified companies, especially those that had diversified broadly into many different industries and lines of business. For instance, one struggling diversified company over a two-year period divested 4 business units, closed down the operations of 4 others, and added 25 new lines of business to its portfolio (16 through acquisition and 9 through internal start-up). PerkinElmer used a series of divestitures and new acquisitions to transform itself from a supplier of low-margin services sold to the government agencies into an innovative high-tech company with operations in over 125 countries and businesses in four industry groups—life sciences (drug research and clinical screening), optoelectronics, instruments, and fluid control and containment (for customers in aerospace, power generation, and semiconductors). Before beginning a restructuring effort in 1995, British-based Hanson PLC owned companies with more than $20 billion in revenues in industries as diverse as beer, exercise equipment, tools, construction cranes, tobacco, cement, chemicals, coal mining, electricity, hot tubs and whirlpools, cookware, rock and gravel, bricks, and asphalt. By early 1997, Hanson had restructured itself into a $3.8 billion enterprise focused more narrowly on gravel, crushed rock, cement, asphalt, bricks, and construction cranes; the remaining businesses were divided into four groups and divested.

During Jack Welch's first four years as CEO of General Electric (GE), the company divested 117 business units, accounting for about 20 percent of GE's assets; these divestitures, coupled with several important acquisitions, provided GE with 14 major business divisions and led to Welch's challenge to the managers of GE's divisions to become number one or number two in their industry. Ten years after Welch became CEO, GE was a different company, having divested operations worth $9 billion, made new acquisitions totaling $24 billion, and cut its workforce by 100,000 people. Then, during the 1990–2001 period, GE continued to reshuffle its business lineup, acquiring over 600 new companies, including 108 in 1998 and 64 during a 90-day period in 1999. Most of the new acquisitions were in Europe, Asia, and Latin America and were aimed at transforming GE into a truly global enterprise. In 2003, GE's new CEO, Jeffrey Immelt, began a further restructuring of GE's business lineup with three initiatives: (1) spending $10 billion to acquire British-based Amersham and extend GE's Medical Systems business into diagnostic pharmaceuticals and biosciences, thereby creating a $15 billion business designated as GE Healthcare; (2) acquiring the entertainment assets of debt-ridden French media conglomerate Vivendi Universal Entertainment (Universal Studios, five Universal theme parks, USA Network, Sci-Fi Channel, the Trio cable channel, and Spanish-language broadcaster Telemundo) and integrating its operations into GE's NBC division (the owner of NBC, 29 television stations, and cable networks CNBC, MSNBC, and Bravo), thereby creating a broad-based $13 billion media business positioned to compete against Walt Disney, Time Warner, Fox, and Viacom; and (3) beginning a withdrawal from the insurance business by divesting several companies in its insurance division and preparing to spin off its remaining life and mortgage insurance businesses through an IPO for a new company called Genworth Financial.

In a study of the performance of the 200 largest U.S. corporations from 1990 to 2000, McKinsey & Company found that those companies that actively managed their business portfolios through acquisitions and divestitures created substantially more shareholder value than those that kept a fixed lineup of businesses.[27]

Multinational Diversification Strategies

The distinguishing characteristics of a multinational diversification strategy are a *diversity of businesses* and a *diversity of national markets.*[28] Such diversity makes multinational diversification a particularly challenging and complex strategy to conceive and execute. Managers have to develop business strategies for each industry (with as many multinational variations as conditions in each country market dictate). Then, they have to pursue and manage opportunities for cross-business and cross-country collaboration and strategic coordination in ways calculated to result in competitive advantage and enhanced profitability.

Moreover, the geographic operating scope of individual businesses within a diversified multinational company (DMNC) can range from only one country to several countries to many countries to global. Thus, each business unit within a DMNC often competes in a somewhat different combination of geographic markets than the other businesses do—adding another element of strategic complexity and perhaps an element of opportunity.

Global Spotlight 6.1 shows the scope of four prominent DMNCs.

The Appeal of Multinational Diversification: More Opportunities for Sustained Growth and Maximum Competitive Advantage Potential Despite their complexity, multinational diversification strategies have great appeal. They contain *two major avenues* for growing revenues and profits: one is to grow by entering additional businesses, and the other is to grow by extending the operations of existing businesses into additional country markets. Moreover, a strategy of multinational diversification also contains six attractive paths to competitive advantage, *all of which can be pursued simultaneously*:

1. *Full capture of economies of scale and experience- and learning-curve effects:* In some businesses, the volume of sales needed to realize full economies of scale and/or benefit fully from experience- and learning-curve effects is rather sizable, often exceeding the volume that can be achieved operating within the boundaries of a single-country market, especially a small one. *The ability to drive down unit costs by expanding sales to additional country markets is one reason why a diversified multinational may seek to acquire a business and then rapidly expand its operations into more and more foreign markets.*

GLOBAL SPOTLIGHT 6.1

The Global Scope of Four Prominent Diversified Multinational Corporations

Company	Global Scope	Businesses into Which the Company Has Diversified
Sony	Operations in more than 100 countries and sales offices in more than 200 countries	■ Televisions, VCRs, DVD players, radios, digital cameras and video equipment, Vaio PCs, Trinitron computer monitors; PlayStation game consoles and video game software; Columbia, Epic, and Sony Classical prerecorded music; Columbia TriStar motion pictures; syndicated television programs; entertainment complexes; and insurance.
Nestlé	Operations in 70 countries and sales offices in more than 200 countries	■ Beverages (Nescafé and Taster's Choice coffees; Nestea, Perrier, Arrowhead, and Calistoga mineral and bottled waters); milk products (Carnation, Gloria, Neslac, Coffee Mate, Nestlé ice cream and yogurt); pet foods (Friskies, Alpo, Fancy Feast, Mighty Dog); Contadina, Libby's, and Stouffer's food products and prepared dishes; chocolate and confectionery products (Nestlé Crunch, Smarties, Baby Ruth, Butterfinger, KitKat); and pharmaceuticals (Alcon opthalmic products, Galderma dermatological products).
Siemens	Operations in 160 countries and sales offices in more than 190 countries	■ Electrical power generation, transmission, and distribution equipment and products; manufacturing automation systems; industrial motors, machinery, and tools; plant construction and maintenance; corporate communication networks; telephones; PCs, mainframes, computer network products, consulting services; mass-transit and light-rail systems, rail cars, locomotives; lighting products (bulbs, lamps, theater and television lighting systems); semiconductors; home appliances; vacuum cleaners; and financial, procurement, and logistics services.
Samsung	Operations in more than 60 countries and sales in more than 200 countries	■ Notebook computers, hard-disk drives, CD/DVD-ROM drives, monitors, printers, and fax machines; televisions (big-screen TVs, plasma-screen TVs, and LCD-screen TVs); DVD and MP3 players; cell phones and various other telecommunications products; compressors; home appliances; DRAM chips, flash memory chips, and graphics memory chip; and optical fibers, fiber-optics cables, and fiber-optics connectors.

Source: Company annual reports and Web sites.

2. *Opportunities to capitalize on cross-business economies of scope:* Diversifying into related businesses offering economies of scope can drive the development of a low-cost advantage over less diversified rivals. For example, a DMNC that uses mostly the same distributors and retail dealers worldwide can diversify into new businesses using these same worldwide distribution channels at relatively little incremental expense. The cost savings of piggybacking distribution activities can be substantial. Moreover, with more businesses selling more products in more countries, a DMNC acquires more bargaining leverage in its purchases from suppliers and more bargaining leverage with retailers in securing attractive display space for its products. Consider, for example, the competitive power that Sony derived from these very sorts of economies of scope when it decided to diversify into the video game business with its PlayStation product line. Sony had in-place capability to go after video game sales in all country markets where it presently did business in other electronics product categories (TVs, computers, DVD players, VCRs, radios, CD players, and camcorders). And it had the marketing clout and brand-name credibility to persuade retailers to give Sony's PlayStation products prime shelf space and visibility. These strategic-fit benefits helped Sony quickly overtake longtime industry leaders Nintendo and Sega and defend its market leadership against Microsoft's new Xbox.

3. *Opportunities to transfer competitively valuable resources both from one business to another and from one country to another:* A company pursuing related diversification can gain a competitive edge over less diversified rivals by transferring competitively valuable resources from one business to another; a multinational company can gain competitive advantage over rivals with narrower geographic coverage by transferring competitively valuable resources from one country to another. But a strategy of multinational diversification enables simultaneous pursuit of both sources of competitive advantage.

4. *Ability to leverage use of a well-known and competitively powerful brand name:* Diversified multinational companies whose businesses have brand names that are well known and respected across the world possess a valuable strategic asset with competitive advantage potential. For example, Sony's well-established global brand-name recognition gives it an important marketing and advertising advantage over rivals with lesser-known brands. When Sony goes into a new marketplace with the stamp of the Sony brand on its product families, it can command prominent display space with retailers. It can expect to win sales and market share simply on the confidence that buyers place in products carrying the Sony name. While Sony may spend money to make consumers aware of the availability of its new products, it does not have to spend nearly as much on achieving brand recognition and market acceptance as would a lesser-known competitor looking at the marketing and advertising costs of entering the same new product/business/country markets and trying to go head-to-head against Sony. Further, if Sony moves into a new country market for the first time and does well selling Sony PlayStations and video games, it is easier to sell consumers in that country Sony TVs, digital cameras, PCs, MP3 players, and so on—plus, the related advertising costs are likely to be less than they would be without having already established the Sony brand strongly in the minds of buyers.

5. *Ability to capitalize on opportunities for cross-business and cross-country collaboration and strategic coordination:*[29] A multinational diversification strategy allows competitively valuable cross-business and cross-country coordination of certain value chain activities. For instance, by channeling corporate resources directly into a combined R&D/technology effort for all related businesses, as opposed to letting each business unit fund and direct its own R&D effort however it sees fit, a DMNC can merge its expertise and efforts *worldwide* to advance core technologies, expedite cross-business and cross-country product improvements, speed the development of new products that complement existing products, and pursue promising technological avenues to create altogether new businesses—all significant contributors to competitive advantage and better corporate performance.[30] Honda has been very successful in building R&D expertise in gasoline engines and transferring the resulting technological advances to its businesses in automobiles, motorcycles, outboard engines, snow blowers, lawn mowers, garden tillers, and portable power generators. Further, a DMNC can reduce costs through cross-business and cross-country coordination of purchasing and procurement from suppliers, from collaborative introduction and shared use of e-commerce technologies and online sales efforts, and from coordinated product introductions and promotional campaigns. Firms that are less diversified and less global in scope have less such cross-business and cross-country collaborative opportunities.

6. *Opportunities to use cross-business or cross-country subsidization to outcompete rivals:* A financially successful DMNC has potentially valuable organizational

resources and multiple profit sanctuaries in both certain country markets and certain business that it can draw on to wage a market offensive. In comparison, a one-business domestic company has only one profit sanctuary—its home market. A diversified one-country competitor may have profit sanctuaries in several businesses, but all are in the same country market. A one-business multinational company may have profit sanctuaries in several country markets, but all are in the same business. All three are vulnerable to an offensive in their more limited profit sanctuaries by an aggressive DMNC willing to lowball its prices and/or spend extravagantly on advertising to win market share at their expense. A DMNC's ability to keep hammering away at competitors with low prices year after year may reflect either a cost advantage growing out of its related diversification strategy or a willingness to accept low profits or even losses in the market being attacked because it has ample earnings from its other profit sanctuaries. For example, Sony's global-scale diversification strategy gives it unique competitive strengths in outcompeting Nintendo and Sega, neither of which are diversified. If need be, Sony can maintain low prices on its PlayStations or fund high-profile promotions for its latest video game products, using earnings from its other business lines to fund its offensive to wrest market share away from Nintendo and Sega in video games. At the same time, Sony can draw on its considerable resources in R&D, its ability to transfer electronics technology from one electronics product family to another, and its expertise in product innovation to introduce better and better video game players, perhaps players that are multifunctional and do more than just play video games. Such competitive actions not only enhance Sony's own brand image but also make it very tough for Nintendo and Sega to match Sony's prices, advertising, and product development efforts and still earn acceptable profits.

Core Concept

A strategy of multinational diversification has more built-in potential for competitive advantage than any other diversification strategy.

The Combined Effects of These Advantages Is Potent   A strategy of diversifying into *related* industries and then competing *globally* in each of these industries thus has great potential for being a winner in the marketplace because of the long-term growth opportunities it offers and the multiple corporate-level competitive advantage opportunities it contains. Indeed, *a strategy of multinational diversification contains more competitive advantage potential* (above and beyond what is achievable through a particular business's own competitive strategy) *than any other diversification strategy.* The strategic key to maximum competitive advantage is for a DMNC to concentrate its diversification efforts in those industries where there are resource-sharing and resource-transfer opportunities and where there are important economies of scope and brand-name benefits. The more a company's diversification strategy yields these kinds of strategic-fit benefits, the more powerful a competitor it becomes and the better its profit and growth performance is likely to be.

However, it is important to recognize that while a DMNC's cross-subsidization capabilities are a potent competitive weapon in theory, in actual practice cross-subsidization can be used only sparingly. It is one thing to *occasionally* divert a portion of the profits and cash flows from existing businesses to help fund entry into a new business or country market or wage a competitive offensive against select rivals. It is quite another thing to *regularly* use cross-subsidization tactics and thereby weaken overall company performance. A DMNC is under the same pressures as any other company to demonstrate consistently acceptable profitability across its whole operation.[31] At some juncture, every business and every country market needs to make a profit contribution or become a candidate for abandonment. As a general rule, *cross-subsidization tactics are justified only when there is a good prospect that the short-term impairment to corporate profitability will be offset by stronger competitiveness and better overall profitability over the long term.*

Key Points

The purpose of diversification is to build shareholder value. Diversification builds shareholder value when a diversified group of businesses can perform better under the auspices of a single corporate parent than they would as independent, stand-alone businesses—the goal is to achieve not just a $1 + 1 = 2$ result but to realize important $1 + 1 = 3$ performance benefits. Whether getting into a new business has potential to enhance shareholder value hinges on whether a company's entry into that business can pass the attractiveness test, the cost-of-entry test, and the better-off test.

There are two fundamental approaches to diversification—into related businesses and into unrelated businesses. The rationale for *related* diversification is *strategic:* diversify into businesses with strategic fits along their respective value chains, capitalize on strategic-fit relationships to gain competitive advantage, and then use competitive advantage to achieve the desired $1 + 1 = 3$ impact on shareholder value.

The basic premise of unrelated diversification is that any business that has good profit prospects and can be acquired on good financial terms is a good business to diversify into. Unrelated diversification strategies surrender the competitive advantage potential of strategic fit in return for such advantages as (1) spreading business risk over a variety of industries and (2) providing opportunities for financial gain (if candidate acquisitions have undervalued assets, are bargain-priced and have good upside potential given the right management, or need the backing of a financially strong parent to capitalize on attractive opportunities).

Analyzing how good a company's diversification strategy involves a six-step process:

Step 1: *Evaluate the long-term attractiveness of the industries into which the firm has diversified.* Industry attractiveness needs to be evaluated from three angles: the attractiveness of each industry on its own, the attractiveness of each industry relative to the others, and the attractiveness of all the industries as a group.

Step 2: *Evaluate the relative competitive strength of each of the company's business units.* The purpose of rating the competitive strength of each business is to gain clear understanding of which businesses are strong contenders in their industries, which are weak contenders, and the underlying reasons for their strength or weakness. The conclusions about industry attractiveness can be joined with the conclusions about competitive strength by drawing an industry attractiveness–competitive strength matrix displaying the positions of each business on a nine-cell grid.

Step 3: *Check for cross-business strategic fits.* A business is more attractive strategically when it has value chain relationships with sister business units that present opportunities to transfer skills or technology, reduce overall costs, share facilities, or share a common brand name—any of which can represent a significant avenue for producing competitive advantage beyond what any one business can achieve on its own.

Step 4: *Check whether the firm's resource strengths fit the resource requirements of its present business lineup.* Resource fit exists when (1) businesses add to a company's resource strengths, either financially or strategically; (2) a company has the resources to adequately support the resource requirements of its businesses as a group without spreading itself too thin; and (3) there are close matches between a company's resources and industry key success factors.

Step 5: *Rank the performance prospects of the businesses from best to worst and determine what the corporate parent's priority should be in allocating resources to its various businesses.* The most important considerations in judging business-unit performance are sales growth, profit growth, contribution to company earnings, and the return on capital invested in the business. Sometimes, cash flow generation is a big consideration. Normally, strong business units in attractive industries have significantly better performance prospects than weak businesses or businesses in unattractive industries. Business subsidiaries with the brightest profit and growth prospects and solid strategic and resource fits generally should head the list for corporate resource support.

Step 6: *Craft new strategic moves to improve overall corporate performance.* This step entails using the results of the preceding analysis as the basis for devising actions to strengthen existing businesses, make new acquisitions, divest weak-performing and unattractive businesses, restructure the company's business lineup, expand the scope of the company's geographic reach multinationally or globally, and otherwise steer corporate resources into the areas of greatest opportunity.

Once a company has diversified, corporate management's task is to manage the collection of businesses for maximum long-term performance. There are four different strategic paths for improving a diversified company's performance: (1) broadening the firm's business base by diversifying into additional businesses, (2) retrenching to a narrower diversification base by divesting some of its present businesses, (3) corporate restructuring, and (4) multinational diversification.

Exercises

1. What do you see as the strategic fits that exist among the value chains of the diversified companies listed in Company Spotlight 6.1?

2. Consider the business lineup of General Electric shown in Company Spotlight 6.2. What problems do you think the top executives at GE encounter in trying to stay on top of all the businesses the company is in? How might they decide the merits of adding new businesses or divesting poorly performing businesses? What types of advice might they be in a position to give to the general managers of each of GE's business units?

3. Go to Johnson & Johnson's Web site at www.jnj.com, click on the "Our Company" link, and review all the different businesses that J&J is in and the variety of products that it produces and markets. Would you characterize the company strategy as one of related or unrelated diversification? What opportunities do you see for cross-business collaboration to capture strategic-fit benefits? Based on the discussion presented in Company Spotlight 6.3, do you see good reason for shareholders to be optimistic about the extent to which cross-business strategic fits might really produce a competitive edge for J&J and lead to added shareholder value?

4. The Walt Disney Company is in the following businesses: theme parks, Disney Cruise Line, resort properties, movie, video, and theatrical productions (for both children and adults), television broadcasting (ABC, Disney Channel, Toon Disney, Classic Sports Network, ESPN and ESPN2, E!, Lifetime, and A&E networks), radio broadcasting (Disney Radio), musical recordings and sales of animation art, Anaheim Mighty Ducks NHL franchise, Anaheim Angels major league baseball franchise (25 percent ownership), books and magazine publishing, interactive software and Internet sites, and The Disney Store retail shops.

Based on the above listing, would you say that Walt Disney's business lineup reflects a strategy of related or unrelated diversification? Be prepared to justify and explain your answer in terms of the extent to which the value chains of Disney's different businesses seem to have competitively valuable cross-business relationships.

CHAPTER 7

Strategy, Ethics, and Social Responsibility

When morality comes up against profit, it is seldom profit that loses.

—*Shirley Chisholm, former congresswoman*

But I'd shut my eyes in the sentry box so I didn't see nothing wrong.

—*Rudyard Kipling, author*

Leaders must be more than individuals of high character. They must "lead" others to behave ethically.

—*Linda K. Treviño and Michael E. Brown, professors*

There is one and only one social responsibility of business—to use its resources and engage in activities designed to increase its profits so long as it stays within the rules of the game, which is to say engages in free and open competition, without deception or fraud.

—*Milton Friedman, Nobel Prize–winning economist*

Corporations are economic entities, to be sure, but they are also social institutions that must justify their existence by their overall contribution to society.

—*Henry Mintzberg, Robert Simons, and Kunal Basu, professors*

Knowing all the moral theory in the world does not equip a person to specify in advance the moral norms of business ethics.

—*Thomas Donaldson and Thomas W. Dunfee, professors*

Clearly, a company has a responsibility to make a profit and grow the business—in capitalistic or market economies, management's fiduciary duty to create value for shareholders is not a matter for serious debate. Just as clearly, a company and its personnel also have a duty to obey the law and play by the rules of fair competition. But does a company have a duty to operate according to the ethical norms of the societies in which it operates—should it be held to some standard of ethical conduct? And does it have a duty or obligation to contribute to the betterment of society independent of the needs and preferences of the customers it serves? Should a company display a social conscience and devote a portion of its resources to bettering society?

The focus of this chapter is to examine what link, if any, there should be between a company's efforts to craft and execute a winning strategy and its duties to (1) conduct its activities in an ethical manner and (2) demonstrate socially responsible behavior by being a committed corporate citizen and directing corporate resources to the betterment of employees, the communities in which it operates, and society as a whole.

What Do We Mean by Business Ethics?

Business ethics is the application of ethical principles and standards to business behavior.[1] Business ethics does not really involve a special set of ethical standards applicable only to business situations. Ethical principles in business are not materially different from ethical principles in general. Why? Because business actions have to be judged in the context of society's ethical standards, not by a special set of rules that businesspeople decide to apply to their own conduct. If dishonesty is considered to be unethical and immoral, then dishonest behavior in business—whether it relates to customers, suppliers, employees, or shareholders—qualifies as equally unethical and immoral. If being ethical entails not deliberately harming others, then recalling a defective or unsafe product is ethically necessary and failing to undertake such a recall or correct the problem in future shipments of the product is unethical. If society deems bribery to be unethical, then it is unethical for company personnel to make payoffs to government officials to facilitate business transactions or bestow gifts and other favors on prospective customers to win or retain their business.

> **Core Concept**
>
> **Business ethics** concerns the application of general ethical principles and standards to the actions and decisions of companies and the conduct of company personnel.

Ethical Standards—Universal or Dependent on Local Norms and Circumstances?

Notions of right and wrong, fair and unfair, moral and immoral, ethical and unethical are present in all societies, organizations, and individuals. But there are three schools of thought about the extent to which the ethical standards travel across cultures and whether multinational companies can apply the same set of ethical standards in any and all of the locations where they operate.

The School of Ethical Universalism

Core Concept

According to the school of **ethical universalism,** the same standards of what's ethical and what's unethical resonate with peoples of most societies regardless of local traditions and cultural norms; hence, common ethical standards can be used to judge the conduct of personnel at companies operating in a variety of country markets and cultural circumstances.

According to the school of **ethical universalism,** some concepts of what is right and what is wrong are *universal* and transcend almost all cultures, societies, and religions. For instance, being truthful (or not lying or not being deliberately deceitful) strikes a chord of what's right in the peoples of all nations. Likewise, demonstrating integrity of character, not cheating, and treating people with dignity and respect are concepts that resonate with people of most cultures and religions. In most societies, people believe that companies should not pillage or degrade the environment in the course of conducting their operations. In most societies, people would concur that it is unethical to knowingly expose workers to toxic chemicals and hazardous materials or to sell products known to be unsafe or harmful to the users. *To the extent there is common moral agreement about right and wrong actions and behaviors across multiple cultures and countries, there exists a set of universal ethical standards to which all societies, all companies, and all individuals can be held accountable.* These universal ethical principles or norms put limits on which actions and behaviors fall inside the boundaries of what is right and which ones fall outside. They set forth the traits and behaviors that are considered virtuous and that a good person is supposed to believe in and to display.

Many ethicists believe that the most important moral standards travel well across countries and cultures and thus are universal—universal norms include being honest or trustworthy, respecting the rights of others, practicing the Golden Rule, avoiding unnecessary harm to workers or to the users of the company's product or service, and respecting the environment.[2] In all such instances where there is cross-cultural agreement as to what actions and behaviors are inside and outside ethical and moral boundaries, adherents of the school of ethical universalism maintain that the conduct of personnel at companies operating in a variety of country markets and cultural circumstances can be judged against the resulting set of common ethical standards.

The strength of ethical universalism is that it draws upon the collective views of multiple societies and cultures to put some clear boundaries on what constitutes ethical business behavior and what constitutes unethical business behavior no matter what country market or culture a company or its personnel are operating in. This means that in those instances where basic moral standards really do not vary significantly according to local cultural beliefs, traditions, religious convictions, or time and circumstance, a multinational company can develop a code of ethics that it applies more or less evenly across its worldwide operations.[3] It can avoid the slippery slope that comes from having different ethical standards for different company personnel depending on where in the world they are working.

The School of Ethical Relativism

But apart from select universal basics—honesty, trustworthiness, fairness, a regard for worker safety, and respect for the environment—there are meaningful variations in what societies generally agree is right and wrong in the conduct of business activities. Divergent religious beliefs, historic traditions, social customs, and prevailing political and economic doctrines (whether a country leans more toward a capitalistic market economy or one heavily dominated by socialistic or communistic principles) frequently produce ethical norms that vary from one country to another. The school of

ethical relativism holds that when there are cross-country or cross-cultural differences in what is deemed fair or unfair, what constitutes proper regard for human rights, and what is considered ethical or unethical in business situations, it is appropriate for local moral standards to take precedence over what the ethical standards may be elsewhere—for instance, in a company's home market. The thesis is that whatever a culture thinks is right or wrong really *is* right or wrong for that culture.[4] Hence, the school of ethical relativism contends that there are important occasions when cultural norms and the circumstances of the situation determine whether certain actions or behaviors are right or wrong. Consider the following examples.

> **Core Concept**
>
> According to the school of **ethical relativism** different societal cultures and customs have divergent values and standards of right and wrong—thus what is ethical or unethical must be judged in the light of local customs and social mores and can vary from one culture or nation to another.

The Use of Underage Labor   In industrialized nations, the use of "underage" workers is considered taboo; social activists are adamant that child labor is unethical and that companies should neither employ children under the age of 18 as full-time employees nor source any products from foreign suppliers that employ underage workers. However, in India, Bangladesh, Botswana, Sri Lanka, Ghana, Somalia, Turkey, and more than 100 other countries, it is customary to view children as potential, even necessary, workers.[5] Many poverty-stricken families cannot subsist without the income earned by young family members, and sending their children to school instead of having them participate in the workforce is not a realistic option. In 2000, the International Labor Organization estimated that 211 million children ages 5 to 14 were working around the world.[6] If such children are not permitted to work—due to pressures imposed by activist groups in industrialized nations—they may be forced to seek work in lower-wage jobs in "hidden" parts of the economy of their countries, be out on the street begging, or even be reduced to trafficking in drugs or engaging in prostitution.[7] So if all businesses succumb to the protests of activist groups and government organizations that, based on their values and beliefs, loudly proclaim that underage labor is unethical, then have either businesses or the protesting groups really done something good on behalf of society in general?

The Payment of Bribes and Kickbacks   A particularly thorny area facing multinational companies is the degree of cross-country variability in paying bribes. In many countries in Eastern Europe, Africa, Latin America, and Asia, it is customary to pay bribes to government officials in order to win a government contract or to facilitate a business transaction. In some developing nations, it is difficult for any company, foreign or domestic, to move goods through customs without paying off low-level officials.[8] Likewise, in many countries it is normal to make payments to prospective customers in order to win or retain their business. According to a 1999 *Wall Street Journal* report, 30 to 60 percent of all business transactions in Eastern Europe involved paying bribes, and the costs of bribe payments averaged 2 to 8 percent of revenues.[9] The 2004 Global Corruption Report, sponsored by Berlin-based Transparency International, found that corruption among public officials and in business transactions is widespread across the world.[10]

Companies that forbid the payment of bribes and kickbacks in their codes of ethical conduct and that are serious about enforcing this prohibition face a formidable challenge in those countries where bribery and kickback payments have been entrenched as a local custom for decades and are not considered unethical by the local population. The same goes for multinational companies that do business in countries where bribery is illegal and also in countries where bribery and kickbacks are tolerated or customary. Some people say that bribing government officials to get goods through customs or giving kickbacks to customers to retain their business or win an order is simply a payment for services rendered, in the same way that people tip for service at restaurants.

U.S. companies are prohibited by the Foreign Corrupt Practices Act (FCPA) from paying bribes to government officials, political parties, political candidates, or others in all countries where they do business; the FCPA requires U.S. companies with foreign operations to adopt accounting practices that ensure full disclosure of a company's transactions so that illegal payments can be detected. The 35 member countries of the Organization for Economic Cooperation and Development (OECD) in 1997 adopted a convention to combat bribery in international business transactions; the Anti-Bribery Convention obligated the countries to criminalize the bribery of foreign public officials, including payments made to political parties and party officials. However, so far there has been only token enforcement of the OECD convention, and the payment of bribes in global business transactions remains a common practice in many countries.

At the level most managers confront it, the custom of paying bribes and kickbacks in certain country markets is a particularly vexing ethical issue and has no satisfactory solution.[11] Refusing to pay bribes or kickbacks is very often tantamount to losing business. Frequently, the sales and profits are lost to more unscrupulous companies, with the result that both ethical companies and ethical individuals are penalized.

> Varying ethical norms across countries and conflicting interpretations of what exactly constitutes honesty, respect for human rights, respect for the environment, and so on, indicate that there are few absolutes when it comes to business ethics and thus few ethical absolutes for consistently judging a company's conduct in various countries and markets.

Other Examples of Varying Ethical Standards   In Japan, China, and other Asian societies, for instance, there's a strong ethic of loyalty to work groups and corporations; such fidelity stems from Confucianism and centuries-long traditions that hold that one's primary obligation is not to oneself but rather to family, clan, government, and employer.[12] In Japan, such beliefs translate into high cultural expectations that company personnel will exhibit strong loyalty to superiors and to their employer. Japanese employees, believing in the importance of loyalty to their employer, are therefore unlikely to blow the whistle when they see their company engage in wrongdoing. Moreover, some Japanese corporations will fire an employee for breach of loyalty if the employee simply interviews for a job with another firm. In China, there's greater societal toleration of child labor, dangerous working conditions, and fake or inferior products than in some other parts of the world. In addition, some Chinese ethicists even contend that traditional concepts of morality are irrelevant insofar as behavior in a market economy is concerned because the manner in which competitive markets operate is inherently amoral.[13]

In Italy, people are relatively carefree; they live for the moment and are generally willing to take chances about what the future will bring. As a consequence, an Italian manager may be disinclined to keep a promise or fulfill long-term contractual obligations; further, there are often low levels of trust between parties in business deals, and honest communications are frequently lacking.[14] In the former Soviet Union, decades of authoritarian government rule and socialistic traditions created a system where Communist party officials issued a blizzard of rules and orders about how industries were to operate in the planned economy. Bribes and favors were frequently used to get government officials to act favorably. Because Soviet managers found it onerous and sometimes impossible to comply with all the various dictates, many of which were conflicting or inefficient, they routinely broke rules, manipulated production data, fabricated accounts, and traded favors in the course of conducting operations. Since the collapse of communist rule and the breakup of the Soviet Union in the late 1980s, many Russian people, long accustomed to the communist idea that people are supposed to work for the collective good of society, have exhibited considerable mistrust of how business is conducted in Russia. Such views are particularly understandable given that the actions of some Russian businesspeople have proved wildly corrupt based on ethical standards in the United States and Western Europe, with unethical practices being more the norm than the exception.

There are also cross-country variations in the *degree* to which certain behaviors are considered unethical. One study revealed that managers in Hong Kong rank taking credit for another's work and accomplishments at the top of a list of unethical behaviors and, in contrast to managers in Western cultures, considered it more unethical than bribery or illicitly obtaining information about competitors.[15] In Mexico, nepotism (favoritism based on family or social ties) is more acceptable than in the United States or many other countries. Ethical standards for gift giving and entertainment commonly vary from one country to another. In the United States, for instance, it is ethically permissible for a company to provide customers with such small favors as tickets to sporting events or take them on golfing or hunting trips (are these not small "bribes" that are calculated to win favor?), but it is considered both unethical and unlawful to give them cash or "large" gifts in return for steering an order to the company.

Ethical Relativism Equates to Multiple Sets of Ethical Standards   The existence of varying ethical norms such as those cited above causes advocates of ethical relativism to maintain that there are comparatively few absolutes when it comes to business ethics and thus comparatively few ethical absolutes for consistently judging a company's conduct in various countries and markets. Indeed, the thesis of ethical relativists is that while there are

> Under ethical relativism, there can be no one-size-fits-all set of authentic ethical norms against which to gauge the conduct of company personnel.

some general moral prescriptions that apply in almost every society and business circumstance, there are plenty of situations where ethical norms must be contoured to fit the local customs, traditions, and notions of fairness shared by the parties involved. A "one-size-fits-all" template for judging the ethical appropriateness of business actions and the behaviors of company personnel simply does not exist—in other words, ethical problems in business cannot be fully resolved without appealing to the shared convictions of the parties in question.[16] European and American managers may want to impose standards of business conduct that give heavy weight to such core human rights as personal freedom, individual security, political participation, the ownership of property, and the right to subsistence, as well as the obligation to respect the dignity of each human person, uphold adequate health and safety standards for all employees, and respect the environment. Japanese managers may prefer ethical standards that show respect for the collective good of society. Muslim managers may wish to apply ethical standards compatible with the teachings of Mohammed. Individual companies may want to give explicit recognition to the importance of company personnel's living up to the company's own espoused values and business principles. Clearly, there is merit in the school of ethical relativism's view that what is deemed right or wrong, fair or unfair, moral or immoral, ethical or unethical in business situations has to be viewed in the context of each country's local customs, religious traditions, and societal norms. Businesses need some room to tailor their ethical standards to fit local situations. A company has to be very cautious about exporting its home-country values and ethics to foreign countries where it operates—"photocopying" ethics is disrespectful of other cultures and neglects the important role of moral free space.

Pushed to Extreme, Ethical Relativism Breaks Down   While the ethical relativism rule of "when in Rome, do as the Romans do" appears reasonable, it nonetheless presents a big problem—when the envelope starts to be pushed, as will inevitably be the case, *it is tantamount to rudderless ethical standards.* Consider, for instance, the following example: In 1992, the owners of the SS *United States,* an aging luxury ocean liner constructed with asbestos in the 1940s, had the liner towed to Turkey, where a contractor had agreed to remove the asbestos for $2 million (versus a far higher cost in the United States, where asbestos removal safety standards were much more stringent).[17] When Turkish officials blocked the asbestos removal because of the dangers to workers of contracting cancer, the owners had the liner towed to the Black Sea port of Sevastopol, in the Crimean Republic, where the asbestos-removal standards were quite lax and where a contractor had agreed to remove more than 500,000 square feet of carcinogenic asbestos for less than $2 million. There are no moral grounds for arguing that exposing workers to carcinogenic asbestos is ethically correct, irrespective of what a country's law allows or the value the country places on worker safety.

A company that adopts the principle of ethical relativism and holds company personnel to local ethical standards necessarily assumes that what prevails as local morality is an adequate guide to ethical behavior. This can be ethically dangerous—it leads to the conclusion that if a country's culture is accepting of bribery or environmental degradation or dangerous working conditions (toxic chemicals or bodily harm), then so much the worse for honest people and protection of the environment and safe working conditions. Such a position is morally unacceptable.

> Managers in multinational enterprises have to figure out how to navigate the gray zone that arises when operating in two cultures with two sets of ethics.

Moreover, from a global markets perspective, ethical relativism results in a maze of conflicting ethical standards for multinational companies wanting to address the very real issue of what ethical standards to enforce companywide. On the one hand, multinational companies need to educate and motivate their employees worldwide to respect the customs and traditions of other nations; on the other hand, they must enforce compliance with the company's own particular code of ethical behavior. It is a slippery slope indeed to resolve such ethical diversity without any kind of higher-order moral compass.

Ethics and Integrative Social Contracts Theory

Core Concept

According to **integrated social contracts theory,** universal ethical principles or norms based on the collective views of multiple cultures and societies combine to form a "social contract" that all individuals in all situations have a duty to observe. Within the boundaries of this social contract, local cultures can specify other impermissible actions; however, universal ethical norms always take precedence over local ethical norms.

Social contracts theory provides yet a middle position between the opposing views of universalism (that the same set of ethical standards should apply everywhere) and relativism (that ethical standards vary according to local custom).[18] According to **integrative social contracts theory,** the ethical standards a company should try to uphold are governed by both (1) a limited number of universal ethical principles that are widely recognized as putting legitimate ethical boundaries on actions and behavior in all situations and (2) the circumstances of local cultures, traditions, and shared values that further prescribe what constitutes ethically permissible behavior and what does not. In other words, universal ethical principles apply when almost all societies—endowed with rationality and moral knowledge—have common moral agreement on what is wrong and thereby put limits on which actions and behaviors fall inside the boundaries of what is right and which ones fall outside. *Universal ethical principles or norms thus establish "moral free space" based on the collective views of multiple societies and cultures; these commonly held views about morality and ethical principles combine to form a "social contract" or contract with society.* This, however, leaves room for societies and national or religious cultures (as well as companies) to make specific interpretations of what other actions may or may not be permissible within the free space defined by universal ethical principles. Where firms, industries, professional associations, and other business-relevant groups have developed ethical codes and norms, then the standards they call for provide appropriate guidance. In all other instances, however, social contracts theory holds that *universal ethical norms take precedence over local ethical norms.*

The strength of integrated social contracts theory is that it accommodates the best parts of ethical universalism and ethical relativism. It is indisputable that cultural differences abound in global business activities and that these cultural differences sometimes give rise to different ethical norms. But it is just as indisputable that some ethical norms are more authentic or universally applicable than others, meaning that in many instances of cross-country differences one side may be more "ethically correct" or "more right" than another. In such instances, resolving cross-cultural differences in what is ethically permissible versus what is not entails applying universal or "first-order" ethical norms and overriding the local or "second-order" ethical norms. A good example is the payment of bribes and kickbacks. Yes, bribes and kickbacks seem to be common in some countries, but does this justify paying them? Just because bribery flourishes in a country does not mean that it is an authentic or legitimate ethical norm. Virtually all of the world's major religions (Buddhism, Christianity, Confucianism, Hinduism, Islam, Judaism, Sikhism, and Taoism) and all moral schools of thought condemn bribery and corruption.[19] Bribery is commonplace in India, but when interviewed, Indian CEOs whose companies constantly engaged in payoffs indicated disgust for the practice and expressed no illusions about its impropriety.[20] Therefore, a multinational company might reasonably conclude that the right ethical standard is one of refusing to condone bribery and kickbacks on the part of company personnel no matter what the local custom is and no matter what the sales consequences are.

Granting an automatic preference to local-country ethical norms presents vexing problems to multinational company managers when the ethical standards followed in a foreign country are lower than those in its home country or in the company's code of ethics. Sometimes there can be no compromise on what is ethically permissible and what is not. *This is precisely what integrated social contracts theory maintains—adherence to universal or first-order ethical norms should always take precedence over local or second-order norms.* Integrated social contracts theory offers managers in multinational companies clear guidance in resolving cross-country ethical differences: those parts of the company's code of ethics that involve universal ethical norms must be enforced worldwide, but within these boundaries there is room for ethical diversity and opportunity for host-country cultures to exert *some* influence in setting their own moral and ethical standards. Such an approach detours the somewhat scary case of a self-righteous multinational company trying to operate as the standard-bearer of moral truth and imposing its interpretation of its code of ethics worldwide no matter what. And it avoids the equally scary case of a company's ethical conduct being no higher than local ethical norms in situations where such norms permit practices that are generally considered immoral or when local norms clearly conflict with a company's code of ethical conduct. But even with the guidance provided by integrated social contracts theory, there are many instances where cross-country differences in ethical norms create all kinds of "gray areas" where it is tough to draw a line in the sand between right and wrong decisions, actions, and business practices.

The Three Categories of Management Morality

Three categories of managers stand out with regard to ethical and moral principles in business affairs:[21]

- *The moral manager:* Moral managers are dedicated to high standards of ethical behavior, both in their own actions and in their expectations of how the company's business is to be conducted. They see themselves as stewards of ethical behavior and believe it is important to exercise ethical leadership. Moral managers may well be ambitious and have a powerful urge to succeed, but they pursue success in business within the confines of both the letter and the spirit of what is ethical and legal—they typically regard the law as an ethical minimum and have a habit of operating well above what the law requires.

- *The immoral manager:* Immoral managers have no regard for so-called ethical standards in business and pay no attention to ethical principles in making decisions and conducting the company's business. Their philosophy is that good business-people cannot spend time watching out for the interests of others and agonizing over "the right thing to do" from an ethical perspective. In the minds of immoral managers, nice guys come in second and the competitive nature of business requires that you either trample on others or get trampled yourself. They believe what really matters is single-minded pursuit of their own best interests—they are living examples of capitalistic greed, caring only about their own or their organization's gains and successes. Immoral managers may even be willing to short-circuit legal and regulatory requirements if they think they can escape detection. And they are always on the lookout for legal loopholes and creative ways to get around rules and regulations that block or constrain actions they deem in their own or their company's self-interest. Immoral managers are thus the bad guys—they have few scruples, have little or no integrity, and are willing to do almost anything they believe they can get away with. It doesn't bother them much to be seen by others as wearing the black hats.

- *The amoral manager:* Amoral managers appear in two forms: the intentionally amoral manager and the unintentionally amoral manager. *Intentionally amoral managers* are of the strong opinion that business and ethics are not to be mixed. They are not troubled by failing to factor ethical considerations into their decisions and actions because it is perfectly legitimate for businesses to do anything they wish as long as they stay within legal and regulatory bounds—in other words, if particular actions and behaviors are legal and comply with existing regulations, then they qualify as permissible and should not be seen as unethical. Intentionally amoral managers view the observance of high ethical standards (doing more than what is required by law) as too Sunday-schoolish for the tough competitive world of business, even though observing some higher ethical considerations may be appropriate in life outside business. Their concept of right and wrong tends to be lawyer-driven—how much can we get by with and can we go ahead even if it is borderline? Thus intentionally amoral managers hold firmly to the view that anything goes, as long as actions and behaviors are not clearly ruled out by prevailing legal and regulatory requirements.

Unintentionally amoral managers do not pay much attention to the concept of business ethics either, but for different reasons. They are simply casual about, careless about, or inattentive to the fact that certain kinds of business decisions or company activities are unsavory or may have deleterious effects on others—in short, they go about their jobs as best they can without giving serious thought to the ethical dimension of decisions and business actions. They are ethically unconscious when it comes to business matters, partly or mainly because they have never stopped to consider whether and to what extent business decisions or company actions sometimes spill over to create adverse impacts on others. Unintentionally amoral managers may even see themselves as people of integrity and as personally ethical. But, like intentionally amoral managers, they are of the firm view that businesses ought to be able to do whatever the current legal and regulatory framework allows them to do without being shackled by ethical considerations.

> **Core Concept**
>
> Amoral managers believe that businesses ought to be able to do whatever current laws and regulations allow them to do without being shackled by ethical considerations—they think that what is permissible and what is not is governed entirely by prevailing laws and regulations, not by societal concepts of right and wrong.

By some accounts, the population of managers is said to be distributed among all three types in a bell-shaped curve, with immoral managers and moral managers occupying the two tails of the curve, and amoral managers (especially intentionally amoral managers) occupying the broad middle ground.[22] Furthermore, within the population of managers, there is experiential evidence to support that while the average manager may be amoral most of the time, he or she may slip into a moral or immoral mode on occasion, based on a variety of impinging factors and circumstances.

A landscape that is apparently so cluttered with amoral and immoral managers does not bode well for the frequency with which company managers ground their strategies on exemplary ethical principles or for the vigor with which they try to ingrain ethical behavior into company personnel. And, as many business school professors have noted, there are considerable numbers of amoral business students in our classrooms. So efforts to root out shady and corrupt business practices and implant high ethical principles into the managerial process of crafting and executing strategy are unlikely to produce an ethically strong global business climate anytime in the near future, barring major effort to address and correct the ethical amorality and immorality of company managers.

Do Company Strategies Need to Be Ethical?

Company managers may formulate strategies that are ethical in all respects, or they may decide to employ strategies that, for one reason or another, have unethical or at least gray-area components. While most company managers are usually careful to ensure that a company's strategy is within the bounds of what is legal, they are not always so careful to ensure that all elements of their strategies are within the bounds of what is generally deemed ethical. Senior executives with strong ethical convictions are proactive in insisting that all aspects of company strategy fall within ethical boundaries. But at other companies, namely those whose senior executives are either immoral or amoral, shady strategies and unethical or borderline business practices may well be utilized, especially if their managers are clever at devising schemes to keep ethically questionable actions hidden from view.

In October 2004, *Wall Street Journal* headlines trumpeted that a cartel among insurance brokers had been busted. Among the ringleaders was worldwide industry leader Marsh & McLennan Cos., Inc., with 2003 revenues of $11.5 billion and a U.S. market share of close to 20 percent. The gist of the cartel was to cheat corporate clients by rigging the bids brokers solicited for insurance policies and thereby collecting big fees (called "contingent commissions") from major insurance companies for steering business their way. Two family members of Marsh & McLennan CEO Jeffrey Greenberg were CEOs of major insurance companies to which Marsh sometimes steered business. Greenberg's father was CEO of insurance giant AIG (which had total revenues of $81 billion and insurance premium revenues of $28 billion in 2003), and Greenberg's younger brother was CEO of ACE, Ltd., the 24th-biggest property-casualty insurer in the United States, with 2003 revenues of $10.7 billion and insurance premium revenues of more than $5 billion worldwide. Prior to joining ACE, Greenberg's younger brother had been president and COO of AIG, headed by his father.

Several months prior to the cartel bust, a Marsh subsidiary, Putnam Investments, had paid a $110 million fine for securities fraud and another Marsh subsidiary, Mercer Consulting, was placed under SEC investigation for engaging in "pay to play" practices that forced investment managers to pay fees to get Mercer's endorsement of them to pension funds.

The cartel scheme arose from the practice of large corporations of hiring the services of such brokers as Marsh & McLennan, Aon Corp., A.J. Gallaher & Co., Wells Fargo, or BB&T Insurance Services to manage their risks and take out appropriate property and casualty insurance on their behalf. The broker's job was to solicit bids from several insurers and obtain the best policies at the lowest prices for the client.

Marsh's insurance brokerage strategy was to solicit artificially high business from some insurance companies so it could guarantee that the bid of a preferred insurer on a given deal would win the business. The scheme involved Marsh brokers' calling underwriters at various insurers, often including AIG and ACE, and asking for "B" quotes—bids that were deliberately high. Insurers that were asked for B quotes knew that Marsh wanted another insurer to win the business, but were willing to participate because Marsh could on other policy solicitations end up steering the business to them via Marsh's B-quote strategy. Sometimes Marsh even asked underwriters that were providing B quotes to attend a meeting with Marsh's client and make a presentation regarding the insurer's policy to help bolster the credibility of the firm's inflated bid.

During the past five years, there has been an ongoing series of revelations where managers at such companies as Enron, Tyco International, HealthSouth, Rite Aid, Citicorp, Bristol-Myers, Adelphia, Royal Dutch/Shell, Parmalat (an Italy-based food products company), Mexican oil giant Pemex, Marsh & McLennan and other insurance brokers, several leading brokerage houses and investment banking firms, and a host of mutual fund companies have ignored ethical standards, deliberately stepped out of bounds, and been called to account by the media, regulators, and the legal system. The consequences of crafting strategies that cannot pass the test of moral scrutiny are manifested in the sharp drops in the stock prices of the guilty companies that have cost shareholders billions of dollars, the frequently devastating public relations hits that the accused companies have taken, the sizes of the fines that have been levied (often amounting to several hundred million dollars), the growing legion of criminal indictments and convictions of company executives, and the numbers of executives who have been dismissed from their jobs, shoved into early retirement, and/or suffered immense public embarrassment. The fallout from all these scandals has resulted in heightened management attention to legal and ethical considerations in crafting strategy. Company Spotlight 7.1 details the ethically flawed strategy at the world's leading insurance broker and the resulting consequences to those concerned.

Since it was widespread practice among insurers to pay brokers contingent commissions based on the volume or profitability of the business the broker directed to them, Marsh's B-quote solicitation strategy allowed it to steer business to those insurers' paying the largest contingent commissions—these commissions were in addition to the fees the broker earned from the corporate client for services rendered in conducting the bidding process for the client. A substantial fraction of the policies that Marsh steered went to two Bermuda-based insurance companies that it helped start up and in which it had ownership interests (some Marsh executives also indirectly owned shares of stock in one of the companies); indeed, these two insurance companies received 30 to 40 percent of their total business from policies that were steered to them by Marsh.

At Marsh, steering business to insurers paying the highest contingent commission was a key component of the company's overall strategy. Marsh's contingent commissions generated revenues of close to $1.5 billion over the 2001–2003 period, including $845 million in 2003 (without these commission revenues, Marsh's $1.5 billion in net profits would have been close to 40 percent lower in 2003).

Within days of headlines about the cartel bust, Marsh's stock price had fallen by 48 percent (costing shareholders about $11.5 billion in market value), and the company was looking down the barrel of a criminal indictment. To stave off the indictment (something no company had ever survived), board members forced Jeffrey Greenberg to resign as CEO. Another top executive was suspended. Criminal charges against several Marsh executives for their roles in the bid-rigging scheme were filed several weeks thereafter.

In an attempt to lead industry reform, Greenberg's successor quickly announced a new business model for Marsh that included not accepting any contingent commissions from insurers. Marsh's new strategy and business model involved charging fees only to its corporate clients for soliciting bids, placing their insurance, and otherwise managing clients' risks and crises. This eliminated the conflict of interest Marsh had in earning fees from both sides of the transactions it made on behalf of its corporate clients. Marsh also committed to provide up-front disclosure to clients of the fees it would earn on their business (in the past such fees had been murky and incomplete). Even so, several lawsuits, some involving class action, were filed against the company.

Meanwhile, all major commercial property-casualty insurers were scrambling to determine whether their payment of contingent commissions was ethical, since such arrangements clearly gave insurance brokers a financial incentive to place insurance with companies paying the biggest contingent commissions, not those with the best prices or terms. Prosecutors of the cartel had referred to the contingent commissions as kickbacks.

Sources: Monica Langley and Theo Francis, "Insurers Reel from Bust of a 'Cartel,'" *The Wall Street Journal*, October 18, 2004, pp. A1, A14; Monica Langley and Ian McDonald, "Marsh Averts Criminal Case with New CEO," *The Wall Street Journal*, October 26, 2004, pp. A1, A10; Christopher Oster and Theo Francis, "Marsh and Aon Have Holdings in Two Insurers," *The Wall Street Journal*, November 1, 2004, p. C1; and Marcia Vickers, "The Secret World of Marsh Mac," *BusinessWeek*, November 1, 2004, pp. 78–89.

What Are the Drivers of Unethical Strategies and Business Behavior?

The apparent pervasiveness of immoral and amoral businesspeople is one obvious reason why ethical principles are an ineffective moral compass in business dealings and why companies may resort to unethical strategic behavior. But apart from "the business of business is business, not ethics" kind of thinking, three other main drivers of unethical business behavior also stand out:[23]

■ Faulty oversight such that overzealous or obsessive pursuit of personal gain, wealth, and other selfish interests is overlooked by or escapes the attention of higher-ups (most usually the board of directors).

■ Heavy pressures on company managers to meet or beat performance targets.

■ A company culture that puts profitability and good business performance ahead of ethical behavior.

Overzealous Pursuit of Personal Gain, Wealth, and Selfish Interests   People who are obsessed with wealth accumulation, greed, power, status, and other selfish interests often push ethical principles aside in their quest for self-gain. Driven by their ambitions, they exhibit few qualms in skirting the rules or doing whatever is necessary to achieve their goals. The first and only priority of such corporate "bad apples" is to look out for their own best interests, and if climbing the ladder of success means having few scruples and ignoring the welfare of others, so be it. A general disregard for business ethics can prompt all kinds of unethical strategic maneuvers and behaviors at companies. Top executives, directors, and majority shareholders at cable TV company Adelphia Communications ripped off the company for amounts totaling well over $1 billion, diverting hundreds of millions of dollars to fund their Buffalo Sabres hockey team, build a private golf course, and buy timber rights—among other things—and driving the company into bankruptcy. Their actions, which represent one of the biggest instances of corporate looting and self-dealing in American business, took place despite the company's public pontifications about the principles it would observe in trying to care for customers, employees, stockholders, and the local communities where it operated. Andrew Fastow, Enron's chief financial officer (CFO), set himself up as the manager of one of Enron's off-the-books partnerships and as the part-owner of another, allegedly earning extra compensation of $30 million for his owner-manager roles in the two partnerships; Enron's board of directors agreed to suspend the company's conflict-of-interest rules designed to protect the company from this kind of executive self-dealing.

According to a civil complaint filed by the Securities and Exchange Commission, the chief executive officer (CEO) of Tyco International, a well-known $35.6 billion manufacturing and services company, conspired with the company's CFO to steal more than $170 million, including a company-paid $2 million birthday party for the CEO's wife held on Sardinia, an island off the coast of Italy; a $7 million Park Avenue apartment for his wife; and secret low-interest and interest-free loans to fund private businesses and investments and purchase lavish artwork, yachts, estate jewelry, and vacation homes in New Hampshire, Connecticut, Nantucket, and Park City, Utah. The CEO allegedly lived rent-free in a $31 million Fifth Avenue apartment that Tyco purchased in his name, directed millions of dollars of charitable contributions in his own name using Tyco funds, diverted company funds to finance his personal businesses and investments, and sold millions of dollars of Tyco stock back to Tyco itself through Tyco subsidiaries located in offshore bank-secrecy jurisdictions. Tyco's CEO and CFO were further charged with conspiring to reap more than $430 million from sales of stock, using questionable accounting to hide their actions, and engaging in deceptive accounting practices to distort the company's financial condition from 1995 to 2002. At the trial on the charges filed by the SEC, the prosecutor told the jury in his opening statement, "This case is about lying, cheating and stealing. These people didn't win the jackpot—they stole it." Defense lawyers countered that "every single transaction…was set down in detail in Tyco's books and records" and that the authorized and disclosed multimillion-dollar compensation packages were merited by the company's financial performance and stock price gains.

Prudential Securities paid a total of about $2 billion in the 1990s to settle misconduct charges relating to practices that misled investors on the risks and rewards of limited-partnership investments. Providian Financial Corporation, despite an otherwise glowing record of social responsibility and corporate citizenship, paid $150 million in 2001 to settle claims that its strategy included systematic attempts to cheat credit card holders. Ten prominent Wall Street securities firms in 2003 paid $1.4 billion to settle charges that they knowingly issued misleading stock research to investors in an effort to prop up the stock prices of client corporations. A host of mutual fund firms made under-the-table arrangements to regularly buy and sell stock for their accounts at special after-hours trading prices that disadvantaged long-term investors, and they had to pay nearly $2 billion in fines and restitution when their unethical practices were discovered by authorities during 2002–2003. Salomon Smith Barney, Goldman Sachs, Credit Suisse First Boston, and several other financial firms were assessed close to $2 billion in fines and restitution for the unethical manner in which they contributed to the scandals at Enron and WorldCom (now MCI) and for the shady practice of allocating shares of hot IPO stocks to a select list of corporate executives who either steered or were in a position to steer investment banking business their way.

Heavy Pressures on Company Managers to Meet or Beat Earnings Targets   When companies find themselves scrambling to achieve ambitious earnings growth and meet the quarterly and annual performance expectations of Wall Street analysts and investors, managers often feel enormous pressure to do whatever it takes to sustain the company's reputation for delivering good financial performance. Executives at high-performing companies know that investors will see the slightest sign of a slowdown in earnings growth as a red flag and unload some of their shares, thus driving down the company's stock price. The company's credit rating could be downgraded if it has used lots of debt to finance its growth. The pressure to watch the scoreboard and "never miss a quarter"—in meeting or beating earnings targets—so as not to upset the expectations of Wall Street analysts and fickle stock market investors—prompts managers to cut costs wherever savings show up immediately, squeeze extra sales out of early deliveries, and engage in other short-term maneuvers to meet earnings expectations. As the pressure builds to keep performance numbers looking good, company personnel start stretching the rules further and further, until the limits of ethical conduct are overlooked.[24] Once ethical boundaries are crossed in efforts to "meet or beat the numbers," the threshold for making more extreme ethical compromises becomes lower.

Several top executives at WorldCom (now MCI), a company built with scores of acquisitions in exchange for WorldCom stock, allegedly concocted a fraudulent $11 billion accounting scheme to hide costs and inflate revenues and profit over several years; the scheme was said to have helped the company keep its stock price propped up high enough to make additional acquisitions, support its nearly $30 billion debt load, and allow executives to cash in on their lucrative stock options. At Qwest Communications, a company created by the merger of a go-go telecom start-up and U.S. West (one of the regional Bell companies), management was charged with scheming to improperly book $2.4 billion in revenues from a variety of sources and deals, thereby inflating the company's profits and thus making it appear that the company's strategy to create a telecommunications company of the future was on track when, in fact, it was faltering badly behind the scenes. Top-level Qwest executives were dismissed and in 2004 new management agreed to $250 million in fines for all the misdeeds.

At Bristol-Myers Squibb, the world's fifth-largest drug maker, management apparently engaged in a series of numbers-game maneuvers to meet earnings targets, including such actions as:

- Offering special end-of-quarter discounts to induce distributors and local pharmacies to stock up on certain prescription drugs—a practice known as "channel stuffing."

- Issuing last-minute price increase alerts to spur purchases and beef up operating profits.

- Setting up excessive reserves for restructuring charges and then reversing some of the charges as needed to bolster operating profits.

- Making repeated asset sales small enough that the gains could be reported as additions to operating profit rather than being flagged as one-time gains. (Some accountants have long used a rule of thumb that says a transaction that alters quarterly profits by less than 5 percent is "immaterial" and need not be disclosed in the company's financial reports.)

Such numbers games were said to be a common "earnings management" practice at Bristol-Myers and, according to one former executive, "sent a huge message across the organization that you make your numbers at all costs."[25]

Company executives often feel pressured to hit financial performance targets because their compensation depends heavily on the company's performance. During the late 1990s, it became fashionable for boards of directors to grant lavish bonuses, stock option awards, and other compensation benefits to executives for meeting specified performance targets. So outlandishly large were these rewards that executives had strong personal incentives to bend the rules and engage in behaviors that allowed the targets to be met. Much of the accounting hocus-pocus at the root of recent corporate scandals has entailed situations in which executives benefited enormously from misleading accounting or other shady activities that allowed them to hit the numbers and receive incentive awards ranging from $10 million to $100 million. At Bristol-Myers Squibb, for example, the pay-for-performance link spawned strong rules-bending incentives. About 94 percent of one top executive's $18.5 million in total compensation in 2001 came from stock option grants, a bonus, and long-term incentive payments linked to corporate performance; about 92 percent of a second executive's $12.9 million of compensation was incentive-based.[26] Company Spotlight 7.2 describes elements of the strategies that three of the world's most prominent investment banking firms employed to gain new business and help meet performance targets—judge for yourself whether their strategies were ethical or shady.

The fundamental problem with a "make the numbers and move on" syndrome is that a company doesn't really serve its customers or its shareholders by putting top priority on the bottom line. In the final analysis, shareholder interests are best served by doing a really good job of serving customers (observing the rule that customers are "king") and by improving the company's competitiveness in the marketplace. Cutting ethical corners or stooping to downright illegal actions in the name of profits first is convoluted and misguided—when the spotlight is shined on such scurrilous behavior, the resulting fallout actually depreciates shareholder value rather than enhancing it.

Company Cultures That Put the Bottom Line Ahead of Ethical Behavior   When a company's culture spawns an ethically corrupt or amoral work climate, people have a company-approved license to ignore "what's right" and engage in almost any behavior or employ almost any strategy they think they can get away with. Such cultural norms as "No one expects strict adherence to ethical standards," "Everyone else does it," and "It is politic to bend the rules to get the job done" permeate the work environment.[27] At such companies, ethically immoral or amoral people are certain to play down observance of ethical strategic actions and business conduct. Moreover, the pressures to conform to cultural norms can prompt otherwise honorable people to make ethical mistakes and succumb to the many opportunities around them to engage in unethical practices.

COMPANY SPOTLIGHT 7.2

Strategies to Gain New Business at Wall Street Investment Banking Firms: Ethical or Unethical?

At Salomon Smith Barney (a subsidiary of Citigroup), Credit Suisse First Boston (CSFB), and Goldman Sachs—three of the world's most prominent investment banking companies—part of the strategy for securing the investment banking business of large corporate clients (to handle the sale of new stock issues or new bond issues or advise on mergers and acquisitions) involved (1) hyping the stocks of companies that were actual or prospective customers of their investment banking services and (2) allocating hard-to-get shares of hot initial public offerings (IPOs) to select executives and directors of existing and potential client companies, who then made millions of dollars in profits when the stocks went up once public trading began. Former World-Com CEO Bernie Ebbers reportedly made more than $11 million in trading profits over a four-year period on shares of IPOs received from Salomon Smith Barney; Salomon served as WorldCom's investment banker on a variety of deals during this period. Jack Grubman, Salomon's top-paid research analyst at the time, enthusiastically touted WorldCom stock and was regarded as the company's biggest cheerleader on Wall Street.

To help draw in business from new or existing corporate clients, CSFB established brokerage accounts for corporate executives who steered their company's investment banking business to CSFB. Apparently, CSFB's strategy for acquiring more business involved promising the CEOs and/or CFOs of companies about to go public for the first time or to issue new long-term bonds that if CSFB was chosen to handle the public offering or bond issue, then it would ensure that they would be allocated shares at the initial offering price of all subsequent IPOs in which CSFB was a participant. During 1999–2000, it was common for the stock of a hot IPO to rise 100 to 500 percent above the initial offering price in the first few days or weeks of public trading; the shares allocated to these executives were then sold for a tidy profit over the initial offering price. According to investigative sources, CSFB increased the number of companies whose executives were allowed to partic-ipate in its IPO offerings from 26 companies in January 1999 to 160 companies in early 2000; executives received anywhere from 200 to 1,000 shares each of every IPO in which CSFB was a participant in 2000. CSFB's accounts for these executives reportedly generated profits of about $80 million for the participants. Apparently, it was CSFB's practice to curtail access to IPOs for some executives if their companies didn't come through with additional securities business for CSFB or if CSFB concluded that other securities offerings by these companies would be unlikely.

Goldman Sachs also used an IPO-allocation scheme to attract investment banking business, giving shares to executives at 21 companies—among the participants were the CEOs of eBay, Yahoo, and Ford Motor Company. The CEO of eBay was a participant in over 100 IPOs managed by Goldman during the 1996–2000 period and was on Goldman's board of directors part of this time; eBay paid Goldman Sachs $8 million in fees for services during the 1996–2001 period.

Questions to Consider

1. If you were a top executive at Salomon Smith Barney, CSFB, or Goldman Sachs, would you be proud to defend your company's actions?

2. Would you want to step forward and take credit for having been a part of the group who designed or approved of the strategy for gaining new business at any of these three firms?

3. Is it accurate to characterize the allocations of IPO shares to "favored" corporate executives as bribes or kickbacks?

Sources: Charles Gasparino, "Salomon Probe Includes Senior Executives," *The Wall Street Journal*, September 3, 2002, p. C1; Randall Smith and Susan Pulliam, "How a Star Banker Pressed for IPOs," *The Wall Street Journal*, September 4, 2002, pp. C1, C14; Randall Smith and Susan Pulliam, "How a Technology-Banking Star Doled Out Shares of Hot IPOs," *The Wall Street Journal*, September 23, 2002, pp. A1, A10; and Randall Smith, "Goldman Sachs Faces Scrutiny for IPO-Allocation Practices," *The Wall Street Journal*, October 3, 2002, pp. A1, A6.

A perfect example of a company culture gone awry on ethics is Enron.[28] Enron's leaders encouraged company personnel to focus on the current bottom line and to be innovative and aggressive in figuring out what could be done to grow current revenues and earnings. Employees were expected to pursue opportunities to the utmost in the electric utility industry, which at the time was undergoing looser regulation. Enron executives viewed the company as a laboratory for innovation; the company hired the best and brightest people and pushed them to be creative, look at problems and opportunities in new ways, and exhibit a sense of urgency in making things happen. Employees were encouraged to make a difference and do their part in creating an entrepreneurial environment where creativity flourished, people could achieve their full potential, and everyone had a stake in the outcome. Enron employees got the message—pushing the limits and meeting one's numbers were viewed as survival skills. Enron's annual "rank and yank" formal evaluation process, where the 15 to 20 percent lowest-ranking employees were let go or encouraged to seek other employment, made it abundantly clear that achieving bottom-line results and being the "mover and shaker" in the marketplace were what counted. The name of the game at Enron became devising clever ways to boost revenues and earnings, even if doing so sometimes meant operating outside established policies and without the knowledge of superiors. In fact, outside-the-lines behavior was celebrated if it generated profitable new business. Enron's energy contracts and its trading and hedging activities grew increasingly more complex and diverse as employees pursued first this avenue and then another to help keep Enron's financial performance looking good.

As a consequence of Enron's well-publicized successes in creating new products and businesses and leveraging the company's trading and hedging expertise into new market arenas, Enron came to be regarded as an exceptionally innovative company. It was ranked by its corporate peers as the most innovative U.S. company for three consecutive years in *Fortune* magazine's annual surveys of the most admired companies. A high-performance–high-rewards climate came to pervade the Enron culture, as the best workers (determined by who produced the best bottom-line results) received impressively large incentives and bonuses (amounting to as much as $1 million for traders and even more for senior executives). On Car Day at Enron, an array of luxury sports cars arrived for presentation to the most successful employees. Understandably, employees wanted to be seen as part of Enron's star team and partake in the benefits that being one of Enron's best and smartest employees entailed. The high monetary rewards, the ambitious and hard-driving people that the company hired and promoted, and the competitive, results-oriented culture combined to give Enron a reputation not only for trampling competitors at every opportunity but also for internal ruthlessness. The company's super-aggressiveness and win-at-all-costs mind-set nurtured a culture that gradually and then more rapidly fostered the erosion of ethical standards, eventually making a mockery of the company's stated values of integrity and respect. When it became evident in the fall of 2001 that Enron was a house of cards propped up by deceitful accounting and a myriad of unsavory practices, the company imploded in a matter of weeks—the biggest bankruptcy of all time cost investors $64 billion in losses (between August 2000, when the stock price was at its five-year high, and November 2001), and Enron employees lost their retirement assets, which were almost totally invested in Enron stock.

More recently, a team investigating an ethical scandal at oil giant Royal Dutch/Shell Group that resulted in the payment of $150 million in fines found that an ethically flawed culture was a major contributor to why managers made rosy forecasts that they couldn't meet and why top executives engaged in maneuvers to mislead investors by overstating Shell's oil and gas reserves by 25 percent (equal to 4.5 billion barrels of oil). The investigation revealed that top Shell executives knew that a variety of internal practices, together with unrealistic and unsupportable estimates submitted by overzealous and bonus-conscious managers in Shell's exploration and production group, were being used to overstate reserves. An e-mail written by Shell's top executive for exploration and production (who was caught up in the ethical misdeeds and later forced to resign) said, "I am becoming sick and tired about lying about the extent of our reserves issues and the downward revisions that need to be done because of our far too aggressive/optimistic bookings."[29]

Approaches to Managing a Company's Ethical Conduct

The stance a company takes in dealing with or managing ethical conduct at any given point can take any of four basic forms:[30]

- The unconcerned or nonissue approach.
- The damage control approach.
- The compliance approach.
- The ethical culture approach.

The differences in these four approaches are discussed briefly below and summarized in Table 7.1.

The Unconcerned or Nonissue Approach

The unconcerned approach is prevalent at companies whose executives are immoral and unintentionally amoral. Senior executives at companies using this approach ascribe to the view that notions of right and wrong in matters of business are defined entirely by government via the prevailing laws and regulations. They maintain that trying to enforce ethical standards above and beyond what is legally required is a nonissue because businesses are entitled to conduct their affairs in whatever manner they wish as long as they comply with the letter of what is legally required. Hence, there is no need to spend valuable management time trying to prescribe and enforce standards of conduct that go above and beyond legal and regulatory requirements. In companies where senior managers are immoral, the prevailing view may well be that under-the-table dealing can be good business if it can be kept hidden or if it can be justified on grounds that others are doing it too. Companies in this mode usually engage in almost any business practices they believe they can get away with, and the strategies they employ may well embrace elements that are either borderline from a legal perspective or ethically shady and unsavory.

The Damage Control Approach

Damage control is favored at companies whose managers are intentionally amoral but who are wary of scandal and adverse public relations fallout that could cost them their jobs or tarnish their careers. Companies using this approach, not wanting to risk tarnishing the reputations of key personnel or the company, usually make some concession to window-dressing ethics, going so far as to adopt a code of ethics—so that their executives can point to it as evidence of good-faith efforts to prevent unethical strategy making or unethical conduct on the part of company personnel. But the code of ethics exists mainly as nice words on paper, and company

> The main objective of the damage control approach is to protect against adverse publicity and any damaging consequences brought on by headlines in the media, outside investigation, threats of litigation, punitive government action, or angry or vocal stakeholders.

Table 7.1   FOUR APPROACHES TO MANAGING BUSINESS ETHICS

	Unconcerned or Nonissue Approach	Damage Control Approach	Compliance Approach	Ethical Culture Approach
Underlying beliefs	■ The business of business is business, not ethics ■ Ethics has no place in the conduct of business ■ Companies should not be morally accountable for their actions	■ Need to make a token gesture in the direction of ethical standards (a code of ethics)	■ Company must be committed to ethical standards and monitoring ethics performance ■ Unethical behavior must be prevented and punished if discovered ■ Important to have a reputation for high ethical standards	■ Ethics is basic to the culture ■ Behaving ethically must be a deeply held corporate value and become a "way of life" ■ Everyone is expected to walk the talk
Ethics management approaches	■ There's no need to make decisions concerning business ethics—if it's legal, it is okay ■ No intervention regarding the ethical component of decisions is needed	■ Act to protect against the dangers of unethical strategies and behavior ■ Ignore unethical behavior or allow it to go unpunished unless the situation is extreme and requires action	■ Establish a clear, comprehensive code of ethics ■ Prevent unethical behavior ■ Provide ethics training for all personnel ■ Have formal ethics compliance procedures, an ethics compliance office, and a chief ethics officer	■ Ethical behavior is ingrained and reinforced as part of the culture ■ Much reliance on coworker peer pressure—"that's not how we do things here" ■ Everyone is an ethics watchdog—whistle-blowing is required ■ Ethics heroes are celebrated; ethics stories are told
Challenges	■ Financial consequences can become unaffordable ■ Some stakeholders are alienated	■ Credibility problems with stakeholders can arise ■ The company is susceptible to ethical scandal ■ The company has a subpar ethical reputation—executives and company personnel don't walk the talk	■ Organization members come to rely on the existing rules for moral guidance—fosters a mentality of what is not forbidden is allowed ■ Rules and guidelines proliferate ■ The locus of moral control resides in the code and in the ethics compliance system rather than in an individual's own moral responsibility for ethical behavior	■ New employees must go through strong ethics induction program ■ Formal ethics management systems can be underutilized ■ Relying on peer pressures and cultural norms to enforce ethical standards can result in eliminating some or many of the compliance trappings and, over time, induce moral laxness

Source: Adapted from Gedeon J. Rossouw and Leon J. van Vuuren, "Modes of Managing Morality: A Descriptive Model of Strategies for Managing Ethics," *Journal of Business Ethics* 46, no. 4 (September 2003), pp. 392–393.

personnel do not operate within a strong ethical context—there's a notable gap between talking ethics and walking ethics. Employees quickly get the message that rule bending is tolerated and may even be rewarded if the company benefits from their actions.

Company executives who practice the damage control approach are prone to look the other way when shady or borderline behavior occurs—adopting a kind of "see no evil, hear no evil, speak no evil" stance (except when exposure of the company's actions puts executives under great pressure to redress any wrongs that have been done). They may even condone questionable actions that help the company reach earnings targets or bolster its market standing—such as pressuring customers to stock up on the company's product (channel stuffing), making under-the-table payments to win new business, stonewalling the recall of products claimed to be unsafe, bad-mouthing the products of rivals, or trying to keep prices low by sourcing goods from disreputable suppliers in low-wage countries that run sweatshop operations or use child labor. But they are usually careful to do such things in a manner that lessens the risks of exposure or damaging consequences. This generally includes making token gestures to police compliance with codes of ethics and relying heavily on all sorts of "spin" to help extricate the company or themselves from claims that the company's strategy has unethical components or that company personnel have engaged in unethical practices.

The Compliance Approach   Anywhere from light to forceful compliance is favored at companies whose managers (1) lean toward being somewhat amoral but are highly concerned about having ethically upstanding reputations or (2) are moral and see strong compliance methods as the best way to impose and enforce ethical rules and high ethical standards. Companies that adopt a compliance mode usually do some or all of the following to display their commitment to ethical conduct: make the code of ethics a visible and regular part of communications with employees, implement ethics training programs, appoint a chief ethics officer or ethics ombudsperson, have ethics committees to give guidance on ethics matters, institute formal procedures for investigating alleged ethics violations, conduct ethics audits to measure and document compliance, give ethics awards to employees for outstanding efforts to create an ethical climate and improve ethical performance, and/or try to deter violations by setting up ethics hotlines for anonymous callers to use in reporting possible violations.

Emphasis here is usually on securing broad compliance and measuring the degree to which ethical standards are upheld and observed. However, violators are disciplined and sometimes subjected to public reprimand and punishment (including dismissal), thereby sending a clear signal to company personnel that complying with ethical standards needs to be taken seriously. The driving force behind the company's commitment to eradicate unethical behavior normally stems from a desire to avoid the cost and damage associated with unethical conduct or from a quest to gain favor with stakeholders (especially ethically conscious customers, employees, and investors) for having a highly regarded reputation for ethical behavior. One of the weaknesses of the compliance approach is that moral control resides in the company's code of ethics and in the ethics compliance system rather than in (1) the strong peer pressures for ethical behavior that come from ingraining a highly ethical corporate culture and (2) an individual's own moral responsibility for ethical behavior.[31]

The Ethical Culture Approach   At some companies, top executives believe that high ethical principles must be deeply ingrained in the corporate culture and function as guides for "how we do things around here." A company using the ethical culture approach seeks to gain employee buy-in to the company's ethical standards, business principles, and corporate values. The ethical principles embraced in the company's code of ethics and/or in its statement of corporate values are seen as integral to the company's identity and ways of operating—they are at the core of the company's soul and are promoted as part of "business as usual." The integrity of the ethical culture approach depends heavily on the ethical integrity of the executives who create and nurture the culture—it is incumbent on them to determine how high the bar is to be set and to exemplify ethical standards in their own decisions and behavior. Further, it is essential that the strategy be ethical in all respects and that ethical behavior be ingrained in the means that company personnel employ to execute the strategy. Such insistence on observing ethical standards is what creates an ethical work climate and a workplace where displaying integrity is the norm.

Many of the trappings used in the compliance approach are also manifest in the ethical culture mode, but one other is added—strong peer pressure from coworkers to observe ethical norms. Thus, responsibility for ethics compliance is widely dispersed throughout all levels of management and the rank and file. Stories of former and current moral heroes are kept in circulation, and the deeds of company personnel who display ethical values and are dedicated to "walking the talk" are celebrated at internal company events. The message that ethics matters—and matters a lot—resounds loudly and clearly throughout the organization and in its strategy and decisions. However, one of the challenges to overcome in the ethical culture approach is relying too heavily on peer pressures and cultural norms to enforce ethics compliance rather than on an individual's own moral responsibility for ethical behavior—in the absence of unrelenting peer pressure or strong internal compliance systems, there is a danger that over time company personnel may become lax about ethical standards. Compliance procedures need to be an integral part of the ethical culture approach to help send the message that management takes the observance of ethical norms seriously and that behavior that falls outside ethical boundaries will have negative consequences.

Why a Company Can Change Its Ethics Management Approach   Regardless of the approach they have used to manage ethical conduct, a company's executives may sense that they have exhausted a particular mode's potential for managing ethics and that they need to become more forceful in their approach to ethics management. Such changes typically occur when the company's ethical failures have made the headlines and created an embarrassing situation for company officials or when the business climate changes. For example, the recent raft of corporate scandals, coupled with aggressive enforcement of anticorruption legislation such as the Sarbanes-Oxley Act of 2002 (which addresses corporate governance and accounting practices), has prompted numerous executives and boards of directors to clean up their acts in accounting and financial reporting, review their ethical standards, and tighten up ethics compliance procedures. Intentionally amoral managers using the unconcerned or nonissue approach to ethics management may see less risk in shifting to the damage control approach (or, for appearance's sake, maybe a "light" compliance mode). Senior managers who have employed the damage control mode may be motivated by bad experiences to mend their ways and shift to a compliance mode. In the wake of so many corporate scandals, companies in the compliance mode may move closer to the ethical culture approach.

Why Should Company Strategies Be Ethical?

There are two reasons why a company's strategy should be ethical: (1) because a strategy that is unethical in whole or in part is morally wrong and reflects badly on the character of the company personnel involved and (2) because an ethical strategy is good business and is in the self-interest of shareholders.

Managers do not dispassionately assess what strategic course to steer. Ethical strategy making generally begins with managers who themselves have strong character (i.e., who are honest, have integrity, are ethical, and truly care about how they conduct the company's business). Managers with high ethical principles and standards are usually advocates of a corporate code of ethics and strong ethics compliance, and they are typically genuinely committed to certain corporate values and business principles. They walk the talk in displaying the company's stated values and living up to its business principles and ethical standards. They understand there's a big difference between adopting values statements and codes of ethics that serve merely as window dressing and adopting those that truly paint the white lines for a company's actual strategy and business conduct. As a consequence, ethically strong managers consciously opt for strategic actions that can pass moral scrutiny—they display no tolerance for strategies with ethically controversial components.

But there are solid business reasons to adopt ethical strategies even if most company managers are not of strong moral character and personally committed to high ethical standards. Pursuing unethical strategies not only damages a company's reputation but can also have costly consequences that are wide-ranging. Some of the costs are readily visible; others are hidden and difficult to track down—as shown in Figure 7.1. The costs of fines and penalties and any declines in the stock price are easy enough to calculate. The administrative "cleanup" (or level 2) costs are usually buried in the general costs of doing business and can be difficult to ascribe to any one ethical misdeed. Level 3 costs can be quite difficult to quantify but can sometimes be the most devastating—the aftermath of the Enron debacle left Arthur Andersen's reputation in shreds and led to the once-revered accounting firm's almost immediate demise. It remains to be seen whether Marsh & McLennan can overcome the problems described in Company Spotlight 7.1 or whether Merck, once one of the world's most respected pharmaceutical firms, can survive the revelation that senior management deliberately concealed that its Vioxx painkiller, which the company pulled off the market in September 2004, was tied to much greater risk of heart attack and strokes—some 20 million people in the United States had taken Vioxx over the years and Merck executives had reason to suspect as early as 2000 (and perhaps earlier) that Vioxx had dangerous side effects.[32]

Rehabilitating a company's shattered reputation is time-consuming and costly. Customers shun companies known for their shady behavior. Companies with reputations for unethical conduct have considerable difficulty in recruiting and retaining talented employees. Most hardworking, ethically upstanding people are repulsed by a work environment where unethical behavior is condoned; they don't want to get entrapped in a compromising situation, nor do they want their personal reputations tarnished by the actions of an unsavory employer. A 1997 survey revealed that 42 percent of the respondents took into account a company's ethics when deciding whether to accept a job.[33] Creditors are usually unnerved by the unethical actions of a borrower because of the potential business fallout and subsequent risk of default on any loans. To some significant degree, therefore, companies recognize that ethical

> Conducting business in an ethical fashion is in a company's enlightened self-interest.

Figure 7.1   **The Business Costs of Ethical Failures**

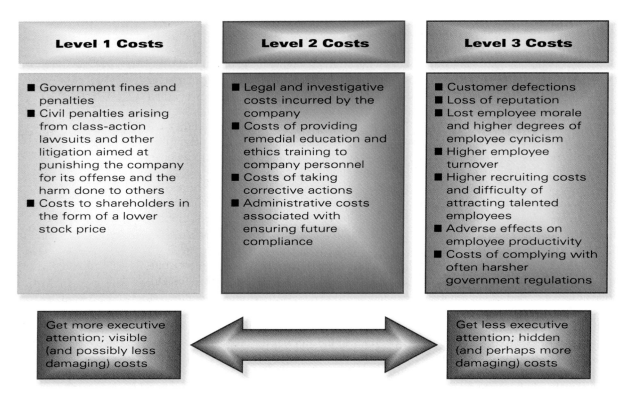

Level 1 Costs	Level 2 Costs	Level 3 Costs
■ Government fines and penalties ■ Civil penalties arising from class-action lawsuits and other litigation aimed at punishing the company for its offense and the harm done to others ■ Costs to shareholders in the form of a lower stock price	■ Legal and investigative costs incurred by the company ■ Costs of providing remedial education and ethics training to company personnel ■ Costs of taking corrective actions ■ Administrative costs associated with ensuring future compliance	■ Customer defections ■ Loss of reputation ■ Lost employee morale and higher degrees of employee cynicism ■ Higher employee turnover ■ Higher recruiting costs and difficulty of attracting talented employees ■ Adverse effects on employee productivity ■ Costs of complying with often harsher government regulations

Get more executive attention; visible (and possibly less damaging) costs	⟺	Get less executive attention; hidden (and perhaps more damaging) costs

Source: Terry Thomas, John R. Schermerhorn, and John W. Dienhart, "Strategic Leadership of Ethical Behavior," *Academy of Management Executive* 18, no. 2 (May 2004), p. 58.

strategies and ethical conduct are good business. Most companies have strategies that pass the test of being ethical, and most companies are aware that both their reputations and their long-term well-being are tied to conducting their business in a manner that wins the approval of suppliers, employees, investors, and society at large.

Strategy and Social Responsibility

The idea that businesses have an obligation to foster social betterment, a much-debated topic in the past 40 years, took root in the 19th century when progressive companies in the aftermath of the industrial revolution began to provide workers with housing and other amenities. The notion that corporate executives should balance the interests of all stakeholders—shareholders, employees, customers, suppliers, the communities in which they operated, and society at large—began to blossom in the 1960s. A group of chief executives of America's 200 largest corporations, calling themselves the Business Roundtable, promoted the concept of corporate social responsibility. In 1981, the Roundtable's "Statement on Corporate Responsibility" said:

Balancing the shareholder's expectations of maximum return against other priorities is one of the fundamental problems confronting corporate management. The shareholder must receive a good return but the legitimate concerns of other constituencies (customers, employees, communities, suppliers and society at large) also must have the appropriate attention. . . . [Leading managers] believe that by giving enlightened consideration to balancing the legitimate claims of all its constituents, a corporation will best serve the interest of its shareholders.[34]

Today, corporate social responsibility is a concept that resonates in Western Europe, the United States, Canada, and such developing nations as Brazil and India.

What Do We Mean by Social Responsibility?

The essence of **social responsibility** as applied to business behavior is that a company should balance strategic actions to benefit shareholders against the *duty* to be a good corporate citizen. Company managers must display a *social conscience* in operating the business and specifically take into account how management decisions and company actions affect the well-being of employees, local communities, the environment, and society at large. Acting in a socially responsible manner thus encompasses more than just participating in community service projects and donating monies to charities and other worthy social causes. Demonstrating social responsibility also entails undertaking actions that earn trust and respect from all stakeholders—operating in an honorable and ethical manner, striving to make the company a great place to work, demonstrating genuine respect for the environment, and trying to make a difference in bettering society. As depicted in Figure 7.2, the menu for demonstrating a social conscience and choosing specific ways to exercise social responsibility includes:

> **Core Concept**
>
> The notion of **social responsibility** as it applies to businesses concerns a company's *duty* to operate in an honorable manner, provide good working conditions for employees, be a good steward of the environment, and actively work to better the quality of life in the local communities where it operates and in society at large.

- *Efforts to employ an ethical strategy and observe ethical principles in operating the business:* A sincere commitment to observing ethical principles is necessary here simply because unethical strategies and conduct are incompatible with the concept of good corporate citizenship and socially responsible business behavior.

- *Making charitable contributions, donating money and the time of company personnel to community service endeavors, supporting various worthy organizational causes, and reaching out to make a difference in the lives of the disadvantaged:* Some companies fulfill their corporate citizenship and community outreach obligations by spreading their efforts over a multitude of charitable and community activities; for instance, Microsoft and Johnson & Johnson support a broad variety of community art, social welfare, and environmental programs. Others prefer to focus their energies more narrowly. McDonald's, for example, concentrates on sponsoring the Ronald McDonald House program (which provides a home away from home for the families of seriously ill children receiving treatment at nearby hospitals), preventing child abuse and neglect, and participating in local community service activities; in 2004, there were 240 Ronald McDonald Houses in 25 countries and more than 6,000 bedrooms available nightly. British Telecom gives 1 percent of its profits directly to communities, largely for education—teacher training, in-school workshops, and digital technology. Leading prescription drug maker GlaxoSmithKline and other pharmaceutical companies either donate or heavily discount medicines for distribution in the least developed nations. Numerous

Figure 7.2   Demonstrating a Social Conscience—The Five Components of Socially Responsible Business Behavior

Source: Adapted from material in Ronald Paul Hill, Debra Stephens, and Iain Smith, "Corporate Social Responsibility: An Examination of Individual Firm Behavior," *Business and Society Review* 108, no. 3 (September 2003), p. 348.

health-related businesses take a leading role in community activities that promote effective health care. Many companies work closely with community officials to minimize the impact of hiring large numbers of new employees (which could put a strain on local schools and utility services) and to provide outplacement services for laid-off workers. Companies frequently reinforce their philanthropic efforts by encouraging employees to support charitable causes and participate in community affairs, often through programs to match employee contributions.

■ *Actions to protect or enhance the environment and, in particular, to minimize or eliminate any adverse impact on the environment stemming from the company's own business activities:* Social responsibility as it applies to environmental protection means doing more than what is legally required. From a social responsibility perspective, companies have an obligation to be stewards of the environment. This means using the best available science and technology to achieve higher-than-required environmental standards. Even more ideally, it means putting time and money into improving the environment in ways that extend past a company's own industry boundaries— such as participating in recycling projects, adopting energy conservation practices, and supporting efforts to clean up local water supplies. Retailers such as Home Depot in the United States and B&Q in the United Kingdom have pressured their suppliers to adopt stronger environmental protection practices.[35]

> Business leaders who want their companies to be regarded as exemplary corporate citizens not only must see that their companies operate ethically but must personally display a social conscience in making decisions that affect employees, the environment, the communities in which they operate, and society at large.

■ *Actions to create a work environment that enhances the quality of life for employees and makes the company a great place to work:* Numerous companies go beyond providing the ordinary kinds of compensation and exert extra efforts to enhance the quality of life for their employees, both at work and at home. This can include varied and engaging job assignments, career development programs and mentoring, rapid career advancement, appealing compensation incentives, ongoing training to ensure future employability, added decision-making authority, onsite day care, flexible work schedules for single parents, workplace exercise facilities, special leaves to care for sick family members, work-at-home opportunities, gender pay equity, showcase plants and offices, special safety programs, and the like.

■ *Actions to build a workforce that is diverse with respect to gender, race, national origin, and perhaps other aspects that different people bring to the workplace:* Most large companies in the United States have established workforce diversity programs, and some go the extra mile to ensure that their workplaces are attractive to ethnic minorities and inclusive of all groups and perspectives. The pursuit of workforce diversity can be good business—Johnson & Johnson, Pfizer, and Coca-Cola believe that a reputation for workforce diversity makes recruiting employees easier (talented employees from diverse backgrounds often seek out such companies). And at Coca-Cola, where strategic success depends on getting people all over the world to become loyal consumers of the company's beverages, efforts to build a public persona of inclusiveness for people of all races, religions, nationalities, interests, and talents have considerable strategic value. Multinational companies are particularly inclined to make workforce diversity a visible strategic component; they recognize that respecting individual differences and promoting inclusiveness resonate well with people all around the world. At a few companies the diversity initiative extends to suppliers—sourcing items from small businesses owned by women or ethnic minorities.

Crafting a Social Responsibility Strategy— The Starting Point for Demonstrating a Social Conscience

While striving to be socially responsible entails choosing from the menu outlined in the preceding section, there's plenty of room for every company to make its own statement about what charitable contributions to make, what kinds of community service projects to emphasize, what environmental actions to support, how to make the company a good place to work, where and how workforce diversity fits into the picture, and what else the company will do to support worthy causes and projects that benefit society. *The particular combination of socially responsible endeavors a company elects to pursue defines its* **social responsibility strategy.** However, unless a company's social responsibility initiatives become part of the way it operates its business every day, the initiatives are unlikely to catch fire and be fully effective. As an executive at Royal Dutch/Shell put it, corporate social responsibility "is not a cosmetic; it must be rooted in our values. It must make a difference to the way we do business."[36] Thus some companies are integrating social responsibility objectives into their missions and overall performance targets—they see social performance and environmental metrics as an essential component of judging the company's overall future performance. Some 2,500 companies around the world are not only articulating their social responsibility strategies and commitments but also issuing annual social responsibility reports (much like an annual report) that set forth their commitments and the progress they are making for all the world to see and evaluate.[37]

At Green Mountain Coffee Roasters, social responsibility includes fair dealing with suppliers and trying to do something about the poverty of small coffee growers; in its dealings with suppliers at small farmer cooperatives in Peru, Mexico, and Sumatra, Green Mountain pays "fair-trade" prices for coffee beans (in 2002, the fair-trade prices were a minimum of $1.26 per pound for conventional coffee and $1.41 for organically grown versus market prices of 24 to 50 cents per pound). Green Mountain also purchases about 25 percent of its coffee direct from farmers so as to cut out intermediaries and see that farmers realize a higher price for their efforts—coffee is the world's second most heavily traded commodity after oil, requiring the labor of some 20 million people, most of whom live at the poverty level.[38] At General Mills the social responsibility focus is on serving the community and bettering the employment opportunities for minorities and women. Stonyfield Farm, a producer of yogurt and ice-cream products, employs a social responsibility strategy focused on wellness, good nutrition, and "earth-friendly" actions (10 percent of profits are donated to help protect and restore the earth, and yogurt lids are used as minibillboards to help educate people about environmental issues); in addition, it is stressing the development of an environmentally friendly supply chain, sourcing from farmers that grow organic products and refrain from using artificial hormones in milk production. Chick-Fil-A, an Atlanta-based fast-food chain with 1,125 outlets, has a charitable foundation, supports 14 foster homes and a summer camp (for some 1,600 campers from 22 states and several foreign countries), funds two scholarship programs (including one for employees that has awarded more than $18 million in scholarships), and has a closed-on-Sunday policy to ensure that every Chick-Fil-A employee and restaurant operator has an opportunity to worship, spend time with family and friends, or just plain rest from the workweek.[39]

It is common for companies engaged in natural resource extraction, electric power production, forestry and paper products, motor vehicles, and chemicals production to place more emphasis on addressing environmental concerns than, say, software and electronics firms or apparel manufacturers. Companies whose business success is heavily dependent on maintaining high employee morale or attracting and retaining the best and brightest employees are somewhat more prone to stress the well-being of their employees and foster a positive, high-energy workplace environment that elicits the dedication and enthusiastic commitment of employees, thus putting real meaning behind the claim "Our people are our greatest asset." Ernst & Young, one of the four largest global accounting firms, stresses its "People First" workforce diversity strategy, which is all about respecting differences, fostering individuality, and promoting inclusiveness, so that its 105,000 employees in 140 countries can feel valued, engaged, and empowered in developing creative ways to serve the firm's clients.

Thus, while the strategies and actions of all socially responsible companies have a sameness in the sense of drawing on the five categories of socially responsible behavior shown in Figure 7.2, each company's version of being socially responsible is unique.

The Moral Case for Corporate Social Responsibility

The moral case for why businesses should actively promote the betterment of society and act in a manner that benefits all of the company's stakeholders—not just the interests of shareholders—boils down to "it's the right thing to do." Ordinary decency, civic-mindedness, and contributions to the well-being of society should be expected of any business. In today's social and political climate most business leaders can be expected to acknowledge that socially responsible actions are important and that businesses have a duty to be good corporate citizens. But there is a complementary school of thought that business operates on the basis of an implied social contract with the members of society. According to this contract, society grants a business the right to conduct its business affairs and agrees not to unreasonably restrain its pursuit of a fair profit for the goods or services it sells; in return for this "license to operate," a business is obligated to act as a responsible citizen and do its fair share to promote the general welfare. Such a view clearly puts a moral burden on a company to take corporate citizenship into consideration and to do what's best for shareholders within the confines of discharging its duties to operate honorably, provide good working conditions to employees, be a good environmental steward, and display good corporate citizenship.

> Every action a company takes can be interpreted as a statement of what it stands for.

The Business Case for Socially Responsible Behavior

Whatever the merits of the moral case for socially responsible business behavior, it has long been recognized that it is in the enlightened self-interest of companies to be good citizens and devote some of their energies and resources to the betterment of employees, the communities in which they operate, and society in general. In short, there are several reasons why the exercise of social responsibility is good business:

■ *It generates internal benefits (particularly as concerns employee recruiting, workforce retention, and training costs).* Companies with deservedly good reputations for contributing time and money to the betterment of society are better able to attract and retain employees compared to companies with tarnished reputations. Some employees just feel better about working for a company committed to improving society.[40] This can contribute to lower turnover and better worker productivity. Other direct and indirect economic benefits include lower costs for staff recruitment and training. For example, Starbucks is said to enjoy much lower rates of employee turnover because of its full benefits package for both full-time and part-time employees, management efforts to make Starbucks a great place to work, and the company's socially responsible practices. When a U.S. manufacturer of recycled paper, taking eco-efficiency to heart, discovered how to increase its fiber recovery rate, it saved the equivalent of 20,000 tons of waste paper—a factor that helped the company become the industry's lowest-cost producer.[41] Various benchmarking and measurement mechanisms have shown that workforce diversity initiatives promote the success of companies that stay behind them. Making a company a great place to work pays dividends in the recruiting of talented workers, more creativity and energy on the part of workers, higher worker productivity, and greater employee commitment to the company's business mission/vision and success in the marketplace.

- *It reduces the risk of reputation-damaging incidents and can lead to increased buyer patronage.* Firms may well be penalized by employees, consumers, and shareholders for actions that are not considered socially responsible. When a major oil company suffered damage to its reputation on environmental and social grounds, the CEO repeatedly said that the most negative impact the company suffered—and the one that made him fear for the future of the company—was that bright young graduates were no longer attracted to work for the company.[42] Consumer, environmental, and human rights activist groups are quick to criticize businesses whose behavior they consider to be out of line, and they are adept at getting their message into the media and onto the Internet. Pressure groups can generate widespread adverse publicity, promote boycotts, and influence like-minded or sympathetic buyers to avoid an offender's products. Research has shown that product boycott announcements are associated with a decline in a company's stock price.[43] Outspoken criticism of Royal Dutch/Shell by environmental and human rights groups and associated boycotts were said to be major factors in the company's decision to tune in to its social responsibilities. For many years, Nike received stinging criticism for not policing sweatshop conditions in the Asian factories of its contractors, causing Nike CEO Phil Knight to observe that "Nike has become synonymous with slave wages, forced overtime, and arbitrary abuse."[44] In 1997, Nike began an extensive effort to monitor conditions in the 800 overseas factories to which it outsourced its shoes; Knight said, "Good shoes come from good factories and good factories have good labor relations." Nonetheless, Nike has continually been plagued by complaints from human rights activists that its monitoring procedures are flawed and that it is not doing enough to correct the plight of factory workers. In contrast, to the extent that a company's socially responsible behavior wins applause from consumers and fortifies its reputation, the company may win additional patron-age; Ben & Jerry's, Whole Foods Market, Stonyfield Farm, and the Body Shop have definitely expanded their customer bases because of their visible and well-publicized activities as socially conscious companies. More and more companies are recognizing the strategic value of social responsibility strategies that reach out to people of all cultures and demographics—in the United States, women are said to have buying power of $3.7 trillion; retired and disabled people, close to $4.1 trillion; Hispanics, nearly $600 billion; African-Americans, some $500 billion; and Asian-Americans, about $255 billion.[45] So reaching out in ways that appeal to such groups can pay off at the cash register. Some observers and executives are convinced that a strong, visible social responsibility strategy gives a company an edge in differentiating itself from rivals and in appealing to those consumers who prefer to do business with companies that are solid corporate citizens. Yet there is only limited evidence that consumers

> The higher the public profile of a company or brand, the greater the scrutiny of its activities and the higher the potential for it to become a target for pressure-group action.

go out of their way to patronize socially responsible companies if doing so means paying a higher price or purchasing an inferior product.[46]

■ *It is in the best interest of shareholders.* Well-conceived social re-sponsibility strategies work to the advantage of shareholders in several ways. Socially responsible business behavior helps avoid or preempt legal and regulatory actions that could prove costly and otherwise burdensome. Increasing numbers of mutual fund and pension benefit managers are restricting their stock purchases to companies that meet social responsibility criteria. According to one survey, one out of every eight dollars under professional man-agement in the United States involved socially responsible investing.[47] Moreover, the growth in socially responsible investing and in identifying socially responsible companies has led to a substantial increase in the number of companies that pub-lish formal reports on their social and environmental activities.[48] The stock prices of companies that rate high on social and environmental performance criteria have been found to perform 35 to 45 percent better than the average of the 2,500 com-panies constituting the Dow Jones Global Index.[49] A two-year study of leading companies found that improving environmental compliance and developing envi-ronmentally friendly products can enhance earnings per share, profitability, and the likelihood of winning contracts.[50] Nearly 100 studies have examined the rela-tionship between corporate citizenship and corporate financial performance over the past 30 years; the majority point to a positive relationship. Of the 80 studies that examined whether a company's social performance is a good predictor of its financial performance, 42 concluded yes, 4 concluded no, and the remainder re-ported mixed or inconclusive findings.[51] To the extent that socially responsible be-havior is good business, then, a social responsibility strategy that packs some punch and is more than rhetorical flourish turns out to be in the best interest of shareholders.

> There's little hard evidence indicating shareholders are disadvantaged in any meaningful way by a company's actions to be socially responsible.

In sum, companies that take social responsibility seriously can improve their busi-ness reputations and operational efficiency while also reducing their risk exposure and encouraging loyalty and innovation. Overall, companies that take special pains to pro-tect the environment (beyond what is required by law), are active in community affairs, and are generous supporters of charitable causes and projects that benefit society are more likely to be seen as good investments and as good companies to work for or do business with. Shareholders are likely to view the business case for social responsibil-ity as a strong one, even though they certainly have a right to be concerned about whether the time and money their company spends to carry out its social responsibility strategy outweighs the benefits and reduces the bottom line by an unjustified amount.

Companies are, of course, sometimes rewarded for bad behavior—a company that is able to shift environmental and other social costs associated with its activities onto society as a whole can reap large short-term profits. The major cigarette producers for many years were able to earn greatly inflated profits by shifting the health-related costs of smoking onto others and escaping any responsibility for the harm their products caused to consumers and the general public. But the profitability of shifting costs onto society is a risky practice because it attracts scrutiny from pressure groups, raises the threat of regulation and/or legislation to correct the inequity, and prompts socially con-scious buyers to take their business elsewhere.

How Much Attention to Social Responsibility Is Enough?

What is an appropriate balance between the imperative to create value for shareholders and the obligation to proactively contribute to the larger social good? What fraction of a company's resources ought to be aimed at addressing social concerns and bettering the well-being of society and the environment? A few companies have a policy of setting aside a specified percentage of their profits (typically 5 percent or maybe 10 percent) to fund their social responsibility strategy; they view such percentages as a fair amount to return to the community as a kind of thank-you or a tithe to the betterment of society. Other companies shy away from a specified percentage of profits or revenues because it entails upping the commitment in good times and cutting back on social responsibility initiatives in hard times (even cutting out social responsibility initiatives entirely if profits temporarily turn into losses). If social responsibility is an ongoing commitment rooted in the corporate culture and enlists broad participation on the part of company personnel, then a sizable portion of the funding for the company's social responsibility strategy has to be viewed as simply a regular and ongoing cost of doing business.

But judging how far a particular company should go in pursuing particular social causes is a tough issue. Consider, for example, Nike's commitment to monitoring the workplace conditions of its contract suppliers.[52] The scale of this monitoring task is significant: Nike has over 800 contract suppliers employing over 600,000 people in 50 countries. How frequently should sites be monitored? How should it respond to the use of underage labor? If children only above a set age are to be employed by suppliers, should suppliers still be required to provide schooling opportunities? At last count, Nike had some 80 people engaged in site monitoring. Should Nike's monitoring budget be $2 million, $5 million, $10 million, or whatever it takes?

Consider another example: If pharmaceutical manufacturers donate or discount their drugs for distribution to low-income people in less developed nations, what safeguards should they put in place to see that the drugs reach the intended recipients and are not diverted by corrupt local officials for reexport to markets in other countries? Should drug manufacturers also assist in drug distribution and administration in these less developed countries? How much should a drug company invest in R&D to develop medicines for tropical diseases commonly occurring in less developed countries when it is unlikely to recover its costs in the foreseeable future?

And how much should a company allocate to charitable contributions? Is it falling short of its responsibilities if its donations are less than 1 percent of profits? Is a company going too far if it allocates 5 percent or even 10 percent of its profits to worthy causes of one kind or another? The point here is that there is no simple or widely accepted standard for judging when a company has or has not gone far enough in fulfilling its citizenship responsibilities.

Linking Social Performance Targets to Executive Compensation

Perhaps the most surefire way to enlist a genuine commitment to corporate social responsibility initiatives is to link the achievement of social performance targets to executive compensation. If a company's board of directors is serious about corporate citizenship, then it will incorporate measures of the company's social and environmental performance into its evaluation of top executives, especially the CEO. And if the CEO uses compensation incentives to further enlist the support of down-the-line company personnel in effectively crafting and executing a social responsibility strategy, the company will over time build a culture rooted in socially responsible and ethical behavior. According to one study, 80 percent of surveyed CEOs believe that environmental and social performance metrics are a valid part of measuring a company's overall performance. At Verizon Communications, 10 percent of the annual bonus of the company's top 2,500 managers is tied directly to the achievement of social responsibility targets; for the rest of the staff, there are corporate recognition awards in the form of cash for employees who have made big contributions toward social causes. The corporate social responsibility reports being issued annually by 2,500 companies across the world that detail social responsibility initiatives and the results achieved are a good basis for compensating executives and judging the effectiveness of their commitment to social responsibility.

Key Points

Ethics involves concepts of right and wrong, fair and unfair, moral and immoral. Beliefs about what is ethical serve as a moral compass in guiding the actions and behaviors of individuals and organizations. Ethical principles in business are not materially different from ethical principles in general.

There are three schools of thought about ethical standards:

■ According to the *school of ethical universalism,* the same standards of what's ethical and what's unethical resonate with peoples of most societies regardless of local traditions and cultural norms; hence, common ethical standards can be used to judge the conduct of personnel at companies operating in a variety of country markets and cultural circumstances.

■ According to the *school of ethical relativism,* different societal cultures and customs have divergent values and standards of right and wrong—thus what is ethical or unethical must be judged in the light of local customs and social mores and can vary from one culture or nation to another.

■ According to *integrated social contracts theory,* universal ethical principles or norms based on the collective views of multiple cultures and societies combine to form a "social contract" that all individuals in all situations have a duty to observe. Within the boundaries of this social contract, local cultures can specify other impermissible actions; however, universal ethical norms always take precedence over local ethical norms.

Three categories of managers stand out in terms of their prevailing beliefs in and commitments to ethical and moral principles in business affairs: the moral manager, the immoral manager, and the amoral manager. By some accounts, the population of managers is said to be distributed among all three types in a bell-shaped curve, with immoral managers and moral managers occupying the two tails of the curve and the amoral managers, especially the intentionally amoral managers, occupying the broad middle ground.

The stance a company takes in dealing with or managing ethical conduct at any given time can take any of four basic forms:

■ The unconcerned or nonissue approach.

■ The damage control approach.

■ The compliance approach.

■ The ethical culture approach.

There are two reasons why a company's strategy should be ethical: (1) because a strategy that is unethical in whole or in part is morally wrong and reflects badly on the character of the company personnel involved and (2) because an ethical strategy is good business and in the self-interest of shareholders.

The term *corporate social responsibility* concerns a company's duty to operate in an honorable manner, provide good working conditions for employees, be a good steward of the environment, and actively work to better the quality of life in the local communities where it operates and in society at large. The menu of actions and behavior for demonstrating social responsibility includes:

■ Employing an ethical strategy and observing ethical principles in operating the business.

■ Making charitable contributions, donating money and the time of company personnel to community service endeavors, supporting various worthy organizational causes, and making a difference in the lives of the disadvantaged. Corporate commitments are further reinforced by encouraging employees to support charitable and community activities.

■ Protecting or enhancing the environment and, in particular, striving to minimize or eliminate any adverse impact on the environment stemming from the company's own business activities.

■ Creating a work environment that makes the company a great place to work.

■ Employing a workforce that is diverse with respect to gender, race, national origin, and perhaps other aspects that different people bring to the workplace.

There's ample room for every company to tailor its social responsibility strategy to fit its core values and business mission, thereby making its own statement about "how we do business and how we intend to fulfill our duties to all stakeholders and society at large."

The moral case for social responsibility boils down to a simple concept: it's the right thing to do. The business case for social responsibility holds that it is in the enlightened self-interest of companies to be good citizens and devote some of their energies and resources to the betterment of such stakeholders as employees, the communities in which they operate, and society in general.

The case for ethical and socially responsible behavior is about attracting and retaining talented staff, about managing risk, and about ensuring a company's reputation with customers, suppliers, local communities, and society.

Exercises

1. Based on the description of Marsh & McLennan's strategy presented in Company Spotlight 7.1, would it be fair to characterize the payment of contingent commissions by property-casualty insurers as nothing more than thinly disguised kickbacks? Why or why not? If you were the manager of a company that hired Marsh & McLennan to provide risk management services, would you see that Marsh had a conflict of interest in steering your company's insurance policies to insurers in which it has an ownership interest? Given Marsh's unethical and illegal foray into rigging the bids on insurance policies for its corporate clients, what sort of fines and penalties would you impose on the company for its misdeeds (assuming you were asked to recommend appropriate penalties by the prosecuting authorities). Using

Internet research tools, determine what Marsh & McLennan ended up paying in fines and restitution for its unethical and illegal strategic behavior and assess the extent to which the conduct of company personnel damaged shareholders.

2. Log on to www.business-ethics.com. Review the companies listed as the "100 Best Corporate Citizens" in the most recent year and the criteria for earning a spot on this list. Do the criteria seem reasonable? Is there ample reason to believe that the 100 companies on this list pursue strategies that are ethical? Or do the criteria used to determine the 100 Best Corporate Citizens point more to companies that have some standout socially responsible practices?

3. Assume you are a manager of a chain of fast-food restaurants in Russia, in partnership with a Russian company. One day you discover that a senior officer of your Russian joint-venture partner has been "borrowing" equipment from the joint-venture company and utilizing it in another of his business ventures. When you confront him, the Russian officer defends his actions, arguing that as an owner of both companies he is entitled to share use of the equipment. What would you say?

CHAPTER 8

Executing the Strategy
Building a Capable Organization and Instilling a Culture

The best game plan in the world never blocked or tackled anybody.

—*Vince Lombardi, NFL Hall of Fame football coach*

Strategies most often fail because they aren't executed well.

—*Larry Bossidy, CEO, Honeywell International, and Ram Charan, author and consultant*

Organizing is what you do before you do something, so that when you do it, it is not all mixed up.

—*A. A. Milne, author*

An organization's capacity to execute its strategy depends on its "hard" infrastructure—its organizational structure and systems—and on its "soft" infrastructure—its culture and norms.

—*Amar Bhide, professor*

The biggest levers you've got to change a company are strategy, structure, and culture. If I could pick two, I'd pick strategy and culture.

—*Wayne Leonard, CEO, Entergy*

Values can't just be words on a page. To be effective, they must shape action.

—*Jeffrey R. Immelt, CEO, General Electric*

Once managers have decided on a strategy, the emphasis turns to converting it into actions and good results. Putting the strategy into place and getting the organization to execute it well call for different sets of managerial skills. Whereas crafting strategy is largely a market-driven activity, executing strategy is primarily an operations-driven activity revolving around the management of people and business processes. Whereas successful strategy making depends on business vision, solid industry and competitive analysis, and shrewd market positioning, successful strategy execution depends on doing a good job of building and strengthening organizational capabilities, motivating and rewarding people in a strategy-supportive manner, and instilling a discipline of getting things done. Executing strategy is an action-oriented, make-things-happen task that tests a manager's ability to direct organizational change, achieve continuous improvement in operations and business processes, create and nurture a strategy-supportive culture, and consistently meet or beat performance targets.

Experienced managers are emphatic in declaring that it is a whole lot easier to develop a sound strategic plan than it is to execute the plan and achieve the desired outcomes. According to one executive, "It's been rather easy for us to decide where we wanted to go. The hard part is to get the organization to act on the new priorities."[1] What makes executing strategy a tougher, more time-consuming management challenge than crafting strategy is the wide array of managerial activities that have to be attended to, the many ways managers can proceed, the demanding people-management skills required, the perseverance necessary to get a variety of initiatives launched and moving, the number of bedeviling issues that must be worked out, the resistance to change that must be overcome, and the difficulties of integrating the efforts of many different work groups into a smoothly functioning whole.

Just because senior managers announce a new strategy doesn't mean that organization members will agree with it or enthusiastically move forward in implementing it. Senior executives cannot simply tell their immediate subordinates to implement new strategic initiatives and expect that the wheels will quickly start grinding and smoothly deliver the intended results. Skeptical managers and employees may see the strategy as contrary to the organization's best interests, unlikely to succeed, or threatening to their departments or careers. Moreover, individual employees may have different ideas about what internal changes are needed to execute the strategy. Long-standing attitudes, vested interests, inertia, and ingrained organizational practices don't melt away when managers decide on a new strategy and begin efforts to implement it—especially when only comparatively few people have been involved in crafting the strategy and when the rationale for strategic change has to be sold to enough organization members to root out the status quo. It takes adept managerial leadership to convincingly communicate the new strategy and the reasons for it, overcome pockets of doubt and disagreement, secure the commitment and enthusiasm of concerned parties, identify and build consensus on all the hows of implementation and execution, and get all the pieces into place and working well. Depending on how much consensus building, motivating, and organizational change is involved, the process of implementing strategy changes can take several months to several years.

Like crafting strategy, executing strategy is a job for the whole management team, not just a few senior managers. While an organization's chief executive officer and the heads of major units (business divisions, functional departments, and key operating units) are ultimately responsible for seeing that strategy is executed successfully, the process typically affects every part of the firm, from the biggest operating unit to the smallest frontline work group. Top-level managers have to rely on the

> ### Core Concept
>
> Implementing and executing a company's strategy is a job for the entire management team, not just a few senior managers.

active support and cooperation of middle and lower managers to push strategy changes into functional areas and operating units and to see that the organization actually operates in accordance with the strategy on a daily basis. Middle and lower-level managers not only are responsible for initiating and supervising the execution process in their areas of authority but also are instrumental in getting subordinates to continuously improve on how strategy-critical value chain activities are being performed and in producing the operating results that allow company performance targets to be met—their role on the company's strategy execution team is by no means minimal. *Strategy execution thus requires every manager to think through the answer to "What does my area have to do to implement its part of the strategic plan, and what should I do to get these things accomplished efficiently and effectively?"* Indeed, the bigger the organization or the more geographically scattered its operating units, the more that *successful strategy execution depends on the cooperation and implementing skills of operating managers who can push needed changes at the lowest organizational levels and consistently deliver good results.* Only in small organizations can top-level managers get around the need for a team effort on the part of management and personally orchestrate the action steps and implementation sequence.

A Framework for Executing Strategy

The first step in implementing strategic changes is for management to communicate the case for organizational change so clearly and persuasively to organization members that a determined commitment takes hold throughout the ranks to find ways to put the strategy into place, make it work, and meet performance targets. The ideal condition is for managers to arouse enough enthusiasm for the strategy to turn the implementation process into a companywide crusade. Then top executives can move to figuring out all the hows—the specific techniques, actions, and behaviors that are needed for a smooth strategy-supportive operation—and then following through to get things done and deliver results.

The Principal Managerial Components of the Strategy Execution Process

While a company's strategy-executing approaches always have to be tailored to the particulars of a company's situation, certain managerial bases have to be covered no matter what the circumstances. Eight managerial tasks crop up repeatedly in company efforts to execute strategy (see Figure 8.1):

1. Building an organization with the competencies, capabilities, and resource strengths to execute strategy successfully.
2. Shaping the work environment and corporate culture to fit the strategy.
3. Allocating ample resources to strategy-critical activities.
4. Ensuring that policies and procedures facilitate rather than impede strategy execution.

Figure 8.1   The Eight Components of the Strategy Execution Process

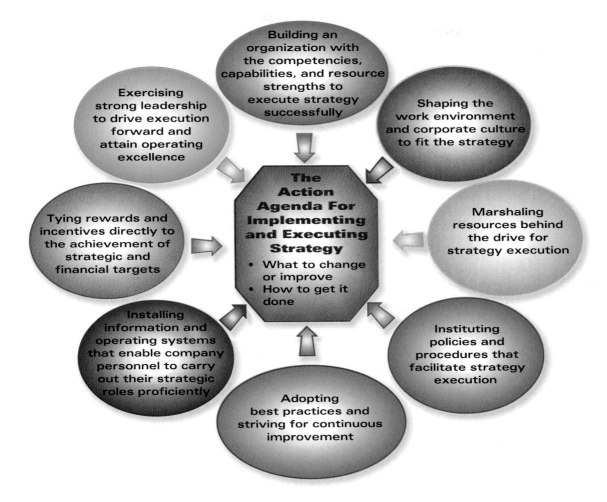

5. Instituting best practices and pushing for continuous improvement in how value chain activities are performed.

6. Installing information and operating systems that enable company personnel to carry out their strategic roles proficiently.

7. Tying rewards directly to the achievement of strategic and financial targets and to good strategy execution.

8. Exercising strong leadership to drive implementation forward, keep improving on how the strategy is being executed, and attain operating excellence.

How well managers perform these eight tasks has a decisive impact on whether the outcome is a spectacular success, a colossal failure, or something in between.

The specific hows of executing a strategy—the exact items that need to be placed on management's action agenda—always have to be customized to fit the particulars

When strategies fail, it is often because of poor execution—things that were supposed to get done slip through the cracks.

of a company's situation. The place for managers to start is with *a probing assessment of what the organization must do differently and better to carry out the strategy successfully.* They should then consider *precisely how to make the necessary internal changes* as rapidly as possible. Successful strategy implementers have a knack for diagnosing what their organizations need to do to execute the chosen strategy well and figuring out how to get things done—they are masters in promoting results-oriented behaviors on the part of company personnel and following through on making the right things happen in a timely fashion.[2] *Management's handling of the strategy implementation process can be considered successful if things go smoothly enough that the company meets or beats its performance targets and shows good progress in achieving its strategic vision.*

Making minor changes in an existing strategy differs from implementing radical strategy changes. The hot buttons for successfully executing a low-cost provider strategy are different from those for executing a high-end differentiation strategy. Implementing and executing a new strategy for a struggling company in the midst of a financial crisis is a different job than improving strategy execution in a company where the execution is already pretty good. Moreover, some managers are more adept than others at using this or that approach to achieving the desired kinds of organizational changes. Hence, there's no definitive recipe for successfully undertaking the eight managerial tasks shown in Figure 8.1.

What's Covered in Chapters 8 and 9   In the remainder of this chapter and the next chapter, we will discuss what is involved in performing the eight key managerial tasks that shape the process of implementing and executing strategy. This chapter explores building a capable organization and instilling a strategy-supportive corporate culture. Chapter 9 looks at the remaining six tasks: marshaling resources, establishing strategy-facilitating policies and procedures, instituting best practices, installing strategy-supportive operating systems, tying rewards to achievement, and exercising strong strategic leadership.

Building an Organization Capable of Proficient Strategy Execution

Proficient strategy execution depends heavily on competent personnel, better-than-adequate competencies and competitive capabilities, and effective internal organization. Building a capable organization is thus always a top priority in strategy execution. As shown in Figure 8.2, three types of organization-building actions are paramount:

1. *Staffing the organization*—putting together a strong management team, and recruiting and retaining employees with the needed experience, technical skills, and intellectual capital.

2. *Building core competencies and competitive capabilities*—developing the skills and expertise that will enable good strategy execution and updating all this know-how as strategy and external conditions change.

3. *Structuring the organization and work effort*—organizing value chain activities and business processes and deciding how much decision-making authority to push down to lower-level managers and frontline employees.

Figure 8.2 The Three Components of Building an Organization Capable of Proficient Strategy Execution

Staffing the Organization

- Putting together a strong management team
- Recruiting and retaining talented employees

Building Core Competencies and Competitive Capabilities

- Developing a set of competencies and capabilities suited to the current strategy
- Updating and revising this set as external conditions and strategy change
- Training and retraining employees as needed to maintain skills-based competencies

Matching the Organization Structure to Strategy

- Instituting organizational arrangements that will facilitate strategy execution
- Deciding how much decision-making authority to push down to lower-level managers and frontline employees

A Company with the Organizational Capability Needed for Proficient Strategy Execution

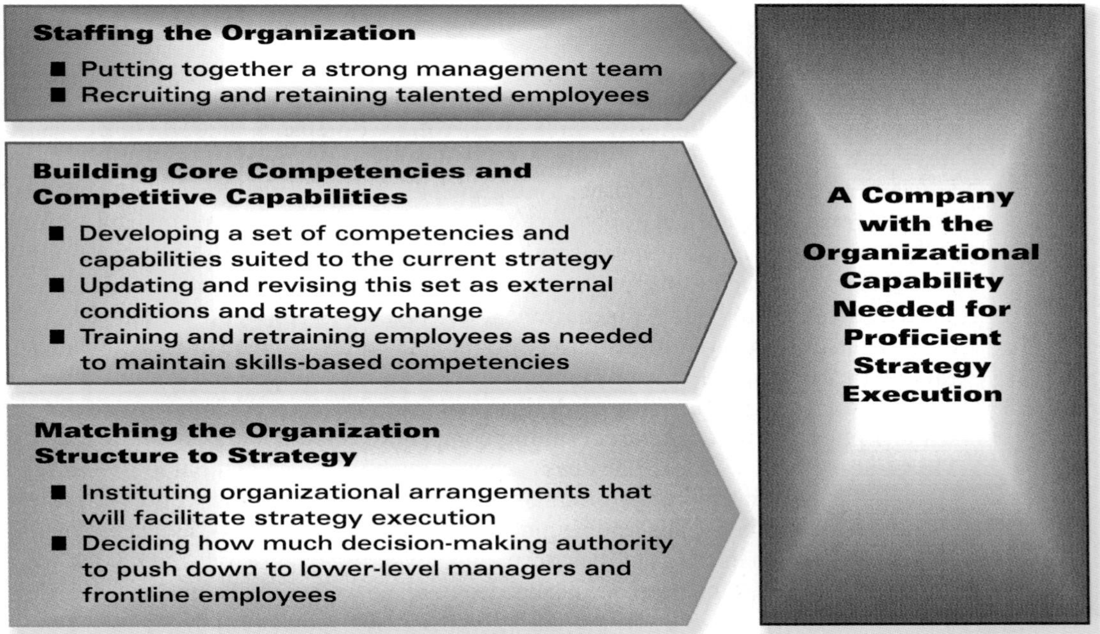

Staffing the Organization

No company can hope to perform the activities required for successful strategy execution without attracting and retaining talented managers and employees who give it suitable skills and *intellectual capital.*

Putting Together a Strong Management Team

Assembling a capable management team is a cornerstone of the organization-building task.[3] Different strategies and company circumstances call for different mixes of managerial backgrounds, experiences, know-how, values, beliefs, management styles, and personalities. The personal chemistry among the members of the management team needs to be right, and the talent base needs to be appropriate for the chosen strategy. But the most important condition is to fill key managerial slots with people who are good at diagnosing what needs to be done and who can be counted on to deliver good results; otherwise, the implementation-execution process can't proceed at full speed.[4] Sometimes the existing management team is suitable; at other times it may need to be strengthened or expanded by promoting qualified people from within or by bringing in outsiders whose experience, skills, and leadership styles better suit the situation. In turnaround and rapid-growth

> **Core Concept**
>
> Putting together a talented management team with the right mix of skills and experiences is one of the first strategy-implementing steps.

situations, and in instances when a company doesn't have insiders with the requisite experience or know-how, filling key management slots from the outside is a fairly standard organization-building approach.

Recruiting and Retaining Capable Employees

Assembling a capable management team is not enough. Staffing the organization with the right kinds of people must go much deeper than managerial jobs in order to build an organization capable of effective strategy execution. Companies like Microsoft, McKinsey & Company, Southwest Airlines, Cisco Systems, Amazon.com, Procter & Gamble, PepsiCo, Nike, Electronic Data Systems (EDS), Google, and Intel make a concerted effort to recruit the best and brightest people they can find and then retain them with excellent compensation packages, opportunities for rapid advancement and professional growth, and challenging and interesting assignments. Having a pool of "A players" with strong skill sets and budding management potential is essential to their business. Microsoft makes a point of hiring the very brightest and most talented programmers it can find and motivating them with both good monetary incentives and the challenge of working on cutting-edge software design projects. McKinsey & Company, one of the world's premier management consulting companies, recruits only cream-of-the-crop MBAs at the nation's top-10 business schools; such talent is essential to McKinsey's strategy of performing high-level consulting for the world's top corporations. The leading global accounting firms screen candidates not only on the basis of their accounting expertise but also on whether they possess the people skills needed to relate well with clients and colleagues. Southwest Airlines goes to considerable lengths to hire people who can have fun and be fun on the job; it uses special interviewing and screening methods to gauge whether applicants for customer-contact jobs have outgoing personality traits that match its strategy of creating a high-spirited, fun-loving, in-flight atmosphere for passengers, and it is so selective that only about 3 percent of the people who apply are offered jobs.

> **Core Concept**
>
> In many industries adding to a company's talent base and building intellectual capital are more important to good strategy execution than additional investments in plants, equipment, and capital projects.

In high-tech companies, the challenge is to staff work groups with gifted, imaginative, and energetic people who can bring life to new ideas quickly and inject into the organization what one Dell Computer executive calls "hum."[5] The saying "People are our most important asset" may seem hollow, but it fits high-technology companies dead-on. Besides checking closely for functional and technical skills, Dell Computer tests applicants for their tolerance of ambiguity and change, their capacity to work in teams, and their ability to learn on the fly. Companies like Amazon.com and Cisco Systems have broken new ground in recruiting, hiring, cultivating, developing, and retaining talented employees—most all of whom are in their 20s and 30s. Cisco goes after the top 10 percent, raiding other companies and endeavoring to retain key people at the companies it acquires so as to maintain a cadre of star engineers, programmers, managers, salespeople, and support personnel in executing its strategy to remain the world's leading provider of Internet infrastructure products and technology.

Where intellectual capital is crucial to good strategy execution, companies have instituted a number of practices in staffing their organizations and developing a strong knowledge base:

1. Spending considerable effort in screening and evaluating job applicants, selecting only those with suitable skill sets, energy, initiative, judgment, and aptitudes for learning and adaptability to the company's work environment and culture.

2. Putting employees through training programs that continue throughout their careers.

3. Providing promising employees with challenging, interesting, and skill-stretching assignments.

4. Rotating people through jobs that not only have great content but also span functional and geographic boundaries. Providing people with opportunities to gain experience in a variety of international settings is increasingly considered an essential part of career development in multinational or global companies.

5. Encouraging employees to be creative and innovative, to challenge existing ways of doing things and offer better ways, and to submit ideas for new products or businesses. Progressive companies work hard at creating an environment in which ideas and suggestions bubble up from below rather than proceed from the top down. Employees are made to feel that their opinions count.

6. Fostering a stimulating and engaging work environment such that employees will consider the company a great place to work.

7. Exerting efforts to retain high-potential, high-performing employees with salary increases, performance bonuses, stock options and equity ownership, and other long-term incentives.

8. Coaching average performers to improve their skills and capabilities, while weeding out underperformers and benchwarmers.

Building Core Competencies and Competitive Capabilities

High among the organization-building priorities in the strategy-implementing/ -executing process is the need to build and strengthen competitively valuable core competencies and organizational capabilities. Whereas managers identify the desired competencies and capabilities in the course of crafting strategy, good strategy execution requires putting the desired competencies and capabilities in place, upgrading them as needed, and then modifying them as market conditions evolve. Sometimes a company already has the needed competencies and capabilities, in which case managers can concentrate on nurturing them to promote better strategy execution. Usually, however, company managers have to add new competencies and capabilities to implement strategic initiatives and promote proficient strategy execution.

A number of prominent companies have succeeded in establishing core competencies and capabilities that have been instrumental in making them winners in the marketplace. Honda's core competence is its depth of expertise in gasoline-engine technology and small-engine design. Intel's is in the design of complex chips for personal computers. Procter & Gamble's core competencies reside in its superb marketing/distribution skills and its R&D capabilities in five core technologies—fats, oils, skin chemistry, surfactants, and emulsifiers. Ciba Specialty Chemicals has technology-based competencies that allow it to quickly manufacture products for customers wanting customized products relating to coloration, brightening and whitening, water treatment and paper processing, freshness, and cleaning. General Electric has a core competence in developing professional managers with broad problem-solving skills and proven ability to grow global businesses.

Disney has core competencies in theme park operation and family entertainment. Sony's core competencies are its expertise in electronic technology and its ability to translate that expertise into innovative products (cutting-edge video game hardware, miniaturized radios and video cameras, TVs and DVDs with unique features, attractively designed PCs). Dell Computer has the capabilities to deliver state-of-the-art products to its customers within days of next-generation components' coming available—and to do so at attractively low costs (it has leveraged its collection of competencies and capabilities into being the global low-cost leader in PCs).

The Three-Stage Process of Developing and Strengthening Competencies and Capabilities

Building core competencies and competitive capabilities is a time-consuming, managerially challenging exercise. While some organization-building assist can be gotten from discovering how best-in-industry or best-in-world companies perform a particular activity, trying to replicate and then improve on the competencies and capabilities of others is much easier said than done—for the same reasons that one is unlikely to ever become a good golfer simply by studying what Tiger Woods does. Putting a new capability in place is more complicated than just forming a new team or department and charging it with becoming highly competent in performing the desired activity, using whatever it can learn from other companies having similar competencies or capabilities. Rather, it takes a series of deliberate and well-orchestrated organizational steps to achieve mounting proficiency in performing an activity. The capability-building process has three stages:

> Building competencies and capabilities is a multi-stage process that occurs over a period of months and years, not something that can be done overnight.

Stage 1: First, the organization must develop the *ability* to do something, however imperfectly or inefficiently. This entails selecting people with the requisite skills and experience, upgrading or expanding individual abilities as needed, and then molding the efforts and work products of individuals into a collaborative effort to create organizational ability.

Stage 2: As experience grows and company personnel learn how to perform the activity *consistently well and at an acceptable cost*, the ability evolves into a tried-and-true *competence* or *capability*.

Stage 3: Should the organization continue to polish and refine its know-how and otherwise sharpen its performance such that it becomes *better than rivals* at performing the activity, the core competence rises to the rank of a *distinctive competence* (or the capability becomes a competitively superior capability), thus providing a path to competitive advantage.

Many companies manage to get through stages 1 and 2 in performing a strategy-critical activity, but comparatively few achieve sufficient proficiency in performing strategy-critical activities to qualify for the third stage.

Managing the Process   Four traits concerning core competencies and competitive capabilities are important in successfully managing the organization-building process:[6]

1. *Core competencies and competitive capabilities are bundles of skills and know-how that most often grow out of the combined efforts of cross-functional work groups and departments performing complementary activities at different locations in the firm's value chain.* Rarely does a core competence or capability consist of narrow skills attached to the work efforts of a single department. For

instance, a core competence in speeding new products to market involves the collaborative efforts of personnel in R&D, engineering and design, purchasing, production, marketing, and distribution. Similarly, the capability to provide superior customer service is a team effort among people in customer call centers (where orders are taken and inquiries are answered), shipping and delivery, billing and accounts receivable, and after-sale support. Complex activities (like designing and manufacturing a sports-utility vehicle or creating the capability for secure credit card transactions over the Internet) usually involve a number of component skills, technological disciplines, competencies, and capabilities—some performed in-house and some provided by suppliers/allies. An important part of the organization-building function is to think about which activities of which groups need to be linked and made mutually reinforcing and then to forge the necessary collaboration both within the company and with outside resource providers.

2. *Normally, a core competence or capability emerges incrementally* out of company efforts either to bolster skills that contributed to earlier successes or to respond to customer problems, new technological and market opportunities, the competitive maneuverings of rivals. Migrating from the one-time ability to do something up the ladder to a core competence or competitively valuable capability is usually an organization-building process that takes months and often years to accomplish—it is definitely not an overnight event.

3. The key to leveraging a core competence into a distinctive competence (or a capability into a competitively superior capability) is *concentrating more effort and more talent than rivals on deepening and strengthening the competence or capability, so as to achieve the dominance needed for competitive advantage.* This does not necessarily mean spending more money on such activities than competitors, but it does mean consciously focusing more talent on them and striving for best-in-industry, if not best-in-world, status. To achieve dominance on lean financial resources, companies like Cray in large computers and Honda in gasoline engines have leveraged the expertise of their talent pool by frequently re-forming high-intensity teams and reusing key people on special projects. The experiences of these and other companies indicate that the usual keys to successfully building core competencies and valuable capabilities are superior employee selection, thorough training and retraining, powerful cultural influences, effective cross-functional collaboration, empowerment, motivating incentives, short deadlines, and good databases—not big operating budgets.

4. Evolving changes in customers' needs and competitive conditions often require *tweaking and adjusting a company's portfolio of competencies and intellectual capital to keep its capabilities freshly honed and on the cutting edge.* This is particularly important in high-tech industries and fast-paced markets where important developments occur weekly. As a consequence, wise company managers work at anticipating changes in customer-market requirements and staying ahead of the curve in proactively building a package of competencies and capabilities that can win out over rivals.

Managerial actions to develop core competencies and competitive capabilities generally take one of two forms: either strengthening the company's base of skills, knowledge, and intellect or coordinating and networking the efforts of the various work groups and departments. Actions of the first sort can be undertaken at all managerial levels, but actions of the second sort are best orchestrated by senior managers who not only appreciate the strategy-executing significance of strong competencies/capabilities but also have the clout to enforce the necessary networking and cooperation among individuals, groups, departments, and external allies.

One organization-building question is whether to develop the desired competencies and capabilities internally or to outsource them by partnering with key suppliers or forming strategic alliances. The answer depends on what can be safely delegated to outside suppliers or allies versus what internal capabilities are key to the company's long-term success. Either way, though, calls for action. Outsourcing means launching initiatives to identify the most attractive providers and to establish collaborative relationships. Developing the capabilities in-house means marshaling personnel with relevant skills and experience, collaboratively networking the individual skills and related cross-functional activities to form organizational capability, and building the desired levels of proficiency through repetition (practice makes perfect).[7]

Sometimes the tediousness of internal organization building can be shortcut by buying a company that has the requisite capability and integrating its competencies into the firm's value chain. Indeed, a pressing need to acquire certain capabilities quickly is one reason to acquire another company—an acquisition aimed at building greater capability can be every bit as competitively valuable as an acquisition aimed at adding new products or services to the company's business lineup. Capabilities-motivated acquisitions are essential (1) when a market opportunity can slip by faster than a needed capability can be created internally and (2) when industry conditions, technology, or competitors are moving at such a rapid clip that time is of the essence. But usually there's no good substitute for ongoing internal efforts to build and strengthen the company's competencies and capabilities in performing strategy-critical value chain activities.

Updating and Reshaping Competencies and Capabilities as External Conditions and Company Strategy Change   Even after core competencies and competitive capabilities are in place and functioning, company managers can't relax. Competencies and capabilities that grow stale can impair competitiveness unless they are refreshed, modified, or even phased out and replaced in response to ongoing market changes and shifts in company strategy. Indeed, the buildup of knowledge and experience over time, coupled with the imperatives of keeping capabilities in step with ongoing strategy and market changes, makes it appropriate to view a company as *a bundle of evolving competencies and capabilities*. Management's organization-building challenge is one of deciding when and how to recalibrate existing competencies and capabilities and when and how to develop new ones. Although the task is formidable, ideally it produces a dynamic organization with "hum" and momentum as well as a distinctive competence.

From Competencies and Capabilities to Competitive Advantage

Core Concept
Building competencies and capabilities has a huge payoff—improved strategy execution and a potential for competitive advantage.

While strong core competencies and competitive capabilities are a major assist in executing strategy, they are an equally important avenue for securing a competitive edge over rivals in situations where it is relatively easy for rivals to copy smart strategies. Any time rivals can readily duplicate successful strategy features, making it difficult or impossible to beat rivals in the marketplace with a superior strategy, the chief way to achieve lasting competitive advantage is to beat them by performing certain value chain activities in superior fashion. Building core competencies, resource strengths, and organizational capabilities that rivals can't match is thus one of the best and most reliable ways to beat them. Moreover, cutting-edge core competencies and organizational capabilities are not easily duplicated by rival firms; thus, any competitive edge they produce is likely to be sustainable, paving the way for above-average organizational performance.

The Strategic Role of Employee Training

Training and retraining are important when a company shifts to a strategy requiring different skills, competitive capabilities, managerial approaches, and operating methods. Training is also strategically important in organizational efforts to build skills-based competencies. And it is a key activity in businesses where technical know-how is changing so rapidly that a company loses its ability to compete unless its skilled people have cutting-edge knowledge and expertise. Successful strategy implementers see to it that the training function is both adequately funded and effective. If the chosen strategy calls for new skills, deeper technological capability, or new capabilities, training should be placed near the top of the action agenda.

The strategic importance of training has not gone unnoticed. Over 600 companies have established internal "universities" to lead the training effort, facilitate continuous organizational learning, and help upgrade company competencies and capabilities. Many companies conduct orientation sessions for new employees, fund an assortment of competence-building training programs, and reimburse employees for tuition and other expenses associated with obtaining additional college education, attending professional development courses, and earning professional certification of one kind or another. A number of companies offer online, just-in-time training courses to employees around the clock. Increasingly, employees at all levels are expected to take an active role in their own professional development, assuming responsibility for keeping their skills and expertise up to date and in sync with the company's needs.

Execution-Related Aspects of Organizing the Work Effort

There are few hard-and-fast rules for organizing the work effort to support good strategy execution. Every firm's organization chart is partly a product of its particular situation, reflecting prior organizational patterns, varying internal circumstances, executive judgments about reporting relationships, and the politics of who gets which assignments. Moreover, every strategy is grounded in its own set of key success factors and value chain activities. But some organizational considerations are common to all companies. These are summarized in Figure 8.3 and discussed in turn in the following sections.

Deciding Which Value Chain Activities to Perform Internally and Which to Outsource

The advantages of a company's having an outsourcing component in its strategy were discussed in Chapter 4 (pages 142–144), but there is also a need to consider the role of outsourcing in executing the strategy. Aside from the fact that an outsider, because of

Figure 8.3   **Structuring the Work Effort to Promote Successful Strategy Execution**

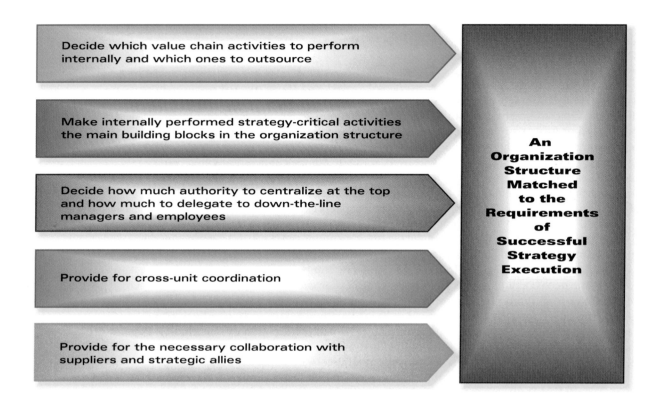

Decide which value chain activities to perform internally and which ones to outsource

Make internally performed strategy-critical activities the main building blocks in the organization structure

Decide how much authority to centralize at the top and how much to delegate to down-the-line managers and employees

Provide for cross-unit coordination

Provide for the necessary collaboration with suppliers and strategic allies

An Organization Structure Matched to the Requirements of Successful Strategy Execution

its expertise and specialized know-how, may be able to perform certain value chain activities better or cheaper than a company can perform them internally, outsourcing can have several organization-related benefits. Managers too often spend inordinate amounts of time, mental energy, and resources haggling with functional support groups and other internal bureaucracies over needed services, leaving less time for them to devote to performing strategy-critical activities in the most proficient manner. One way to reduce such distractions is to outsource the performance of assorted administrative support functions and perhaps even selected core or primary value chain activities to outside vendors, thereby enabling the company to *heighten its strategic focus and concentrate its full energies and resources on even more competently performing those value chain activities that are at the core of its strategy and for which it can create unique value.* For example, E. & J. Gallo Winery outsources 95 percent of its grape production, letting farmers take on the weather and other grape-growing risks while it concentrates its full energies on wine production and sales.[8] A number of PC makers outsource the mundane and highly specialized task of PC assembly, concentrating their energies instead on product design, sales and marketing, and distribution.

When a company uses outsourcing to zero in on ever better performance of those truly strategy-critical activities where its expertise is most needed, then it may be able to realize three very positive benefits:

1. *The company improves its chances for outclassing rivals in the performance of these activities and turning a core competence into a distinctive competence.* At the very least, the heightened focus on performing a select few value chain activities should meaningfully strengthen the company's existing core competencies and promote more innovative performance of those activities—either of which could lower costs or materially improve competitive capabilities. Eastman Kodak, Ford, ExxonMobil, Merrill Lynch, and Chevron have outsourced their data processing activities to computer service firms, believing that outside specialists can perform the needed services at lower costs and equal or better quality. A relatively large number of companies outsource the operation of their Web sites to Web design and hosting enterprises. Many businesses that get a lot of inquiries from customers or that have to provide 24/7 technical support to users of their products across the world have found that it is considerably less expensive to outsource these functions to specialists (often located in foreign countries where skilled personnel are readily available and worker compensation costs are much lower) than to operate their own call centers.

2. *The streamlining of internal operations that flows from outsourcing often acts to decrease internal bureaucracies, flatten the organizational structure, speed internal decision making, and shorten the time it takes to respond to changing market conditions.*[9] In consumer electronics, where advancing technology drives new product innovation, organizing the work effort in a manner that expedites getting next-generation products to market ahead of rivals is a critical competitive capability. The world's motor vehicle manufacturers have found that they can shorten the cycle time for new models, improve the quality and performance of those models, and lower overall production costs by outsourcing the big majority of their parts and components from independent suppliers and then working closely with their vendors to advance the design and functioning of the items being supplied, to swiftly incorporate new technology, and to better integrate individual parts and components to form engine cooling systems, transmission systems, and electrical systems.

3. *Partnerships can add to a company's arsenal of capabilities and contribute to better strategy execution.* By building, continually improving, and then leveraging partnerships, a company enhances its overall organizational capabilities and builds resource strengths—strengths that deliver value to customers and consequently pave the way for competitive success. Soft-drink and beer manufacturers all cultivate their relationships with their bottlers and distributors to strengthen access to local markets and build loyalty, support, and commitment for corporate marketing programs, without which their own sales and growth are weakened. Similarly, fast-food enterprises like McDonald's and Taco Bell find it essential to work hand-in-hand with franchisees on outlet cleanliness, consistency of product quality, in-store ambience, courtesy and friendliness of store personnel, and other aspects of store operations. Unless franchisees continuously deliver sufficient customer satisfaction to attract repeat business, a fast-food chain's sales and competitive standing will suffer quickly. Companies like Boeing, Aerospatiale, Verizon Communications, and Dell Computer have learned that their central R&D groups cannot begin to match the innovative capabilities of a well-managed network of supply chain partners having the ability to advance the technology, lead the development of next-generation parts and components, and supply them at a relatively low price.[10]

> **Core Concept**
>
> Wisely choosing which activities to perform internally and which to outsource can lead to several strategy-executing advantages— lower costs, heightened strategic focus, less internal bureaucracy, speedier decision making, and a better arsenal of competencies and capabilities.

As a general rule, companies refrain from outsourcing those value chain activities over which they need direct strategic and operating control in order to build core competencies, achieve competitive advantage, and effectively manage key customer-supplier-distributor relationships. It is the strategically less important activities—like handling customer inquiries and providing technical support, doing the payroll, administering employee benefit programs, providing corporate security, managing stockholder relations, maintaining fleet vehicles, operating the company's Web site, conducting employee training, and managing an assortment of information and data processing functions—for which outsourcing is most used.

However, a number of companies have found ways to successfully rely on outside vendors to perform strategically significant value chain activities.[11] For years Polaroid Corporation bought its film from Eastman Kodak, its electronics from Texas Instruments, and its cameras from Timex and others, while it concentrated on producing its unique self-developing film packets and designing its next-generation cameras and films. Nike concentrates on design, marketing, and distribution to retailers, while outsourcing virtually all production of its shoes and sporting apparel. Cisco Systems outsources virtually all manufacturing of its routers, switches, and other Internet gear; yet it protects its market position by retaining tight internal control over product design, and it closely monitors the daily operations of its manufacturing vendors. So while performing core value chain activities in-house normally makes good sense, there can be times when outsourcing some of them works to good advantage.

The Dangers of Excessive Outsourcing   Critics contend that a company can go overboard on outsourcing and so hollow out its knowledge base and capabilities as to leave itself at the mercy of outside suppliers and short of the resource strengths needed to be master of its own destiny.[12] The point is well taken. Outsourcing strategy-critical activities must be done judiciously and with safeguards against losing control over the performance of key value chain activities and becoming overly dependent on outsiders. Thus, many companies refuse to source key components from a single supplier, opting to use two or three suppliers as a way to avoid becoming overly dependent on any one supplier and giving any one supplier too much bargaining power. Moreover, they regularly evaluate their suppliers, looking not only at the supplier's overall performance but also at whether they should switch to another supplier or even bring the activity back in-house. To avoid loss of control, companies typically work closely with key suppliers, endeavoring to make sure that suppliers' activities are closely integrated with their own requirements and expectations. Most companies appear alert to the primary danger of taking outsourcing to an extreme and finding themselves without the internal capabilities needed to be a master of their own destiny and protect their well-being in the marketplace.

Making Strategy-Critical Activities the Main Building Blocks of the Organizational Structure

In any business, some activities in the value chain are always more critical to strategic success and competitive advantage than others. For instance, hotel/motel enterprises have to be good at fast check-in/checkout, housekeeping and facilities maintenance, food service, and creating a pleasant ambience. For a manufacturer of chocolate bars, buying quality cocoa beans at low prices is vital and reducing production costs by a fraction of a cent per bar can mean a seven-figure improvement in the bottom line. In discount stock brokerage, the strategy-critical activities are fast access to information, accurate order execution, efficient record keeping and transactions processing, and good customer service. In specialty chemicals, the critical activities are R&D, product innovation, getting new products onto the market quickly, effective marketing, and expertise in assisting customers. Where such is the case, it is important for management to build its organizational structure around proficient performance of these activities, making them the centerpieces or main building blocks on the organization chart.

The rationale for making strategy-critical activities the main building blocks in structuring a business is compelling: if activities crucial to strategic success are to have the resources, decision-making influence, and organizational impact they need, they have to be centerpieces in the organizational scheme. Plainly, implementing a new or changed strategy is likely to entail new or different key activities, competencies, or capabilities and therefore to require new or different organizational arrangements. If workable organizational adjustments are not forthcoming, the resulting mismatch between strategy and structure can open the door to execution and performance problems.[13] Hence, attempting to carry out a new strategy with an old organizational structure is usually unwise.

The primary organizational building blocks within a business are usually *traditional functional departments* (R&D, engineering and design, production and operations, sales and marketing, information technology, finance and accounting, and human resources) and *process-complete departments* (supply chain management, customer order fulfillment, customer service, quality control, direct sales via the company's Web site). For instance, a technical instruments manufacturer may be organized around research and development, engineering, supply chain management, assembly, quality control, marketing, technical services, and corporate administration. A hotel may have a functional organization based on front-desk operations, housekeeping, building maintenance, food service, convention services and special events, guest services, personnel and training, and accounting. A discount retailer may organize around such functional units as purchasing, warehousing and distribution, store operations, advertising, merchandising and promotion, customer service, and corporate administrative services.

In enterprises with operations in various countries around the world (or with geographically scattered organizational units within a country), the basic building blocks may also include *geographic organizational units*, each of which has profit/loss responsibility for its assigned geographic area. In vertically integrated firms, the major building blocks are *divisional units performing one or more of the major processing steps along the value chain* (raw materials production, components manufacture, assembly, wholesale distribution, retail store operations); each division in the value chain may operate as a profit center for performance measurement purposes. The typical building blocks of a diversified company are its *individual businesses*, with each business unit usually operating as an independent profit center and with corporate headquarters performing assorted support functions for all of its business units.

Determining the Degree of Authority and Independence to Give Each Unit and Each Employee

In executing the strategy and conducting daily operations, companies must decide how much authority to delegate to the managers of each organizational unit—especially the

Table 8.1   ADVANTAGES AND DISADVANTAGES OF CENTRALIZED VERSUS DECENTRALIZED DECISION MAKING

Centralized Organizational Structures	Decentralized Organizational Structures
Basic Tenets ■ Decisions on most matters of importance should be pushed to managers up the line who have the experience, expertise, and judgment to decide what is the wisest or best course of action. ■ Frontline supervisors and rank-and-file employees can't be relied upon to make the right decisions—because they seldom know what is best for the organization and they do not have the time or the inclination to properly manage the tasks they are performing (letting them decide "what to do" is thus risky). **Chief Advantage** ■ Tight control from the top fixes accountability. **Primary Disadvantages** ■ Lengthens response times because management bureaucracy must decide on a course of action. ■ Does not encourage responsibility among lower-level managers and rank-and-file employees. ■ Discourages lower-level managers and rank-and-file employees from exercising any initiative—they are expected to wait to be told what to do.	**Basic Tenets** ■ Decision-making authority should be put in the hands of the people closest to and most familiar with the situation, and these people should be trained to exercise good judgment. ■ A company that draws on the combined intellectual capital of all its employees can outperform a command-and-control company. **Chief Advantages** ■ Encourages lower-level managers and rank-and-file employees to exercise initiative and act responsibly. ■ Promotes greater motivation and involvement in the business on the part of more company personnel. ■ Spurs new ideas and creative thinking. ■ Allows fast response times. ■ Entails fewer layers of management. **Primary Disadvantages** ■ Puts the organization at risk if many "bad" decisions are made at lower levels—top management lacks "full control." ■ Impedes cross-unit coordination and capture of strategic fits.

heads of business subsidiaries, functional and process departments, plants, sales offices, distribution centers, and other operating units—and how much decision-making latitude to give individual employees in performing their jobs. The two extremes are to *centralize decision making* at the top (the CEO and a few close lieutenants) or to *decentralize decision making* by giving managers and employees considerable decision-making latitude in their areas of responsibility. As shown in Table 8.1, the two approaches are based on sharply different underlying principles and beliefs, with each having its pros and cons.

Centralized Decision Making: Pros and Cons   *In a highly centralized organizational structure, top executives retain authority for most strategic and operating decisions and keep a tight rein on business-unit heads, department heads, and the managers of key operating units; comparatively little discretionary authority is granted to frontline supervisors and rank-and-file employees.* The command-and-control paradigm of centralized structures is based on the underlying assumption that frontline personnel have neither the time nor the inclination to direct and properly control the work they are performing and that they lack the knowledge and judgment to make wise decisions about how best to do it—hence the need for managerially prescribed policies and procedures, close supervision, and tight control. The thesis underlying authoritarian structures is that strict enforcement of detailed procedures backed by rigorous managerial oversight is the most reliable way to keep the daily execution of strategy on track.

> There are disadvantages to having a small number of top-level managers micromanage the business either by personally making decisions or by requiring lower-level subordinates to gain approval before taking action.

The big advantage of an authoritarian structure is tight control by the manager in charge—it is easy to know who is accountable when things do not go well. But there are some serious disadvantages. Hierarchical command-and-control structures make an organization sluggish in responding to changing conditions because of the time it takes for the review/approval process to run up all the layers of the management bureaucracy. Furthermore, to work well, centralized decision making requires top-level managers to gather and process whatever information is relevant to the decision. When the relevant knowledge resides at lower organizational levels (or is technical, detailed, or hard to express in words), it is difficult and time-consuming to get all of the facts and nuances in front of a high-level executive located far from the scene of the action—full understanding of the situation cannot be readily copied from one mind to another. Hence, centralized decision making is often impractical—the larger the company and the more scattered its operations, the more that decision-making authority has to be delegated to managers closer to the scene of the action.

Decentralized Decision Making: Pros and Cons *In a highly decentralized organization, decision-making authority is pushed down to the lowest organizational level capable of making timely, informed, competent decisions.* The objective is to put adequate decision-making authority in the hands of the people closest to and most familiar with the situation and train them to weigh all the factors and exercise good judgment. Decentralized decision making means that the managers of each organizational unit are delegated lead responsibility for deciding how best to execute it (as well as some role in shaping the strategy for the units they head). Decentralization thus requires selecting strong managers to head each organizational unit and holding them accountable for crafting and executing appropriate strategies for their units. Managers who consistently produce unsatisfactory results have to be weeded out.

The case for empowering down-the-line managers and employees to make decisions related to daily operations and execution of the strategy is based on the belief that a company that draws on the combined intellectual capital of all its employees can outperform a command-and-control company.[14] Decentralized decision making means, for example, that in a diversified company the various business-unit heads have broad authority to execute the agreed-on business strategy with comparatively little interference from corporate headquarters; moreover, the business-unit heads delegate considerable decision-making latitude to functional and process department heads and the heads of the various operating units (plants, distribution centers, sales offices) in implementing and executing their pieces of the strategy. In turn, work teams may be empowered to manage and improve their assigned value chain activities, and employees with customer contact may be empowered to do what it takes to please customers. At Starbucks, for example, employees are encouraged to exercise initiative in promoting customer satisfaction—there's the story of a store employee who, when the computerized cash register system went offline, enthusiastically offered free coffee to waiting customers.[15] *With decentralized decision making, top management maintains control by limiting empowered managers' and employees' discretionary authority and holding people accountable for the decisions they make.*

> The ultimate goal of decentralized decision making is to put decision-making authority in the hands of those persons or teams closest to and most knowledgeable about the situation.

Decentralized organizational structures have much to recommend them. Delegating greater authority to subordinate managers and employees creates a more horizontal organizational structure with fewer management layers. Whereas in a centralized vertical structure managers and workers have to go up the ladder of authority for an answer, in a decentralized horizontal structure they develop their own answers and action plans—making decisions in their areas of responsibility and being accountable for results is an integral part of their job. Pushing decision-making authority down to middle and lower-level managers and then further on to work teams and individual employees shortens organizational response times and spurs new ideas, creative thinking, innovation, and greater involvement on the part of subordinate managers and employees. In worker-empowered structures, jobs can be defined more broadly, several tasks can be integrated into a single job, and people can direct their own work. Fewer managers are needed because deciding how to do things becomes part of each person's or team's job. Further, today's electronic communication systems make it easy and relatively inexpensive for people at all organizational levels to have direct access to data, other employees, managers, suppliers, and customers. They can access information quickly (via the Internet or company intranet), readily check with superiors or whomever else as needed, and take responsible action. Typically, there are genuine gains in morale and productivity when people are provided with the tools and information they need to operate in a self-directed way. Decentralized decision making can not only shorten organizational response times but also spur new ideas, creative thinking, innovation, and greater involvement on the part of subordinate managers and employees.

The past decade has seen a growing shift from authoritarian, multilayered hierarchical structures to flatter, more decentralized structures that stress employee empowerment. There's strong and growing consensus that authoritarian, hierarchical organizational structures are not well suited to implementing and executing strategies in an era when extensive information and instant communication are the norm and when a big fraction of the organization's most valuable assets consists of intellectual capital and resides in the knowledge and capabilities of its employees. Many companies have therefore begun empowering lower-level managers and employees throughout their organizations, giving them greater discretionary authority to make strategic adjustments in their areas of responsibility and to decide what needs to be done to put new strategic initiatives into place and execute them proficiently.

Maintaining Control in a Decentralized Organizational Structure   Pushing decision-making authority deep down into the organizational structure and empowering employees presents its own organizing challenge: *how to exercise adequate control over the actions of empowered employees so that the business is not put at risk at the same time that the benefits of empowerment are realized.*[16] Maintaining adequate organizational control over empowered employees is generally accomplished by placing limits on the authority that empowered personnel can exercise, holding people accountable for their decisions, instituting compensation incentives that reward people for doing their jobs in a manner that contributes to good company performance, and creating a corporate culture where there's strong peer pressure on individuals to act responsibly.

Capturing Strategic Fits in a Decentralized Structure   Diversified companies striving to capture cross-business strategic fits have to beware of giving business heads full rein to operate independently when cross-business collaboration is essential in order to gain strategic-fit benefits. Cross-business strategic fits typically have to be captured either by enforcing close cross-business collaboration or by centralizing performance of functions having strategic fits at the corporate level.[17] For example, if businesses with overlapping process and product technologies have their own independent R&D departments—each pursuing its own priorities, projects, and strategic agenda—it's hard for the corporate parent to prevent duplication of effort, capture either economies of scale or economies of scope, or broaden the company's R&D efforts to embrace new technological paths, product families, end-use applications, and customer groups. Where cross-business R&D fits exist, the best solution is usually to centralize the R&D function and have a coordinated corporate R&D effort that serves the interests of both individual businesses and the company as a whole. Likewise, centralizing the related activities of separate businesses makes sense when there are opportunities to share a common sales force, use common distribution channels, rely on a common field service organization to handle customer requests for technical assistance or provide maintenance and repair services, use common e-commerce systems and approaches, and so on.

The point here is that efforts to decentralize decision making and give organizational units leeway in conducting operations have to be tempered with the need to maintain adequate control and cross-unit coordination—decentralization doesn't mean delegating authority in ways that allow organizational units and individuals to do their own thing. There are numerous instances when decision-making authority must be retained at high levels in the organization and ample cross-unit coordination strictly enforced.

Providing for Internal Cross-Unit Coordination

The classic way to coordinate the activities of organizational units is to position them in the hierarchy so that the most closely related ones report to a single person (a functional department head, a process manager, a geographic area head, a senior executive). Managers higher up in the ranks generally have the clout to coordinate, integrate, and arrange for the cooperation of units under their supervision. In such structures, the chief executive officer, chief operating officer, and business-level managers end up as central points of coordination because of their positions of authority over the whole unit. When a firm is pursuing a related diversification strategy, coordinating the related activities of independent business units often requires the centralizing authority of a single corporate-level officer. Also, diversified companies commonly centralize such staff support functions as public relations, finance and accounting, employee benefits, and information technology at the corporate level both to contain the costs of support activities and to facilitate uniform and coordinated performance of such functions within each business unit.

But, as explained earlier, close cross-unit collaboration is usually needed to build core competencies and competitive capabilities in such strategically important activities as speeding new products to market and providing superior customer service. To achieve the desired degree of cross-unit cooperation and collaboration, most companies supplement their functional organizational structures. Sometimes this takes the form of creating process departments to bring together the pieces of strategically important activities previously performed in separate functional units. And sometimes the coordinating mechanisms involve the use of cross-functional task forces, dual reporting relationships, informal organizational networking, voluntary cooperation, incentive compensation tied to group performance measures, and strong executive-level insistence on teamwork and cross-department cooperation (including removal of recalcitrant managers who stonewall collaborative efforts). At one European-based company, a top executive promptly replaced the managers of several plants who were not fully committed to collaborating closely on eliminating duplication in product development and production efforts among plants in several different countries. Earlier, the executive, noting that negotiations among the managers had stalled on which labs and plants to close, had met with all the managers, asked them to cooperate to find a solution, discussed with them which options were unacceptable, and given them a deadline to find a solution. When the asked-for teamwork wasn't forthcoming, several managers were replaced.

Providing for Collaboration with Outside Suppliers and Strategic Allies

Someone or some group must be authorized to collaborate as needed with each major outside constituency involved in strategy execution. Forming alliances and cooperative relationships presents immediate opportunities and opens the door to future possibilities, but nothing valuable is realized until the relationship grows, develops, and blossoms. Unless top management sees that constructive organizational bridge building with strategic partners occurs and that productive working relationships emerge, the value of alliances is lost and the company's power to execute its strategy is weakened. If close working relationships with suppliers are crucial, then supply chain management must be given formal status on the company's organization chart and a significant position in the pecking order. If distributor/dealer/franchisee relationships are important, someone must be assigned the task of nurturing the relationships with forward channel allies. If working in parallel with providers of complementary products and services contributes to enhanced organizational capability, then cooperative organizational arrangements have to be put in place and managed to good effect.

Building organizational bridges with external allies can be accomplished by appointing "relationship managers" with responsibility for making particular strategic partnerships or alliances generate the intended benefits. Relationship managers have many roles and functions: getting the right people together, promoting good rapport, seeing that plans for specific activities are developed and carried out, helping adjust internal organizational procedures and communication systems, ironing out operating dissimilarities, and nurturing interpersonal cooperation. Multiple cross-organization ties have to be established and kept open to ensure proper communication and coordination.[18] There has to be enough information sharing to make the relationship work and periodic frank discussions of conflicts, trouble spots, and changing situations.[19]

Instilling a Corporate Culture That Promotes Good Strategy Execution

Core Concept

Corporate culture refers to the character of a company's internal work climate and personality—as shaped by its core values, beliefs, business principles, traditions, ingrained behaviors, and style of operating.

Every company has its own unique culture. The character of a company's culture or work climate is a product of the core values and business principles that executives espouse, the standards of what is ethically acceptable and what is not, the operating practices and behaviors that define "how we do things around here," the company's approach to people management, the "chemistry" and the "personality" that permeate its work environment, and the stories that get told over and over to illustrate and reinforce the company's values, business practices, and traditions. The meshing together of stated beliefs, business principles, style of operating, ingrained behaviors and attitudes, and work climate define a company's **corporate culture.**

Corporate cultures vary widely. For instance, the bedrock of Wal-Mart's culture is dedication to customer satisfaction, zealous pursuit of low costs and frugal operating practices, a strong work ethic, ritualistic Saturday-morning headquarters meetings to exchange ideas and review problems, and company executives' commitment to visiting stores, listening to customers, and soliciting suggestions from employees. At Nordstrom, the corporate culture is centered on delivering exceptional service to customers; the company's motto is "Respond to unreasonable customer requests"—each out-of-the-ordinary request is seen as an opportunity for a "heroic" act by an employee that can further the company's reputation for a customer-pleasing shopping environment. Nordstrom makes a point of promoting employees noted for their heroic acts and dedication to outstanding service; the company motivates its salespeople with a commission-based compensation system that enables Nordstrom's best salespeople to earn more than double what other department stores pay. General Electric's culture is founded on a hard-driving, results-oriented atmosphere (where all of the company's business divisions are held to a standard of being number one or two in their industries as well as achieving good business results); extensive cross-business sharing of ideas, best practices, and learning; reliance on "workout sessions" to identify, debate, and resolve burning issues; a commitment to Six Sigma quality; and globalization of the company. At Microsoft, there are stories of the long hours programmers put in, the emotional peaks and valleys in encountering and overcoming coding problems, the exhilaration of completing a complex program on schedule, the satisfaction of working on cutting-edge projects, the rewards of being part of a team responsible for a popular new software program, and the tradition of competing aggressively. Enron's collapse in 2001 was partly the product of a flawed corporate culture—one based on the positives of product innovation, aggressive risk taking, and a driving ambition to lead global change in the energy business but also on the negatives of arrogance, ego, greed, deliberately obscure accounting practices, and an "ends-justify-the-means" mentality in pursuing stretch revenue and profitability targets. In the end, Enron came unglued because a few top executives chose unethical and illegal paths to pursue corporate revenue and profitability targets—in a company that publicly preached integrity and other notable corporate values but was lax in making sure that key executives walked the talk.

Company Spotlight 8.1 presents Alberto-Culver's description of its corporate culture.

What to Look For in Identifying a Company's Corporate Culture

The taproot of corporate culture is the organization's values, beliefs, and business principles that set forth how its affairs ought to be conducted—the reasons why it does things the way it does. A company's culture is manifested in the values and business principles that management preaches and practices, in official policies and procedures, in its revered traditions and oft-repeated stories, in the attitudes and behaviors of employees, in the peer pressures that exist to do things in particular ways, in the organization's politics, in its approaches to people management and problem solving, in its relationships with external stakeholders (particularly vendors and local communities where it has operations), and in the "chemistry" and the "personality" that permeates its work environment. Some of these sociological forces are readily apparent, and others operate quite subtly.

The values, beliefs, and practices that undergird a company's culture can come from anywhere in the organization hierarchy, sometimes representing the philosophy of an influential executive and sometimes resulting from exemplary actions on the part of company personnel or a particular organizational unit.[20] Most often, key elements of the culture originated with a founder or certain strong leaders who articulated them as a set of business principles, company policies, or ways of dealing with employees, customers, vendors, shareholders, and the communities in which it operated. Over time, these cultural underpinnings take root, become embedded in how the company conducts its business, come to be accepted and shared by company managers and employees, and then persist as new employees are encouraged to adopt and follow the professed values and practices.

The Role of Stories Frequently, a significant part of a company's culture is captured in the stories that get told over and over again to illustrate to newcomers the importance of certain values and the depth of commitment that various company personnel have displayed. One of the folktales at FedEx, world renowned for the reliability of its next-day package delivery guarantee, is about a deliveryman who had been given the wrong key to a FedEx drop box. Rather than leave the packages in the drop box until the next day when the right key was available, the deliveryman unbolted the drop box from its base, loaded it into the truck, and took it back to the station. There, the box was pried open and the contents removed and sped on their way to their destination the next day. Nordstrom keeps a scrapbook commemorating the heroic acts of its employees and uses it as a regular reminder of the above-and-beyond-the-call-of-duty behaviors that employees are encouraged to display. At Frito-Lay, there are dozens of stories about truck drivers who went to extraordinary lengths in overcoming adverse weather conditions in order to make scheduled deliveries to retail customers and keep store shelves stocked with Frito-Lay products. Such stories serve the valuable purpose of illustrating the kinds of behavior the company encourages and reveres. Moreover, each retelling of a legendary story puts a bit more peer pressure on company personnel to display core values and do their part in keeping the company's traditions alive.

Perpetuating the Culture   Once established, company cultures are perpetuated in six important ways: (1) by screening and selecting new employees who will mesh well with the culture, (2) by systematic indoctrination of new members in the culture's fundamentals, (3) by the efforts of senior group members to reiterate core values in daily conversations and pronouncements, (4) by the telling and retelling of company legends, (5) by regular ceremonies honoring members who display desired cultural behaviors, and (6) by visibly rewarding those who display cultural norms and penalizing those who don't.[21] The more new employees a company is hiring, the more important it becomes to screen job applicants every bit as much for how well their values, beliefs, and personalities match up with the culture as for their technical skills and experience. For example, a company that stresses operating with integrity and fairness has to hire people who themselves have integrity and place a high value on fair play. A company whose culture revolves around creativity, product innovation, and leading change has to screen new hires for their ability to think outside the box, generate new ideas, and thrive in a climate of rapid change and ambiguity. Southwest Airlines, whose two core values—"LUV" and fun—permeate the work environment and whose objective is to ensure that passengers have a positive and enjoyable flying experience, goes to considerable lengths to hire flight attendants and gate personnel who are witty, cheery, and outgoing and who display "whistle while you work" attitudes. Fast-growing companies risk creating a culture by chance rather than by design if they rush to hire employees mainly for their talents and credentials and neglect to screen out candidates whose values, philosophies, and personalities aren't a good fit with the organizational character, vision, and strategy being articulated by the company's senior executives.

As a rule, companies are attentive to the task of hiring people who will fit in and who will embrace the prevailing culture. And, usually, job seekers lean toward accepting jobs at companies where they feel comfortable with the atmosphere and the people they will be working with. Employees who don't hit it off at a company tend to leave quickly, while employees who thrive and are pleased with the work environment stay on, eventually moving up the ranks to positions of greater responsibility. The longer people stay at an organization, the more that they come to embrace and mirror the corporate culture—their values and beliefs tend to be molded by mentors, coworkers, company training programs, and the reward structure. Normally, employees who have worked at a company for a long time play a major role in indoctrinating new employees into the culture.

Forces That Cause a Company's Culture to Evolve   However, even stable cultures aren't static—just like strategy and organizational structure, they evolve. New challenges in the marketplace, revolutionary technologies, and shifting internal conditions—especially eroding business prospects, an internal crisis, or top-executive turnover—tend to breed new ways of doing things and, in turn, cultural evolution. An incoming CEO who decides to shake up the existing business and take it in new directions often triggers a cultural shift, perhaps one of major proportions. Likewise, diversification into new businesses, expansion into foreign countries, rapid growth, an influx of new employees, and merger with or acquisition of another company can all precipitate cultural changes of one kind or another.

Company Subcultures: The Problems Posed by New Acquisitions and Multinational Operations   Although it is common to speak about corporate culture in the singular, companies typically have multiple cultures (or subcultures).[22] Values, beliefs, and practices within a company sometimes vary significantly by department, geographic location, division, or business unit. A company's subcultures can clash, or at least not mesh well, if they embrace conflicting business philosophies or operating approaches, if key executives employ different approaches to people management, or if important differences between a company's culture and those of recently acquired companies have not yet been ironed out. *Global and multinational companies tend to be at least partly multicultural* because cross-country organization units have different operating histories and work climates, as well as members who have grown up under different social customs and traditions and who have different sets of values and beliefs. The human resources manager of a global pharmaceutical company who took on an assignment in the Far East discovered, to his surprise, that one of his biggest challenges was to persuade his company's managers in China, Korea, Malaysia, and Taiwan to accept promotions—their cultural values were such that they did not believe in competing with their peers for career rewards or personal gain, nor did they relish breaking ties with their local communities to assume cross-national responsibilities.[23] Many companies that have merged with or acquired foreign companies have to deal with language- and custom-based cultural differences.

Nonetheless, the existence of subcultures does not preclude important areas of commonality and compatibility. For example, General Electric's cultural traits of boundarylessness, workout, and Six Sigma quality can be implanted and practiced successfully in different countries. AES, a global power company with operations in over 20 countries, has found that the four core values of integrity, fairness, fun, and social responsibility underlying its culture are readily embraced by people in most countries. Moreover, AES tries to define and practice its cultural values the same way in all of its locations while still being sensitive to differences that exist among various people groups across the world; top managers at AES express the views that people across the world are more similar than different and that the company's culture is as meaningful in Buenos Aires or Kazakhstan as in Virginia.

In today's globalizing world, multinational companies are learning how to make strategy-critical cultural traits travel across country boundaries and create a workably uniform culture worldwide. Likewise, company managements are quite alert to the importance of cultural compatibility in making acquisitions and the need to address how to merge and integrate the cultures of newly acquired companies—cultural due diligence is often as important as financial due diligence in deciding whether to go forward on an acquisition or merger. On a number of occasions, companies have decided to forgo acquiring particular companies because of culture conflicts that they believed would be hard to resolve.

Culture: Ally or Obstacle to Strategy Execution?

A company's present culture and work climate may or may not be compatible with what is needed for effective implementation and execution of the chosen strategy. *When a company's present work climate promotes attitudes and behaviors that are well suited to first-rate strategy execution, its culture functions as a valuable ally in the strategy execution process.* When the culture is in conflict with some aspect of the company's direction, performance targets, or strategy, the culture becomes a stumbling block.[24]

How Culture Can Promote Better Strategy Execution A culture grounded in strategy-supportive values, practices, and behavioral norms adds significantly to the power and effectiveness of a company's strategy execution effort. For example, a culture where frugality and thrift are values widely shared by organization members nurtures employee actions to identify cost-saving opportunities—the very behavior needed for successful execution of a low-cost leadership strategy. A culture built around such business principles as customer satisfaction, fair treatment, operating excellence, and employee empowerment promotes employee behaviors and an esprit de corps that facilitate execution of strategies keyed to high product quality and superior customer service. A culture in which taking initiative, challenging the status quo, exhibiting creativity, embracing change, and teamwork pervade the work climate promotes creative collaboration on the part of employees and organization drive to lead market change—outcomes that are very conducive to successful execution of product innovation and technological leadership strategies.[25]

A tight culture-strategy alignment furthers a company's strategy execution effort in two ways:[26]

1. *A culture that encourages actions supportive of good strategy execution not only provides company personnel with clear guidance regarding what behaviors and results constitute good job performance but also produces significant peer pressure from coworkers to conform to culturally acceptable norms.* The tighter the strategy-culture fit, the more that the culture pushes people to display behaviors and observe operating practices that are conducive to good strategy execution. A strategy-supportive culture thus funnels organizational energy toward getting the right things done and delivering positive organizational results. In a company where strategy and culture are misaligned, some of the very behaviors needed to execute strategy successfully run contrary to the behaviors and values embedded in the prevailing culture. Such a clash nearly always produces resistance from employees who have strong allegiance to the present culture. Culture-bred resistance to the actions and behaviors needed for good execution, if strong and widespread, poses a formidable hurdle that has to be cleared for strategy execution to get very far.

2. *A culture embedded with values and behaviors that facilitate strategy execution promotes strong employee identification with and commitment to the company's vision, performance targets, and strategy.* When a company's culture is grounded in many of the needed strategy-executing behaviors, employees feel genuinely better about their jobs, the company they work for, and the merits of what the company is trying to accomplish. As a consequence, company personnel are more inclined to exhibit some passion and exert their best efforts in making the strategy work, trying to achieve the targeted performance, and moving the company closer to realizing its strategic vision.

This says something important about the task of managing the strategy-executing process: *Closely aligning corporate culture with the requirements for proficient strategy execution merits the full attention of senior executives.* The managerial objective is to create and nurture a work culture that mobilizes organizational energy squarely behind efforts to execute strategy. A good job of culture building on management's part promotes can-do attitudes and acceptance of change, instills strong peer pressures for behaviors conducive to good strategy execution, and enlists more enthusiasm and dedicated effort among company personnel for achieving company objectives.

Core Concept

Because culturally approved behavior thrives and culturally disapproved behavior gets squashed, company managers are well advised to spend time creating a culture that supports and encourages the behaviors conducive to good strategy execution.

The Perils of Strategy-Culture Conflict   Conflicts between behaviors approved by the culture and behaviors needed for good strategy execution send mixed signals to organization members, forcing an undesirable choice. Should organization members be loyal to the culture and company traditions (as well as to their own personal values and beliefs, which are likely to be compatible with the culture) and thus resist or be indifferent to actions and behaviors that will promote better strategy execution? Or should they support the strategy execution effort and engage in actions and behaviors that run counter to the culture?

When a company's culture is out of sync with what is needed for strategic success, the culture has to be changed as rapidly as can be managed—this, of course, presumes that it is one or more aspects of the culture that are out of whack rather than the strategy. While correcting a strategy-culture conflict can occasionally mean revamping strategy to produce cultural fit, more usually it means revamping the mismatched cultural features to produce strategy fit. The more entrenched the mismatched aspects of the culture, the greater the difficulty of implementing new or different strategies until better strategy-culture alignment emerges. A sizable and prolonged strategy-culture conflict weakens and may even defeat managerial efforts to make the strategy work.

Strong versus Weak Cultures

Company cultures vary widely in the degree to which they are embedded in company practices and behavioral norms. Strongly embedded cultures go directly to a company's heart and soul; those with shallow roots provide little in the way of a definable corporate character.

Strong-Culture Companies   A company's culture can be strong and cohesive in the sense that the company conducts its business according to a clear and explicit set of principles and values, that management devotes considerable time to communicating these principles and values to organization members and explaining how they relate to its business environment, and that the values are shared widely across the company—by senior executives and rank-and-file employees alike.[27]

> In a strong-culture company, values and behavioral norms are like crabgrass: deeply rooted and hard to weed out.

Strong-culture companies have a well-defined corporate character, typically underpinned by a creed or values statement. Executives regularly stress the importance of using company values and business principles as the basis for decisions and actions taken throughout the organization. In strong-culture companies, values and behavioral norms are so deeply rooted that they don't change much when a new CEO takes over—although they can erode over time if the CEO ceases to nurture them. And they may not change much as strategy evolves and the organization acts to make strategy adjustments, either because the new strategies are compatible with the present culture or because the dominant traits of the culture are somewhat strategy-neutral and compatible with evolving versions of the company's strategy.

Three factors contribute to the development of strong cultures: (1) a founder or strong leader who establishes values, principles, and practices that are consistent and sensible in light of customer needs, competitive conditions, and strategic requirements; (2) a sincere, long-standing company commitment to operating the business according to these established traditions, thereby creating an internal environment that supports decision making and strategies based on cultural norms; and (3) a genuine concern for the well-being of the organization's three biggest constituencies—customers, employees, and shareholders. Continuity of leadership, small group size, stable group membership, geographic concentration, and considerable organizational success all contribute to the emergence and sustainability of a strong culture.[28]

During the time a strong culture is being implanted, there's nearly always a good strategy-culture fit (which partially accounts for the organization's success). Mismatches between strategy and culture in a strong-culture company tend to occur when a company's business environment undergoes significant change, prompting a drastic strategy revision that clashes with the entrenched culture. A strategy-culture clash can also occur in a strong-culture company whose business has gradually eroded; when a new leader is brought in to revitalize the company's operations, he or she may push the company in a strategic direction that requires substantially different cultural and behavioral norms. In such cases, a major culture-changing effort has to be launched.

One of the best examples of an industry in which strategy changes have clashed with deeply implanted cultures is the electric utility industry. Most electric utility companies, long used to operating as slow-moving regulated monopolies with captive customers, are now confronting the emergence of a vigorously competitive market in wholesale power generation and growing freedom on the part of industrial, commercial, and residential customers to choose their own energy supplier (in much the same way as customers choose their long-distance telephone carriers—an industry that once was a heavily regulated market). These new market circumstances are prompting electric companies to shift away from cultures predicated on risk avoidance, centralized control of decision making, and the politics of regulatory relationships and toward cultures aimed at entrepreneurial risk taking, product innovation, competitive thinking, greater attention to customer service, cost reduction, and competitive pricing.

Weak-Culture Companies   In direct contrast to strong-culture companies, weak-culture companies are fragmented in the sense that no one set of values is consistently preached or widely shared, few behavioral norms are evident in operating practices, and few traditions are widely revered or proudly nurtured by company personnel. Because top executives don't repeatedly espouse any particular business philosophy or exhibit long-standing commitment to particular values or extol particular operating practices and behavioral norms, organization members at weak-culture companies typically lack any deeply felt sense of corporate identity. While employees may have some bonds of identification with and loyalty toward their department, their colleagues, their union, or their boss, a weak company culture breeds no strong employee allegiance to what the company stands for or to operating the business in well-defined ways. Such lack of a definable corporate character results in many employees' viewing their company as just a place to work and their job as just a way to make a living—there's neither passion about the company nor emotional commitment to what it is trying to accomplish. Very often, cultural weakness stems from moderately entrenched subcultures that block the emergence of a well-defined companywide work climate.

As a consequence, *weak cultures provide little or no strategy-implementing assistance* because there are no traditions, beliefs, values, common bonds, or behavioral norms that management can use as levers to mobilize commitment to executing the chosen strategy. While a weak culture does not usually pose a strong barrier to strategy execution, it also provides no support. Absent a work climate that channels organizational energy in the direction of good strategy execution, managers are left with the options of either using compensation incentives and other motivational devices to mobilize employee commitment or trying to establish cultural roots that will in time start to nurture the strategy execution process.

Unhealthy Cultures

The distinctive characteristic of an unhealthy corporate culture is the presence of counterproductive cultural traits that adversely impact the work climate and company performance.[29] The following three traits are particularly unhealthy:

1. A highly politicized internal environment in which many issues get resolved and decisions are made on the basis of which individuals or groups have the most political clout to carry the day.

2. Hostility to change and a general wariness of people who champion new ways of doing things.

3. A "must-be-invented-here" mind-set that makes company personnel averse to looking outside the company for best practices, new managerial approaches, and innovative ideas.

What makes a politicized internal environment so unhealthy is that political infighting consumes a great deal of organizational energy, often with the result that what's best for the company takes a backseat to political maneuvering. In companies where internal politics pervades the work climate, empire-building managers jealously guard their decision-making prerogatives. They have their own agendas and operate the work units under their supervision as autonomous "fiefdoms," and the positions they take on issues are usually aimed at protecting or expanding their turf. Collaboration with other organizational units is viewed with suspicion (What are "they" up to? How can "we" protect "our" flanks?), and cross-unit cooperation occurs grudgingly. When an important proposal moves to the front burner, advocates try to ram it through and opponents try to alter it in significant ways or else kill it altogether. The support or opposition of politically influential executives and/or coalitions among departments with vested interests in a particular outcome typically weigh heavily in deciding what actions the company takes. All this maneuvering takes away from efforts to execute strategy with real proficiency and frustrates company personnel who are less political and more inclined to do what is in the company's best interests.

In less adaptive cultures where skepticism about the importance of new developments and resistance to change are the norm, managers prefer waiting until the fog of uncertainty clears before steering a new course, making fundamental adjustments to their product line, or embracing a major new technology. They believe in moving cautiously and conservatively, preferring to follow others rather than take decisive action to be in the forefront of change. Change-resistant cultures place a premium on not making mistakes, thus prompting managers to lean toward safe, don't-rock-the-boat options that will have only a ripple effect on the status quo, protect or advance their own careers, and guard the interests of their immediate work groups.

Change-resistant cultures encourage a number of undesirable or unhealthy behaviors—avoiding risks, not making bold proposals to pursue emerging opportunities, taking a lax approach to both product innovation and continuous improvement in performing value chain activities, and following rather than leading market change. In change-resistant cultures, word quickly gets around that proposals to do things differently face an uphill battle and that people who champion them may be seen as either something of a nuisance or a troublemaker. Executives who don't value managers or employees with initiative and new ideas put a damper on product innovation, experimentation, and efforts to improve. At the same time, change-resistant companies have little appetite for being first-movers or fast-followers, believing that being in the forefront of change is too risky and that acting too quickly increases vulnerability to costly mistakes. They are more inclined to adopt a wait-and-see posture, carefully analyze several alternative responses, learn from the missteps of early-movers, and then move forward cautiously and conservatively with initiatives that are deemed safe. Hostility to change is most often found in companies with multilayered management bureaucracies that have enjoyed considerable market success in years past and that are wedded to the "we have done it this way for years" syndrome.

When such companies encounter business environments with accelerating change, going slow on altering traditional ways of doing things can be a liability rather than an asset. General Motors, IBM, Sears, and Eastman Kodak are classic examples of companies whose change-resistant bureaucracies were slow to respond to fundamental changes in their markets; clinging to the cultures and traditions that had made them successful, they were reluctant to alter operating practices and modify their business approaches. As strategies of gradual change won out over bold innovation and being an early-mover, all four lost market share to rivals that quickly moved to institute changes more in tune with evolving market conditions and buyer preferences. These companies are now struggling to recoup lost ground with cultures and behaviors more suited to market success—the kinds of fit that caused them to succeed in the first place.

The third unhealthy cultural trait—the must-be-invented-here mind-set—tends to develop when a company reigns as an industry leader or enjoys great market success for so long that its personnel start to believe they have all the answers or can develop them on their own. Such confidence in the correctness of how the company does things and in its skills and capabilities breeds arrogance—there's a strong tendency for company personnel to discount the merits or significance of what outsiders are doing and what can be learned by studying best-in-class performers. Benchmarking and searching for the best practices of outsiders are seen as offering little payoff. Any market share gains on the part of up-and-coming rivals are regarded as temporary setbacks, soon to be reversed by the company's own forthcoming initiatives. Insular thinking, internally driven solutions, and a must-be-invented-here mind-set come to permeate the corporate culture. An inwardly focused corporate culture gives rise to managerial inbreeding and a failure to recruit people who can offer fresh thinking and outside perspectives. The big risk of insular cultural thinking is that the company can underestimate the competencies and accomplishments of rival companies and overestimate its own progress—with a resulting loss of competitive advantage over time.

Unhealthy cultures typically impair company performance. Avon, BankAmerica, Citicorp, Coors, Ford, General Motors, Kmart, Kroger, Sears, and Xerox are examples of companies whose unhealthy cultures during the late 1970s and early 1980s contributed to ho-hum performance on the bottom line and in the marketplace.[30] General Motors, Kmart, and Sears are still struggling to uproot problematic cultural traits and replace them with behaviors having a more suitable strategy-culture fit.

Adaptive Cultures

The hallmark of adaptive corporate cultures is willingness on the part of organization members to accept change and take on the challenge of introducing and executing new strategies.[31] Company personnel share a feeling of confidence that the organization can deal with whatever threats and opportunities come down the pike; they are receptive to risk taking, experimentation, innovation, and changing strategies and practices. In direct contrast to change-resistant cultures, adaptive cultures are very supportive of managers and employees at all ranks who propose or help initiate useful change. Internal entrepreneurship on the part of individuals and groups is encouraged and rewarded.

Core Concept

In adaptive cultures, there's a spirit of doing what's necessary to ensure long-term organizational success provided the new behaviors and operating practices that management is calling for are seen as legitimate and consistent with the core values and business principles underpinning the culture.

Senior executives seek out, support, and promote individuals who exercise initiative, spot opportunities for improvement, and display the skills to implement them. Managers habitually fund product development initiatives, evaluate new ideas openly, and take prudent risks to create new business positions. As a consequence, the company exhibits a proactive approach to identifying issues, evaluating the implications and options, and implementing workable solutions. Strategies and traditional operating practices are modified as needed to adjust to or take advantage of changes in the business environment.

But why is change so willingly embraced in an adaptive culture? Why are organization members not fearful of how change will affect them? Why does an adaptive culture not become unglued with ongoing changes in strategy, operating practices, and behavioral norms? The answers lie in two distinctive and dominant traits of an adaptive culture: (1) Any changes in operating practices and behaviors must *not* compromise core values and long-standing business principles, and (2) the changes that are instituted must satisfy the legitimate interests of stakeholders—customers, employees, shareowners, suppliers, and the communities where the company operates.[32] In other words, what sustains an adaptive culture is that organization members perceive the changes that management is trying to institute as being legitimate and in keeping with the core values and business principles that form the heart and soul of the culture.

Thus, for an adaptive culture to remain intact over time, top management must orchestrate the responses in a manner that demonstrates genuine care for the well-being of all key constituencies and tries to satisfy all their legitimate interests simultaneously. Unless fairness to all constituencies is a decision-making principle and a commitment to doing the right thing is evident to organization members, the changes are not likely to be seen as legitimate and thus be readily accepted and implemented.[33] Making changes that will please customers and/or that protect, if not enhance, the company's long-term well-being is generally seen as legitimate and is often seen as the best way of looking out for the interests of employees, stockholders, suppliers, and communities where the company operates. At companies with adaptive cultures, management concern for the well-being of employees is nearly always a big factor in gaining employee support for change—company personnel are usually receptive to change as long as employees understand that changes in their job assignments are part of the process of adapting to new conditions and that their employment security will not be threatened unless the company's business unexpectedly reverses direction. In cases where workforce downsizing becomes necessary, management concern for employees dictates that separation be handled humanely, making employee departure as painless as possible. Management efforts to make the process of adapting to change fair and equitable for customers, employees, stockholders, suppliers, and communities where the company operates, keeping adverse impacts to a minimum insofar as possible, breeds acceptance of and support for change among all organization stakeholders.

Technology companies, software companies, and today's dot-com companies are good illustrations of organizations with adaptive cultures. Such companies thrive on change—driving it, leading it, and capitalizing on it (but sometimes also succumbing to change when they make the wrong move or are swamped by better technologies or the superior business models of rivals). Companies like Microsoft, Intel, Nokia, Amazon.com, and Dell Computer cultivate the capability to act and react rapidly. They are avid practitioners of entrepreneurship and innovation, with a demonstrated willingness to take bold risks to create altogether new products, new businesses, and new industries. To create and nurture a culture that can adapt rapidly to changing or shifting business conditions, they make a point of staffing their organizations with people who are proactive, who rise to the challenge of change, and who have an aptitude for adapting.

In fast-changing business environments, a corporate culture that is receptive to altering organizational practices and behaviors is a virtual necessity. However, adaptive cultures work to the advantage of all companies, not just those in rapid-change environments. Every company operates in a market and business climate that is changing to one degree or another and that, in turn, requires internal operating responses and new behaviors on the part of organization members. As a company's strategy evolves, an adaptive culture is a definite ally in the strategy-implementing, strategy-executing process as compared to cultures that have to be coaxed and cajoled to change. This constitutes a good argument for why managers should strive to build a strong, adaptive corporate culture.

> A good case can be made that a strongly planted, adaptive culture is the best of all corporate cultures.

Creating a Strong Fit between Strategy and Culture

It is the *strategy maker's* responsibility to select a strategy compatible with the sacred or unchangeable parts of the organization's prevailing corporate culture. It is the *strategy implementer's* task, once strategy is chosen, to change whatever facets of the corporate culture hinder effective execution.

Changing a Problem Culture   Changing a company's culture to align it with strategy is among the toughest management tasks because of the heavy anchor of deeply held values and habits—people cling emotionally to the old and familiar. It takes concerted management action over a period of time to replace an unhealthy culture with a healthy culture or to root out certain unwanted behaviors and instill ones that are more strategy-supportive. *The single most visible factor that distinguishes successful culture-change efforts from failed attempts is competent leadership at the top.* Great power is needed to force major cultural change—to overcome the springback resistance of entrenched cultures—and great power normally resides only at the top.

As shown in Figure 8.4, the first step in fixing a problem culture is to identify those facets of the present culture that are dysfunctional and explain why they pose obstacles to executing new strategic initiatives and achieving company performance targets. Second, managers have to clearly define the desired new behaviors and specify the key features of the culture they want to create. Third, managers have to talk openly and forthrightly to all concerned about problematic aspects of the culture and why and how new behaviors will improve company performance—the case for cultural change has to be persuasive and the benefits of a reformed culture made convincing to all concerned. Finally, and most important, the talk has to be followed swiftly by visible, aggressive actions to promote the desired new behaviors—actions that everyone will understand are intended to produce behaviors and practices conducive to good strategy execution.

> Once a culture is established, it is difficult to change.

The menu of actions management can take to change a problem culture includes the following:[34]

1. Making a compelling case for why the company's new direction and a different cultural atmosphere are in the organization's best interests and why individuals and groups should commit themselves to making it happen despite the obstacles.

Figure 8.4   Changing a Problem Culture

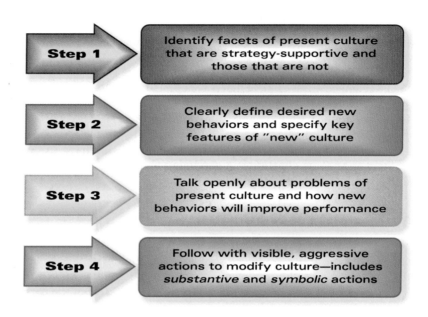

Skeptics have to be convinced that all is not well with the status quo. This can be done by:

- Challenging the status quo with very basic questions: Are we giving customers what they really need and want? Why aren't we taking more business away from rivals? Why do our rivals have lower costs than we do? How can we drive costs out of the business and be more competitive on price? Why can't design-to-market cycle time be halved? Why aren't we moving faster to make better use of the Internet and e-commerce technologies and practices? How can we grow company revenues at 15 percent instead of 10 percent? What can we do to speed up our decision making and shorten response times?

- Creating events where everyone in management is forced to listen to angry customers, dissatisfied strategic allies, alienated employees, or disenchanted stockholders.

2. Repeating at every opportunity the message of why cultural change is good for company stakeholders (particularly customers, employees, and shareholders). Effective culture-change leaders are good at telling stories to convey new values and connect the case for change to organization members.

3. Visibly praising and generously rewarding people who display newly advocated cultural norms and who participate in implementing the desired kinds of operating practices.

4. Altering incentive compensation to reward the desired cultural behavior and deny rewards to those who resist change.

5. Recruiting and hiring new managers and employees who have the desired cultural values and can serve as role models for the desired cultural behavior.

6. Replacing key executives who are strongly associated with the old culture.

7. Revising policies and procedures in ways that will help drive cultural change.

Only with bold leadership and concerted action on many fronts can a company succeed in tackling so large and difficult a task as major cultural change. When only strategic fine-tuning is being implemented, it takes less time and effort to bring values and culture into alignment with strategy, but there is still a lead role for the manager to play in communicating the need for new cultural behaviors and personally launching actions to prod the culture into better alignment with strategy.

Symbolic Culture-Changing Actions Managerial actions to tighten the strategy-culture fit need to be both symbolic and substantive. Symbolic actions are valuable for the signals they send about the kinds of behavior and performance strategy implementers wish to encourage. The most important symbolic actions are those that top executives take to *lead by example*. For instance, if the organization's strategy involves a drive to become the industry's low-cost producer, senior managers must display frugality in their own actions and decisions: inexpensive decorations in the executive suite, conservative expense accounts and entertainment allowances, a lean staff in the corporate office, scrutiny of budget requests, few executive perks, and so on. If the culture-change imperative is to work harder and smarter to please customers, the CEO can instill greater attention to customer satisfaction by requiring all officers and executives to spend a significant portion of each week talking with customers about their needs.

Another category of symbolic actions includes the ceremonial events organizations hold to designate and honor people whose actions and performance exemplify what is called for in the new culture. Many universities give outstanding-teacher awards each year to symbolize their commitment to good teaching and their esteem for instructors who display exceptional classroom talents. Numerous businesses have employee-of-the-month awards. The military has a long-standing custom of awarding ribbons and medals for exemplary actions. Mary Kay Cosmetics awards an array of prizes—from ribbons to pink automobiles—to its beauty consultants for reaching various sales plateaus.

The best companies and the best executives expertly use symbols, role models, ceremonial occasions, and group gatherings to tighten the strategy-culture fit. Low-cost leaders like Wal-Mart and Nucor are renowned for their spartan facilities, executive frugality, intolerance of waste, and zealous control of costs. Nucor executives make a point of flying coach class and using taxis at airports rather than limousines. Executives sensitive to their role in promoting strategy-culture fits make a habit of appearing at ceremonial functions to praise individuals and groups that get with the program. They honor individuals who exhibit cultural norms and reward those who achieve strategic milestones. They participate in employee training programs to stress strategic priorities, values, ethical principles, and cultural norms. Every group gathering is seen as an opportunity to repeat and ingrain values, praise good deeds, reinforce cultural norms, and promote changes that assist strategy execution. Sensitive executives make sure that current decisions and policy changes will be construed by organization members as consistent with cultural values and supportive of the company's new strategic direction.[35]

Substantive Culture-Changing Actions While symbolically leading the push for new behaviors and communicating the reasons for new approaches is crucial, strategy implementers have to convince all those concerned that the culture-changing effort is more than cosmetic. Talk and symbolism have to be complemented by substantive actions and real movement. The actions taken have to be credible, highly visible, and unmistakably indicative of the seriousness of management's commitment to new strategic initiatives and the associated cultural changes. There are several ways to accomplish this. One is to engineer some quick successes that highlight the benefits of the proposed changes, thus making enthusiasm for them contagious. However, achieving instant results is usually not as important as having the will and patience to create a solid, competent team psychologically committed to pursuing the strategy in a superior fashion. The strongest signs that management is truly committed to creating a new culture include replacing old-culture traditionalist managers with new-breed managers, changing dysfunctional policies and operating practices, instituting new compensation incentives visibly tied to the achievement of freshly set performance targets, and making major budgetary reallocations that shift substantial resources from old-strategy projects and programs to new-strategy projects and programs.

Implanting the needed culture-building values and behavior depends on a sincere, sustained commitment by the chief executive coupled with extraordinary persistence in reinforcing the culture at every opportunity through both word and deed. Neither charisma nor personal magnetism is essential. However, personally talking to many departmental groups about the reasons for change *is* essential; organizational changes are seldom accomplished successfully from an office. Moreover, creating and sustaining a strategy-supportive culture is a job for the whole management team. Major cultural change requires many initiatives from many people. Senior officers, department heads, and middle managers have to reiterate valued behaviors and translate the organization's core values and business principles into everyday practice. In addition, for the culture-building effort to be successful, strategy implementers must enlist the support of frontline supervisors and employee opinion leaders, convincing them of the merits of practicing and enforcing cultural norms at the lowest levels in the organization. Until a big majority of employees join the new culture and share an emotional commitment to its basic values and behavioral norms, there's considerably more work to be done in both instilling the culture and tightening the strategy-culture fit.

Changing culture to support strategy is not a short-term exercise. It takes time for a new culture to emerge and prevail. Overnight transformations simply don't occur. The bigger the organization and the greater the cultural shift needed to produce a strategy-culture fit, the longer it takes. In large companies, fixing a problem culture and instilling a new set of attitudes and behaviors can take two to five years. In fact, it is usually tougher to reform an entrenched problematic culture than it is to instill a strategy-supportive culture from scratch in a brand-new organization. Sometimes executives succeed in changing the values and behaviors of small groups of managers and even whole departments or divisions, only to find the changes eroded over time by the actions of the rest of the organization—what is communicated, praised, supported, and penalized by an entrenched majority undermines the new emergent culture and halts its progress. Executives, despite a series of well-intended actions to reform a problem culture, are likely to fail at weeding out embedded cultural traits when widespread employee skepticism about the company's new directions and culture-change effort spawns covert resistance to the cultural behaviors and operating practices advocated by top management. This is why management must take every opportunity to convince employees of the need for culture change and communicate to them how new attitudes, behaviors, and operating practices will benefit the interests of organizational stakeholders.

A company that has done a good job of fixing its problem culture is Alberto-Culver—see Company Spotlight 8.2.

COMPANY SPOTLIGHT 8.2

The Culture-Change Effort at Alberto-Culver's North American Division

In 1993, Carol Bernick—vice chairperson of Alberto-Culver, president of its North American division, and daughter of the company's founders—concluded that her division's existing culture had four problems: Employees dutifully waited for marching orders from their bosses, workers put pleasing their bosses ahead of pleasing customers, some company policies were not family-friendly, and there was too much bureaucracy and paperwork. What was needed, in Bernick's opinion, was a culture in which company employees had a sense of ownership and an urgency to get things done, welcomed innovation, and were willing to take risks.

To change the culture, Alberto-Culver's management undertook a series of actions:

- In 1993, a new position, called growth development leader (GDL), was created to help orchestrate the task of fixing the culture deep in the ranks (there were 70 GDLs in Alberto-Culver's North American division). GDLs came from all ranks of the company's managerial ladder and were handpicked for such qualities as empathy, communication skills, positive attitude, and ability to let their hair down and have fun. GDLs performed their regular jobs in addition to taking on the GDL role; it was considered an honor to be chosen. Each GDL mentored about 12 people from both a career and a family standpoint. GDLs met with senior executives weekly, bringing forward people's questions and issues and then, afterward, sharing with their groups the topics and solutions that were discussed. GDLs brought a group member as a guest to each meeting. One meeting each year is devoted to identifying "macros and irritations"—attendees are divided into four subgroups and given 15 minutes to identify the company's four biggest challenges (the macros) and the four most annoying aspects of life at the company (the irritations); the whole group votes on which four deserve the company's attention. Those selected are then addressed, and assignments made for follow-up and results.

- Changing the culture was made an issue across the company, starting in 1995 with a two-hour State of the Company presentation to employees that covered where the company was and where it wanted to be. The State of the Company address was made an annual event.

- Management created ways to measure the gains in changing the culture. One involved an annual all-employee survey to assess progress against cultural goals and to get 360-degree feedback—the 2000 survey had 180 questions, including 33 relating to the performance of each respondent's GDL. A bonfire celebration was held in the company parking lot to announce that paperwork would be cut 30 percent.

- A list of 10 cultural imperatives was formalized in 1998—honesty, ownership, trust, customer orientation, commitment, fun, innovation, risk taking, speed and urgency, and teamwork. These imperatives came to be known internally as HOT CC FIRST.

- Extensive celebrations and awards programs were instituted. Most celebrations are scheduled, but some are spontaneous (an impromptu thank-you party for a good fiscal year). Business Builder awards (initiated in 1997) are given to individuals and teams that make a significant impact on the company's growth and profitability. The best-scoring GDLs on the annual employee surveys are awarded shares of company stock. The company notes all work anniversaries and personal milestones with "Alberto-appropriate" gifts; appreciative company employees sometimes give thank-you gifts to their GDLs. According to Carol Bernick, "If you want something to grow, pour champagne on it. We've made a huge effort—maybe even an over-the-top effort—to celebrate our successes and, indeed, just about everything we'd like to see happen again."

The culture-change effort at Alberto-Culver North America was viewed as a major contributor to improved performance. From 1993, when the effort first began, to 2001, the division's sales increased from just under $350 million to over $600 million and pretax profits rose from $20 million to almost $50 million. Carol Bernick was elevated to chairman of Alberto-Culver's board of directors in 2004.

Source: Reprinted by permission of *Harvard Business Review,* from "When Your Culture Needs a Makeover," by Carol Lavin Bernick, June 2001. Copyright © 2001 by the President and Fellows of Harvard College, all rights reserved.

Table 8.2   THE CONTENT OF COMPANY VALUES STATEMENTS AND CODES OF ETHICS

Topics Commonly Appearing in Values Statements	Topics Commonly Appearing in Codes of Ethics
■ Commitment to such outcomes as customer satisfaction and customer service, quality, product innovation, and/or technological leadership ■ Commitment to achievement, excellence, and results ■ Importance of demonstrating such qualities as honesty, integrity, trust, fairness, quality of life, pride of workmanship, and ethics ■ Importance of being creative, taking initiative, and accepting responsibility ■ Importance of teamwork and a cooperative attitude ■ Importance of Golden Rule behavior and respect for coworkers ■ Making the company a great place to work ■ Importance of having fun and creating a fun work environment ■ Duty to stakeholders—customers, employees, suppliers, shareholders, communities where the company operates, and society at large ■ Commitment to exercising social responsibility and being a good community citizen ■ Commitment to protecting the environment ■ Commitment to workforce diversity	■ Mandates that company personnel will display honesty and integrity in their actions ■ An expectation that all company personnel will comply fully with all laws and regulations, specifically: ■ Antitrust laws prohibiting anticompetitive practices, conspiracies to fix prices, or attempts to monopolize ■ Foreign Corrupt Practices Act ■ Securities laws and prohibitions against insider trading ■ Environmental and workplace safety regulations ■ Discrimination and sexual harassment regulations ■ Prohibitions against giving or accepting bribes, kickbacks, or gifts ■ Avoiding conflicts of interest ■ Fairness in selling and marketing practices ■ Supplier relationships and procurement practices ■ Acquiring and using competitively sensitive information about rivals and others ■ Political contributions, activities, and lobbying ■ Avoiding use of company assets, resources, and property for personal or other inappropriate purposes ■ Responsibility to protect proprietary information and not divulge trade secrets

Grounding the Culture in Core Values and Ethics

A corporate culture grounded in socially approved values and ethical business principles is a vital ingredient in a company's long-term strategic success.[36] Unless a company's executives genuinely care about how the company's business affairs are conducted, the company's reputation and ultimately its performance are put at risk. While there's no doubt that some companies and some company personnel knowingly engage in shady business practices and have little regard for ethical standards, one must be cautious about assuming that a company's core values and ethical standards are meaningless window dressing. Executives at many companies genuinely care about the values and ethical standards that company personnel exhibit in conducting the company's business; they are aware that their own reputations, as well as the company's reputation, hang on whether outsiders see the company's actions as ethical or honest or socially acceptable. At such companies, values statements and codes of ethics matter, and they are ingrained to one degree or another in the company's culture—see Table 8.2 for the kinds of topics that are commonly found in values statements and codes of ethics.

Indeed, at companies where executives are truly committed to practicing the values and ethical standards that have been espoused, *the stated core values and ethical principles are the cornerstones of the corporate culture.* As depicted in Figure 8.5, a company that works hard at putting its stated core values and ethical principles into practice fosters a work climate where company personnel share common convictions

Figure 8.5   **The Two Culture-Building Roles of a Company's Core Values and Ethical Standards**

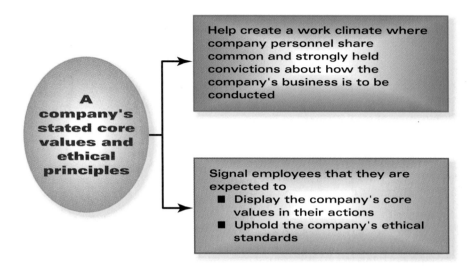

about how the company's business is to be conducted and where they are expected to act in accord with stated values and ethical standards. By promoting behaviors that mirror the values and ethics standards, a company's stated values and ethical standards nurture the corporate culture in three highly positive ways: (1) They communicate the company's good intentions and validate the integrity and aboveboard character of its business principles and operating methods, (2) they steer company personnel toward both doing the right thing and doing things right, and (3) they establish a "corporate conscience" and provide yardsticks for gauging the appropriateness of particular actions, decisions, and policies (see Figure 8.6).[37]

Companies ingrain their values and ethical standards in a number of different ways.[38] Tradition-steeped companies with a rich folklore rely heavily on word-of-mouth indoctrination and the power of tradition to instill values and enforce ethical conduct. But many companies today convey their values and codes of ethics to stakeholders and interested parties in their annual reports, on their Web sites, and in internal communications to all employees. The standards are hammered in at orientation courses for new employees and in training courses for managers and employees. The trend of making stakeholders aware of a company's commitment to core values and ethical business conduct is attributable to three factors: (1) greater management understanding of the role these statements play in culture building, (2) a renewed focus on ethical standards stemming from the corporate scandals that came to light in 2001–2004, and (3) the growing numbers of consumers who prefer to patronize ethical companies with ethical products.

> A company's values statement and code of ethics communicate expectations of how employees should conduct themselves in the workplace.

However, there is a considerable difference between saying the right things (having a well-articulated corporate values statement or code of ethics) and truly managing a company in an ethical and socially responsible way. Companies that are truly

Figure 8.6   How a Company's Core Values and Ethical Principles Positively Impact the Corporate Culture

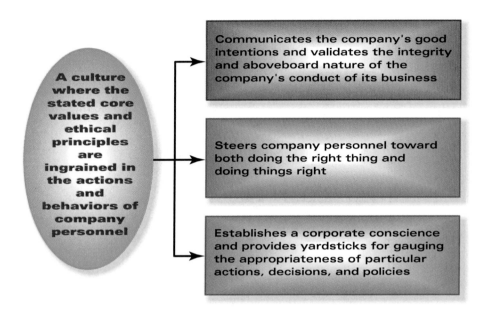

committed to the stated core values and to high ethical standards make ethical behavior *a fundamental component of their corporate culture.* They put a stake in the ground, making it unequivocally clear that company personnel are expected to live up to the company's values and ethical standards—how well individuals display core values and adhere to ethical standards is often part of their job performance evaluations. Peer pressures to conform to cultural norms are quite strong, acting as an important deterrent to outside-the-lines behavior. Moreover, values statements and codes of ethical conduct are used as benchmarks for judging the appropriateness of company policies and operating practices.

At Darden Restaurants—a $5 billion casual-dining company with over 1,300 company-owned Red Lobster, Olive Garden, Bahama Breeze, Seasons 52, and Smokey Bones BBQ Sports Bar restaurants—the core values are operating with integrity and fairness, treating people fairly and with respect, being "of service," engaging in teamwork, promoting innovation and excellence, and welcoming and celebrating workforce diversity. The company's practice of these values has been instrumental in creating a culture characterized by trust, exciting jobs and career opportunities for employees, and a passion to be the best in casual dining.[39]

Once values and ethical standards have been formally adopted, they must be institutionalized in the company's policies and practices and embedded in the conduct of company personnel. Deeply rooting values and ethical standards into how the company conducts its business entails several actions:

■   Incorporating the statement of values and the code of ethics into employee training and educational programs.

- Giving explicit attention to values and ethics in recruiting and hiring to screen out applicants who do not exhibit compatible character traits.

- Having senior executives frequently reiterate the importance and role of company values and ethical principles at company events and in internal communications to employees.

- Making sure that managers, from the CEO down to frontline supervisors, are diligent in stressing the importance of values and ethical conduct and in overseeing the compliance process.

- Periodically having ceremonial occasions to recognize individuals and groups who display the values and ethical principles.

- Instituting ethics enforcement procedures.

In the case of codes of ethics, special attention must be given to sections of the company that are particularly vulnerable—procurement, sales, and political lobbying. Employees who deal with external parties are in ethically sensitive positions and often are drawn into compromising situations. Company personnel assigned to subsidiaries in foreign countries can find themselves trapped in ethical dilemmas if bribery and corruption of public officials are common practices or if suppliers or customers are accustomed to kickbacks of one kind or another. Mandatory ethics training for such personnel is usually desirable.

Structuring the Ethics Compliance and Enforcement Process
If a company's executives truly aspire for company personnel to behave ethically, then procedures for enforcing ethical standards and handling potential violations have to be developed. Even in an ethically strong company, there can be bad apples—and some of the bad apples may even rise to the executive ranks. So it is rarely enough to rely on an ethically strong culture to produce ethics compliance.

The compliance effort must permeate the company, extending to every organizational unit. The attitudes, character, and work history of prospective employees must be scrutinized. Company personnel have to be educated about what is ethical and what is not; this means establishing ethics training programs and discussing what to do in gray areas. Everyone must be encouraged to raise issues with ethical dimensions, and such discussions should be treated as a legitimate topic. Line managers at all levels must give serious and continuous attention to the task of explaining how the values and ethical code apply in their areas. In addition, they must insist that company values and ethical standards become a way of life. In general, instilling values and insisting on ethical conduct must be looked on as a continuous culture-building, culture-nurturing exercise. Whether the effort succeeds or fails depends largely on how well corporate values and ethical standards are visibly integrated into company policies, managerial practices, and actions at all levels.

A company's formal ethics compliance and enforcement mechanisms can entail such actions as forming an ethics committee to give guidance on ethics matters, appointing an ethics officer to head the compliance effort, establishing an ethics hotline or Web site that employees can use to either anonymously report a possible violation or get confidential advice on a troubling ethics-related situation, and having an annual ethics audit to measure the extent of ethical behavior and identify problem areas. Increasing numbers of companies, wary of the damage to their reputations from public exposure of unethical behavior by company personnel, have begun openly encouraging employees to blow the whistle on possible ethical violations via toll-free hotlines, e-mail, and special Web sites. If a company is really serious about enforcing ethical behavior, it probably needs to do four things:[40]

1. Have mandatory ethics training programs for employees.
2. Conduct an annual audit of each manager's efforts to uphold ethical standards and require formal reports on the actions taken by managers to remedy deficient conduct.
3. Require all employees to sign a statement annually certifying that they have complied with the company's code of ethics.
4. Openly encourage company personnel to report possible infractions via anonymous calls to a hotline or posting to a special company Web site.

While these actions may seem extreme or objectionable, they leave little room to doubt the seriousness of a company's commitment to ethics compliance. And most company personnel will think twice about knowingly engaging in unethical conduct when they know their actions will be audited and/or when they have to sign statements certifying compliance with the company's code of ethics. Ideally, the company's commitment to its stated values and ethical principles will instill not only a corporate conscience but also a conscience on the part of company personnel that prompts them to report possible ethical violations. While ethically conscious companies have provisions for disciplining violators, *the main purpose of the various means of enforcement is to encourage compliance rather than administer punishment.* Thus, the reason for openly encouraging people to report possible ethical violations is not so much to get someone in trouble as to *prevent further damage* and heighten awareness of operating within ethical bounds.

As was discussed in Chapter 5, transnational companies face a host of challenges in enforcing a common set of ethical standards because what is considered ethical often varies substantially or subtly from country to country. While there are a number of mostly universal and cross-cultural ethical standards—as concerns honesty, trustworthiness, fairness, avoidance of unnecessary harm to individuals, and respect for the environment—there are shades and variations in what societies generally agree to be "right" and "wrong" based on the prevailing circumstances, local customs, and predominant religious convictions. And certainly there are cross-country variations in the *degree* or *severity* with which certain behaviors are considered unethical.[41] Thus transnational companies have to make a fundamental decision whether to try to enforce common ethical standards and interpretation of what is ethically right and wrong across their operations in all countries or whether to permit selected "rules bending" on a case-by-case basis.

Establishing a Strategy-Culture Fit in Multinational and Global Companies

In multinational and global companies, where some cross-border diversity in the corporate culture is normal, efforts to establish a tight strategy-culture fit are complicated by the diversity of societal customs and lifestyles from country to country. Company personnel in different countries sometimes fervently insist on being treated as distinctive individuals or groups, making a one-size-fits-all culture potentially inappropriate. Leading cross-border culture-change initiatives requires sensitivity to prevailing cultural differences; managers must discern when diversity has to be accommodated and when cross-border differences can be and should be narrowed.[42] Cross-country cultural diversity in a multinational enterprise is more tolerable if the company is pursuing a multicountry strategy and if the company's culture in each country is well aligned with its strategy in that country. But significant cross-country differences in a company's culture are likely to impede execution of a global strategy and have to be addressed.

As discussed earlier in this chapter, the trick to establishing a workable strategy-culture fit in multinational companies is to ground the culture in strategy-supportive values and operating practices that travel well across country borders and strike a chord with managers and workers in many different areas of the world, despite the diversity of local customs and traditions. A multinational enterprise with a misfit between its strategy and culture in certain countries where it operates can attack the problem by reinterpreting or deemphasizing or even abandoning those values and cultural traits that it finds inappropriate for some countries where it operates. Problematic values and operating principles can be replaced with values and operating approaches that travel well across country borders but that are still strategy-supportive. Many times a company's values statement only has to be reworded so as to express existing values in ways that have more universal appeal. Sometimes certain offending operating practices can be modified to good advantage in all locations where the company operates.

Aside from trying to ground the culture in a set of core values and operating principles that have universal appeal, management can seek to minimize the existence of subcultures and cross-country cultural diversity by:

- Instituting training programs to communicate the meaning of core values and explain the case for common operating principles and practices.

- Drawing on the full range of motivational and compensation incentives to induce personnel to adopt and practice the desired behaviors.

- Allowing *some leeway* for certain core values and principles to be interpreted and applied somewhat differently, if necessary, to accommodate local customs and traditions.

Generally, a high degree of cross-country cultural homogeneity is desirable and has to be pursued. Having too much variation in the culture from country to country not only makes it difficult to use the culture in helping drive the strategy execution process but also works against the establishment of a one-company mind-set and a consistent corporate identity.

Key Points

The job of strategy implementation and execution is to convert strategic plans into actions and good results. The test of successful strategy execution is whether actual organization performance matches or exceeds the targets spelled out in the strategic plan. Shortfalls in performance signal weak strategy, weak execution, or both.

In deciding how to implement a new or revised strategy, managers have to determine what internal conditions are needed to execute the strategic plan successfully. Then they must create these conditions as rapidly as practical. The process of implementing and executing strategy involves:

1. Building an organization with the competencies, capabilities, and resource strengths to execute strategy successfully.

2. Allocating ample resources to strategy-critical activities.

3. Ensuring that policies and procedures facilitate rather than impede strategy execution.

4. Instituting best practices and pushing for continuous improvement in how value chain activities are performed.

5. Installing information and operating systems that enable company personnel to carry out their strategic roles proficiently.

6. Tying rewards and incentives directly to the achievement of strategic and financial targets and to good strategy execution.

7. Shaping the work environment and corporate culture to fit the strategy.

8. Exerting the internal leadership needed to drive implementation forward and to keep improving on how the strategy is being executed.

Building a capable organization is always a top priority in strategy execution; three types of organization-building actions are paramount: (1) *staffing the organization*—putting together a strong management team and recruiting and retaining employees with the needed experience, technical skills, and intellectual capital, (2) *building core competencies and competitive capabilities* that will enable good strategy execution and updating them as strategy and external conditions change, and (3) *structuring the organization and work effort*—organizing value chain activities and business processes and deciding how much decision-making authority to push down to lower-level managers and frontline employees.

Building core competencies and competitive capabilities is a time-consuming, managerially challenging exercise that involves three stages: (1) developing the ability to do something, however imperfectly or inefficiently, by selecting people with the requisite skills and experience, upgrading or expanding individual abilities as needed, and then molding the efforts and work products of individuals into a collaborative group effort; (2) coordinating group efforts to learn how to perform the activity *consistently well and at an acceptable cost*, thereby transforming the ability into a tried-and-true *competence* or *capability*; and (3) continuing to polish and refine the organization's know-how and otherwise sharpen performance such that the company becomes *better than rivals* at performing the activity, thus raising the core competence (or capability) to the rank of a *distinctive competence* (or competitively superior capability) and opening an avenue to competitive advantage. Many companies manage to get through stages 1 and 2 in performing a strategy-critical activity but comparatively few achieve sufficient proficiency in performing strategy-critical activities to qualify for the third stage.

Structuring the organization and organizing the work effort in a strategy-supportive fashion has five aspects: (1) deciding which value chain activities to perform internally and which ones to outsource; (2) making internally performed strategy-critical activities the main building blocks in the organization structure; (3) deciding how much authority to centralize at the top and how much to delegate to down-the-line managers and employees; (4) providing for internal cross-unit coordination and collaboration to build and strengthen internal competencies/capabilities; and (5) providing for the necessary collaboration and coordination with suppliers and strategic allies.

A company's culture is manifested in the values and business principles that management preaches and practices, in the tone and philosophy of official policies and procedures, in its revered traditions and oft-repeated stories, in the attitudes and behaviors of employees, in the peer pressures that exist to display core values, in the organization's politics, in its approaches to people management and problem solving, in its relationships with external stakeholders (particularly vendors and the communities in which it operates), and in the atmosphere that permeates its work environment. Culture thus concerns the personality a company has and the style in which it does things.

Changing a company's culture, especially a strong one with traits that don't fit a new strategy's requirements, is one of the toughest management challenges. Changing a culture requires competent leadership at the top. It requires symbolic actions and substantive actions that unmistakably indicate serious commitment on the part of top management. The more that culture-driven actions and behaviors fit what's needed for good strategy execution, the less managers have to depend on policies, rules, procedures, and supervision to enforce what people should and should not do.

To be effective, corporate ethics and values programs have to become a way of life through training, strict compliance and enforcement procedures, and reiterated management endorsements. Moreover, top managers must practice what they preach, serving as role models for ethical behavior, values-driven decision making, and a social conscience.

Exercises

1. Go to www.hermanmiller.com and read what the company has to say about its corporate culture in the careers sections of the Web site. Do you think this statement is just nice window dressing and PR, or—based on what else you can learn about the Herman Miller Company from browsing this Web site—is there reason to believe that management has truly built a culture that makes the stated values and principles come alive?

2. Go to the careers section at www.qualcomm.com and see what Qualcomm, one of the most prominent companies in mobile communications technology, has to say about "life at Qualcomm." Is what's on this Web site just recruiting propaganda, or does it convey the type of work climate that management is actually trying to create? If you were a senior executive at Qualcomm, would you see merit in building and nurturing a culture like that described in the section on life at Qualcomm? Would such a culture represent a tight fit with Qualcomm's high-tech business and strategy (you can get an overview of Qualcomm's strategy by exploring the section for investors and some of the recent press releases)? Is your answer consistent with what is presented in the "Awards and Honors" menu selection in the "About Qualcomm" portion of the Web site?

3. Go to www.jnj.com, the Web site of Johnson & Johnson, and read the "J&J Credo," which sets forth the company's responsibilities to customers, employees, the community, and shareholders. Then read the "Our Company" section. Why do you think the credo has resulted in numerous awards and accolades that recognize the company as a good corporate citizen?

CHAPTER 9

Managing Internal Operations in Ways That Promote Good Strategy Execution

Winning companies know how to do their work better.

—*Michael Hammer and James Champy*

If you talk about change but don't change the reward and recognition system, nothing changes.

—*Paul Allaire, former CEO, Xerox Corporation*

If you want people motivated to do a good job, give them a good job to do.

—*Frederick Herzberg*

You ought to pay big bonuses for premier performance. . . . Be a top payer, not in the middle or low end of the pack.

—*Lawrence Bossidy, CEO, Honeywell International*

Weak leadership can wreck the soundest strategy; forceful execution of even a poor plan can often bring victory.

—*Sun Zi*

Leadership is accomplishing something through other people that wouldn't have happened if you weren't there. . . . Leadership is being able to mobilize ideas and values that energize other people. . . . Leaders develop a story line that engages other people.

—*Noel Tichy*

In Chapter 8 we emphasized why and how the task of executing strategy is facilitated by conscious managerial efforts to strengthen organizational capabilities and instill a strategy-supportive culture. In this chapter we discuss six additional managerial actions that promote the success of a company's strategy execution efforts:

1. Marshaling resources behind the strategy execution effort.
2. Instituting policies and procedures that facilitate strategy execution.
3. Adopting best practices and striving for continuous improvement in how value chain activities are performed.
4. Installing information and operating systems that enable company personnel to better carry out their strategic roles proficiently.
5. Tying rewards and incentives directly to the achievement of strategic and financial targets and to good strategy execution.
6. Exercising strong leadership to drive implementation forward, keep improving on how the strategy is being executed, and attain operating excellence.

Marshaling Resources behind the Drive for Strategy Execution

Early in the process of implementing and executing a new or different strategy, managers need to determine what resources will be needed and then consider whether the current budgets of organizational units are suitable. Plainly, organizational units must have the budgets and resources for executing their parts of the strategic plan effectively and efficiently. Developing a strategy-driven budget requires top management to determine what funding is needed to execute new strategic initiatives and to strengthen or modify the company's competencies and capabilities. This includes careful screening of requests for more people and more or better facilities and equipment, approving those that hold promise for making a cost-justified contribution to strategy execution and turning down those that don't. Should internal cash flows prove insufficient to fund the planned strategic initiatives, then management must raise additional funds through borrowing or selling additional shares of stock to willing investors.

A company's ability to marshal the resources needed to support new strategic initiatives and steer them to the appropriate organizational units has a major impact on the strategy execution process. Too little funding (stemming either from constrained financial resources or from sluggish management action to adequately increase the budgets of strategy-critical organizational units) slows progress and impedes the efforts of organizational units to execute their pieces of the strategic plan proficiently. Too much funding wastes organizational resources and reduces financial performance. Both outcomes argue for managers to be deeply involved in reviewing budget proposals and directing the proper kinds and amounts of resources to strategy-critical organizational units.

A change in strategy nearly always calls for budget reallocations. Units important in the prior strategy but having a lesser role in the new strategy may need downsizing. Units that now have a bigger and more critical strategic role may need more people, new equipment, additional facilities, and above-average increases in their operating budgets. Strategy implementers need to be active and forceful in shifting resources, downsizing some areas and upsizing others, not only to amply fund activities with a critical role in the new strategy but also to avoid inefficiency and achieve profit projections. They have to exercise their power to put enough resources behind new strategic initiatives to make things happen, and they have to make the tough decisions to kill projects and activities that are no longer justified.

Visible actions to reallocate operating funds and move people into new organizational units signal a determined commitment to strategic change and frequently are needed to catalyze the implementation process and give it credibility. Microsoft has made a practice of regularly shifting hundreds of programmers to new high-priority programming initiatives within a matter of weeks or even days. At Harris Corporation, where the strategy was to diffuse research ideas into areas that were commercially viable, top management regularly shifted groups of engineers out of government projects and into new commercial venture divisions. Fast-moving developments in many markets are prompting companies to abandon traditional annual or semiannual budgeting and resource allocation cycles in favor of cycles that match the strategy changes a company makes in response to newly developing events.

Just fine-tuning the execution of a company's existing strategy, however, seldom requires big movements of people and money from one area to another. The desired improvements can usually be accomplished through above-average budget increases to organizational units where new initiatives are contemplated and below-average increases (or even small cuts) for the remaining organizational units. The chief exception occurs where all the strategy changes need to be made within the existing budget. Then managers have to squeeze savings out of some areas to fund the new strategic initiatives.

Instituting Policies and Procedures That Facilitate Strategy Execution

Changes in strategy generally call for some changes in work practices and operations. Asking people to alter established procedures always upsets the internal order of things. It is normal for pockets of resistance to develop and for people to exhibit some degree of stress and anxiety about how the changes will affect them, especially when the changes may eliminate jobs. Questions are also likely to arise over what activities need to be rigidly prescribed and where there ought to be leeway for independent action.

As shown in Figure 9.1, prescribing new policies and operating procedures designed to facilitate strategy execution has merit from several angles:

1. *It provides top-down guidance regarding how certain things now need to be done.* New policies and operating practices can help align actions with strategy throughout the organization, placing limits on independent behavior and channeling individual and group efforts along a path in tune with the new strategy. They also help counteract tendencies for some people to resist change—most people refrain from violating company policy or going against recommended practices and procedures without first gaining clearance or having strong justification.

Figure 9.1   How Prescribed Policies and Procedures Facilitate Strategy Execution

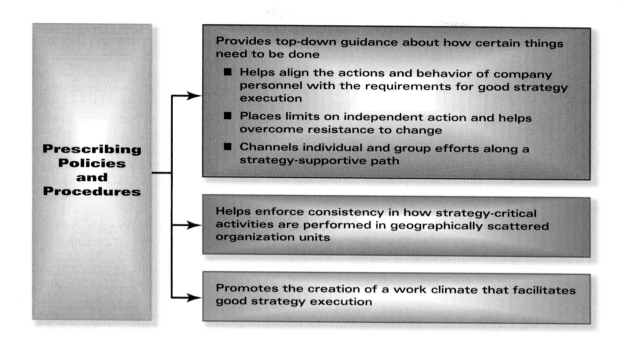

Prescribing Policies and Procedures

Provides top-down guidance about how certain things need to be done
- Helps align the actions and behavior of company personnel with the requirements for good strategy execution
- Places limits on independent action and helps overcome resistance to change
- Channels individual and group efforts along a strategy-supportive path

Helps enforce consistency in how strategy-critical activities are performed in geographically scattered organization units

Promotes the creation of a work climate that facilitates good strategy execution

2. *It helps enforce needed consistency in how particular critical activities are performed in geographically scattered operating units.* Eliminating significant differences in the operating practices of different plants, sales regions, customer service centers, or the individual outlets in a chain operation is frequently desirable to avoid sending mixed messages to internal personnel and to customers who do business with the company at multiple locations.

3. *It promotes the creation of a work climate that facilitates strategy execution.* Because dismantling old policies and procedures and instituting new ones invariably alter the internal work climate, strategy implementers can use the policy-changing process as a powerful lever for changing the corporate culture in ways that produce a stronger fit with the new strategy.

Company managers therefore need to be inventive in devising policies and practices that can provide vital support to effective strategy implementation and execution.

In an attempt to steer "crew members" into stronger quality and service behavior patterns, McDonald's policy manual spells out procedures in detail; for example, "Cooks must turn, never flip, hamburgers. If they haven't been purchased, Big Macs must be discarded in 10 minutes after being cooked and French fries in 7 minutes. Cashiers must make eye contact with and smile at every customer." Hewlett-Packard requires R&D people to make regular visits to customers to learn about their problems, talk about new product applications, and in general keep the company's R&D programs customer-oriented.

> **Core Concept**
> Well-conceived policies and procedures aid strategy execution; out-of-sync ones are barriers.

Granite Construction, a California company that consistently appears on Fortune's annual list of the "100 Best Companies to Work For," has a strategy aimed at total customer satisfaction and outstanding customer service; to signal both employees and customers that it was deadly serious about these two strategic commitments, it created what it called a "short-pay" policy that appeared on the bottom of every Granite construction invoice: "If you are not satisfied for any reason, don't pay us for it. Simply scratch out the line item, write a brief note about the problem, and return a copy of this invoice along with your check for the balance." Customers do not have to call and complain and are not expected to return the product. They are given complete discretionary power to decide whether and how much to pay based on their satisfaction level. Granite's short-pay policy has worked exceptionally well, providing unmistakable feedback and spurring company managers to correct any problems quickly in order to avoid repeated short payments.[1] Five years after instituting the policy, Granite won the prestigious Malcolm Baldrige National Quality Award. In addition Granite construction has a no-layoff policy (in 82 years, Granite has never had a lay off), provides employees with 12 massages a year, and sends positive customer comments about employees home for families to read.

Thus, wisely constructed policies and procedures help channel actions, behavior, decisions, and practices in directions that promote good strategy execution and push the company to achieve operating excellence. When policies and practices aren't strategy-supportive, they become a barrier to the kinds of attitudinal and behavioral changes strategy implementers are trying to promote. Sometimes people hide behind or vigorously defend long-standing policies and operating procedures in an effort to stall new strategic initiatives or force them to take a different form. Anytime a company alters its strategy, managers should review existing policies and operating procedures, proactively revise or discard those that are out of sync, and formulate new ones to facilitate execution and support the achievement of performance targets.

None of this implies that companies need thick policy manuals to direct the strategy execution process and prescribe exactly how daily operations are to be conducted. Too much policy can erect as many obstacles as wrong policy or be as confusing as no policy. There is wisdom in a middle approach: *Prescribe enough policies to give organization members clear direction in implementing strategy and to place desirable boundaries on their actions; then empower them to act within these boundaries however they think makes sense.* Allowing company personnel to act anywhere between the "white lines" is especially appropriate when individual creativity and initiative are more essential to good strategy execution than standardization and strict conformity. Instituting strategy-facilitating policies can therefore mean more policies, fewer policies, or different policies. It can mean policies that require things to be done a certain way or policies that give employees leeway to do activities the way they think best.

Adopting Best Practices and Striving for Continuous Improvement

Company managers can significantly advance the cause of competent strategy execution by pushing organizational units and company personnel to identify and adopt the best practices for performing value chain activities and, further, insisting on continuous improvement in how internal operations are conducted. One of the most widely used and effective tools for gauging how well a company is executing pieces of its strategy entails benchmarking the company's performance of particular activities and business processes against "best-in-industry" and "best-in-world" performers.[2] It can also be useful to look at "best-in-company" performers of an activity if a company has a number of different organizational units performing much the same function at different locations. Identifying, analyzing, and understanding how top companies or individuals perform particular value chain activities and business processes provides useful yardsticks for judging the effectiveness and efficiency of internal operations and setting performance standards for organizational units to meet or beat.

> **Core Concept**
>
> Managerial efforts to identify and adopt best practices are a powerful tool for promoting operating excellence and better strategy execution.

How the Process of Identifying and Incorporating Best Practices Works

A **best practice** is a technique for performing an activity or business process that at least one company has demonstrated works particularly well. To qualify as a legitimate best practice, the technique must have a proven record in significantly lowering costs, improving quality or performance, shortening time requirements, enhancing safety, or delivering some other highly positive operating outcome. Best practices thus identify a path to operating excellence. For a best practice to be valuable and transferable, it must demonstrate success over time, deliver quantifiable and highly positive results, and be repeatable.

> **Core Concept**
>
> A **best practice** is any practice that at least one company has proved works particularly well.

Benchmarking is the backbone of the process of identifying, studying, and implementing outstanding practices. A company's benchmarking effort looks outward to find best practices and then proceeds to develop the data for measuring how well a company's own performance of an activity stacks up against the best-practice standard. Informally, benchmarking involves being humble enough to admit that others have come up with world-class ways to perform particular activities yet wise enough to try to learn how to match, and even surpass, them. But, as shown in Figure 9.2, the payoff of benchmarking comes from adapting the top-notch approaches pioneered by other companies in the company's own operation and thereby boosting, perhaps dramatically, the proficiency with which value chain tasks are performed.

However, benchmarking is more complicated than simply identifying which companies are the best performers of an activity and then trying to imitate their approaches—

Figure 9.2   From Benchmarking and Best-Practice Implementation to Operating Excellence

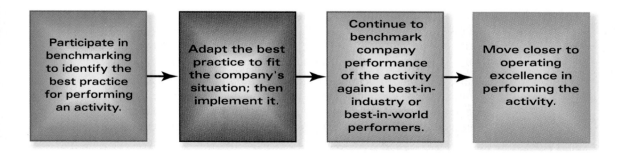

especially if these companies are in other industries. Normally, the outstanding practices of other organizations have to be *adapted* to fit the specific circumstances of a company's own business and operating requirements. Since most companies believe "our work is different" or "we are unique," the telling part of any best-practice initiative is how well the company puts its own version of the best practice into place and makes it work.

Indeed, a best practice remains little more than another company's interesting success story unless company personnel buy into the task of translating what can be learned from other companies into real action and results. The agents of change must be frontline employees who are convinced of the need to abandon the old ways of doing things and switch to a best-practice mind-set. The more that organizational units use best practices in performing their work, the closer a company moves toward performing its value chain activities as effectively and efficiently as possible. This is what operational excellence is all about.

Legions of companies across the world now engage in benchmarking to improve their strategy execution efforts and, ideally, gain a strategic, operational, and financial advantage over rivals. Scores of trade associations and special-interest organizations have undertaken efforts to collect best-practice data relevant to a particular industry or business function and make their databases available online to members—good examples include The Benchmarking Exchange (www.benchnet.com); Best Practices, LLC (www.best-in-class.com); and the American Productivity and Quality Center (www.apqc.org). Benchmarking and best-practice implementation have clearly emerged as legitimate and valuable managerial tools for promoting operational excellence.

Business Process Reengineering, Six Sigma Quality Programs, and TQM: Additional Tools for Promoting Operating Excellence

In striving for operating excellence, many companies have also come to rely on three other potent management tools: business process reengineering, Six Sigma quality control techniques, and total quality management (TQM) programs. Indeed, these three tools have become globally pervasive techniques for implementing strategies keyed to cost reduction, defect-free manufacture, superior product quality, superior customer service, and total customer satisfaction. The following sections describe how business process reengineering, Six Sigma, and TQM can contribute to operating excellence and better strategy execution.

Business Process Reengineering   Companies scouring for ways to improve their operations have sometimes discovered that organizing around traditional functional departments results in higher costs and poses cross-department coordination problems because having pieces of strategically relevant activities and capabilities performed in several different functional departments creates inefficiencies and because no one group or functional manager is thus accountable for optimum performance of the entire activity. Strategy-critical value chain activities where various components are typically scattered across several functional departments include:

- *Filling customer orders accurately and promptly*—a process that cuts across sales (which wins the order), finance (which may have to check credit terms or approve special financing), production (which must produce the goods and replenish warehouse inventories as needed), warehousing (which has to verify whether the items are in stock, pick the order from the warehouse, and package it for shipping), and shipping (which has to choose a carrier to deliver the goods and release the goods to the carrier).[3]

■ *Speeding new products to market*—a cross-functional process involving personnel in R&D, design and engineering, purchasing, manufacturing, and sales and marketing.

■ *Improving product quality*—a process that often involves the collaboration of personnel in R&D, engineering and design, components purchasing from suppliers, in-house components production, manufacturing, and assembly.

■ *Managing the supply chain*—a collaborative process that cuts across such functional areas as purchasing, engineering and design, components purchasing, inventory management, manufacturing and assembly, and warehousing and shipping.

■ *Building the capability to conduct business via the Internet*—a process that involves personnel in information technology, supply chain management, production, sales and marketing, warehousing and shipping, customer service, finance, and accounting.

■ *Obtaining feedback from customers and making product modifications to meet their needs*—a process that involves personnel in customer service and after-sale support, R&D, engineering and design, components purchasing, manufacturing and assembly, and marketing research.

To address the problem of inefficiency and curtail the time and effort that went into coordinating the efforts of different work groups, many companies during the past decade have opted to reengineer the work effort and create *process departments* or *teams*. Pulling the pieces of strategy-critical processes out of the functional silos and creating process departments or cross-functional work groups charged with performing all the steps needed to produce a strategy-critical result is called **business process reengineering**.[4] It involves reorganizing the people who performed the pieces in functional departments into a close-knit group that has charge over the whole process and that can be held accountable for performing the activity in a cheaper, better, and/or more strategy-supportive fashion.

> **Core Concept**
>
> **Business process reengineering** involves reorganizing the fragmented tasks of a strategy-critical activity into a close-knit group that has charge over the whole process and can be held accountable for performing the activity in a cheaper, better, and/or more strategy-supportive fashion.

When done properly, business process reengineering can produce dramatic operating benefits. In the order-processing section of General Electric's circuit breaker division, elapsed time from order receipt to delivery was cut from three weeks to three days by consolidating six production units into one, reducing a variety of former inventory and handling steps, automating the design system to replace a human custom-design process, and cutting the organizational layers between managers and workers from three to one. Productivity rose 20 percent in one year, and unit manufacturing costs dropped 30 percent. Northwest Water, a British utility, used business process reengineering to eliminate 45 work depots that served as home bases to crews who installed and repaired water and sewage lines and equipment. Now crews work directly from their vehicles, receiving assignments and reporting work completion from computer terminals in their trucks. Crew members are no longer employees but contractors to Northwest Water. These reengineering efforts not only eliminated the need for the work depots but also allowed Northwest Water to eliminate a big percentage of the bureaucratic personnel and supervisory organization that managed the crews.[5]

Since the early 1990s, reengineering of value chain activities has been undertaken at many companies in many industries all over the world, with excellent results being achieved at some companies.[6] While reengineering has produced only modest results in some instances, usually because of ineptness and/or lack of wholehearted commitment, reengineering has nonetheless proven itself as a useful tool for streamlining a company's work effort and moving closer to operational excellence.

Total Quality Management Programs   Total quality management (TQM) *is a philosophy of managing a set of business practices that emphasizes continuous improvement in all phases of operations, 100 percent accuracy in performing tasks, involvement and empowerment of employees at all levels, team-based work design, benchmarking, and total customer satisfaction.*[7] While TQM concentrates on producing quality goods and fully satisfying customer expectations, it achieves its biggest successes when it is extended to employee efforts in *all departments*—human resources, billing, R&D, engineering, accounting and records, and information systems—that may lack pressing, customer-driven incentives to improve. It involves reforming the corporate culture and shifting to a total quality/continuous improvement business philosophy that permeates every facet of the organization.[8] TQM aims at instilling enthusiasm and commitment to doing things right from the top to the bottom of the organization. Management's job is to kindle an organizationwide search for ways to improve, a search that involves all company personnel exercising initiative and using their ingenuity. TQM doctrine preaches that there's no such thing as "good enough" and that everyone has a responsibility to participate in continuous improvement. TQM is thus a race without a finish. Success comes from making little steps forward each day, a process that the Japanese call *kaizen*.

> **Core Concept**
> TQM entails creating a total quality culture bent on continuously improving the performance of every task and value chain activity.

TQM takes a fairly long time to show significant results—very little benefit emerges within the first six months. The long-term payoff of TQM, if it comes, depends heavily on management's success in implanting a culture within which TQM philosophies and practices can thrive. TQM is a managerial tool that has attracted numerous users and advocates over several decades, and it can deliver good results when used properly.

Six Sigma Quality Control   *Six Sigma quality control consists of a disciplined, statistics-based procedure aimed at producing not more than 3.4 defects per million iterations for any business process—from manufacturing to customer transactions.*[9] The Six Sigma process of define, measure, analyze, improve, and control (DMAIC) is an improvement system for *existing* processes falling below specification and needing incremental improvement. The Six Sigma process of define, measure, analyze, design, and verify (DMADV) is used to develop *new* processes or products at Six Sigma quality levels. Both Six Sigma processes are executed by personnel who have earned Six Sigma "green belts" and Six Sigma "black belts" and are overseen by personnel who have completed Six Sigma "master black belt" training. According to the Six Sigma Academy, personnel with black belts can save companies approximately $230,000 per project and can complete four to six projects a year.[10]

The statistical thinking underlying Six Sigma is based on the following three principles: All work is a process, all processes have variability, and all processes create data that explain variability.[11] To illustrate how these three principles drive the metrics of DMAIC, consider the case of a janitorial company that wants to improve the caliber of work done by its cleaning crews and thereby boost customer satisfaction. The janitorial company's Six Sigma team can pursue quality enhancement and continuous improvement via the DMAIC process as follows:

- *Define.* Because Six Sigma is aimed at reducing defects, the first step is to define what constitutes a defect. Six Sigma team members might decide that leaving streaks on windows is a defect because it is a source of customer dissatisfaction.

- *Measure.* The next step is to collect data to find out why, how, and how often this defect occurs. This might include a process flow map of the specific ways that cleaning crews go about the task of cleaning a commercial customer's windows. Other metrics may include recording what tools and cleaning products the crews use to clean windows.

- *Analyze.* After the data are gathered and the statistics analyzed, the company's Six Sigma team discovers that the tools and window-cleaning techniques of certain employees are better than those of other employees because their tools and procedures leave no streaked windows—a "best practice" for avoiding window streaking is thus identified and documented.

- *Improve.* The Six Sigma team implements the documented best practice as a standard way of cleaning windows.

- *Control.* The company teaches new and existing employees the best-practice technique for window cleaning. Over time, there's significant improvement in customer satisfaction and increased business.

Six Sigma's DMAIC process is a particularly good vehicle for improving performance when there are *wide variations* in how well an activity is performed.[12] For instance, airlines striving to improve the on-time performance of their flights have more to gain from actions to curtail the number of flights that are late by more than 30 minutes than from actions to reduce the number of flights that are late by less than 5 minutes. Likewise, FedEx might have a 16-hour average delivery time for its overnight package service operation, but if the actual delivery time varies around the 16-hour average from a low of 12 hours to a high of 26 hours such that 10 percent of its packages are delivered over 6 hours late, then it has a huge reliability problem.

A problem tailor-made for Six Sigma occurs in the insurance industry, where it is common for top agents to outsell poor agents by a factor of 10 to 1 or more. If insurance executives offer a trip to Hawaii in a monthly contest to motivate low-performing agents, the typical result is that top agents are motivated to be even more productive, thus making the performance gap even wider. A DMAIC Six Sigma project to reduce the variation in the performance of agents and correct the problem of so many low-performing agents would begin by measuring the performance of all agents, perhaps discovering that the top 20 percent sell seven times more policies than the bottom 40 percent. Six Sigma analysis would then consider such steps as mapping how top agents spend their day, investigating the factors that distinguish top performers from low performers, learning what techniques training specialists have employed in converting low-performing agents into high performers, and examining how the hiring process could be improved to avoid hiring underperformers in the first place.

The next step would be to test proposed solutions—better training methods or psychological profiling to identify and weed out candidates likely to be poor performers—to identify and measure which alternative solutions really work, which don't, and why. Only those actions that prove statistically beneficial are then introduced on a wide scale. The DMAIC method thus entails empirical analysis to diagnose the problem *(design, measure, analyze),* test alternative solutions *(improve),* and then *control* the variability in how well the activity is performed by implementing actions shown to truly fix the problem.

COMPANY SPOTLIGHT 9.1
Whirlpool's Use of Six Sigma to Promote Operating Excellence

Top management at Whirlpool Corporation, the leading global manufacturer and marketer of home appliances in 2003 with production operations in 14 countries and sales in some 170 countries, has a vision of Whirlpool appliances in "Every Home, Everywhere." One of management's chief objectives in pursuing this vision is to build unmatched customer loyalty to the Whirlpool brand. Whirlpool's strategy to win the hearts and minds of appliance buyers the world over has been to produce and market appliances with top-notch quality and innovative features that users will find appealing. In addition, Whirlpool's strategy has been to offer a wide selection of models (recognizing that buyer tastes and needs differ) and to strive for low-cost production efficiency, thereby enabling Whirlpool to price its products very competitively. Executing this strategy at Whirlpool's operations in North America (where it is the market leader), Latin America (where it is also the market leader), Europe (where it ranks third), and Asia (where it is number one in India and has a foothold with huge growth opportunities elsewhere) has involved a strong focus on continuous improvement and a drive for operating excellence. To marshal the efforts of its 68,000 employees in executing the strategy successfully, management developed a comprehensive Operational Excellence program with Six Sigma as one of the centerpieces.

The Operational Excellence initiative, which began in the 1990s, incorporated Six Sigma techniques to improve the quality of Whirlpool products and at the same time lower costs and trim the time it took to get product innovations into the marketplace. The Six Sigma program helped Whirlpool save $175 million in manufacturing costs in its first three years.

To sustain the productivity gains and cost savings, Whirlpool embedded Six Sigma practices within each of its manufacturing facilities worldwide and instilled a culture based on Six Sigma and lean manufacturing skills and capabilities. In 2002, each of Whirlpool's operating units began taking the Six Sigma initiative to a higher level by first placing the needs of the customer at the center of every function—R&D, technology, manufacturing, marketing, and administrative support—and then striving to consistently improve quality levels while eliminating all unnecessary costs. The company has systematically gone through every aspect of its business with the view that company personnel should perform every activity at every level in a manner that focuses on delivering value to the customer and that leads to continuous improvement on how things are done. Whirlpool management believes that the company-wide Six Sigma program and emphasis on continuous improvement has been a major contributor in sustaining the company's global leadership in appliances.

Source: www.whirlpool.com, accessed September 25, 2003.

General Electric, one of the most successful companies implementing Six Sigma training and pursuing Six Sigma perfection, estimated benefits on the order of $10 billion during the first five years of implementation. GE first instituted the use of Six Sigma in 1995 after Motorola and Allied Signal blazed the Six Sigma trail. Since the mid-1990s, thousands of companies and nonprofit organizations around the world have begun utilizing Six Sigma programs to promote operating excellence. Company Spotlight 9.1 describes Whirlpool's use of Six Sigma in its appliance business.

Six Sigma is, however, not just a quality-enhancing tool for manufacturers. At one company, product sales personnel typically wined and dined customers to close their deals.[13] But the costs of such entertaining were viewed as excessively high in many instances. A Six Sigma project that examined sales data found that although face time with customers was important, wining, dining, and other types of entertainment were not. The data showed that regular face time helped close sales but that time could be spent over a cup of coffee instead of golfing at a resort or taking clients to expensive restaurants. In addition, analysis showed that too much face time with customers was counterproductive. A regularly scheduled customer picnic was found to be detrimental to closing sales because it was held at a busy time of year, when customers preferred not to be away from their offices. Changing the manner in which prospective customers were wooed resulted in a 10 percent increase in sales. One of GE's successes was in its Lighting division, where Six Sigma was used to cut invoice defects and disputes by 98 percent, a particular benefit to Wal-Mart, the division's largest customer. GE Capital Mortgage improved the chances of a caller's reaching a "live" GE person from 76 to 99 percent.[14] A Milwaukee hospital used Six Sigma to map the process in which prescriptions originated with a doctor's write-up, were filled by the hospital pharmacy, and then were administered by nurses. DMAIC analysis revealed that most mistakes came from misreading the doctor's handwriting.[15] The hospital implemented a program requiring doctors to type the prescription into a computer, and this slashed the number of errors dramatically.

A company that systematically applies Six Sigma methods to its value chain, activity by activity, can make major strides in improving the proficiency with which its strategy is executed. As is the case with TQM, obtaining managerial commitment, establishing a quality culture, and fully involving employees are the three most intractable challenges encountered in the implementation of Six Sigma quality programs.[16]

The Difference between Business Process Reengineering and Continuous Improvement Programs Like Six Sigma and TQM   Business process reengineering and continuous improvement efforts like TQM and Six Sigma both aim at improved efficiency and reduced costs, better product quality, and greater customer satisfaction. The essential difference between business process reengineering and continuous improvement programs is that reengineering aims at *quantum gains* on the order of 30 to 50 percent or more whereas total quality programs stress *incremental progress*, striving for inch-by-inch gains again and again in a never-ending stream. The two approaches to improved performance of value chain activities and operating excellence are not mutually exclusive; it makes sense to use them in tandem. Reengineering can be used first to produce a good basic design that yields quick, dramatic improvements in performing a business process. Total quality programs like TQM and Six Sigma can then be used as a follow-on to reengineering and/or best-practice implementation, delivering gradual improvements. Such a two-pronged approach to implementing operational excellence is like a marathon race in which you run the first 4 miles as fast as you can and then gradually pick up speed the remainder of the way.

> Business process reengineering aims at one-time quantum improvement; continuous improvement programs like TQM and Six Sigma aim at ongoing incremental improvements.

Capturing the Benefits of Initiatives to Improve Operations

Usually, the biggest beneficiaries of benchmarking and best-practice initiatives, reengineering, TQM, and Six Sigma are companies that view such programs not as ends in themselves but as tools for implementing and executing company strategy more effectively. The skimpiest payoffs occur when company managers seize these programs as something worth trying—novel ideas that could improve things. In most such instances, they result in strategy-blind efforts to simply manage better. There's an important lesson here. Best practices, TQM, Six Sigma quality, and reengineering all need to be seen and used as part of a bigger-picture effort to execute strategy proficiently. Only strategy can point to which value chain activities matter and what performance targets make the most sense. Without a strategic framework, managers lack the context in which to fix things that really matter to business-unit performance and competitive success.

To get the most from initiatives to better execute strategy, managers must have a clear idea of what specific outcomes really matter. Is it a Six Sigma or lower defect rate, high on-time delivery percentages, low overall costs relative to rivals, high percentages of pleased customers and few customer complaints, shorter cycle times, a higher percentage of revenues coming from recently introduced products, or what? Benchmarking best-in-industry and best-in-world performance of most or all value chain activities provides a realistic basis for setting internal performance milestones and longer-range targets.

Then comes the managerial task of building a total quality culture that is genuinely committed to achieving the performance outcomes that strategic success requires.[17] Managers can take the following action steps to realize full value from TQM or Six Sigma initiatives:[18]

1. Visible, unequivocal, and unyielding commitment to total quality and continuous improvement, including a quality vision and specific, measurable objectives for boosting quality and making continuous improvement.

2. Nudging people toward quality-supportive behaviors by:
   a) Screening job applicants rigorously and hiring only those with attitudes and aptitudes right for quality-based performance.
   b) Providing quality training for most employees.
   c) Using teams and team-building exercises to reinforce and nurture individual effort (the creation of a quality culture is facilitated when teams become more cross-functional, multitask-oriented, and increasingly self-managed).
   d) Recognizing and rewarding individual and team efforts regularly and systematically.
   e) Stressing prevention (doing it right the first time), not inspection (instituting ways to correct mistakes).

3. Empowering employees so that authority for delivering great service or improving products is in the hands of the doers rather than the overseers—*improving quality has to be seen as part of everyone's job.*

4. Using online systems to provide all relevant parties with the latest best practices and actual experiences with them, thereby speeding the diffusion and adoption of best practices throughout the organization and also allowing the parties to exchange data and opinions about how to upgrade the prevailing best practices.

5. Preaching that performance can, and must, be improved because competitors are not resting on their laurels and customers are always looking for something better.

Core Concept

The purpose of using benchmarking, best practices, business process reengineering, TQM, Six Sigma, or other operational improvement programs is to improve the performance of critical activities and enhance strategy execution.

If the targeted performance measures are appropriate to the strategy and if all organization members (top executives, middle managers, professional staff, and line employees) buy into a culture of operating excellence, then a company's work climate becomes decidedly more conducive to proficient strategy execution. Benchmarking, best-practices implementation, reengineering, TQM, and Six Sigma initiatives can greatly enhance a company's product design, cycle time, production costs, product quality, service, customer satisfaction, and other operating capabilities—and they can even deliver competitive advantage.[19] Not only do improvements from such initiatives add up over time and strengthen organizational capabilities, but the benefits they produce have hard-to-imitate aspects. While it is relatively easy for rivals to undertake benchmarking, process improvement, and quality training, it is much more difficult and time-consuming for them to instill a deeply ingrained culture of operating excellence (as occurs when such techniques are religiously employed and top management exhibits lasting commitment to operational excellence throughout the organization).

Installing Information and Operating Systems

Company strategies can't be executed well without a number of internal systems for business operations. Southwest, American, Northwest, Delta, and other major airlines cannot hope to provide passenger-pleasing service without a user-friendly online reservation system, an accurate and speedy baggage handling system, and a strict aircraft maintenance program that minimizes equipment failures requiring at-the-gate service and delaying plane departures. FedEx has internal communication systems that allow it to coordinate its over 70,000 vehicles in handling an average of 5.5 million packages a day. Its leading-edge flight operations systems allow a single controller to direct as many as 200 of FedEx's 650 aircraft simultaneously, overriding their flight plans should weather or other special emergencies arise. In addition, FedEx has created a series of e-business tools for customers that allow them to ship and track packages online (either at FedEx's Web site or on their own company intranets or Web sites), create address books, review shipping history, generate custom reports, simplify customer billing, reduce internal warehousing and inventory management costs, purchase goods and services from suppliers, and respond quickly to changing customer demands. All of FedEx's systems support the company's strategy of providing businesses and individuals with a broad array of package delivery services (from premium next-day to economical five-day deliveries) and boosting its competitiveness against United Parcel Service, Airborne Express, and the U.S. Postal Service.

Otis Elevator has a 24-hour centralized communications center called OtisLine to coordinate its maintenance efforts in North America.[20] Trained operators take all trouble calls, input critical information on a computer screen, and dispatch people directly via a beeper system to the local trouble spot. Also, much of the information needed for faulty elevator and escalator repairs is accessed directly from electronic monitors installed on each user's site. The OtisLine system helps keep outage times to less than two and a half hours. All the trouble-call data are automatically relayed to design and manufacturing personnel, allowing them to quickly alter design specifications or manufacturing procedures when needed to correct recurring problems. All customers have online access to performance data on each of their Otis elevators and escalators.

Wal-Mart is generally considered to have the most sophisticated retailing systems of any company in the world. For example, Wal-Mart's computers transmit daily sales data to Wrangler, a supplier of blue jeans; Wrangler then uses a model that interprets the data, and software applications that act on these interpretations, in order to ship specific quantities of specific sizes and colors to specific stores from specific warehouses—the system lowers logistics and inventory costs and leads to fewer stockouts.[21] Domino's Pizza has computerized systems at each outlet to facilitate ordering, inventory, payroll, cash flow, and work control functions, thereby freeing managers to spend more time on supervision, customer service, and business development activities.[22] Most telephone companies, electric utilities, and TV broadcasting systems have online monitoring systems to spot transmission problems within seconds and increase the reliability of their services. At eBay, there are systems for real-time monitoring of new listings, bidding activity, Web site traffic, and page views.

Amazon.com ships customer orders from fully computerized, 1,300- by 600-foot warehouses containing about 3 million books, CDs, toys, and houseware items.[23] The warehouses are so technologically sophisticated that they require about as many lines of code to run as Amazon's Web site does. Using complex picking algorithms, computers initiate the order-picking process by sending signals to workers' wireless receivers, telling them which items to pick off the shelves in which order. Computers also generate data on misboxed items, chute backup times, line speed, worker productivity, and shipping weights on orders. Systems are upgraded regularly, and productivity improvements are aggressively pursued. In 2003 Amazon's six warehouses were able to handle three times the volume handled in 1999 at costs averaging 10 percent of revenues (versus 20 percent in 1999); in addition, they turned their inventory over 20 times annually in an industry whose average was 15 turns. Amazon's warehouse was so efficient and its cost per order filled was so low that one of the fastest-growing and most profitable parts of Amazon's business was using its warehouses to run the e-commerce operations of Toys "R" Us and Target.

In businesses such as public accounting and management consulting, where large numbers of professional staff need cutting-edge technical know-how, companies need well-functioning systems for training and retraining employees regularly and keeping them supplied with up-to-date information. Companies that rely on empowered customer service employees to act promptly and creatively in pleasing customers need state-of-the-art information systems that put essential data in front of employees with a few keystrokes. Many companies have cataloged best-practice information on their intranets to promote faster transfer and implementation organizationwide.[24]

Well-conceived state-of-the-art operating systems not only enable better strategy execution but also strengthen organizational capabilities—perhaps enough to provide a competitive edge over rivals. For example, a company with a differentiation strategy based on superior quality has added capability if it has systems for training personnel in quality techniques, tracking product quality at each production step, and ensuring that all goods shipped meet quality standards. A company striving to be a low-cost provider is competitively stronger if it has a benchmarking system that identifies opportunities to implement best practices and drive costs out of the business. Fast-growing companies get an important assist from having capabilities in place to recruit and train new employees in large numbers and from investing in infrastructure that gives them the capability to handle rapid growth as it occurs. It is nearly always better to put infrastructure and support systems in place before they are actually needed than to have to scramble to catch up to customer demand.

> **Core Concept**
>
> State-of-the-art support systems can be a basis for competitive advantage if they give a firm capabilities that rivals can't match.

Instituting Adequate Information Systems, Performance Tracking, and Controls

Accurate and timely information about daily operations is essential if managers are to gauge how well the strategy execution process is proceeding. Information systems need to cover five broad areas: (1) customer data, (2) operations data, (3) employee data, (4) supplier/partner/collaborative ally data, and (5) financial performance data.

All key strategic performance indicators have to be tracked and reported as often as practical. Monthly profit-and-loss statements and monthly statistical summaries, long the norm, are fast being replaced by daily statistical updates and even up-to-the-minute performance monitoring that online technology makes possible. Many retail companies have automated online systems that generate daily sales reports for each store and maintain up-to-the-minute inventory and sales records on each item. Manufacturing plants typically generate daily production reports and track labor productivity on every shift. Many retailers and manufacturers have online data systems connecting them with their suppliers that monitor the status of inventories, track shipments and deliveries, and measure defect rates.

Real-time information systems permit company managers to stay on top of implementation initiatives and daily operations and to intervene if things seem to be drifting off course. Tracking key performance indicators, gathering information from operating personnel, quickly identifying and diagnosing problems, and taking corrective actions are all integral pieces of the process of managing strategy implementation and execution and exercising adequate organization control. Telephone companies have elaborate information systems to measure signal quality, connection times, interrupts, wrong connections, billing errors, and other measures of reliability that affect customer service and satisfaction. To track and manage the quality of passenger service, airlines have information systems that monitor gate delays, on-time departures and arrivals, baggage handling times, lost baggage complaints, stockouts on meals and drinks, overbookings, and maintenance delays and failures. Virtually all companies now provide customer-contact personnel with computer access to customer databases so that they can respond effectively to customer inquiries and deliver personalized customer service.

Statistical information gives managers a feel for the numbers, briefings and meetings provide a feel for the latest developments and emerging issues, and personal contacts add a feel for the people dimension. All are good barometers. Managers have to identify problem areas and deviations from plan before they can take actions to get the organization back on course, by either improving the approaches to strategy execution or fine-tuning the strategy. Jeff Bezos, Amazon's CEO, is an ardent proponent of managing by the numbers—as he puts it, "Math-based decisions always trump opinion and judgment. . . . The trouble with most corporations is that they make judgment-based decisions when data-based decisions could be made."[25]

> **Core Concept**
> Having good information systems and operating data is integral to the managerial task of executing strategy successfully and achieving greater operating excellence.

Exercising Adequate Controls over Empowered Employees

Another important aspect of effectively managing and controlling the strategy execution process is monitoring the performance of empowered workers to see that they are acting within the specified limits.[26] Leaving empowered employees to their own devices in meeting performance standards without appropriate checks and balances can expose an organization to excessive risk.[27] Instances abound of employees' decisions or behavior having gone awry, sometimes costing a company huge sums or producing lawsuits aside from just generating embarrassing publicity.

Managers can't devote big chunks of their time to making sure that the decisions and behavior of empowered employees stay between the white lines—this would defeat the major purpose of empowerment and, in effect, lead to the reinstatement of a managerial bureaucracy engaged in constant over-the-shoulder supervision. Yet management has a clear responsibility to exercise sufficient control over empowered employees to protect the company against out-of-bounds behavior and unwelcome surprises. Scrutinizing daily and weekly operating statistics is one of the important ways in which managers can monitor the results that flow from the actions of empowered subordinates—if the operating results flowing from the actions of empowered employees look good, then it is reasonable to assume that empowerment is working.

One of the main purposes of tracking daily operating performance is to relieve managers of the burden of constant supervision and give them time for other issues. But managerial control is only part of the answer. Another valuable lever of control in companies that rely on empowered employees, especially in those that use self-managed work groups or other such teams, is peer-based control. Most team members feel responsible for the success of the whole team and tend to be relatively intolerant of any team member's behavior that weakens team performance or puts team accomplishments at risk. Because peer evaluation is such a powerful control device, companies organized into teams can remove some layers of the management hierarchy. This is especially true when a company has the information systems capability to monitor team performance daily or in real time.

Tying Rewards and Incentives to Strategy Execution

It is important for both organization units and individuals to be enthusiastically committed to executing strategy and achieving performance targets. Company managers typically use an assortment of motivational techniques and rewards to enlist organizationwide commitment to executing the strategic plan. A manager has to do more than just talk to everyone about how important new strategic practices and performance targets are to the organization's well-being. No matter how inspiring, talk seldom commands people's best efforts for long. *To get employees' sustained, energetic commitment, management has to be resourceful in designing and using motivational incentives—both monetary and nonmonetary.* The more a manager understands what motivates subordinates and the more he or she relies on motivational incentives as a tool for achieving the targeted strategic and financial results, the greater will be employees' commitment to good day-in, day-out strategy execution and achievement of performance targets.[28]

> **Core Concept**
>
> A properly designed reward structure is management's most powerful tool for mobilizing organizational commitment to successful strategy execution.

Strategy-Facilitating Motivational Practices

Financial incentives generally head the list of motivating tools for trying to gain wholehearted employee commitment to good strategy execution and operating excellence. Monetary rewards generally include some combination of base pay increases, performance bonuses, profit sharing plans, stock awards, company contributions to employee 401(k) or retirement plans, and piecework incentives (in the case of production workers). But successful companies and managers normally make extensive use of such nonmonetary carrot-and-stick incentives as frequent words of praise (or constructive criticism), special recognition at company gatherings or in the company newsletter, more (or less) job security, stimulating assignments, opportunities to transfer to attractive locations, increased (or decreased) autonomy, and rapid promotion (or the risk of being sidelined in a routine or dead-end job). In addition, companies use a host of other motivational approaches to spur stronger employee commitment to the strategy execution process; the following are some of the most important:[29]

> **Core Concept**
>
> One of management's biggest strategy-executing challenges is to employ motivational techniques that build wholehearted commitment to operating excellence and winning attitudes among employees.

- *Providing attractive perks and fringe benefits*—The various options here include full coverage of health insurance premiums, full tuition reimbursement for work on college degrees, paid vacation time of three or four weeks, on-site child care at major facilities, on-site gym facilities and massage therapists, getaway opportunities at company-owned recreational facilities (beach houses, ranches, resort condos), personal concierge services, subsidized cafeterias and free lunches, casual dress every day, personal travel services, paid sabbaticals, maternity leaves, paid leaves to care for ill family members, telecommuting, compressed workweeks (four 10-hour days instead of five 8-hour days), reduced summer hours, college scholarships for children, on-the-spot bonuses for exceptional performance, and relocation services.

- *Relying on promotion from within whenever possible*—This practice helps bind workers to their employer and employers to their workers; plus, it is an incentive for good performance. Promotion from within also helps ensure that people in positions of responsibility actually know something about the business, technology, and operations they are managing.

- *Making sure that the ideas and suggestions of employees are valued and respected*—Research indicates that the moves of many companies to push decision making down the line and empower employees increase employee motivation and satisfaction, as well as boost their productivity. The use of self-managed teams has much the same effect.

- *Creating a work atmosphere in which there is genuine sincerity, caring, and mutual respect among workers and between management and employees*—A "family" work environment where people are on a first-name basis and there is strong camaraderie promotes teamwork and cross-unit collaboration.

- *Stating the strategic vision in inspirational terms that make employees feel they are a part of doing something very worthwhile in a larger social sense*—There's strong motivating power associated with giving people a chance to be part of something exciting and personally satisfying. Jobs with noble purpose tend to turn employees on. At Pfizer, Merck, and most other pharmaceutical companies, it is the notion of helping sick people get well and restoring patients to full life. At Whole Foods Market (a natural-foods grocery chain), it is helping customers discover good eating habits and thus improving human health and nutrition.

- *Sharing information with employees about financial performance, strategy, operational measures, market conditions, and competitors' actions*—Broad disclosure and prompt communication send the message that managers trust their workers. Keeping employees in the dark denies them information useful to performing their job, prevents them from being "students of the business," and usually turns them off.

- *Having knockout facilities*—An impressive corporate facility for employees to work in usually has decidedly positive effects on morale and productivity.

■ *Being flexible in how the company approaches people management (motivation, compensation, recognition, recruitment) in multinational, multicultural environments*—Managers and employees in countries whose customs, habits, values, and business practices vary from those at the home office often become frustrated with insistence on consistent people-management practices worldwide. But the one area where consistency is essential is conveying the message that the organization values people of all races and cultural backgrounds and that discrimination of any sort will not be tolerated.

For specific examples of the motivational tactics employed by several prominent companies, see Company Spotlight 9.2.

Striking the Right Balance between Rewards and Punishment

While most approaches to motivation, compensation, and people management accentuate the positive, companies also embellish positive rewards with the risk of punishment. At General Electric, McKinsey & Company, several global public accounting firms, and other companies that look for and expect top-notch individual performance, there's an "up-or-out" policy—managers and professionals whose performance is not good enough to warrant promotion are first denied bonuses and stock awards and eventually weeded out. A number of companies deliberately give employees heavy workloads and tight deadlines—personnel are pushed hard to achieve "stretch" objectives and expected to put in long hours (nights and weekends if need be). At most companies, senior executives and key personnel in underperforming units are pressured to boost performance to acceptable levels and keep it there or risk being replaced.

As a general rule, it is unwise to take off the pressure for good individual and group performance or play down the stress, anxiety, and adverse consequences of shortfalls in performance. There is no evidence that a no-pressure/no-adverse-consequences work environment leads to superior strategy execution or operating excellence. As the CEO of a major bank put it, "There's a deliberate policy here to create a level of anxiety. Winners usually play like they're one touchdown behind."[30] *High-performing organizations nearly always have a cadre of ambitious people who relish the opportunity to climb the ladder of success, love a challenge, thrive in a performance-oriented environment, and find some competition and pressure useful to satisfy their own drives for personal recognition, accomplishment, and self-satisfaction.*

However, if an organization's motivational approaches and reward structure induce too much stress, internal competitiveness, and job insecurity and too many unpleasant consequences, the impact on workforce morale and strategy execution can be counterproductive. Evidence shows that managerial initiatives to improve strategy execution should incorporate more positive than negative motivational elements because when cooperation is positively enlisted and rewarded, rather than strong-armed by orders and threats (implicit or explicit), people tend to respond with more enthusiasm, dedication, creativity, and initiative. Something of a middle ground is generally optimal—not only handing out decidedly positive rewards for meeting or beating performance targets but also imposing sufficiently negative consequences (if only withholding rewards) when actual performance falls short of the target. But the negative consequences of underachievement should never be so severe or demoralizing as to impede a renewed and determined effort to overcome existing obstacles and hit the targets in upcoming periods.

COMPANY SPOTLIGHT 9.2
Techniques Companies Use to Motivate and Reward Employees

Companies have come up with an impressive variety of motivational and reward practices to help create a work environment that energizes employees and promotes better strategy execution. Here's a sampling of what companies are doing:

- Google has a sprawling four-building complex known as the Googleplex where the roughly 1,000 employees are provided with free food, unlimited ice cream, pool and Ping-Pong tables, and complimentary massages—management built the Googleplex to be "a dream environment." Moreover, the company allows its employees to spend 20 percent of their work time on any outside activity.

- Lincoln Electric, widely known for its piecework pay scheme and incentive bonus plan, rewards individual productivity by paying workers for each nondefective piece produced. Workers have to correct quality problems on their own time—defects in products used by customers can be traced back to the worker who caused them. Lincoln's piecework plan motivates workers to pay attention to both quality and volume produced. In addition, the company sets aside a substantial portion of its profits above a specified base for worker bonuses. To determine bonus size, Lincoln Electric rates each worker on four equally important performance measures: dependability, quality, output, and ideas and cooperation. The higher a worker's merit rating, the higher the incentive bonus earned; the highest-rated workers in good profit years receive bonuses of as much as 110 percent of their piecework compensation.

- At JM Family Enterprises, a Toyota distributor in Florida, employees get a great lease on new Toyotas and are flown to the Bahamas for cruises on the company yacht, plus the company's office facility has such amenities as a heated lap pool, a fitness center, and a free nail salon.

- Amazon.com hands out Just Do It awards to employees who do something they think will help Amazon *without* getting their boss's permission. The action has to be well thought through but doesn't have to succeed.

- Nordstrom, widely regarded for its superior in-house customer service experience, typically pays its retail salespeople an hourly wage higher than the prevailing rates paid by other department store chains plus a commission on each sale. Spurred by a culture that encourages salespeople to go all-out to satisfy customers and to seek out and promote new fashion ideas, Nordstrom salespeople often earn twice the average incomes of sales employees at competing stores. Nordstrom's rules for employees are simple: "Rule #1: Use your good judgment in all situations. There will be no additional rules."

- At W. L. Gore (the maker of Gore-Tex), employees get to choose what project/team they work on, and each team member's compensation is based on other team members' rankings of his or her contribution to the enterprise.

- At Ukrop's Super Markets, a family-owned chain, stores stay closed on Sunday; the company pays out 20 percent of pretax profits to employees in the form of quarterly bonuses; and the company picks up the membership tab for employees if they visit their health club 30 times a quarter.

- At biotech leader Amgen, employees get 16 paid holidays, generous vacation time, tuition reimbursements up to $10,000, on-site massages, a discounted car wash, and the convenience of shopping at on-site farmers' markets.

- At Synovus, a financial services and credit card company, the company adds 21 percent to employees' salaries with "wealth-building" programs like a 401(k) and profit sharing, plus it holds an annual bass fishing tournament.

- At specialty chip maker Xilinx, new hires receive stock option grants; the CEO responds promptly to employee e-mails, and during hard times management takes a 20 percent pay cut instead of laying off employees.

Source: *Fortune*'s lists of the 100 best companies to work for in America, both the February 4, 2002, and January 12, 2004 issues; Jefferson Graham, "The Search Engine That Could," *USA Today*, August 26, 2003, p. B3; and Fred Vogelstein, "Winning the Amazon Way," *Fortune*, May 26, 2003, p.73.

Linking the Reward System to Strategically Relevant Performance Outcomes

The most dependable way to keep people focused on strategy execution and the achievement of performance targets is to generously reward and recognize individuals and groups who meet or beat performance targets and to deny rewards and recognition to those who don't. *The use of incentives and rewards is the single most powerful tool management has to win strong employee commitment to diligent, competent strategy execution and operating excellence.* Decisions on salary increases, incentive compensation, promotions, key assignments, and the ways and means of awarding praise and recognition are potent attention-getting, commitment-generating devices. Such decisions seldom escape the closest employee scrutiny, as they say more about what is expected and who is considered to be doing a good job than about any other factor. Hence, when achievement of the targeted strategic and financial outcomes becomes the dominating basis for designing incentives, evaluating individual and group efforts, and handing out rewards, company personnel quickly grasp that it is in their own self-interest to do their best in executing the strategy competently and achieving key performance targets.[31] Indeed, it is usually through the company's system of incentives and rewards that workforce members emotionally ratify their commitment to the company's strategy execution effort.

> **Core Concept**
>
> A properly designed reward system aligns the well-being of organization members with their contributions to competent strategy execution and the achievement of performance targets.

Strategy-driven performance targets need to be established for every organizational unit, every manager, every team or work group, and perhaps every employee—targets that measure whether strategy execution is progressing satisfactorily. If the company's strategy is to be a low-cost provider, the incentive system must reward actions and achievements that result in lower costs. If the company has a differentiation strategy predicated on superior quality and service, the incentive system must reward such outcomes as Six Sigma defect rates, infrequent need for product repair, low numbers of customer complaints, and speedy order processing and delivery. If a company's growth is predicated on a strategy of new product innovation, incentives should be tied to factors such as the percentages of revenues and profits coming from newly introduced products.

Company Spotlight 9.3 provides two vivid examples of how companies have designed incentives linked directly to outcomes reflecting good strategy execution.

The Importance of Basing Incentives on Achieving Results, Not on Performing Assigned Duties

To create a strategy-supportive system of rewards and incentives, a company must emphasize rewarding people for accomplishing results, not for just dutifully performing assigned tasks. Focusing jobholders' attention and energy on what to *achieve* as opposed to what to *do* makes the work environment results-oriented. It is flawed management to tie incentives and rewards to satisfactory performance of duties and activities in hopes that the by-products will be the desired business outcomes and company achievements.[32] In any job, performing assigned tasks is not equivalent to achieving intended outcomes.

> It is folly to reward one outcome in hopes of getting another outcome.

Diligently showing up for work and attending to job assignments does not, by itself, guarantee results. As any student knows, the fact that an instructor teaches and students go to class doesn't necessarily mean that the students are learning. The enterprise of education would no doubt take on a different character if teachers were rewarded for the result of student learning rather than for the activity of teaching.

Nucor and Bank One: Two Companies That Tie Incentives Directly to Strategy Execution

The strategy at Nucor Corporation, now the biggest steel producer in the United States, is to be *the* low-cost producer of steel products. Because labor costs are a significant fraction of total cost in the steel business, successful implementation of Nucor's low-cost leadership strategy entails achieving lower labor costs per ton of steel than competitors' costs. Nucor management uses an incentive system to promote high worker productivity and drive labor costs per ton below rivals'. Each plant's workforce is organized into production teams (each assigned to perform particular functions), and weekly production targets are established for each team. Base pay scales are set at levels comparable to wages for similar manufacturing jobs in the local areas where Nucor has plants, but workers can earn a 1 percent bonus for each 1 percent that their output exceeds target levels. If a production team exceeds its weekly production target by 10 percent, team members receive a 10 percent bonus in their next paycheck; if a team exceeds its quota by 20 percent, team members earn a 20 percent bonus. Bonuses, paid every two weeks, are based on the prior two weeks' actual production levels measured against the targets.

Nucor's piece-rate incentive plan has resulted in labor productivity levels 10 to 20 percent above the average of the unionized workforces of several of its largest rivals, given Nucor a cost advantage over most rivals, and made Nucor workers among the highest-paid in the U.S. steel industry.

At Bank One (recently acquired by JP Morgan Chase), management believed it was strategically important to boost its customer satisfaction ratings in order to enhance its competitiveness vis-à-vis rivals. Targets were set for customer satisfaction, and monitoring systems for measuring customer satisfaction at each branch office were put in place. Then, to motivate branch office personnel to be more attentive in trying to please customers and also to signal that top management was truly committed to achieving higher levels of overall customer satisfaction, top management opted to tie pay scales in each branch office to that branch's customer satisfaction rating—the higher the branch's ratings, the higher that branch's pay scales. Management believed its shift from a theme of equal pay for equal work to one of equal pay for equal performance contributed significantly to its customer satisfaction priority.

Incentive compensation for top executives is typically tied to such financial measures as revenue and earnings growth, stock price performance, return on investment, and creditworthiness and perhaps such strategic measures as market share, product quality, or customer satisfaction. However, incentives for department heads, teams, and individual workers may be tied to performance outcomes more closely related to their strategic area of responsibility. In manufacturing, incentive compensation may be tied to unit manufacturing costs, on-time production and shipping, defect rates, the number and extent of work stoppages due to labor disagreements and equipment breakdowns, and so on. In sales and marketing, there may be incentives for achieving dollar sales or unit volume targets, market share, sales penetration of each target customer group, the fate of newly introduced products, the frequency of customer complaints, the number of new accounts acquired, and customer satisfaction. Which performance measures to base incentive compensation on depends on the situation—the priority placed on various financial and strategic objectives, the requirements for strategic and competitive success, and what specific results are needed in different facets of the business to keep strategy execution on track.

> **Core Concept**
>
> The role of the reward system is to align the well-being of organization members with realizing the company's vision so that organization members benefit by helping the company execute its strategy competently and fully satisfy customers.

Guidelines for Designing Incentive Compensation Systems

The concepts and company experiences discussed above yield the following prescriptive guidelines for creating an incentive compensation system to help drive successful strategy execution:

1. *Make the performance payoff a major, not minor, piece of the total compensation package.* Payoffs must be at least 10 to 12 percent of base salary to have much impact. Incentives that amount to 20 percent or more of total compensation are big attention getters, likely to really drive individual or team effort; incentives amounting to less than 5 percent of total compensation have comparatively weak motivational impact. Moreover, the payoff for high-performing individuals and teams must be meaningfully greater than the payoff for average performers, and the payoff for average performers meaningfully bigger than that for below-average performers.

2. *Have incentives that extend to all managers and all workers, not just top management.* It is a gross miscalculation to expect that lower-level managers and employees will work their hardest to hit performance targets just so a few senior executives can get lucrative rewards.

3. *Administer the reward system with scrupulous objectivity and fairness.* If performance standards are set unrealistically high or if individual/group performance evaluations are not accurate and well documented, dissatisfaction with the system will overcome any positive benefits.

4. *Tie incentives to performance outcomes directly linked to good strategy execution and financial performance.* Incentives should never be paid just because people are thought to be "doing a good job" or because they "work hard." Performance evaluation based on factors not tightly related to good strategy execution signal that either the strategic plan is incomplete (because important performance targets were left out) or management's real agenda is something other than the stated strategic and financial objectives.

5. *Make sure that the performance targets each individual or team is expected to achieve involve outcomes that the individual or team can personally affect.* The role of incentives is to enhance individual commitment and channel behavior in beneficial directions. This role is not well served when the performance measures by which company personnel are judged are outside their arena of influence.

6. *Keep the time between achieving the target performance outcome and the payment of the reward as short as possible.* Companies like Nucor and Continental Airlines have discovered that weekly or monthly payments for good performance work much better than annual payments. Nucor pays weekly bonuses based on prior-week production levels; Continental awards employees a monthly bonus for each month that on-time flight performance meets or beats a specified percentage companywide. Annual bonus payouts work best for higher-level managers and for situations where target outcome relates to overall company profitability or stock price performance.

7. *Make liberal use of nonmonetary rewards; don't rely solely on monetary rewards.* When used properly, money is a great motivator, but there are also potent advantages to be gained from praise, special recognition, handing out plum assignments, and so on.

8. *Absolutely avoid skirting the system to find ways to reward effort rather than results.* Whenever actual performance falls short of targeted performance, there's merit in determining whether the causes are attributable to subpar individual/group performance or to circumstances beyond the control of those responsible. It can be argued that exceptions should be made in giving rewards to people who've tried hard, gone the extra mile, yet still come up short because of circumstances beyond

their control. The problem with making exceptions for unknowable, uncontrollable, or unforeseeable circumstances is that once good excuses start to creep into justifying rewards for subpar results, the door is open for all kinds of reasons why actual performance failed to match targeted performance. A "no excuses" standard is more evenhanded and certainly easier to administer.

Once the incentives are designed, they have to be communicated and explained. Everybody needs to understand how his or her incentive compensation is calculated and how individual/group performance targets contribute to organizational performance targets. The pressure to achieve the targeted strategic and financial performance and continuously improve on strategy execution should be unrelenting, with few (if any) loopholes for rewarding shortfalls in performance. People at all levels have to be held accountable for carrying out their assigned parts of the strategic plan, and they have to understand that their rewards are based on the caliber of results achieved.

> **Core Concept**
>
> The unwavering standard for judging whether individuals, teams, and organizational units have done a good job must be whether they achieve performance targets consistent with effective strategy execution.

But with the pressure to perform should come meaningful rewards. Without an ample payoff, the system breaks down, and managers are left with the less workable options of barking orders, trying to enforce compliance, and depending on the goodwill of employees.

Performance-Based Incentives and Rewards in Multinational Enterprises   In some foreign countries, incentive pay runs counter to local customs and cultural norms. Professor Steven Kerr cites the time he lectured an executive education class on the need for more performance-based pay and a Japanese manager protested, "You shouldn't bribe your children to do their homework, you shouldn't bribe your wife to prepare dinner, and you shouldn't bribe your employees to work for the company."[33] Singling out individuals and commending them for unusually good effort can also be a problem; Japanese culture considers public praise of an individual an affront to the harmony of the group. In some countries, employees have a preference for nonmonetary rewards—more leisure time, important titles, access to vacation villages, and nontaxable perks. Thus, multinational companies have to build some degree of flexibility into the design of incentives and rewards in order to accommodate cross-cultural traditions and preferences.

Leading the Strategy Execution Process

The litany of managing the strategy process is simple enough: craft a sound strategic plan, implement it, execute it to the fullest, adjust it as needed, and win! But the leadership challenges are significant and diverse. To achieve results, a manager must take on a variety of leadership roles in managing the strategy execution process: resource acquirer and allocator, capabilities builder, motivator, policy maker, policy enforcer, head cheerleader, crisis solver, decision maker, and taskmaster, to mention a few. There are times when leading the strategy execution process entails being authoritarian and hard-nosed, times when it is best to be a perceptive listener and a compromising decision maker, times when matters are best delegated to people closest to the scene of the action, and times when being a coach is the proper role. Many occasions call for the manager in charge to assume a highly visible role and put in long hours guiding the process, while others entail only a brief ceremonial performance with the details delegated to subordinates.

For the most part, leading the strategy execution process has to be top-down and driven by mandates to get things on the right track and show good results. The specifics of leading organization efforts to put a strategy in place and deliver the intended results should start with understanding the requirements for good strategy execution, followed by diagnosing the organization's capabilities and preparedness to execute the necessary strategic initiatives, and then deciding which of several ways to proceed to get things done and achieve the targeted results.[34] In general, leading the drive for good strategy execution and operating excellence calls for several actions on the part of the manager in charge:

1. Staying on top of what is happening, closely monitoring progress, ferreting out issues, and learning what obstacles lie in the path of good execution.

2. Putting constructive pressure on the organization to achieve good results and operating excellence.

3. Leading the development of stronger core competencies and competitive capabilities.

4. Displaying ethical integrity and leading social responsibility initiatives.

5. Pushing corrective actions to improve strategy execution and achieve the targeted results.

Staying on Top of How Well Things Are Going

To stay on top of how well the strategy execution process is going, a manager needs to develop a broad network of contacts and sources of information, both formal and informal. The regular channels include talking with key subordinates, attending presentations and meetings, reading reviews of the latest operating results, talking to customers, watching the competitive reactions of rival firms, exchanging e-mail and holding telephone conversations with people in outlying locations, making on-site visits, and listening to rank-and-file employees. However, some information is more trustworthy than the rest, and the views and perspectives offered by different people can vary widely. Presentations and briefings by subordinates may be colored by wishful thinking or shoddy analysis rather than representing the unvarnished truth. Bad news or problems are sometimes filtered, minimized, or distorted by people pursuing their own agendas; in some cases they are not reported at all, as subordinates delay conveying failures and problems in hopes that they can turn things around in time. Hence, managers have to make sure that they get their information directly from the source and have an accurate feel for the existing situation. They have to confirm whether things are on track, identify problems, learn what obstacles lie in the path of good strategy execution, ruthlessly assess whether the organization has the talent and attitude needed to drive the required changes, and develop a basis for determining what, if anything, they can personally do to move the process along.[35]

One of the best ways for executives to stay on top of the strategy execution process is by making regular visits to the field and talking with many different people at many different levels—a technique often labeled **managing by walking around (MBWA).** Wal-Mart executives have had a long-standing practice of spending two to three days every week visiting Wal-Mart's stores and talking with store managers and employees. Sam Walton, Wal-Mart's founder, insisted, "The key is to get out into the store and listen to what the associates have to say." Jack Welch, the highly effective CEO of General Electric from

Core Concept

Management by walking around (MBWA) is one of the techniques that effective leaders use to stay informed about how well the strategy execution process is progressing.

1980 to 2001, not only spent several days each month personally visiting GE operations and talking with major customers but also arranged his schedule so that he could spend time exchanging information and ideas with GE managers from all over the world who were attending classes at the company's leadership development center near GE's headquarters.

Often, customers and suppliers can provide valuable perspectives on how well a company's strategy execution process is going. Joe Tucci, COO at data-storage leader EMC, when confronted with an unexpected dropoff in EMC's sales in 2001 and not sure whether the downturn represented a temporary slump or a structural market change, went straight to the source for hard information: the CEOs and CFOs to whom CIOs at customer companies reported and to the consultants who advised them. The information he got was eye-opening—fundamental market shifts were occurring and the rules of market engagement now called for major strategy changes at EMC followed by quick implementation.

To keep their fingers on the company's pulse, managers at some companies host weekly get-togethers (often on Friday afternoons) to create a regular opportunity for tidbits of information to flow freely between down-the-line employees and executives. Many manufacturing executives make a point of strolling the factory floor to talk with workers and of meeting regularly with union officials. Some managers operate out of open cubicles in big spaces populated with open cubicles for other personnel so that they can interact easily and frequently with coworkers. Jeff Bezos, Amazon.com's CEO, is noted for his practice of MBWA, firing off a battery of questions when he tours facilities and insisting that Amazon managers spend time in the trenches with their people to avoid abstract thinking and getting disconnected from the reality of what's happening.[36]

Most managers rightly attach great importance to spending time with people at various company facilities and gathering information and opinions firsthand from diverse sources about how well different aspects of the strategy execution process are going. Such contacts give managers a feel for what progress is being made, what problems are being encountered, and whether additional resources or different approaches may be needed. Just as important, MBWA provides opportunities for managers to talk informally to many different people at different organizational levels, give encouragement, lift spirits, shift attention from the old to the new priorities, and create some excitement—all of which generate positive energy and help mobilize organizational efforts behind strategy execution.

Putting Constructive Pressure on the Organization to Achieve Good Results and Operating Excellence

Managers have to be out front in mobilizing organizational energy behind the drive for good strategy execution and operating excellence. Part of the leadership requirement here entails nurturing a results-oriented work climate. A culture where there's constructive pressure to achieve good results is a valuable contributor to good strategy execution and operating excellence. Results-oriented cultures are permeated with a spirit of achievement and have a good track record in meeting or beating performance targets. If management wants to drive the strategy execution effort by instilling a results-oriented work climate, then senior executives have to take the lead in promoting certain enabling cultural drivers: a strong sense of involvement on the part of company personnel, emphasis on individual initiative and creativity, respect for the contribution of individuals and groups, and pride in doing things right.

Organization leaders who succeed in creating a results-oriented work climate typically are intensely people-oriented, and they are skilled users of people-management practices that win the emotional commitment of company personnel and inspire them to do their best.[37] They understand that treating employees well generally leads to increased teamwork, higher morale, greater loyalty, and increased employee commitment to making a contribution. All of these foster an esprit de corps that energizes organization members to contribute to the drive for operating excellence and proficient strategy execution.

Successfully leading the effort to instill a spirit of high achievement into the culture generally entails such leadership actions and managerial practices as:

- Treating employees with dignity and respect. This often includes a strong company commitment to training each employee thoroughly, providing attractive career opportunities, emphasizing promotion from within, and providing a high degree of job security. Some companies symbolize the value of individual employees and the importance of their contributions by referring to them as cast members (Disney), crew members (McDonald's), coworkers (Kinko's and CDW Computer Centers), job owners (Graniterock), partners (Starbucks), or associates (Wal-Mart, Lenscrafters, W. L. Gore, Edward Jones, Publix Supermarkets, and Marriott International). At a number of companies, managers at every level are held responsible for developing the people who report to them.

- Making champions out of the people who turn in winning performances—but doing so in ways that promote teamwork and cross-unit collaboration as opposed to spurring an unhealthy footrace among employees to best one another. Would-be champions who advocate radical or different ideas must not be looked on as disruptive or troublesome. The best champions and change agents are persistent, competitive, tenacious, committed, and fanatical about seeing their idea through to success. It is particularly important that people who champion an unsuccessful idea not be punished or sidelined but, rather, be encouraged to try again—encouraging lots of "tries" is important since many ideas won't pan out.

- Encouraging employees to use initiative and creativity in performing their work. Operating excellence requires that everybody be expected to contribute ideas, exercise initiative, and pursue continuous improvement. The leadership trick is to keep a sense of urgency alive in the business so that people see change and innovation as necessities. Moreover, people with maverick ideas or out-of-the-ordinary proposals have to be tolerated and given room to operate; anything less tends to squelch creativity and initiative.

- Setting stretch objectives and clearly communicating an expectation that company personnel are to give their best in achieving performance targets.

- Using the tools of benchmarking, best practices, business process reengineering, TQM, and Six Sigma quality to focus attention on continuous improvement. These are proven approaches to getting better operating results and facilitating better strategy execution.

- Using the full range of motivational techniques and compensation incentives to inspire company personnel, nurture a results-oriented work climate, and enforce high-performance standards. Managers cannot mandate innovative improvements by simply exhorting people to "be creative," nor can they make continuous progress toward operating excellence with directives to "try harder." Rather, they have to foster a culture where innovative ideas and experimentation with new ways of doing things can blossom and thrive. Individuals and groups need to be strongly encouraged to brainstorm, let their imaginations fly in all directions, and come up with proposals for improving how things are done. This means giving company personnel enough autonomy to stand out, excel, and contribute. And it means that the rewards for successful champions of new ideas and operating improvements should be large and visible.

■ Celebrating individual, group, and company successes. Top management should miss no opportunity to express respect for individual employees and appreciation of extraordinary individual and group effort.[38] Companies like Mary Kay Cosmetics, Tupperware, and McDonald's actively seek out reasons and opportunities to give pins, buttons, badges, and medals for good showings by average performers—the idea being to express appreciation and give a motivational boost to people who stand out in doing ordinary jobs. General Electric and 3M Corporation make a point of ceremoniously honoring individuals who believe so strongly in their ideas that they take it on themselves to hurdle the bureaucracy, maneuver their projects through the system, and turn them into improved services, new products, or even new businesses.

While leadership efforts to instill a results-oriented culture usually accentuate the positive, negative consequences are sometimes needed. Managers whose units consistently perform poorly have to be replaced. Low-performing workers and people who reject the results-oriented cultural emphasis have to be weeded out or at least moved to out-of-the-way positions. Average performers have to be candidly counseled that they have limited career potential unless they show more progress in the form of more effort, better skills, and ability to deliver better results.

Leading the Development of Better Competencies and Capabilities

A third avenue to better strategy execution and operating excellence is proactively strengthening organizational competencies and competitive capabilities. This often requires top management intervention. Senior management usually has to lead the strengthening effort because core competencies and competitive capabilities typically reside in the combined efforts of different work groups, departments, and strategic allies. The tasks of managing human skills, knowledge bases, and intellect and then integrating them to forge competitively advantageous competencies and capabilities is an exercise best orchestrated by senior managers who appreciate their strategy-implementing significance and who have the clout to enforce the necessary networking and cooperation among individuals, groups, departments, and external allies. Stronger competencies and capabilities can not only lead to better performance of value chain activities but also pave the way for better bottom-line results. Also, in today's globalizing economy, strategy leaders are well positioned to spot opportunities to leverage existing competencies and competitive capabilities across geographic borders.

Aside from leading efforts to strengthen existing competencies and capabilities, effective strategy leaders try to anticipate changes in customer-market requirements and proactively build new competencies and capabilities that offer a competitive edge over rivals. Senior managers are in the best position to see the need and potential of new capabilities and then to play a lead role in the capability-building, resource-strengthening process. Proactively building new competencies and capabilities ahead of rivals to gain a competitive edge is strategic leadership of the best kind, but strengthening the company's resource base in reaction to newly developed capabilities of pioneering rivals occurs more frequently.

Displaying Ethical Integrity and Leading Social Responsibility Initiatives

For an organization to avoid the pitfalls of scandal and disgrace and consistently display the intent to conduct its business in a principled manner, the CEO and those around the CEO must be openly and unswervingly committed to ethical conduct and socially redeeming business principles and core values. Leading the effort to operate the company's business in an ethically principled fashion has three pieces. First and foremost, the CEO and other senior executives must set an excellent example in their own ethical behavior, demonstrating character and personal integrity in their actions and decisions. The behavior of senior executives is always watched carefully, sending a clear message to company personnel regarding what the "real" standards of personal conduct are. Moreover, the company's strategy and operating decisions have to be seen as ethical—actions speak louder than words here. Second, top management must declare unequivocal support of the company's ethical code and take an uncompromising stand on expecting all company personnel to conduct themselves in an ethical fashion at all times. This means iterating and reiterating to employees that it is their duty to observe the company's ethical code. Third, top management must be prepared to act as the final arbiter on hard calls; this means removing people from key positions or terminating them when they are guilty of a violation. It also means reprimanding those who have been lax in monitoring and enforcing ethical compliance. Failure to act swiftly and decisively in punishing ethical misconduct is interpreted as a lack of real commitment.

Demonstrating Genuine Commitment to a Strategy of Social Responsibility

As was discussed in Chapter 7, business leaders who want their companies to be regarded as exemplary corporate citizens must not only see that their companies operate ethically but also take a lead role in crafting a social responsibility strategy that positively improves the well-being of employees, the environment, the communities in which they operate, and society at large. The CEO and other senior executives must insist that the company go past the rhetoric and cosmetics of corporate citizenship and employ a genuine strategy of social responsibility. *What separates companies that make a sincere effort to carry their weight in being good corporate citizens from companies that are content to do only what is legally required of them are company leaders who believe strongly that just making a profit is not good enough. Such leaders are committed to a higher standard of performance that includes social and environmental metrics as well as financial and strategic metrics.*

> Companies with socially conscious strategy leaders and a core value of corporate social responsibility move beyond the rhetorical flourishes of corporate citizenship and enlist the full support of company personnel behind social responsibility initiatives.

One of the leadership responsibilities of the CEO and other senior managers, therefore, is to step out front, wave the flag of socially responsible behavior for all to see, marshal the support of company personnel, and transform social responsibility initiatives into an everyday part of how the company conducts its business affairs. Strategy leaders have to insist on the use of social and environmental metrics in evaluating performance, and, ideally, the company's board of directors will elect to tie the company's social and environmental performance to executive compensation—a surefire way to make sure that social responsibility efforts are more than window dressing. To help ensure that it has commitment from senior managers, Verizon Communications ties 10 percent of the annual bonus of the company's top 2,500 managers directly to the achievement of social responsibility targets. One survey found over 60 percent of senior managers believed that a portion of executive compensation should be linked to a company's performance on social and environmental measures. The strength of the commitment from the top—typically a company's CEO and board of directors—ultimately determines whether a company will pursue a genuine, full-fledged strategy of social responsibility that embraces some customized combination of actions to protect the environment (beyond what is required by law), actively participate in community affairs, be a generous supporter of charitable causes and projects that benefit society, and have a positive impact on workforce diversity and the overall well-being of employees.

Leading the Process of Making Corrective Adjustments

The leadership challenge of making corrective adjustments is twofold: deciding when adjustments are needed and deciding what adjustments to make. Both decisions are a normal and necessary part of managing the strategy execution process, since no scheme for implementing and executing strategy can foresee all the events and problems that will arise. There comes a time at every company when managers have to fine-tune or overhaul the approaches to strategy execution and push for better results. Clearly, when a company's strategy execution effort is not delivering desired results and making measurable progress toward operating excellence, it is the leader's responsibility to step forward and push corrective actions.

The *process* of making corrective adjustments varies according to the situation. In a crisis, it is typical for leaders to have key subordinates gather information, identify and evaluate options (crunching whatever numbers may be appropriate), and perhaps prepare a preliminary set of recommended actions for consideration. The organization leader then usually meets with key subordinates and personally presides over extended discussions of the proposed responses, trying to build a quick consensus among members of the executive inner circle. If no consensus emerges and action is required immediately, the burden falls on the manager in charge to choose the response and urge its support.

When the situation allows managers to proceed more deliberately in deciding when to make changes and what changes to make, most managers seem to prefer a process of incrementally solidifying commitment to a particular course of action.[39] The process that managers go through in deciding on corrective adjustments is essentially the same for both proactive and reactive changes: they sense needs, gather information, broaden and deepen their understanding of the situation, develop options and explore their pros and cons, put forth action proposals, generate partial (comfort-level) solutions, strive for a consensus, and finally formally adopt an agreed-on course of action.[40] The time frame for deciding what corrective changes to initiate can take a few hours, a few days, a few weeks, or even a few months if the situation is particularly complicated.

Success in initiating corrective actions usually hinges on thorough analysis of the situation, the exercise of good business judgment in deciding what actions to take, and good implementation of the corrective actions that are initiated. Successful managers are skilled in getting an organization back on track rather quickly; they (and their staffs) are good at discerning what actions to take and in ramroding them through to a successful conclusion. Managers who struggle to show measurable progress in generating good results and improving the performance of strategy-critical value chain activities are candidates for being replaced.

The challenges of leading a successful strategy execution effort are, without question, substantial.[41] But the job is definitely doable. Because each instance of executing strategy occurs under different organizational circumstances, the managerial agenda for executing strategy always needs to be situation-specific—there's no neat generic procedure to follow. And, as we said at the beginning of Chapter 8, executing strategy is an action-oriented, make-the-right-things-happen task that challenges a manager's ability to lead and direct organizational change, create or reinvent business processes, manage and motivate people, and achieve performance targets. If you now better understand what the challenges are, what approaches are available, which issues need to be considered, and why the action agenda for implementing and executing strategy sweeps across so many aspects of administrative and managerial work, then we will look on our discussion in Chapters 8 and 9 as a success.

A Final Word on Managing the Process of Crafting and Executing Strategy   In practice, it is hard to separate the leadership requirements of executing strategy from the other pieces of the strategy process. As we emphasized in Chapter 1, the job of crafting, implementing, and executing strategy is a five-task process with much looping and recycling to fine-tune and adjust strategic visions, objectives, strategies, capabilities, implementation approaches, and cultures to fit one another and to fit changing circumstances. The process is continuous, and the conceptually separate acts of crafting and executing strategy blur together in real-world situations. The best tests of good strategic leadership are whether the company has a good strategy and whether the strategy execution effort is delivering the intended results. If these two conditions exist, the chances are excellent that the company has good strategic leadership.

Key Points

Managers implementing and executing a new or different strategy must identify the resource requirements of each new strategic initiative and then consider whether the current pattern of resource allocation and the budgets of the various subunits are suitable.

Anytime a company alters its strategy, managers should review existing policies and operating procedures, proactively revise or discard those that are out of sync, and formulate new ones to facilitate execution of new strategic initiatives. Prescribing new or freshly revised policies and operating procedures aids the task of strategy execution (1) by providing top-down guidance to operating managers, supervisory personnel, and employees regarding how certain things need to be done and what the boundaries are on independent actions and decisions; (2) by enforcing consistency in how particular strategy-critical activities are performed in geographically scattered operating units; and (3) by promoting the creation of a work climate and corporate culture that fosters good strategy execution.

Competent strategy execution entails visible, unyielding managerial commitment to best practices and continuous improvement. Benchmarking, the discovery and adoption of best practices, reengineering core business processes, and continuous improvement initiatives like total quality management (TQM) or Six Sigma programs all aim at improved efficiency, lower costs, better product quality, and greater customer satisfaction. *These initiatives are important tools for learning how to execute a strategy more proficiently.*

Company strategies can't be implemented or executed well without a number of support systems to carry on business operations. Well-conceived state-of-the-art support systems can not only facilitate better strategy execution but also strengthen organizational capabilities enough to provide a competitive edge over rivals.

Strategy-supportive motivational practices and reward systems are powerful management tools for gaining employee commitment. The key to creating a reward system that promotes good strategy execution is to make strategically relevant measures of performance *the dominating basis* for designing incentives, evaluating individual and group efforts, and handing out rewards. Positive motivational practices generally work better than negative ones, but there is a place for both. There's also a place for both monetary and nonmonetary incentives.

Successful managers do several things in leading the drive for good strategy execution and operating excellence. First, they stay on top of things. They keep a finger on the organization's pulse by spending considerable time outside their offices, listening and talking to organization members, coaching, cheerleading, and picking up important information. Second, they are active and visible in putting constructive pressure on the organization to achieve good results and operating excellence. This entails (1) promoting an esprit de corps that mobilizes and energizes organization members to execute strategy in a competent fashion and deliver the targeted results and (2) championing innovative ideas for improvement and promoting the use of best practices and benchmarking to measure the progress being made in performing value chain activities in first-rate fashion. Third, wise leaders exert their clout in developing competencies and competitive capabilities that enable better execution. Fourth, they serve as a role model in displaying high ethical standards, and they insist that company personnel conduct the company's business ethically and in a socially responsible manner. They demonstrate unequivocal and visible commitment to the ethics enforcement process. Fifth and finally, when a company's strategy execution effort is not delivering good results and the organization is not making measurable progress toward operating excellence, it is the leader's responsibility to step forward and push corrective actions.

Exercises

1. Go to www.google.com and, using the advanced search feature, enter "best practices." Browse through the search results to identify at least five organizations that have gathered a set of best practices and are making the best-practice library they have assembled available to members. Explore at least one of the sites to get an idea of the kind of best-practice information that is available.

2. Using the Internet search engine at www.google.com, do a search on "Six Sigma" quality programs. Browse through the search results and (a) identify several companies that offer Six Sigma training and (b) find lists of companies that have implemented Six Sigma programs in their pursuit of operational excellence. In particular, you should go to www.isixsigma.com and explore the "Six Sigma Q&A" menu option.

3. Using the Internet search engine at www.google.com, do a search on "total quality management." Browse through the search results and (a) identify companies

that offer TQM training, (b) identify some books on TQM programs, and (c) find lists of companies that have implemented TQM programs in their pursuit of operational excellence.

4. Consult the most recent issue of *Fortune* containing the annual "100 Best Companies to Work For" list (usually a late-January or early-February issue). Identify at least 5 (preferably 10) compensation incentives that these companies use to enhance employee motivation and reward employees for good strategic and financial performance.

Readings in Strategy

What Is Strategy and How Do You Know If You Have One?

Costas Markides
London Business School

What is strategy, *really?* Despite the obvious importance of a superior strategy to the success of an organization and despite decades of research on the subject, there is little agreement among academics as to what strategy really is. From notions of strategy as positioning to strategy as visioning, several possible definitions are fighting for legitimacy. Lack of an acceptable definition has opened up the field to an invasion of sexy slogans and terms, all of which add to the confusion and state of unease.

Not that the confusion is restricted to academics. If asked, most practicing executives would define strategy as "how I could achieve my company's objectives." Although this definition is technically correct, it is so general that it is practically meaningless.

Needless to say, this state of affairs is unfortunate. Perhaps nothing highlights better the sad (comical?) state of affairs surrounding strategy than the following.

In November 1996, the most prominent strategy academic, Michael Porter of Harvard, published a *Harvard Business Review* article grandly entitled "What is strategy?" (*Harvard Business Review,* Nov–Dec 1996). This was followed only a few months later by another famous academic, Gary Hamel of London Business School, with an equally impressively titled article, "The search for strategy" (London Business School working paper, 1997). That after 40 years of academic research on the subject, two of the most prominent academics in the field felt the need to go out of their way and start searching for strategy goes to show how much confusion we have managed to create regarding such a crucial business decision.

Although part of the confusion is undoubtedly self-inflicted, a major portion of it also stems from an honest lack of understanding as to the content of strategy. I would like to propose a view of strategy that is based on my research on companies that have strategically innovated in their industries. These are companies that not only developed strategies that are fundamentally different from the strategies of their competitors but whose strategies also turned out to be tremendously successful.

Based on my research on these successful strategists, I'd like to propose that there are certain simple but fundamental principles underlying every successful strategy. When one goes beyond the visible differences among strategies and probes deeper into the roots of these strategies, one cannot fail but notice that all successful strategies share the same underlying principles or building blocks. Thus, the building blocks of

"What is Strategy and How Do You Know if You Have One?," Costas Markides, *Business Strategy Review,* Vol. 15, Issue 2 (Summer 2004), p. 5–12. Reprinted with permission of Blackwell Publishing Ltd.

Microsoft's successful strategy are the same as the building blocks of the strategy that propelled Sears to industry leadership 100 years ago. My argument is that by understanding what these building blocks are, an organization can use them to develop its own successful strategy. The building blocks are:

Strategy Must Decide on a Few Parameters

In today's uncertain and ever-changing environment strategy is all about making some very difficult decisions on a *few* parameters. It is absolutely essential that the firm decides on these parameters because they become the boundaries within which people are given the freedom and the autonomy to operate and try things out. They also define the company's *strategic position* in its industry. Without clear decisions on these parameters, the company will drift like a rudderless ship in the open seas.

What Are These Parameters?

A company has to decide on three main issues: *who* will be its targeted customers and who it will *not* target; *what* products or services it will offer its chosen customers and what it will *not* offer them; and *how* it will go about achieving all this—what activities it will perform and what activities it will not perform.

These are not easy decisions to make and each question has many possible answers, all of them *ex-ante* possible and logical. As a result, these kinds of decisions will unavoidably be preceded with debates, disagreements, politicking and indecision. Yet, at the end of the day, a firm cannot be everything to everybody; so clear and explicit decisions must be made. These choices may turn out to be wrong but that is not an excuse for not deciding.

It is absolutely essential that an organization make clear and explicit choices on these three dimensions because the choices made become the parameters within which people are allowed to operate with autonomy. Without these clear parameters, the end result can be chaos. Seen in another way, it would be foolish and dangerous to allow people to take initiatives without some clear parameters guiding their actions.

Not only must a company make clear choices on these parameters, it must also attempt to make choices that are different from the choices its competitors have made. A company will be successful if it chooses a *distinctive* (that is, different from competitors) strategic position. Sure, it may be impossible to come up with answers that are 100 percent different from those of competitors but the ambition should be to create as much differentiation as possible.

Given the importance of coming up with clear answers to these three issues, the question is: who comes up with possible answers to these questions; who decides what to do out of the many possibilities; and how long do the decisions remain unchanged?

Who Comes Up with Ideas?

Given the right organizational context, strategic ideas (on who to target, what to sell and how to do it) can come from anybody, anywhere, anytime. They may emerge through trial and error or because somebody has a "gut feeling" or because somebody "got lucky" and stumbled across a good idea. They may even emerge out of a formal strategic planning session. (However dismissive we can be of the modern corporation's formal planning process, the possibility still exists that some good ideas can come out of such a process.) No matter how the ideas are conceived, it is unlikely that they will be perfect from the start. The firm must therefore be willing and ready to modify or change its strategic ideas as it receives feedback from the market.

In general, there are numerous tactics at our disposal to enhance creativity at the idea-generation stage. Let me list a few of them:

- Encourage everyone in the organization to question the firm's implicit assumptions and beliefs (its sacred cows) as to who our customers really are, what we are really offering to them and how we do these things. Also, encourage a fundamental questioning of the firm's accepted answer to the question: "what business are we in?"

- To facilitate this questioning, create a positive crisis. If done correctly, this will galvanize the organization into active thinking. If done incorrectly, it will demoralize everybody and create confusion and disillusionment throughout the organization.

- Develop processes in the organization to collect and utilize ideas from everybody—employees, customers, distributors and so on. At Lan & Spar Bank, for example, every employee is asked to contribute ideas through a strategy workbook; Schlumberger has an internal venturing unit; Bank One has a specific customer center where all customers are encouraged to phone and express their complaints; at my local supermarket, there is a customer suggestion box. Different organizations have come up with different tactics but the idea is the same: allow everybody to contribute ideas and make it easy for them to communicate their ideas to the decision makers in the organization.

- Create variety in the thinking that takes place in formal planning processes. This can be achieved not only by using a diverse team of people but also by utilizing as many thinking approaches as possible.

- Institutionalize a culture of innovation. The organization must create the organizational environment (culture/structure/incentives/people) that promotes and supports innovative behaviors.

This is not an exhaustive list of tactics that could be used to increase creativity in strategy making. I am sure that other tactics and processes exist or can be thought of. The principle, though, remains the same: at this stage of crafting an innovative strategy, the goal must be to generate as many strategic ideas as possible so that we have the luxury of choosing.

Who Decides?

Even though anyone in an organization can come up with new strategic ideas (and everybody should be *encouraged* to do so), it is the responsibility of top management to make the final choices.

There have been many calls lately to make the process of strategy development "democratic" and "flexible"—to bring everybody in the organization into the process. The thinking here is that the odds of conceiving truly innovative ideas are increased if thousands of people rather than just 5 or 10 senior managers put their minds to work. And this much is true.

But the job of choosing the ideas that the firm will actually pursue must be left to top management. Otherwise, the result is chaos, confusion and ultimately a demotivated workforce. After all is said and done, it is the leaders of an organization, not every single employee, who must choose which ideas will be pursued.

Choosing is difficult. At the time of choosing no one knows for sure whether a particular idea will work nor does anyone know if the choices made are really the most appropriate ones.

One could reduce the uncertainty at this stage by either evaluating each idea in a rigorous way or by experimenting with the idea in a limited way to see if it works. However, it is crucial to understand that uncertainty can be reduced but not limited. No matter how much experimentation we carry out and no matter how much thinking goes into it, the time will come when a firm must decide one way or another. Choices have to be made and these choices may turn out to be wrong. However, lack of certainty is no excuse for indecision.

Not only must a firm choose what to do but it must also make it clear what it will *not* do. The worst strategic mistake possible is to choose something but also keep our options open by doing other things as well. Imagine an organization where the CEO proclaims that "our strategy is crystal clear: we will do ABC" and at the same time the employees of the organization see the firm doing XYZ as well as ABC. In their eyes, this means one of two things: either we don't really have a strategy, or top management is totally confused. Either way, the organization is left demoralized and confidence in senior management is shattered. Organizations that say one thing and then do another are those that have failed to make clear choices about what they will do and what they will not do with their strategy.

The difficult choices made by Canon in attacking Xerox highlight the importance of choosing in an explicit way what to do and what not to do. At the time of the attack, Xerox had a lock on the copier market by following a well-defined and successful strategy, the main elements of which were the following: having segmented the market by volume, Xerox decided to go after the corporate reproduction market by concentrating on copiers designed for high-speed, high-volume needs. This inevitably defined Xerox's customers as big corporations, which in turn determined its distribution method: the direct sales force. At the same time, Xerox decided to lease rather than sell its machines, a strategic choice that had worked well in the company's earlier battles with 3M. Xerox's strategy proved to be so successful that several new competitors, among them IBM and Kodak, tried to enter the market by adopting the same or similar tactics.

Canon, on the other hand, chose to play the game differently. Having determined in the early 1960s to diversify out of cameras and into copiers, Canon segmented the market by end-user and decided to target small and medium-sized businesses while also producing PC copiers for individuals. At the same time, Canon decided to sell its machines through a dealer network rather than lease them. And while Xerox emphasized the speed of its machines, Canon elected to concentrate on quality and price as its differentiating features.

Cutting the story short, where IBM's and Kodak's assault on the copier market failed, Canon's succeeded. Within 20 years of attacking Xerox, Canon emerged as the market leader in volume terms.

There are many reasons behind the success of Canon. Notice, however, that just as Xerox did 20 years before it, Canon created for itself a *distinctive strategic position* in the industry—a position that was different from Xerox's. Whereas Xerox targeted big corporations as its customers, Canon went after small companies and individuals; while Xerox emphasized the speed of its machines, Canon focused on quality and price; and whereas Xerox used a direct sales force to lease its machines, Canon used its dealer network to sell its copiers. Rather than try to beat Xerox at its own game, Canon triumphed by creating its own unique strategic position.

As in the case of Xerox, these were *not* the only choices available to Canon. Serious debates and disagreements must undoubtedly have taken place within Canon as to whether these were the right choices to pursue. Yet choices were made and a clear strategy with sharp and well-defined boundaries was put in place. As in the case of Xerox, Canon was successful because it chose a unique and well-defined strategic position in the industry—one with distinctive customers, products and activities.

Strategy Must Put All Our Choices Together to Create a Reinforcing Mosaic

Choosing what to do and what not to do is certainly an important element of strategy. However, strategy is much more than this. Strategy is all about *combining* these choices into a *system* that creates the requisite *fit* between what the environment needs and what the company does. It is the combining of a firm's choices into a well-balanced system that's important, not the individual choices.

The importance of conceptualizing the company *as a combination of activities* cannot be overemphasized. In this perspective, a firm is a complex system of interrelated and interdependent activities, each affecting the other: decisions and actions in one part of the business affect other parts, directly or indirectly. This means that unless we take a holistic, big-picture approach in designing the activities of our company, our efforts will backfire. Even if each individual activity is optimally crafted, the whole may still suffer unless we take interdependencies into consideration. The numerous local optima almost always undermine the global optimum.

The problem is that human beings can never really comprehend all the complexity embedded in our companies. We therefore tend to focus on one or two aspects of the system and try to optimize these sub-systems independently. By doing so, we ignore the interdependencies in the system and we are therefore making matters worse. Since it takes time for the effect of our actions to show up, we do not even see that we are the source of our problems. When the long-term effects of our short-sighted actions hit home, we blame other people and especially outside forces for our problems (we had no forecasts, demand is unpredictable, the economy is not growing and so on).

In designing a company's system of activities, managers must bear four principles in mind:

- First, the individual activities we choose to do must be the ones that are demanded by the market.
- Second, the activities we decide to perform must fit with each other.
- Third, activities must not only fit but must also be in *balance* with each other.
- Finally, in designing these activities, it is important to keep in mind that the collection of these activities will form an interrelated system.

Not only should we pay particular attention to the interrelationships in this system but we should also be aware that the *structure* of this system will drive behavior in it. What people do in a firm is conditioned by this underlying structure. Therefore, if we want to change behavior, we will have to change the structure of the system.

Strategy Must Achieve Fit without Losing Flexibility

Creating the right fit between what the market needs and what a firm does can backfire if the environment changes and the firm does not respond accordingly. We are all familiar with the story of the frog.

When a frog is put in a pot of boiling water, it jumps out; when, instead, the same frog is put in a pot of cold water and the water is slowly brought to a boil, the frog stays in the pot and boils to death.

In the same manner, if a company does not react to the constant changes taking place in its environment, it will find itself boiled to death.

This implies that a company needs to create the requisite fit with its current environment while remaining flexible enough to respond to (or even create) changes in this environment. But what does it mean when we say that a firm *must remain flexible?*

The way I use the term here, I imply three things: a firm must first be able to identify changes in its environment *early enough;* it must then have the *cultural* readiness to embrace change and respond to it; and it must have the requisite *skills and competencies* to compete in whatever environment emerges after the change. Thus, flexibility has a cultural element to it (being willing to change) as well as a competence element to it (being able to change).

Strategy Needs to Be Supported by the Appropriate Organizational Environment

Any strategy, however brilliant, needs to be implemented properly if it is to deliver the desired results. However, implementation does not take place in a vacuum. It takes place within an *organizational environment,* which we, as managers, create. It is this organizational environment that produces the behavior that we observe in companies. Therefore, to secure the desired strategic behavior by employees, a firm must first create the appropriate environment—that is, the environment that promotes and supports its chosen strategy.

By environment, I mean four elements: an organization's culture; its incentives; its structure; and its people. (What I call here "environment" is what is widely known as the 7S framework developed by McKinsey and Co. The 7S are: style, strategy, structure, systems, skills, staff and superordinate goals.)

A company that wants to put into action a certain strategy must first ask the question: "what kind of culture, incentives, structure and people do we need to implement the strategy?"

In other words, to create a superior strategy, a company must think beyond customers, products and activities. It must also decide what underlying environment to create and how exactly to create it so as to facilitate the implementation of its strategy.

However, deciding on what kind of culture, structure, incentives and people to have is not enough. The challenge for strategy is to develop these four elements of organizational environment and then put them together so that on one hand they support and complement each other while on the other they collectively support and promote the chosen strategy. As was the case with the activities I described above, this is the real challenge for strategy: not only to create the correct individual parts but to combine them to create a strong and reinforcing system.

Achieving internal and external fits will only bring short-term success. Inevitably, fit will create contentment, overconfidence and inertia. Therefore, while a company aims to achieve fit it must also create enough slack in the system so that, as it grows or as the external environment changes, the organizational environment can remain flexible and responsive.

Finally, if business conditions oblige a strategic change of direction, the internal context of an organization must change them. This is extremely difficult. Not only do we need to change the individual pieces that make up the organizational environment but we must also put them together to form an overall organizational environment that will again fit with the new strategy.

No Strategy Remains Unique Forever

There is no question that success stems from the exploitation of a distinctive or unique strategic position. Unfortunately, no position will remain unique or attractive forever. Not only do attractive positions get imitated by aggressive competitors but also—and perhaps more importantly—*new* strategic positions keep emerging all the time. A new strategic position is simply a new, viable who-what-how combination—perhaps a new customer segment (a new who), or a new value proposition (a new what), or a new way of distributing or manufacturing the product (a new how). Over time, these new positions may grow to challenge the attractiveness of our own position.

You see this happening in industry after industry. Once formidable companies that built their success on what seemed to be unassailable strategic positions find themselves humbled by relatively unknown companies that base their attacks on creating and exploiting new strategic positions in the industry.

New strategic positions—that is new who-what-how combinations—emerge all around us all the time. As industries change, new strategic positions emerge to challenge existing positions for supremacy. Changing industry conditions, changing customer needs or preferences, countermoves by competitors and a company's own evolving competencies give rise to new opportunities and the potential for new ways of playing the game. Unless a company continuously questions its accepted norms and behaviors, it will never discover what else has become available. It will miss these new combinations and other, more agile, players will jump in and exploit the gaps left behind. Therefore, a company must never settle for what it has. While fighting it out in its current position, it must continuously search for new positions to colonize and new opportunities to take advantage of.

Simple as this may sound, it contrasts sharply with the way most companies compete in their industries: most of them take the established rules of the game as given and spend all their time trying to become *better* than each other in their existing positions—usually through cost or differentiation strategies.

Little or no emphasis is placed on becoming *different* from competitors. This is evidenced from the fact that the majority of companies that strategically innovate by breaking the rules of the game tend to be small niche players or new market entrants. It is indeed rare to find a strategic innovator that is also an established industry big player—a fact that hints at the difficulties of risking the sure thing for something uncertain.

There are many reasons why established companies find it hard to become strategic innovators. Compared to new entrants or niche players, leaders are weighed down by *structural* and *cultural* inertia, internal politics, complacency, fear of cannibalizing existing products, fear of destroying existing competencies, satisfaction with the status quo and a general lack of incentives to abandon a certain present for an uncertain future. In addition, since there are fewer industry leaders than potential new entrants, the chances that the innovator will emerge from the ranks of the leaders is inevitably small.

Despite such obstacles, established companies cannot afford not to innovate strategically. As already pointed out, dramatic shifts in company fortunes can only take place if a company succeeds in not only playing its game better than its rivals but in also designing and playing a different game from its competitors.

Strategic innovation has the potential to take third-rate companies and elevate them to industry leadership status; and it can take established industry leaders and destroy them in a short period of time. Even if established players do not want to innovate strategically (for fear of destroying their existing profitable positions), somebody else will. Established players might as well pre-empt that from happening.

The culture that established players must develop is that *strategies are not cast in concrete*. A company needs to remain flexible and ready to adjust its strategy if the feedback from the market is not favorable. More importantly, a company needs to continuously question the way it operates in its current position *while* still fighting it out in its current position against existing competitors.

Continuously questioning one's accepted strategic position serves two vital purposes: first, it allows a company to identify early enough whether its current position in the business is losing its attractiveness to others (and so decide what to do about it); second, and more importantly, it gives the company the opportunity to proactively explore the emerging terrain and hopefully be the first to discover new and attractive strategic positions to take advantage of.

This is no guarantee: questioning one's accepted answers will not automatically lead to new unexploited goldmines. But a remote possibility of discovering something new will never even come up if the questions are never asked.

Resources

Ansoff, H Igor, *Implanting Strategic Management,* Prentice Hall, 1984 (2nd edition, 1990).

Markides, Costas, *Diversification, Refocusing and Economic Performance,* MIT Press, 1995.

Markides, Costas, *All the Right Moves,* Harvard Business School Press 1999.

Mintzberg, Henry, *The Rise and Fall of Strategic Planning,* Prentice Hall, 1994.

Nadler, David and **Tushman, Michael,** *Competing by Design: The Power of Organizational Architecture,* New York: Oxford University Press, 1997.

Markides, Costas, "Strategic innovation," *Sloan Management Review,* Spring 1997.

Markides, Costas, "Strategic innovation in established companies," *Sloan Management Review,* Spring 1998.

Slywotzky, Adrian J, *Value Migration: How to Think Several Moves Ahead of the Competition,* Harvard Business School Press, 1996.

Walking the Talk (Really!)
Why Visions Fail

Mark Lipton
New School University

Leaders may be able to articulate a vision, but very few actually live the vision each day. However, as this author writes, a leader who lives, breathes and weaves the vision into the fabric of an organization inspires everyone to a higher performance every day.

Some executives are not reluctant to say that vision is a "squishy" concept and nearly impossible to quantify. But research and experiences over the past decade make a nearly incontrovertible case that the vision process has a profound impact on organizational performance. As well, that performance is measurable. So what's the problem? Or, why do so many CEOs *believe* in the need for vision, yet *fail* to carry through on the process to develop and implement one. The reason there is cynicism about "the vision thing" is less about the actual failure of a vision, than it is about a leadership failing I call The Believing-Doing Gap: While there's a lot of talk about vision, few at the helm actually follow through on the work required to bring a vision to life.

The vision process—when fully executed—evokes a considerable amount of emotion, and the Believing-Doing (B-D) Gap exists because executives are ill prepared for the emotional engagement that this process actually demands. Many executives become myopic when it comes to vision. A "successful" vision is not simply a question of crafting a few paragraphs of verbiage that sound as though they were excerpted from a Dilbert comic strip. Nor is success how John Rock, once the general manager of General Motors' Oldsmobile division, so eloquently put it, "a bunch of guys taking off their ties and coats, going into a motel room for three days, and putting a bunch of friggen' words on a piece of paper—and then going back to business as usual." A vision is about personal passion. Without substantive ideas and concrete actions, the process becomes a joke, often backfiring on the leader responsible, as others turn into cynics. When the B-D Gap persists, there's rarely a full-range vision that organizational members are able to buy into and use to guide the growth of the firm.

A vision is successful when it "speaks" to a wide audience, tells an engaging story that people want to be a part of, challenges people, and creates a sense of urgency. Success occurs when the vision becomes embedded in the daily decisions and actions taken of those you want to lead. A vision is not merely an extended strategic plan or "mission." When we see a vision that is working, guiding an organization to sustained growth, we know that behind it are leaders who are comfortable leading with their hearts as well as their heads. This article describes what a leader needs to do to sustain a vision—and the growth of an organization.

Believing Is Not the Problem; It's in the Doing

It's worth considering two data points that seem, at first blush, to be contradictory. One study found that 94 percent of CEOs report "a great deal of discomfort working with the vision process." A second study, conducted by The Conference Board, polled 700 global CEOs and found, for the past three years, that the number one marketplace and management issue was "engaging employees in the vision." Perhaps what both studies are saying, from the executive perspective, is that "I believe in the need for vision but I cannot get my 'internal mechanism' in gear to make it happen. I can't connect my desire to create and implement it with the internal energy necessary to get over all the barriers. I'm frustrated!"

At a dinner during the first week of 2004, the chief marketing officer of a *Fortune* 50 company confided to me how alone he felt at the top:

> We're hitting our revenue targets, we have obscene share of market in most of the areas in which we operate, but our stock price doesn't reflect how well we're doing. The outside world doesn't understand who we are, why we're unique, how all our pieces fit together, and what we stand for. On the inside, we're operating like 60 different silos. My CEO says our vision is to provide shareholder return . . . but that's no vision, shareholder return is something that we get rewarded for as a result of executing against a proper vision. I've got to believe he has some vision of who we are. (long pause) But he can't unlock his thoughts and feelings about it to us. And if he can't begin to get us thinking about a real vision, then I'm afraid of what lies ahead.

Believe in Vision: It Works

I didn't believe in "the vision thing." A decade ago I considered the notion of organizational vision to be just another fad. I'm inherently skeptical of any new silver bullet that promises to cure a range of organizational ills and, in the late 1980s, vision made the list. Yet, after a few years as a cynical consultant, I found myself intrigued by the paucity of analytic research that would support this gut-level belief. Broad studies analyzing the impact of visions were nonexistent. I, too, thought vision was too "squishy," but I didn't have the data to prove it.

As a management professor, I decided it was time to make the case that vision didn't really matter. After one year into the first leg of the research project on the impact of vision, I began to see some very surprising data. My hypothesis, I realized, was dead wrong.

I found that a well-articulated vision, when implemented throughout an organization, had a profoundly positive impact. The data didn't lie and I found myself a convert from skeptic to born-again believer. Once my research was complete, I began testing some of the best-practices results with a range of organizations in the private, non-profit and public sectors. Consistently, I found that once senior executives were able to break through the natural barriers of resistance that often bring this process to a screeching halt, they too became believers.

Publicly owned firms that use a vision to guide their growth have significantly higher market-cap growth, top-line and bottom-line growth in comparison to their competitors who aren't driven by the vision process. Firms with a vision were twice as profitable as the S&P 500 as a group, and their stock price grew nearly 3 times the rate of others. An analysis of Average Compounded Total Return found the vision-driven firms earning their investors 17.69 percent more than the S&P 500 overall.

A well-conceived and -implemented vision doesn't yield this kind of bottom-line performance magically. It comes from the people who are challenged by the vision and remain focused on a clear, yet distant, target. These firms had higher productivity per employee, greater levels of employee commitment, increased loyalty to the firm, greater esprit de corps, clearer departmental and/or organizational values, and a greater sense of pride in their organization.

Vision provides direction and nourishment for sustained growth

Find the Appetite for Vision

Over the past decade, I've found that leaders who overcame the B-D Gap became adept at stretching their time horizons; they also "saw" into and pondered their own thoughts and feelings as the vision evolved. Passion characterized their vision for their organization. They could articulate it to themselves and to others. They were willing to face the reality that, if the vision process at their organization stalled, it was perhaps because they succumbed to a form of inertia. And, most important, they were willing to be true to their own values and refrain from placing blame for inaction on some institutional imperative. They explored the vision not dispassionately from the outside, but with a full-range view of how they thought and felt about that distant future and what would be required of them to implement it.

Ask yourself: "Where does my appetite for vision, with all the risk inherent in its development, come from?"

The "appetite" starts from living. It comes from feeling the bumps and bangs and pain of life that create emotional jolts that stay with us consciously and unconsciously. It comes from living through life-changing events that trigger unique personal insights, and emerging with a new resolve. It comes from finding the passion on a personal level, and harnessing it to hold onto, even before the vision development process gets under way.

Many people have been forced to look inward for meaning in response to an emotionally charged event such as the death or serious illness of a loved one, a divorce, growing up poor or discriminated against, consequences from the September 11 terrorist attack, rejection by a role model—things that are beyond their control.

Some struggle to sort out the meaning of the experience, which may have left them with feelings of profound separateness, perhaps anger, and most likely, disorientation. For these people, what often emerges is the need to examine goals, values and norms of conduct. The question, "Why did this happen to me?" evokes emotional energy, which can either be turned on oneself in a counterproductive way or applied in a creative burst of productive energy.

Two clear examples are Andy Grove and Dave Thomas. Grove is the former CEO and current Chairman of Intel. He escaped Nazi Europe with his parents, learned new languages to survive, came to the United States with virtually nothing, worked his way through college and a doctoral program, and waged a winning fight against prostate cancer. Thomas, founder of Wendy's, was an adopted orphan and high school dropout who ended up leading a chain of six thousand restaurants. He had the audacity to think that square hamburgers would taste better and the commitment to dedicate his life to helping abandoned children.

Theories and research that have tried to explain the success of organizational leaders express a similar theme. Leadership is less about sheer talent than about introspection forged from events that caused great discomfort, if not suffering. It is more than a coincidence that so many people who have successfully built and run complex organizations have had this leadership-shaping experience. At one time or another they have had to let go of something they thought was important.

Now, they seek to clarify for others the "abyss"—the difference between a highly defined and desirable future, matched by dissatisfaction with the status quo. Perhaps they can do this for others because they have had to do it for themselves. They have the capacity to speak to the depths of another person because they are in touch with their own deeper conflicts. They found support along the way through the intensity of their convictions and their awareness of the impressions they left on others.

In 1987, Elisabet Eklind got married and moved to the United States from Stockholm, Sweden, where she had lived all her life. In March 1993, her husband died after a long battle with cancer. As she sat in her home after her husband's death, she told me, she realized that she could either "die" then and there as well—simply continue going through the motions of living—or she could rebuild herself. Start again, in other words, and work through the pain. She chose the latter and, as she says, has emerged "a stronger, better person for the effort."

> A fish doesn't know what water is until it is out of water. And before (those two experiences), I was like a fish. I didn't know what "water" was. I was not aware, in a truly meaningful sense, of how the nuances of my surroundings affected me and how I responded to them.
>
> Now I know what water is. I know when I'm out of it. I am much more aware of my needs, and I believe these experiences also helped me to understand the needs of others—and this includes people in my organization.

Eklind's effort to find a new awareness has shaped her life in ways she never imagined. It has also shaped the way she approaches her work as executive director of HIPPY USA, a non-profit whose purpose is to enhance the potential for the educational success of low-income children. She realized that to truly realign the values of her organization, she would have to bring the effects of her own very personal journey to bear on the effort.

"You carry significant experiences with you, and they shape the way you look at the world," she said. "And if you let them, they shape the way you approach your work and think about what your organization or company needs. My own personal experiences helped me see HIPPY with greater clarity than I ever could have before."

Those who create and implement visions that serve as engines for guided corporate growth know who they are and what they want their organizations to be. Their articulated vision comes alive from a conviction that not only meets their personal need for action but is also part of a much larger purpose.

Vision Failure from Myopia

When it comes to executing a plan for growth, most CEOs talk the talk. Vision committees crank out visions and post them on their Web sites and on the walls of conference rooms. Usually, however, the process doesn't go far beyond that. And that is where cynicism for the concept of corporate vision takes root. Having a page that articulates a vision is far different from weaving that vision into the daily fabric of organizational life.

When relatively superficial—what I call myopic—visions are used as a rallying cry for the troops, the vision *process* is rarely unleashed with the full force and power it's capable of achieving. Sadly, executive groups take too little advantage of a vision's ability to transform their organizations into one whose actions are driven and directed by that vision.

My experiences with CEOs and executive groups have made me realize that it is difficult for them to stretch their thinking toward the future. They're "grounded," realistic people. They are drawn toward a "mission," which enables them to describe what an organization does now, rather than toward a vision, which forces them to describe why their organization actually engages in these activities.

My Fortune 50 dinner companion commiserated further:

> Just because we're so obsessed with planning, tinkering with our plans every year, and holding division leaders accountable for achieving their plan, the executive suite has a collective mentality that we're very strategic. Because the culture has us so focused on planning, they think that's visionary! As head of marketing, I need to position the corporate brand with a far longer horizon but I'm clueless how to do that when everyone's thinking about next year or barely five years out.

Henry Mintzberg, a management professor at McGill University, found that strategic plans invariably fail when there is no over-arching vision driving them. Not only do they fail to motivate others to reach further and become innovative, to pull together far-flung units, but they also fail as analytic planning documents (*The Rise and Fall of Strategic Planning*, Free Press: 1994).

Visions, therefore, must describe the desired long-term future of the organization—a future that typically is not quite achievable, but also not so fantastic as to seem like a ridiculous pipedream. Visioning requires imagination, a mental capacity for synthesis, a trust in intuition, and a deep *emotional* commitment to that desired future. And this is partially why the vision-development process is such a leadership balancing act—and another reason why the B-D Gap exists. Visions need to challenge people, evoke feelings that draw people toward wanting to be a part of something quite special.

When a vision is framed as something that is achievable within a set amount of years, then it falls into the terrain of a strategic plan. That is why the overwhelming majority of organizational visions fail to deliver the impact: they are rational, time-bound and highly impersonal.

Shrinking the Believing-Doing Gap

I have found that there are three particular areas of emotional dissonance in the vision process. Too much time can be lost, and the quality of the final result will be compromised, if each key participant in the process isn't mindful of these three dynamics from the start:

1. *Live in the past, present and future, simultaneously.*

Visions work in part because those who develop them are able to constantly juggle the past, present and future. A study of firms with rapid, sustained growth found that their senior-most executives seem to stay focused on the state of the firm's desired future. Yet they are also attentive to the day-to-day activities that continually reinforce the vision and the philosophy that guides their internal context (e.g. organizational processes like the structure, culture and people processes); what I call the Vision Framework. With a robust vision as their beacon, they modify or supplement existing structures and processes rather than completely replace old techniques that worked well in the past. The overriding characteristic here is their ability to continually analyze and reconcile the firms' recent past with its intended future.

2. *Acknowledge emotion and disorientation.*

Strategic vision depends on the ability *to feel.* It cannot be developed by looking coldly at words and numbers on pieces of paper or computer screens. We have found in our work with the executives who truly desire to create adaptive, growth-oriented organizations that they begin the process first by looking deep within themselves. They need to know who they are and what they want their organizations to be. That way, when they articulate a vision, it comes from a conviction that meets their personal need for action, but is also part of a larger purpose. A deep, visceral commitment signals to themselves and everyone around them that they are open to changing the way they see and think of themselves and the company. This is far from easy and, for most, it can be scary as hell.

After a divisional leader in one of the world's largest consulting firms completed the final outline of his unit's vision, he remarked to me that,

> It was like putting together a tough puzzle, only more difficult. You don't see all the pieces, know how many there are, or even where we can go to find them. Then, we found that some of the pieces can change shape as a result of other pieces we were playing around with afterwards. God, I'm glad we went through this, but it was the most nerve-wracking, soul-searching, sobering thing I've ever done professionally.

Leaders who close the B-D Gap don't simply think about themselves in the context of the future they are defining. They allow themselves to feel enthusiasm, even passion for that future. When this excitement courses through them, it leads in turn to higher levels of commitment and determination. These characteristics make it easier to overcome the often-daunting challenges and roadblocks that prevent the vision from becoming a living reality.

Niall Fitzgerald, co-chairman of Unilever and co-creator of its vision-driven transformation process, spoke openly about the abyss for him. "You feel anticipation, even deep uneasiness, but the excitement of the vision calls on you to take that leap, then build a bridge for others . . . At Unilever, the bridge we needed to build was all about people: we needed to tap into their passion; we needed them to see their business in entirely new ways; and we needed them to develop very different leadership styles."

Antony Burgmans, Fitzgerald's counterpart as co-chairman, reflected similarly, "As we launched into our growth strategy, I realized that I didn't feel right: something was missing . . . What I saw was that even though we had an excellent change strategy, and an inspiring vision, what was really required to bring about change at Unilever was a new culture, a new leadership mindset, and new behaviors."

"A new leadership mindset." In other words, as Burgmans was to discover, what Unilever needed was the passion at the top to fuel the change process throughout the organization. Innovation and the risk taking necessary for closing the abyss, and bringing the vision to life, require the same level of passion for overcoming the Believing-Doing Gap.

Another load of emotional baggage that travels with this process is an executive's comfort level with setting goals and trying to achieve them. Conceptualizing a vision raises goal thinking to a far higher level—one that may easily induce feelings of inadequacy. Visions are like dreams—dreams of the kind of life we want, the things we want to create, or the part of the world we want to change. When the goal-driven executive begins connecting vision to dreams, he or she may relegate it to fantasy. Too often, business is a place reserved only for cold, practical reality and dealing with the problems of the present.

3. *Accept that the process is, by nature, imprecise, frustrating and sometimes tedious.*

The process of developing a vision runs counter to the way most people in organizations actually operate. Visioning cannot occur without starts, stops and some confusion. A natural reaction when one's mental map is triggered by new external or unexpected inputs is to be confused. It's a sign that the brain is trying to process new information. Unfortunately, those in senior-most positions too often relate confusion to information not mastered, to not being professional, to something one should avoid doing. Acknowledgement that visioning is not a "clean," easy process will help overcome resistance to a full-range vision.

You're Making Progress When . . .

An organization's vision should provide both movement and direction for shaping the culture, people processes, structure, and how the executive group's decisions will continually reinforce the vision. It should rally energies, galvanize aspirations and commitment from people in the organization, and mobilize them into determined action toward a desire future that includes growth.

As you work through the vision development process, pause frequently and ask yourself if what you're creating will do the following:

- Would it motivate you to join this organization and continue to motivate you once you are there?
- Does it provide a beacon for guiding the kinds of adaptation and change required for continual growth?
- Will it challenge you?
- Can it serve as the basis to formulate strategy that can be acted on?
- Will it serve as the framework to keep all strategic decision making in context?

Well-conceptualized visions, those that come from the heart as well as the head, accomplish all of these. Quantitative, impersonal goals cannot create purpose in a process that has none. Organizations do not become great by having a quest for more of anything, since merely wanting more is inherently unsatisfying. Increasing shareholder return, reaching for other financial metrics, or wanting to be number one falls flat as vision material. It's myopic. If there is no point in what you are doing, if a vision does not evoke emotion, then just measuring your progress can't make it anymore worthwhile.

Organizing people around purpose is the most powerful form of leadership. But leaders who create and implement the visions that impact long-run performance can define their organization's raison d'être, a far-reaching strategy that sets its distinctive competencies and competitive advantages apart from others, and the values that give it a soul. These are the leaders who look outward, to a distant future, and declare how their firms will change the world. They can do this because they have also looked inward, to understand how personal discomfort can be converted to commitment, clarity and courage to create the bridge from believing to doing.

The Motivational Benefits of Goal-Setting

Gary P. Latham
Rotman School of Management

One beauty of valid theories in the behavioral sciences is that they facilitate predicting, understanding, and influencing one's own actions as well as the actions of others. An excellent example is goal-setting theory. Its underlying premise is that one's conscious goals affect what one achieves.[1] This is because a goal is the object or aim of an action—for example, to attain a specific standard of proficiency within a specified time limit. Having a specific goal improves performance. Goal-setting theory also asserts that people with specific hard goals (often called "stretch" goals) perform better than those with vague goals such as "do your best" or specific easy goals. Further, the theory states that a goal is a standard for assessing one's satisfaction. To say that one is trying to increase revenue by 30 percent means that one will not be fully satisfied until that goal is attained. To the extent that the goal is met or exceeded, satisfaction increases; and conversely, to the extent that performance falls short of the goal, one's satisfaction decreases. The more goal successes, the higher the person's satisfaction. In short, employees who are committed to attaining high goals are high performers, because they are not satisfied with less. Working with Edwin Locke as well as my former graduate students Dennis Dossett, Collette Frayne, Lise Saari, Gerrard Seijts, and Dawn Winters, we found that the application of goal-setting theory is highly beneficial in organizational settings.

Applications of Goal-Setting Theory

The American Pulpwood Association was searching for ways in which pulpwood producers, that is, independent loggers, could increase their productivity (cords per employee hour). The majority of the employees were uneducated, unskilled laborers who were paid on a piece-rate basis. Cutting pine trees in the southern United States can be tiring, monotonous work. Based on goal-setting theory, pulpwood crew supervisors assigned a specific high goal, gave out tally meters to enable people to keep count of the number of trees that they cut down, and then stood back and watched.

The people who were assigned goals started bragging to one another as well as to family members as to their effectiveness as loggers. Productivity soared relative to those crews who were urged to do their best. Goal-setting instilled purpose, challenge,

---

"The Motivational Benefits of Goal-Setting," Gary P. Latham, *Academy of Management Executive*, Vol. 18, No. 4, November 2004. Reprinted by permission of the Academy of Management via The Copyright Clearance Center.

and meaning into what had been perceived previously as a tedious and physically tiresome task. A by-product of the goal intervention was that within the week, employee attendance soared relative to attendance in those crews who were randomly assigned to the condition where no goals were set. Why? Because the psychological outcomes of setting and attaining high goals include enhanced task interest, pride in performance, a heightened sense of personal effectiveness, and, in most cases, many practical life benefits such as better jobs and higher pay.

What is wrong with urging people to "do their best," especially when they are paid on a piece-rate basis? The answer is that people simply do not do their best because this exhortation is too vague, too abstract. There is no external referent for evaluation. Consequently, it is defined idiosyncratically. It allows for a wide range of performance levels that are acceptable to different people. Setting a specific high goal, on the other hand, makes explicit for people what needs to be attained.

Causal Mechanisms

Why is goal-setting effective? What are the causal mechanisms? The answer to this question is four-fold.[2] First, in committing to a goal, a person chooses to divert attention toward goal-relevant activities and away from goal-irrelevant activities. Second, goals energize people. Challenging goals lead to higher effort than easy goals. This is true regardless of whether goal attainment requires physical or cognitive effort. Third, goals affect persistence. High goals prolong effort; tight deadlines lead to a more rapid work pace than loose deadlines. Fourth, goals motivate people to use the knowledge they have that will help them to attain the goal or to discover the knowledge needed to do so.

Conditions for Effectiveness

What conditions increase or decrease the benefits of goal-setting? Here the answer is five-fold. First, as implied above, the person must have the ability and knowledge to attain the goal. If the goal is a performance outcome (e.g., increase market share by 20 percent within the next twelve months), and employees lack the knowledge to attain it, urging them to do their best can sometimes be even more effective than setting a specific performance-outcome goal. An outcome goal can make people so anxious to succeed that they scramble to discover strategies in an unsystematic way and hence fail to learn what is effective. This in turn leads to evaluation apprehension and anxiety. The antidote for this problem is to set a specific high-learning goal rather than an outcome goal (e.g., discover five ways to master this task). A learning goal requires people to focus on understanding the task that is required of them and to develop a plan for performing it correctly. In short, when behavioral routines have yet to be developed, a specific high-learning goal focuses attention on systematic problem solving and ultimately on high performance.[3]

Second, the person must be committed to the goal, especially if the goal is difficult. Achieving a difficult goal requires a great deal of effort, with low probability of success. Goal commitment is likely if the outcome of the goal is important to the person, and the person believes that the goal is indeed attainable. With regard to importance,

(a) Making one's goal public enhances commitment because striving to attain it enhances one's integrity in one's own eyes as well as in the eyes of others.

(b) To the extent that a leader is supportive, goals that are assigned create "demand characteristics" in that they are an implicit expression of the leader's confidence in the person that the goal can and will be attained.

(c) A vision provided by a leader that galvanizes and inspires people is likely to increase goal commitment to the extent that the goal leads to concrete action steps toward the attainment of the vision.

(d) Monetary incentives can be tied to goals, but to do so is tricky. . . .

Third, people need feedback on their progress toward the goal. Feedback enables them to adjust the level or direction of their effort and the strategy necessary for goal attainment. When people discover that they are below their goal, they typically increase their effort and/or modify their strategy. As people attain their goal, they generally set an even higher goal because the goal attained diminishes in its effectiveness for inducing pride in one's performance.

Fourth, tasks that are complex for a person, where strategy and behavioral routines have yet to become automatized, mitigate the normally positive effects of setting a specific high goal. Training is obviously one solution here. A second solution, as previously noted, is to set a learning rather than an outcome goal. A third solution is to set subgoals. In a manufacturing simulation, when people were paid on a piece-rate basis to make toys but market conditions changed unexpectedly, the people who were urged to do their best had higher paychecks than those with a specific high-outcome goal. However, those who had subgoals in addition to a long-term outcome goal had the highest paychecks of all. This is because in dynamic situations, it is important to search actively for feedback and react quickly to it. Subgoals yield information for people as to whether their progress is consistent with what is required for them to attain their goal.[4]

Fifth, situational constraints can make goal attainment difficult. A primary role of a leader is (1) to ensure that people have the resources to attain their objectives and (2) to take the steps necessary to remove obstacles in the way of accomplishing those objectives.

Goal-Setting on Complex Jobs

Do goals work on highly complex tasks? The Weyerhaeuser Company was impressed by the results of goal-setting obtained with loggers on the West Coast. Increases in productivity were as impressive as those obtained in the South even though the loggers in the West were hourly paid unionized employees.[5] The question remained whether something as straightforward as goal-setting is effective with highly educated employees performing complex work. The answer came as a result of a Weyerhaeuser task force consisting of line managers who recommended laying off engineers and scientists as a way of responding to an economic downturn. The task force failed to take into account the fact that the senior vice president of R&D car-pooled to work with George Weyerhaeuser, the CEO!

The R&D vice president subsequently set up an R&D taskforce to find ways to motivate engineers/scientists to attain excellence. Step 1 involved job analysis to gain consensus on the organization's definition of excellence in R&D. Step 2 serendipitously involved a dispute among the four R&D directors, who reported to the senior VP, as to what would motivate engineers/scientists to attain excellence. One director advocated assigned goals "because that is what we receive from the senior VP." Another director, an avid reader of management journals, advocated participatively set goals. Still another believed that goal-setting was appropriate only for lower-level employees in the company such as loggers. Goals were said to be unnecessary for scientists/engineers who were already highly goal oriented. This director advocated instead a monetary bonus system. This suggestion added fuel to the argument among the four directors as to what motivated their workforce. One director stressed the need for public recognition within the company rather than a bonus. Another poignantly stated that the unspoken philosophy in the company during that time period was "If you screw up, you will hear from us; if you don't hear from us, assume you are doing well. Think," he exclaimed, "what might occur if the reverse were true. If you hear from us, you are doing well; if you don't hear from us, assume you are not."

Bets were made as to who was right. The following experiment was launched. Some scientists/engineers were given an assigned goal and received praise, public recognition, or a monetary bonus for achieving it. Others participated in setting their own goals and received one of these same three rewards. Still others were urged to do their best and given one of the same three rewards. This created nine experimental conditions. Because everyone knew who was doing what in terms of type of goal set (assigned, participative, do your best) and type of reward that was to be administered (praise, public recognition, and money), a tenth group of scientists was added to the experiment. This group was "kept in the dark."

The results? Those who were urged to do their best performed no better than those who were "kept in the dark," despite the fact that those who were urged to do their best received either praise, public recognition, or a monetary bonus. Goal commitment was the same regardless of the method by which the goal was set. However, those with participatively set goals had higher performance than those with assigned goals. Why? Because they set higher goals than was the case when the supervisor set the goal unilaterally. Consistent with goal-setting theory, higher goals led to higher performance. The performance of those who received a monetary bonus versus those who received praise was a virtual tie. Both methods of acknowledging high performance were more effective than providing people with public recognition.[6]

The outcome of this study led to a series of experiments which showed that when goal difficulty is held constant, performance is usually the same regardless of whether the goal is assigned or set participatively.[7] An exception is when the task is complex. When working smarter rather than harder, when one's knowledge rather than one's effort (motivation) is required, participation in decision-making leads to higher performance if it increases the probability of finding an appropriate strategy for performing the task, and if it increases the confidence of people that the strategy can be implemented effectively.[8]

Self-Management

Motivation of oneself is arguably as important as, if not more important than, motivating the behavior of others. Goal-setting is a key mechanism for self-management. The job attendance of unionized, state government employees in one American agency was abysmal. An analysis of the reasons for low attendance revealed that people lacked confidence that they could overcome problems that they perceived as preventing them from coming to work. The problems included family issues such as caring for a sick child and meeting with school teachers, as well as coping with conflicts in the work place.

A training program in self-management was initiated that included self-set goals for job attendance and keeping a weekly attendance record. The latter was done because there is overwhelming data showing that "what gets measured in relation to goals gets done." In addition, people self-selected rewards (e.g., going to a sports event and punishments (e.g., cleaning out the attic) to self-administer. Finally, people met in groups to discuss strategies for coping with job-attendance issues. The outcome was a dramatic increase in attendance. When several months later those in the control group (so named because to control for alternative explanations as to why job attendance increased, this group was identical in all respects except that it did not participate in the initial training program) were also given training in self-management, their job attendance increased to the same high level as the originally trained group.[9]

Downsides and Risks

Virtually all techniques have drawbacks, including goal-setting. People may try too hard for quantity at the expense of quality or vice versa. Those who are highly committed to their goals may be less likely to help others to attain their goals. Hence Scott Paper Company, prior to being bought by Kimberly Clark, set goals for both performance quantity and quality, as well as behavioral goals for team playing that were assessed by peers.

When there are two or more goals, goal conflict may occur in the absence of employee participation in the process. Performance on both goals may suffer. People can, however, pursue more than one goal effectively when goals are prioritized. Challenging goals over an extended time period, without sufficient time periods between them, can lead to exhaustion. In knowledge-based firms where employees lack the requisite information, specific high learning rather than outcome goals should be set. As noted earlier, performance-outcome goals in this setting sometimes result in worse performance than an abstract goal of "do your best" and, worse, may also stifle innovation. If innovation is needed, goals should be set for innovation itself (e.g., discover ten new products in the next twelve months) rather than just for performance output.

If employees are forced to try for hard goals, especially in a punitive environment, some may be tempted to fudge the figures. Organizations require ethical climates as well as controls to detect and prevent cheating by employees.[10] If goal failure is judged severely, employees are also likely to find ingenious ways to set easy goals that appear difficult to their managers. In contrast, if the anticipated outcome for employees who fail to meet goals is that organizational decision-makers will view the failure as transitory and part of the learning process (especially in high-innovation firms), employees will be more willing to risk setting goals that "stretch" them, and the positive benefits of goal setting will occur.

Endnotes

[1]Latham, G. P., & Locke, E. A. 1991. Self regulation through goal setting. *Organizational Behavior and Human Decision Processes*, 50(2): 212–247.
[2]Locke, E. A., & Latham, G. P. 1990. *A theory of goal setting and task performance.* Englewood Cliffs, NJ: Prentice Hall.
[3]Winters, D., & Latham, G. P. 1996. The effect of learning versus outcome goals on a simple versus a complex task. *Group and Organization Management,* 21: 236–250.
[4]Latham, G. P., & Seijts, G. H. 1999. The effects of proximal and distal goals on performance on a moderately complex task. *Journal of Organizational Behavior,* 20(4): 421–429.

[5]Latham, G. P., & Saari, L. M. 1982. The importance of union acceptance for productivity improvement through goal setting. *Personnel Psychology,* 35: 781–787.

[6]Latham, G. P., Mitchell, T. R., & Dossett, D. L. 1978. The importance of participative goal setting and anticipated rewards on goal difficulty and job performance. *Journal of Applied Psychology,* 63: 163–171.

[7]Latham, G. P., & Saari, L. M. 1979. The effects of holding goal difficulty constant on assigned and participatively set goals. *Academy of Management Journal,* 22(March): 163–168.

[8]Latham, G. P., Winters, D. C., & Locke, E. A. 1994. Cognitive and motivational effects of participation: A mediator study. *Journal of Organizational Behavior,* 15(1): 49–63; Seijts, G. H., & Latham, G. P. 2001. The effect of learning, outcome, and proximal goals on a moderately complex task. *Journal of Organizational Behavior,* 22: 291–307.

[9]Frayne, C. A., & Latham, G. P. 1987. The application of social learning theory to employee self management of attendance. *Journal of Applied Psychology,* 72(3): 387–392; Latham, G. P., & Frayne, C. A. 1989. Self management training for increasing job attendance: A follow-up and a replication. *Journal of Applied Psychology,* 74(3): 411–416.

[10]Jensen, M. C. 2001. Corporate budgeting is broken—let's fix it. *Harvard Business Review,* 79(November): 94–101.

How Industries Change

Anita M. McGahan
Boston University

You can't make intelligent investments within your organization unless you understand how your whole industry is changing. If the industry is in the midst of radical change, you'll eventually have to dismantle old businesses. If the industry is experiencing incremental change, you'll probably need to reinvest in your core. The need to understand change in your industry may seem obvious, but such knowledge is not always easy to come by. Companies misread clues and arrive at false conclusions all the time. Sotheby's, for example, invested in online auctions (its own Web site as well as a venture with Amazon) as if the Internet were just another channel; in truth, the new technology represented a fundamental shock to the industry's structure.

To truly understand where your industry is headed, you have to shut out the noise from the popular business press and the pressure of immediate competitive threats to take a longer-term look at the context in which you do business. That is what some of my colleagues and I did. The research described in this article is based on a high-level look at a variety of businesses from a broad cross section of U.S. industries. The research, which began in the early 1990s and continues today, originally focused on how industry structure affects business profitability and investor returns. This statistical analysis yielded several hypotheses about how industries evolve, which were then tested and refined in a series of case studies on industry structure, industry change, and competitive advantage.

The conclusion, which I'll oversimplify here for the sake of clarity, is that industries evolve along four distinct trajectories—radical, progressive, creative, and intermediating.[1] Moreover, a firm's strategy—its plan for achieving a return on invested capital—cannot succeed unless it is aligned with the industry's change trajectory. The four trajectories set boundaries on what will generate profits in a business. Many companies have incurred losses because they tried to innovate outside of those boundaries. One of the most famous examples is Xerox, which is legendary for its innovations and for its struggle to harvest profits from them. By the mid 1980s, the copier manufacturing industry had matured around a business model that emphasized creative "hit products." Meanwhile, the personal computing industry was in its infancy, and even though Xerox PARC had pioneered PC inventions such as the graphical user interface and the mouse, the company was unable to make inroads in this burgeoning industry that required an entirely new set of business activities.

No innovation strategy works for every company in every industry. But if you understand the nature of change in your industry, you can determine which strategies are likely to succeed and which will backfire.

Four Trajectories of Change

Before we look at the four trajectories of industry evolution in depth, it is worthwhile to recognize that they are defined by two types of threats of obsolescence. The first is a threat to the industry's core activities—the activities that have historically generated profits for the industry. These are threatened when they become less relevant to suppliers and customers because of some new, outside alternative. In the auto industry, for example, many dealerships are finding that their traditional sales activities are less valued by consumers, who are going online for data on the characteristics, performance, and prices of the cars they want. The second is a threat to the industry's core assets—the resources, knowledge, and brand capital that have historically made the organization unique. These are threatened if they fail to generate value as they once did. In the pharmaceutical industry, for instance, blockbuster drugs are constantly under threat as patents expire and new drugs are developed.

The exhibit "Trajectories of Industry Change" maps the relationships between these two threats and the following four change trajectories. *Radical* change occurs when an industry's core assets and core activities are both threatened with obsolescence. This trajectory is closest to the concept of disruptive change that Harvard's Clayton M. Christensen discusses. Under this scenario, the knowledge and brand capital built up in the industry erode, and so do customer and supplier relationships. During the 1980s and 1990s, an estimated 19% of U.S. industries went through some stage of radical change. A good example is the travel business. Agencies' core activities and core assets came under fire as the airlines implemented systems to enhance direct price competition (such as SABRE and other reservations systems) and as the agencies' clients turned to Web-enabled systems (such as Expedia, Orbitz, and Travelocity) that offered new value (online monitoring of available flights and fares, for instance).

When neither core assets nor core activities are threatened, the industry's change trajectory is *progressive*. Over the past 20 years, this has been by far the most common trajectory; about 43% of U.S. industries were changing progressively, including long-haul trucking and commercial airlines. In those industries, the basic assets, activities, and underlying technologies remained stable. Innovators like Yellow Roadway, Southwest, and JetBlue succeeded not because the incumbents' strengths became obsolete but because the upstart firms had smart insights about how to optimize efficiency.

The other two change trajectories—*creative* and *intermediating*—have been neglected in the management literature, possibly because of their nuances. Creative change occurs when core assets are under threat but core activities are stable. This means that companies must continually find ways to restore their assets while protecting ongoing customer and supplier relationships; think of movie studios churning out new films or oil companies mining for new wells. About 6% of all U.S. industries are on a creative change trajectory.

Intermediating change occurs when core activities are threatened with obsolescence—customer and supplier relationships are stretched and fragile—while core assets retain their capacity to create value. Sotheby's, for instance, is as good as it ever was at assessing fine works of art, but, because of the technology that made eBay possible, the auction house's matchmaking activity no longer creates as much value. The

TRAJECTORIES OF INDUSTRY CHANGE

When determining which type of change your industry is going through—and, no doubt, it is going through some type of transformation—you need to consider whether there are threats to your industry's *core activities* (the recurring actions your company performs that attract and retain suppliers and buyers) and to your industry's *core assets* (the durable resources, including intangibles, that make your company more efficient at performing core activities).

		Core Activities	
		Threatened	**Not Threatened**
Core Assets	**Threatened**	**Radical Change** *Everything is up in the air.* Examples: makers of landline telephone handsets, overnight letter-delivery carriers, and travel agencies	**Creative Change** *The industry is constantly redeveloping assets and resources.* Examples: the motion picture industry, sports team ownership, and investment banking
	Not Threatened	**Intermediating Change** *Relationships are fragile.* Examples: automobile dealerships, investment brokerages, and auction houses	**Progressive Change** *Companies implement incremental testing and adapt to feedback.* Examples: online auctions, commercial airlines, and long-haul trucking

challenge under intermediating change is to find ways to preserve knowledge, brand capital, and other valuable assets while fundamentally changing relationships with customers and with suppliers. During the 1980s and 1990s, approximately 32% of U.S. industries went through some form of intermediating change.

Radical Change

Radical transformation occurs when both core activities and core assets are threatened with obsolescence. The relevance of an industry's established capabilities and resources is diminished by some outside alternative; relationships with buyers and suppliers come under attack; and companies are eventually thrown into crisis. Radical industry evolution is relatively unusual. It normally occurs following the mass introduction of some new technology. It can also happen when there are regulatory changes (as in the long-haul, trunk-route airline industry of the 1970s, for example) or simply because of changes in taste (U.S. consumers' retreat from cigarettes over the past 20 years, for instance).

An industry on a radical change trajectory is entirely transformed—but not overnight. It usually takes decades for change to become clear and play out. The end result is a completely reconfigured—usually diminished—industry. The overnight letter-delivery business is currently in the early phases of a radical transformation that began about ten years ago. As Internet usage has become more prevalent, e-mail (especially securely encrypted e-mail) has loomed as a threat to this industry. Yet the volume of overnight letters is increasing; business is still thriving, because the threat is still in its infancy.

That is part of the good news associated with radical transformation: Industries that are on a radical change trajectory often remain profitable for a long time, especially if the companies in these industries scale back their commitments accordingly.

A Fair Share?

The four change trajectories are not at all evenly distributed among industries. Surprisingly, given the time and attention much of the management literature devotes to it, radical change affects less than one-fifth of all industries. More prevalent are progressive and inter-mediating change. The percentages shown are estimates of the distribution of change trajectories among U.S. industries between 1980 and 1999, based on variability in revenues and assets among large firms.

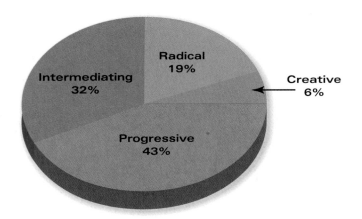

Businesses also have time to develop strategic options that can be exercised in the future if they recognize the trajectory they are on early enough. For example, Federal Express's acquisition of Kinko's will help FedEx create deeper relationships with small and midsize businesses that need document storage, management, and dissemination services.

The only reasonable approach to radical change is to focus on the endgame and its implications for your company's current strategy. Exiting isn't the sole option; sometimes a few survivors can sustain profitable positions after others leave the industry. The computer mainframe business, for example, is still quite large despite the threat from PC and workstation manufacturers.

To consider the best strategy when your industry is on a radical change trajectory, look at your productivity figures, the pace and timing of the transition in the industry, and buyers' switching costs. Early-moving companies might employ a staggered strategy—pursuing incremental improvements to established businesses' activities and conducting selective experiments in developing new assets. That is how encyclopedia companies responded to the radical threat that online search engines posed: They experimented with new electronic products and services while creating new distribution channels, marketing their existing products aggressively, and updating their inventory management systems.

Historically, many organizations confronted with radical change in their industries have abandoned their established positions and moved into emerging lines of business—incurring enormous risk in the process. Several typewriter makers, for instance, attempted to enter the PC manufacturing business only to cut short their efforts as the demands of the emerging industry became clearer. (IBM succeeded with this strategy, but its success in the PC industry was closely related to its experience in other areas of computing.) The alternative—reinvesting in the established industry—is also risky because it commits the firm to an approach that may become unprofitable. Companies dealing with radical transformation must accept the inevitability of the change and chart a course that maximizes returns without accelerating commitment to the troubled business—much easier said than done.

Intermediating Change

Intermediating change is more common than radical industry evolution. It typically occurs when buyers and suppliers have new options because they have gained unprecedented access to information. The core activities of industries on an intermediating change trajectory are threatened. But the core assets of these industries—knowledge, brand capital, patents, or even specialized factory equipment—retain most of their value if they are used in new ways. In effect, industries are on an intermediating change trajectory when their business activities for dealing in both downstream and upstream markets are simultaneously threatened. Intermediating change is occurring in auto dealerships, for example, for a number of reasons. First, traditional auto sales activities are becoming less relevant because of the Internet and because vehicles now last so long that consumers buy cars less frequently. Second, car manufacturers are seeking closer relationships with drivers and, as a result, are starting to share the management of customer relations with their dealers; in some cases, they're trying to take over customer relations completely. Finally, individual dealers are losing control of inventory management as IT and sophisticated financing create economies of scope that can be exploited only by larger, integrated companies.

Managing a company in an industry that is experiencing intermediating change is extraordinarily difficult. Of all the change trajectories described in this article, this one is perhaps the most challenging because companies must simultaneously preserve their valuable assets and restructure their key relationships.

Executives tend to underestimate the threat to their core activities by assuming that longtime customers are still satisfied and that old supplier relationships are still relevant. In reality, these relationships have probably become fragile. The value of core assets often escalates, which compounds managers' confusion. For example, auction houses initially had a flurry of heightened interest in their accumulated appraisal experience because eBay had created so much excitement about auctioning.

During periods of intermediating change, pressure in the industry tends to build until it hits a breaking point, and then relationships break down dramatically only to be temporarily reconstituted until the cycle is repeated. Consider large brokerage firms. They had long confronted criticism about conflicts of interest in their analyst organizations. But the straws that broke the camel's back were the recent market downturn and accounting scandals—both of which were tied to fundamental changes in the information available to investors and companies seeking investment capital. The core assets in investment brokerage—including the systems for evaluating securities and for processing trades—retained their value, yet old relationships no longer offered the same opportunities to generate profits.

Companies facing intermediating change must find unconventional ways to extract value from their core resources. They may diversify by entering a new business or even a new industry. Or they may sell off assets or services to former competitors. In the music industry, for instance, recording companies are beginning to sell their services à la carte to aspiring musicians rather than make huge investments in the artists up front and incur all the costs of artist development (radio promotions, choreography, and image management, among other expenses). The customer and the activities have changed, but the core resource—the recording companies' ability to develop new artists—retains its value. In another example, some traditional auctioneers, threatened by eBay, have capitalized on their appraisal expertise online; for a fee, they will certify the value of the wares being exchanged on the Internet. By reconfiguring old assets in new ways, these companies are dealing effectively with intermediation.

Initial returns under this change trajectory may be relatively high and then drop dramatically only to recover temporarily. The recording companies' profits, for example, have been volatile as the companies adapt to intermediation with varying levels of success. A plateau in performance can create the illusion that reinvestment in the business as usual is a good idea. But organizations that recognize the trajectory their industry is on can turn relatively calm periods into opportunities for strategic transformation.

Creative Change

In industries on a creative change trajectory, relationships with customers and suppliers are generally stable, but assets turn over constantly. The film production industry is a good example. Larger production companies enjoy ongoing relationships with actors, agents, theater owners, and cable television executives. Within this network, they produce and distribute new films all the time. This combination of unstable assets (new films) and stable relationships (with buyers and suppliers) makes it possible to deliver superior performance over the long term. Indeed, the top companies in creative change industries usually retain their standing for long periods.

Other industries evolving on creative trajectories include pharmaceuticals, oil and gas exploration, and prepackaged software. In pharmaceuticals, companies research, develop, and test new drugs and then use their administrative and marketing skills to commercialize them. In oil and gas exploration, companies manage their portfolios of exploration ventures and maintain relationships with refineries and distributors. In the prepackaged software industry, developers create and test multiple applications in the hopes that one or more will become a killer app. By applying well-honed user-testing and marketing skills, the industry leaders perpetuate their success.

The creative change trajectory, like the intermediating trajectory, has not been studied extensively. It is easy to mistake it for radical change, despite the stability of relationships within the network. When this mistake is made, companies can overreact and neglect important relationships that are critical to their profitability. For example, some pharmaceutical companies became so focused on emerging methods of drug discovery that they invested capital exclusively in new research relationships and did not develop appropriate sales forces in new markets.

Innovation under creative change occurs in fits and starts. Although there are several long-standing formulas for making hit movies, for example, occasionally a new genre or technical approach to filmmaking emerges. Similarly, companies in the pharmaceutical industry have been experimenting with new methods of drug discovery over the last 15 years. Despite these changes, the companies that lead these industries are not new entrants. They have retained their strength by capitalizing on their networks of relationships.

There are many ways for companies in an industry on a creative change trajectory to generate strong returns on invested capital. For instance, the leading companies in these industries tend to spread the risk of new-project development over a portfolio of initiatives. As a result, their returns are less volatile than those of smaller competitors. Other tactics include outsourcing project management and development tasks.

Progressive Change

Progressive evolution is like creative evolution in that buyers, suppliers, and the industry's incumbents have incentives to preserve the status quo. The difference is that core assets are not threatened with obsolescence under progressive change, so industries on this trajectory are more stable than those on a creative change trajectory. Today's discount retailing, long-haul trucking, and commercial airline industries are evolving in this way.

Progressive evolution is most similar to the kind of change that Christensen refers to as "sustaining." Progress occurs, and technology can have an enormous impact, but it happens within the existing framework of the business. Core resources tend to appreciate rather than depreciate over time. Progressive change doesn't mean that change is minor or even that it is slow. Over time, incremental changes can lead to major improvements and major changes. Think of what has happened in discount retailing over the last ten years. Wal-Mart's cumulative impact has been extraordinary, and the company has developed unprecedented clout. But the retailer developed that advantage by deepening existing customer and supplier relationships, not by seeking out entirely new ones.

The most profitable corporate strategies in progressive change industries generally involve carving out distinct positions based on geographic, technical, or marketing expertise. The goal is to build resources and capabilities steadily and incrementally. Companies rarely get into brinkmanship or eyeball-to-eyeball competition, and they don't have to put large amounts of capital at risk before learning whether an innovation creates value. Instead, their performance depends on their quick responses to feedback. Southwest Airlines, for instance, tests new flight routes but isn't afraid to pull out if a route ultimately doesn't work under the company's approach to air travel.

Successful companies in progressive change industries tend to be viewed by the financial community as minimally risky with the potential for only moderate returns. Over the long run, though, these companies can actually create very large total returns for investors. *Money* has reported that the two companies that had generated the greatest total return to shareholders during the magazine's 25-year history were none other than Wal-Mart and Southwest.

Which Trajectory Are You On?

Identifying your industry's evolutionary trajectory on the fly is difficult. It is easy to become distracted or confused by conventional wisdom, customer demands, and competitors' moves. To ensure accuracy, your analysis must be focused and systematic.

The first step is to define your industry. You can begin by identifying the companies in your industry that share common buyers and suppliers. Many economists use a 5% rule to assess whether the commonality is sufficient to qualify the firms as direct competitors: If a 5% price fluctuation by one company causes customers or suppliers to switch to another company, the businesses qualify as direct competitors. When a group of companies intend to appeal to the same buyers and rely on the same suppliers, you have additional evidence that they are direct competitors. And when companies use similar technologies to create value, it is likely that they qualify as direct competitors.

The second step is to define the industry's core assets and activities. Here is an easy way to test whether something is core: If it were eradicated today, would profits be lower a year from now, despite efforts to work around what's missing? If the answer is yes, then it definitely qualifies. In the auctioneering industry, for example, the capacity to evaluate works of art is a core activity. In the soft-drink industry, Coca-Cola's brand is a core asset. The disappearance of either of these capabilities would seriously damage profitability in their respective industries.

The third step is to determine whether the core assets and activities are threatened with obsolescence. To qualify, the threat must make core assets and activities potentially irrelevant to profitability. It must be significant enough to jeopardize the survival of at least one industry leader and widespread enough to influence every company in the industry. Once you know whether core activities and assets are threatened, you can identify which of the four trajectories applies to the industry you are studying.

The final step in the diagnosis is to evaluate the phase of the evolutionary trajectory. This step is important: Industry change generally takes place over a long period, and the options for dealing with change typically drop off sharply through each phase. (See the sidebar "The Industry Life Cycle Revisited.")

It is also essential to note that an industry generally evolves along just one trajectory at a time. It almost always starts out on either a progressive or creative trajectory because, collectively, companies in the industry can't capture value without a clear model for organizing their core activities. Over time, the industry may feel pressure to change these activities—driven by, for example, customer demands and new technologies. The threat of obsolescence can catapult the industry on to either a radical or an intermediating trajectory. As the industry restructures its core activities and assets, the threat of obsolescence may fade, marking the industry's transition back to a progressive or creative trajectory. A company that has survived these transitions can sometimes retain profitability, although it almost always must operate at a smaller scale and with a very different approach.

Industries do not shift their trajectories very often; no industry that I have studied has shifted between evolutionary paths more than once in ten years. So it is a good bet that a given industry has been on a single evolutionary trajectory for at least a few years. And while it is sometimes possible for individual companies to influence the trajectory of an entire industry, the effort required is almost always too great to be worthwhile, and failure can be devastating to the company's profitability or even its survival.

Capitalizing on Industry Evolution

Understanding industry change can do more than help you avoid mistakes. The rules under each trajectory can help you forecast early on how change will occur in your industry—and help you determine how to exploit change as it occurs. It would be impossible to list here all the possible contingencies for change on each trajectory and at each stage. But here are a few general insights:

Analyzing Radical and Intermediating Change

As noted earlier, companies operating in an industry that is on a radical or intermediating change trajectory must perform a balancing act—aggressively pursuing profits in the near term while avoiding investments that could later prevent them from ramping down their commitments. To get the right balance, put yourself in the suppliers' shoes as well as in those of the buyers. What new options are emerging?

THE INDUSTRY LIFE CYCLE REVISITED

Once you've determined which change trajectory your industry is on, you'll need to figure out which phase of change the industry is experiencing. The classic industry life cycle model is relevant for understanding the phases of progressive and creative change. But this model does not apply to industries that are experiencing radical or intermediating change.

In the traditional life cycle model, industries begin in a period *of fragmentation* as companies experiment with different approaches to a market. The companies offer a variety of products and operate at low volumes. They tend to be entrepreneurial, private, and focused on serving narrow geographic areas. Over time, the industry experiences a *shakeout,* usually because a specific business model achieves greater legitimacy than any other. Competitors become more efficient, the volume of sales increases, and the industry generates unprecedented value for suppliers and buyers. When industries reach *maturity,* sales growth slows, and leaders often lock their positions. As the volume of sales drops, industries move into *decline.* In this phase, companies often search for incremental improvements in efficiency to recover profitability. (See "The Tradition Model" below.)

But if you apply this model in industries that are experiencing radical or intermediating change, you may end up trying to renew your position in an industry that will no longer generate significant returns. Or you may end up missing opportunities in both the established and emerging industries.

A more accurate model for those on radical or intermediating trajectories is the one below, which reflects changes in the ways buyers and suppliers respond to the level of the threat of obsolescence. (See "An Alternate Model.") During an initial period of *emergence,* upstart firms warrant attention but may not be significant enough to prompt established companies to restructure. As the new approach *converges* in volume, established companies may react by reconfiguring some of their activities. During a period *of coexistence,* buyers and suppliers become increasingly sophisticated at evaluating the new approach, and as a result, new opportunities for value creation may emerge even in the old industry. During a final phase of *dominance,* the industry's products and services are evaluated on new criteria that reflect the popularity of the new approach.

The Traditional Model

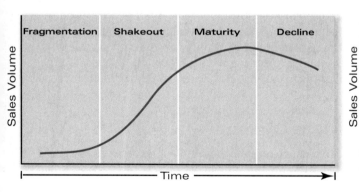

An Alternate Model

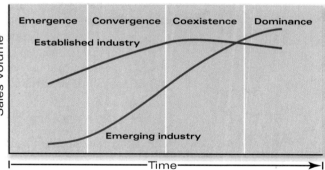

Take the example of auto dealerships, which are on an intermediating change trajectory. They are locked into multiyear pacts with the manufacturers, their suppliers. Yet the intermediation of the dealers presents new opportunities for the automakers to relate to consumers: What are the trade-offs for the manufacturers if they advertise collaboratively with the dealerships rather than directly to consumers? How can the carmakers pull off something like this without violating their contracts with the dealers? Only with unconventional thinking—beyond standard market research and advertising plans—can the manufacturers find answers to these questions.

Radical and intermediating change also calls for new ways of dealing with competitive threats. Instead of viewing rivals in conventional terms, consider whether you can use alliances to protect common interests and defend against new competition from outsiders—or to facilitate consolidation. When some regions of the U.S. became overcrowded with auto dealerships, affiliated car lots (Honda dealers in adjacent towns, for instance) merged.

Under radical and intermediating change, it is also important to interpret conflict within your organization in a new way. "Civil wars" can emerge within an organization as divisions with exposure to different segments of the business develop opposing views about the nature and pace of change. It is uncanny how frequently this happens. Strong, central leadership is required to deal with the problem effectively.

Surviving Radical and Creative Change

Under these conditions, it is smart to evaluate how quickly your core assets are depreciating. The easiest way to do this is to identify how much you are spending to renew them. Investing in a full-blown cost-accounting effort is worthwhile since the value of your assets may vary across different segments of the business in surprising ways. The goal of this analysis should be to distinguish the segments in which you can protect your competitive position from those in which your position will erode quickly. Often, this assessment yields important information about the value of intellectual property and how it can be guarded more intensively. For example, a film studio might discover that, in some geographies, losses from video piracy outweigh the potential profits from distributing content, at retail, on videotape or DVD.

To navigate radical and creative change trajectories successfully, companies must have the mettle to disappoint some buyers and suppliers, regardless of their track records, if the risks are too high. Despite Marlon Brando's box-office successes during the 1950s, film studios were reluctant to work with him because of his personal idiosyncrasies. The stakes in developing new films are simply too great for producers to take many risks. Because of the volatility of new-asset development, it is also crucial to cultivate relationships with investors to ensure quick access to capital when a worthwhile project comes around.

Managing Progressive Change

Progressive change is not simple to manage, despite the fact that neither core assets nor core activities are threatened. The accumulated impact of incremental changes can raise the standards for doing business to the point where only a handful of companies are competitive. For example, the standard-bearers in discount retailing (Wal-Mart and Target among them) have relentlessly managed incremental changes in activities for decades. As a result, only a few national retailers have competitive cost structures on a large scale. Ultimately, one of the most successful strategies for companies in industries on a progressive change trajectory is to develop a system of interrelated activities that are defensible because of their compounding effects on profits, not because they are hard to understand or replicate. Consider that very little about Wal-Mart's approach is secret. The company's efficiencies have accumulated ever since Sam Walton built his first distribution centers decades ago.

Adapting to the Stages of Change

As we've noted, all four trajectories typically unfold over decades, which means organizations have time to outline strategic options for the future. As change happens, fighting it is almost always too costly to be worthwhile. In the late stages, companies invite trouble by sticking with outdated budget systems and cost-accounting processes. Organizations must reconfigure themselves for lower revenue growth and develop the ability to move activities and resources out of the business.

Diversifying Your Business

Some of the most exciting opportunities associated with industry evolution relate to diversification across industries. By participating in more than one industry on a progressive trajectory, Wal-Mart has enhanced the effects of its powerful distribution systems. And with its acquisition of Kinko's, FedEx has diversified in response to radical change. Some of the major challenges of diversification have to do with sharing core activities and core assets across divisions on different trajectories, and developing clear lines of authority for resolving disputes between divisions as their industries create different investment requirements. It is virtually impossible to diversify profitably without understanding the differences in the trajectories and phases of industry change.

The trajectories outlined above can help you anticipate how change will unfold in your industry—and how to take advantage of opportunities as they emerge. To get out from under industry threats, your company must cultivate a deep understanding of how changes to the industry will unfold over time. How will buyer and seller relationships be affected? And are intangible assets like brand capital and knowledge capital truly adaptable across industries? The work of systematically analyzing the business environment is not easy, but the payoff is great: better strategic decision-making for your company.

Endnote

1. This article builds on the author's "How Industries Evolve," *Business Strategy Review,* Autumn 2000.

Five Killer Strategies for Trouncing the Competition

George Stalk, Jr.
Boston Consulting Group

Rob Lachenauer
Boston Consulting Group

Winners in business play rough and don't apologize for it. Toyota has steadily attacked the Big Three where their will to defend was weakest, moving up the line from compact cars to mid- and full-size vehicles and on to Detroit's last remaining profit centers, light trucks and SUVs. All the while, Toyota has dared its rivals to duplicate a production system that gives the company unmatchable productivity and quality.

Dell is similarly relentless, and ruthless, in dealing with competitors. Last summer, the day after Hewlett-Packard announced weak results because of price competition in PCs, Dell announced a further across-the-board cut—delivering a swift kick to a tough rival when it was down.

Wal-Mart is well known for its uncompromising stance toward suppliers. In 1996, Rubbermaid, a $2 billion business that a few years earlier had been *Fortune*'s most admired company, ventured to contest Wal-Mart's pressure on suppliers to lower their prices—and Wal-Mart simply cut Rubbermaid off. (Newell acquired a struggling Rubbermaid in 1999.) Wal-Mart doesn't pull punches with competitors, either. In recent years, as Kmart floundered in bankruptcy proceedings, Wal-Mart rolled out a knockoff of Kmart's Martha Stewart product line, putting pressure on one of the tottering retailer's few areas of success.

Hardly anyone would dispute that Toyota, Dell, and Wal-Mart have epitomized corporate success over the past decade. But the raised eyebrows they provoke—recent *BusinessWeek* cover articles have included "Can Anything Stop Toyota?" "Is Wal-Mart Too Powerful?" and "What You Don't Know About Dell"—suggest there's something not quite kosher about the way they achieve that success.

That's because Toyota, Dell, and Wal-Mart play hardball. What do we mean by this? Hardball players pursue with a single-minded focus competitive advantage and the benefits it offers—leading market share, great margins, rapid growth, and all the intangibles of being in command. They pick their shots, seek out competitive encounters, set the pace of innovation, test the edges of the possible. They play to win. And they do.

Softball players, by contrast, may look good—they may report decent earnings and even get favorable ink in the business press—but they aren't *intensely* serious about winning. They don't accept that you sometimes must hurt your rivals, and risk being hurt yourself, to get what you want. Instead of running smart and hard, they seem almost to be standing around and watching. They play to play. And though they may not end up out-and-out losers, they certainly don't win.

This may reflect the recent emphasis of management science, which itself has gone soft. Indeed, the discourse around a constellation of squishy issues—leadership, corporate culture, customer care, knowledge management, talent management, employee empowerment, and the like—has encouraged the making of softball players.

Look at the titles of some recent business books. *Who Moved My Cheese?* (Come on, what are you, a man or a mouse?) Or *Fish! A Remarkable Way to Boost Morale and Improve Results.* Or *Servant Leader.* Or *Hug Your Customers.* Softball books accounted for probably four out of five of the titles on the business best-seller list in the last ten years—and even more in the past five years. This trend is not good for the people in your organization who read this stuff or are sent to hear the authors speak.

Now, the word "hardball" may be difficult for some people to swallow. In business, it smacks of corporate moguls and robber barons—Andrew Carnegie sending armed Pinkerton's men and gunboats into mill towns to fight the unions. It sounds like the kind of game played by former Sunbeam CEO "Chainsaw" Al Dunlap, whose memoirs were entitled *Mean Business* and who was eventually barred by the SEC from ever again being an officer of a public company.

But hardball is *not* about playing beyond the lines of legality. Enron and World-Com may have appeared to be hardball competitors, but they in fact used a classic softball tactic: manipulating (whether legally or illegally) results to make yourself look better. Hardball players don't cheat.

But they can cause discomfort. In sports, after all, playing hardball means brushing back an aggressive batter with a 100-mile-an-hour pitch. It means bare-knuckle boxing, John L. Sullivan–style. It means giving someone a head fake in a pickup basketball game on a city court littered with broken glass—and leaving him sitting on his rear.

Hardball is not only intense, it's efficient. It cleanses the market. It makes companies strong and vibrant. It results in more affordable products and services, as well as more satisfied customers. It makes competitors sweat. Flabby rivals will sometimes gasp that hardball players are playing *too* hard, that their advantages are "unfair" or "anticompetitive." Softball players may demand trade restrictions or take their complaints to the press—or to the courts. They will posture and pout. Meanwhile, they will let billions of dollars of shareholder wealth drip, drip, drip into oblivion.

Hardball players are immune to this sort of thing. In fact, they have a name for it. They call it whining.

The Hardball Manifesto

We believe the time has come to rebalance the hard and the soft. Softball players that have survived until now—think of most airlines, the U.S. auto industry, the recording industry, to name a few examples—are in deep trouble. Hardball players are taking their places at an unprecedented rate. Companies join and fly off the *Fortune* 100 list faster than ever before. In this quicker, tougher world of business, playing hardball is not an option; it is a requirement for winning.

Ready to relearn the fundamentals of winning and losing? Start with the Hardball Manifesto. It lays out the keys to becoming an effective hardball player.

HARDBALL

The Manifesto

Relearn the fundamental behaviors of winning:
- Focus relentlessly on competitive advantage.
- Strive for "extreme" competitive advantage.
- Avoid attacking directly.
- Exploit people's will to win.
- Know the caution zone.

The Strategies

Deploy these in bursts of ruthless intensity:
- Devastate rivals' profit sanctuaries.
- Plagiarize with pride.
- Deceive the competition.
- Unleash massive and overwhelming force.
- Raise competitors' costs.

Focus Relentlessly on Competitive Advantage

The history of business is littered with the remains of companies whose competitive advantages, once robust, simply withered away. Hardball players, by contrast, strive to widen the performance gap between themselves and competitors. They are not satisfied with today's competitive advantage—they want tomorrow's.

Although a lot of companies talk about competitive advantage, few are able to put a finger on exactly what theirs is, and fewer still can quantify it. Hardball players know—empirically—what theirs is and exploit it ruthlessly.

Companies that relentlessly pursue competitive advantage are wonders to behold. Wal-Mart is first and foremost a logistics company, and it established its competitive advantage in discount retailing in the 1970s with a network of "cross-docking" warehouses. Goods from suppliers were accepted only in full truckload quantities. They were then moved across the dock and loaded onto other trucks that later departed fully loaded with a variety of goods going to stores.

But Wal-Mart didn't stop with this drastic reduction in its transportation costs. It went to "everyday low prices" to stabilize demand and thereby further reduce costs. Supercomputers were installed to track and analyze consumer purchases, competitor prices, and other information. Satellites beamed the data from stores to suppliers and on to warehouses, helping to keep inbound and outbound trucks full and shelves stocked. Suppliers were told exactly when to deliver shipments to warehouses; if they missed the window, their shipments might be returned until the next window opened—or rejected altogether. Wal-Mart also used sales and inventory data to tell companies like Rubbermaid which products it would carry—no matter what the companies thought was the appropriate merchandising of their lines.

Wal-Mart continues to tighten the bolts on this system, so far without any signs of shearing. In Wal-Mart's intense and relentless effort to further increase efficiency, suppliers' costs and consumer prices are, apparently, expected to decline forever.

Strive for "Extreme" Competitive Advantage

To hardball players, there's something far more important than competitive advantage. It is, in effect, extreme competitive advantage, which is the ultimate endgame. Unlike plain old competitive advantage, which can be fleeting, this is something that puts you out of the reach of your competitors. They're likely to cry that such an advantage is unfair—not because it's unjust, but because no matter how hard they try, they cannot match it. Often, the hardball competitor has an economic system that is unassailable. Or a relationship with a customer or a supplier that is not available to its competitors. Or capabilities such as fast product development or superior customer knowledge that others cannot replicate.

Toyota's production system, for example, is so much better than any other automaker's that the company practically flaunts it. The system lets Toyota produce, at both high and low volumes, a great variety of high-quality vehicles at very low cost. Toyota is so confident that its system cannot be replicated that it has welcomed competitors into its factories. "Study us all you want," the company has said. Despite decades of trying, no rival has matched Toyota's system. Toyota continues to push the boundaries of its advantage with a new type of flexible assembly line—dubbed the Global Body Line—that costs 50% less to install and can be changed to accommodate a new model for 70% less than Toyota's previous production system.

The rewards to Toyota have been spectacular. Its global market share has steadily risen from 5% in 1980 to more than 10% today, with each point of market share worth about $10 billion in revenue. Toyota, which recently overtook Ford as the world's second-largest automaker (in terms of volume), says its global market share goal is 15% by 2010. Does anyone want to bet against it?

Avoid Attacking Directly

Perhaps paradoxically, hardball players avoid direct confrontation. That's because they're smart. History shows that for a military force to be reasonably assured of success in a direct attack, its strength must be several times greater than its opponent's. That's not a prospect hardball players like. Even if they have the strength, they prefer the economies of force inherent in the indirect attack.

Southwest Airlines' unusual but highly successful route strategy is a classic indirect attack. Traditional airlines built huge competitive strengths in their hubs; for example, United has nearly 1,000 flights in and out of Chicago's O'Hare airport every day. Southwest chose not to attack the major airlines on their well-defended turf. Instead, it opened operations in small, out-of-the-way airports. For instance, bypassing Boston, it offered service out of Manchester, New Hampshire, and Providence, Rhode Island. Instead of trying to get slots at O'Hare or New York's LaGuardia airport, it set up operations at Chicago's Midway airport and at Islip on Long Island. Not surprisingly, there were no bloody battles with the major airlines for control of these locations.

Once Southwest was established in the smaller airports, the major carriers faced a dilemma. How could they respond to Southwest's small-airport success without stepping out of their well-protected foxholes at the major airports? Should they compete directly with Southwest in smaller airports where Southwest had built a competitive advantage? Or should they create their own non-hub-based airlines to compete with Southwest? With either response, the major carriers would be playing into Southwest's game. And, in fact, no major carrier has yet resolved this dilemma. Numerous attempts to confront Southwest directly—for example, Continental Lite—have failed. Meanwhile, Southwest continues to push into small cities. Its well-documented success as other airline companies teetered after the September 11, 2001, tragedy only confirms just how savvy Southwest was.

Exploit People's Will to Win

Hardball requires guts as well as smarts. Victory often belongs to those who want it the most. Southwest's founder, Herb Kelleher, despite his aw-shucks persona, is a hardball player, and Southwest is a hardball team. Don't be fooled by its touchy-feely image in the media—or by its stock ticker symbol, LUV. Sure, in a syrupy training video, one animated character tells employees, "Spirit is engaging our minds and our hearts and our souls to do the right thing. Southwest spirit is you." But in an advertisement for the whole world to see—including employees—Southwest once crowed: "We came. We saw. We kicked tail."

This is a great mantra for hardball players. To achieve competitive advantage and drive toward extreme competitive advantage, hardball players must be action oriented, constantly impatient with the status quo. Fortunately, one can foster this will to win and turn softball players into hardball players.

One way to do this is by adopting hardball strategies of the kind we describe below. These by themselves can help release people's natural desire to win. But to really turn softball players into hardball players, you need to create and maintain in people a hardball attitude. This becomes more difficult as your advantage over competitors grows and people become complacent. As Kelleher said in a letter to all employees in the early 1990s, "The number one threat is us." He added: "We must not let success breed complacency; cockiness; greediness; laziness; indifference; preoccupation with nonessentials; bureaucracy; hierarchy; quarrelsomeness; or obliviousness to threats posed by the outside world."

To avoid such complacency, you need to foster a sense of urgency. Once, in response to United's launch of a competing service in several California cities that were served by Southwest, Kelleher dispatched a letter to employees with the headline "Commencement of Hostilities." Noting that United had more than 100 planes that could be "hurled against us" on the contested routes, he warned that "our stock price, our wages, our benefits, our job security, our expansion opportunities…are all on the line." In several cities where the competition was fiercest, Southwest employees came to work wearing camouflage outfits and battle helmets.

Know the Caution Zone

Hardball involves playing the edges, probing that narrow strip of territory—so rich in possibilities—between the places where society clearly says you can play the game of business and those where society clearly says you can't. The hardball player ventures closer to the boundary, whether it be established by law or social conventions, than competitors would ever dare.

But to play the edges, you have to know where the edges are. This is perhaps the most complex and daunting aspect of hardball. So hardball players do their homework. They know their industries cold. They have the legal and accounting counsel to help them determine what they can and can't do. But the answers often are far from clear.

A few guidelines can help you navigate your way through the caution zone when considering an action:

■   Does it break any existing laws? It goes without saying that hardball isn't about playing dirty: You brush a batter back but you don't aim for his head; you throw hard but you don't doctor the ball with spit. Keep in mind, though, that a legal standard is often less than crystal clear. By aggressively pushing the limits of existing regulations, a hardball player can sometimes win tremendous competitive advantages.

■   Is the action good for the customer? If so, a move otherwise subject to challenge may be found acceptable by the courts or legislators. If it isn't, you may be creating an army of malcontents eager to assist in your downfall.

■   Will competitors be directly hurt by it? Putting competitors in situations in which they inflict damages on themselves is acceptable—for example, enticing a rival to invest in an area where it has no hope of winning. Overtly hurting a competitor by, say, buying a key supplier and then cutting off your rival may win you the wrath of others you do business with, even if the move is legal.

■   Will the action touch a nerve in special-interest groups? Organizations of people who don't want to be customers but want to impose their point of view on those who might be customers—think, for example, of the ecoterrorists who have set fire to Hummers and other sport-utility vehicles—can create costly public relations disasters for companies.

Microsoft regularly plays in the caution zone, to its benefit and detriment. The company's seeming disregard for the damage it can inflict on competitors by refusing to share ownership of the PC desktop has mired it in lawsuits. At the same time, its assertion that customers benefit from its approach—a view shared by many—has undoubtedly reduced the impact of the numerous legal attacks by competitors and regulators.

At the risk of repetition, let us stress once again that hardball is not about breaking, or even bending, the law. It is not about crooked accounting, breaching contracts, stealing trade secrets, or predatory pricing. It's not about being mean.

Well, not too mean. The nicest part of playing hardball is watching your competitors squirm.

Five Hardball Strategies

How do you become a hardball player? While there are countless ways to play hardball, a handful of classic strategies are timelessly effective in generating competitive advantage. These methods are best employed in bursts of ruthless intensity. The aim: a dramatic shift in your competitive position, followed by consolidation of the gains and preparation for the next attack.

Devastate Rivals' Profit Sanctuaries

Profit sanctuaries are the parts of a business where a company makes the most money, where it can quietly accumulate wealth, like a bear storing up fat for winter. If a rival starts pushing into one of your territories, you respond by attacking his plump underbelly. He should get the message, fast.

There are numerous ways to devastate a competitor's profit sanctuary—for example, flooding the market with advertising or making across-the-board price cuts—but the most effective strikes are surgical. Some of these can take you deep into the caution zone, and the legality of each must be considered. Given the competitive sensitivity of this strategy, companies that have successfully employed it are rarely willing to describe it in detail. The following disguised example is one such case.

A few years ago, vacuum cleaner maker VacuCorp was having a problem with a rival. SweepCo was cutting into VacuCorp's fattest profit sanctuary—its product range sold to national retail accounts—by lowballing its products to the same buyers.

VacuCorp did a competitive deconstruction of SweepCo's business. The company's managers looked at everything—products, pricing, design, distribution—and finally found what they were looking for at a SweepCo plant in Iowa. Here, SweepCo made the canister type of vacuum cleaner, the kind that rests horizontally on wheels and has a long hose and a cord that always seems to be tangled. Most manufacturers had stopped making canisters. As a result, they were a rich profit sanctuary for SweepCo. VacuCorp estimated that canisters, which accounted for only 25% of SweepCo's revenue, produced 80% of the company's profits.

That's all VacuCorp needed to know. VacuCorp designed a canister with fewer parts and less expensive components than SweepCo's. VacuCorp then set the new canister's price below SweepCo's—and waited. When SweepCo attempted to lowball one of VacuCorp's national accounts, VacuCorp went after one of Sweep major accounts with its own low-priced canister. After several of these skirmishes, SweepCo figured out what going on. SweepCo stopped lowballing VacuCorp's customers. Peace settled over the vacuum cleaner industry.

Knowledge is the key to devastating a competitor's profit sanctuary. You need to know, among other things, your own and your competitor's costs and profitability—by category, by geography, and by account. This will allow you to hone your attack strategy, adjusting prices to inflict the most pain.

You also need to be alert to the legal limits on pricing strategies. There's a fine but real line between aggressive and predatory pricing. Above all, recognize that an attack on your competitor's profit sanctuary is liable to provoke a strong response. Be hypervigilant, therefore, for early warning signs of failure or success. Your competitor may attack your profit sanctuaries in response. He may have greater financial resources than you thought or a "sugar daddy" to protect him. When you decide to gut the bear, don't be reckless.

Plagiarize with Pride

Softball competitors like to think that their bright ideas are sacred. But hardball players know better. They're willing to steal any good idea they see—as long as it isn't nailed down by a robust patent—and use it for themselves. Ray Kroc didn't invent McDonald's; he took the idea from brothers Dick and Maurice McDonald when he bought their small chain of burger joints. Home Depot founders Arthur Blank and Bernie Marcus didn't invent the first warehouse-outlet hardware chain; they got the "big box" concept from their earlier employer, Handy Dan Home Improvement.

But hardball plagiarism involves much more than appropriating a good idea. You have to improve on it. As Harry Cunningham, the founder of Kmart, is reported to have conceded, Sam Walton "not only copied our concepts, he strengthened them."

It's also important that you make the idea your own, grafting it onto your organization and getting your people to buy into it. Simply replicating the details isn't enough. Just ask the airlines that have tried—and failed—to copy Southwest. All of this means that plagiarizing is not as easy as it may seem.

In the late 1990s, Ford dealers were losing business at their service bays. Ford—which enjoyed particularly high margins on the replacement parts installed by dealers' service technicians—couldn't figure out why. So it sent a team to look at the competition. The team discovered that one carmaker, Honda, had built a particularly strong service business. Honda's secret had two parts: tying a new vehicle's purchase to its after-sales service and boiling down the car's hundreds of servicing needs into a simple, customer-friendly menu. Based on their preferences and mileage, Honda customers could choose a bundled package of maintenance tasks as easily as they could order a Happy Meal at McDonald's. Ford decided to do the same thing.

The problem, however, was that Ford's dealers and engineers were entrenched groups. Some powerful engineers felt that if a part needed servicing at 33,603 miles, then that was it. No lumping of servicing intervals into a menu of Happy Meal programs for them! Meanwhile, the dealers, an equally independent lot, had a single-minded focus on selling new cars and thus generally neglected their service business. In the end, Ford did copy Honda's program and improved upon it, marketing it aggressively to new-car buyers. But it wasn't the details of the program that made it successful. It was Ford's effort to win over its engineers and, most important, its massive network of 5,000 dealers.

Some people might recoil when competitors or the media call them copycats. Hardball players couldn't care less. They know that if Steve Jobs had ignored the graphical user interface he saw at Xerox PARC, Apple Computer would never have been born. If Kiichiro Toyoda hadn't learned the forerunner of just-in-time techniques from Ford, Toyota wouldn't have surpassed rival Nissan in the 1950s and later become such a formidable challenger to U.S. automakers.

And you needn't imitate just your competitors. You can take ideas from one geographic market and transplant them in another, as Ryanair has done with Southwest's model in Europe. You can also transplant between industries, as casket maker Hillenbrand has done: It applied the methods of the Toyota production system to casket making and transformed its industry.

Deceive the Competition

Do you have a great strategy but worry that you lack the time to get it in place before competitors can blunt or otherwise resist it? Hardball players will mislead rivals to buy time—or to gain any other kind of competitive advantage.

Think of the "fake" that is a fundamental—and legal—tactic in any number of sports: the head fake in basketball, the fake handoff in football, a pitcher's fake pickoff throw in baseball. The aim of all these feints is the same: getting your rival to set up or move in a way that puts him off balance and reduces his ability to meet your attack.

Similar moves occur in business, although no one says much about them. The high-technology industry has employed fakes for years—for example, to attract potential customers and distract competitors, a software company will announce "vaporware" that isn't ready for prime time. In the auto industry, prototypes are sometimes doctored up to throw off the competition.

Pushing this tactic too far—beyond the caution zone—could spell trouble, especially if it deceives investors as well as competitors. But certain types of fakes, particularly those that distort rivals' understanding of what you're up to, represent a key hardball strategy.

Wausau Papers was a poorly performing manufacturer of uncoated paper, with outdated machines and high production costs. When a new president of the company learned that Wausau had an unusually large share of business in Chicago, he began asking questions. It turned out that Wausau's share was high there because, with a factory nearby, it could service its distributor daily. This became the foundation for a new strategy: Wausau would offer next-day service to its distributors in the major midwestern cities and encourage them to order small quantities, some with custom specifications.

Wausau's customers responded enthusiastically to this offering of better service and greater choice. Frustration over long and unreliable lead times, poor service, and limited choice from traditional suppliers was so high that distributors eagerly switched to Wausau, even if they had to pay a premium price. Indeed, some ordered Wausau's traditional commodity products along with its new customized ones because of its speedy service.

Wausau had to move fast to lock up its customers before competitors caught on and copied the strategy. To buy time, the company decided to try a little sleight of hand. Wausau was helped by the traditional mind-set of the industry. Its competitors, used to keeping their prices down by producing standard products in large quantities on very fast machines, were initially confused by customers' willingness to pay a premium for significantly better service and choice.

Wausau needed to prolong this confusion so that rivals would take no action—or the wrong action—while the company executed its new strategy. So Wausau executives told the trade press that the company had been able to speed deliveries by holding large inventories of finished goods and by working longer hours—both of which were true. But the company didn't signal that it had also undertaken a major shift in strategy and operations. As Wausau hoped, competitors for the most part chose to ignore Wausau's moves.

In addition to this active deception, the company employed passive deception, allowing competitors to think that they were continuing to win against their historically weak rival. Although Wausau rapidly captured the business of service-sensitive distributors that needed high-margin specialty products, many of those distributors continued buying competitively priced commodity products from less service-oriented suppliers. The suppliers saw this new segmentation as entirely acceptable; why would they want to undermine their own performance by introducing costly small production runs?

Furthermore, to meet the demand of customers who wanted to continue buying its commodity products, Wausau began buying commodity papers in rolls from its competitors, cutting and repackaging them as part of its overall offering—which delighted the competitors. Wausau thus reduced its production of commodity papers and boosted its rivals' reliance on those low-margin products.

Unleash Massive and Overwhelming Force

Although hardball players prefer the indirect attack, sometimes they beat their competitors with the polar opposite.

Massive and overwhelming force must be the equivalent of a hammer blow: focused, direct, and swift. Consequently, a company must be darn sure it is ready to employ it. Substantial competitive advantage may exist on paper, but is that advantage readily and quickly available? The sum of the company's divisions may be greater than the sum of a competitor's, but can those divisions act as one in battle?

Thus, a company choosing massive force must be ready to completely overhaul its business. Because the company may not face the immediate competitive pressure that typically forces this kind of massive revamping, the process can have the feel of a turnaround of a successful company. This paradoxical situation makes the strategy uncomfortable for entrenched leaders who don't have the vision and courage to engage in hardball competition.

In the early 1990s, Anheuser-Busch attacked Frito-Lay's leadership in salty snacks—potato, corn, and tortilla chips. The big brewer had noticed that Frito-Lay, a division of PepsiCo, had been distracted by its expansion into cookies and crackers. So, in a classic indirect attack, Anheuser-Busch began to slip its new Eagle brand salty snacks onto the shelves of its traditional beer outlets—supermarkets and liquor stores—where Frito-Lay was comparatively weak.

Unfortunately for Anheuser-Busch, Roger Enrico, toughened by a stint battling Coke as the head of Pepsi-Cola North America, had just taken the helm at Frito-Lay. He realized that Frito-Lay's strong brands and huge size gave it a clear economic advantage over Anheuser-Busch in the salty-snack business. But to get the full benefit of this competitive advantage, Enrico had to get Frito-Lay into fighting shape by massively redirecting investments within the company.

He cut the number of offerings in Frito-Lay's product line by half—no more cookies, no more crackers—and concentrated the company's energy, not to mention its 10,000 route drivers, on America's salty-snack aisles. He took Frito-Lay's considerable ad budget, which had been balkanized into regional fiefdoms, and rolled it back up into a single blockbuster sum.

He heavily invested in product quality, which had slipped below Eagle's. In a turning-point meeting, he directed his operations people to bury in the ground $30 million worth of inferior potatoes rather than put them into Frito-Lay products. He ordered the first layoffs in Frito-Lay's history—but hired additional salespeople. And because he had cut costs, he was able to cut prices.

Armed with this superior offering—better chips, better service, and lower prices—Enrico began to put pressure on one of Eagle's profit sanctuaries: potato chips in supermarkets. Frito-Lay sent its salespeople streaming in; some even stayed at the largest supermarkets full time, continually restocking the Frito-Lay products.

When the dust had settled in 1996, Anheuser-Busch had shuttered its Eagle snack business. In the end, Frito-Lay even bought four of Eagle's plants—at very attractive prices.

To use this kind of strategy, a company often unleashes forces that are latent in its organization, as Enrico did at Frito-Lay. But those forces must represent a real, if unrealized, competitive advantage. For example, you must have a clear cost advantage before attacking; otherwise, competitors can counter with price cuts that blunt the attack.

Of course, seldom do you want to eliminate your competitors. Weak competitors are better than those that may emerge from bankruptcy fit and ready to fight. Also, you must be prepared for public scrutiny; Frito-Lay's sales practices in supermarkets were investigated and cleared by the FTC. After all, your competitors may scream loudly on the way down.

Raise Competitors' Costs

If you have a superior understanding of your costs, you can use pricing to maneuver your competitors into believing that they are making profitable moves, when in fact their costs are increasing. Implausible as it sounds, successfully driving up a competitor's costs without his knowing is one of the marks of a true hardball competitor.

Some years back, automotive components maker Federal-Mogul began to see its profits slide. Then-CEO Dennis Gormley decided to look closely at the company's cost and pricing structures. Until that point, top management had assumed that Federal-Mogul's low-volume sales of engine bearings to Caterpillar, Cummins, and John Deere were much more profitable, because of their high gross margins, than the company's high-volume sales of bearings to Ford, GM, and other carmakers.

Gormley was in for a shock. Contrary to the reports of the company's standard costing system, low-volume parts generated far more indirect costs per unit than did high-volume parts—that is, the costs of low-volume parts had been understated and their profits overstated. This meant that Federal-Mogul's strategy of increasing profitability through the sales of more low-volume parts was having an effect exactly the opposite of what was intended. In fact, for some low-volume parts, Federal-Mogul was "shipping cash."

The company could have addressed the problem by simply ceding the low-volume business to a competitor, JP Industries, which was weaker than Federal-Mogul in high-volume bearings and stronger in the low-volume end—and also apparently unaware of how little profit was to be made in low-volume sales. But doing so would have handed the rival company a profit sanctuary from which to launch attacks on Federal-Mogul's now more attractive position in the high-volume business.

So Gormley hatched a plan to cede the low-volume segment in such a way as to keep JPI unwittingly enmeshed in that business. The strategy: overprice Federal-Mogul's bids for the low-volume business, setting them just high enough that Federal-Mogul lost most competitions but low enough to keep JPI's profit margins slim. JPI repeatedly won these bidding contests, to its detriment. Its victories both distracted JPI from any thoughts it might have had about attacking Federal-Mogul's high-volume business and reduced its financial ability to launch an attack if it had been inclined to do so.

Of course, Federal-Mogul didn't want JPI to drive itself into a destructive cycle of higher costs and lower margins. That might have led it in desperation to try boosting its high-volume sales to generate cash. So every now and then, to keep JPI from running itself into the ground or catching on to the deception, Federal-Mogul would take a win in the low-volume business and give JPI a win in the high-volume business.

Raising your competitors' costs works well in certain situations, primarily when the complexities of a business introduce costs that can be misallocated. For example, large volume differences between a company's highest- and lowest-selling products or services—as was the case for Federal-Mogul and JPI—can result in such misallocations.

This is a risky, bet-the-company strategy. There is lots of room for error. Your analysis of the actual versus apparent costs associated with a product, service, or customer—and the strategy that grows out of that analysis—had better be right.

A Hardball State of Mind

These five strategies don't constitute a comprehensive hardball strategy playbook; there are others. Indeed, any strategy that provides you with an extreme but legal competitive advantage is a hardball move. But it's important to emphasize that hardball isn't only about the moves you make. It's also about the attitude you bring to them. A hardball playbook won't do you any good if you feel squeamish about using it.

Look first at how tough you are on yourself. Do you demand to hear the truth from customers, suppliers, business partners, shareholders, and employees? Do you look without flinching at the problems most likely to bring your company down? Are you constantly dissatisfied with the status quo, no matter how fine things may seem?

If you play hardball at home, then you're ready to go after competitors. Again, we're not talking about cruelty here: Hardball is tough, not sadistic. Yes, you want rivals to squirm, but not so visibly that you are viewed as a bully. In fact, you want the people in your world—the same ones you demand straight answers from—to cheer you on. And many of them will, as they share the riches your strategies generate.

A few of them may even come to share your intense passion for winning in ways that can seem unfair to competitors. That kind of mind-set isn't something most people have these days, when apologizing for victory is about as common as celebrating it. So, how do you feel?

Do you have what it takes to play hardball?

Racing to Be 2nd
Conquering the Industries of the Future

Costas Markides
London Business School

Paul A. Geroski
London Business School

M a n y ideas have been developed in the last fifty years on how big established companies could create entirely new markets. This advice has been hungrily consumed by large, established corporations as well as smaller firms. After all, which company does not want to become more innovative and which CEO does not dream about leading their organization into virgin territories, discovering in the process exciting new markets?

Yet despite all this advice and good intentions, it is very rare to find a big, established company among the innovators that create radical new markets. Why not?

The simple answer is that the advice given is either inadequate or plainly wrong. What people often forget is that "innovation" is not one entity. There are different kinds of innovations, with different competitive effects. For example, what a firm needs to do to achieve product innovation may be entirely different from what it needs to do to achieve process innovation. Lumping the two kinds of innovation together is like mixing oil with water.

What this implies is that the generic question, "How can the modern corporation be more innovative and create new markets?" only gets us generic answers—and these answers may or may not help the company achieve the kind of innovation that creates radical new markets. In other words, prescriptions to help a firm become more "innovative" may or may not be the ones that lead to radical new market creation.

It's virtually impossible to offer proper advice on how to create or colonize radical new markets without first understanding where these kinds of markets come from, what they look like and what it takes to succeed in them. A better opening question is, "Where do radical new markets come from, what are their structural characteristics, and what skills are needed to create and compete effectively in them?" This helps us identify the skills and competences needed—and the strategies that must be adopted—if a firm is to be a successful colonizer of radical new markets.

In fact, as we show in our book *Fast Second: How Smart Companies Bypass Radical Innovation to Enter and Dominate New Markets,* the full extent of what established companies need to change to be successful pioneers is such a formidable challenge that many of them are better off not even trying.

"Racing to Be 2nd: Conquering the Industries of the Future," Costas Markides, Paul A. Geroski, *Business Strategy Review,* Vol. 15, Issue 4 (winter 2004), p. 25–31. Reprinted with permission of Blackwell Publishing Ltd.

Where Do Radical New Markets Come From?

Radical new markets get created through radical innovation. It's important to appreciate this point because it is only by promoting this specific type of innovation inside a firm that the company can hope to create radical new markets.

Innovations are considered radical if they meet two conditions: first, they introduce major new value propositions that disrupt existing consumer habits and behaviors—what on earth did our ancestors do in the evenings without television?—and second, the markets they create undermine the competences and complementary assets on which existing competitors have built their success.

Not all innovations are radical. When we classify innovations along the two dimensions mentioned above—disrupting customers' activities and undermining competitors—we get four types of innovation, as shown in Figure 1. The dividing points in the matrix are subjective and our intention is not to defend the boundaries of a particular definition. Rather, our goal is to simply suggest that innovation can mean different things to different people, that different types of innovation exist and that one particular innovation may be more or less radical than another.

We focus on radical innovations here because these are the kind of innovations that give rise to brand new markets. They are innovations that disrupt both customers and producers. They are based on a different set of scientific principles from the prevailing set, create radical new markets, demand new consumer behaviors and present major challenges to the existing competitors. The introduction of the car at the end of the 19th century is an example of radical innovation.

Academic researchers have been studying radical innovation for the past fifty years. As a result, we know many things about this kind of innovation. Specifically, we have learned the following about radical innovation over the years:

■ Radical innovations that create new-to-the-world markets are disruptive for both customers and producers.

Figure 1   Different Types of Innovation

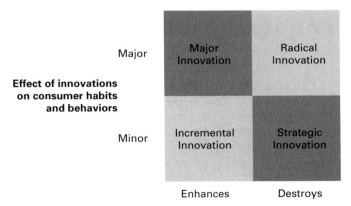

Effect of innovation on established firms' competences and complementary assets

- As a result, these kinds of innovations are rarely driven by demand or immediate customer needs. Instead, they result from a supply-push process that originates from those responsible for developing the new technology.

- Such innovations typically lack champions, either in the form of lead consumers or existing market leaders.

- Supply-push innovations share certain characteristics: they are developed in a haphazard manner without a clear customer need driving them; they emerge from the efforts of a large number of scientists working independently on totally unrelated research projects who devise the technology for their own uses; and they go through a long gestation process when seemingly nothing happens until they suddenly explode onto the market.

- These kinds of innovation create small niches on the periphery of well-established markets. This makes them unattractive to established firms.

The fact that radical innovations result from a haphazard supply-push process has a serious implication for the modern corporation. Specifically, since this process cannot be easily replicated in the R&D facility of a single firm, it is highly unlikely that brand-new markets will be created by a single firm.

Consider the development of the Internet over the last forty years. The associated technology, both hardware and software, was developed in a haphazard way without a clear customer need driving it. No one involved with the technology in the early days had any idea that things would end up where they are today; there was no master plan linking the development of new client-server relations between users and mainframe computers to the possibility of booking a hotel room by computer from a mobile phone.

This unplanned, unsystematic development of the underlying technology seems to have largely been a consequence of how the work was done, and by whom—scientists and engineers in research institutes and universities in this case. Even the major early user, the US Department of Defense, took a remarkably hands-off attitude toward the research work sponsored by DARPA, rarely insisting that it be linked explicitly to defense needs but instead giving it a blue skies mandate. Furthermore, the research efforts that "suddenly" culminated in the Internet were undertaken by a host of scientists from a number of institutions and government agencies over a very long period of time. Such a process can hardly be planned or coordinated.

Supply Push and the Emergence of New Markets

Different innovations produce different kinds of markets. Figure 2 lists a number of markets that have been created through innovation. Those on the left came about through radical innovation, while those on the right came about through strategic innovation. Our interest here is with the markets that are created through the supply-push process of radical innovation—how and when they emerge and how firms ought to compete in these markets.

So what kind of markets do supply-push innovation processes produce? What are their structural characteristics and what skills and competences are needed to compete effectively?

Figure 2   NEW MARKETS CREATED THROUGH INNOVATION

New Markets Created through Radical Innovation	New Markets Created through Strategic Innovation
Television	Internet Banking
Personal Computers	Low-Cost Flights
Personal Digital Assistants (PDAs)	Private Label Consumer Goods
Cars	Screen-Based Electronic Trading Systems
Supercomputers	Generic Drugs
Semiconductors	Online Distribution of Groceries
Mobile Phones	Catalogue Retailing
Video Cassette Recorders (VCRs)	Department Stores
Medical Diagnostic Imaging	Steel Minimills
Computer Operating System	Online Universities

Supply-push innovation processes have one very important property and this property has a profound impact on how new markets develop. Since the ultimate consumers of the new products or services which embody a new radical technology typically have very little knowledge of what the products have to offer them and how they would feel about them, the race to bring the fruits of the new technology to market is wide open.

No one knows what consumers really want and no one knows just what new technology can do; nor how to produce economically whatever it is that results from the innovation. Your guess is, therefore, as good as ours. Since there are no real barriers to entry into the (as yet) underdeveloped new market, there will not in principle be any shortage of entrepreneurs who are willing to try out their own particular vision of what the new technology has to offer. Anyone who understands the new technology is a potential entrant; anyone sufficiently enthused by what the new technology might ultimately offer will try to become an actual entrant.

This is what happens in all new markets created by radical innovation. Consider the television market. Thirty firms were producing television sets in the US in 1947, 40 more entered the following year and another 71 entered between 1949 and 1953. The peak population of television producers in the US was 71 in 1951, a number larger than the entire number of TV manufacturers that exist today. This massive wave of entry is a phenomenon that always happens in the early days of new markets. Since all of these entrants bring their own product variants to the market, the massive swelling in the population of producers is usually matched by a widening in the range of product variety which is wholly unmatched by anything that happens later on.

Eventually the wave of entry subsides and is in turn followed by what is sometimes a sharp, sudden and very sizable shakeout that leads to the death of most of the early pioneers. The shakeout is associated with the emergence of a dominant design in the market; this is an event that signals the beginning of growth in the industry.

The dominant design is a basic template or core product that defines what the product is and what it does. It is a consensus good that commands the support of a wide range of early consumers (even if it is not their first preference). It is a product standard that sends signals to suppliers upstream, retailers downstream and producers of complementary goods everywhere. Finally, it is a platform good that allows different manufacturers to offer differentiated versions of the product without destroying the consensus or requiring new complementary goods.

The emergence of a dominant design is the decisive step in establishing a new market. It signals the emergence of a standard product that is capable of forming the basis of a mass market. For the many potential consumers who have yet to enter and make a choice, it signals the end of choice and therefore reduces their risk. A successful dominant design almost always triggers massive entry by consumers into the market, and ushers in the early heavy growth phase that most markets undergo.

The emergence of a dominant design is important for a second reason. The hundreds of early pioneers who entered the new market on the basis of different product designs die soon after the dominant design emerges. On the other hand, the champion whose product forms the basis of the dominant design often develops substantial and very long lived first mover advantages from being the product champion. Notice that most of these so-called "first movers" were not, in fact, the first into the market. All of them were preceded by many, now forgotten, entrepreneurial start-ups whose work formed the foundation upon which these slightly later entrants built. These "first movers" were first only in the sense that they were the first to champion the particular product variant that became the dominant design. They were first when the market, not the product, emerged—and this is why they ended up with most of the profits.

It is important to emphasize three points that emerge from this.

- Very few of the original entrants (the pioneers) survive the consolidation of the market. Most disappear, never to be heard of again.

- The consolidators who ultimately win are rarely the first in the new market. Their success is based precisely on not moving fast—but by choosing the right time to move.

- Consolidators' activities—entering at the right time, standardizing the product, cutting prices, scaling up production, creating distribution networks, segmenting the market, investing in advertising and marketing—are the activities that create what we somewhat inaccurately call "first mover advantages." Consolidators' shrewd movements create buyer loyalty, obtain preemptive control of scarce assets, go down the learning curve, create brands and reputation and enjoy economies of scale benefits—all of which give them advantages that potential new entrants don't have. Thus, even though pioneers are chronologically first to market, consolidators are the "real" first movers. They are the first to the market that counts—the mass market!

The upshot of all this is that the companies that end up capturing and dominating the new-to-the-world markets are almost never the ones that created these markets. Henry Ford did not create the car market, but his company ended up capturing most of the value in that market in its first century of existence. Procter & Gamble did not create the market for disposable nappies, but it harvested most of the value from the mass market. And General Electric did not create the CAT scanner market, yet it was GE that made most of the money.

It turns out that when it comes to radical new markets, this is more the norm than the exception. So—given this fact—why would any company want to create a new market? Surely, the advice we should be giving companies is how to scale up and consolidate new markets, not how to create them.

How to "Create" the Industries of the Future

All this has serious implications for big, established companies. Specifically:

- The innovation process that creates radical new markets cannot be replicated inside the modern corporation.
- The companies that create brand-new markets are almost never the ones that end up consolidating and dominating these markets.

These two facts suggest to us that big, established firms should leave the task of creation to "the market"—the thousands of small, start-up firms around the world that have the requisite skills and attitudes to succeed at this game. Established firms should, instead, concentrate on what they are good at—which is to consolidate young markets into big mass markets.

They could do this by creating a network of feeder firms—young, entrepreneurial companies that are busy colonizing new niches. Through its business development function, the established company could serve as a venture capitalist to these feeder firms. It may also help them with their own R&D, more to keep close to technological developments than for any other reason. Then, when it is time to consolidate the market, it could build a new mass-market business on the platform that these feeder firms have provided. Since the younger firms do not have the resources, power, marketing and distribution to scale up their creations, they should—in principle—be happy to subcontract this activity to the bigger firms, subject to a fair division of the spoils.

What we are proposing here is for the modern corporation to subcontract the creation of radical new products to the market and for start-up firms to subcontract the consolidation of these products to big established firms. This will strike some people as too radical an idea, but it is in fact a business model that is widely accepted in industries where companies live and die on their ability to bring creative new products continuously to the market. We are talking about creative industries such as movies, plays, art galleries, book publishing and music publishing.

Think about it. A major book publisher does not try to create any of its "new products" (the books) internally. It could, of course, attempt to do so. It would involve hiring thousands of employees, giving them an office and a computer and asking them to produce new books in return for a fixed salary. But how silly does that sound? An organizational structure like that would be the fastest way to destroy the very creativity and innovation it seeks to generate!

Instead of attempting to do everything internally, a major book publisher goes out in the market, identifies potential product creators (authors) and signs them up to deliver their product. Once the product is created (outside the bureaucracy of the big firm), the author subcontracts the marketing, promotion and distribution of their creation to the book publisher. Just as it would be silly for the big publisher to attempt to create the new products internally, it would be a similar act of folly for an individual author to attempt to sell and promote their book on their own. The division of labor builds upon the strengths of each participant and is a solution that maximizes the welfare of everyone involved. There may be disagreements and problems between publisher and author, but that's what management is there for.

Professor Richard Caves is to be thanked for this insight. Caves alerted us to the striking similarity between what we are proposing (division of labor between young and established firms) and what he was observing in his study of creative industries. This is an arrangement which appears to be the norm in several creative industries. How many art galleries do you know that create their own "products" (paintings) every year? Equally, how many famous painters do you know who used to be full-time employees of major art houses? The image of Picasso or van Gogh laboring away in the R&D lab of a major gallery, straining to create their next masterpiece, is so laughable that no one would take it seriously. Yet this is exactly how we have organized the modern corporation to deliver new radical products.

As a final example, consider the record industry. It would be hard to imagine any famous singers actually working as full-time employees of the big record companies. Professor Caves' research on the subject has shown that there is a very clear division of labor in this market: "Large and small firms play different roles in the recruitment of performers and promotion of their albums. The large companies' distinctive competence lies in promotion and record distribution on a large—increasingly international—scale. The small or independent company performs the gatekeeping function of recruiting new artists and, particularly, identifies and promotes new styles of music and types of performers. The distinction closely parallels that between contemporary art galleries that focus on identifying and developing artists with promise and those devoted to promoting successful artists."

A similar proposition to ours was developed by Reid McRae Watts. In *The Slingshot Syndrome,* he makes the same link between creative industries and the creation of new radical products, showing how the modern corporation could structure itself along the lines that one sees in creative industries. The interested reader is directed to both books.

Some people might object that the division of labor between creators and promoters that we see in creative industries is easy to achieve because the creators of the product are mostly individuals (authors, singers, painters). Therefore, the argument goes, it is easy to allow them to operate as free agents and simply sign them up whenever they have something to offer. By contrast, the creation of a new radical product often requires many scientists to work together, usually in the same laboratory, building upon the knowledge and expertise of the organization. This requires some coordination and supervision of the work.

Although this is a valid concern, we only have to look at the film industry to understand how the division of labor that we are advocating here could be achieved even when there are many people involved in the creation of the product and coordination is necessary. In the film business, a new product (a movie) starts with a screenplay, often written by an independent agent (the writer). The writer approaches several producers to seek financing. The producers may be independent or employed by distribution companies such as Disney, Sony, or Time-Warner. Once a producer acquires the rights to the screenplay, it is their job to provide the financing as well as the director and the actors to make the movie.

Once again, these are all independent agents, willing to offer their services to a specific project for a specific fee. It is only when the product is finally created that the big established firm—the studio—moves into action. The studio acquires the rights to distribute the new product and uses its massive marketing power and existing distribution infrastructure to sell, promote and distribute the film.

Therefore, in several creative industries we see a clear separation between those who create the product and those who promote, distribute and sell it. Needless to say, the "promoters" must be knowledgeable about the latest technology and products so that they can make an intelligent assessment of whether a painting, book or record is good enough for them to promote. But they do not have to be actively involved in its creation. If this organization of work functions well in creative industries, shouldn't we at least attempt to import it into other industries that aspire to become more creative?

In fact, when we compare the basic economic properties of creative industries with the features that characterize new radical markets, the two types of market are amazingly similar. Given this fact, we would be surprised if the organizational structure that characterizes creative industries cannot be readily imported into any industry that aspires to create radical new markets.

Resources

Markides, Costas, and Geroski, Paul A. (2004), *Fast Second: How Smart Companies Bypass Radical Innovation to Enter and Dominate New Markets,* Jossey Bass.
Caves, Richard (2000), *Creative Industries: Contracts between Art and Commerce,* Harvard University Press.
Watts, Reid McRae (2000), *The Slingshot Syndrome: Why America's Leading Technology Firms Fail at Innovation,* Writers Club Press.

Outsourcing Strategies
Opportunities and Risks

Brian Leavy
Dublin City University Business School

A characteristic of corporate strategy in developed countries in the last 20 years has been an increasing interest in outsourcing as a potential source of competitiveness and value creation. The earliest outsourcing strategies were largely driven by the desire to lower costs in the face of intensifying global competition, typically by moving low-skilled, labor-intensive, activities offshore to South-East Asia and other low cost locations. In more recent years, there has been a growing awareness of the potential of outsourcing to support a range of strategies beyond that of lower cost

Corporate strategists may not be fully familiar with four of the most promising opportunities for using outsourcing strategies—focus, scale without mass, disruptive innovation, and strategic repositioning. While assessing the potential of those opportunities in specific corporate situations, strategists also need to look at two of the most significant associated risks—the risk of losing skills that could be key to competing in the future, and the risk of turning to outsourcing at the wrong stage in an industry's evolution. My goal is to widen managers' views of the strategic alternatives that outsourcing can be used to support, while making managers aware of the main risks to be weighed in the balance.

Four Promising Outsourcing Strategies

Focus—Nike and Dell

In intensely competitive environments, many companies see outsourcing as a way to hire "best in class" companies to perform routine business functions and then focus corporate resources on key activities in their value chain where the impact will be felt the most by the customer. This is the strategy that has helped Nike to capture and sustain leadership in the athletic footwear and apparel industry for most of the last three decades.

Nike's business started as a company of athletes selling imported performance Japanese shoes to other athletes, and by the end of its first decade in 1972, sales had reached just $2 million. Despite the relatively slow growth of these early years, the founders continued to experiment with new performance designs and prototypes, based on their intimate knowledge of the market. By the end of their first decade they had already developed the core competencies in brand building and design that were

---

soon to become the foundation for Nike's rapid growth. The company decided to focus primarily on these activities and outsource most of its production and much of its sales and distribution. As a consequence, by the end of its second decade Nike sales had rocketed to $700 million, with gross margins running at nearly 40 percent. Even before the notion of focused outsourcing was generally understood, Nike had demonstrated the potential power of such a strategy. It continues to do so today, retaining a 39 percent share of the $7.8 billion US market for branded athletic footwear, and doing so in the face of very determined competition.

The strategy of focusing corporate resources mainly on those activities where clear differentiation can be developed and outsourcing much of the rest has also served many other companies well. The key often lies in knowing which of the main value drivers to concentrate on—customer intimacy, product leadership or operational excellence. All three are key to delivering value to customers, but the organizational capabilities and cultures that promote them are not the same, and often tend to pull in different directions.[1] So, for example, Nike has tended to focus primarily on product leadership and Dell on operational excellence and customer relationship management, and both rely on the competencies of others to help them deliver value in other areas. The appeal of such a strategy continues to widen, even into some of the most traditional sectors. Today, for example, many newspapers now tend to concentrate mainly on the customer relationship area, outsourcing much of their content and most of their printing and distribution.

Scaling without Mass—Nokia and Nortel

Another attractive feature of outsourcing is that it offers companies the opportunity to grow in market presence without a corresponding expansion in organizational size or bureaucracy. Strategic outsourcing can help a rapidly growing company avoid a premature internal transition from its informal entrepreneurial phase to a more bureaucratic mode of operation. In this way, outsourcing allows firms to retain their entrepreneurial speed and agility, which they would otherwise sacrifice in order to become efficient as they greatly expanded.

This is one of the primary benefits that companies like Nike, opting initially for a focused strategy with extensive outsourcing, tend to enjoy from the outset. For example, over the 1978–82 period, during the steepest phase in Nike's early growth, revenue scaled up nearly ten-fold from $71 million to $690 million, while the employee population grew from 720 to 3,600, just half the growth rate of revenue. In fact, Nike continued to retain many of the characteristics of an entrepreneurial firm until it was almost a $1 billion company. It was not until it reached billionaire status that the lack of formal management systems became a serious impediment to the company's further development.

However, the prospect of being able to scale up without a pro-rata increase in organizational mass and complexity is an attractive reason to consider outsourcing at any stage in a company's development, not just at start-up. For example, in early 2000, when employee numbers at Nokia were increasing at the rate of 1,000 per month, and approaching the 60,000 mark, CEO Jorma Ollila decided to outsource a significant portion of its production in both its network equipment and mobile handset businesses in order to help slow down the growth in number of employees without impeding the company's momentum in the marketplace. It was a strategy that helped cushion the effects of a subsequent downturn, but the main consideration was the fear that too-rapid growth would dilute the Nokia spirit and undermine organizational coherence. At the time, Nokia was widely known as one of the least bureaucratic of global corporations, and Ollila embraced outsourcing to keep it that way.

For another large corporate example, at Nortel Networks in 1999 management recognized they were on the cusp of a "once-in-a-lifetime" market shift, with the opportunity to double their company's revenue from $20 billion to $40 billion within 24 months, if they could get their business model right. They also realized that they could not hope to avail themselves of this opportunity by remaining a traditional manufacturer. The realization produced a managerial mantra—"Why do companies fail? They fail because their processes don't scale." This insight led the Nortel management team to conclude that "we'd never be a $40B company with our existing processes" as Frank Dunn, the company's chief financial officer, later recalled. At the time, the company's return on invested capital was running at just about half that of market leader, Cisco. Over the 1999–2001 period, Nortel divested 15 manufacturing sites and transferred 9,000 employees to contract manufacturers such as Solectron and Sanmina. This was part of a wider move toward a more customer-centric strategy, outsourcing production while creating in-house supply chain management teams for each major customer. The entire system was dedicated to improving end-to-end fulfillment using Internet-enabled resource management systems.[2]

Disruptive Innovation—IKEA, Canon and Ryanair

Outsourcing is a key element in many of the most impressive examples of disruptive innovation to date. Typical examples include IKEA's entry into furniture retailing, Canon's into the photocopying market, and Ryanair's into the European airline industry. The primary aim of most disruptive innovation is to create a whole new segment at a price point well below the bottom of the current market and then to dominate this segment as it grows. This usually requires the development of an innovative business model capable of producing overall returns at least as good as those of the leading incumbents, but doing it at significantly lower cost through much higher asset productivity.[3] IKEA, Canon and Ryanair were all late entrants into their respective industries, but all succeeded in building substantial market positions through such a strategy, and outsourcing was a common element in the development of a distinctive lower-cost/higher-asset productivity formula in all three cases.

At the time of IKEA's founding in the early 1950s, the European furniture industry was highly fragmented geographically. National department stores established exclusive relationships with local manufacturers to allow them to offer distinctive product lines, reflective of local tastes and traditions. Quality new furniture was typically priced beyond the reach of all but the relatively prosperous, and most young people setting out to furnish their first home had to rely on the secondhand market or hand-me-downs from parents. Ingvar Kamprad, and his company IKEA, set out to "democratize" this marketplace by bringing quality new furniture within reach of the many, not just the few. IKEA developed a range of simple, elegant, "modern" designs, using light-colored quality woods. This appealed to young customers of all nations. The key to delivering such attractive furniture at prices well below prevailing norms was designing for manufacturability and transportability, not just consumer appeal. IKEA revolutionized the European furniture industry with a novel "production-oriented retailing" business model, the competitiveness of which depended not only on the careful outsourcing of production, but also on "outsourcing" final assembly and delivery to the customers themselves. The "production-oriented retailing" principle remains fundamental to the IKEA business model as the company continues to expand internationally, and, no matter how strong the pull at the retail end, the company will only enter new lines of furniture that fit with its production-oriented economics.

Outsourcing has been a prominent feature in the business models of other classic disruptive innovators over the years, not just IKEA. For example, in the case of Canon, outsourcing has always been a major element in the company's strategy in the copier market, with 80 percent of product assembled from purchased parts and only drums and toner manufactured in-house. Outsourcing is also prominent in the business model of Ryanair, the disruptive innovator in the European airline industry (the self-styled "Southwest Airlines of Europe"), where the company contracts out most of its aircraft handling, heavy maintenance and baggage handling as part of its strategy to avoid complexity, keep cost down and maintain productivity at levels well above industry norms.

Strategic Repositioning—IBM

Strategic repositioning is rarely easy, especially when you are a long-time industry leader like IBM. Yet, one of the biggest strategic bets that Lou Gerstner made as part of the turnaround at IBM in the mid-1990s was that services, not technology, would be the major growth area going forward, particularly in the corporate computing market. As he saw it then: "If customers were going to look to an integrator to help them envision, design, and build end-to-end solutions, then the companies playing that role would exert tremendous influence over the full range of technology decisions—from architecture and applications to hardware and software choices."[4] Traditionally IBM's strategy had always stressed service as a distinguishing feature of its value proposition, but this was service tied to products. What Gerstner had in mind was consultancy and solutions integration services as a major business driver in its own right. In 1992, services was a $9.2 billion business at IBM—within ten years IBM Global Services had grown into a $30 billion business, employing half the corporation's human resources. Recently, IBM has intensified its commitment to this strategic repositioning, as part of CEO Sam Palmisano's e-business "on-demand" vision.

Outsourcing is central to IBM's repositioning—both as a driver and an enabler. Under the new strategy IBM has become both an extensive provider of outsourcing services to others as part of its offering as a solutions integrator (primarily in the IT area), while at the same time becoming a more extensive user of outsourcing services itself (primarily in the product area from contract manufacturers). For example, IBM's own IT outsourcing services is now one of the main revenue drivers in the company's new e-business on demand strategy and one that generated $13 billion in the European market alone in 2002. Further back its value chain, IBM's decision to outsource a growing share of its own production is helping it accelerate its ongoing migration to a services-led model and reconfigure its resources to support this strategy. Within the last two years the company has entered into a $5 billion outsourcing contract with Sanmina-SCI Corporation to manufacture its NetVista line of desktop computers, later expanded to include a significant portion of its low- to mid-range server and workstation lines, along with some distribution and fulfillment activities. Substantial transfers of assets and overheads have been involved in both of these deals, which the company sees as allowing it to "leverage the skills of the industry where it makes sense to improve our costs, and focus our own investments on areas that deliver the highest value to our customers."[5]

The Risks of Outsourcing

Outsourcing also increases certain strategic risks. Two of the most important are the risk of losing skills key to competing for the future and the risk of making the outsourcing move at the least suitable time in an industry's evolution.

Mortgaging the Future: Losing Key Skills and Capabilities

Companies can often be attracted to outsourcing as a means to relieve intensifying competitive pressure. However, if they fail to consider the long-term implications, they may unwittingly mortgage their future opportunities for short-term advantage. For example, not too many years ago Eastman Kodak executives made a decision to exit the camcorder business because the investment challenge at the time looked too steep to stay in the game. Years later, however, they came to recognize that the skills and knowledge they would have developed in the manufacture of the major sub-components could have been used to support a wider range of applications of the core technologies beyond the consumer market into medical imaging and other areas. In a similar way, Bulova was slow to see the wider applications that the manufacturing skills developed in the area of miniature tuning fork technology might have beyond the watch market, an insight not lost on Citizen. In contrast, Canon chose to take a longer view and remain in the semiconductor business following its failure to make the hoped-for impact in the calculator market, a decision that in time would leave it well positioned to play in the office products market when electronic imaging later emerged as a key technology.

Like prematurely exiting a market, hasty and near-sighted outsourcing may result in the loss or unintended transfer of critical learning opportunities, as happened to General Electric in its outsourcing arrangement with Samsung in the microwave market. In the early 1980s General Electric was still investing heavily in its own manufacturing capability in Columbia, Maryland, when it decided to outsource the production of some of its models at the small to medium end of the market to Samsung, then just a modest enterprise little known outside of Korea. The initial contract was for just 15,000 units. However, GE quickly found itself on a steep dependence spiral that ultimately saw it ceding most of the investment and skills development initiative in microwave production to its outsourcer within just two years. For Samsung, the arrangement allowed it to scale up its production and engineering to levels that would not have been possible without access to GE's American consumers. This one small outsourcing contract set the stage for Samsung's emergence as a global powerhouse in consumer appliances.[6] The lesson from this and similar examples is that it pays to be mindful that strategic capabilities are rarely synonymous with discrete functions like engineering or production but tend to be deeply embedded in the collective know-how that reflects their integration.[7] That is why many extensive outsourcers like Nike still wish to retain some manufacturing activity and closely tie it to engineering and marketing in order to preserve the multifunctional capabilities they see as key to their future success.

Choosing to Outsource at the Wrong Time in a Market's Evolution

Strategists also need to know when in an industry's evolution and where along its value chain the economics favor outsourcing. They also need to be aware how this tends to change over time, particularly in technology markets. According to disruptive innovation authority, Clayton Christensen, the critical transition is when the market changes from the stage where most customers continue to desire more functionality than is currently offered to the point where the majority of customers come to see themselves as being over-served with features. This is the juncture at which the product rapidly becomes a commodity and where the primary basis of competition shifts to aspects of the value proposition beyond technology—such as price, speed, convenience and customization.

In the PC market, for example, it is widely recognized today that IBM outsourced too early because of its anxiety to slow down the progress of Apple Computer, and in doing so allowed the initiative at the features-driven stage of the market's evolution to flow mainly to Intel and Microsoft. Later, when the personal computer became a commodity, the market favored the business model of Dell, which focused largely on customer relationship management and efficient fulfillment and used extensive outsourcing. Indeed, in migrating its model to other segments, Dell's success continues to rely on recognizing when a market's evolution has progressed beyond the features-led, technology-driven stage. To date, it has managed to get this right in the personal computer and mid-range server markets. It now believes the time is more than ripe to apply its model to inkjet printers, where market leader Hewlett Packard continues to place its bets on its superior technological capabilities and on proprietary features. When deciding whether to make such a wager, it is important for managers to recognize that core competence, as understood in many businesses, can be "a dangerously inward-looking notion." Managers are much more likely to win their bet if they understand that competitiveness "is far more about doing what customers value than what you think you are good at."[8] Knowing the difference is one of the secrets to getting the timing of outsourcing strategy right, as the following insight from a senior supply chain executive at Hewlett Packard makes clear:

> How do you spot early that you are losing your protected differentiation with the customer in terms of product, process or performance? Every company likes to believe that it has a superior product. It takes skill to recognize that others are catching up. In the inkjet printer market we always have to ask ourselves are we still producing products that the customer values on an ongoing basis? Are things going horizontal? Sooner or later, you get to a point of diminishing returns where the market no longer fully values say an improvement in speed from 25 to 30 pages per minute or where the next improvement in photo quality resolution reaches the point where only a measuring instrument will detect it. When further improvements have a negligible impact on the customer, in terms of perceived value, you are not too far from being commoditized or horizontalized. How do you then operate in a different mode? How do you transition to a different model? This is when outsourcing tends to become a serious option for a business to consider.[9]

Know Your Options and Consider the Timing and Risk

Outsourcing as a strategy has the potential to drive competitiveness and value creation in many ways beyond the narrow goal of cost reduction alone. Achieving greater focus, scaling without mass, fueling disruptive innovation and enabling strategic repositioning are just four of the many promising options that outsourcing as a strategy can offer and support. However, managers considering any such outsourcing options will always need to ask themselves whether the timing is right and also what strategic skills and capabilities they might be putting at risk.

Notes

1. For a full discussion of these value drivers see Treacy, M. and Wiersema, F. (1993), "Customer intimacy and other value disciplines," *Harvard Business Review,* January–February, pp. 84–93. For a closer look at the inherent tensions among them, see also Hagel, J. and Singer, M. (1999), "Unbundling the corporation," *Harvard Business Review,* March–April, pp. 133–41.

2. For more on the Nortel case see Fisher, L. M. (2001), "From vertical to virtual: how Nortel's supplier alliances extend the enterprise," *Strategy + Business,* Quarter 1.

3. The term disruptive innovation is used here in the sense defined by Clay Christensen—see Christensen, C. M. and Raynor, M. E. (2003), *The Innovator's Solution,* Harvard Business School Press, Boston, MA.

4. Quote from Gerstner, L. V. (2003), *Who Says Elephants Can't Dance?* HarperBusiness, New York, NY.

5. Bob Moffat, general manager of IBM's Personal & Printing Systems Group, quoted in an IBM press release, "IBM signs agreement with Sanmina-SCI to manufacture its NetVista desktop PCs in US and Europe," January 8, 2002.

6. For more on the GE/Samsung case see Magaziner, I. C. and Patinkin, M. (1989), "Fast heat: how Korea won the microwave war," *Harvard Business Review,* January–February, pp. 83–91. For more examples of the risk of losing key skills and learning opportunities, see Lei, D. and Slocum, J. W. (1992), "Global strategy, competence-building and strategic alliances," *California Management Review,* Fall, pp. 81–97.

7. For more on the embedded and integrated nature of core competencies see Prahalad, C. K., Fahey, L. and Randall, R. M. (2001), "Creating and leveraging core competencies," in Fahey, L. and Randall, R. M. (Eds), *The Portable MBA in Strategy,* 2nd ed, Wiley, New York, NY, pp. 236–52.

8. For more on this risk, see Christensen, C. M. and Raynor, M. E. (2003), *The Innovator's Solution,* Harvard Business School Press, Boston, MA (especially chapters 5 and 6—the quote comes from Chapter 6).

9. Maurice O'Connell, Materials Director of Hewlett Packard's inkjet printer business, in conversation with the author at the HP plant in Dublin, July 2, 2004.

Increasing the Odds of Successful Growth

The Critical Prelude to Moving "Beyond the Core"

Chris Zook
Bain & Company

From a multi-study Bain & Company search to identify the most reliable principles on which to base a strategy for profitable growth, two key insights emerged. The first is that the most promising growth opportunities tend to lie adjacent to the core business. Indeed, the farther away from the core business companies extend themselves in pursuit of growth, the worse they tend to fare. The second insight, and the one focused on here, is that the competitive strength of the core business itself is a crucial factor in the success of growth initiatives. The principal message of this article is that companies should first re-examine the strength of their core business before they attempt to expand beyond it. Even if the core business is a market leader, it may need to seek even greater competitive advantage before essaying major growth initiatives. If it's well behind the market leaders, its position can be greatly strengthened through consolidation, upwards or downwards. The result will be a sounder, more reliable base for growth. The cases featured here help show the way.

A chief concern of senior executives these days is finding new sources of sustained and profitable growth. Yet choosing between investing in a proven business versus a potential one requires careful analysis and study of both successful and failed attempts. Recent Bain & Company research shows that overreaching for growth in areas adjacent to a firm's core business is often destructive.

To put the successful and failed attempts into historical perspective, consider the starkly contrasting investment choices on expansion into markets adjacent to their core businesses taken by Kmart and Wal-Mart in the 42 years after both chain stores opened their first stores in 1962. Wal-Mart made a series of methodical moves into such adjacencies as Sam's Club, electronics, and overseas stores, one by one. Kmart overreached with adjacency moves ranging from books (Walden) to sporting goods (Sports Authority) and a chain of department stores in Czechoslovakia. Though there are many causes of the two firm's different fortunes, over the decades Wal-Mart became the largest company in the *Fortune* 500, while Kmart descended into bankruptcy.

When Bain examined the top 25 non-Internet business calamities between 1997 and 2002, we concluded that a failed strategy to grow into a new adjacency around a once-successful core business was a critical factor in 80 percent of these cases. In total, these companies experienced an 88 percent loss in value, totaling $1.1 trillion. On the other hand, successful adjacency moves fueled some of the same period's greatest

Exhibit 1   Market Leadership Drives Adjacency Success

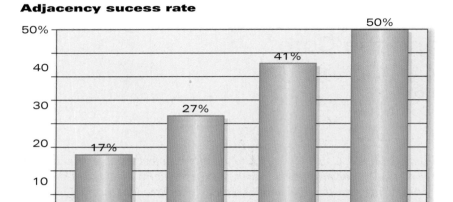

growth stories, such as IBM's move into services and Nike's remarkable string of product extensions from jogging gear into new sporting venues such as volleyball, tennis, basketball, soccer and finally golf.

In short, adjacency judgments are among the most difficult and critical decisions senior executives face. They can make or break a company. According to Bain's recent five-year study of 1,850 companies, the chances for success in growth initiatives were nearly three times higher for companies moving into adjacencies from strong leadership positions in their core business (see Exhibit 1).

Accurate determination of core strength is challenging. The three critical dimensions are competitive position, market dynamics and financial performance (see Exhibit 2). Competitive position can range all the way from a weak follower to strong market leader, with parity or weak leadership common states in between. Market dynamics range from strong growth to stable low growth to total meltdown. Financial performance can vary from full potential to underperformance. Executives need to take a hard and detailed look at the state of their cores along these three dimensions when considering the challenge of targeting and pursuing promising adjacencies. For leaders and followers alike, the first priority is to define, secure, and if necessary, fix the core business.

Boosting an Underperforming Core— the Case of AmBev

One of the most striking findings from our study is the frequency with which executives underestimate the full potential of their core and prematurely abandon the business (see Exhibit 3).

AmBev, the Brazilian-based beer company, is a case that demonstrates how to boost an underperforming core. In 1989, a group of private investors led by AmBev's current CEO, Marcel Telles, purchased what was then called Brahma. At the time, the

Exhibit 2   Core Situations

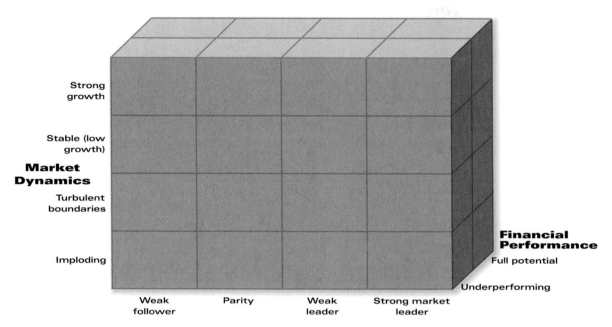

Exhibit 3   Exact Signs of Value Opportunities in the Core

1. Poorly defined core, no consensus
2. Declining core customer "share of wallet"
3. Flattening unit cost experience curves
4. Increasing competitor reinvestment rates or market share up
5. Disappointing recent adjacency attempts
6. Increasing product and process complexity
7. Varying and unexplained performance differences across units
8. Neglecting to revise customer segments

company was one of the top two competitors in its domestic market. Telles and his colleagues might well have decided that the business was maxing out and used its extensive distribution network as the basis for diversification into related or adjacent products or segments. Instead, they decided to concentrate on boosting the performance of the core business. From 1989 to 2001, the company posted an annual growth rate of 20.4 percent in a low-growth market, fueling a year-on-year rise in its stock valuation of 34.4 percent. Today, AmBev is the leading brewer in South America. And with its recent combination with Belgium's Interbrew, it will also take over Canada's number two brand, Labatt, to move into North America.

Telles describes the turnaround this way: "The growth story of AmBev actually begins with ten years of cost cutting and cultural rebuilding in the core business. This takes time. We instilled a culture . . . of being intensely dissatisfied with anything less

THE VOCABULARY OF ADJACENCY EXPANSION

There are six primary ways to push out the boundaries of a business:

1. *Product adjacencies:* Selling a new product or new services to core customers is one of the most commonly pursued and highest-potential adjacencies. The creation of IBM Global Services for IBM's hardware customers illustrates one of the most successful growth strategies triggered by a product adjacency. Global Services now constitutes 40 percent of the company.

2. *Geographic adjacencies:* Moving into a new geographic area is a type of adjacency move that companies consistently underestimate in complexity, hence the lower-than-average success rate. An example is Vodafone's expansion from the UK into Europe, into the USA through the AirTouch merger, into Germany through the purchase of Manesmann, and into Japan through the acquisition of a majority share in Japan Telecom and its J-Phone subsidiary.

3. *Value chain adjacencies:* Going up or down the value chain into an entirely new set of activities is one of the most difficult forms of adjacency expansion. Merck's acquisition and recent divestiture of Medco, a mail-order drug distributor, illustrates a value chain adjacency. Another example is the entrance of LVMH, the luxury goods company that owns 25 fashion brands, from Fendi to Louis Vuitton, into the retail business by the purchase of Sephora and Duty Free Shoppers in 1996. At the time, LVMH announced that these purchases were complementary to its activities. In 2001, the company changed its point of view and announced that these units would be divested, indicating that this retail segment was found to be "noncore."

4. *Channel adjacencies:* If successful, the move into a new channel can produce an enormous source of new value. If not, it can turn into a true Waterloo. For example, Experimental and Applied Science (EAS), the leading sports-supplement company, has had great success in making minor changes in the formulation, packaging, and celebrity sponsorship of its Myoplex sports bars, originally sold in specialty nutrition stores, and quickly becoming a leader in its category selling to Wal-Mart. By contrast, the entry of Dell into the mass retail channel with personal computers caused massive disruption in pricing, factory processes, marketing, and sales and led to the only time in which Dell lost money—1993, when it lost $36 million. In June of 1994, Dell made the courageous decision to exit the indirect retail channel even though at the time it was building a large warehouse to serve Wal-Mart. This exit move allowed Dell to resume its trajectory to become the best-performing company in the United States during the 1990s.

5. *Customer adjacencies:* Modifying a proven product or technology to enter a totally new customer segment is a major adjacency move for many companies. Examples include the creation of Kids "R" Us by Toys "R" Us, the move by Staples from retail into the delivery of office products to small businesses, and Charles Schwab's expansion of advisory services to target high-net-worth individuals.

6. *New business adjacencies:* Building a new business around a strong capability, essentially repurposing it, is the rarest form of adjacency move—and the most difficult to pull off. The classic example is when American Airlines created the Sabre reservation system, which grew into a spin-off now worth more than the airline itself. Sabre, in turn, went on to create a new business adjacency of its own in Travelocity.

than full potential and results. . . . We discovered that we could constantly turn the screw more and more in the core business to extract much more than ever seemed (possible) at first glance. In 1989, AmBev had productivity of 1,200 hectoliters per employee. Today it has productivity of 8,200 hectoliters per employee. . . . It is the power of these core economics that is now allowing us to drive into new adjacencies successfully."

The new strength in its core allowed the then-Brahma to overtake and wear down its long-standing domestic competitor, leading to a merger ten years after the Brahma buyout. The new combination, renamed AmBev, now controls close to 70 percent of the Brazilian market. More than a decade of sustained productivity improvement and market consolidation has helped AmBev to drive up its pretax profit margin from 8.7

percent to 30.5 percent, giving it a very strong position in a core market that is set for further growth (one study estimates that 42 percent of new growth in the world profit pool for beer will come from Brazil).

The company was wise to delay diversification until it had boosted its underperforming core. By waiting until it had trimmed its cost structure, AmBev has been able to move into market after market beyond Brazil. At each step, it used its low-cost operations to build share through lower prices and to gain competitive advantage through higher margins and greater levels of reinvestment. Through its superior operating economics, AmBev has taken leadership market positions in Uruguay, Paraguay, Bolivia, and Argentina, along with establishing a strong beachhead in Venezuela and Chile. It is now the largest brewer in South America, and the most profitable in the world. It is well positioned there for expansion into further adjacencies—including the market for beverages like "guarana," which is a major non-cola soft-drink flavor category in the South American market. Moreover, AmBev's latest deal with Interbrew will make it part of the world's largest brewer.

Strengthening a Weak Core

Companies with relatively weak core positions face an uphill struggle when pursuing profitable growth. However, the situation is not without hope. Consider the strategies of companies like US Foodservice (USF) and MBNA (credit cards). The most reliable route is through consolidation—upward, like USF, to improve its leadership position in the market as a whole—or downward, like MBNA, in pursuit of a stronger position within a more narrowly defined market boundary.

Consolidating Upward—USF

According to Bain data, more than 45 percent of companies that succeeded in improving the strength of their core businesses did so by moving up their industry rankings through merger or acquisition, consolidating upward.

A good example is US Foodservice (USF). In 1989, Sara Lee spun off USF in a leveraged buyout. At the time, the business was number six in the US market as a whole, and number three in its principal regional markets in the Midwest and Northeast. USF's strategy of consolidation began by building up stronger regional market shares, followed by a series of equity offerings that enabled it to make 17 acquisitions in its core business area over a six-year period.

The focus was threefold: the improvement of operations; the introduction of proprietary, higher-margin, private-label and signature brands; and the rapid integration of back-office activities into the core. Over the next 11 years, from the time of the buyout to its eventual takeover by Royal Ahold in 2000, USF revenues grew from $0.89 billion to $6.9 billion, while operating profits rose from $26 million to $250 million. Though we estimate the odds of executing a consolidation roll-up strategy are less than 40 percent, it can be a very effective way to secure a leadership position and the economic benefits that flow from it. To be successful, such a strategy requires four critical elements:

- A stable platform on which to bolt on acquisitions.
- A method to achieve real economies of scale.
- Realistic acquisition costs.
- Superb execution of the integration process.

Consolidating Downward—the Case of MBNA

Our data also shows that 20 percent of companies improve the position of their core businesses by consolidating downward into market leadership within a narrower and more finely drawn market boundary. This creates a smaller, but more promising, platform for robust expansion later down the line, and might be termed a "shrink to grow" strategy.

The credit card issuer MBNA is a good example of this type of strategy. The business was founded in 1982 as the credit card subsidiary of a US regional savings bank, Maryland National. The bank, however, did not survive the real estate loan crisis of the late 1980s. The distressed parent was acquired by what is now Bank of America, and the MBNA division was spun off.

Lou Gerstner on Renewal of the Base Business

"In my 35-year business career I have seen many companies, when the going gets tough in their base business, decide to try their luck in new industries. . . . Too many executives don't want to fight the tough battles of resurrecting, resuscitating, and strengthening their base businesses—or they simply give up on their base business too soon. . . . History shows that truly great and successful companies go through constant and sometimes difficult self-renewal of the base business. They don't jump into new pools where they have no sense of the depth or temperature of the water."

Who Says Elephants Can't Dance by Louis V. Gerstner (HarperBusiness, 2002)

At the time of its acquisition, Maryland National was a weak follower. However, time revealed it actually contained a smaller, specialized, alternative core business with much greater growth potential. MBNA built its latent core strength by focusing on the credit card customer base segmented by profession and affinity group, and by concentrating on customers with the best economics and the greatest potential for loyalty. It found that the best way to reach this market-within-a-market was through zeroing in on affinity groups like universities and the National Education Association. The practice went back to the company's first core customer in 1982, the Alumni Association of Georgetown. Though other credit card companies competed for this business, MBNA established a lead in know-how regarding customer segmentation and in servicing the needs of specific groups to ensure their retention. Over the following 20 years, MBNA grew to become the third-largest credit card issuer. It entered the new millennium with $7.9 billion in revenue and $1.3 billion in profit. All that was built on an obscure initiative within a weak follower that led to a smaller, stronger, more specialized core business platform for significant future growth.

Escaping from a Declining Core—the Case of Imation

The least promising basis for future growth is a core market in inexorable decline. Fortunately, this condition is a rarity, represented by no more than 2 to 3 percent of the examples in our study, and severe market decline is most often a process of erosion, rather than one of sudden collapse.

Our research revealed that only 12 percent of the 1,000 distant followers that we analyzed actually achieved significant improvements in financial performance or market positioning. Virtually none of these improved through entering adjacencies. But a few found ways to fix their core business.

Some companies have found ways to rehabilitate their core business and expand into adjacent businesses even though their market is in precipitous decline. One of the most interesting examples involved transferring skills to a new core, a strategy used effectively by Imation.

When the company's core floppy-disk business began to disappear and be replaced by optical storage media, the company decided to use its value chain reputation, expertise and infrastructure to build a new core business from the ashes of the old. Created in 1996, as one of six businesses spun off by 3M, Imation has since become, by necessity, a master at creating new growth opportunities through strategic partnership. According to CEO Bill Monahan, the "ability to set up joint venture partnerships that work is a core skill in our company, has taken a long time to develop, and is now the primary engine for our expansion into new products and adjacencies."

At the time of the spin off, Imation had built a leading position as a manufacturer of floppy disks. But even though the floppy disk has rapidly declined as the medium of choice for data storage, Imation continues to possess a strong industry position, thanks to its successful partnership with a world-class manufacturer of optical storage media. The relationship gives Imation access to a quality product line at low cost, while its partner gains access to worldwide markets, through Imation's branding, customer relationships and distribution infrastructure. As Monahan now describes it, this new concentration on marketing and distribution "will ultimately become a total replacement of a major piece of our core and possibly our largest core business."

It is not easy to build a new core business from the ashes of an old one, and odds against it being successful are quite high. Nevertheless, Imation's recovery suggests that for companies in such a difficult situation, it's well worth emulating.

Synthesizing the lessons from our research, we've discovered that there are four reasons why executives frequently misjudge their companies' ability to support an adjacency:

1. Believing a major adjacency move will transform a follower situation, or create parity—unfortunately, the odds are minuscule.

2. Abandoning the core business before reaching its full potential—businesses nearly always underestimate their true capacity; this is particularly true for leaders.

3. Misjudging the adjacency gap—the difference between an adjacency and a leap into the unknown can be measured in the number of steps outward from the core.

4. Misunderstanding their company's strength—the best adjacency moves grow out of a minute understanding of the core business.

Management Is the Art of Doing and Getting Done

Heike Bruch
University of St. Gallen

Sumantra Ghoshal
London Business School

"Management was, is, and always will be the same thing: the art of getting things done," wrote Harvard Business School professors Bob Eccles and Nitin Nohria in their book *Beyond the Hype*. "And to get things done, managers must act themselves and mobilize collective action on the part of others."[1]

Almost ten years later, lamenting what they described as the pervasive "knowing-doing gap" in companies, Jeffrey Pfeffer and Bob Sutton of Stanford posed the question: "Did you ever wonder why so much education and training, management consultation, organizational research, and so many books and articles produce so few changes in actual management practice?. . . Why knowledge of what needs to be done frequently fails to result in action or behavior consistent with that knowledge."[2]

Our own research in companies mirrors Pfeffer and Sutton's observations. Most companies, including those that are very successful, can be visualized as a few isolated islands of action amid an ocean of inaction. There are a few managers in them who take decisive, purposeful action, while the vast majority does not. What we found in our research surprised us. Only about 10 percent of the managers took purposeful action.

One of the companies in which we conducted a detailed study on action-taking is Lufthansa, a highly successful organization. From a crisis situation in 1991, when it was close to bankruptcy, it had pulled itself up to record profits of close to a billion marks in 1997. Beyond the dramatic change in financial performance, the company was also seen as extremely energetic and vigorous, being the primary engine of restructuring the airlines industry, for example, by creating the Star Alliance. Jürgen Weber, Lufthansa's charismatic and highly regarded CEO, had dismantled the company's historically strong central hierarchy and had also declared war on its traditional bureaucratic culture, creating freedom for managers at the operating levels to take bold action. These were the managers we wanted to study, to see the why and how of their action-taking.

So, it was not that only a limited number of managers took purposeful action in a poorly managed, poor performing company. This was the situation in a highly successful, high performance company. We repeated the same study in Conoco, the US oil company, surveying 250 managers. The percentage of purposeful action-takers was about the same.

"Management is the Art of Doing and Getting Done," Heike Bruch, Sumantra Ghoshal, *Business Strategy Review*, Vol. 15, Issue 3, Fall 2004, p. 4–13. Reprinted with permission of Blackwell Publishing Ltd.

It is not that the other 90 percent of managers did not know what to do. Most of them had clearly defined projects and goals, and had all the knowledge necessary to take action. The real problem for those managers was not the lack of knowledge or even resources. The real problem was that even though they knew what to do, they simply did not do those things. The real gap was between knowledge and action.

Also, it is not true that those who did not take action were lazy people who were shirking from their work. They worked very hard. They were extremely busy, attending meetings, making phone calls, conducting reviews—they were running all the time. But not purposefully. They were spinning wheels and no real progress came out of all their busyness.

What are the causes of this pervasive lack of purposeful action-taking among managers? What is different about those who do take purposeful action? What can managers do to enhance their personal action-taking ability? And what can corporate leaders do to create an organizational context in which others can take purposeful action? What can they do to develop managers who can and do act?

These are the research questions we have pursued over the last five years. We started in 1998, following the 130 managers in Lufthansa over a two-year period and observing what they did to pursue specific projects they had committed to execute. We also carried out a questionnaire survey, covering the same 130 managers, to test with some quantitative rigor some ideas we had developed from the interview-based qualitative data. Then we replicated the survey to Conoco, to check if the patterns revealed in the Lufthansa survey also held in another company with a very different industrial and organizational background.

Beyond these two studies, we have also written detailed case studies on 12 companies—Goldman Sachs, Oracle and Sun Microsystems in the United States; BP, Hilti, Micro Mobility Systems and Siemens in Europe; and Sony, the LG Group and Infosys in Asia. Each focused on managerial action-taking in the context of a specific project or initiative. Finally, in the last phase of our study, we identified 20 managers from different companies and at different levels of seniority—people whom we knew very well including several ex-students—and interviewed them at length (some up to 20 hours and none less than 4 hours) to document their own experiences of both action-taking and non-action.

Based on these different pieces of work, we have developed a set of answers to the research questions we posed. Our data and analysis is presented in our book, *A Bias for Action*. Here, we provide a broad overview of some of our key findings, summarizing what we believe we have learnt from our investigation of the phenomenon of managerial action-taking.

Action Must Not Be Confused with Being Active

One of the most common misunderstandings about action is that it is confused with being active or doing something. This misunderstanding is the central reason why effective and persistent action is so rare in companies.

In *In Search of Excellence* (1982), Tom Peters and Robert Waterman identified "a bias for action" as the one attribute of excellent companies that underpins all their other attributes. "Ready, Fire, Aim" was their prescription for building a bias for action. Experimentation, "make a little, sell a little," remaining flexible to disengage quickly—these were the things they saw as the essence of action-taking in companies.

What we mean by purposeful action is very different from what Peters and Waterman described as action. Purposeful action is determined, persistent and relentless action-taking to achieve a goal or a purpose, against all odds. It is driven by a deep personal commitment to the goal that cuts out all distractions and overcomes all difficulties. It is not a quick shuffle, not flirtation with ideas, not the dilettante behavior of management butterflies. It is not the superficial attempt to do something. It is action-taking to succeed, no matter what.

Experimentation is important for companies. The flexibility of dipping toes in the water to test the temperature is sometimes useful. But, in our observation, the most critical challenge for companies is relentless execution, and purposeful action-taking lies at the heart of relentless execution. Behind every significant improvement in productivity, every new product, and every successful strategic or organizational change lies a set of disciplined, persistent and purposeful actions taken by specific individuals, both separately and together.

Purposeful action, as we use the term, is based on two traits—energy and focus. Action is particularly energetic in the sense that it implies a level of personal involvement that is more than "just doing something." Action is subjectively meaningful; it genuinely matters to the action-taker. Also, such action demands effort. It involves a certain amount of exertion. The need for effort is not only a result of external pressures but also of forces within the action-taker: action is self-generated, engaged and self-driven behavior.

Purposeful action is focused, i.e. conscious, intentional and goal-directed behavior. It is guided by a person's intention to achieve a particular goal. This purposefulness of action is demonstrated when attainment of the goal requires discipline to resist distraction, overcome problems and persist in the face of unanticipated setbacks. In other words, purposeful action is different from impulsive behavior—it does not emerge out of the moment but involves thought, analysis and planning.

Very Few Managers Take Purposeful Action

Typical managers are not passive or lazy. On the contrary, looking at what managers do shows that their day is usually busy and there is seldom any relief from the workload—managers are permanently facing requests. There is practically no interruption in doing. During a typical day, managers face a constant stream of demands for their time and attention. They are very active.

However, only a small minority use their time to make a real difference, to get things done that matter. As we have indicated earlier, only about 10 percent of the managers we studied took purposeful action. It is possible that in a particular company the fraction can be a little higher but, in all likelihood, not a lot higher.

The awareness that unproductive activity—what we call active non-action—is a hazard to effective management is not new.[3] In fact, managers themselves bemoan the problem; but the underlying dynamics of the behavior are less well understood. Undoubtedly, managers are under incredible pressure to perform, and they have far too much to do, even if they work twelve-hour days. However, the reason why many managers spin their wheels without much progress very rarely lies in contextual conditions. Rather, in most cases the reason lies in the way managers deal with their jobs.

Diagnosing the causes of non-action as well as the basis for purposeful action-taking, our research shows four types of managerial behavior:

Figure 1

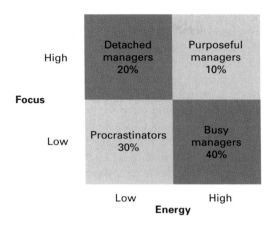

While 10 percent of managers take purposeful action—a behavior that relies on a combination of high energy and high focus, 30 percent of managers procrastinate—they hesitate and fail to take initiative because they suffer from low-level energy and focus. While 20 percent of managers show detached behavior—they are highly focused but have little energy, 40 percent exhibit distracted behavior—busyness—a highly energetic but unfocused activity.

Busyness Is the Central Hazard to Purposeful Action

The most dangerous hazard to managerial action is busyness—high energy with low focus. There are three reasons why. First, busy managers are usually highly motivated and well-intended. They are enthusiastic about their work, identify strongly with their jobs and could achieve a lot if they would consciously concentrate their force on purposeful action.

Second, the largest group of managers suffer from busyness. The reason is that the nature of managerial work makes focusing extremely difficult. The typical managerial job requires multiple activities, implies numerous interruptions and makes it extremely difficult to concentrate attention and energy on selected goals.[4] Managers need discipline in order to prevent themselves from falling victim to the omnipresent trap of busyness.

Third, and most critical, is a culture of frenzy and unreflected activity that dominates most organizations. Presence-cultures, cultures of speed and the rhetoric of instant decisions force managers into mindless busyness. Taking time for reflection, seriously reviewing and questioning projects are simply neither the usual practice nor well perceived in many organizations. Rather, the implicit expectation is that managers must do everything quickly, must be permanently active and must not "hesitate" to take immediate actions. Being motivated and engaged, busy managers are particularly prone to meeting these expectations. A culture of busyness makes it hard for them to escape from the trap of busyness. By creating such cultures, senior executives virtually drive their managers into busyness.

The problem is not only that busyness is the most pervasive trap of managerial jobs but also that it is the most costly form of managerial non-action—from both a personal and a company perspective. Busyness is costly for the individual because busy managers spend a lot of time, energy and emotions on their jobs and yet are not really effective. Due to their strong identification, busy managers tend to get frustrated or hurt more easily when confronted with setbacks, criticism or mediocre performance. Often they have difficulties dealing with the higher effectiveness and, eventually, the greater success of their more reflective and purposeful colleagues. Many managers who have become chronic procrastinators were once busy managers.[5]

Busyness is also costly for companies not only because the immense potential of these managers is not effectively used, but also because it can cause serious damage. Distracted managers—especially when under pressure or in times of crisis—act in extremely short-sighted ways. Because they do not take sufficient time for reflection, they typically deal with immediate problems while neglecting long-term issues, underestimate the necessary time-spans for implementing strategies and start activities without adequate analysis and consideration of the risks and long-term implications. Busy managers demonstrate a well-intentioned but desperate need to do something, anything—and they become as potentially destructive as the proverbial bull in the china shop.

Purposeful Action Requires Deliberate Management of Demands, Constraints and Choices

Most managers who fail to take purposive action do so because they fall victim to one or more of three traps of non-action.

The first is the trap of *overwhelming demands*. Many managers get caught in webs of expectations that completely overwhelm them. The second is the trap of *unbearable constraints*. In this trap, managers feel squeezed by narrow constraints of rules, regulations, budget restrictions and so on and come to believe that they have no space for autonomous action. The third trap of non-action is *unexplored choices*. Focused on the demands and constraints of their jobs, managers develop a tunnel vision and concentrate on immediate needs and requirements. They do not perceive or exploit their freedom to make choices about what they would do and how they would do it.[6]

Managers who overcome these traps of non-action actively manage their jobs and their work environments. To overcome the trap of overwhelming demands, they develop an explicit personal agenda that helps them link short-term, medium-term and long-term goals and also shape the expectations of others inside and outside the organization. They learn to manage their time to create the slack necessary for pursuing their long-term goals. They build in time for reflection and develop personal discipline to reduce, prioritize and organize the demands they face. Above all, they do not attempt to become indispensable and thus avoid getting caught up at the center of frantic activity.

Most organizational constraints are real, but they are rarely as absolute as some managers make them out to be. To unshackle themselves from the trap of unbearable constraints, purposeful action-takers consciously map the relevant constraints. What they often discover is that not all the constraints are relevant in terms of their personal action-taking agenda, and so they can focus on overcoming only those that are. They also learn to accept trade offs, sacrificing some "nice to have" aspects of their projects while intensely fighting for the "must have" aspects. They selectively break rules and develop the capacity to tolerate conflicts and ambiguity in the course of making progress on their chosen tasks.

Finally, to overcome the trap of unexplored choices, purposeful managers learn to become aware of their choices. They consistently expand their opportunities and their freedom to take autonomous action on the choices they have, and they develop personal competencies that both create choice and enhance their ability to make things happen. Above all else, they learn to enjoy choices—to thrive in the context of freedom and derive energy and excitement from that pleasure.

Willpower, Not Motivation, Drives Purposeful Action

Why are some managers highly energetic and focused, whereas others procrastinate, disengage, or dissipate their energy in unfocused busyness? What distinguishes managers who take purposeful action from those who do not? Most top-level leaders will tend to ascribe the difference to "motivation" or the lack thereof.

Our research does indeed indicate that motivation enables managers to perform routine tasks well.

But it is not sufficient for making things happen that would otherwise not happen. Unfortunately, managers are not the maintainers of routine; they are not paid to make the inevitable happen. Their tasks are usually complex and innovative, dealing with long-term objectives. In everyday jobs, managers commonly strive for multiple—often conflicting—goals, many of which are not simple one-shot affairs but long-term projects that require sustained effort. Ambitious goals, long-term projects, high uncertainty, extreme opposition—these are the circumstances when the limitations of motivation become critical. Managers who make things happen under these circumstances rely on a different force: the power of their will.[7]

Motivation is usually driven by external variables or triggered by the expectation of some reward. Yes, theoretical concepts as well as management practice acknowledge the role of intrinsic motivation—the internally driven desire to do something. But motivation remains in the volatile state of wishing to engage, feeling attracted by certain opportunities, or being tempted to act out certain behaviors. Ultimately, both intrinsic and extrinsic motivations are volatile because they are susceptible to changes in either the external context or inner preferences or both. Since the expectation of some reward drives extrinsically motivated behavior, a more attractive opportunity can always come along or obstacles can appear that reduce the perceived value of the reward. Similarly, the desires and enjoyment that drive intrinsic motivation can always change and fade.

Typical managerial deficiencies in taking purposeful action, such as difficulties in getting started, being too easily distracted from goal pursuit, not resuming action after disruptions, losing interest and excitement as the project evolves, and giving up in the face of obstacles, are the consequences of this fragility and volatility of motivation.

Willpower goes a decisive step further than motivation. It implies the commitment that comes only from a deep personal attachment to a certain intention. Willpower springs from a conscious choice to make a concrete thing happen. This commitment to a certain end—not to doing something but to achieving something—represents the engagement of the human will.[5]

While motivation ultimately remains in the superficial and volatile state of wishing, willpower enables managers to execute disciplined action even when they lack the desire to do something, do not feel excited by the work at hand, or feel tempted by alternative opportunities. The force of their will enables them to fight the headwind that comes with change. Their will gives them the power to overcome barriers, to deal with setbacks, to persevere through the energy-demanding long journey from a vision to its realization. With willpower, abandoning an intention is not an option—subjectively, there is no way back. Willful managers are determined to achieve their intention, no matter what.

The Foremost Task of Leaders Is to Engage Their Own Willpower

Top level leaders of companies are often not in the position to give direction to others, to enthuse them or to encourage them simply because they themselves have not engaged their personal willpower. Managers who are distracted or disengaged, as well as those who procrastinate or take purposeful action only occasionally, aren't good leaders, and they know that they are not. The subjective feeling of unease in their leadership role is neither an exception nor a surprise. How could they energize others when they themselves feel exhausted or even burnt out? How could they provide orientation and meaning when they are carried along by inertia and much of their capacity is absorbed in fire fighting? How could they encourage others when they themselves are insecure about the right way to go?

We have come to the conclusion that effective leadership is impossible without the force of personal energy and focus. Being the central source of managers' energy and focus, willpower is the basis for effective leadership. The first and foremost task of a leader is to engage his or her willpower, and then to unleash the power of the will in others.

Willpower Is Not a Personality Trait

While only a minority of managers actually form and use the power of the will, the good news is that every manager can actively engage his or her willpower. We have seen many managers who take purposeful action in one situation while taking a reactive and will-less stance in another situation. We have also observed that in similar situations, while many managers have problems in taking purposeful action, others pursue their goals vigorously, persist in the face of obstacles, and are able to resume their action even after disruptions. As a result, it is clear to us that willpower is neither linked to a stable set of personality traits nor is it the product of certain contextual conditions. Each individual manager can activate the force of his and her volition.

How can managers harness the power of their will? Many managers have never had the experience of volitional action at work. Some others may have accidentally got into situations that set free their volitional force, but they do not know how to deliberately activate and use it. Our research shows that to build willpower, managers have to undertake a personal journey through three overlapping phases.

The perception of an exciting opportunity—something that will make a difference, nothing routine—triggers the first phase of *intention formation*. An emotional dimension gives the intention meaning; a purely rational calculation of costs and benefits of pursuing a goal never leads to volition.

During this first stage, attention is unfocused, perceptions are undirected and judgments are unbiased.[8] Gradually, managers acquire the focus that precedes the leap to commitment that defines the second phase of *engaging willpower.* In this phase, managers make a choice, which is a prerequisite for the engagement of willpower. When there is no choice—in reality or in perception—there can be no free will, no volition. Also essential is acceptance of personal responsibility. The decision to commit comes with the resolve to bear full responsibility.

In this phase managers go through a process of inner consensus building to resolve anxiety, conflicting feelings and doubts. Few managers confront conflicting feelings about work, a costly mistake that blocks real commitment. By facing their concerns, volitional managers avoid later hesitations and develop the apparently unreasonable belief in success which helps them accomplish feats that others would find impossible.

Finally, the third phase is one of *intention protection.* Homer tells the story of Odysseus' escape from the Sirens—sea nymphs whose singing made sailors leap overboard and drown. Odysseus bound himself to the mast of the ship, ordered his men to plug their ears with wax, and forbade them from freeing him from the mast until the ship had safely passed beyond the Sirens' island. As the singing began, he struggled to release himself, begging to be untied. But deaf to his entreaties, his men stayed on course, saving themselves, Odysseus and the ship.

Companies are full of Sirens—distractions that take attention and energy away from purposive action. Willful managers adopt a variety of ways to protect their intention through the action-taking process.[9] They create social pressures by making public commitments, for example, or by setting challenging deadlines and having relevant stakeholders monitor their progress. They deliberately enhance the cost of abandoning their goals. Some reward themselves for passing certain mileposts. Initially exciting projects can become boring or difficult in advanced stages; so they set up increased interactions such as review meetings at later stages in order to keep energy flowing and to shield their intentions.

Most Motivational Techniques Generate Superficiality, not Willful Commitment

Most executives see themselves as motivators of their managers. They coax and cajole, they seduce and incentivize, and they try to enthuse their managers to persuade them to engage in particular activities. Many leaders do these things quite well; they actually build up the motivation of their people and feel good as a result. But the perspective utterly changes when the focus shifts from intention to action. Many managers who are motivated to do something and achieve their goals do not actually make things happen. Leaders may create motivation but they rarely unleash the power of volition.

Helping people engage their willpower is a completely different process from motivating. Leadership that focuses on motivating managers is often superficial and even counter-productive. The same leadership practices that lead to high motivation often destroy the willpower of middle managers. To engage willpower behind particular projects or goals, leaders need to do precisely the opposite of what they typically do. They need to create a desire for action without encouraging superficial acquiescence.

They need to make commitment more difficult and build in barriers rather than trying to get quick buy-ins. They need to make their people consider conflicts, doubts, anxieties and emotional ambivalence. They need to tell them about difficulties, costs and privations rather then painting rosy pictures of the tasks.

Overall, leadership that counts on unleashing willpower is a much more difficult way of winning people over. But, it is much more effective and, in the end, less risky than motivating managers and counting on their half-hearted acceptance.

Organizations Can Be Designed to Support Volitional Action

Volition-supportive leadership involves more than a certain way of directly influencing managers. Unleashing managers' willpower also includes the task of creating an organizational context that does not suppress volitional action but leaves enough room and gives sufficient reason for it. Again, creating a volitional company is far from easy. Our observations show that executives who seriously foster managerial volition concentrate on a combination of three contextual principles: creating space for autonomous action; building processes for providing professional, social and emotional support; and developing a culture that fosters the exercise of responsible willpower.

To exercise their willpower, managers must have sufficient freedom to take action. To develop a sense of personal ownership, they must not only have the space to take action but also perceive and feel it. It is only within such space that their ability to take self-initiated and purposeful action comes into full force.[10]

The second principle is that the main benefits of organizational scale and diversity lie in the ability to support individual action. Our research indicates that managers need three forms of support to be able to exercise volitional action. First, they need supervisory support which is the central source of inspiration, intellectual stimulation, backing and encouragement. Second, they need personal relationships that provide both professional and emotional support. Professional support involves cooperative work as well as information or advice and is primarily problem-focused. Emotional support, on the other hand, plays an important role in coping with stress or negative feelings as well as for building up action-inducing emotions such as courage, pride and enthusiasm for the job.

Organizational structures and management processes by themselves, however, cannot create volitional action and sustain it over long periods of time. In most companies, the rhetoric of leaders emphasizes empowerment of people and celebrates autonomous action of managers. The reality, however, is often exactly the opposite. The third principle for designing the organization to facilitate volitional action, therefore, is to build a supporting culture. To unleash the willpower of their managers, leaders have to—and this is ultimately both the more difficult and the more important task—embed volitional behavior as a central element of the company's core values and habits. Ultimately, it is the culture, not structure, that stimulates and sustains a manager's courage to exercise choice and his or her ability to enjoy freedom.

While the requirements of autonomy, support and a volitional culture are pretty straight-forward, the challenge of effectively developing them lies in the tensions that exist across them. At the extreme, personal freedom and shared support are difficult to combine: highly autonomous managers focus only on their own goals and tasks and tend to be unwilling to share knowledge or resources with others, or to invest their own time and energy in helping others succeed. There are no quick-fixes for creating a volitional culture—it is the product of a long journey of continuously living and uncompromisingly demanding the values of action, willpower, and personal responsibility. Yet, these tensions can be reconciled but such reconciliation requires both an enormous amount of courage on the part of organizational leaders and persistent and patient work over long periods of time.

Organizational Energy Drives Persistent, Collective Action

In thinking about organization design and management, most senior leaders focus on the intellectual and cognitive dimensions: how decisions must be taken, how resources should be allocated, how strategies should be made, and so on. Few pay explicit attention to the emotional features of their organizations. Yet, the most important driver of organization-wide action is organizational energy—which, in turn, is also a manifestation of the organization's emotional state. To build the capacity for determined, persistent and collective action, a key leadership task is to create the force of strong, constructive energy in the company.

Many executives neglect this leadership task although most of them have experienced the decisive difference in the productivity and momentum of highly energetic companies compared to their inactive or inert counterparts. Many have seen the symptoms of a lack of organizational energy: apathy and inertia, tiredness, inflexibility and cynicism. And they know that highly energetic organizations can be ineffective if their energy turns corrosive: their force is invested in selfish or destructive actions. By contrast, some have experienced the momentum of positively energized organizations which have fully activated their potential in the pursuit of their business goals.

In our research we have found that leaders have two critical tasks in managing the energy of their companies. First, they must mobilize organizational energy and focus it on key strategic initiatives. We have discovered three different ways in which leaders can unleash and leverage the energy of their companies. The first, which we have labeled *killing the dragon* strategy, focuses the organization on a clear and unambiguous threat and channels the energy created in response to the threat to a highly disciplined process of executing concrete projects that would overcome the threat. The second way, which we describe as *winning the princess* strategy, creates energy by drawing the organization's attention to an exciting vision and enabling people to take self-initiated actions to pursue the dream. The third strategy combines these two approaches—essentially creating a vision the pursuit of which will also automatically involve dealing with short-term problems or challenges.

At the same time, we have also observed the fallacies of trying to continuously drive a company to higher and higher levels of energy. No organization can exist in a state of permanent acceleration. The second leadership task in managing organizational energy, therefore, is to sustain corporate vitality and momentum over long periods of time.

Leaders Must Create a Desire for the Sea

The French World War II pilot and philosopher Antoine de Saint-Exupéry wrote: "If you want to build a ship, don't drum up your men to go to the forest to gather wood, saw it, and nail the planks together. Instead, teach them the desire for the sea."

This metaphor reflects an enduring truth about willpower: Leaders must create in their people the capacity to dream. Most managers are prisoners of routines. They do not have the time to dream. Some lack the openness of mind necessary for visualizing an exciting future and the opportunities that may lie there. Others may dream but kill those dreams immediately because they cannot imagine stepping outside the cage of their daily habits. Indeed, through their own efforts to systematize things, senior leaders often reinforce habitual work and prevent their people from taking the first necessary step toward building collective commitment and organizational energy: the ability to develop ideas and the capacity to imagine.

There is no recipe for creating dreams: how can one find a formula for crafting a seductive picture in managers' hearts, a space for adventurous exploration? And yet, leaders can follow some general guidelines for allowing dreams to emerge. The first requirement is to provide some open space—not only to provide managers with the freedom to act but also to help them see and use that freedom. A second requirement is to provide people with a challenge—a difficult and stretching goal. Easy problems do not seduce or excite. Difficult challenges do.[11] Finally, leaders must make the goal personally meaningful to people. To inspire managers, a "desire for the sea" cannot be abstract or mundane; it must be subjectively meaningful and emotionally captivating.

Ultimately, what distinguishes human beings from almost all other species are two things—imagination and willpower. These two wonderful capacities have allowed the enormous progress that human society has forged over time. Corporate leaders have many resources at their disposal—money, technology, equipment—but none as valuable as their ability to use their own imagination and will, and enable others to do the same. As we move forward into the future, this is the task of the purposeful leader.

Notes

1. Eccles, Robert G., & Nohria, Nitin (1992), *Beyond the Hype*. Harvard Business School Press.
2. Pfeffer, Jeffrey, & Sutton, Robert I. (2000), *The Knowing-Doing Gap*. Harvard Business School Press.
3. See for example Kotter, John P. (1995), "Leading change: Why transformation efforts fail." *Harvard Business Review*, 73(2).
4. Mintzberg, Henry (1973), *The Nature of Managerial Work*. Harper Collins. Also see Colin P. Hales (1986), "What do managers do? A critical review of the evidence," *Journal of Management Studies*, 23(1).
5. See for example, Hallsten, L. (1993), "Burning out: A framework." In W. B. Schaufeli, C. Maslach, & T. Mazek, (Eds.), *Professional Burnout: Recent Developments in Theory and Research*. Taylor and Francis.
6. Rosemary Stewart (1967) suggested the framework of demands, constraints and choices in her book *Managers and Their Jobs*. Macmillan. See also her 1982 book *Choices for Managers*. Prentice Hall.
7. Narziss Ach's research showed that, before a person's intention could become a deep, personal commitment, he or she had to cross an emotional threshold. He distinguished motivation, the state of desire before crossing the threshold, from volition, the state beyond it, when the individual has converted the wish of motivation to the will of unwavering resolute engagement. See Narziss Ach (1935), *Analyse des Willens (Analysis of the Will)*. Urban and Schwarzenberg.
8. This three stage model of developing and sustaining volitional action-taking was proposed by Heinz Heckhausen and his colleagues. For one of the foundational pieces in this stream of work, see Heckhausen, Heinz, & Kuhl, J. (1985), "From wishes to action: The dead ends and short cuts on the long way to action." In M. Frese & J. Sabini, (Eds.), *The Concept of Action in Psychology*. Erlbaum.
9. Julias Kuhl and his colleagues have developed a theory of action control which identifies different strategies for shielding an intention during the process of enactment: See Kuhl, Julias, & Fuhrmann, A. (1998), "Decomposing self-regulation and self-control: The volitional components inventory." In J. Heckhausen and C. S. Dweck (Eds.), *Motivation and Self-Regulation Across the Lifespan*. Cambridge University Press. And Kuhl, Julias (1987), "Action control: The maintenance of motivational states." In F. Halish & J. Kuhl (Eds.), *Motivational Intention and Volition*. Springer.
10. See Deci, E. L., & Ryan, R. H. (1988), "The support of autonomy and the control of behaviour." *Journal of Personality and Social Psychology*, 53(6).
11. Only ambitious goals energize individuals and are likely to influence their will to enact intentions; goals that are considered "easy" are unlikely to do so: See E. A. Locke et al. (1984), "Effect of self-efficacy, goal and task strategies on task performance." *Journal of Applied Psychology*, 69(2). For a more detailed analysis, see Locke, E. A., & Latham, G. P. (1990), *A Theory of Goal Setting and Task Performance*. Prentice Hall.

Some Pros and Cons of Six Sigma

An Academic Perspective

Jiju Antony
Caledonian Business School

Introduction

Six Sigma is a business strategy that seeks to identify and eliminate causes of errors or defects or failures in business processes by focusing on outputs that are critical to customers (Snee, 1999). It is also a measure of quality that strives for near elimination of defects using the application of statistical methods. A defect is defined as anything which could lead to customer dissatisfaction. The fundamental objective of the Six Sigma methodology is the implementation of a measurement-based strategy that focuses on process improvement and variation reduction. A number of papers and books have been published showing the fundamentals of Six Sigma, such as, what is Six Sigma (Hoerl, 1998; Breyfogle III, 1999; Harry and Schroeder, 1999), why do we need Six Sigma (Snee, 2000; Pande et al., 2001), what makes Six Sigma different from other quality initiatives (Pyzdek, 2001; Snee and Hoerl, 2003), Six Sigma deployment (Keller, 2001; Adams et al., 2003), critical success factors of Six Sigma implementation (Antony and Banuelas, 2002), Six Sigma project selection process (Snee, 2002) and organizational infrastructure required for implementing Six Sigma (Adams et al., 2003; Snee and Hoerl, 2003).

I personally have experienced that senior management in many organizations view Six Sigma as another quality improvement initiative or flavor of the month in their list. I am often told by many engineers and managers, in small and big companies, that there is nothing really new in Six Sigma compared to other quality initiatives we have witnessed in the past. In response, I often ask a simple question to people in organizations who practice TQM, "What do you understand by the term TQM?" I often get many varying answers to this question. However if I ask a bunch of Six Sigma practitioners, "What do you know of the term Six Sigma?" I often get an answer which means more or less the same thing and concurs with what I would have expected. The following aspects of the Six Sigma strategy are not accentuated in previous quality improvement initiatives:

- Six Sigma strategy places a clear focus on achieving measurable and quantifiable financial returns to the bottom-line of an organization. No Six Sigma project is approved unless the bottom-line impact has been clearly identified and defined.

- Six Sigma strategy places an unprecedented importance on strong and passionate leadership and the support required for its successful deployment.

- Six Sigma methodology of problem solving integrates the human elements (culture change, customer focus, belt system infrastructure, etc.) and process elements (process management, statistical analysis of process data, measurement system analysis, etc.) of improvement.

- Six Sigma methodology utilizes the tools and techniques for fixing problems in business processes in a sequential and disciplined fashion. Each tool and technique within the Six Sigma methodology has a role to play and when, where, why and how these tools or techniques should be applied is the difference between success and failure of a Six Sigma project.

- Six Sigma creates an infrastructure of champions, master black belts (MBBs), black belts (BBs) and green belts (GBs), that lead, deploy and implement the approach.

- Six Sigma emphasizes the importance of data and decision making based on facts and data rather than assumptions and hunches! Six Sigma forces people to put measurements in place. Measurement must be considered as a part of the culture change.

- Six Sigma utilizes the concept of statistical thinking and encourages the application of well-proven statistical tools and techniques for defect reduction through process variability reduction methods (e.g. statistical process control and design of experiments).

Just like any other quality improvement initiatives we have seen in the past, Six Sigma has its own limitations. The following are some of the limitations of Six Sigma which create opportunities for future research:

- The challenge of having quality data available, especially in processes where no data is available to begin with (sometimes this task could take the largest proportion of the project time).

- In some cases, there is frustration as the solutions driven by the data are expensive and only a small part of the solution is implemented at the end.

- The right selection and prioritization of projects is one of the critical success factors of a Six Sigma program. The prioritization of projects in many organizations is still based on pure subjective judgment. Very few powerful tools are available for prioritizing projects and this should be a major thrust for research in the future.

- The statistical definition of Six Sigma is 3.4 defects or failures per million opportunities. In service processes, a defect may be defined as anything which does not meet customer needs or expectations. It would be illogical to assume that all defects are equally good when we calculate the sigma capability level of a process. For instance, a defect in a hospital could be a wrong admission procedure, lack of training required by a staff member, misbehavior of staff members, unwillingness to help patients when they have specific queries, etc.

- The calculation of defect rates or error rates is based on the assumption of normality. The calculation of defect rates for non-normal situations is not yet properly addressed in the current literature of Six Sigma.

- Due to dynamic market demands, the critical-to-quality characteristics (CTQs) of today would not necessarily be meaningful tomorrow. All CTQs should be critically examined at all times and refined as necessary (Goh, 2002).

- Very little research has been done on the optimization of multiple CTQs in Six Sigma projects.

- Assumption of a 1.5 sigma shift for all service processes does not make much sense. This particular issue should be the major thrust for future research, as a small shift in sigma could lead to erroneous defect calculations.

- Non-standardization procedures in the certification process of black belts and green belts is another limitation. This means not all black belts or green belts are equally capable. Research has shown that the skills and expertise developed by black belts are inconsistent across companies and are dependent to a great extent on the certifying body. For more information on this aspect, readers are advised to refer to Hoerl (2001). Black belts believe they know all the practical aspects of advanced quality improvement methods such as design of experiments, robust design, response surface methodology, statistical process control and reliability, when in fact they have barely scratched the surface.

- The start-up cost for institutionalizing Six Sigma into a corporate culture can be a significant investment. This particular feature would discourage many small and medium size enterprises from the introduction, development and implementation of Six Sigma strategy.

- Six Sigma can easily digress into a bureaucratic exercise if the focus is on such things as the number of trained black belts and green belts, number of projects completed, etc., instead of bottom-line savings.

- There is an overselling of Six Sigma by too many consulting firms. Many of them claim expertise in Six Sigma when they barely understand the tools and techniques and the Six Sigma roadmap.

- The relationship between cost of poor quality (COPQ) and process sigma quality level requires more justification.

- The linkage between Six Sigma and organizational culture and learning is not addressed properly in the existing literature.

- The "five sigma" wall proposed in Mikel Harry's book, *Six Sigma: The Breakthrough Management Strategy Revolutionizing the World's Top Corporations,* is questionable. Companies might redesign their processes well before even four sigma quality level. Moreover, it is illogical to assume that the "five sigma" wall approach is valid for all processes (manufacturing, service or transactional). Moreover, the decision of re-design efforts over continuous improvement depends on a number of other variables such as risk, technology, cost, customer demands, time, complexity, etc.

What Does the Future Hold for Six Sigma?

In my opinion, Six Sigma will be around as long as the projects yield measurable or quantifiable bottom-line results in monetary or financial terms. When Six Sigma projects stop yielding bottom-line results, it might disappear. I also feel that while Six Sigma will evolve in the forthcoming years, there are some core elements or principles within Six Sigma that will be maintained, irrespective of the "next big thing." One of the real dangers of Six Sigma has to do with the capability of black belts (the so-called technical experts) who tackle challenging projects in organizations. We cannot simply assume that all black belts are equally good, and their capabilities vary enormously across industries (manufacturing or service), depending a great deal on the certifying body. Another danger is the attitude of many senior managers in organizations that Six Sigma is "an instant pudding" solving all their ever-lasting problems.

I also believe that the Six Sigma toolkit will continue to add new tools, especially from other disciplines such as healthcare, finance, sales and marketing. Having a core set of tools and techniques is an advantage of Six Sigma that brings speed to fix problems and its ease of accessibility to black belts and green belts.

I would like to raise the point that Six Sigma does provide an effective means for deploying and implementing statistical thinking (Snee, 1990; 2002) which is based on the following three rudimentary principles:

1. All work occurs in a system of interconnected processes.
2. Variation exists in all processes.
3. Understanding and analyzing the variation are keys to success.

Statistical thinking can also be defined as thought processes, which recognize that variation is all around us and present in everything we do. All work is a series of interconnected processes, and identifying, characterizing, quantifying, controlling and reducing variation provide opportunities for improvement (Snee, 1990). The above principles of statistical thinking within Six Sigma are robust and therefore it is fair to say that Six Sigma will continue to grow in the forthcoming years. In other words, statistical thinking may be used to create a culture that should be deeply embedded in every employee within any organization embarking on Six Sigma programs. However the total package may change in the evolutionary process. It is important to remember that Six Sigma has a better record than total quality management (TQM) and business process re-engineering (BPR), since its inception in the mid–late 1980s. The ever-changing need to improve will no doubt create needs to improve the existing Six Sigma methodology and hence develop better products and provide better services in the future. As a final note, the author believes that companies implementing or contemplating embarking on Six Sigma programs should not view it as an advertising banner for promotional purposes.

Conclusion

Six Sigma as a powerful business strategy has been well recognized as an imperative for achieving and sustaining operational and service excellence. While the original focus of Six Sigma was on manufacturing, today it has been widely accepted in both service and transactional processes. This paper highlights the pros and cons of Six Sigma from the viewpoint of an academician. Although the total package may change as part of the evolutionary process, the core principles of Six Sigma will continue to grow in the future. Six Sigma has made a huge impact on industry and yet the academic community lags behind in its understanding of this powerful strategy. It will therefore be incumbent on academic fraternity to provide well-grounded theories to explain the phenomena of Six Sigma. In other words, Six Sigma lacks a theoretical underpinning and hence it is our responsibility as academicians to bridge the gap between the theory and practice of Six Sigma.

References

Adams, C., Gupta, P. and Wilson, C. (2003), *Six Sigma Deployment,* Butterworth-Heinemann, Burlington, MA.

Antony, J. and Bañuelas, R. (2002), "Key ingredients for the effective implementation of Six Sigma program," *Measuring Business Excellence,* Vol. 6 No. 4, pp. 20–7.

Breyfogle, F. W. III (1999), *Implementing Six Sigma: Smarter Solutions Using Statistical Methods,* John Wiley & Sons, New York, NY.

Goh, T. N. (2002), "A strategic assessment of Six Sigma," *Quality and Reliability Engineering International,* Vol. 18 No. 2, pp. 403–10.

Harry, M. J. and Schroeder, R. (1999), *Six Sigma: The Breakthrough Management Strategy Revolutionizing the World's Top Corporations,* Doubleday, New York, NY.

Hoerl, R. W. (1998), "Six sigma and the future of the quality profession," *Quality Progress,* Vol. 31 No. 6, pp. 35–42.

Hoerl, R. W. (2001), "Six sigma black belts: what do they need to know?" *Journal of Quality Technology,* Vol. 33 No. 4, pp. 391–406.

Keller, P. A. (2001), *Six Sigma Deployment,* Quality Publishing, Tucson, AZ.

Pande, P., Neuman, R. and Cavanagh, R. (2001), *The Six Sigma Way,* McGraw-Hill, New York, NY.

Pyzdek, T. (2001), *The Six Sigma Handbook: A Complete Guide for Greenbelts, Blackbelts and Managers at All Levels,* McGraw-Hill, New York, NY.

Snee, R. D. (1990), "Statistical thinking and its contribution to total quality," *The American Statistician,* Vol. 44 No. 2, pp. 116–21.

Snee, R. D. (1999), "Why should statisticians pay attention to Six Sigma?" *Quality Progress,* September, pp. 100–3.

Snee, R. D. (2000), "Impact of Six Sigma on quality engineering," *Quality Engineering,* Vol. 12 No. 3, pp. 9–14.

Snee, R. D. (2002), "The project selection process," *Quality Progress,* September, pp. 78–80.

Snee, R. D. and Hoerl, R. W. (2003), *Leading Six Sigma Companies,* FT Prentice-Hall, Upper Saddle River, NJ.

Further Reading

ASQ (1996), *Glossary and Tables for SQC,* Quality Press, Milwaukee, WI.

READING 11

Linking Goals to Monetary Incentives

Edwin A. Locke
University of Maryland

Every experienced executive knows the importance of rewarding good performance and also how difficult it is to design an incentive system that works as it is supposed to. A recent article in the *Wall Street Journal*[1] reported that Hewitt Associates found that 83 percent of companies with a pay-for-performance system said that their incentive plan was "only somewhat successful or not working at all."

Consider just some of the ideas that must be addressed in designing an incentive system:

- What should be the form of the incentive plan? That is, how, specifically, should pay be tied to performance?

- How do you keep employees from shortcutting or cheating in order to get their bonus?

- Which actions or outcomes should you pay bonuses for?

- What will be the effect of incentives on actions or outcomes that are not included in the incentive plan?

- How many different actions or outcomes can an employee actually manage?

- If more than one action or outcome is part of the plan, how should they all be combined or weighted?

- What do you do when market conditions change radically and make the incentive system ineffective or meaningless?

It is no accident that most companies constantly tinker with, and often radically overhaul, their incentive plans. Many can never seem to get it quite right. This article will try to provide some answers to the above questions, but I will start by addressing one fundamental issue. Hewitt's research indicates that one major cause of the failure of incentive plans is the lack of clear goals.

Goal-setting theory, as summarized by Gary Latham . . . , asserts that people must have goals that are both clear and challenging in order to motivate high performance. The question then arises: How do you combine goal setting with incentives?

I will describe four different methods and the pros and cons of each.

"Linking Goals to Monetary Incentives," Edwin A. Locke, *Academy of Management Executive,* Vol. 18, No. 4, 2004. Reprinted by permission of the Academy of Management via the Copyright Clearance Center.

Method 1: Stretch Goals with Bonuses for Success

This method involves assigning people difficult or stretch goals, giving them a substantial bonus if they reach them and no bonus if they do not. The respective advantages and disadvantages of this method include the following.

Pros

This method provides a strong incentive to attain the goals. There is a huge difference in reward between attaining the goals and failing, even by a small amount, to attain the goals. Further, it leaves no ambiguity about what is required of the person to receive the bonus.

Cons

A weakness of this method is ironically the result of its strength. Precisely because the motivation for goal attainment is so high, there is considerable temptation for the person to think short range, e.g., pile up excess inventory with customers (which will come back to haunt the company in the next quarter), take shortcuts (e.g., lower quality, ignore maintenance, increase risk), and cheat (e.g., exaggerate or make up totally fake results, cook the books) in order to receive the bonus.

To prevent these and other dysfunctional outcomes, the organization needs rules of conduct: ethical norms or standards that are clearly communicated and consistently enforced. The moral atmosphere or climate of an organization is set by the CEO and the senior management team, who must not only be impeccable role models but who must make certain that the company's ethical standards are strictly enforced (e.g., those who flout them must be fired). If the CEO and top managers are not personally honest, it leads to demoralization and cynicism among employees. This, in turn, can lead to a whole culture of dishonesty.

Another downside of this method is that performance which is very high but just misses the goal yields no bonus at all. This can be very demoralizing to competent, hard-working employees. It can lay the seeds for future dishonesty.

Method 2: Multiple Goal Levels with Multiple Bonus Levels

This method avoids some of the problems of method 1. Instead of a single goal level with the bonus being "all or none," there are multiple goal levels (for example, five), and a different bonus level is attached to each—the higher the goal level attained, the higher the reward.

Pros

There is less temptation for employees to shortcut or cheat here, because even if they do not attain the top goal level, they can get a bonus for making the next lower level. Highly competent employees who just miss a high-level goal still get rewarded.

Cons

Because there are multiple goal and bonus levels, employees may be less motivated to try for the highest level than in the case of method 1. A problem can occur if employees are content to try for the lowest goal level that is rewarded. For this bonus system to be effective, the CEO or senior management must set some minimum goal below which performance is considered inadequate. Then the multiple-goal level can start from a level above this minimum. However, this approach still does not push everyone to try for the highest goal. Furthermore, there is no tangible motivation to exceed the top goal because no further bonus would be forthcoming. Of course, pride and recognition are powerful motivators independent of money, but most employees want consistency between tangible and intangible rewards.

Method 3: A Linear System

This method is recommended by Michael Jensen of the Harvard Business School.[2] It is a variation on method 2, which involves increments. Consider five levels of sales goals, e.g., +5%, +10%, +15%, +20%, +25%. The employee who makes 24.5% will get rewarded, but only for reaching the 20% goal, so may still feel disappointed at coming close to, but just missing, the 25% goal. The simplest solution here is to make this a continuous bonus system, e.g., a 2% bonus for every 1% increase in sales. (Obviously 1% is still an increment but a very small one.)

Pros

This method eliminates two disadvantages of methods 1 and 2. First, there is no "loss" for getting close to a higher goal level and just missing it; an employee gets paid for exactly what is achieved. This, according to Jensen, further decreases the temptation to cheat or take shortcuts. Second, there is no upper limit on the bonus. Under methods 1 and 2 if a person attained the top goal for an increase in sales (say 25%), the employee would get the same bonus even if that person achieved a +50% or +100% sales increase. So there would be little tangible incentive to exceed +25%. Under method 3, however, if the person gets a 50% sales increase, the bonus would be 2 × 50% or 100%.

Cons

There is still the problem inherent in method 2: less pressure for the employee to "stretch." Setting a minimum goal would help as with method 2, but many people might not be financially motivated to go far beyond the minimum. Also some companies could have a problem with unlimited compensation for employees; it might seem unfair to people in other parts of the company (e.g., non-sales jobs) where a meaningful linear system would be hard to design.

Method 4: Motivate by Goals but Pay for Performance

This method, suggested by Gary Latham of the Rotman Business School (University of Toronto), makes the tie between goals and performance a little looser than under the other methods. The employee is given specific, challenging goals, but the decision about bonus awards is made after the fact so as to take account of the full context in which the goal is pursued. The relevant context factors might include, e.g., how much was actually achieved regardless of what the goals were, how the company as a whole did, how difficult the goals *really* were, in the light of such factors as resources, obstacles, and market conditions, as well as the methods the employee used to attain the goals (e.g., ethical behavior). Often the bonus decisions will be made by a management team because they may have more knowledge than any one executive.

Pros

The main benefit of this method is its flexibility and comprehensiveness. For example, an employee who tries for a hard goal under very difficult circumstances but does not quite reach it can still be well rewarded, whereas an employee who attains an allegedly hard goal which turned out not to be so hard in hindsight would get less (or be penalized or fired if the goal was attained unethically). This method, of course, is similar to what is called "merit based pay," but it would require that clear goals be set for every action or outcome that was important to the organization.

Cons

This method requires the boss to be knowledgeable about the full context and also to be objective in order to minimize favoritism or bias. Many people at the CEO and top-management levels lack these qualities. Of course, with poor quality leadership, the other incentive plans may not work either, because no method is better than the people who use it.

Which Method Is Best?

To the author's knowledge, there have been no published field studies or laboratory experiments comparing the effectiveness of the four systems described above or even comparing any two of them. Thus there is no basis for claiming that one is necessarily better than others. Much may depend on the nature of the business and the quality of the management. This topic is ripe for further study and experimentation.

Observe . . . that GE decided to make a distinction between goals that were absolutely essential to the organization and goals that were not. Stretch goals, which allowed credit for failure, were used mainly in the latter case. This implies that different incentive rules could be applied to each type of goal.

Cheating or shortcutting can occur under any incentive system; thus, as noted earlier, all companies need a strict (and enforced) code of ethics and well-designed control systems. (GE was known for having excellent control systems.)

What Activities Should Goals Be Set For?

For whatever is important. This will certainly involve performance outcomes and often goal-setting for the critical actions that lead to those outcomes. For example, sales, specifically repeat sales, depend on customer satisfaction, and there are specific actions that can be taken to satisfy customers (e.g., on-time delivery, high-quality products, changing policies as a result of customer feedback, etc.). Customer satisfaction is a "soft" measure, yet it can be measured quantitatively. Information-sharing with other managers, executives, employees, and so forth is another desirable action that often can benefit the entire company. Information-sharing could be measured by means of peer assessments. Developing subordinates is another important activity required for long-term organizational success.

It is possible to make causal maps that show the relationship between behaviors and outcomes. Consider this example: knowledge sharing within the company and with customers Æ improved customer service and better products Æ improved customer satisfaction Æ improved customer retention and sales Æ increase in profits. Note that goals can be set for any part or all parts of this sequence. Observe also that the benefit of the causal map is that it forces one to formulate the plan for improving the final outcome: profits. The causal inputs constitute a plan.

Actions and outcomes for which goals are not set and which are not rewarded monetarily will probably get minimum attention unless they are causally connected to the actions and outcomes that are measured and rewarded. A poorly devised bonus system can create "tunnel vision"—a focus only on what gets rewarded to the neglect of other important outcomes. Of course, bonus systems are *supposed* to focus attention and effort in a certain direction to the exclusion of others. Thus it is critical to do a lot of thinking about which actions and outcomes are important before creating a goal and reward system.

How Many Goals Should There Be?

It is important to avoid cognitive overload. No one manager, for example, could make good progress toward achieving 17 different goals, unless most of them could be delegated, nor would the manager even have the time to track progress. One person alone could probably handle somewhere between three and seven goals, depending on how difficult and complex they were and how much time was allowed for completion.

If employees are trying to achieve multiple goals, this presents a problem with respect to designing the reward system. *Ideal reward systems are simple,* and the simplest system has only one rewarded outcome or goal. The problem is that a one-goal system is usually too narrow in scope for a job. When a one-goal system is not adequate, there is an advantage to method 4, since it can take account of as many goals as the boss or top-management team considers relevant. If methods 1, 2, or 3 are used with multiple goals, then the goals have to be weighted in terms of importance.

Goal Integration

In any organization virtually everything that happens affects everything else, for better or for worse. Ideally, goals should be integrated across the entire organization, but this is usually impossible due to time constraints. However, through knowledge sharing within and across organizational levels and departments, it is possible to coordinate essential activities (e.g., sales, marketing, and production all need to be involved if a new product is contemplated). Such coordination is what cross-functional teams are designed to achieve.

Goal integration, including knowledge sharing, may be facilitated if part of the bonus is paid on the basis of peer ratings of knowledge sharing and/or on how well the company as a whole does.

Should Goals Be Changed When Conditions Change?

If goals are changed constantly (e.g., every three months), the danger is that no one will take them seriously. But if the strategic direction of a company changes, the goals need to reflect such changes. For example, when Jack Welch decided that GE would embrace the Six Sigma quality-control process, every executive was given goals to train employees in Six Sigma principles and to initiate Six Sigma projects. Bonuses were based, in part, on performance in relation to those goals.

What if the economy or industry turns bad? At Nucor, plant workers get paid by team productivity. If steel demand goes down, they get paid less. The same principle holds for Nucor's plant managers and executives. In some years profits drop, and no bonuses are distributed. Nucor's philosophy is: Why should plant employees and executives get bonuses when the stockholders are losing money? At Nucor they have to tough it out until business increases. A business downturn could be a signal to develop better business strategies, to cut costs, and to set new goals.

The Effective Incentive System

Effective bonus plans are extraordinarily difficult to set up and to maintain. It has been said that it is better to have no bonus system at all, other than simply merit pay, than to have a bad one. Bad incentive plans encourage people to do the wrong things in the wrong way, and they lead to cynicism, anger, and indifference. The first step that should be taken when considering setting up a bonus system is to ask: What do we really want people to do or accomplish? As Steve Kerr, a former GE executive, said many years ago, there is no point in rewarding A if what you want is B.[3] This issue probably takes more thought than any other aspect of an incentive system.

The second step is to set goals for desired outcomes. Make them clear and challenging. If needed, include goals for the actions that lead to the desired outcomes and not just the outcomes themselves. Make sure the number of goals assigned is doable. And do not change the goals too readily.

The third step is to consider which goals will need to be integrated within and across levels and divisions.

The fourth step is to pick the type of bonus system that is right for your company considering what you came up with in the first three steps, with full awareness of all the pros and cons of each method.

Following these steps will not guarantee that you will devise a successful bonus system, but it will definitely increase the odds.

Endnotes

[1]Chu, K. Firms report lackluster results from pay-for-performance plans. *Wall Street Journal,* 15 June 2004: D-1.
[2]Jensen, M. 2002. Paying people to lie: The truth about the budgeting process. Harvard Business School Working Paper 01-072.
[3]Kerr, S. 1995. On the folly of rewarding A, while hoping for B. *Academy of Management Executive,* 9(1): 7–14.

The Seven Habits of Spectacularly Unsuccessful Executives

Sydney Finkelstein
Dartmouth College

The past few years have witnessed some admirable business successes—and some exceptional failures. Among the companies that have hit hard times are a few of the most storied names in business—think Arthur Andersen, Rubbermaid and Schwinn Bicycle—as well as a collection of former high flyers like Enron, Tyco and WorldCom. Behind each of these failures stands a towering figure, a CEO or business leader who will long be remembered for being spectacularly unsuccessful.

The truth is, it takes some special personal qualities to be spectacularly unsuccessful. I'm talking about people who took world-renowned business operations and made them almost worthless. What's remarkable is that the individuals who possess the personal qualities that make this magnitude of destruction possible usually possess other, genuinely admirable qualities. It makes sense: Hardly anyone gets a chance to destroy so much value without demonstrating the potential for creating it. Most of the great destroyers of value are people of unusual intelligence and talent who display personal magnetism. They are the leaders who appear on the covers of *Fortune* and *Forbes*.

Still, when it comes to the crunch, these people fail—and fail monumentally. What's the secret of their destructive powers? After spending six years studying more than 50 companies and conducting some 200 interviews, I found that spectacularly unsuccessful people had seven characteristics in common. Nearly all of the leaders who preside over major business failures exhibit four or five of these habits. The truly gifted ones exhibit all seven. But here's what's really remarkable: Each of these seven habits represents a quality that is widely admired in the business world. Business not only tolerates the qualities that make these leaders spectacularly unsuccessful, it celebrates them.

Here, then, are seven habits of spectacularly unsuccessful people, along with some warning signs to look out for. These habits are most destructive when a CEO exhibits them, but any manager who has these habits can do terrible harm—including you. Study them. Learn to recognize them. And try to catch these red flags before spectacular failure finds you!

Habit #1: They See Themselves and Their Companies as Dominating Their Environment

This first habit may be the most insidious, since it appears to be highly desirable. Shouldn't a company try to dominate its business environment, shape the future of its markets and set the pace within them? Yes, but there's a catch. Unlike successful leaders, failed leaders who never question their dominance fail to realize they are at the mercy of changing circumstances. They vastly overestimate the extent to which they actually control events and vastly underestimate the role of chance and circumstance in their success.

CEOs who fall prey to this belief suffer from the illusion of personal preeminence: Like certain film directors, they see themselves as the *auteurs* of their companies. As far as they're concerned, everyone else in the company is there to execute their personal vision for the company. Samsung's CEO Kun-Hee Lee was so successful with electronics that he thought he could repeat this success with automobiles. He invested $5 billion in an already oversaturated auto market. Why? There was no business case. Lee simply loved cars and had dreamed of being in the auto business.

Warning Sign: A Lack of Respect

Leaders who suffer from the illusion of personal pre-eminence tend to believe that their companies are indispensable to their suppliers and customers. Rather than looking to satisfy customer needs, CEOs who believe they run pre-eminent companies act as if their customers were the lucky ones. When asked how Johnson & Johnson lost its seemingly insurmountable lead in the medical stent business, cardiologists and hospital administrators pointed to the company's arrogance and lack of respect for customers' ideas. Motorola exhibited the same arrogance when it continued to build fancy analogue phones, rather than the digital variety its customers were clamoring for.

Habit #2: They Identify So Completely with the Company That There Is No Clear Boundary between Their Personal Interests and Their Corporation's Interests

Like the first habit, this one seems innocuous, perhaps even beneficial. We want business leaders to be completely committed to their companies, with their interests tightly aligned with those of the company. But digging deeper, you find that failed executives weren't identifying too little with the company, but rather too much. Instead of treating companies as enterprises that they needed to nurture, failed leaders treated them as extensions of themselves. And with that, a "private empire" mentality took hold.

CEOs who possess this outlook often use their companies to carry out personal ambitions. The most slippery slope of all for these executives is their tendency to use corporate funds for personal reasons. CEOs who have a long or impressive track record may come to feel that they've made so much money for the company that the expenditures they make on themselves, even if extravagant, are trivial by comparison. This twisted logic seems to have been one of the factors that shaped the behavior of Dennis Kozlowski of Tyco. His pride in his company and his pride in his own extravagance seem to have reinforced each other. This is why he could sound so sincere making speeches about ethics while using corporate funds for personal purposes. Being the CEO of a sizable corporation today is probably the closest thing to being king of your own country, and that's a dangerous title to assume.

Warning Sign: A Question of Character

When it comes right down to it, the biggest warning sign of CEO failure is a question of character. We might want to believe that leaders at companies like Adelphia, Tyco and ImClone were trustworthy stewards of those companies, but their behavior suggests otherwise. But questions about character need not be limited to dubious or unethical acts. In fact, most leaders I studied were scrupulously honest. Rather, it is denial and defensiveness that are the critical warning signs. As Tony Galban, a D&O underwriter at Chubb, told me, "Always listen to the analysts' calls because that gives you a sense of how an individual thinks on their feet. They give you a sense of whether they're in denial or whether they're being professional." It gets down to this: Do you really trust this person?

Habit #3: They Think They Have All the Answers

Here's the image of executive competence that we've been taught to admire for decades: a dynamic leader making a dozen decisions a minute, dealing with many crises simultaneously, and taking only seconds to size up situations that have stumped everyone else for days. The problem with this picture is that it's a fraud. Leaders who are invariably crisp and decisive tend to settle issues so quickly they have no opportunity to grasp the ramifications. Worse, because these leaders need to feel they have all the answers, they aren't open to learning new ones.

CEO Wolfgang Schmitt of Rubbermaid was fond of demonstrating his ability to sort out difficult issues in a flash. A former colleague remembers that under Schmitt, "the joke went, 'Wolf knows everything about everything.' In one discussion, where we were talking about a particularly complex acquisition we made in Europe, Wolf, without hearing different points of view, just said, 'Well, this is what we are going to do.'" Leaders who need to have all the answers shut out other points of view. When your company or organization is run by someone like this, you'd better hope the answers he comes up with are going to be the right ones. At Rubbermaid they weren't. The company went from being Fortune's most admired company in America in 1993 to being acquired by the conglomerate Newell a few years later.

Warning Sign: A Leader without Followers

John Keogh, another big-time underwriter of D&O insurance, pointed out what he looks for when CEOs are being interviewed by analysts: "[Was] the management team incredibly arrogant? [Did the CEO or CFO] have all the answers and is [he or she] pretty [much] on top of his or her game?" CEOs who believe they have all the answers don't really need other people, except to do what they want them to do. One of the critical side effects of a CEO's fixation on being right is that opposition can go underground, effectively closing down dissent. As middle management begins to realize that their personal contributions aren't important, an entire organization can grind to a halt. When a leader's perspective and the management team's perspective drastically differ, take note. The difference in perception between Schmitt and his staff at Rubbermaid was striking, and was characteristic of many executives' predicament. He was a leader without followers.

Habit #4: They Ruthlessly Eliminate Anyone Who Isn't Completely behind Them

CEOs who think their job is to instill belief in their vision also think that it is their job to get everyone to buy into it. Anyone who doesn't rally to the cause is undermining the vision. Hesitant managers have a choice: Get with the plan or leave.

The problem with this approach is that it's both unnecessary and destructive. CEOs don't need to have everyone unanimously endorse their vision to have it carried out successfully. In fact, by eliminating all dissenting and contrasting viewpoints, destructive CEOs cut themselves off from their best chance of seeing and correcting problems as they arise. Sometimes CEOs who seek to stifle dissent only drive it underground. Once this happens, the entire organization falters. At Mattel, Jill Barad removed her senior lieutenants if she thought they harbored serious reservations about the way that she was running things. Schmitt created such a threatening atmosphere at Rubbermaid that firings were often unnecessary. When new executives realized that they'd get no support from the CEO, many of them left almost as fast as they'd come on board. Eventually, these CEOs had everyone on their staff completely behind them. But where they were headed was toward disaster. And no one was left to warn them.

CONVERSATIONS WITH MYSELF: SEVEN DISASTROUS THOUGHTS OF UNSUCCESSFUL LEADERS

Habit #1: "Our products are superior, and so am I. We're untouchable. My company is successful because of my leadership and intellect—I made it happen."

Habit #2: "I am the sole proprietor. This company is my baby. Obviously, my wants and needs are in the best interest of my company and stockholders."

Habit #3: "I'm a genius. I believe in myself and you should too. Don't worry, I know all the answers. I'm not micro-managing; I'm being attentive. I don't need anyone else, certainly not a team."

Habit #4: "If you're not with me, you're against me! Get with the plan, or get out of the way. Where's your loyalty?"

Habit #5: "I'm the spokesperson. It's all about image. I'm a promotions and public relations genius. I love making public appearances; that's why I star in our commercials. It's my job to be socially visible; that's why I give frequent speeches and have regular media coverage."

Habit #6: "It's just a minor roadblock. Full steam ahead! Let's call that division a 'partner company' so we don't have to show it on our books."

Habit #7: "It has always worked this way in the past. We've done it before, and we can do it again."

Warning Sign: Executive Departures

A revolving door at the top is one of the strongest signals that there has been executive failure at a company. Whether executives leave under "false pretenses," or are sent to some distant outpost where they'll have no further influence at headquarters, a pattern of executive departures speaks volumes for what is going on at a company. At Mattel, along with firing senior lieutenants on a moment's notice, Jill Barad drove six direct reports to resign for "personal reasons." The same thing has happened at Sun Microsystems over the last year. A mass exodus may be an indication that the CEO is out to eliminate any contrary opinions, or it may reflect inside information senior executives are acting on. In either case, it's a powerful warning sign. Analysts and many investors regularly track insider sales of stock, but executive departures may provide an even clearer window on the company. After all, what stronger statement can an executive make than to leave his or her job and the company entirely?

Habit #5: They Are Consummate Spokespersons, Obsessed with the Company Image

You know these CEOs: high-profile executives who are constantly in the public eye. The problem is that amid all the media frenzy and accolades, these leaders' management efforts become shallow and ineffective. Instead of actually accomplishing things, they often settle for the appearance of accomplishing things.

Behind these media darlings is a simple fact of executive life: CEOs don't achieve a high level of media attention without devoting themselves assiduously to public relations. When CEOs are obsessed with their image, they have little time for operational details. Tyco's Dennis Kozlowski sometimes intervened in remarkably minor matters, but left most of the company's day-to-day operations unsupervised.

As a final negative twist, when CEOs make the company's image their top priority, they run the risk of using financial-reporting practices to promote that image. Instead of treating their financial accounts as a control tool, they treat them as a public relations tool. The creative accounting that was apparently practiced by such executives as Enron's Jeffrey Skilling or Tyco's Kozlowski is as much or more an attempt to promote the company's image as it is to deceive the public: In their eyes, everything that the company does is public relations.

Warning Sign: Blatant Attention-Seeking

The types of behavior exhibited by Napoleonic CEOs tend to be so blatant that they can't be missed. Warning signs begin with the executive lifestyle—they may start to run with a very cool crowd, buy expensive art, and hobnob with political dignitaries and celebrities. The CEO will seem to spend more time with PR personnel and making public appearances than doing something as mundane as visiting customers. Other times, a company will build a striking new headquarters, designed to serve as a corporate symbol. In more extreme cases, the CEO will try to acquire the naming rights for a new sports arena or stadium.

Habit #6: They Underestimate Obstacles

Part of the allure of being a CEO is the opportunity to espouse a vision. Yet, when CEOs become so enamored of their vision, they often overlook or underestimate the difficulty of actually getting there. And when it turns out that the obstacles they casually waved aside are more troublesome than they anticipated, these CEOs have a habit of plunging full-steam into the abyss. For example, when Webvan's core business was racking up huge losses, CEO George Shaheen was busy expanding those operations at an awesome rate.

Why don't CEOs in this situation re-evaluate their course of action, or at least hold back for a while until it becomes clearer whether their policies will work? Some feel an enormous need to be right in every important decision they make, because if they admit to being fallible, their position as CEO might seem precarious. Once a CEO admits that he or she made the wrong call, there will always be people who say the CEO wasn't up to the job. These unrealistic expectations make it exceedingly hard for a CEO to pull back from any chosen course of action, which not surprisingly causes them to push that much harder. That's why leaders at Iridium and Motorola kept investing billions of dollars to launch satellites even after it had become apparent that land-based cellphones were a better alternative.

Warning Sign: Excessive Hype

One of the things we learned from the Internet bubble is the danger of hype, which can hide problems or mask intentions that, if known, would lead people to make different decisions. Simply stated: When something sounds too good to be true . . . it usually is. One of the best signs of a company relying on hype is the missed milestone. Whenever a company announces that its quarterly earnings are below forecast, the market reacts negatively to the news. Another important warning sign to look out for is when companies avoid looking at persuasive market data. When Barneys was planning its doomed geographic expansion, someone suggested that it do a market study to make sure that its offerings could work outside New York. CEO Bob Pressman thought the idea was ludicrous. "Market studies?" he exclaimed, incredulously. "Why do we have to do market studies? We're Barneys!"

Habit #7: They Stubbornly Rely on What Worked for Them in the Past

Many CEOs on their way to becoming spectacularly unsuccessful accelerate their company's decline by reverting to what they regard as tried-and-true methods. In their desire to make the most of what they regard as their core strengths, they cling to a static business model. They insist on providing a product to a market that no longer exists, or they fail to consider innovations in areas other than those that made the company successful in the past. Instead of considering a range of options that fit new circumstances, they use their own careers as the only point of reference and do the things that made them successful in the past. For example, when Jill Barad was trying to promote educational software at Mattel, she used the promotional techniques that had been effective for her when she was promoting Barbie dolls, despite the fact that software is not distributed or bought the way dolls are.

Frequently, CEOs who fall prey to this habit owe their careers to some "defining moment," a critical decision or policy choice that resulted in their most notable success. It's usually the one thing that they're most known for and the thing that gets them all of their subsequent jobs. The problem is that after people have had the experience of that defining moment, if they become the CEO of a large company, they allow their defining moment to define the company as well—no matter how unrealistic it has become.

Warning Sign: Constantly Referring to What Worked in the Past

When CEOs continually use the same model or repeatedly make the same decision, despite its inappropriateness, it can lead to significant failure. This type of thinking is often evident in the comments of senior executives who focus on similarities across situations while ignoring the sometimes more momentous differences. Take the case of Quaker Oats' acquisition of Snapple. Quaker paid $1.7 billion for Snapple, mistakenly assuming that the drink would be another smash hit like Gatorade. The beverage division president said things such as, "We have an excellent sales and marketing team here at Gatorade. We believe we do know how to build brands; we do know how to advance Snapple as well as Gatorade to the next level." Unfortunately, they didn't realize that Snapple was not a traditional mass-market beverage, but a "quirky, cult" drink. What's more, while Gatorade was distributed via a warehouse system, Snapple relied on family-run distributorships that had little interest in cooperating with Quaker. In 1997, Quaker sold Snapple for a paltry $300 million.

These seven habits of spectacularly unsuccessful people are powerful reminders of how organizational leaders are not only instruments of growth and success, but sometimes also architects of failure. That each of the habits has elements that are valuable for leaders only serves to point out how vigilant people who enter a leader's orbit must be, whether they are other executives, board members, lower-level managers and employees, regulators, or even suppliers, customers and competitors. In small doses, each of the habits can be part of a winning formula, but when executives overdose, the habits can quickly become toxic. That is a lesson all leaders and would-be leaders should take to heart.

Corporate Social Responsibility

Why Good People Behave Badly in Organizations

Pratima Bansal
University of Western Ontario

Sonia Kandola
University of Western Ontario

What Is Corporate Social Irresponsibility?

It is not difficult to identify socially irresponsible companies. Examples that come to mind easily include Enron, Arthur Andersen, Philip Morris and Union Carbide. In fact, it is much easier to identify firms that are irresponsible than those that are responsible. Most people agree that firms should operate within legal parameters and not knowingly harm stakeholders. Yet despite the risks and consequences, some firms still operate outside of these parameters. Take the cases of Enron and Arthur Andersen.

On Nov. 8, 2001, following the Securities and Exchange Commission's investigations into its accounting irregularities, Enron was forced to write down its earnings dating back to 1997 by 20 percent, and reduce its retained earnings by $2.2 billion (all currency in U.S. dollars). Enron had excluded its partnerships with Chewco and Joint Energy Development Investments from its consolidated financial statements. By keeping the $600-million debt associated with these partnerships off of the balance sheet, Enron had been able to maintain its strong credit rating and share price. It was clear, however, that this practice was improper; Enron had a large stake in these partnerships, and several senior Enron officials were part of their management.

This accounting practice clearly misled shareholders, analysts and creditors. Andrew Fastow, the ex-CFO of Enron, was accused of knitting together this complex web of transactions and earning about $30 million in management fees in addition to his Enron salary. He has been indicted by a federal grand jury on 78 counts of fraud, money laundering and conspiracy. Because of the erosion of investor and public confidence, Enron filed for bankruptcy on Dec. 2, 2001.

Arthur Andersen, Enron's auditors for over 16 years, should have caught this malpractice. Sherry Watkins, the Enron employee who brought the accounting irregularities to the attention of Kenneth Lay, Enron's then-CEO and a former Andersen employee, stated that "[Andersen] should have known what they were signing off." Outsiders have stated that the audit team, led by Andersen's Houston partner, David Duncan, should have questioned the exclusion of the partnerships from the beginning. Why it didn't is open to speculation, but the matter of conflict of interest is inevitably raised; Andersen earned $25 million in revenues for auditing Enron and $27 million in revenues for consulting. Its actions have led to a criminal charge for obstructing justice and to the sale of its foreign branches and non-tax divisions.

Enron's and Arthur Andersen's actions were unquestionably irresponsible. It is important to ask, then, what caused such behavior and disregard for ethical principles. We discuss those causes in this article.

Why Firms Act Irresponsibly: The Role of Individuals

For organizations to act irresponsibly, individuals must act irresponsibly. When individual irresponsible actions become systemic and significant, the problem then becomes an organizational one. The fact that some people in organizations act irresponsibly is not surprising. While most people resist the temptation to become involved in illegitimate activities, some inevitably succumb.

While it is possible to understand why some individuals act badly, it is more difficult to explain why other individuals, especially senior management, condone or even become involved in such actions, especially given that the consequences are often serious and can lead to the company's failure. After all, everything that we know about good leadership suggests that leaders must demonstrate integrity.

In the case of Arthur Andersen, the behavior of senior management, David Duncan and his audit team all contributed to organizational failure. It was clear that Duncan benefited financially from managing the lucrative and prestigious Enron account, though he did seem to have some misgivings about Enron's accounting irregularities. In 1997, Andersen appointed Duncan to be its lead partner for Enron's global engagement; in addition, as the firm's lead partner on the Enron audit, he was responsible for all of the accounting team's decisions.

Managing the account proved challenging for Duncan. He continued to uncover accounting irregularities and brought these to the attention of Andersen's professional standards board. However, Enron management and Andersen's senior managers pressured him to accept the accounting practices, likely because of the revenues generated from the audit and non-audit work. Once the SEC had uncovered Enron's misdemeanors and the spotlight had moved to Arthur Andersen, Duncan sent an e-mail message to his staff that he knew would result in the destruction of documents that the SEC would soon request. On May 13, 2002, although he knew that his confession could lead to a sentence of 10 years in prison, and that Arthur Andersen would be held criminally liable, Duncan admitted to obstructing justice. During these proceedings, several people indicated that they were aware of the accounting irregularities but could nevertheless not curb the malpractice.

Why Good People Behave Badly in Organizations: The Perspective of Social Psychology

Psychologists often argue that our personality traits or dispositions govern our behavior. In other words, people act in similar ways in different situations. While our dispositions are formed by socialization, some may be genetically coded. It could be argued, then, that if people are honest and trustworthy in their personal life, they will be so in their professional life. However, considerable research shows that situational factors are more relevant than personal dispositions in explaining individuals' actions. People who act responsibly in one situation may act irresponsibly in another because of the context in which their actions occur. Just what is it about the organizational context that can lead good people to behave badly? Social psychologists have looked for answers.

Consider the situation of Kitty Genovese, a 28-year-old woman who was murdered in Queens, N.Y., in 1964. Thirty-eight witnesses watched the assault. The assailant returned to the scene of the crime three times over a period of 30 minutes, but it was not until the final stabbing that an observer finally called the police; they arrived within two minutes. The community was shocked that not one of the 38 witnesses had attempted to stop the killing. This behavior, commonly called the "bystander effect," was explained by researchers John Darley and Bibb Latané, who found that people have a tendency to not intervene in emergency situations. In fact, the more bystanders there are, the longer it takes for someone to intervene. Extending the research of Darley and Latané, we suggest three ways in which the bystander effect can explain how individual actions contribute to corporate social irresponsibility.

Watching Other Bystanders

Individuals are guided in their behavior by observing other bystanders. They may be aware that the individuals they are observing are acting irresponsibly, yet they may do nothing to intervene because they assume that keeping silent is the norm. The more people, especially senior management, who are aware of the situation, the longer the irresponsible practices will continue. In the case of Arthur Andersen, most of the audit team was likely aware of the accounting irregularities, and the anomalies were reported to the firm's professional standards board. Yet ironically, as more people became aware of the situation, it became less likely that something would be done, because the actions were seemingly deemed acceptable by the organization.

The Ambiguity of Irresponsible Actions

Second, the ambiguity contributes to bystander apathy. If it is not absolutely clear that the action is unacceptable, or it is not clear who is responsible for resolving the problem, the issue is less likely to be addressed. It is ultimately the responsibility of the CEO to ensure that the firm operates within legal parameters, but if an infraction is not addressed, there will inevitably arise much uncertainty about when it occurred, how serious it is, and whether it is illegal or just bad practice. If ambiguity exists, employees will often continue to engage in the irresponsible practice, not admitting that there really is a problem.

In the case of Arthur Andersen, David Duncan and the audit team may have initially been uncertain about the seriousness of the problem. As evidence mounted about the accounting irregularity, Duncan attempted to reduce the ambiguity by taking it to Andersen's professional standards board. Given that the board did not rule that the practices should be discontinued, the acceptability of the situation continued to remain an unanswered question.

Diffused Responsibility

Responsibility for addressing ethical issues is diffused among the people involved in the situation. In larger organizations, responsibility for bad organizational behavior lies with all employees, so it is assumed that everyone in the organization will share the consequences of irresponsible actions—despite the fact that only a few individuals may be rewarded. David Duncan earned $700,000 in the year prior to his indictment, and Andersen's senior management profited even more from the lucrative audit and non-audit contracts with Enron. These individuals had little incentive to expose the scandal. Those that did not profit likely did not believe it was their responsibility to report the problem or did not know to whom they should go.

Consequences of Irresponsible Actions

Most of us would like to believe that we would not behave irresponsibly in organizations. Yet, there is considerable evidence to suggest that many people just like us do behave irresponsibly. At some time or other, every general manager will likely be placed in a situation requiring them to decide whether to engage in a practice that compromises what they deem to be acceptable. If they make the wrong choice, there are consequences for the individual and the organization.

Employee Commitment and Turnover

First, and maybe most importantly, employees who engage in irresponsible actions, or merely stand by watching, often experience guilt and anxiety. These feelings could influence their relationships with their staff, colleagues and family members. Ultimately, the commitment of these employees to the organization will wane, leading to poor personal performance and, potentially, their departure.

Corporate Norms

Second, employees who act irresponsibly will likely influence those around them. Those who observe the behavior start to treat it as the norm. Irresponsible actions often beget further irresponsible actions, which can cause a contagion of irresponsibility.

While individuals initiate irresponsible actions, it is the organization that will ultimately be labeled as socially irresponsible, especially as the number of actions and degree of harm mount. While a few isolated incidents may be blamed on individuals, the legitimacy of the organization will be challenged as the number of bystanders increases or the actions become systemic. The share price of such firms experiences greater volatility, and ultimately, the organization may fail, as was the case with Enron and Arthur Andersen.

Preventing Corporate Social Irresponsibility

Two conditions are necessary to prevent corporate social irresponsibility: a set of strong and consistent organizational values that espouse corporate social responsibility, and employee empowerment that permits and encourages individuals to express their concerns to senior management.

Organizational Values

Organizations need to adhere to a set of values that dictate appropriate individual actions. These values establish a framework for what is considered to be acceptable

ENRON'S VALUES

Communication

We have an obligation to communicate. Here, we take the time to talk with one another . . . and to listen. We believe that information is meant to move and that information moves people.

Respect

We treat others as we would like to be treated ourselves. We do not tolerate abusive or disrespectful treatment.

Integrity

We work with customers and prospects openly, honestly and sincerely. When we say we will do something, we will do it; when we say we cannot or will not do something, then we won't do it.

Excellence

We are satisfied with nothing less than the very best in everything we do. We will continue to raise the bar for everyone. The great fun here will be for all of us to discover just how good we can really be.

within the organization. Employees will often turn to these values to determine how they should act. As a result, the values must be clear and consistent. If the firm espouses shareholder wealth as an important value, it must be framed in the context of the firm's commitment to social responsibility. Further, it is important that the firm actually practices its values, rather than merely list them in the annual reports and elsewhere. The organization's actions must be framed in the context of the value statements, and all of the values must be exercised throughout the year. Activities that do not support those values must be stopped.

Ironically, Enron espoused a set of values that clearly articulated integrity (see box). It is clear that Enron articulated appropriate values, but did not exercise them. The company also did not provide a mechanism for employees to express their concerns, which is the second necessary condition to prevent corporate social irresponsibility.

Individual Concerns

Employee empowerment is necessary so that employees can express their concerns to senior management. Employees need to be able to voice ideas that support the organization's values or warn of violations. Individuals will naturally be concerned about issues that interest them personally, such as the impact of the firm's operations on the environment, or about an issue that has arisen on the job, such as the way in which a client's account is being handled. By enabling employees to express their concerns, the organization can prevent corporate social irresponsibility and instill responsibility.

Employees may perceive issues that others miss and issues that may have compromised the health and reputation of the organization. They will make those issues part of their own agenda and attempt to initiate corporate action. If the organization acts on those concerns, bystander apathy can be at least partially curbed. Such individual actions can take place at all levels of the organization, and will reflect well on the company as a whole.

Take, for example, Johnson & Johnson and its reaction to the Tylenol incident. Seven people died in the Chicago area in 1982 after reportedly taking Extra Strength Tylenol capsules. Because Johnson & Johnson suspected product tampering on store shelves, it could have chosen to deny responsibility, which was the financially prudent decision at that time. But, Johnson & Johnson's credo states:

We believe our first responsibility is to the doctors, nurses and patients, to mothers and fathers and all others who use our products and services. In meeting their needs we must do everything of high quality.

The CEO, James Burke, used the credo to govern the company's response to the crisis. To reflect its concern for consumers of the Tylenol brand, Johnson & Johnson recalled more than 31 million bottles of the drug at a cost of more than $100 million. The speed with which Johnson & Johnson addressed the issue serves as an example of a company standing firmly by the values it espouses. Although the crisis could have destroyed the Tylenol brand, sales of the product rebounded after an initial loss to capture more than its original 32 percent market share of over-the-counter pain medication. These actions are typical of decision-making at Johnson & Johnson, which first enunciated its credo in 1943. The firm has a strong tradition of developing products and policies that positively influence its consumers, employees, communities and, ultimately, its shareholders.

From Irresponsibility to Responsibility

The practice of developing a strong organizational value system while giving employees and management the opportunity to express their concerns not only prevents corporate social irresponsibility; it promotes corporate social responsibility. Corporate social responsibility is defined as meeting the needs or expectations of all stakeholders. Employees provide a window into what stakeholders desire. Employee relationships with customers, investors, suppliers, the local community and other employees give them insights into significant issues that should be addressed. Senior management needs to respond to the most significant issues that threaten the organization's values.

By implementing easy actions that fit with organizational values and address the concerns of a large number of employees, the organization will build commitment. For example, Xerox encourages all employees to participate in Earth Day activities. Such activities fuel personal initiatives because people attach environmental concerns to their daily activities. The organization also has a mechanism that enables employees to suggest ways in which environmental initiatives can extend to organizational-level actions. Through these initiatives, Xerox has shown leadership in its response to environmental issues.

The corporate accounting scandals in recent years are notable for the bystander apathy that permitted widespread and significant accounting irregularities. The resulting corporate failures have underlined the importance of keeping corporate social irresponsibility in check. By subscribing to a set of consistent organizational values that attempt to safeguard both financial and social performance, and by empowering and enabling employees to articulate their concerns, organizations can prevent corporate social irresponsibility, and promote responsibility.

Good Governance and the Misleading Myths of Bad Metrics

Jeffrey Sonnenfeld
Yale School of Management

In the aftermath of the well-publicized corruption and malfeasance in several large public corporations, especially at the executive and board levels, investors and analysts are searching for management tools to measure the vulnerability of firms to dishonesty, fraud, and corruption. While this effort to improve governance through uniform guidelines is understandable, at times boards and companies are reaching out for any life preserver that comes along. Some firms are capitalizing on this desperation by setting themselves up as corporate governance experts. In 1999, when William Donaldson was chairman of Aetna, he said prophetically, "I fear that there is a growing cottage industry of superficial thought about corporate governance."[1] The swelling number of governance consultants has made Donaldson's statement truer than ever. The vogue in the consulting world, in fact, is governance—supplanting business process reengineering, the "new economy," transformational leadership, diversity training, right-sizing, total quality management, and the like.

Some of what is being sold by the close to 100 governance training programs offered by consulting firms and universities is truly disturbing because it is often anchored more in clichés and myths than in careful research. In a recent review of academic studies on governance, the *Financial Times* suggested that many of the supposedly preventive practices advocated are not truly related to better performance and concluded, "Perhaps it is time the corporate governance activists came under the sort of scrutiny to which they subject listed companies."[2]

The Metrics Rating Services

The problematic nature of what is often being sold by commercial governance consultants is epitomized by the offerings of the powerful and feared governance metrics ratings services, the best known of which are Institutional Shareholder Services (ISS) and Governance Metrics International (GMI). While firms such as Moody's and The Corporate Library use a wide mix of criteria to evaluate companies, including their openly qualitative judgment, ISS and GMI rely more on crisp numerical scoring systems. Some even believe that it is dangerous for firms to challenge the influential ISS and GMI ratings services, given the attention paid to them by credit analysts, institutional portfolio managers, and liability underwriters.[3]

ISS and GMI look at public records to score firms on their governance effectiveness by using simplistic checklists of standards or metrics based heavily upon clichés and myths, rather than on genuine research. They also may cross the line from being independent raters to becoming active consultants for the firms they study in ways which lead to questions about their objective credibility. Finally and most importantly, their methods do not work; reliable, accurate governance ratings are not really produced despite all the charts and lists published. These three aspects of corporate governance ratings services—using evaluation standards based on Wall Street superstitions rather than research, potential conflicts of interest, and providing ratings that don't work—are discussed in the following sections.

Governance Expertise: Mixing Fact and Fiction in Measurement

Certainly the ratings services examine such worthwhile factors as financial disclosure, shareholder rights, related-party transactions, and executive compensation. These are sensible, research-supported dimensions to include in measures of the effectiveness of corporate governance.[4] But ISS and GMI blend these dimensions with superstitious ones to create checklists of highly stringent standards, regardless of the genuine research foundation to support them. They cite the collapsed firms of Enron and Worldcom as examples of poor governance without demonstrating how well these firms met many prominent structural dimensions of supposed good governance.

They perpetuate unfounded myths and clichés by downgrading firms for such reasons as failing to have a retirement age for directors and failing to separate the chairman and CEO roles. They claim that the downfall of many corporations has resulted from a lack of financial expertise on the board. Other reasons for poor ratings are failing to require that managers and directors have a formally set amount of equity holdings; prior history of service on boards of firms suffering financial distress; failure to have a formal retirement age, board size, and code of conduct; allowing a former CEO to serve on the firm's board; failing to have a separate chairman and CEO; and failing to have a supermajority of outside, independent directors. In sum, the ratings services evaluate the corporate governance of firms by mixing together empirically based standards and the myths and clichés of "the Street." Let us examine some of these myths and superstitions on which many corporations are measured, to see how wrong they can be.

The Structure Myth

One problem is that certain studies not actually showing a relationship between board structure and performance are often cited as justification for structural reform, while true structural studies do not find relationships that matter between structure and performance. While a frequently cited McKinsey study suggests that investors were willing to pay an 18 percent premium for a well-governed firm, such "good governance" was not defined in terms of any explicit board structure requirements.[5]

Millstein and MacAvoy studied the relationship between board independence and corporate performance to suggest that an active board made a difference. A board was deemed active if it met any one of the following criteria: (a) a non-executive chairman or lead director; (b) scheduled meetings of outside/independent directors without management present; or (c) substantial adherence to the well-known General Motors guidelines for corporate governance. This was thus not a study of the structural attributes of boards.[6] A recent study by Paul Gompers, Joy Ishii, and Andrew Metrick found that companies with strong shareholder rights had higher annual returns, profits, and sales growth than companies with weak rights. But again, though sometimes offered as substantiation for the need to reform board structure, this was not a study of structure.[7]

Finance studies by Sunil Wahal and Michael Smith suggest that even when shareholder activists have been able to change firm governance structures, the changes have not translated into improvements in operating performance.[8] Similarly, in research I have been doing with Sanjay Bhagat of Colorado and Dick Wittink of Yale on 1500 public companies, we are finding no support for a relationship between structural dimensions of board governance and company performance.

The Age Myth

There is no research suggesting that increased director age leads to impaired judgment. In fact, experience is often found to be advantageous in decision-making. Cognitive and developmental psychologists have mapped a strong correspondence between age, wisdom, and judgment on and off the job.[9] In particular, these studies have indicated an age-related strength in competency in the face of uncertainty and in perceiving others' intentions, as well as stronger communications skills. Term limits and age limits for board members are commonly discussed, but age-biased policies for board turnover lack genuine validation.

The Split CEO/Board Chairman Myth

The Conference Board recommended either splitting the CEO and chairman roles or using lead directors or presiding directors.[10] The metrics services also favor firms that divide these functions. And yet, many if not most of the highest-profile scandals in the US and Europe (e.g., Enron, Worldcom, Vivendi, Adecco, Royal Ahold, ABB, Manesmann, Deutsche Telecom) involved firms that had separated the CEO and chairman roles, but the split hardly prevented subsequent scandals. Accordingly, there is no research that has established a link between the split leadership roles and firm performance.

The Financial Expertise Myth

A recent advertisement I received suggested a higher level of financial literacy as the solution to governance crises such as those experienced at Enron, Worldcom, the New York Stock Exchange, and Freddie Mac, despite the fact that these and many other struggling and collapsed firms had boards dominated by wide-ranging financial wizards including Ph.D. academicians in finance. Insufficient financial expertise has rarely been the point of vulnerability for firms suffering from executive corruption. Despite Enron's good fortune in having on the board an accounting professor and former Stanford Business School dean along with international bankers, former financial market regulars, and current financial service firm leaders, they claimed not to have understood their firm's activities in international financial markets. Thus they initially named a tainted executive as the successor CEO until he was forced out by public pressure several months later.

Similarly, the Freddie Mac board included one of the world's leading financial economists, several prominent mortgage experts, and a former Big Four accounting firm CEO, yet still lacked confidence and felt compelled to nominate a knowingly tainted executive as CEO who better understood the mathematics of their market exposures.[11] He too was forced out by external pressure several months later. The Board of the New York Stock Exchange had twelve investment bankers, plus commercial bankers, mutual fund managers, and CEOs; yet they claimed they could not understand the finances of their own CEO compensation plan. Similarly, investor loss of trust in troubled mutual funds such as those of Strong Fund, Putnam, and Pilgrim Baxter did not occur because their boards lacked financial savvy.

The Director Equity Myth

One dimension or standard said to promote good governance is for directors to own significant amounts of stock in their firms, the thinking being that directors with an ownership stake will have a heightened incentive to govern well. There is research in support of this theory by Sanjay Bhagat, Dennis Carey, and Charles Elson.[12] In their study of 4874 directors from the 1994 proxies of 449 firms, their results showed a significant correlation between the amount of stock owned by individual outside directors and firm performance as well as an increased likelihood that CEOs would be terminated in poor-performing firms. Since this was not a longitudinal study, however, the findings are suggestive but do not prove causality.

Moreover, how much stock is enough, and does it matter if the policy is observed but not codified in a formal written mandate? Equity holdings by directors in firms such as Enron have been very high, with directors overseeing the loss of billions of dollars' worth of stock that they personally owned or controlled. Furthermore, many great firms, such as UPS, where the average director owns millions of dollars in company equity, just do not require arbitrary formal levels of equity holdings in written policies and consequently suffer in the ratings.

The Former CEO Myth

Some ratings firms downgrade boards if the former CEO remains on the board, the fear being that the person will exert undue influence and perhaps have a negative effect on the independence of the current CEO. On the contrary, a former CEO on the board can provide valuable "ambassadorial service"[13] as is seen today in Intel's Andy Grove, Southwest Airlines' Herb Kelleher, Jim Kelly of UPS, and Microsoft's Bill Gates. Rather than intimidate or collude with their successors, they serve as invaluable public spokespersons and private advisors to the new CEO.

The Independent Board Myth

While the stock exchanges call for a majority of independent directors, they do not call for "supermajorities" as the governance metrics firms generally do. In the aftermath of its own governance difficulties, in late 2003 the NYSE also recommended that its own board be independent from its management and members, and from listed companies. A common standard used by firms rating corporate governance suggests that having a supermajority of independent, outside members with only one or two inside directors is a step toward good governance. The conventional wisdom has come to be that an independent board is preferable to a board made up mainly of company insiders.

Although an independent board of directors has many advantages, it is clearly not a panacea. A board comprised mainly of inside members may have more knowledge of the business and more motivation to help it succeed. Several studies, such as those by Victor Dulewicz and Peter Herbert as well as by Sanjay Bhagat and Bernard Black, indicate that having larger numbers of non-executive directors may correspond with worse performance. According to Bhagat and Black, "There is no convincing evidence that greater board independence correlates with greater firm profitability or faster growth. In particular, there is no empirical support for current proposals that firms should have 'supermajority-independent boards' with only one or two inside directors. To the contrary, there is some evidence that firms with supermajority-independent boards are less profitable than other firms."[14] In fact, research by April Klein on all directors from S&P 500 firms suggested that affiliated directors are not puppets of management. She found a positive correlation between the percentage of insiders on board finance and investment committees and both stock market performance and return on investments.[15]

Outmoded Standards: Attendance, Size, and Others

Other dimensions frequently measured, such as director attendance, codes of conduct, board size, and number of other boards on which directors serve, rarely matter as much as they may have in the past. For example, in several troubled firms such as Enron, director attendance had been nearly perfect. Similarly, the findings of research on board size are contrary to the beliefs of governance reformers and metrics firms who advance a template favoring smaller boards. In fact, David Yermack's study of 452 large firms found that the complex associations with other variables such as firm growth make it unclear if board size corresponds with higher or lower market values. Similar studies by Dan Dalton and Catherine Daily could not support the thesis that smaller boards are better performing boards.[16]

Ethics and Independence: Conflicts of Interest

Reports in such publications as the *Wall Street Journal* and *Fortune* have revealed how market-leading metrics firm Institutional Shareholder Services sells governance consulting advice to investors and to corporate management as well as to some firms they also evaluate, ironically thus potentially compromising their own objectivity and independence.[17] If ISS sees what they believe to be an improper transfer of shareholder wealth in your compensation plan, you have to become their client to find out what they do not like, in order to improve your scores.

Their major competitor, GMI, tries to avoid such criticism by maintaining that it makes its money by advising investors and not management. GMI states on its website, "We will not provide corporate governance consulting services to any company that is part of our research universe. . . . To do so would in our opinion impinge on our reputation and credibility." However, on this website GMI also describes their Comprehensive Rating of governance practices in a way which may encourage rated firms to become clients. This Comprehensive Rating is a "level of review possible only at the invitation of the company, which is required to pay a fee to GMI." It would be hard to imagine that *Consumer Reports,* JD Power, or the Academy Awards could maintain their credibility as independent evaluators with similar practices.

Efficacy and Accountability: Do The Governance Metrics Work?

ISS claims to have created governance metrics "that allow investors to quickly and accurately identify the relative performance of companies." When ISS launched their Corporate Governance Quotient in the summer of 2002, they trumpeted their prior low rating of Adelphia and stated that investors could have used their metrics to be wary of this coming governance fiasco. However, they did not publish the fact that they gave high scores to firms where similar train wrecks subsequently occurred.

For example, according to the ISS analysis of HealthSouth, its governance in early 2003 outperformed 64.3 percent of S&P 500 companies and 92.3 percent of its industry peers—just months before its own massive scandals were revealed.[18] In fact, ISS's proprietary evaluation praised HealthSouth's specific governance features such as: a supermajority of independent outside directors, nominating and compensation committees comprised solely of independent outside directors, annual election of the full board, no former CEO of the company on its board, the CEO does not serve on more than two other boards, there are between nine and twelve directors on the board, and all directors attended at least 75 percent of the board meetings. Apparently measuring up well on so many structural dimensions advocated by ISS did not prevent the board's scandals. To the credit of ISS, they have begun to list top-ten performers in different size groupings with continual updating—but then of course that makes ISS accountability for past predictions tough to track.

Similarly, while competitor GMI's concerns over independence recently anticipated some serious governance problems at Adecco, their mistaken early 2003 positive assessments of such firms as Boeing, AMR, Merrill Lynch, Bristol-Myers, Delta, EDS, Citigroup, and Xerox as "Above Average" preceded the revelations of governance crises resulting in subsequent leadership changes and board overhauls of the qualities reviewed so highly by GMI. Their early 2003 "Average Ratings" of HealthSouth, Tenet Healthcare, and AOL all occurred just months before these companies generally made sweeping governance changes in response to the revelations of scandals and performance problems. Perhaps most disappointing of all were their "Below Average Ratings" of such widely admired, top-performing firms as Dell, Southwest Airlines, Wal-Mart, UPS, Starbucks, and eBay. Hopefully not too many investors or regulators relied upon these ratings as guidelines.

GMI has recently simply stopped publishing ratings on their website, thereby avoiding the same easy public accountability for significant miscalls. At about the same time, in September 2003 GMI released a "performance study" and heavily promoted it in the media, stating that they had found "a substantive link between investor-friendly governance practices and shareholder returns." Unfortunately, their study creates statistical confusion by comparing the handful of top-rated firms to 1500 others, resulting in problems of unmeasured within-group variance, regression toward the mean, and other distortions arising from comparing populations that are wildly unequal in size.[19]

The agreement between the ratings firms is not high nor are they always kind towards each other as evidenced by GMI's rating of Moody's, which also evaluates governance effectiveness. GMI protects itself by putting a disclaimer in its confidentiality agreement which states: "GMI makes no guarantees or warranties as to the accuracy or completeness of the GMI rating report or the overall rating or subcategory ratings." So much for confidence and accountability.

Some newer governance ratings firms such as The Corporate Library are making far more cautious claims about governance links to financial performance and are looking beyond simple public documents and governance clichés about board structure to examine actual governance conduct in making their assessments and have produced more accurate assessments.[20]

The Missing Ingredient: The Human Side of Governance

Such attempts at improving corporate governance procedures as new legal and accounting mandates and the use of metrics have addressed only part of the governance challenge. At least as important are the human dynamics of boards as social systems where leadership character, individual values, decision-making processes, conflict management, and strategic thinking will truly differentiate a firm's governance.[21] Can fellow directors be trusted? Does management provide the full story? Is there enough time for advance reading and full discussion of materials? Is dissent encouraged? Are people well prepared? Does management allow themselves to be vulnerable? How are board members kept accountable for their preparation and decisions? How is assessment conducted so board members can learn and improve? Wayne Cascio's "Executives Ask" article . . . on boards as social systems sheds light on some of these questions.

In 2003 former Aetna chairman William Donaldson, now Securities and Exchange Commission chairman, captured the essence of the problem with the emerging governance industry's laundry-list approach:

> Such a "check the box" approach to good corporate governance will not inspire a true sense of ethical obligation. It could merely lead to an array of inhibiting, "politically correct" dictates. Instead of striving to meet higher standards, corporations would only strain under new costs associated with fulfilling a mandated process that could produce little of the desired effect. They would lose the freedom to make innovative decisions that an ethically sound entrepreneurial culture requires. . . .
>
> [Determining criteria for corporate governance] is not a one-size-fits-all exercise . . . we should go slowly in mandating specific structures and committees for all corporations. . . . There are vast differences in the function, structure, and business mandate of the thousands of corporations struggling with the issues of good corporate governance. . . . there is no one answer to these hotly debated questions. . . . [22]

Endnotes

[1]Donaldson, W. Legend in Leadership Award remarks. Yale School of Management CEO Leadership Summit, 17 December 1999.

[2]*Financial Times.* Lex: Talking in codes. 30 December 2003, 19–23.

[3]Lashinsky, A. ISS wants business both ways: The firm that got its start serving shareholders is now catering to big business. *Fortune.* 3 June 2003, 12; Langley, M. ISS rates firms—and sells roadmaps to boosting score. *Wall Street Journal.* 6 June 2003, 1; Sonnenfeld, J. Meet our corporate governance watchdogs. *Wall Street Journal.* 11 March 2003, B-2.

[4]As an example of such research support, see la Porta, R., et al. 2000. Investor protection and corporate governance. *Journal of Financial Economics*, 58(1): 1–25.

[5]Coombes, P., & Watson, M. 2000. Three surveys on corporate governance. *McKinsey Quarterly*, 4: 74–77.

[6]Millstein, I., & MacAvoy, P. 1998. Active board of directors and performance of the large publicly traded corporation. *Columbia Law Journal,* June: 1283–1322.

[7]Gompers, P. A., Ishii, J., & Metrick, A. 2003. Corporate governance and equity prices. *Quarterly Journal of Economics,* 118(1): 107–155.

[8]Wahal, S. 1996. Pension fund activism and firm performance. *Journal of Financial and Quantitative Analysis,* March: 1–23; Smith, M. P. 1996. Shareholder activism by institutional investors: Evidence from CalPERS. *Journal of Finance,* 51(1): 227–252.

[9]Sonnenfeld, J. 1978. Dealing with an aging work force. *Harvard Business Review,* 56(6): 81–92. Reprinted in M. C. Gentile (Ed.). 1996. *Differences that work: Organizational excellence through diversity.* Cambridge, MA: Harvard Business Review; Birren, J. E., & Fisher, L. M. 1990. The elements of wisdom: Overview and integration. In R. J. Sternberg (Ed.), *Wisdom: Its nature, origins, and development.* New York: Cambridge University Press; Clayton, V. P., & Birren, J. E. 1980. The development of wisdom across life-span: A re-examination of an ancient topic. *Life-Span Development and Behavior,* 3: 103–125; Denney, N. W., Dew, J. R., & Kroupa, S. L. 1995. Perceptions of wisdom. *Journal of Adult Development,* 2: 37–47; Erikson, E. H. 1959. Identity and the life cycle. *Psychology Issues Monograph I.* New York: International University Press.

[10]The Conference Board. 2003. Commission on Public Trust and Private Enterprise Report, Part II. January.

[11]Sonnenfeld, J. 2003. Hit the road, Mac. *Wall Street Journal.* 26 August 2003, B-2.

[12]Bhagat, S., Cary, D., & Elson, C. 1999. Director ownership, corporate performance, and management turnover. *Business Lawyer,* 54(3): 45–61.

[13]Sonnenfeld, J. 1988. *The hero's farewell: What happens when CEOs retire.* New York: Oxford University Press.

[14]Dulewicz, V., & Herbert, P. 2003. Does the composition and practice of UK boards bear any relationship to the performance of listed companies? Henley Working Papers, 1861811586; Bhagat, S., & Black, B. 2002. Board independence and long-term performance. *Journal of Corporation Law,* 27: 231–273; Bhagat, S., & Black, B. 1999. The uncertain relationship between board composition and firm performance. *Business Lawyer,* 54: 921–963.

[15]Klein, A. 1998. Firm performance and board committee structure. *The Journal of Law and Economics,* 20: 493–502.

[16]Yermack, D. 1996. Higher market valuation of companies with a small board of directors. *Journal of Financial Economics,* 40: 185–211; Dalton, D., & Daily, C. 2000. Board and financial performance: Bigger is better. *Director's Monthly,* August; Dalton, D., et al. 1998. Meta-analytic reviews of board composition, leadership structure, and financial performance. *Strategic Management Journal,* 19 (3): 269–290.

[17]Lashinsky. A., & Langley, M. ISS rates firms—and sells roadmaps to boosting score. *Wall Street Journal.* 6 June 2003, 1; Sonnenfeld, J. Meet our corporate governance watchdogs. *Wall Street Journal.* 11 March 2003, B-2.

[18]From ISS records as acknowledged by ISS vice president Patrick McGurn, Tuesday October 21, 2003, Annual Meeting of the National Association of Corporate Directors, Washington DC.

[19]Brown, K. Weak boardrooms and weak stocks go hand in hand. *Wall Street Journal.* 9 September 2003, C-9.

[20]Langley. M. Big companies get low marks for lavish pay to executives. *Wall Street Journal.* 7 June 2003, C-1.

[21]Sonnenfeld, J. 2002. What makes great boards great. *Harvard Business Review,* 80(9): 106–113; Westphal, J. D., & Poonam, K. 2004. Keeping directors in line: Social distancing as a control mechanism in the corporate elite. *Administrative Sciences Quarterly,* forthcoming.

[22]Donaldson, W. H. 2003. Corporate governance: What has happened and where we need to go. *Business Economics,* 38(3). A transcript of an address at the national Association for Business Economics Washington Economic Policy Conference, March 24, 2003.

Endnotes

Chapter 1

[1]For a discussion of the different ways that companies can position themselves in the marketplace, see Michael E. Porter, "What Is Strategy?" *Harvard Business Review* 74, no. 6 (November-December 1996), pp. 65–67.

[2]W. Chan Kim and Renée Mauborgne, "Blue Ocean Strategy," *Harvard Business Review* 82, no. 10 (October 2004), pp. 76–84.

[3]See Henry Mintzberg and Joseph Lampel, "Reflecting on the Strategy Process," *Sloan Management Review* 40, no. 3 (Spring 1999), pp. 21–30; Henry Mintzberg and J. A. Waters, "Of Strategies, Deliberate and Emergent," *Strategic Management Journal* 6 (1985), pp. 257–272; Costas Markides, "Strategy as Balance: From 'Either-Or' to 'And,'" *Business Strategy Review* 12, no. 3 (September 2001), pp. 1–10; Henry Mintzberg, Bruce Ahlstrand, and Joseph Lampel, *Strategy Safari: A Guided Tour through the Wilds of Strategic Management* (New York: Free Press, 1998), chaps. 2, 5, and 7; and C. K. Prahalad and Gary Hamel, "The Core Competence of the Corporation," *Harvard Business Review* 70, no. 3 (May-June 1990), pp. 79–93.

[4]For an excellent treatment of the strategic challenges posed by high-velocity changes, see Shona L. Brown and Kathleen M. Eisenhardt, *Competing on the Edge: Strategy as Structured Chaos* (Boston: Harvard Business School Press, 1998), chap. 1.

[5]Joseph L. Badaracco, "The Discipline of Building Character," *Harvard Business Review* 76, no. 2 (March-April 1998), pp. 115–124.

[6]Joan Magretta, "Why Business Models Matter," *Harvard Business Review* 80, no. 5 (May 2002), p. 87.

[7]For a more in-depth discussion of the challenges of developing a well-conceived vision, as well as some good examples, see Hugh Davidson, *The Committed Enterprise: How to Make Vision and Values Work* (Oxford: Butterworth Heinemann, 2002), chap. 2; W. Chan Kim and Renée Mauborgne, "Charting Your Company's Future," *Harvard Business Review* 80, no. 6 (June 2002), pp. 77–83; James C. Collins and Jerry I. Porras, "Building Your Company's Vision," *Harvard Business Review* 74, no. 5 (September-October 1996), pp. 65–77; and Michel Robert, *Strategy Pure and Simple II* (New York: McGraw-Hill, 1998), chap. 2, 3, and 6.

[8]Davidson, *The Committed Enterprise,* pp. 20, 54.

[9]Ibid., pp. 36, 54.

[10]As quoted in Charles H. House and Raymond L. Price, "The Return Map: Tracking Product Teams," *Harvard Business Review* 60, no. 1 (January-February 1991), p. 93.

[11]The concept of strategic intent is described in more detail in Gary Hamel and C. K. Pralahad, "Strategic Intent," *Harvard Business Review* 89, no. 3 (May-June 1989), pp. 63–76; this section draws on their pioneering discussion. See also Michael A. Hitt, Beverly B. Tyler, Camilla Hardee, and Daewoo Park, "Understanding Strategic Intent in the Global Marketplace," *Academy of Management Executive* 9, no. 2 (May 1995), pp. 12–19.

[12]For a fuller discussion of strategy as an entrepreneurial process, see Mintzberg, Ahlstrand, and Lampel, *Strategy Safari,* chap. 5. Also see Bruce Barringer and Allen C. Bluedorn, "The Relationship between Corporate Entrepreneurship and Strategic Management," *Strategic Management Journal* 20 (1999), pp. 421–444, and Jeffrey G. Covin and Morgan P. Miles, "Corporate Entrepreneurship and the Pursuit of Competitive Advantage," *Entrepreneurship: Theory and Practice* 23, no. 3 (Spring 1999), pp. 47–63.

[13]The strategy-making, strategy-implementing roles of middle managers are thoroughly discussed and documented in Steven W. Floyd and Bill Wooldridge, *The Strategic Middle Manager* (San Francisco: Jossey-Bass, 1996), chaps. 2 and 3.

[14]For more discussion of this point, see Orit Gadiesh and James L. Gilbert, "Transforming Corner-Office Strategy into Frontline Action," *Harvard Business Review* 79, no. 5 (May 2001), pp. 72–79, and Kathleen M. Eisenhardt and Donald N. Sull, "Strategy as Simple Rules," *Harvard Business Review* 79, no. 1 (January 2001), pp. 106–116.

[15]For an excellent discussion of why a strategic plan needs to be more than a list of bullet points and should in fact tell an engaging, insightful, stage-setting story that lays out the industry and competitive situation as well as the vision, objectives, and strategy, see Gordon Shaw, Robert Brown, and Philip Bromiley, "Strategic Stories: How 3M Is Rewriting Business Planning," *Harvard Business Review* 76, no. 3 (May-June 1998), pp. 41–50.

[16]For a discussion of what it takes for the corporate governance system to function properly, see David A. Nadler, "Building Better Boards," *Harvard Business Review* 82, no. 5 (May 2004), pp. 102–105. See also Cynthia A. Montgomery and Rhonda Kaufman, "The Board's Missing Link," *Harvard Business Review* 81, no. 3 (March 2003), pp. 86–93; John Carver, "What Continues to Be Wrong with Corporate Governance and How to Fix It," *Ivey Business Journal* 68, no. 1 (September-October 2003), pp. 1–5; and Gordon Donaldson, "A New Tool for Boards: The Strategic Audit," *Harvard Business Review* 73, no. 4 (July-August 1995), pp. 99–107.

Chapter 2

[1]A large number of studies have examined the size of the cost reductions associated with experience; the median cost reduction associated with a doubling of cumulative production volume is approximately 15 percent, but there

is a wide variation from industry to industry. In semiconductors, strong *learning and experience* effects in manufacturing cause unit costs to decline about 20 percent each time *cumulative* production volume doubles. In other words, if the first 1 million chips cost $100 each to produce, by a production volume of 2 million chips costs would drop to $80 each (80 percent of $100), by a production volume of 4 million each chip would cost $64 to produce (80 percent of $80), and so on.

[2]The five-forces model of competition is the creation of Professor Michael Porter of the Harvard Business School. For his original presentation of the model, see Michael E. Porter, "How Competitive Forces Shape Strategy," *Harvard Business Review* 57, no. 2 (March-April 1979), pp. 137–145. A more thorough discussion can be found in Michael E. Porter, *Competitive Strategy: Techniques for Analyzing Industries and Competitors* (New York: Free Press, 1980), chap. 1.

[3]Adapted with permission of the Free Press, a division of Simon & Schuster Adult Publishing Group, from *Competitive Advantage: Creating and Sustaining Superior Performance,* by Michael Porter, Copyright © 1995, 1998 by Michael E. Porter. All rights reserved.

[4]Ibid., pp. 7–17.

[5]When profits are sufficiently attractive, entry barriers are unlikely to be an effective entry deterrent. At most, they limit the pool of candidate entrants to enterprises with the requisite competencies and resources and with the creativity to fashion a strategy for competing with incumbent firms. For a good discussion of this point, see George S. Yip, "Gateways to Entry," *Harvard Business Review* 60, no. 5 (September-October 1982), pp. 85–93.

[6]Porter, "How Competitive Forces Shape Strategy," p. 140, and Porter, *Competitive Strategy,* pp. 14–15.

[7]Porter, "How Competitive Forces Shape Strategy," p. 142, and Porter, *Competitive Strategy,* pp. 22–24.

[8]Porter, *Competitive Strategy,* p. 10.

[9]Ibid., pp. 27–28.

[10]Ibid., pp. 24–27.

[11]For a more extended discussion of the problems with the life-cycle hypothesis, see Porter, *Competitive Strategy,* pp. 157–162.

[12]Porter, *Competitive Strategy,* p. 162.

[13]Ibid., pp. 164–183.

[14]For an excellent discussion of the different patterns of change in industries, see Anita M. McGahan, "How Industries Change," *Harvard Business Review* 82, no. 10 (October 2004), pp. 87–94.

[15]Porter, *Competitive Strategy,* chap. 7.

[16]Ibid., pp. 129–130.

[17]For an excellent discussion of how to identify the factors that define strategic groups, see Mary Ellen Gordon and George R. Milne, "Selecting the Dimensions That Define Strategic Groups: A Novel Market-Driven Approach," *Journal of Managerial Issues* 11, no. 2 (Summer 1999), pp. 213–233.

[18]Porter, *Competitive Strategy,* pp. 152–154.

[19]Ibid., pp. 130, 132–138, 154–155.

[20]Strategic groups act as good reference points for predicting the evolution of an industry's competitive structure. See Avi Fiegenbaum and Howard Thomas, "Strategic Groups as Reference Groups: Theory, Modeling and Empirical Examination of Industry and Competitive Strategy," *Strategic Management Journal* 16 (1995), pp. 461–476. For a study of how strategic group analysis helps identify the variables that lead to sustainable competitive advantage, see S. Ade Olusoga, Michael P. Mokwa, and Charles H. Noble, "Strategic Groups, Mobility Barriers, and Competitive Advantage," *Journal of Business Research* 33 (1995), pp. 153–164.

[21]For a discussion of legal ways of gathering competitive intelligence on rival companies, see Larry Kahaner, *Competitive Intelligence* (New York: Simon & Schuster, 1996).

[22]Kahaner, *Competitive Intelligence,* pp. 84–85.

[23]Some experts dispute the strategy-making value of key success factors. Professor Ghemawat has claimed that the "whole idea of identifying a success factor and then chasing it seems to have something in common with the ill-considered medieval hunt for the *philosopher's stone,* a substance which would transmute everything it touched into gold." Pankaj Ghemawat, *Commitment: The Dynamic of Strategy* (New York: Free Press, 1991), p. 11.

Chapter 3

[1]Many business organizations are coming to view cutting-edge knowledge and intellectual resources as valuable competitive assets and have concluded that explicitly managing these assets is an essential part of their strategy. See Michael H. Zack, "Developing a Knowledge Strategy," *California Management Review* 41, no. 3 (Spring 1999), pp. 125–145 and Shaker A. Zahra, Anders P. Nielsen, and William C. Bogner, "Corporate Entrepreneurship, Knowledge, and Competence Development," *Entrepreneurship Theory and Practice,* Spring 1999, pp. 169–189.

[2]In the past decade, there's been considerable research into the role a company's resources and competitive capabilities play in crafting strategy and in determining company profitability. The findings and conclusions have coalesced into what is called the *resource-based view* of the firm. Among the most insightful articles are Birger Wernerfelt, "A Resource-Based View of the Firm," *Strategic Management Journal,* September-October 1984, pp. 171–180; Jay Barney, "Firm Resources and Sustained Competitive Advantage," *Journal of Management* 17, no. 1 (1991), pp. 99–120; Margaret A. Peteraf, "The Cornerstones of Competitive Advantage: A Resource-Based View," *Strategic Management Journal,* March 1993, pp. 179–191; Birger Wernerfelt, "The Resource-Based View of the Firm: Ten Years After," *Strategic Management Journal* 16 (1995), pp. 171–174; Jay B. Barney, "Looking Inside for Competitive Advantage," *Academy of Management Executive* 9, no. 4 (November 1995), pp. 49–61; Christopher A. Bartlett and Sumantra Ghoshal, "Building Competitive Advantage through

People," *MIT Sloan Management Review* 43, no. 2 (Winter 2002), pp. 34–41; and Danny Miller, Russell Eisenstat, and Nathaniel Foote, "Strategy from the Inside Out: Building Capability-Creating Organizations," *California Management Review* 44, no. 3 (Spring 2002), pp. 37–54.

[3]George Stalk, Jr., and Rob Lachenauer, "Hard Ball: Five Killer Strategies for Trouncing the Competition," *Harvard Business Review* 82, no. 4 (April 2004), p. 65.

[4]For a more extensive discussion of how to identify and evaluate the competitive power of a company's capabilities, see David W. Birchall and George Tovstiga, "The Strategic Potential of a Firm's Knowledge Portfolio," *Journal of General Management* 25, no. 1 (Autumn 1999), pp. 1–16, and Nick Bontis, Nicola C. Dragonetti, Kristine Jacobsen, and Goran Roos, "The Knowledge Toolbox: A Review of the Tools Available to Measure and Manage Intangible Resources," *European Management Journal* 17, no. 4 (August 1999), pp. 391–401. Also see David Teece, "Capturing Value from Knowledge Assets: The New Economy, Markets for Know-How, and Intangible Assets," *California Management Review* 40, no. 3 (Spring 1998), pp. 55–79.

[5]See David J. Collis and Cynthia A. Montgomery, "Competing on Resources: Strategy in the 1990s," *Harvard Business Review* 73, no. 4 (July-August 1995), pp. 120–123.

[6]See Jack W. Duncan, Peter Ginter, and Linda E. Swayne, "Competitive Advantage and Internal Organizational Assessment," *Academy of Management Executive* 12, no. 3 (August 1998), pp. 6–16.

[7]Value chains and strategic cost analysis are described at greater length in Michael E. Porter, *Competitive Advantage* (New York: Free Press, 1985), chaps. 2 and 3; Robin Cooper and Robert S. Kaplan, "Measure Costs Right: Make the Right Decisions," *Harvard Business Review* 66, no. 5 (September-October, 1988), pp. 96–103; and John K. Shank and Vijay Govindarajan, *Strategic Cost Manage-*ment (New York: Free Press, 1993), especially chaps. 2–6 and 10.

[8]Porter, *Competitive Advantage,* p. 36.

[9]Ibid., p. 34.

[10]The strategic importance of effective supply chain management is discussed in Hau L. Lee, "The Triple-A Supply Chain," *Harvard Business Review* 82, no. 10 (October 2004), pp. 102–112.

[11]M. Hegert and D. Morris, "Accounting Data for Value Chain Analysis," *Strategic Management Journal* 10 (1989), p. 180.

[12]For more on how and why the clustering of suppliers and other support organizations matters to a company's costs and competitiveness, see Michael E. Porter, "Clusters and the New Economics of Competition," *Harvard Business Review* 76, no. 6 (November-December 1998), pp. 77–90.

[13]For discussions of the accounting challenges in calculating the costs of value chain activities, see Shank and Govindarajan, *Strategic Cost Management,* pp. 62–72 and chap. 5, and Hegert and Morris, "Accounting Data for Value Chain Analysis," pp. 175–188.

[14]Porter, *Competitive Advantage,* p. 45.

[15]For a discussion of activity-based cost accounting, see Cooper and Kaplan, "Measure Costs Right"; Shank and Govindarajan, *Strategic Cost Management,* chap. 11; and Joseph A. Ness and Thomas G. Cucuzza, "Tapping the Full Potential of ABC," *Harvard Business Review* 73, no. 4 (July-August 1995), pp. 130–138.

[16]Shank and Govindarajan, *Strategic Cost Management,* p. 62.

[17]For more details, see Gregory H. Watson, *Strategic Benchmarking: How to Rate Your Company's Performance against the World's Best* (New York: Wiley, 1993); Robert C. Camp, *Benchmarking: The Search for Industry Best Practices That Lead to Superior Performance* (Milwaukee: ASQC Quality Press, 1989); Christopher E. Bogan and Michael J. English, *Benchmarking for Best Practices: Winning through Innovative Adaptation* (New York: McGraw-Hill, 1994); and Dawn Iacobucci and Christie Nordhielm, "Creative Benchmarking," *Harvard Business Review* 78, no. 6 (November-December 2000), pp. 24–25.

[18]Jeremy Main, "How to Steal the Best Ideas Around," *Fortune,* October 19, 1992, pp. 102–103.

[19]Shank and Govindarajan, *Strategic Cost Management,* p. 50.

[20]Ibid., chap. 3.

[21]An example of how Whirlpool Corporation transformed its supply chain from a competitive liability to a competitive asset is discussed in Reuben E. Stone, "Leading a Supply Chain Turnaround," *Harvard Business Review* 82, no. 10 (October 2004), pp. 114–121.

[22]James Brian Quinn, *Intelligent Enterprise* (New York: Free Press, 1993), p. 54.

[23]Ibid., p. 34.

Chapter 4

[1]This classification scheme is an adaption of one presented in Michael E. Porter, *Competitive Strategy: Techniques for Analyzing Industries and Competitors* (New York: Free Press, 1980), chap. 2, especially pp. 35–40 and 44–46. For a discussion of the different ways that companies can position themselves in the marketplace, see Michael E. Porter, "What Is Strategy?" *Harvard Business Review* 74, no. 6 (November-December 1996), pp. 65–67.

[2]Porter, *Competitive Advantage,* p. 97.

[3]The items and explanations in this listing are condensed from ibid., pp. 70–107.

[4]Ibid., pp. 135–138.

[5]For a more detailed discussion, see George Stalk, Philip Evans, and Lawrence E. Schulman, "Competing on Capabilities: The New Rules of Corporate Strategy," *Harvard Business Review* 70, no. 2 (March-April 1992), pp. 57–69.

[6]Porter, *Competitive Advantage,* pp. 160–162.

[7]Gary Hamel, "Strategy as Revolution," *Harvard Business Review* 74, no. 4 (July-August 1996), p. 72. For an interesting and entertaining presentation

of Trader Joe's mission, strategy, and operating practices, see the information the company has posted at www.trader-joes.com.

[8]Yves L. Doz and Gary Hamel, *Alliance Advantage: The Art of Creating Value through Partnering* (Boston: Harvard Business School Press, 1998), pp. xiii, xiv.

[9]Jason Wakeam, "The Five Factors of a Strategic Alliance," *Ivey Business Journal* 68, no 3 (May-June 2003), pp. 1–4.

[10]Jeffrey H. Dyer, Prashant Kale, and Harbir Singh, "When to Ally and When to Acquire," *Harvard Business Review* 82, no. 7/8 (July-August 2004), p. 109.

[11]Salvatore Parise and Lisa Sasson, "Leveraging Knowledge Management across Strategic Alliances," *Ivey Business Journal* 67, no. 2 (March-April 2002), p. 42.

[12]Michael E. Porter, *The Competitive Advantage of Nations* (New York: Free Press, 1990), p. 66. For a discussion of how to realize the advantages of strategic partnerships, see Nancy J. Kaplan and Jonathan Hurd, "Realizing the Promise of Partnerships," *Journal of Business Strategy* 23, no. 3 (May-June 2002), pp. 38–42.

[13]Doz and Hamel, *Alliance Advantage,* pp. 16–18.

[14]Dyer, Kale, and Singh, "When to Ally and When to Acquire," p. 109.

[15]For an excellent discussion of the pros and cons of alliances versus acquisitions, see Dyer, Kale, and Singh, "When to Ally and When to Acquire," pp. 109–115.

[16]For an excellent review of the strategic objectives of various types of mergers and acquisitions and the managerial challenges that different kinds of mergers and acquisitions present, see Joseph L. Bower, "Not All M&As Are Alike-And That Matters," *Harvard Business Review* 79, no. 3 (March 2001), pp. 93–101.

[17]For a more expansive discussion, see Dyer, Kale, and Singh, "When to Ally and When to Acquire," pp. 109–110.

[18]See Kathryn R. Harrigan, "Matching Vertical Integration Strategies to Competitive Conditions," *Strategic Management Journal* 7, no. 6 (November-December 1986), pp. 535–556. For a more extensive discussion of the advantages and disadvantages of vertical integration, see John Stuckey and David White, "When and When Not to Vertically Integrate," *Sloan Management Review,* Spring 1993, pp. 71–83.

[19]The resilience of vertical integration strategies despite the disadvantages is discussed in Thomas Osegowitsch and Anoop Madhok, "Vertical Integration Is Dead or Is It?" *Business Horizons* 46, no. 2 (March-April 2003), pp. 25–35.

[20]For more details, see James Brian Quinn, "Strategic Outsourcing: Leveraging Knowledge Capabilities," *Sloan Management Review* 40, no. 4 (Summer 1999), pp. 9–21.

[21]Dean Foust, "Big Brown's New Bag," *BusinessWeek,* July 19, 2004, pp. 54–55.

[22]"The Internet Age," *BusinessWeek,* October 4, 1999, p. 104.

[23]For a good discussion of the problems that can arise from outsourcing, see Jérôme Barthélemy, "The Seven Deadly Sins of Outsourcing," *Academy of Management Executive* 17, no. 2 (May 2003), pp. 87–100.

[24]For an excellent discussion of aggressive offensive strategies, see George Stalk, Jr., and Rob Lachenauer, "Hardball: Five Killer Strategies for Trouncing the Competition," *Harvard Business Review* 82, no. 4 (April 2004), pp. 62–71. A discussion of offensive strategies particularly suitable for industry leaders is presented in Richard D'Aveni, "The Empire Strikes Back: Counterrevolutionary Strategies for Industry Leaders," *Harvard Business Review* 80, no. 11 (November 2002), pp. 66–74.

[25]Ian C. MacMillan, "How Long Can You Sustain a Competitive Advantage?" in *The Strategic Planning Management Reader,* ed. Liam Fahey (Englewood Cliffs, NJ: Prentice Hall, 1989), pp. 23–24.

[26]Ian C. MacMillan, Alexander B. van Putten, and Rita Gunther McGrath, "Global Gamesmanship," *Harvard Business Review* 81, no. 5 (May 2003), pp. 66–67; also see Askay R. Rao, Mark E. Bergen, and Scott Davis, "How to Fight a Price War," *Harvard Business Review* 78, no. 2 (March-April, 2000), pp. 107–116.

[27]Stalk and Lachenauer, "Hardball," p. 64.

[28]Ibid., p. 67.

[29]A good example of the use of this type of strategic offensive in the battle between Netscape and Microsoft over Internet browsers is presented in David B. Yoffie and Michael A. Cusumano, "Judo Strategy: The Competitive Dynamics of Internet Time," *Harvard Business Review* 77, no. 1 (January-February 1999), pp. 70–81.

[30]For an interesting study of how small firms can successfully employ guerrilla-style tactics, see Ming-Jer Chen and Donald C. Hambrick, "Speed, Stealth, and Selective Attack: How Small Firms Differ from Large Firms in Competitive Behavior," *Academy of Management Journal* 38, no. 2 (April 1995), pp. 453–482. Other discussions of guerrilla offensives can be found in Ian MacMillan, "How Business Strategists Can Use Guerrilla Warfare Tactics," *Journal of Business Strategy* 1, no. 2 (Fall 1980), pp. 63–65; William E. Rothschild, "Surprise and the Competitive Advantage," *Journal of Business Strategy* 4, no. 3 (Winter 1984), pp. 10–18; Kathryn R. Harrigan, *Strategic Flexibility* (Lexington, MA: Lexington Books, 1985), pp. 30–45; and Liam Fahey, "Guerrilla Strategy: The Hit-and-Run Attack," in *The Strategic Management Planning Reader,* ed. Liam Fahey (Englewood Cliffs, NJ: Prentice Hall, 1989), pp. 194–197.

[31]The use of preemptive strike offensives is treated comprehensively in Ian MacMillan, "Preemptive Strategies," *Journal of Business Strategy* 14, no. 2 (Fall 1983), pp. 16–26.

[32]For an excellent discussion of how to wage offensives against strong rivals, see David B. Yoffie and Mary Kwak, "Mastering Balance: How to Meet and Beat a Stronger Opponent," *California Management Review* 44, no. 2 (Winter 2002), pp. 8–24.

[33]Porter, *Competitive Advantage,* pp. 489–494.

[34]Ibid., pp. 495–497. The list here is selective; Porter offers a greater number of options.

[35]For a more extensive discussion of how the Internet impacts strategy, see Michael E. Porter, "Strategy and the Internet," *Harvard Business Review* 79, no. 3 (March 2001), pp. 63–78.

[36]Porter, *Competitive Advantage,* pp. 232–233.

[37]For research evidence on the effects of pioneering versus following, see Jeffrey G. Covin, Dennis P. Slevin, and Michael B. Heeley, "Pioneers and Followers: Competitive Tactics, Environment, and Growth," *Journal of Business Venturing* 15, no. 2 (March 1999), pp. 175–210, and Christopher A. Bartlett and Sumantra Ghoshal, "Going Global: Lessons from Late-Movers," *Harvard Business Review* 78, no. 2 (March-April 2000), pp. 132–145.

[38]Gary Hamel, "Smart Mover, Dumb Mover," *Fortune,* September 3, 2001, p. 195.

[39]Ibid., p. 192.

Chapter 5

[1]For an insightful discussion of how much significance these kinds of demographic and market differences have, see C. K. Prahalad and Kenneth Lieberthal, "The End of Corporate Imperialism," *Harvard Business Review* 76, no. 4 (July-August 1999), pp. 68–79.

[2]Michael E. Porter, *The Competitive Advantage of Nations* (New York: Free Press, 1990), pp. 53–54.

[3]Ibid., p. 61.

[4]For more details on the merits of and opportunities for cross-border transfer of successful strategy experiments, see C. A. Bartlett and S. Ghoshal, *Managing across Borders: The Transnational Solution,* 2d ed. (Boston: Harvard Business School Press, 1998), pp. 79–80 and chap. 9.

[5]H. Kurt Christensen, "Corporate Strategy: Managing a Set of Businesses," in *The Portable MBA in Strategy,* ed.

Liam Fahey and Robert M. Randall (New York: Wiley, 2001), p. 42.

[6]Porter, *The Competitive Advantage of Nations,* pp. 53–55.

[7]Ibid., pp. 55–58.

[8]C. K. Prahalad and Yves L. Doz, *The Multinational Mission* (New York: Free Press, 1987), p. 60.

[9]Porter, *The Competitive Advantage of Nations,* p. 57.

[10]Ibid., pp. 58–60.

[11]Ian C. MacMillan, Alexander B. van Putten, and Rita Gunther McGrath, "Global Gamesmanship," *Harvard Business Review* 81, no. 5 (May 2003), pp. 63–68.

[12]Porter, *The Competitive Advantage of Nations,* p. 66; see also Yves L. Doz and Gary Hamel, *Alliance Advantage* (Boston: Harvard Business School Press, 1998), especially chaps. 2–4.

[13]Christensen, "Corporate Strategy," p. 43.

[14]For an excellent discussion of company experiences with alliances and partnerships, see Doz and Hamel, *Alliance Advantage,* chaps. 2–7, and Rosabeth Moss Kanter, "Collaborative Advantage: The Art of the Alliance," *Harvard Business Review* 72, no. 4 (July-August 1994), pp. 96–108.

[15]Jeremy Main, "Making Global Alliances Work," *Fortune,* December 19, 1990, p. 125.

[16]Details of the disagreements are reported in Shawn Tully, "The Alliance from Hell," *Fortune,* June 24, 1996, pp. 64–72.

[17]Doz and Hamel, *Alliance Advantage,* chaps. 4–8.

[18]Much of this section is based on Prahalad and Lieberthal, "The End of Corporate Imperialism," pp. 68–79, and David J. Arnold and John A. Quelch, "New Strategies in Emerging Markets," *Sloan Management Review* 40, no. 1 (Fall 1998), pp. 7–20. For a more extensive discussion of strategy in emerging markets, see C. K. Prahalad, *The Fortune at the Bottom of the Pyramid: Eradicating Poverty through Profits* (Upper Saddle River, NJ: Wharton, 2005), especially chaps. 1–3.

[19]Brenda Cherry, "What China Eats (and Drinks and . . .)" *Fortune,* October 4, 2004, pp. 152–153.

[20]Prahalad and Lieberthal, "The End of Corporate Imperialism," pp. 72–73.

[21]Niroj Dawar and Tony Frost, "Competing with Giants: Survival Strategies for Local Companies in Emerging Markets," *Harvard Business Review* 77, no. 1 (January-February 1999), p. 122; see also Guitz Ger, "Localizing in the Global Village: Local Firms Competing in Global Markets," *California Management Review* 41, no. 4 (Summer 1999), pp. 64–84.

[22]Dawar and Frost, "Competing with Giants," p. 124.

[23]Ibid., p. 125.

[24]Steve Hamm, "Tech's Future," *BusinessWeek,* September 27, 2004, p. 88.

[25]Dawar and Frost, "Competing with Giants," p. 126.

[26]Hamm, "Tech's Future," p. 89.

Chapter 6

[1]For a further discussion of when diversification makes good strategic sense, see Constantinos C. Markides, "To Diversify or Not to Diversify," *Harvard Business Review* 75, no. 6 (November-December 1997), pp. 93–99.

[2]Michael E. Porter, "From Competitive Advantage to Corporate Strategy," *Harvard Business Review* 45, no. 3 (May-June 1987), pp. 46–49.

[3]Michael E. Porter, *Competitive Strategy: Techniques for Analyzing Industries and Competitors* (New York: Free Press, 1980), pp. 354–355.

[4]Ibid., pp. 344–345.

[5]Yves L. Doz and Gary Hamel, *Alliance Advantage: The Art of Creating Value through Partnering* (Boston: Harvard Business School Press, 1998), chaps. 1 and 2.

[6]Michael E. Porter, *Competitive Advantage* (New York: Free Press, 1985), pp. 318–319, 337–353, and Porter, "From Competitive Advantage to Corporate Strategy," pp. 53–57. For an empirical study confirming that strategic fits are capable of enhancing performance

(provided the resulting resource strengths are competitively valuable and difficult to duplicate by rivals), see Constantinos C. Markides and Peter J. Williamson, "Corporate Diversification and Organization Structure: A Resource-Based View," *Academy of Management Journal* 39, no. 2 (April 1996), pp. 340–367.

[7]For a discussion of the strategic significance of cross-business coordination of value chain activities and insight into how the process works, see Jeanne M. Liedtka, "Collaboration across Lines of Business for Competitive Advantage," *Academy of Management Executive* 10, no. 2 (May 1996), pp. 20–34.

[8]"Beyond Knowledge Management: How Companies Mobilize Experience," *The Financial Times,* February 8, 1999, p. 5.

[9]For a discussion of what is involved in actually capturing strategic-fit benefits, see Kathleen M. Eisenhardt and D. Charles Galunic, "Coevolving: At Last, a Way to Make Synergies Work," *Harvard Business Review* 78, no. 1 (January-February 2000), pp. 91–101. Adeptness at capturing cross-business strategic fits positively impacts performance; see Constantinos C. Markides and Peter J. Williamson, "Related Diversification, Core Competences and Corporate Performance," *Strategic Management Journal* 15 (Summer 1994), pp. 149–165.

[10]Peter Drucker, *Management: Tasks, Responsibilities, Practices* (New York: Harper & Row, 1974), pp. 692–693.

[11]While arguments that unrelated diversification is a superior way to diversify financial risk have logical appeal, there is research showing that related diversification is less risky from a financial perspective than is unrelated diversification; see Michael Lubatkin and Sayan Chatterjee, "Extending Modern Portfolio Theory into the Domain of Corporate Diversification: Does It Apply?" *Academy of Management Journal* 37, no. 1 (February 1994), pp. 109–136.

[12]For a review of the experiences of companies that have pursued unrelated diversification successfully, see Patricia L. Anslinger and Thomas E.

Copeland, "Growth through Acquisitions: A Fresh Look," *Harvard Business Review* 74, no. 1 (January-February 1996), pp. 126–135.

[13]Of course, management may be willing to assume the risk that trouble will not strike before it has had time to learn the business well enough to bail it out of almost any difficulty. But there is research that shows this is very risky from a financial perspective; see, for example, Lubatkin and Chatterjee, "Extending Modern Portfolio Theory," pp. 132–133.

[14]For research evidence of the failure of broad diversification and the trend of companies to focus their diversification efforts more narrowly, see Lawrence G. Franko, "The Death of Diversification? The Focusing of the World's Industrial Firms, 1980–2000," *Business Horizons* 47, no. 4 (July-August 2004), pp. 41–50.

[15]For an excellent discussion of what to look for in assessing these fits, see Andrew Campbell, Michael Gould, and Marcus Alexander, "Corporate Strategy: The Quest for Parenting Advantage," *Harvard Business Review* 73, no. 2 (March-April 1995), pp. 120–132.

[16]Ibid., p. 128.

[17]Ibid., p. 123.

[18]A good discussion of the importance of having adequate resources, and also the importance of upgrading corporate resources and capabilities, can be found in David J. Collis and Cynthia A. Montgomery, "Competing on Resources: Strategy in the 90s," *Harvard Business Review* 73, no. 4 (July-August 1995), pp. 118–128.

[19]Ibid., pp. 121–122.

[20]Drucker, *Management: Tasks, Responsibilities, Practices,* p. 709.

[21]See, for example, Constantinos C. Markides, "Diversification, Restructuring, and Economic Performance," *Strategic Management Journal* 16 (February 1995), pp. 101–118.

[22]For a discussion of why divestiture needs to be a standard part of any company diversification strategy, see Lee Dranikoff, Tim Koller, and Antoon Schneider, "Divestiture: Strategy's

Missing Link," *Harvard Business Review* 80, no. 5 (May 2002), pp. 74–83.

[23]Drucker, *Management: Tasks, Responsibilities, Practices,* p. 94.

[24]See David J. Collis and Cynthia A. Montgomery, "Creating Corporate Advantage," *Harvard Business Review* 76, no. 3 (May-June 1998), pp. 72–80.

[25]Drucker, *Management: Tasks, Responsibilities, Practices,* p. 719.

[26]Evidence that restructuring strategies tend to result in higher levels of performance is contained in Markides, "Diversification, Restructuring, and Economic Performance," pp. 101–118.

[27]Dranikoff, Koller, and Schneider, "Divestiture: Strategy's Missing Link," p. 76.

[28]C. K. Pralahad and Yves L. Doz, *The Multinational Mission* (New York: Free Press, 1987), p. 2.

[29]Ibid., p. 15.

[30]Ibid., pp. 62–63.

[31]For a fascinating discussion of the chess match in strategy that can unfold when two DMNCs go head-to-head in a global marketplace, see Ian C. MacMillan, Alexander B. van Putten, and Rita Gunther McGrath, "Global Gamesmanship," *Harvard Business Review* 81, no. 5 (May 2003), pp. 62–71.

Chapter 7

[1]James E. Post, Anne T. Lawrence, and James Weber, *Business and Society: Corporate Strategy, Public Policy, Ethics,* 10th ed. (Burr Ridge, IL: McGraw-Hill Irwin, 2002), p. 103.

[2]See, for instance, Mark. S. Schwartz, "A Code of Ethics for Corporate Codes of Ethics," *Journal of Business Ethics* 41, nos. 1–2 (November-December 2002), pp. 27–43.

[3]For more discussion of this point, see ibid., pp. 29–30.

[4]T. L. Beauchamp and N. E. Bowie, *Ethical Theory and Business* (Upper Saddle River, NJ: Prentice-Hall, 2001), p. 8.

[5]Based on information in U.S. Department of Labor, "The Department of Labor's 2002 Findings on the Worst Forms

of Child Labor," 2003, accessible at www.dol.gov/ILAB/media/reports.

[6]ILO-IPEC (SIMPOC), "Every Child Counts: New Global Estimates on Child Labour," Geneva, April 2002, available from www.ilo.org/public/english/standards/ipec/simpoc/othersglobalest.pdf. The estimate of the number of working children is based on the definition of the "economically active population," which restricts the labor force activity of children to "paid" or "unpaid" employment, military personnel, and the unemployed. The definition does not include children in informal work settings, noneconomic activities, "hidden" forms of work, or work that is defined by ILO Convention 182 as the worst forms of child labor.

[7]W. M. Greenfield, "In the Name of Corporate Social Responsibility," *Business Horizons* 47, no. 1 (January-February 2004), p. 22.

[8]Thomas Donaldson and Thomas W. Dunfee, "When Ethics Travel: The Promise and Peril of Global Business Ethics," *California Management Review* 41, no. 4 (Summer 1999), p. 53.

[9]John Reed and Erik Portanger, "Bribery, Corruption Are Rampant in Eastern Europe, Survey Finds," *The Wall Street Journal,* November 9, 1999, p. A21.

[10]Transparency International, *2004 Global Corruption Report,* www.globalcorruptionreport.org, accessed at November 2, 2004; in particular, see pp. 277–294 and secs. 8 and 9.

[11]Donaldson and Dunfee, "When Ethics Travel," p. 59.

[12]George A. Steiner and John F. Steiner, Business, Government, and Society: *A Managerial Perspective* (Burr Ridge, IL: McGraw-Hill/Irwin, 2003), p. 213.

[13]See John. J. Hannifin, "Morality and the Market in China: Some Contemporary Views," *Business Ethics Quarterly* 12, no. 1 (January 2002), pp. 6–9.

[14]Stephen J. Carroll and Martin J. Gannon, *Ethical Dimensions of International Management* (Thousand Oaks, CA: Sage Publications, 1997), p. 9.

[15]For more documentation of cross-country differences in what is considered ethical, see Robert D. Hirsch, Branko Bucar, and Sevgi Oztark, "A Cross-Cultural Comparison of Business Ethics: Cases of Russia, Slovenia, Turkey, and United States," *Cross Cultural Management* 10, no. 1 (2003), pp. 3–28; P. Maria Joseph Christie, Ik-Whan G. Kwan, Philipp A. Stoeberl, and Raymond Baumhart, "A Cross-Cultural Comparison of Ethical Attitudes of Business Managers: India, Korea, and the United States," *Journal of Business Ethics* 46, no. 3 (September 2003), pp. 263–287; and Turgut Guvenli and Rajib Sanyal, "Ethical Concerns in International Business: Are Some Issues More Important than Others?" *Business and Society Review* 107, no. 2 (June 2002), pp. 195–206.

[16]Thomas Donaldson and Thomas W. Dunfee, *Ties That Bind: A Social Contracts Approach to Business Ethics* (Boston: Harvard Business School Press, 1999), pp. 35, 83.

[17]Based on a report in M. J. Satchell, "Deadly Trade in Toxics," *U.S. News and World Report,* March 7, 1994, p. 64, and cited in Donaldson and Dunfee, "When Ethics Travel," p. 46.

[18]Two of the definitive treatments of integrated social contracts theory as applied to ethics are Thomas Donaldson and Thomas W. Dunfee, "Towards a Unified Conception of Business Ethics: Integrative Social Contracts Theory," *Academy of Management Review* 19, no. 2 (April 1994), pp. 252–284, and Donaldson and Dunfee, *Ties That Bind,* especially chaps. 3, 4, and 6. See also Andrew Spicer, Thomas W. Dunfee, and Wendy J. Bailey, "Does National Context Matter in Ethical Decision Making? An Empirical Test of Integrative Social Contracts Theory," *Academy of Management Journal* 47, no. 4 (August 2004), p. 610.

[19]P. M. Nichols, "Outlawing Transnational Bribery through the World Trade Organization," *Law and Policy in International Business* 28, no. 2 (1997), pp. 321–322.

[20]Donaldson and Dunfee, "When Ethics Travel," pp. 55–56.

[21]Archie B. Carroll, "Models of Management Morality for the New Millennium," *Business Ethics Quarterly* 11, no. 2 (April 2001), pp. 367–369.

[22]Ibid., pp. 369–370.

[23]For survey data on what managers say about why they sometimes behave unethically, see John F. Veiga, Timothy D. Golden, and Kathleen Dechant, "Why Managers Bend Company Rules," *Academy of Management Executive* 18, no. 2 (May 2004), pp. 84–89.

[24]For more details, see Ronald R. Sims and Johannes Brinkmann, "Enron Ethics (Or: Culture Matters More than Codes)," *Journal of Business Ethics* 45, no. 3 (July 2003), pp. 244–246.

[25]As reported in Gardiner Harris, "At Bristol-Myers, Ex-Executives Tell of Numbers Games," *The Wall Street Journal,* December 12, 2002, pp. A1, A13.

[26]Ibid., p. A13.

[27]Veiga, Golden, and Dechant, "Why Managers Bend Company Rules," p. 36.

[28]The following account is based largely on the discussion and analysis in Sims and Brinkmann, "Enron Ethics," pp. 245–252.

[29]Chip Cummins and Almar Latour, "How Shell's Move to Revamp Culture Ended in Scandal," *The Wall Street Journal,* November 2, 2004, p. A14.

[30]Gedeon J. Rossouw and Leon J. van Vuuren, "Modes of Managing Morality: A Descriptive Model of Strategies for Managing Ethics," *Journal of Business Ethics* 46, no. 4 (September 2003), pp. 389–400.

[31]Empirical evidence that an ethical culture approach produces better results than the compliance approach is presented in Terry Thomas, John R. Schermerhorn, and John W. Dienhart, "Strategic Leadership of Ethical Behavior," *Academy of Management Executive* 18, no. 2 (May 2004), p. 64.

[32]Anna Wilde Mathews and Barbara Martinez, "E-Mails Suggest Merck Knew Vioxx's Dangers at Early Stage," *The Wall Street Journal,* November 1, 2004, pp. A1, A10.

[33]Archie B. Carroll, "The Four Faces of Corporate Citizenship," *Business*

and *Society Review* 100–101 (September 1998), p. 6.

[34]Business Roundtable, "Statement of Corporate Responsibility," New York, October 1981, p. 9.

[35]Sarah Roberts, Justin Keeble, and David Brown, "The Business Case for Corporate Citizenship," a study for the World Economic Forum, accessed at www.weforum.org/corporatecitizenship, October 14, 2003, p. 3.

[36]N. Craig Smith, "Corporate Responsibility: Whether and How," *California Management Review* 45, no. 4 (Summer 2003), p. 63.

[37]Jeffrey Hollender, "What Matters Most: Corporate Values and Social Responsibility," *California Management Review* 46, no. 4 (Summer 2004), p. 112.

[38]World Business Council for Sustainable Development, "Corporate Social Responsibility: Making Good Business Sense," January 2000, p. 7, accessed at www.wbscd.ch, October 10, 2003. For a discussion on how companies are connecting social initiatives to their core values, see David Hess, Nikolai Rogovsky, and Thomas W. Dunfee, "The Next Wave of Corporate Community Involvement: Corporate Social Initiatives," *California Management Review* 44, no. 2 (Winter 2002), pp. 110–125. See also Susan Ariel Aaronson, "Corporate Responsibility in the Global Village: The British Role Model and the American Laggard," *Business and Society Review* 108, no. 3 (September 2003), p. 323.

[39]www.chick-fil-a.com, accessed October 16, 2003.

[40]Smith, "Corporate Responsibility," p. 63; see also World Economic Forum, "Findings of a Survey on Global Corporate Leadership," accessed at www.weforum.org/corporatecitizenship, October 11, 2003.

[41]Roberts, Keeble, and Brown, "The Business Case for Corporate Citizenship," p. 6.

[42]Ibid., p.3.

[43]Wallace N. Davidson, Abuzar El-Jelly, and Dan L. Worrell, "Influencing Managers to Change Unpopular Corporate Behavior through Boycotts and Divestitures: A Stock Market Test," *Business and Society* 34, no. 2 (1995), pp. 171–196.

[44]Tom McCawley, "Racing to Improve Its Reputation: Nike Has Fought to Shed Its Image as an Exploiter of Third-World Labor yet It Is Still a Target of Activists," *Financial Times,* December 2000, p. 14, and Smith, "Corporate Social Responsibility," p. 61.

[45]Based on data in Amy Aronson, "Corporate Diversity, Integration, and Market Penetration," *BusinessWeek,* October 20, 2003, pp. 138ff.

[46]Smith, "Corporate Social Responsibility," p. 62.

[47]See Social Investment Forum, 2001 Report on Socially Responsible Investing Trends in the United States (Washington, DC: Social Investment Forum, 2001).

[48]Smith, "Corporate Social Responsibility," p. 63.

[49]See James C. Collins and Jerry I. Porras, *Built to Last: Successful Habits of Visionary Companies,* 3d ed. (London: HarperBusiness, 2002); Roberts, Keeble, and Brown, "The Business Case for Corporate Citizenship," p. 4; and Smith, "Corporate Social Responsibility," p. 63.

[50]Roberts, Keeble, and Brown, "The Business Case for Corporate Citizenship," p. 4.

[51]Smith, "Corporate Social Responsibility," p. 65; Lee E. Preston and Douglas P. O'Bannon, "The Corporate Social-Financial Performance Relationship," *Business and Society* 36, no. 4 (December 1997), pp. 419–429; Ronald M. Roman, Sefa Hayibor, and Bradley R. Agle, "The Relationship between Social and Financial Performance: Repainting a Portrait," *Business and Society* 38, no. 1 (March 1999), pp. 109–125; and Joshua D. Margolis and James P. Walsh, *People and Profits* (Mahwah, NJ: Lawrence Erlbaum, 2001).

[52]Smith, "Corporate Social Responsibility," p. 70.

Chapter 8

[1]As quoted in Steven W. Floyd and Bill Wooldridge, "Managing Strategic Consensus: The Foundation of Effective Implementation," *Academy of Management Executive* 6, no. 4 (November 1992), p. 27.

[2]For an excellent and very pragmatic discussion of this point, see Larry Bossidy and Ram Charan, *Execution: The Discipline of Getting Things Done* (New York: Crown Business, 2002), chap. 1.

[3]For an insightful discussion of how important staffing an organization with the right people is, see Christopher A. Bartlett and Sumantra Ghoshal, "Building Competitive Advantage through People," *MIT Sloan Management Review* 43, no. 2 (Winter 2002), pp. 34–41.

[4]See Bossidy and Charan, *Execution: The Discipline of Getting Things Done,* chap. 1.

[5]John Byrne, "The Search for the Young and Gifted," *Business Week,* October 4, 1999, p. 108.

[6]James Brian Quinn, *Intelligent Enterprise* (New York: Free Press, 1992), pp. 52–53, 55, 73–74, 76. Also see Christine Soo, Timothy Devinney, David Midgley, and Anne Deering, "Knowledge Management: Philosophy, Processes, and Pitfalls," *California Management Review* 44, no. 4 (Summer 2002), pp. 129–151, and Julian Birkinshaw, "Why Is Knowledge Management So Difficult?" *Business Strategy Review* 12, no. 1 (March 2001), pp. 11–18. Adapted with permission of the Free Press, a division of Simon & Schuster Adult Publishing Group, from *Intelligent Enterprise,* by James Brian Quinn, Copyright © 1992, 1992 by James Brian Quinn, All rights reserved.

[7]Robert H. Hayes, Gary P. Pisano, and David M. Upton, *Strategic Operations: Competing through Capabilities* (New York: Free Press, 1996), pp. 503–507. Also see Jonas Ridderstråle, "Cashing In on Corporate Competencies," *Business Strategy Review* 14, no. 1 (Spring 2003), pp. 27–38, and Danny Miller, Russell Eisenstat, and Nathaniel Foote,

"Strategy from the Inside Out: Building Capability-Creating Organizations," *California Management Review* 44, no. 3 (Spring 2002), pp. 37–55.

[8]Quinn, *Intelligent Enterprise,* p. 43.

[9]Quinn, *Intelligent Enterprise,* pp. 33, 89; James Brian Quinn and Frederick G. Hilmer, "Strategic Outsourcing," *Sloan Management Review* 35, no. 4 (Summer 1994), pp. 43–55; and James Brian Quinn, "Strategic Outsourcing: Leveraging Knowledge Capabilities," *Sloan Management Review* 40, no. 4 (Summer 1999), pp. 9–22. See also Jussi Heikkilä and Carlos Cordon, "Outsourcing: A Core or Non-Core Strategic Management Decision," *Strategic Change* 11, no. 3 (June-July 2002), pp. 183–193. For a discussion of why outsourcing initiatives fall short of expectations, see Jérôme Barthélemy, "The Seven Deadly Sins of Outsourcing," *Academy of Management Executive* 17, no. 2 (May 2003), pp. 87–98.

[10]Quinn, "Strategic Outsourcing: Leveraging Knowledge Capabilities," p. 17.

[11]For a more extensive discussion of the reasons for building cooperative, collaborative alliances and partnerships with other companies, see James F. Moore, *The Death of Competition* (New York: HarperBusiness, 1996), especially chap. 3; Quinn and Hilmer, "Strategic Outsourcing"; and Quinn, "Strategic Outsourcing: Leveraging Knowledge Capabilities," pp. 9–22.

[12]Quinn, *Intelligent Enterprise,* pp. 39–40; also see Barthélemy, "The Seven Deadly Sins of Outsourcing."

[13]The importance of matching organizational design and structure to the particular needs of strategy was first brought to the forefront in a landmark study of 70 large corporations conducted by Professor Alfred Chandler of Harvard University. Chandler's research revealed that changes in an organization's strategy bring about new administrative problems that, in turn, require a new or refashioned structure for the new strategy to be successfully implemented. He found that structure tends to follow the growth strategy of the firm—but often not until inefficiency and internal operating problems provoke a structural adjustment. The experiences of these firms followed a consistent sequential pattern: new strategy creation, emergence of new administrative problems, a decline in profitability and performance, a shift to a more appropriate organizational structure, and then recovery to more profitable levels and improved strategy execution. See Alfred Chandler, *Strategy and Structure* (Cambridge, MA: MIT Press, 1962).

[14]The importance of empowering workers in executing strategy and the value of creating a great working environment are discussed in Stanley E. Fawcett, Gary K. Rhoads, and Phillip Burnah, "People as the Bridge to Competitiveness: Benchmarking the 'ABCs' of an Empowered Workforce," *Benchmarking: An International Journal* 11, no. 4 (2004), pp. 346–360.

[15]Iain Somerville and John Edward Mroz, "New Competencies for a New World," in *The Organization of the Future,* ed. Frances Hesselbein, Marshall Goldsmith, and Richard Beckard (San Francisco: Jossey-Bass, 1997), p. 70.

[16]Exercising adequate control over empowered employees is a serious issue. For example, a prominent Wall Street securities firm lost $350 million when a trader allegedly booked fictitious profits; Sears took a $60 million write-off after admitting that employees in its automobile service departments recommended unnecessary repairs to customers. For a discussion of the problems and possible solutions, see Robert Simons, "Control in an Age of Empowerment," *Harvard Business Review* 73 (March-April 1995), pp. 80–88.

[17]For a discussion of the importance of cross-business coordination, see Jeanne M. Liedtka, "Collaboration across Lines of Business for Competitive Advantage," *Academy of Management Executive* 10, no. 2 (May 1996), pp. 20–34.

[18]Rosabeth Moss Kanter, "Collaborative Advantage: The Art of the Alliance," *Harvard Business Review* 72, no. 4 (July-August 1994), pp. 105–106.

[19]For an excellent review of ways to effectively manage the relationship between alliance partners, see ibid., pp. 96–108.

[20]John P. Kotter and James L. Heskett, *Corporate Culture and Performance* (New York: Free Press, 1992), p. 7. See also Robert Goffee and Gareth Jones, *The Character of a Corporation* (New York: HarperCollins, 1998).

[21]Kotter and Heskett, *Corporate Culture and Performance,* pp. 7–8.

[22]Ibid., p. 5.

[23]John Alexander and Meena S. Wilson, "Leading across Cultures: Five Vital Capabilities," in *The Organization of the Future,* ed. Frances Hesselbein, Marshall Goldsmith, and Richard Beckard (San Francisco: Jossey-Bass, 1997), pp. 291–292.

[24]Kotter and Heskett, *Corporate Culture and Performance,* p. 5.

[25]Avan R. Jassawalla and Hemant C. Sashittal, "Cultures That Support Product-Innovation Processes," *Academy of Management Executive* 16, no. 3 (August 2002), pp. 42–54.

[26]Kotter and Heskett, *Corporate Culture and Performance,* pp. 15–16. Also see Jennifer A. Chatham and Sandra E. Cha, "Leading by Leveraging Culture," *California Management Review* 45, no. 4 (Summer 2003), pp. 20–34.

[27]Terrence E. Deal and Allen A. Kennedy, *Corporate Cultures* (Reading, MA: Addison-Wesley, 1982), p. 22. See also Terrence E. Deal and Allen A. Kennedy, *The New Corporate Cultures: Revitalizing the Workplace after Downsizing, Mergers, and Reengineering* (Cambridge, MA: Perseus, 1999).

[28]Vijay Sathe, *Culture and Related Corporate Realities* (Homewood, IL: Irwin, 1985).

[29]Kotter and Heskett, *Corporate Culture and Performance,* chap. 6.

[30]Ibid., p. 68.

[31]This section draws heavily on the discussion in ibid., chap. 4.

[32]There's no inherent reason why new strategic initiatives should conflict with core values and business principles.

While conflict is always possible, most strategy makers lean toward choosing strategic initiatives that are compatible with the company's character and culture and that don't go against ingrained values and beliefs. After all, the company's culture is usually something that strategy makers have had a hand in building and perpetuating, so they are not often anxious to undermine core values and business principles without serious soul-searching and compelling business reasons.

[33]Kotter and Heskett, *Corporate Culture and Performance,* p. 52. Adapted with permission of the Free Press, a division of Simon & Schuster Adult Publishing Group, from *Corporate Culture and Performance,* by John P. Kotter and James L. Heskett, Copyright © 1992, 1992 by James Brian Quinn, All rights reserved.

[34]Ibid., pp. 84, 144, 148.

[35]Judy D. Olian and Sara L. Rynes, "Making Total Quality Work: Aligning Organizational Processes, Performance Measures, and Stakeholders," *Human Resource Management* 30, no. 3 (Fall 1991), p. 324.

[36]For several perspectives on the role and importance of core values and ethical behavior, see Joseph L. Badaracco, *Defining Moments: When Managers Must Choose between Right and Wrong* (Boston: Harvard Business School Press, 1997); Joe Badaracco and Allen P. Webb. "Business Ethics: A View from the Trenches," *California Management Review* 37, no. 2 (Winter 1995), pp. 8–28; Patrick E. Murphy, "Corporate Ethics Statements: Current Status and Future Prospects," *Journal of Business Ethics* 14 (1995), pp. 727–740; and Lynn Sharp Paine, "Managing for Organizational Integrity," *Harvard Business Review* 72, no. 2 (March-April 1994), pp. 106–117.

[37]See Mark S. Schwartz, "A Code of Ethics for Corporate Codes of Ethics," *Journal of Business Ethics* 41, nos. 1–2 (November-December 2002), p. 27.

[38]For a study of the status of formal codes of ethics in large corporations, see Emily F. Carasco and Jang B. Singh, "The Content and Focus of the Codes of Ethics of the World's Largest Transnational Corporations," *Business and Society Review* 108, no. 1 (January 2003), pp. 71–94, and Patrick E. Murphy, "Corporate Ethics Statements: Current Status and Future Prospects," *Journal of Business Ethics* 14 (1995), pp. 727–740. For a discussion of the strategic benefits of formal statements of corporate values, see John Humble, David Jackson, and Alan Thomson, "The Strategic Power of Corporate Values," *Long Range Planning* 27, no. 6 (December 1994), pp. 28–42. An excellent discussion of whether one should assume that company codes of ethics are always ethical is presented in Schwartz, "A Code of Ethics for Corporate Codes of Ethics," pp. 27–43.

[39]www.dardenrestaurants.com, accessed October 2004, and Robert C. Ford, "Darden Restaurants CEO Joe Lee on the Importance of Core Values: Integrity and Fairness," *Academy of Management Executive* 16, no. 1 (February 2002), pp. 31–36.

[40]For some cautions on implementing ethics compliance, see Robert J. Rafalko, "A Caution about Trends in Ethics Compliance Programs," *Business and Society Review* 108, no. 1 (January 2003), pp. 115–126. A good discussion of the failures of ethics compliance programs can be found in Megan Barry, "Why Ethics and Compliance Programs Can Fail," *Journal of Business Strategy* 26, no. 6 (November-December 2002), pp. 37–40.

[41]For documentation of cross-country differences in what is considered ethical, see Robert D. Hirsch, Branko Bucar, and Sevgi Oztark, "A Cross-Cultural Comparison of Business Ethics: Cases of Russia, Slovenia, Turkey, and United States," *Cross Cultural Management* 10, no. 1 (2003), pp. 3–28, and P. Maria Joseph Christie, Ik-Whan G. Kwan, Philipp A. Stoeberl, and Raymond Baumhart, "A Cross-Cultural Comparison of Ethical Attitudes of Business Managers: India, Korea, and the United States," *Journal of Business Ethics* 46, no. 3 (September 2003), pp. 263–287.

[42]Ford, "Darden Restaurants CEO Joe Lee on the Importance of Core Values."

Chapter 9

[1]Jim Collins, "Turning Goals into Results: The Power of Catalytic Mechanisms," *Harvard Business Review* 77, no. 4 (July-August 1999), pp. 72–73; Robert Levering and Milton Moskowitz, "The 100 Best Companies to Work For," *Fortune,* February 4, 2004, p. 73; and Robert Levering and Milton Moskowitz, "The 100 Best Companies to Work For," *Fortune,* January 12, 2004, p. 78.

[2]For a discussion of the value of benchmarking in implementing strategy, see Christopher E. Bogan and Michael J. English, *Benchmarking for Best Practices: Winning through Innovative Adaptation* (New York: McGraw-Hill, 1994), chaps. 2 and 6; Mustafa Ungan, "Factors Affecting the Adoption of Manufacturing Best Practices," *Benchmarking: An International Journal* 11, no. 5 (2004), pp. 504–520; Paul Hyland and Ron Beckett, "Learning to Compete: The Value of Internal Benchmarking," *Benchmarking: An International Journal* 9, no. 3 (2002), pp. 293–304; and Yoshinobu Ohinata, "Benchmarking: The Japanese Experience," *Long-Range Planning* 27, no. 4 (August 1994), pp. 48–53.

[3]Michael Hammer and James Champy, *Reengineering the Corporation* (New York: HarperBusiness, 1993), pp. 26–27.

[4]Ibid.

[5]Gene Hall, Jim Rosenthal, and Judy Wade, "How to Make Reengineering Really Work," *Harvard Business Review* 71, no. 6 (November-December 1993), pp. 119–131.

[6]For more information on business process reengineering and how well it has worked in various companies, see James Brian Quinn, *Intelligent Enterprise* (New York: Free Press, 1992), p. 162; Ann Majchrzak and Qianwei Wang, "Breaking the Functional Mind-Set in Process Organizations," *Harvard Business Review* 74, no. 5 (September-October 1996), pp. 93–99; Stephen L. Walston, Lawton R. Burns, and John R. Kimberly, "Does Reengineering Really Work? An Examination of the Context and Outcomes of Hospital Reengineer-

ing Initiatives," *Health Services Research* 34, no. 6 (February 2000), pp. 1363–1388; and Allessio Ascari, Melinda Rock, and Soumitra Dutta, "Reengineering and Organizational Change: Lessons from a Comparative Analysis of Company Experiences," *European Management Journal* 13, no. 1 (March 1995), pp. 1–13. For a review of why some company personnel embrace process reengineering and some don't, see Ronald J. Burke, "Process Reengineering: Who Embraces It and Why?" *TQM Magazine* 16, no. 2 (2004), pp. 114–119.

[7]For some of the seminal discussions of what TQM is and how it works written by ardent enthusiasts of the technique, see M. Walton, *The Deming Management Method* (New York: Pedigree, 1986); J. Juran, *Juran on Quality by Design* (New York: Free Press, 1992); Philip Crosby, *Quality Is Free: The Act of Making Quality Certain* (New York: McGraw-Hill, 1979); and S. George, *The Baldrige Quality System* (New York: Wiley, 1992). For a critique of TQM, see Mark J. Zbaracki, "The Rhetoric and Reality of Total Quality Management," *Administrative Science Quarterly* 43, no 3 (September 1998), pp. 602–636.

[8]For a discussion of the shift in work environment and culture that TQM entails, see Robert T. Amsden, Thomas W. Ferratt, and Davida M. Amsden, "TQM: Core Paradigm Changes," *Business Horizons* 39, no. 6 (November-December 1996), pp. 6–14.

[9]For easy-to-understand overviews of what six sigma is all about, see Peter S. Pande and Larry Holpp, *What Is Six Sigma?* (New York: McGraw-Hill, 2002); Jiju Antony, "Some Pros and Cons of Six Sigma: An Academic Perspective," *TQM Magazine* 16, no. 4 (2004), pp. 303–306; Peter S. Pande, Robert P. Neuman, and Roland R. Cavanagh, *The Six Sigma Way: How GE, Motorola and Other Top Companies Are Honing Their Performance* (New York: McGraw-Hill, 2000); and Joseph Gordon and M. Joseph Gordon, Jr., *Six Sigma Quality for Business and Manufacture* (New York: Elsevier, 2002). For how six sigma can be used in

smaller companies, see Godecke Wessel and Peter Burcher, "Six Sigma for Small and Medium-Sized Enterprises," *TQM Magazine* 16, no. 4 (2004), pp. 264–272.

[10]Based on information posted at www.isixsigma.com, November 4, 2002.

[11]Kennedy Smith, "Six Sigma for the Service Sector," *Quality Digest Magazine,* May 2003, posted at www.qualitydigest.com, accessed September 28, 2003.

[12]Del Jones, "Taking the Six Sigma Approach," *USA Today,* October 31, 2002, p. 5B.

[13]Smith, "Six Sigma for the Service Sector."

[14]Pande, Neuman, and Cavanagh, *The Six Sigma Way,* pp. 5–6.

[15]Jones, "Taking the Six Sigma Approach."

[16]Terry Nels Lee, Stanley E. Fawcett, and Jason Briscoe, "Benchmarking the Challenge to Quality Program Implementation," *Benchmarking: An International Journal* 9, no. 4 (2002), pp. 374–387.

[17]For a recent study documenting the imperatives of establishing a supportive culture, see Milan Ambrož, "Total Quality System as a Product of the Empowered Corporate Culture," *TQM Magazine* 16, no. 2 (2004), pp. 93–104. Research confirming the factors that are important in making TQM programs successful in both Europe and the U.S. is presented in Nick A. Dayton, "The Demise of Total Quality Management," *TQM Magazine* 15, no. 6 (2003), pp. 391–396.

[18]Judy D. Olian and Sara L. Rynes, "Making Total Quality Work: Aligning Organizational Processes, Performance Measures, and Stakeholders," *Human Resource Management* 30, no. 3 (Fall 1991), pp. 310–311, and Paul S. Goodman and Eric D. Darr, "Exchanging Best Practices Information through Computer-Aided Systems," *Academy of Management Executive* 10, no. 2 (May 1996), p. 7.

[19]Thomas C. Powell, "Total Quality Management as Competitive Advan-

tage," *Strategic Management Journal* 16 (1995), pp. 15–37. See also Richard M. Hodgetts, "Quality Lessons from America's Baldrige Winners," *Business Horizons* 37, no. 4 (July-August 1994), pp. 74–79, and Richard Reed, David J. Lemak, and Joseph C. Montgomery, "Beyond Process: TQM Content and Firm Performance," *Academy of Management Review* 21, no. 1 (January 1996), pp. 173–202.

[20]Based on information at www.otiselevator.com, accessed October 14, 2004.

[21]Stephan H. Haeckel and Richard L. Nolan, "Managing by Wire," *Harvard Business Review* 75, no. 5 (September-October 1993), p. 129.

[22]Quinn, *Intelligent Enterprise,* p. 181.

[23]Fred Vogelstein, "Winning the Amazon Way," *Fortune,* May 26, 2003, pp. 70, 74.

[24]Such systems speed organizational learning by providing fast, efficient communication, creating an organizational memory for collecting and retaining best-practice information, and permitting people all across the organization to exchange information and updated solutions. See Goodman and Darr, "Exchanging Best Practices Information through Computer-Aided Systems," pp. 7–17.

[25]Vogelstein, "Winning the Amazon Way," p. 64.

[26]For a discussion of the need for putting appropriate boundaries on the actions of empowered employees and possible control and monitoring systems that can be used, see Robert Simons, "Control in an Age of Empowerment," *Harvard Business Review* 73 (March-April 1995), pp. 80–88.

[27]Ibid. See also David C. Band and Gerald Scanlan, "Strategic Control through Core Competencies," *Long Range Planning* 28, no. 2 (April 1995), pp. 102–114.

[28]The importance of motivating and empowering workers so as to create a working environment that is highly conducive to good strategy execution is discussed in Stanley E. Fawcett,

Gary K. Rhoads, and Phillip Burnah, "People as the Bridge to Competitiveness: Benchmarking the 'ABCs' of an Empowered Workforce," *Benchmarking: An International Journal* 11, no. 4 (2004), pp. 346–360.

[29]Jeffrey Pfeffer and John F. Veiga, "Putting People First for Organizational Success," *Academy of Management Executive* 13, no. 2 (May 1999), pp. 37–45; Linda K. Stroh and Paula M. Caliguiri, "Increasing Global Competitiveness through Effective People Management," *Journal of World Business* 33, no. 1 (Spring 1998), pp. 1–16; and articles in *Fortune* on the 100 best companies to work for (1998, 1999, 2000, and 2001).

[30]As quoted in John P. Kotter and James L. Heskett, *Corporate Culture and Performance* (New York: Free Press, 1992), p. 91.

[31]For a provocative discussion of why incentives and rewards are actually counterproductive, see Alfie Kohn, "Why Incentive Plans Cannot Work," *Harvard Business Review* 71, no. 6 (September-October 1993), pp. 54–63.

[32]See Steven Kerr, "On the Folly of Rewarding A While Hoping for B," *Academy of Management Executive* 9, no. 1 (February 1995), pp. 7–14; Steven Kerr, "Risky Business: The New Pay Game," *Fortune,* July 22, 1996, pp. 93–96; and Doran Twer, "Linking Pay to Business Objectives," *Journal of Business Strategy* 15, no. 4 (July-August 1994), pp. 15–18.

[33]Kerr, "Risky Business." p. 96.

[34]For excellent discussions of the problems and pitfalls in leading the transition to a new strategy and to fundamentally new ways of doing business, see Larry Bossidy and Ram Charan, *Confronting Reality: Doing What Matters to Get Things Right* (New York: Crown Business, 2004); Larry Bossidy and Ram Charan, *Execution: The Discipline of Getting Things Done* (New York: Crown Business, 2002), especially chaps. 3 and 5; John P. Kotter, "Leading Change: Why Transformation Efforts Fail," *Harvard Business Review* 73, no. 2 (March-April 1995), pp. 59–67; Thomas M. Hout and John C. Carter, "Getting It Done: New Roles for Senior Executives," *Harvard Business Review* 73, no. 6 (November-December 1995), pp. 133–145; and Sumantra Ghoshal and Christopher A. Bartlett, "Changing the Role of Top Management: Beyond Structure to Processes," *Harvard Business Review* 73, no. 1 (January-February 1995), pp. 86–96.

[35]For a pragmatic, cut-to-the-chase treatment of why some leaders succeed and others fail in executing strategy, especially in a period of rapid market change or organizational crisis, see Bossidy and Charan, *Confronting Reality.*

[36]Vogelstein, "Winning the Amazon Way," p. 64.

[37]For a more in-depth discussion of the leader's role in creating a results-oriented culture that nurtures success, see Benjamin Schneider, Sarah K. Gunnarson, and Kathryn Niles-Jolly, "Creating the Climate and Culture of Success," *Organizational Dynamics,* Summer 1994, pp. 17–29.

[38]Jeffrey Pfeffer, "Producing Sustainable Competitive Advantage through the Effective Management of People," *Academy of Management Executive* 9, no. 1 (February 1995), pp. 55–69.

[39]James Brian Quinn, *Strategies for Change: Logical Incrementalism* (Homewood, IL: Irwin, 1980), pp. 20–22.

[40]Ibid., p. 146.

[41]For a good discussion of the challenges, see Daniel Goleman, "What Makes a Leader," *Harvard Business Review* 76, no. 6 (November-December 1998), pp. 92–102; Ronald A. Heifetz and Donald L. Laurie, "The Work of Leadership," *Harvard Business Review* 75, no. 1 (January-February 1997), pp. 124–134; and Charles M. Farkas and Suzy Wetlaufer, "The Ways Chief Executive Officers Lead," *Harvard Business Review* 74, no. 3 (May-June 1996), pp. 110–122. See also Michael E. Porter, Jay W. Lorsch, and Nitin Nohria, "Seven Surprises for New CEOs," *Harvard Business Review* 82, no. 10 (October 2004), pp. 62–72.

Name Index

Organization Index

Subject Index